# BROOSE: Literally More Imagery

By Broose Dickinson

TheBROOSE Museum
Bath, England


ISBN #: 978-0-578-17195-1

# CONTENTS

# Literary Imagery©

The text in this book is visually poetic in the sense that if entered into an internet browser an image will appear. Yet, the image is not actually a picture… It is text telling an internet browser where to place 1x1 cells within a table, and what background color to assign each cell. The resulting "images" are stealth, meaning they cannot be detected by search engines, nor can they be right clicked and saved… However, the text can be copied from the effected web page. Having exclusive rights to the literary imagery, Broose has questioned copyright, and what makes a picture a picture? The QR code at the beginning of each chapter will take you to the corresponding webpage of the literary image.

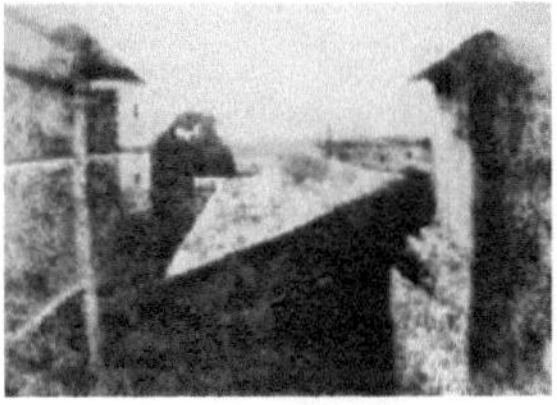

Niépce's Photo

```
<html>
<head><title>Niépce's Photo, written by Broose G. Dickinson</title></head>
<body>
<table border=0 cellpadding=0 cellspacing=0>
  <tr>
    <td width="1" height="1" bgcolor=#cecece></td>
    <td width="1" height="1" bgcolor=#d0d0d0></td>
    <td width="1" height="1" bgcolor=#d5d5d5></td>
    <td width="1" height="1" bgcolor=#d6d6d6></td>
    <td width="1" height="1" bgcolor=#dedede></td>
    <td width="1" height="1" bgcolor=#dadada></td>
    <td width="1" height="1" bgcolor=#dddddd></td>
    <td width="1" height="1" bgcolor=#dcdcdc></td>
    <td width="1" height="1" bgcolor=#dddddd></td>
    <td width="1" height="1" bgcolor=#dcdcdc></td>
    <td width="1" height="1" bgcolor=#dedede></td>
    <td width="1" height="1" bgcolor=#e0e0e0></td>
    <td width="1" height="1" bgcolor=#e2e2e2></td>
    <td width="1" height="1" bgcolor=#e0e0e0></td>
    <td width="1" height="1" bgcolor=#e3e3e3></td>
    <td width="1" height="1" bgcolor=#e4e4e4></td>
    <td width="1" height="1" bgcolor=#e3e3e3></td>
    <td width="1" height="1" bgcolor=#e2e2e2></td>
    <td rowspan="4" colspan="1" width="1" height="1" bgcolor=#e1e1e1></td>
    <td rowspan="2" colspan="1" width="1" height="1" bgcolor=#e2e2e2></td>
    <td width="1" height="1" bgcolor=#e4e4e4></td>
    <td width="1" height="1" bgcolor=#e6e6e6></td>
    <td width="1" height="1" bgcolor=#e5e5e5></td>
    <td width="1" height="1" bgcolor=#e4e4e4></td>
    <td width="1" height="1" bgcolor=#e5e5e5></td>
    <td width="1" height="1" bgcolor=#e6e6e6></td>
    <td width="1" height="1" bgcolor=#e7e7e7></td>
    <td width="1" height="1" bgcolor=#e6e6e6></td>
    <td width="1" height="1" bgcolor=#e7e7e7></td>
    <td width="1" height="1" bgcolor=#e8e8e8></td>
    <td rowspan="1" colspan="2" width="1" height="1" bgcolor=#e7e7e7></td>
    <td rowspan="1" colspan="2" width="1" height="1" bgcolor=#e6e6e6></td>
    <td rowspan="1" colspan="2" width="1" height="1" bgcolor=#e7e7e7></td>
    <td width="1" height="1" bgcolor=#e6e6e6></td>
    <td width="1" height="1" bgcolor=#e5e5e5></td>
    <td width="1" height="1" bgcolor=#e3e3e3></td>
    <td rowspan="5" colspan="1" width="1" height="1" bgcolor=#e2e2e2></td>
    <td width="1" height="1" bgcolor=#e1e1e1></td>
    <td width="1" height="1" bgcolor=#e2e2e2></td>
    <td width="1" height="1" bgcolor=#e4e4e4></td>
    <td width="1" height="1" bgcolor=#e6e6e6></td>
    <td rowspan="1" colspan="2" width="1" height="1" bgcolor=#e7e7e7></td>
    <td width="1" height="1" bgcolor=#e6e6e6></td>
    <td rowspan="1" colspan="2" width="1" height="1" bgcolor=#e5e5e5></td>
    <td width="1" height="1" bgcolor=#e6e6e6></td>
    <td width="1" height="1" bgcolor=#e4e4e4></td>
    <td width="1" height="1" bgcolor=#e5e5e5></td>
    <td width="1" height="1" bgcolor=#e6e6e6></td>
    <td rowspan="2" colspan="1" width="1" height="1" bgcolor=#e4e4e4></td>
    <td width="1" height="1" bgcolor=#e2e2e2></td>
    <td width="1" height="1" bgcolor=#e5e5e5></td>
    <td width="1" height="1" bgcolor=#e4e4e4></td>
    <td width="1" height="1" bgcolor=#e7e7e7></td>
    <td width="1" height="1" bgcolor=#dfdfdf></td>
    <td width="1" height="1" bgcolor=#e7e7e7></td>
    <td width="1" height="1" bgcolor=#e5e5e5></td>
    <td width="1" height="1" bgcolor=#e0e0e0></td>
    <td width="1" height="1" bgcolor=#e3e3e3></td>
    <td width="1" height="1" bgcolor=#e0e0e0></td>
    <td width="1" height="1" bgcolor=#e1e1e1></td>
    <td rowspan="1" colspan="2" width="1" height="1" bgcolor=#dfdfdf></td>
    <td width="1" height="1" bgcolor=#dadada></td>
    <td width="1" height="1" bgcolor=#d9d9d9></td>
    <td width="1" height="1" bgcolor=#d7d7d7></td>
    <td width="1" height="1" bgcolor=#d2d2d2></td>
    <td width="1" height="1" bgcolor=#d4d4d4></td>
```

```
  </tr>
  <tr>
    <td width="1" height="1"
bgcolor=#bdbdbd></td>
    <td width="1" height="1"
bgcolor=#afafaf></td>
    <td width="1" height="1"
bgcolor=#c0c0c0></td>
    <td width="1" height="1"
bgcolor=#cacaca></td>
    <td width="1" height="1"
bgcolor=#d0d0d0></td>
    <td rowspan="1"
colspan="2" width="1"
height="1"
bgcolor=#d7d7d7></td>
    <td width="1" height="1"
bgcolor=#dadada></td>
    <td width="1" height="1"
bgcolor=#dbdbdb></td>
    <td width="1" height="1"
bgcolor=#dfdfdf></td>
    <td width="1" height="1"
bgcolor=#e2e2e2></td>
    <td width="1" height="1"
bgcolor=#dcdcdc></td>
    <td width="1" height="1"
bgcolor=#dadada></td>
    <td rowspan="1"
colspan="2" width="1"
height="1"
bgcolor=#dddddd></td>
    <td width="1" height="1"
bgcolor=#e1e1e1></td>
    <td rowspan="3"
colspan="1" width="1"
height="1"
bgcolor=#e2e2e2></td>
    <td rowspan="6"
colspan="1" width="1"
height="1"
bgcolor=#e1e1e1></td>
    <td rowspan="1"
colspan="3" width="1"
height="1"
bgcolor=#e2e2e2></td>
    <td rowspan="1"
colspan="2" width="1"
height="1"
bgcolor=#e3e3e3></td>
    <td width="1" height="1"
bgcolor=#e4e4e4></td>
    <td rowspan="1"
colspan="3" width="1"
height="1"
bgcolor=#e5e5e5></td>
    <td rowspan="1"
colspan="2" width="1"
height="1"
bgcolor=#e6e6e6></td>
    <td width="1" height="1"
bgcolor=#e5e5e5></td>
    <td rowspan="1"
colspan="3" width="1"
height="1"
bgcolor=#e4e4e4></td>
    <td rowspan="1"
colspan="3" width="1"
height="1"
bgcolor=#e3e3e3></td>
    <td width="1" height="1"
bgcolor=#e2e2e2></td>
    <td width="1" height="1"
bgcolor=#dfdfdf></td>
    <td width="1" height="1"
bgcolor=#e0e0e0></td>
    <td rowspan="3"
colspan="1" width="1"
height="1"
bgcolor=#e2e2e2></td>
    <td width="1" height="1"
bgcolor=#e3e3e3></td>
    <td rowspan="1"
colspan="3" width="1"
height="1"
bgcolor=#e4e4e4></td>
    <td rowspan="2"
colspan="1" width="1"
height="1"
bgcolor=#e3e3e3></td>
    <td rowspan="2"
colspan="1" width="1"
height="1"
bgcolor=#e2e2e2></td>
    <td rowspan="1"
colspan="2" width="1"
height="1"
bgcolor=#e3e3e3></td>
    <td rowspan="2"
colspan="1" width="1"
height="1"
bgcolor=#e4e4e4></td>
    <td width="1" height="1"
bgcolor=#e5e5e5></td>
    <td width="1" height="1"
bgcolor=#e3e3e3></td>
    <td width="1" height="1"
bgcolor=#e4e4e4></td>
    <td rowspan="1"
colspan="2" width="1"
height="1"
bgcolor=#e0e0e0></td>
    <td width="1" height="1"
bgcolor=#e9e9e9></td>
    <td width="1" height="1"
bgcolor=#dfdfdf></td>
    <td width="1" height="1"
bgcolor=#e0e0e0></td>
    <td width="1" height="1"
bgcolor=#dddddd></td>
    <td width="1" height="1"
bgcolor=#e1e1e1></td>
    <td width="1" height="1"
bgcolor=#dddddd></td>
    <td width="1" height="1"
bgcolor=#dbdbdb></td>
    <td rowspan="2"
colspan="1" width="1"
height="1"
bgcolor=#dddddd></td>
    <td width="1" height="1"
bgcolor=#d9d9d9></td>
    <td width="1" height="1"
bgcolor=#dbdbdb></td>
    <td width="1" height="1"
bgcolor=#d6d6d6></td>
    <td width="1" height="1"
bgcolor=#d1d1d1></td>
    <td width="1" height="1"
bgcolor=#d7d7d7></td>
    <td width="1" height="1"
bgcolor=#d0d0d0></td>
  </tr>
  <tr>
    <td width="1" height="1"
bgcolor=#cbcbcb></td>
    <td width="1" height="1"
bgcolor=#c3c3c3></td>
    <td width="1" height="1"
bgcolor=#b0b0b0></td>
    <td width="1" height="1"
bgcolor=#afafaf></td>
    <td width="1" height="1"
bgcolor=#bcbcbc></td>
    <td width="1" height="1"
bgcolor=#d2d2d2></td>
    <td width="1" height="1"
bgcolor=#dcdcdc></td>
    <td width="1" height="1"
bgcolor=#d4d4d4></td>
    <td rowspan="1"
colspan="2" width="1"
height="1"
bgcolor=#c9c9c9></td>
    <td width="1" height="1"
bgcolor=#dadada></td>
    <td rowspan="2"
colspan="1" width="1"
height="1"
bgcolor=#e2e2e2></td>
    <td width="1" height="1"
bgcolor=#dbdbdb></td>
    <td rowspan="2"
colspan="1" width="1"
```

```
height="1"
bgcolor=#dcdcdc></td>
    <td width="1" height="1"
bgcolor=#e0e0e0></td>
    <td width="1" height="1"
bgcolor=#e3e3e3></td>
    <td rowspan="4"
colspan="1" width="1"
height="1"
bgcolor=#e1e1e1></td>
    <td width="1" height="1"
bgcolor=#e1e1e1></td>
    <td rowspan="1"
colspan="2" width="1"
height="1"
bgcolor=#e0e0e0></td>
    <td rowspan="1"
colspan="2" width="1"
height="1"
bgcolor=#e2e2e2></td>
    <td rowspan="1"
colspan="4" width="1"
height="1"
bgcolor=#e3e3e3></td>
    <td rowspan="2"
colspan="2" width="1"
height="1"
bgcolor=#e4e4e4></td>
    <td rowspan="2"
colspan="2" width="1"
height="1"
bgcolor=#e3e3e3></td>
    <td rowspan="7"
colspan="1" width="1"
height="1"
bgcolor=#e2e2e2></td>
    <td rowspan="2"
colspan="1" width="1"
height="1"
bgcolor=#e1e1e1></td>
    <td rowspan="2"
colspan="2" width="1"
height="1"
bgcolor=#e0e0e0></td>
    <td rowspan="3"
colspan="1" width="1"
height="1"
bgcolor=#e1e1e1></td>
    <td width="1" height="1"
bgcolor=#e1e1e1></td>
    <td rowspan="1"
colspan="2" width="1"
height="1"
bgcolor=#e1e1e1></td>
    <td rowspan="2"
colspan="1" width="1"
height="1"
bgcolor=#e2e2e2></td>
    <td rowspan="1"
colspan="2" width="1"
height="1"
bgcolor=#e3e3e3></td>
    <td width="1" height="1"
bgcolor=#e2e2e2></td>
    <td width="1" height="1"
bgcolor=#e2e2e2></td>
    <td rowspan="2"
colspan="1" width="1"
height="1"
bgcolor=#e4e4e4></td>
    <td rowspan="1"
colspan="2" width="1"
height="1"
bgcolor=#e3e3e3></td>
    <td width="1" height="1"
bgcolor=#e4e4e4></td>
    <td width="1" height="1"
bgcolor=#e2e2e2></td>
    <td width="1" height="1"
bgcolor=#e4e4e4></td>
    <td width="1" height="1"
bgcolor=#e3e3e3></td>
    <td width="1" height="1"
bgcolor=#e0e0e0></td>
    <td rowspan="2"
colspan="1" width="1"
height="1"
bgcolor=#e5e5e5></td>
    <td width="1" height="1"
bgcolor=#e1e1e1></td>
    <td width="1" height="1"
bgcolor=#e5e5e5></td>
    <td rowspan="2"
colspan="1" width="1"
height="1"
bgcolor=#e0e0e0></td>
    <td width="1" height="1"
bgcolor=#ececec></td>
    <td width="1" height="1"
bgcolor=#e5e5e5></td>
    <td width="1" height="1"
bgcolor=#dcdcdc></td>
    <td rowspan="2"
colspan="1" width="1"
height="1"
bgcolor=#d7d7d7></td>
    <td width="1" height="1"
bgcolor=#d7d7d7></td>
    <td width="1" height="1"
bgcolor=#d8d8d8></td>
    <td width="1" height="1"
bgcolor=#d0d0d0></td>
    <td width="1" height="1"
bgcolor=#d2d2d2></td>
  </tr>
  <tr>
    <td width="1" height="1"
bgcolor=#cecece></td>
    <td width="1" height="1"
bgcolor=#c6c6c6></td>
    <td width="1" height="1"
bgcolor=#c8c8c8></td>
    <td width="1" height="1"
bgcolor=#bebebe></td>
    <td width="1" height="1"
bgcolor=#a6a6a6></td>
    <td width="1" height="1"
bgcolor=#acacac></td>
    <td width="1" height="1"
bgcolor=#a6a6a6></td>
    <td width="1" height="1"
bgcolor=#9e9e9e></td>
    <td rowspan="1"
colspan="2" width="1"
height="1"
bgcolor=#8e8e8e></td>
    <td width="1" height="1"
bgcolor=#b5b5b5></td>
    <td width="1" height="1"
bgcolor=#e1e1e1></td>
    <td width="1" height="1"
bgcolor=#e2e2e2></td>
    <td width="1" height="1"
bgcolor=#e0e0e0></td>
    <td rowspan="1"
colspan="2" width="1"
height="1"
bgcolor=#e2e2e2></td>
    <td width="1" height="1"
bgcolor=#e1e1e1></td>
    <td rowspan="2"
colspan="1" width="1"
height="1"
bgcolor=#e0e0e0></td>
    <td rowspan="2"
colspan="1" width="1"
height="1"
bgcolor=#e1e1e1></td>
    <td rowspan="2"
colspan="1" width="1"
height="1"
bgcolor=#e2e2e2></td>
    <td rowspan="2"
colspan="1" width="1"
height="1"
bgcolor=#e3e3e3></td>
    <td rowspan="1"
colspan="2" width="1"
height="1"
bgcolor=#e3e3e3></td>
    <td rowspan="3"
colspan="1" width="1"
height="1"
bgcolor=#e2e2e2></td>
```

```
    <td rowspan="1"
colspan="2" width="1"
height="1"
bgcolor=#e3e3e3></td>
    <td width="1" height="1"
bgcolor=#e2e2e2></td>
    <td rowspan="1"
colspan="2" width="1"
height="1"
bgcolor=#e1e1e1></td>
    <td width="1" height="1"
bgcolor=#e2e2e2></td>
    <td width="1" height="1"
bgcolor=#e4e4e4></td>
    <td width="1" height="1"
bgcolor=#e3e3e3></td>
    <td rowspan="2"
colspan="1" width="1"
height="1"
bgcolor=#e3e3e3></td>
    <td rowspan="2"
colspan="1" width="1"
height="1"
bgcolor=#e1e1e1></td>
    <td width="1" height="1"
bgcolor=#e3e3e3></td>
    <td rowspan="2"
colspan="1" width="1"
height="1"
bgcolor=#e5e5e5></td>
    <td rowspan="2"
colspan="1" width="1"
height="1"
bgcolor=#e3e3e3></td>
    <td width="1" height="1"
bgcolor=#e2e2e2></td>
    <td rowspan="2"
colspan="1" width="1"
height="1"
bgcolor=#e4e4e4></td>
    <td width="1" height="1"
bgcolor=#e6e6e6></td>
    <td width="1" height="1"
bgcolor=#e4e4e4></td>
    <td width="1" height="1"
bgcolor=#e7e7e7></td>
    <td width="1" height="1"
bgcolor=#b5b5b5></td>
    <td width="1" height="1"
bgcolor=#c6c6c6></td>
    <td width="1" height="1"
bgcolor=#e2e2e2></td>
    <td width="1" height="1"
bgcolor=#dfdfdf></td>
    <td width="1" height="1"
bgcolor=#d8d8d8></td>
    <td width="1" height="1"
bgcolor=#d7d7d7></td>
    <td width="1" height="1"
bgcolor=#d4d4d4></td>
    <td width="1" height="1"
bgcolor=#d6d6d6></td>
  </tr>
  <tr>
    <td width="1" height="1"
bgcolor=#c6c6c6></td>
    <td width="1" height="1"
bgcolor=#cccccc></td>
    <td width="1" height="1"
bgcolor=#cdcdcd></td>
    <td width="1" height="1"
bgcolor=#c8c8c8></td>
    <td width="1" height="1"
bgcolor=#c1c1c1></td>
    <td width="1" height="1"
bgcolor=#b0b0b0></td>
    <td width="1" height="1"
bgcolor=#7a7a7a></td>
    <td width="1" height="1"
bgcolor=#5c5c5c></td>
    <td width="1" height="1"
bgcolor=#747474></td>
    <td width="1" height="1"
bgcolor=#707070></td>
    <td width="1" height="1"
bgcolor=#606060></td>
    <td width="1" height="1"
bgcolor=#8e8e8e></td>
    <td width="1" height="1"
bgcolor=#d0d0d0></td>
    <td width="1" height="1"
bgcolor=#e2e2e2></td>
    <td rowspan="2"
colspan="1" width="1"
height="1"
bgcolor=#dcdcdc></td>
    <td width="1" height="1"
bgcolor=#e3e3e3></td>
    <td width="1" height="1"
bgcolor=#dedede></td>
    <td width="1" height="1"
bgcolor=#e2e2e2></td>
    <td width="1" height="1"
bgcolor=#e1e1e1></td>
    <td rowspan="1"
colspan="2" width="1"
height="1"
bgcolor=#e3e3e3></td>
    <td rowspan="4"
colspan="1" width="1"
height="1"
bgcolor=#e2e2e2></td>
    <td rowspan="1"
colspan="3" width="1"
height="1"
bgcolor=#e3e3e3></td>
    <td rowspan="3"
colspan="1" width="1"
height="1"
bgcolor=#e2e2e2></td>
    <td width="1" height="1"
bgcolor=#e3e3e3></td>
    <td rowspan="4"
colspan="2" width="1"
height="1"
bgcolor=#e2e2e2></td>
    <td width="1" height="1"
bgcolor=#e1e1e1></td>
    <td width="1" height="1"
bgcolor=#e1e1e1></td>
    <td width="1" height="1"
bgcolor=#e0e0e0></td>
    <td width="1" height="1"
bgcolor=#dfdfdf></td>
    <td rowspan="2"
colspan="1" width="1"
height="1"
bgcolor=#e0e0e0></td>
    <td width="1" height="1"
bgcolor=#e0e0e0></td>
    <td width="1" height="1"
bgcolor=#dfdfdf></td>
    <td width="1" height="1"
bgcolor=#e0e0e0></td>
    <td width="1" height="1"
bgcolor=#e1e1e1></td>
    <td rowspan="2"
colspan="1" width="1"
height="1"
bgcolor=#e3e3e3></td>
    <td rowspan="2"
colspan="1" width="1"
height="1"
bgcolor=#e2e2e2></td>
    <td width="1" height="1"
bgcolor=#e3e3e3></td>
    <td width="1" height="1"
bgcolor=#e2e2e2></td>
    <td width="1" height="1"
bgcolor=#e3e3e3></td>
    <td width="1" height="1"
bgcolor=#e0e0e0></td>
    <td width="1" height="1"
bgcolor=#eaeaea></td>
    <td width="1" height="1"
bgcolor=#e2e2e2></td>
    <td width="1" height="1"
bgcolor=#959595></td>
    <td width="1" height="1"
bgcolor=#4d4d4d></td>
    <td width="1" height="1"
bgcolor=#333333></td>
    <td width="1" height="1"
bgcolor=#4a4a4a></td>
```

```
    <td width="1" height="1"
bgcolor=#9a9a9a></td>
    <td width="1" height="1"
bgcolor=#c8c8c8></td>
    <td width="1" height="1"
bgcolor=#d4d4d4></td>
    <td width="1" height="1"
bgcolor=#d6d6d6></td>
    <td width="1" height="1"
bgcolor=#d9d9d9></td>
    <td width="1" height="1"
bgcolor=#d6d6d6></td>
    <td width="1" height="1"
bgcolor=#d2d2d2></td>
  </tr>
  <tr>
    <td width="1" height="1"
bgcolor=#c2c2c2></td>
    <td width="1" height="1"
bgcolor=#c7c7c7></td>
    <td width="1" height="1"
bgcolor=#cbcbcb></td>
    <td width="1" height="1"
bgcolor=#cfcfcf></td>
    <td width="1" height="1"
bgcolor=#cecece></td>
    <td width="1" height="1"
bgcolor=#cccccc></td>
    <td width="1" height="1"
bgcolor=#b0b0b0></td>
    <td width="1" height="1"
bgcolor=#8a8a8a></td>
    <td width="1" height="1"
bgcolor=#787878></td>
    <td width="1" height="1"
bgcolor=#606060></td>
    <td width="1" height="1"
bgcolor=#2a2a2a></td>
    <td width="1" height="1"
bgcolor=#4a4a4a></td>
    <td width="1" height="1"
bgcolor=#a9a9a9></td>
    <td width="1" height="1"
bgcolor=#e0e0e0></td>
    <td width="1" height="1"
bgcolor=#d6d6d6></td>
    <td width="1" height="1"
bgcolor=#dcdcdc></td>
    <td width="1" height="1"
bgcolor=#e3e3e3></td>
    <td width="1" height="1"
bgcolor=#dfdfdf></td>
    <td rowspan="2"
colspan="1" width="1"
height="1"
bgcolor=#e1e1e1></td>
    <td rowspan="1"
colspan="2" width="1"
height="1"
bgcolor=#e2e2e2></td>
    <td rowspan="2"
colspan="1" width="1"
height="1"
bgcolor=#e0e0e0></td>
    <td width="1" height="1"
bgcolor=#e1e1e1></td>
    <td rowspan="2"
colspan="1" width="1"
height="1"
bgcolor=#e2e2e2></td>
    <td rowspan="2"
colspan="1" width="1"
height="1"
bgcolor=#e2e2e2></td>
    <td rowspan="3"
colspan="2" width="1"
height="1"
bgcolor=#e3e3e3></td>
    <td rowspan="2"
colspan="1" width="1"
height="1"
bgcolor=#e2e2e2></td>
    <td rowspan="4"
colspan="1" width="1"
height="1"
bgcolor=#e2e2e2></td>
    <td rowspan="2"
colspan="1" width="1"
height="1"
bgcolor=#e2e2e2></td>
    <td width="1" height="1"
bgcolor=#e1e1e1></td>
    <td width="1" height="1"
bgcolor=#e0e0e0></td>
    <td rowspan="1"
colspan="2" width="1"
height="1"
bgcolor=#dedede></td>
    <td width="1" height="1"
bgcolor=#e1e1e1></td>
    <td width="1" height="1"
bgcolor=#e0e0e0></td>
    <td width="1" height="1"
bgcolor=#e1e1e1></td>
    <td width="1" height="1"
bgcolor=#e2e2e2></td>
    <td rowspan="1"
colspan="2" width="1"
height="1"
bgcolor=#e4e4e4></td>
    <td width="1" height="1"
bgcolor=#e2e2e2></td>
    <td rowspan="1"
colspan="3" width="1"
height="1"
bgcolor=#e0e0e0></td>
    <td width="1" height="1"
bgcolor=#dedede></td>
    <td width="1" height="1"
bgcolor=#dddddd></td>
    <td width="1" height="1"
bgcolor=#ededed></td>
    <td width="1" height="1"
bgcolor=#d3d3d3></td>
    <td width="1" height="1"
bgcolor=#717171></td>
    <td width="1" height="1"
bgcolor=#313131></td>
    <td width="1" height="1"
bgcolor=#252525></td>
    <td width="1" height="1"
bgcolor=#3f3f3f></td>
    <td width="1" height="1"
bgcolor=#484848></td>
    <td width="1" height="1"
bgcolor=#7b7b7b></td>
    <td width="1" height="1"
bgcolor=#acacac></td>
    <td rowspan="1"
colspan="2" width="1"
height="1"
bgcolor=#c1c1c1></td>
    <td width="1" height="1"
bgcolor=#cdcdcd></td>
    <td width="1" height="1"
bgcolor=#d2d2d2></td>
    <td width="1" height="1"
bgcolor=#dadada></td>
  </tr>
  <tr>
    <td width="1" height="1"
bgcolor=#bfbfbf></td>
    <td width="1" height="1"
bgcolor=#b7b7b7></td>
    <td rowspan="1"
colspan="2" width="1"
height="1"
bgcolor=#c8c8c8></td>
    <td width="1" height="1"
bgcolor=#cccccc></td>
    <td width="1" height="1"
bgcolor=#c6c6c6></td>
    <td width="1" height="1"
bgcolor=#afafaf></td>
    <td width="1" height="1"
bgcolor=#b1b1b1></td>
    <td width="1" height="1"
bgcolor=#acacac></td>
    <td width="1" height="1"
bgcolor=#6e6e6e></td>
    <td rowspan="1"
colspan="2" width="1"
height="1"
bgcolor=#383838></td>
```

```
    <td width="1" height="1"
bgcolor=#5f5f5f></td>
    <td width="1" height="1"
bgcolor=#aeaeae></td>
    <td width="1" height="1"
bgcolor=#dddddd></td>
    <td rowspan="1"
colspan="2" width="1"
height="1"
bgcolor=#e1e1e1></td>
    <td rowspan="1"
colspan="2" width="1"
height="1"
bgcolor=#e2e2e2></td>
    <td width="1" height="1"
bgcolor=#e1e1e1></td>
    <td rowspan="2"
colspan="1" width="1"
height="1"
bgcolor=#e1e1e1></td>
    <td width="1" height="1"
bgcolor=#e2e2e2></td>
    <td rowspan="4"
colspan="1" width="1"
height="1"
bgcolor=#e2e2e2></td>
    <td rowspan="1"
colspan="2" width="1"
height="1"
bgcolor=#e3e3e3></td>
    <td width="1" height="1"
bgcolor=#e2e2e2></td>
    <td width="1" height="1"
bgcolor=#e0e0e0></td>
    <td width="1" height="1"
bgcolor=#e1e1e1></td>
    <td rowspan="1"
colspan="2" width="1"
height="1"
bgcolor=#e3e3e3></td>
    <td rowspan="1"
colspan="2" width="1"
height="1"
bgcolor=#e2e2e2></td>
    <td width="1" height="1"
bgcolor=#e3e3e3></td>
    <td width="1" height="1"
bgcolor=#e4e4e4></td>
    <td rowspan="1"
colspan="2" width="1"
height="1"
bgcolor=#e3e3e3></td>
    <td width="1" height="1"
bgcolor=#e4e4e4></td>
    <td rowspan="2"
colspan="1" width="1"
height="1"
bgcolor=#e3e3e3></td>
    <td width="1" height="1"
bgcolor=#dfdfdf></td>
    <td width="1" height="1"
bgcolor=#dedede></td>
    <td width="1" height="1"
bgcolor=#e1e1e1></td>
    <td width="1" height="1"
bgcolor=#e6e6e6></td>
    <td width="1" height="1"
bgcolor=#e4e4e4></td>
    <td width="1" height="1"
bgcolor=#aaaaaa></td>
    <td width="1" height="1"
bgcolor=#464646></td>
    <td rowspan="1"
colspan="2" width="1"
height="1"
bgcolor=#2f2f2f></td>
    <td width="1" height="1"
bgcolor=#282828></td>
    <td width="1" height="1"
bgcolor=#292929></td>
    <td width="1" height="1"
bgcolor=#595959></td>
    <td width="1" height="1"
bgcolor=#6d6d6d></td>
    <td width="1" height="1"
bgcolor=#848484></td>
    <td width="1" height="1"
bgcolor=#b3b3b3></td>
    <td width="1" height="1"
bgcolor=#bfbfbf></td>
    <td width="1" height="1"
bgcolor=#c0c0c0></td>
    <td width="1" height="1"
bgcolor=#cdcdcd></td>
    <td width="1" height="1"
bgcolor=#d2d2d2></td>
  </tr>
  <tr>
    <td width="1" height="1"
bgcolor=#a5a5a5></td>
    <td width="1" height="1"
bgcolor=#a8a8a8></td>
    <td width="1" height="1"
bgcolor=#c5c5c5></td>
    <td width="1" height="1"
bgcolor=#c9c9c9></td>
    <td width="1" height="1"
bgcolor=#bbbbbb></td>
    <td width="1" height="1"
bgcolor=#a3a3a3></td>
    <td width="1" height="1"
bgcolor=#939393></td>
    <td width="1" height="1"
bgcolor=#878787></td>
    <td width="1" height="1"
bgcolor=#8c8c8c></td>
    <td width="1" height="1"
bgcolor=#5b5b5b></td>
    <td width="1" height="1"
bgcolor=#282828></td>
    <td width="1" height="1"
bgcolor=#181818></td>
    <td width="1" height="1"
bgcolor=#313131></td>
    <td width="1" height="1"
bgcolor=#6f6f6f></td>
    <td width="1" height="1"
bgcolor=#9c9c9c></td>
    <td width="1" height="1"
bgcolor=#cbcbcb></td>
    <td width="1" height="1"
bgcolor=#e8e8e8></td>
    <td width="1" height="1"
bgcolor=#e2e2e2></td>
    <td width="1" height="1"
bgcolor=#dfdfdf></td>
    <td width="1" height="1"
bgcolor=#e2e2e2></td>
    <td width="1" height="1"
bgcolor=#e5e5e5></td>
    <td width="1" height="1"
bgcolor=#e3e3e3></td>
    <td rowspan="1"
colspan="2" width="1"
height="1"
bgcolor=#e1e1e1></td>
    <td width="1" height="1"
bgcolor=#e3e3e3></td>
    <td width="1" height="1"
bgcolor=#e3e3e3></td>
    <td rowspan="2"
colspan="2" width="1"
height="1"
bgcolor=#e3e3e3></td>
    <td rowspan="2"
colspan="1" width="1"
height="1"
bgcolor=#e3e3e3></td>
    <td rowspan="2"
colspan="1" width="1"
height="1"
bgcolor=#e4e4e4></td>
    <td width="1" height="1"
bgcolor=#e5e5e5></td>
    <td rowspan="3"
colspan="1" width="1"
height="1"
bgcolor=#e4e4e4></td>
    <td rowspan="3"
colspan="1" width="1"
height="1"
bgcolor=#e2e2e2></td>
    <td width="1" height="1"
bgcolor=#e3e3e3></td>
```

```
<td rowspan="1" colspan="2" width="1" height="1" bgcolor=#e4e4e4></td>
<td width="1" height="1" bgcolor=#e1e1e1></td>
<td width="1" height="1" bgcolor=#e0e0e0></td>
<td rowspan="3" colspan="1" width="1" height="1" bgcolor=#e2e2e2></td>
<td width="1" height="1" bgcolor=#e3e3e3></td>
<td width="1" height="1" bgcolor=#e2e2e2></td>
<td rowspan="2" colspan="1" width="1" height="1" bgcolor=#e0e0e0></td>
<td rowspan="2" colspan="1" width="1" height="1" bgcolor=#e2e2e2></td>
<td width="1" height="1" bgcolor=#e0e0e0></td>
<td width="1" height="1" bgcolor=#e1e1e1></td>
<td width="1" height="1" bgcolor=#e8e8e8></td>
<td width="1" height="1" bgcolor=#c9c9c9></td>
<td width="1" height="1" bgcolor=#828282></td>
<td width="1" height="1" bgcolor=#393939></td>
<td rowspan="1" colspan="2" width="1" height="1" bgcolor=#2b2b2b></td>
<td width="1" height="1" bgcolor=#1d1d1d></td>
<td width="1" height="1" bgcolor=#161616></td>
<td width="1" height="1" bgcolor=#212121></td>
<td width="1" height="1" bgcolor=#3d3d3d></td>
<td width="1" height="1" bgcolor=#474747></td>
<td width="1" height="1" bgcolor=#5b5b5b></td>
<td width="1" height="1" bgcolor=#888888></td>
<td width="1" height="1" bgcolor=#a1a1a1></td>
<td width="1" height="1" bgcolor=#b2b2b2></td>
<td width="1" height="1" bgcolor=#c0c0c0></td>
<td width="1" height="1" bgcolor=#d4d4d4></td>
</tr>
<tr>
<td width="1" height="1" bgcolor=#787878></td>
<td width="1" height="1" bgcolor=#585858></td>
<td width="1" height="1" bgcolor=#7d7d7d></td>
<td width="1" height="1" bgcolor=#808080></td>
<td width="1" height="1" bgcolor=#7c7c7c></td>
<td width="1" height="1" bgcolor=#7e7e7e></td>
<td width="1" height="1" bgcolor=#969696></td>
<td width="1" height="1" bgcolor=#aaaaaa></td>
<td width="1" height="1" bgcolor=#7d7d7d></td>
<td width="1" height="1" bgcolor=#363636></td>
<td width="1" height="1" bgcolor=#141414></td>
<td width="1" height="1" bgcolor=#010101></td>
<td width="1" height="1" bgcolor=#000000></td>
<td width="1" height="1" bgcolor=#0d0d0d></td>
<td width="1" height="1" bgcolor=#272727></td>
<td width="1" height="1" bgcolor=#3b3b3b></td>
<td width="1" height="1" bgcolor=#888888></td>
<td width="1" height="1" bgcolor=#e0e0e0></td>
<td rowspan="1" colspan="2" width="1" height="1" bgcolor=#d9d9d9></td>
<td width="1" height="1" bgcolor=#e2e2e2></td>
<td width="1" height="1" bgcolor=#e1e1e1></td>
<td width="1" height="1" bgcolor=#dcdcdc></td>
<td width="1" height="1" bgcolor=#e3e3e3></td>
<td width="1" height="1" bgcolor=#dfdfdf></td>
<td rowspan="2" colspan="1" width="1" height="1" bgcolor=#e2e2e2></td>
<td width="1" height="1" bgcolor=#e4e4e4></td>
<td width="1" height="1" bgcolor=#e0e0e0></td>
<td width="1" height="1" bgcolor=#e2e2e2></td>
<td width="1" height="1" bgcolor=#e6e6e6></td>
<td rowspan="1" colspan="2" width="1" height="1" bgcolor=#e1e1e1></td>
<td width="1" height="1" bgcolor=#e4e4e4></td>
<td width="1" height="1" bgcolor=#e1e1e1></td>
<td rowspan="1" colspan="3" width="1" height="1" bgcolor=#e2e2e2></td>
<td width="1" height="1" bgcolor=#e1e1e1></td>
<td rowspan="3" colspan="1" width="1" height="1" bgcolor=#e1e1e1></td>
<td width="1" height="1" bgcolor=#e4e4e4></td>
<td width="1" height="1" bgcolor=#e4e4e4></td>
<td width="1" height="1" bgcolor=#e6e6e6></td>
<td width="1" height="1" bgcolor=#d8d8d8></td>
<td width="1" height="1" bgcolor=#929292></td>
<td width="1" height="1" bgcolor=#323232></td>
<td width="1" height="1" bgcolor=#060606></td>
<td width="1" height="1" bgcolor=#0f0f0f></td>
<td width="1" height="1" bgcolor=#363636></td>
<td width="1" height="1" bgcolor=#404040></td>
<td width="1" height="1" bgcolor=#141414></td>
<td width="1" height="1" bgcolor=#101010></td>
<td width="1" height="1" bgcolor=#1c1c1c></td>
<td width="1" height="1" bgcolor=#2f2f2f></td>
<td width="1" height="1" bgcolor=#2a2a2a></td>
```

```
    <td width="1" height="1"
bgcolor=#2d2d2d></td>
    <td width="1" height="1"
bgcolor=#313131></td>
    <td width="1" height="1"
bgcolor=#656565></td>
    <td width="1" height="1"
bgcolor=#a3a3a3></td>
    <td width="1" height="1"
bgcolor=#ababab></td>
    <td width="1" height="1"
bgcolor=#c4c4c4></td>
  </tr>
  <tr>
    <td rowspan="2"
colspan="1" width="1"
height="1"
bgcolor=#b6b6b6></td>
    <td width="1" height="1"
bgcolor=#7b7b7b></td>
    <td width="1" height="1"
bgcolor=#4f4f4f></td>
    <td width="1" height="1"
bgcolor=#2f2f2f></td>
    <td width="1" height="1"
bgcolor=#333333></td>
    <td width="1" height="1"
bgcolor=#373737></td>
    <td width="1" height="1"
bgcolor=#565656></td>
    <td width="1" height="1"
bgcolor=#5a5a5a></td>
    <td width="1" height="1"
bgcolor=#464646></td>
    <td width="1" height="1"
bgcolor=#323232></td>
    <td rowspan="1"
colspan="2" width="1"
height="1"
bgcolor=#212121></td>
    <td width="1" height="1"
bgcolor=#3c3c3c></td>
    <td width="1" height="1"
bgcolor=#444444></td>
    <td width="1" height="1"
bgcolor=#3c3c3c></td>
    <td width="1" height="1"
bgcolor=#353535></td>
    <td width="1" height="1"
bgcolor=#2d2d2d></td>
    <td width="1" height="1"
bgcolor=#757575></td>
    <td width="1" height="1"
bgcolor=#cfcfcf></td>
    <td width="1" height="1"
bgcolor=#e3e3e3></td>
    <td width="1" height="1"
bgcolor=#dbdbdb></td>
    <td width="1" height="1"
bgcolor=#dedede></td>
    <td width="1" height="1"
bgcolor=#dfdfdf></td>
    <td width="1" height="1"
bgcolor=#e2e2e2></td>
    <td width="1" height="1"
bgcolor=#e0e0e0></td>
    <td width="1" height="1"
bgcolor=#e0e0e0></td>
    <td width="1" height="1"
bgcolor=#e4e4e4></td>
    <td width="1" height="1"
bgcolor=#e5e5e5></td>
    <td width="1" height="1"
bgcolor=#dfdfdf></td>
    <td rowspan="4"
colspan="1" width="1"
height="1"
bgcolor=#e2e2e2></td>
    <td width="1" height="1"
bgcolor=#e4e4e4></td>
    <td width="1" height="1"
bgcolor=#e3e3e3></td>
    <td rowspan="1"
colspan="2" width="1"
height="1"
bgcolor=#e2e2e2></td>
    <td rowspan="2"
colspan="1" width="1"
height="1"
bgcolor=#e4e4e4></td>
    <td rowspan="1"
colspan="3" width="1"
height="1"
bgcolor=#e5e5e5></td>
    <td width="1" height="1"
bgcolor=#e0e0e0></td>
    <td width="1" height="1"
bgcolor=#e1e1e1></td>
    <td rowspan="2"
colspan="2" width="1"
height="1"
bgcolor=#e2e2e2></td>
    <td width="1" height="1"
bgcolor=#e2e2e2></td>
    <td width="1" height="1"
bgcolor=#e3e3e3></td>
    <td width="1" height="1"
bgcolor=#e2e2e2></td>
    <td width="1" height="1"
bgcolor=#e5e5e5></td>
    <td width="1" height="1"
bgcolor=#e3e3e3></td>
    <td width="1" height="1"
bgcolor=#c0c0c0></td>
    <td width="1" height="1"
bgcolor=#8c8c8c></td>
    <td width="1" height="1"
bgcolor=#545454></td>
    <td width="1" height="1"
bgcolor=#0d0d0d></td>
    <td width="1" height="1"
bgcolor=#050505></td>
    <td width="1" height="1"
bgcolor=#0a0a0a></td>
    <td width="1" height="1"
bgcolor=#202020></td>
    <td width="1" height="1"
bgcolor=#252525></td>
    <td width="1" height="1"
bgcolor=#1d1d1d></td>
    <td width="1" height="1"
bgcolor=#171717></td>
    <td width="1" height="1"
bgcolor=#1b1b1b></td>
    <td width="1" height="1"
bgcolor=#1f1f1f></td>
    <td width="1" height="1"
bgcolor=#252525></td>
    <td width="1" height="1"
bgcolor=#1d1d1d></td>
    <td width="1" height="1"
bgcolor=#191919></td>
    <td width="1" height="1"
bgcolor=#3c3c3c></td>
    <td width="1" height="1"
bgcolor=#565656></td>
    <td width="1" height="1"
bgcolor=#a2a2a2></td>
    <td width="1" height="1"
bgcolor=#c3c3c3></td>
  </tr>
  <tr>
    <td width="1" height="1"
bgcolor=#b3b3b3></td>
    <td width="1" height="1"
bgcolor=#9a9a9a></td>
    <td width="1" height="1"
bgcolor=#666666></td>
    <td width="1" height="1"
bgcolor=#3a3a3a></td>
    <td width="1" height="1"
bgcolor=#363636></td>
    <td width="1" height="1"
bgcolor=#202020></td>
    <td width="1" height="1"
bgcolor=#1a1a1a></td>
    <td width="1" height="1"
bgcolor=#0c0c0c></td>
    <td width="1" height="1"
bgcolor=#424242></td>
    <td width="1" height="1"
bgcolor=#545454></td>
    <td width="1" height="1"
bgcolor=#898989></td>
```

```
    <td width="1" height="1" bgcolor=#c6c6c6></td>
    <td width="1" height="1" bgcolor=#c0c0c0></td>
    <td width="1" height="1" bgcolor=#bdbdbd></td>
    <td width="1" height="1" bgcolor=#c6c6c6></td>
    <td width="1" height="1" bgcolor=#c2c2c2></td>
    <td width="1" height="1" bgcolor=#afafaf></td>
    <td width="1" height="1" bgcolor=#cecece></td>
    <td width="1" height="1" bgcolor=#dddddd></td>
    <td width="1" height="1" bgcolor=#e3e3e3></td>
    <td width="1" height="1" bgcolor=#e2e2e2></td>
    <td width="1" height="1" bgcolor=#e4e4e4></td>
    <td rowspan="2" colspan="1" width="1" height="1" bgcolor=#e0e0e0></td>
    <td rowspan="2" colspan="1" width="1" height="1" bgcolor=#e3e3e3></td>
    <td width="1" height="1" bgcolor=#e3e3e3></td>
    <td width="1" height="1" bgcolor=#e0e0e0></td>
    <td width="1" height="1" bgcolor=#e2e2e2></td>
    <td width="1" height="1" bgcolor=#e3e3e3></td>
    <td width="1" height="1" bgcolor=#e0e0e0></td>
    <td width="1" height="1" bgcolor=#e5e5e5></td>
    <td width="1" height="1" bgcolor=#e3e3e3></td>
    <td width="1" height="1" bgcolor=#e2e2e2></td>
    <td rowspan="2" colspan="1" width="1" height="1" bgcolor=#e1e1e1></td>
    <td rowspan="2" colspan="1" width="1" height="1" bgcolor=#e2e2e2></td>
    <td rowspan="2" colspan="2" width="1" height="1" bgcolor=#e4e4e4></td>
    <td rowspan="2" colspan="1" width="1" height="1" bgcolor=#e3e3e3></td>
    <td width="1" height="1" bgcolor=#e3e3e3></td>
    <td width="1" height="1" bgcolor=#e0e0e0></td>
    <td rowspan="2" colspan="1" width="1" height="1" bgcolor=#dfdfdf></td>
    <td rowspan="2" colspan="1" width="1" height="1" bgcolor=#e0e0e0></td>
    <td rowspan="3" colspan="1" width="1" height="1" bgcolor=#e1e1e1></td>
    <td rowspan="2" colspan="1" width="1" height="1" bgcolor=#e1e1e1></td>
    <td width="1" height="1" bgcolor=#e2e2e2></td>
    <td width="1" height="1" bgcolor=#e3e3e3></td>
    <td width="1" height="1" bgcolor=#dfdfdf></td>
    <td width="1" height="1" bgcolor=#e1e1e1></td>
    <td width="1" height="1" bgcolor=#d9d9d9></td>
    <td width="1" height="1" bgcolor=#d7d7d7></td>
    <td width="1" height="1" bgcolor=#e7e7e7></td>
    <td width="1" height="1" bgcolor=#6a6a6a></td>
    <td width="1" height="1" bgcolor=#020202></td>
    <td width="1" height="1" bgcolor=#000000></td>
    <td width="1" height="1" bgcolor=#1c1c1c></td>
    <td width="1" height="1" bgcolor=#313131></td>
    <td width="1" height="1" bgcolor=#262626></td>
    <td width="1" height="1" bgcolor=#131313></td>
    <td rowspan="1" colspan="2" width="1" height="1" bgcolor=#191919></td>
    <td width="1" height="1" bgcolor=#212121></td>
    <td width="1" height="1" bgcolor=#2e2e2e></td>
    <td width="1" height="1" bgcolor=#1c1c1c></td>
    <td width="1" height="1" bgcolor=#323232></td>
    <td width="1" height="1" bgcolor=#6e6e6e></td>
    <td width="1" height="1" bgcolor=#b3b3b3></td>
    <td width="1" height="1" bgcolor=#bbbbbb></td>
  </tr>
  <tr>
    <td width="1" height="1" bgcolor=#b8b8b8></td>
    <td width="1" height="1" bgcolor=#a1a1a1></td>
    <td width="1" height="1" bgcolor=#bababa></td>
    <td width="1" height="1" bgcolor=#9f9f9f></td>
    <td width="1" height="1" bgcolor=#808080></td>
    <td width="1" height="1" bgcolor=#848484></td>
    <td width="1" height="1" bgcolor=#686868></td>
    <td width="1" height="1" bgcolor=#3e3e3e></td>
    <td width="1" height="1" bgcolor=#1d1d1d></td>
    <td width="1" height="1" bgcolor=#3e3e3e></td>
    <td width="1" height="1" bgcolor=#383838></td>
    <td width="1" height="1" bgcolor=#303030></td>
    <td width="1" height="1" bgcolor=#414141></td>
    <td width="1" height="1" bgcolor=#343434></td>
    <td width="1" height="1" bgcolor=#5d5d5d></td>
    <td width="1" height="1" bgcolor=#cecece></td>
    <td width="1" height="1" bgcolor=#d4d4d4></td>
    <td width="1" height="1" bgcolor=#e1e1e1></td>
    <td width="1" height="1" bgcolor=#dfdfdf></td>
    <td width="1" height="1" bgcolor=#d7d7d7></td>
    <td width="1" height="1" bgcolor=#dadada></td>
    <td width="1" height="1" bgcolor=#dbdbdb></td>
```

```
    <td width="1" height="1"
bgcolor=#dfdfdf></td>
    <td width="1" height="1"
bgcolor=#dedede></td>
    <td width="1" height="1"
bgcolor=#e1e1e1></td>
    <td width="1" height="1"
bgcolor=#dfdfdf></td>
    <td width="1" height="1"
bgcolor=#e1e1e1></td>
    <td width="1" height="1"
bgcolor=#e2e2e2></td>
    <td width="1" height="1"
bgcolor=#e1e1e1></td>
    <td rowspan="1"
colspan="2" width="1"
height="1"
bgcolor=#e1e1e1></td>
    <td rowspan="2"
colspan="1" width="1"
height="1"
bgcolor=#e3e3e3></td>
    <td width="1" height="1"
bgcolor=#e1e1e1></td>
    <td rowspan="3"
colspan="1" width="1"
height="1"
bgcolor=#dfdfdf></td>
    <td rowspan="2"
colspan="1" width="1"
height="1"
bgcolor=#e1e1e1></td>
    <td width="1" height="1"
bgcolor=#e1e1e1></td>
    <td width="1" height="1"
bgcolor=#e4e4e4></td>
    <td width="1" height="1"
bgcolor=#e0e0e0></td>
    <td width="1" height="1"
bgcolor=#e2e2e2></td>
    <td rowspan="2"
colspan="1" width="1"
height="1"
bgcolor=#e0e0e0></td>
    <td width="1" height="1"
bgcolor=#e0e0e0></td>
    <td width="1" height="1"
bgcolor=#dfdfdf></td>
    <td width="1" height="1"
bgcolor=#dddddd></td>
    <td width="1" height="1"
bgcolor=#e6e6e6></td>
    <td width="1" height="1"
bgcolor=#9f9f9f></td>
    <td width="1" height="1"
bgcolor=#181818></td>
    <td width="1" height="1"
bgcolor=#0e0e0e></td>
    <td width="1" height="1"
bgcolor=#2d2d2d></td>
    <td width="1" height="1"
bgcolor=#3a3a3a></td>
    <td width="1" height="1"
bgcolor=#242424></td>
    <td width="1" height="1"
bgcolor=#101010></td>
    <td width="1" height="1"
bgcolor=#0f0f0f></td>
    <td width="1" height="1"
bgcolor=#1b1b1b></td>
    <td width="1" height="1"
bgcolor=#333333></td>
    <td width="1" height="1"
bgcolor=#272727></td>
    <td width="1" height="1"
bgcolor=#2f2f2f></td>
    <td width="1" height="1"
bgcolor=#393939></td>
    <td width="1" height="1"
bgcolor=#636363></td>
    <td width="1" height="1"
bgcolor=#838383></td>
    <td width="1" height="1"
bgcolor=#a0a0a0></td>
  </tr>
  <tr>
    <td width="1" height="1"
bgcolor=#afafaf></td>
    <td width="1" height="1"
bgcolor=#aeaeae></td>
    <td width="1" height="1"
bgcolor=#bdbdbd></td>
    <td rowspan="2"
colspan="1" width="1"
height="1"
bgcolor=#a6a6a6></td>
    <td width="1" height="1"
bgcolor=#a0a0a0></td>
    <td width="1" height="1"
bgcolor=#a5a5a5></td>
    <td width="1" height="1"
bgcolor=#a6a6a6></td>
    <td width="1" height="1"
bgcolor=#828282></td>
    <td width="1" height="1"
bgcolor=#555555></td>
    <td width="1" height="1"
bgcolor=#7f7f7f></td>
    <td width="1" height="1"
bgcolor=#6f6f6f></td>
    <td width="1" height="1"
bgcolor=#404040></td>
    <td width="1" height="1"
bgcolor=#2e2e2e></td>
    <td width="1" height="1"
bgcolor=#0f0f0f></td>
    <td width="1" height="1"
bgcolor=#424242></td>
    <td width="1" height="1"
bgcolor=#cacaca></td>
    <td width="1" height="1"
bgcolor=#dcdcdc></td>
    <td width="1" height="1"
bgcolor=#d8d8d8></td>
    <td width="1" height="1"
bgcolor=#e1e1e1></td>
    <td width="1" height="1"
bgcolor=#dadada></td>
    <td width="1" height="1"
bgcolor=#e0e0e0></td>
    <td width="1" height="1"
bgcolor=#e3e3e3></td>
    <td width="1" height="1"
bgcolor=#dbdbdb></td>
    <td width="1" height="1"
bgcolor=#dddddd></td>
    <td width="1" height="1"
bgcolor=#e1e1e1></td>
    <td width="1" height="1"
bgcolor=#e5e5e5></td>
    <td width="1" height="1"
bgcolor=#dfdfdf></td>
    <td width="1" height="1"
bgcolor=#dcdcdc></td>
    <td rowspan="2"
colspan="1" width="1"
height="1"
bgcolor=#e3e3e3></td>
    <td width="1" height="1"
bgcolor=#dddddd></td>
    <td rowspan="2"
colspan="1" width="1"
height="1"
bgcolor=#e0e0e0></td>
    <td rowspan="1"
colspan="3" width="1"
height="1"
bgcolor=#e0e0e0></td>
    <td width="1" height="1"
bgcolor=#e1e1e1></td>
    <td rowspan="1"
colspan="2" width="1"
height="1"
bgcolor=#e3e3e3></td>
    <td width="1" height="1"
bgcolor=#e2e2e2></td>
    <td width="1" height="1"
bgcolor=#dfdfdf></td>
    <td rowspan="2"
colspan="1" width="1"
height="1"
bgcolor=#e0e0e0></td>
    <td rowspan="2"
colspan="1" width="1"
```

```
height="1"
bgcolor=#e1e1e1></td>
    <td width="1" height="1"
bgcolor=#e0e0e0></td>
    <td rowspan="2"
colspan="1" width="1"
height="1"
bgcolor=#e2e2e2></td>
    <td rowspan="3"
colspan="1" width="1"
height="1"
bgcolor=#dfdfdf></td>
    <td rowspan="1"
colspan="2" width="1"
height="1"
bgcolor=#e3e3e3></td>
    <td rowspan="1"
colspan="2" width="1"
height="1"
bgcolor=#dbdbdb></td>
    <td rowspan="2"
colspan="1" width="1"
height="1"
bgcolor=#dcdcdc></td>
    <td width="1" height="1"
bgcolor=#dedede></td>
    <td width="1" height="1"
bgcolor=#d3d3d3></td>
    <td width="1" height="1"
bgcolor=#7b7b7b></td>
    <td width="1" height="1"
bgcolor=#4b4b4b></td>
    <td width="1" height="1"
bgcolor=#5b5b5b></td>
    <td width="1" height="1"
bgcolor=#4c4c4c></td>
    <td width="1" height="1"
bgcolor=#1e1e1e></td>
    <td width="1" height="1"
bgcolor=#0a0a0a></td>
    <td width="1" height="1"
bgcolor=#111111></td>
    <td width="1" height="1"
bgcolor=#222222></td>
    <td width="1" height="1"
bgcolor=#4a4a4a></td>
    <td width="1" height="1"
bgcolor=#2c2c2c></td>
    <td width="1" height="1"
bgcolor=#404040></td>
    <td width="1" height="1"
bgcolor=#4e4e4e></td>
    <td width="1" height="1"
bgcolor=#606060></td>
    <td width="1" height="1"
bgcolor=#7e7e7e></td>
    <td width="1" height="1"
bgcolor=#8e8e8e></td>
  </tr>
  <tr>
    <td width="1" height="1"
bgcolor=#bfbfbf></td>
    <td width="1" height="1"
bgcolor=#c4c4c4></td>
    <td width="1" height="1"
bgcolor=#c2c2c2></td>
    <td width="1" height="1"
bgcolor=#9e9e9e></td>
    <td width="1" height="1"
bgcolor=#bababa></td>
    <td width="1" height="1"
bgcolor=#c4c4c4></td>
    <td width="1" height="1"
bgcolor=#9e9e9e></td>
    <td width="1" height="1"
bgcolor=#686868></td>
    <td width="1" height="1"
bgcolor=#6f6f6f></td>
    <td width="1" height="1"
bgcolor=#5f5f5f></td>
    <td width="1" height="1"
bgcolor=#232323></td>
    <td width="1" height="1"
bgcolor=#323232></td>
    <td width="1" height="1"
bgcolor=#2c2c2c></td>
    <td width="1" height="1"
bgcolor=#4a4a4a></td>
    <td width="1" height="1"
bgcolor=#d1d1d1></td>
    <td width="1" height="1"
bgcolor=#d8d8d8></td>
    <td width="1" height="1"
bgcolor=#b3b3b3></td>
    <td width="1" height="1"
bgcolor=#dcdcdc></td>
    <td width="1" height="1"
bgcolor=#e0e0e0></td>
    <td rowspan="2"
colspan="1" width="1"
height="1"
bgcolor=#dbdbdb></td>
    <td width="1" height="1"
bgcolor=#dedede></td>
    <td width="1" height="1"
bgcolor=#e4e4e4></td>
    <td width="1" height="1"
bgcolor=#dedede></td>
    <td width="1" height="1"
bgcolor=#d0d0d0></td>
    <td width="1" height="1"
bgcolor=#d6d6d6></td>
    <td width="1" height="1"
bgcolor=#e3e3e3></td>
    <td width="1" height="1"
bgcolor=#e2e2e2></td>
    <td width="1" height="1"
bgcolor=#dedede></td>
    <td rowspan="1"
colspan="3" width="1"
height="1"
bgcolor=#dddddd></td>
    <td rowspan="1"
colspan="2" width="1"
height="1"
bgcolor=#dedede></td>
    <td rowspan="1"
colspan="4" width="1"
height="1"
bgcolor=#dfdfdf></td>
    <td rowspan="2"
colspan="1" width="1"
height="1"
bgcolor=#dedede></td>
    <td width="1" height="1"
bgcolor=#e0e0e0></td>
    <td width="1" height="1"
bgcolor=#dfdfdf></td>
    <td width="1" height="1"
bgcolor=#e0e0e0></td>
    <td rowspan="2"
colspan="1" width="1"
height="1"
bgcolor=#e5e5e5></td>
    <td width="1" height="1"
bgcolor=#dcdcdc></td>
    <td width="1" height="1"
bgcolor=#dddddd></td>
    <td width="1" height="1"
bgcolor=#e0e0e0></td>
    <td width="1" height="1"
bgcolor=#dedede></td>
    <td rowspan="2"
colspan="1" width="1"
height="1"
bgcolor=#dcdcdc></td>
    <td width="1" height="1"
bgcolor=#dcdcdc></td>
    <td width="1" height="1"
bgcolor=#b0b0b0></td>
    <td width="1" height="1"
bgcolor=#8f8f8f></td>
    <td width="1" height="1"
bgcolor=#888888></td>
    <td width="1" height="1"
bgcolor=#6e6e6e></td>
    <td width="1" height="1"
bgcolor=#2d2d2d></td>
    <td width="1" height="1"
bgcolor=#111111></td>
    <td width="1" height="1"
bgcolor=#151515></td>
    <td width="1" height="1"
bgcolor=#1e1e1e></td>
```

```
    <td width="1" height="1" bgcolor=#414141></td>
    <td width="1" height="1" bgcolor=#3d3d3d></td>
    <td width="1" height="1" bgcolor=#3a3a3a></td>
    <td width="1" height="1" bgcolor=#616161></td>
    <td width="1" height="1" bgcolor=#858585></td>
    <td width="1" height="1" bgcolor=#bdbdbd></td>
    <td width="1" height="1" bgcolor=#b7b7b7></td>
  </tr>
  <tr>
    <td width="1" height="1" bgcolor=#c5c5c5></td>
    <td width="1" height="1" bgcolor=#b5b5b5></td>
    <td width="1" height="1" bgcolor=#c0c0c0></td>
    <td width="1" height="1" bgcolor=#a8a8a8></td>
    <td width="1" height="1" bgcolor=#b6b6b6></td>
    <td width="1" height="1" bgcolor=#c8c8c8></td>
    <td width="1" height="1" bgcolor=#b4b4b4></td>
    <td width="1" height="1" bgcolor=#8f8f8f></td>
    <td width="1" height="1" bgcolor=#525252></td>
    <td width="1" height="1" bgcolor=#939393></td>
    <td width="1" height="1" bgcolor=#868686></td>
    <td width="1" height="1" bgcolor=#2a2a2a></td>
    <td width="1" height="1" bgcolor=#3a3a3a></td>
    <td width="1" height="1" bgcolor=#404040></td>
    <td width="1" height="1" bgcolor=#6a6a6a></td>
    <td rowspan="1" colspan="2" width="1" height="1" bgcolor=#d2d2d2></td>
    <td width="1" height="1" bgcolor=#bebebe></td>
    <td width="1" height="1" bgcolor=#dfdfdf></td>
    <td width="1" height="1" bgcolor=#d8d8d8></td>
    <td width="1" height="1" bgcolor=#e7e7e7></td>
    <td width="1" height="1" bgcolor=#c7c7c7></td>
    <td width="1" height="1" bgcolor=#929292></td>
    <td width="1" height="1" bgcolor=#767676></td>
    <td width="1" height="1" bgcolor=#848484></td>
    <td width="1" height="1" bgcolor=#aaaaaa></td>
    <td width="1" height="1" bgcolor=#b7b7b7></td>
    <td width="1" height="1" bgcolor=#d7d7d7></td>
    <td width="1" height="1" bgcolor=#e5e5e5></td>
    <td width="1" height="1" bgcolor=#dbdbdb></td>
    <td width="1" height="1" bgcolor=#e1e1e1></td>
    <td rowspan="1" colspan="5" width="1" height="1" bgcolor=#dddddd></td>
    <td rowspan="1" colspan="3" width="1" height="1" bgcolor=#dcdcdc></td>
    <td rowspan="1" colspan="3" width="1" height="1" bgcolor=#dddddd></td>
    <td width="1" height="1" bgcolor=#dedede></td>
    <td width="1" height="1" bgcolor=#dddddd></td>
    <td width="1" height="1" bgcolor=#dedede></td>
    <td width="1" height="1" bgcolor=#dfdfdf></td>
    <td rowspan="1" colspan="2" width="1" height="1" bgcolor=#dedede></td>
    <td rowspan="3" colspan="1" width="1" height="1" bgcolor=#dcdcdc></td>
    <td width="1" height="1" bgcolor=#dadada></td>
    <td width="1" height="1" bgcolor=#d8d8d8></td>
    <td width="1" height="1" bgcolor=#dddddd></td>
    <td width="1" height="1" bgcolor=#d3d3d3></td>
    <td width="1" height="1" bgcolor=#cbcbcb></td>
    <td width="1" height="1" bgcolor=#838383></td>
    <td width="1" height="1" bgcolor=#4b4b4b></td>
    <td width="1" height="1" bgcolor=#222222></td>
    <td width="1" height="1" bgcolor=#161616></td>
    <td width="1" height="1" bgcolor=#131313></td>
    <td width="1" height="1" bgcolor=#1d1d1d></td>
    <td width="1" height="1" bgcolor=#363636></td>
    <td width="1" height="1" bgcolor=#2f2f2f></td>
    <td width="1" height="1" bgcolor=#1e1e1e></td>
    <td width="1" height="1" bgcolor=#464646></td>
    <td width="1" height="1" bgcolor=#666666></td>
    <td width="1" height="1" bgcolor=#a1a1a1></td>
    <td width="1" height="1" bgcolor=#b2b2b2></td>
  </tr>
  <tr>
    <td width="1" height="1" bgcolor=#c3c3c3></td>
    <td width="1" height="1" bgcolor=#a0a0a0></td>
    <td width="1" height="1" bgcolor=#adadad></td>
    <td width="1" height="1" bgcolor=#9d9d9d></td>
    <td width="1" height="1" bgcolor=#8c8c8c></td>
    <td width="1" height="1" bgcolor=#c3c3c3></td>
    <td width="1" height="1" bgcolor=#bebebe></td>
    <td width="1" height="1" bgcolor=#a1a1a1></td>
    <td width="1" height="1" bgcolor=#6b6b6b></td>
    <td width="1" height="1" bgcolor=#aaaaaa></td>
    <td width="1" height="1" bgcolor=#939393></td>
    <td width="1" height="1" bgcolor=#2f2f2f></td>
    <td width="1" height="1" bgcolor=#474747></td>
    <td width="1" height="1" bgcolor=#464646></td>
    <td width="1" height="1" bgcolor=#6c6c6c></td>
```

```
    <td width="1" height="1" bgcolor=#d1d1d1></td>
    <td width="1" height="1" bgcolor=#dbdbdb></td>
    <td rowspan="2" colspan="1" width="1" height="1" bgcolor=#cecece></td>
    <td width="1" height="1" bgcolor=#d8d8d8></td>
    <td width="1" height="1" bgcolor=#d5d5d5></td>
    <td width="1" height="1" bgcolor=#e1e1e1></td>
    <td width="1" height="1" bgcolor=#d4d4d4></td>
    <td width="1" height="1" bgcolor=#7f7f7f></td>
    <td width="1" height="1" bgcolor=#6a6a6a></td>
    <td width="1" height="1" bgcolor=#616161></td>
    <td width="1" height="1" bgcolor=#8d8d8d></td>
    <td width="1" height="1" bgcolor=#777777></td>
    <td width="1" height="1" bgcolor=#959595></td>
    <td width="1" height="1" bgcolor=#dfdfdf></td>
    <td width="1" height="1" bgcolor=#dddddd></td>
    <td width="1" height="1" bgcolor=#e1e1e1></td>
    <td width="1" height="1" bgcolor=#e0e0e0></td>
    <td rowspan="2" colspan="1" width="1" height="1" bgcolor=#dfdfdf></td>
    <td rowspan="1" colspan="2" width="1" height="1" bgcolor=#e0e0e0></td>
    <td width="1" height="1" bgcolor=#dfdfdf></td>
    <td width="1" height="1" bgcolor=#dedede></td>
    <td rowspan="1" colspan="4" width="1" height="1" bgcolor=#dddddd></td>
    <td width="1" height="1" bgcolor=#dadada></td>
    <td rowspan="1" colspan="2" width="1" height="1" bgcolor=#d9d9d9></td>
    <td rowspan="1" colspan="3" width="1" height="1" bgcolor=#dbdbdb></td>
    <td width="1" height="1" bgcolor=#dcdcdc></td>
    <td width="1" height="1" bgcolor=#dedede></td>
    <td width="1" height="1" bgcolor=#e0e0e0></td>
    <td width="1" height="1" bgcolor=#e1e1e1></td>
    <td width="1" height="1" bgcolor=#e2e2e2></td>
    <td width="1" height="1" bgcolor=#dfdfdf></td>
    <td width="1" height="1" bgcolor=#dbdbdb></td>
    <td width="1" height="1" bgcolor=#dadada></td>
    <td width="1" height="1" bgcolor=#d9d9d9></td>
    <td width="1" height="1" bgcolor=#dbdbdb></td>
    <td width="1" height="1" bgcolor=#d4d4d4></td>
    <td width="1" height="1" bgcolor=#989898></td>
    <td width="1" height="1" bgcolor=#505050></td>
    <td width="1" height="1" bgcolor=#242424></td>
    <td width="1" height="1" bgcolor=#111111></td>
    <td width="1" height="1" bgcolor=#121212></td>
    <td width="1" height="1" bgcolor=#2f2f2f></td>
    <td width="1" height="1" bgcolor=#444444></td>
    <td width="1" height="1" bgcolor=#3e3e3e></td>
    <td width="1" height="1" bgcolor=#252525></td>
    <td width="1" height="1" bgcolor=#434343></td>
    <td width="1" height="1" bgcolor=#898989></td>
    <td width="1" height="1" bgcolor=#929292></td>
    <td width="1" height="1" bgcolor=#7c7c7c></td>
  </tr>
  <tr>
    <td width="1" height="1" bgcolor=#bcbcbc></td>
    <td width="1" height="1" bgcolor=#9f9f9f></td>
    <td width="1" height="1" bgcolor=#b8b8b8></td>
    <td width="1" height="1" bgcolor=#8d8d8d></td>
    <td width="1" height="1" bgcolor=#6c6c6c></td>
    <td width="1" height="1" bgcolor=#909090></td>
    <td width="1" height="1" bgcolor=#939393></td>
    <td width="1" height="1" bgcolor=#919191></td>
    <td width="1" height="1" bgcolor=#9b9b9b></td>
    <td width="1" height="1" bgcolor=#c2c2c2></td>
    <td width="1" height="1" bgcolor=#838383></td>
    <td width="1" height="1" bgcolor=#2d2d2d></td>
    <td width="1" height="1" bgcolor=#3f3f3f></td>
    <td width="1" height="1" bgcolor=#363636></td>
    <td width="1" height="1" bgcolor=#515151></td>
    <td width="1" height="1" bgcolor=#cecece></td>
    <td width="1" height="1" bgcolor=#dadada></td>
    <td width="1" height="1" bgcolor=#d5d5d5></td>
    <td width="1" height="1" bgcolor=#dddddd></td>
    <td width="1" height="1" bgcolor=#c4c4c4></td>
    <td width="1" height="1" bgcolor=#636363></td>
    <td width="1" height="1" bgcolor=#6b6b6b></td>
    <td width="1" height="1" bgcolor=#dddddd></td>
    <td width="1" height="1" bgcolor=#aeaeae></td>
    <td width="1" height="1" bgcolor=#afafaf></td>
    <td width="1" height="1" bgcolor=#5e5e5e></td>
    <td width="1" height="1" bgcolor=#7e7e7e></td>
    <td width="1" height="1" bgcolor=#e3e3e3></td>
    <td width="1" height="1" bgcolor=#e0e0e0></td>
    <td rowspan="1" colspan="2" width="1" height="1" bgcolor=#dfdfdf></td>
```

```
    <td width="1" height="1" bgcolor=#dfdfdf></td>
    <td width="1" height="1" bgcolor=#e1e1e1></td>
    <td width="1" height="1" bgcolor=#e2e2e2></td>
    <td width="1" height="1" bgcolor=#dcdcdc></td>
    <td width="1" height="1" bgcolor=#e1e1e1></td>
    <td width="1" height="1" bgcolor=#dcdcdc></td>
    <td width="1" height="1" bgcolor=#dfdfdf></td>
    <td width="1" height="1" bgcolor=#dedede></td>
    <td width="1" height="1" bgcolor=#e1e1e1></td>
    <td width="1" height="1" bgcolor=#c9c9c9></td>
    <td width="1" height="1" bgcolor=#d3d3d3></td>
    <td width="1" height="1" bgcolor=#dcdcdc></td>
    <td width="1" height="1" bgcolor=#dbdbdb></td>
    <td width="1" height="1" bgcolor=#d9d9d9></td>
    <td width="1" height="1" bgcolor=#d7d7d7></td>
    <td width="1" height="1" bgcolor=#dbdbdb></td>
    <td width="1" height="1" bgcolor=#dcdcdc></td>
    <td width="1" height="1" bgcolor=#d8d8d8></td>
    <td width="1" height="1" bgcolor=#d9d9d9></td>
    <td width="1" height="1" bgcolor=#dadada></td>
    <td width="1" height="1" bgcolor=#dfdfdf></td>
    <td width="1" height="1" bgcolor=#dcdcdc></td>
    <td width="1" height="1" bgcolor=#d8d8d8></td>
    <td width="1" height="1" bgcolor=#d6d6d6></td>
    <td width="1" height="1" bgcolor=#c8c8c8></td>
    <td width="1" height="1" bgcolor=#6d6d6d></td>
    <td width="1" height="1" bgcolor=#4f4f4f></td>
    <td width="1" height="1" bgcolor=#2a2a2a></td>
    <td width="1" height="1" bgcolor=#121212></td>
    <td width="1" height="1" bgcolor=#080808></td>
    <td width="1" height="1" bgcolor=#252525></td>
    <td width="1" height="1" bgcolor=#4f4f4f></td>
    <td width="1" height="1" bgcolor=#404040></td>
    <td width="1" height="1" bgcolor=#2d2d2d></td>
    <td width="1" height="1" bgcolor=#5e5e5e></td>
    <td width="1" height="1" bgcolor=#888888></td>
    <td width="1" height="1" bgcolor=#919191></td>
    <td width="1" height="1" bgcolor=#828282></td>
  </tr>
  <tr>
    <td width="1" height="1" bgcolor=#acacac></td>
    <td width="1" height="1" bgcolor=#b9b9b9></td>
    <td width="1" height="1" bgcolor=#bebebe></td>
    <td width="1" height="1" bgcolor=#909090></td>
    <td width="1" height="1" bgcolor=#6a6a6a></td>
    <td width="1" height="1" bgcolor=#5e5e5e></td>
    <td width="1" height="1" bgcolor=#4b4b4b></td>
    <td width="1" height="1" bgcolor=#3e3e3e></td>
    <td width="1" height="1" bgcolor=#686868></td>
    <td width="1" height="1" bgcolor=#b7b7b7></td>
    <td width="1" height="1" bgcolor=#8d8d8d></td>
    <td rowspan="1" colspan="2" width="1" height="1" bgcolor=#383838></td>
    <td rowspan="2" colspan="1" width="1" height="1" bgcolor=#2c2c2c></td>
    <td width="1" height="1" bgcolor=#4f4f4f></td>
    <td width="1" height="1" bgcolor=#cdcdcd></td>
    <td rowspan="1" colspan="2" width="1" height="1" bgcolor=#dbdbdb></td>
    <td width="1" height="1" bgcolor=#e0e0e0></td>
    <td width="1" height="1" bgcolor=#bcbcbc></td>
    <td width="1" height="1" bgcolor=#505050></td>
    <td width="1" height="1" bgcolor=#2f2f2f></td>
    <td width="1" height="1" bgcolor=#444444></td>
    <td width="1" height="1" bgcolor=#7a7a7a></td>
    <td width="1" height="1" bgcolor=#7d7d7d></td>
    <td width="1" height="1" bgcolor=#606060></td>
    <td width="1" height="1" bgcolor=#464646></td>
    <td width="1" height="1" bgcolor=#4f4f4f></td>
    <td width="1" height="1" bgcolor=#969696></td>
    <td width="1" height="1" bgcolor=#d6d6d6></td>
    <td width="1" height="1" bgcolor=#d8d8d8></td>
    <td width="1" height="1" bgcolor=#d9d9d9></td>
    <td width="1" height="1" bgcolor=#d6d6d6></td>
    <td width="1" height="1" bgcolor=#d7d7d7></td>
    <td width="1" height="1" bgcolor=#d8d8d8></td>
    <td width="1" height="1" bgcolor=#cecece></td>
    <td width="1" height="1" bgcolor=#d8d8d8></td>
    <td width="1" height="1" bgcolor=#d3d3d3></td>
    <td width="1" height="1" bgcolor=#d1d1d1></td>
    <td width="1" height="1" bgcolor=#cccccc></td>
    <td width="1" height="1" bgcolor=#c5c5c5></td>
    <td width="1" height="1" bgcolor=#b3b3b3></td>
    <td width="1" height="1" bgcolor=#8e8e8e></td>
    <td width="1" height="1" bgcolor=#a0a0a0></td>
    <td width="1" height="1" bgcolor=#979797></td>
    <td rowspan="1" colspan="2" width="1" height="1" bgcolor=#939393></td>
```

```
    <td width="1" height="1" bgcolor=#969696></td>
    <td rowspan="1" colspan="2" width="1" height="1" bgcolor=#a9a9a9></td>
    <td width="1" height="1" bgcolor=#9b9b9b></td>
    <td width="1" height="1" bgcolor=#858585></td>
    <td width="1" height="1" bgcolor=#848484></td>
    <td width="1" height="1" bgcolor=#a0a0a0></td>
    <td width="1" height="1" bgcolor=#868686></td>
    <td width="1" height="1" bgcolor=#636363></td>
    <td width="1" height="1" bgcolor=#bbbbbb></td>
    <td width="1" height="1" bgcolor=#dcdcdc></td>
    <td rowspan="2" colspan="1" width="1" height="1" bgcolor=#cbcbcb></td>
    <td width="1" height="1" bgcolor=#9f9f9f></td>
    <td width="1" height="1" bgcolor=#797979></td>
    <td width="1" height="1" bgcolor=#323232></td>
    <td width="1" height="1" bgcolor=#161616></td>
    <td width="1" height="1" bgcolor=#151515></td>
    <td width="1" height="1" bgcolor=#141414></td>
    <td width="1" height="1" bgcolor=#3e3e3e></td>
    <td width="1" height="1" bgcolor=#3c3c3c></td>
    <td width="1" height="1" bgcolor=#303030></td>
    <td width="1" height="1" bgcolor=#737373></td>
    <td width="1" height="1" bgcolor=#7a7a7a></td>
    <td width="1" height="1" bgcolor=#878787></td>
    <td width="1" height="1" bgcolor=#8a8a8a></td>
  </tr>
  <tr>
    <td width="1" height="1" bgcolor=#b1b1b1></td>
    <td width="1" height="1" bgcolor=#b0b0b0></td>
    <td width="1" height="1" bgcolor=#bababa></td>
    <td width="1" height="1" bgcolor=#a7a7a7></td>
    <td width="1" height="1" bgcolor=#858585></td>
    <td width="1" height="1" bgcolor=#5c5c5c></td>
    <td width="1" height="1" bgcolor=#3c3c3c></td>
    <td width="1" height="1" bgcolor=#333333></td>
    <td width="1" height="1" bgcolor=#4b4b4b></td>
    <td width="1" height="1" bgcolor=#bbbbbb></td>
    <td width="1" height="1" bgcolor=#a3a3a3></td>
    <td width="1" height="1" bgcolor=#202020></td>
    <td width="1" height="1" bgcolor=#2a2a2a></td>
    <td width="1" height="1" bgcolor=#373737></td>
    <td width="1" height="1" bgcolor=#818181></td>
    <td width="1" height="1" bgcolor=#adadad></td>
    <td width="1" height="1" bgcolor=#959595></td>
    <td width="1" height="1" bgcolor=#9e9e9e></td>
    <td rowspan="2" colspan="1" width="1" height="1" bgcolor=#636363></td>
    <td width="1" height="1" bgcolor=#212121></td>
    <td width="1" height="1" bgcolor=#1b1b1b></td>
    <td width="1" height="1" bgcolor=#1a1a1a></td>
    <td width="1" height="1" bgcolor=#1b1b1b></td>
    <td width="1" height="1" bgcolor=#282828></td>
    <td width="1" height="1" bgcolor=#343434></td>
    <td width="1" height="1" bgcolor=#414141></td>
    <td width="1" height="1" bgcolor=#4e4e4e></td>
    <td width="1" height="1" bgcolor=#515151></td>
    <td width="1" height="1" bgcolor=#8c8c8c></td>
    <td width="1" height="1" bgcolor=#c7c7c7></td>
    <td width="1" height="1" bgcolor=#bbbbbb></td>
    <td width="1" height="1" bgcolor=#c1c1c1></td>
    <td width="1" height="1" bgcolor=#c4c4c4></td>
    <td width="1" height="1" bgcolor=#c6c6c6></td>
    <td rowspan="1" colspan="2" width="1" height="1" bgcolor=#cbcbcb></td>
    <td width="1" height="1" bgcolor=#c5c5c5></td>
    <td width="1" height="1" bgcolor=#cbcbcb></td>
    <td width="1" height="1" bgcolor=#c7c7c7></td>
    <td width="1" height="1" bgcolor=#c4c4c4></td>
    <td width="1" height="1" bgcolor=#959595></td>
    <td rowspan="1" colspan="2" width="1" height="1" bgcolor=#4e4e4e></td>
    <td width="1" height="1" bgcolor=#474747></td>
    <td width="1" height="1" bgcolor=#5a5a5a></td>
    <td width="1" height="1" bgcolor=#6d6d6d></td>
    <td width="1" height="1" bgcolor=#717171></td>
    <td width="1" height="1" bgcolor=#858585></td>
    <td width="1" height="1" bgcolor=#838383></td>
    <td width="1" height="1" bgcolor=#9f9f9f></td>
    <td width="1" height="1" bgcolor=#999999></td>
    <td width="1" height="1" bgcolor=#858585></td>
    <td rowspan="1" colspan="2" width="1" height="1" bgcolor=#979797></td>
    <td width="1" height="1" bgcolor=#464646></td>
    <td width="1" height="1" bgcolor=#a0a0a0></td>
    <td width="1" height="1" bgcolor=#d8d8d8></td>
    <td width="1" height="1" bgcolor=#c5c5c5></td>
    <td width="1" height="1" bgcolor=#c0c0c0></td>
```

```
    <td width="1" height="1"
bgcolor=#6b6b6b></td>
    <td width="1" height="1"
bgcolor=#111111></td>
    <td rowspan="1"
colspan="2" width="1"
height="1"
bgcolor=#1c1c1c></td>
    <td width="1" height="1"
bgcolor=#303030></td>
    <td width="1" height="1"
bgcolor=#2e2e2e></td>
    <td width="1" height="1"
bgcolor=#363636></td>
    <td width="1" height="1"
bgcolor=#7e7e7e></td>
    <td width="1" height="1"
bgcolor=#757575></td>
    <td width="1" height="1"
bgcolor=#818181></td>
    <td width="1" height="1"
bgcolor=#909090></td>
  </tr>
  <tr>
    <td width="1" height="1"
bgcolor=#aeaeae></td>
    <td width="1" height="1"
bgcolor=#9b9b9b></td>
    <td width="1" height="1"
bgcolor=#8b8b8b></td>
    <td width="1" height="1"
bgcolor=#878787></td>
    <td width="1" height="1"
bgcolor=#808080></td>
    <td width="1" height="1"
bgcolor=#636363></td>
    <td width="1" height="1"
bgcolor=#5a5a5a></td>
    <td width="1" height="1"
bgcolor=#5b5b5b></td>
    <td width="1" height="1"
bgcolor=#5c5c5c></td>
    <td width="1" height="1"
bgcolor=#969696></td>
    <td width="1" height="1"
bgcolor=#a8a8a8></td>
    <td width="1" height="1"
bgcolor=#7e7e7e></td>
    <td width="1" height="1"
bgcolor=#848484></td>
    <td width="1" height="1"
bgcolor=#939393></td>
    <td width="1" height="1"
bgcolor=#999999></td>
    <td width="1" height="1"
bgcolor=#bfbfbf></td>
    <td width="1" height="1"
bgcolor=#cecece></td>
    <td width="1" height="1"
bgcolor=#bfbfbf></td>
    <td width="1" height="1"
bgcolor=#d5d5d5></td>
    <td width="1" height="1"
bgcolor=#1d1d1d></td>
    <td width="1" height="1"
bgcolor=#232323></td>
    <td width="1" height="1"
bgcolor=#212121></td>
    <td rowspan="1"
colspan="2" width="1"
height="1"
bgcolor=#292929></td>
    <td width="1" height="1"
bgcolor=#1e1e1e></td>
    <td width="1" height="1"
bgcolor=#303030></td>
    <td width="1" height="1"
bgcolor=#383838></td>
    <td width="1" height="1"
bgcolor=#303030></td>
    <td width="1" height="1"
bgcolor=#454545></td>
    <td width="1" height="1"
bgcolor=#b1b1b1></td>
    <td width="1" height="1"
bgcolor=#c5c5c5></td>
    <td width="1" height="1"
bgcolor=#c4c4c4></td>
    <td width="1" height="1"
bgcolor=#c8c8c8></td>
    <td width="1" height="1"
bgcolor=#cfcfcf></td>
    <td width="1" height="1"
bgcolor=#c3c3c3></td>
    <td width="1" height="1"
bgcolor=#b1b1b1></td>
    <td width="1" height="1"
bgcolor=#a8a8a8></td>
    <td width="1" height="1"
bgcolor=#9d9d9d></td>
    <td width="1" height="1"
bgcolor=#a9a9a9></td>
    <td width="1" height="1"
bgcolor=#b9b9b9></td>
    <td width="1" height="1"
bgcolor=#b8b8b8></td>
    <td width="1" height="1"
bgcolor=#7d7d7d></td>
    <td width="1" height="1"
bgcolor=#7b7b7b></td>
    <td width="1" height="1"
bgcolor=#464646></td>
    <td width="1" height="1"
bgcolor=#676767></td>
    <td width="1" height="1"
bgcolor=#7b7b7b></td>
    <td width="1" height="1"
bgcolor=#939393></td>
    <td width="1" height="1"
bgcolor=#a0a0a0></td>
    <td width="1" height="1"
bgcolor=#6a6a6a></td>
    <td width="1" height="1"
bgcolor=#8e8e8e></td>
    <td width="1" height="1"
bgcolor=#bebebe></td>
    <td width="1" height="1"
bgcolor=#a8a8a8></td>
    <td width="1" height="1"
bgcolor=#959595></td>
    <td rowspan="2"
colspan="1" width="1"
height="1"
bgcolor=#bdbdbd></td>
    <td width="1" height="1"
bgcolor=#8a8a8a></td>
    <td width="1" height="1"
bgcolor=#a9a9a9></td>
    <td width="1" height="1"
bgcolor=#cecece></td>
    <td width="1" height="1"
bgcolor=#d0d0d0></td>
    <td rowspan="1"
colspan="2" width="1"
height="1"
bgcolor=#cfcfcf></td>
    <td width="1" height="1"
bgcolor=#8f8f8f></td>
    <td width="1" height="1"
bgcolor=#151515></td>
    <td width="1" height="1"
bgcolor=#111111></td>
    <td width="1" height="1"
bgcolor=#1b1b1b></td>
    <td width="1" height="1"
bgcolor=#343434></td>
    <td width="1" height="1"
bgcolor=#3d3d3d></td>
    <td width="1" height="1"
bgcolor=#414141></td>
    <td width="1" height="1"
bgcolor=#565656></td>
    <td width="1" height="1"
bgcolor=#606060></td>
    <td width="1" height="1"
bgcolor=#7c7c7c></td>
    <td width="1" height="1"
bgcolor=#979797></td>
  </tr>
  <tr>
    <td width="1" height="1"
bgcolor=#c2c2c2></td>
    <td rowspan="2"
colspan="1" width="1"
```

```
height="1"
bgcolor=#c1c1c1></td>
    <td width="1" height="1"
bgcolor=#c6c6c6></td>
    <td width="1" height="1"
bgcolor=#c4c4c4></td>
    <td width="1" height="1"
bgcolor=#c1c1c1></td>
    <td width="1" height="1"
bgcolor=#c5c5c5></td>
    <td width="1" height="1"
bgcolor=#d7d7d7></td>
    <td width="1" height="1"
bgcolor=#c7c7c7></td>
    <td width="1" height="1"
bgcolor=#a1a1a1></td>
    <td width="1" height="1"
bgcolor=#ababab></td>
    <td width="1" height="1"
bgcolor=#939393></td>
    <td width="1" height="1"
bgcolor=#4f4f4f></td>
    <td width="1" height="1"
bgcolor=#636363></td>
    <td width="1" height="1"
bgcolor=#656565></td>
    <td width="1" height="1"
bgcolor=#818181></td>
    <td width="1" height="1"
bgcolor=#c7c7c7></td>
    <td width="1" height="1"
bgcolor=#d7d7d7></td>
    <td width="1" height="1"
bgcolor=#d9d9d9></td>
    <td width="1" height="1"
bgcolor=#d8d8d8></td>
    <td width="1" height="1"
bgcolor=#757575></td>
    <td width="1" height="1"
bgcolor=#1c1c1c></td>
    <td width="1" height="1"
bgcolor=#242424></td>
    <td width="1" height="1"
bgcolor=#1c1c1c></td>
    <td width="1" height="1"
bgcolor=#1d1d1d></td>
    <td width="1" height="1"
bgcolor=#222222></td>
    <td width="1" height="1"
bgcolor=#0c0c0c></td>
    <td rowspan="1"
colspan="2" width="1"
height="1"
bgcolor=#1f1f1f></td>
    <td width="1" height="1"
bgcolor=#1e1e1e></td>
    <td width="1" height="1"
bgcolor=#121212></td>
    <td width="1" height="1"
bgcolor=#919191></td>
    <td width="1" height="1"
bgcolor=#d5d5d5></td>
    <td width="1" height="1"
bgcolor=#bdbdbd></td>
    <td width="1" height="1"
bgcolor=#c5c5c5></td>
    <td width="1" height="1"
bgcolor=#d6d6d6></td>
    <td width="1" height="1"
bgcolor=#cccccc></td>
    <td width="1" height="1"
bgcolor=#b6b6b6></td>
    <td width="1" height="1"
bgcolor=#979797></td>
    <td width="1" height="1"
bgcolor=#8a8a8a></td>
    <td width="1" height="1"
bgcolor=#757575></td>
    <td width="1" height="1"
bgcolor=#7b7b7b></td>
    <td width="1" height="1"
bgcolor=#949494></td>
    <td width="1" height="1"
bgcolor=#acacac></td>
    <td width="1" height="1"
bgcolor=#c9c9c9></td>
    <td width="1" height="1"
bgcolor=#b0b0b0></td>
    <td width="1" height="1"
bgcolor=#a2a2a2></td>
    <td width="1" height="1"
bgcolor=#999999></td>
    <td width="1" height="1"
bgcolor=#898989></td>
    <td width="1" height="1"
bgcolor=#9c9c9c></td>
    <td width="1" height="1"
bgcolor=#8a8a8a></td>
    <td width="1" height="1"
bgcolor=#939393></td>
    <td width="1" height="1"
bgcolor=#b4b4b4></td>
    <td width="1" height="1"
bgcolor=#b0b0b0></td>
    <td width="1" height="1"
bgcolor=#a8a8a8></td>
    <td width="1" height="1"
bgcolor=#aeaeae></td>
    <td width="1" height="1"
bgcolor=#b3b3b3></td>
    <td width="1" height="1"
bgcolor=#d1d1d1></td>
    <td width="1" height="1"
bgcolor=#cfcfcf></td>
    <td width="1" height="1"
bgcolor=#cdcdcd></td>
    <td width="1" height="1"
bgcolor=#cecece></td>
    <td width="1" height="1"
bgcolor=#999999></td>
    <td width="1" height="1"
bgcolor=#282828></td>
    <td width="1" height="1"
bgcolor=#080808></td>
    <td width="1" height="1"
bgcolor=#0b0b0b></td>
    <td width="1" height="1"
bgcolor=#181818></td>
    <td width="1" height="1"
bgcolor=#323232></td>
    <td width="1" height="1"
bgcolor=#434343></td>
    <td width="1" height="1"
bgcolor=#3a3a3a></td>
    <td rowspan="1"
colspan="2" width="1"
height="1"
bgcolor=#373737></td>
    <td width="1" height="1"
bgcolor=#414141></td>
  </tr>
  <tr>
    <td width="1" height="1"
bgcolor=#d5d5d5></td>
    <td width="1" height="1"
bgcolor=#cecece></td>
    <td width="1" height="1"
bgcolor=#c5c5c5></td>
    <td width="1" height="1"
bgcolor=#adadad></td>
    <td width="1" height="1"
bgcolor=#969696></td>
    <td width="1" height="1"
bgcolor=#7d7d7d></td>
    <td width="1" height="1"
bgcolor=#4c4c4c></td>
    <td width="1" height="1"
bgcolor=#595959></td>
    <td width="1" height="1"
bgcolor=#c7c7c7></td>
    <td width="1" height="1"
bgcolor=#8e8e8e></td>
    <td width="1" height="1"
bgcolor=#262626></td>
    <td width="1" height="1"
bgcolor=#292929></td>
    <td width="1" height="1"
bgcolor=#333333></td>
    <td width="1" height="1"
bgcolor=#5d5d5d></td>
    <td width="1" height="1"
bgcolor=#c3c3c3></td>
    <td width="1" height="1"
bgcolor=#d4d4d4></td>
```

```
<td width="1" height="1"
bgcolor=#bababa></td>
<td width="1" height="1"
bgcolor=#d5d5d5></td>
<td width="1" height="1"
bgcolor=#646464></td>
<td width="1" height="1"
bgcolor=#171717></td>
<td width="1" height="1"
bgcolor=#252525></td>
<td width="1" height="1"
bgcolor=#222222></td>
<td width="1" height="1"
bgcolor=#181818></td>
<td width="1" height="1"
bgcolor=#1d1d1d></td>
<td width="1" height="1"
bgcolor=#1c1c1c></td>
<td width="1" height="1"
bgcolor=#1a1a1a></td>
<td width="1" height="1"
bgcolor=#242424></td>
<td width="1" height="1"
bgcolor=#1b1b1b></td>
<td width="1" height="1"
bgcolor=#0c0c0c></td>
<td width="1" height="1"
bgcolor=#474747></td>
<td width="1" height="1"
bgcolor=#8c8c8c></td>
<td width="1" height="1"
bgcolor=#8d8d8d></td>
<td width="1" height="1"
bgcolor=#adadad></td>
<td width="1" height="1"
bgcolor=#d0d0d0></td>
<td rowspan="2"
colspan="1" width="1"
height="1"
bgcolor=#dddddd></td>
<td width="1" height="1"
bgcolor=#b8b8b8></td>
<td width="1" height="1"
bgcolor=#8b8b8b></td>
<td width="1" height="1"
bgcolor=#747474></td>
<td width="1" height="1"
bgcolor=#737373></td>
<td rowspan="1"
colspan="2" width="1"
height="1"
bgcolor=#797979></td>
<td width="1" height="1"
bgcolor=#a0a0a0></td>
<td width="1" height="1"
bgcolor=#c8c8c8></td>
<td width="1" height="1"
bgcolor=#c2c2c2></td>
<td width="1" height="1"
bgcolor=#b9b9b9></td>
<td width="1" height="1"
bgcolor=#c6c6c6></td>
<td width="1" height="1"
bgcolor=#c7c7c7></td>
<td width="1" height="1"
bgcolor=#bebebe></td>
<td rowspan="1"
colspan="2" width="1"
height="1"
bgcolor=#aeaeae></td>
<td width="1" height="1"
bgcolor=#acacac></td>
<td width="1" height="1"
bgcolor=#626262></td>
<td width="1" height="1"
bgcolor=#212121></td>
<td width="1" height="1"
bgcolor=#4e4e4e></td>
<td width="1" height="1"
bgcolor=#7a7a7a></td>
<td width="1" height="1"
bgcolor=#acacac></td>
<td width="1" height="1"
bgcolor=#d7d7d7></td>
<td rowspan="2"
colspan="1" width="1"
height="1"
bgcolor=#d3d3d3></td>
<td width="1" height="1"
bgcolor=#d0d0d0></td>
<td width="1" height="1"
bgcolor=#d7d7d7></td>
<td width="1" height="1"
bgcolor=#a3a3a3></td>
<td width="1" height="1"
bgcolor=#323232></td>
<td width="1" height="1"
bgcolor=#070707></td>
<td width="1" height="1"
bgcolor=#0a0a0a></td>
<td width="1" height="1"
bgcolor=#0f0f0f></td>
<td width="1" height="1"
bgcolor=#2f2f2f></td>
<td width="1" height="1"
bgcolor=#373737></td>
<td width="1" height="1"
bgcolor=#313131></td>
<td width="1" height="1"
bgcolor=#212121></td>
<td width="1" height="1"
bgcolor=#232323></td>
<td width="1" height="1"
bgcolor=#2a2a2a></td>
</tr>
<tr>
<td width="1" height="1"
bgcolor=#bdbdbd></td>
<td width="1" height="1"
bgcolor=#a1a1a1></td>
<td width="1" height="1"
bgcolor=#cccccc></td>
<td width="1" height="1"
bgcolor=#a4a4a4></td>
<td width="1" height="1"
bgcolor=#9a9a9a></td>
<td width="1" height="1"
bgcolor=#8c8c8c></td>
<td width="1" height="1"
bgcolor=#4c4c4c></td>
<td width="1" height="1"
bgcolor=#636363></td>
<td width="1" height="1"
bgcolor=#777777></td>
<td width="1" height="1"
bgcolor=#bebebe></td>
<td width="1" height="1"
bgcolor=#9c9c9c></td>
<td rowspan="2"
colspan="1" width="1"
height="1"
bgcolor=#303030></td>
<td width="1" height="1"
bgcolor=#343434></td>
<td width="1" height="1"
bgcolor=#3c3c3c></td>
<td width="1" height="1"
bgcolor=#494949></td>
<td width="1" height="1"
bgcolor=#b4b4b4></td>
<td width="1" height="1"
bgcolor=#cdcdcd></td>
<td width="1" height="1"
bgcolor=#858585></td>
<td width="1" height="1"
bgcolor=#d8d8d8></td>
<td width="1" height="1"
bgcolor=#585858></td>
<td width="1" height="1"
bgcolor=#111111></td>
<td width="1" height="1"
bgcolor=#171717></td>
<td width="1" height="1"
bgcolor=#1a1a1a></td>
<td width="1" height="1"
bgcolor=#252525></td>
<td width="1" height="1"
bgcolor=#3e3e3e></td>
<td rowspan="1"
colspan="2" width="1"
height="1"
bgcolor=#b5b5b5></td>
<td width="1" height="1"
bgcolor=#bababa></td>
```

```
    <td width="1" height="1" bgcolor=#afafaf></td>
    <td width="1" height="1" bgcolor=#929292></td>
    <td width="1" height="1" bgcolor=#a2a2a2></td>
    <td width="1" height="1" bgcolor=#aeaeae></td>
    <td width="1" height="1" bgcolor=#cacaca></td>
    <td width="1" height="1" bgcolor=#d7d7d7></td>
    <td width="1" height="1" bgcolor=#e1e1e1></td>
    <td rowspan="2" colspan="1" width="1" height="1" bgcolor=#c1c1c1></td>
    <td width="1" height="1" bgcolor=#a7a7a7></td>
    <td width="1" height="1" bgcolor=#646464></td>
    <td width="1" height="1" bgcolor=#838383></td>
    <td width="1" height="1" bgcolor=#ababab></td>
    <td width="1" height="1" bgcolor=#9f9f9f></td>
    <td width="1" height="1" bgcolor=#b9b9b9></td>
    <td width="1" height="1" bgcolor=#b7b7b7></td>
    <td width="1" height="1" bgcolor=#bababa></td>
    <td width="1" height="1" bgcolor=#afafaf></td>
    <td width="1" height="1" bgcolor=#cccccc></td>
    <td width="1" height="1" bgcolor=#d9d9d9></td>
    <td width="1" height="1" bgcolor=#d0d0d0></td>
    <td width="1" height="1" bgcolor=#cbcbcb></td>
    <td width="1" height="1" bgcolor=#adadad></td>
    <td width="1" height="1" bgcolor=#898989></td>
    <td width="1" height="1" bgcolor=#545454></td>
    <td rowspan="2" colspan="1" width="1" height="1" bgcolor=#080808></td>
    <td width="1" height="1" bgcolor=#070707></td>
    <td width="1" height="1" bgcolor=#171717></td>
    <td width="1" height="1" bgcolor=#858585></td>
    <td width="1" height="1" bgcolor=#c6c6c6></td>
    <td width="1" height="1" bgcolor=#d4d4d4></td>
    <td width="1" height="1" bgcolor=#d0d0d0></td>
    <td rowspan="2" colspan="1" width="1" height="1" bgcolor=#a5a5a5></td>
    <td width="1" height="1" bgcolor=#393939></td>
    <td width="1" height="1" bgcolor=#161616></td>
    <td width="1" height="1" bgcolor=#0d0d0d></td>
    <td width="1" height="1" bgcolor=#1e1e1e></td>
    <td width="1" height="1" bgcolor=#353535></td>
    <td width="1" height="1" bgcolor=#282828></td>
    <td width="1" height="1" bgcolor=#333333></td>
    <td width="1" height="1" bgcolor=#313131></td>
    <td width="1" height="1" bgcolor=#464646></td>
    <td width="1" height="1" bgcolor=#404040></td>
  </tr>
  <tr>
    <td width="1" height="1" bgcolor=#aeaeae></td>
    <td width="1" height="1" bgcolor=#b1b1b1></td>
    <td width="1" height="1" bgcolor=#ababab></td>
    <td width="1" height="1" bgcolor=#878787></td>
    <td width="1" height="1" bgcolor=#848484></td>
    <td width="1" height="1" bgcolor=#6b6b6b></td>
    <td width="1" height="1" bgcolor=#525252></td>
    <td width="1" height="1" bgcolor=#585858></td>
    <td width="1" height="1" bgcolor=#757575></td>
    <td width="1" height="1" bgcolor=#c5c5c5></td>
    <td width="1" height="1" bgcolor=#727272></td>
    <td width="1" height="1" bgcolor=#505050></td>
    <td width="1" height="1" bgcolor=#2c2c2c></td>
    <td width="1" height="1" bgcolor=#1d1d1d></td>
    <td width="1" height="1" bgcolor=#898989></td>
    <td width="1" height="1" bgcolor=#adadad></td>
    <td width="1" height="1" bgcolor=#a5a5a5></td>
    <td width="1" height="1" bgcolor=#c9c9c9></td>
    <td width="1" height="1" bgcolor=#5d5d5d></td>
    <td rowspan="1" colspan="2" width="1" height="1" bgcolor=#1b1b1b></td>
    <td width="1" height="1" bgcolor=#212121></td>
    <td width="1" height="1" bgcolor=#1f1f1f></td>
    <td width="1" height="1" bgcolor=#2d2d2d></td>
    <td width="1" height="1" bgcolor=#7d7d7d></td>
    <td width="1" height="1" bgcolor=#818181></td>
    <td width="1" height="1" bgcolor=#878787></td>
    <td width="1" height="1" bgcolor=#e0e0e0></td>
    <td rowspan="2" colspan="1" width="1" height="1" bgcolor=#c9c9c9></td>
    <td width="1" height="1" bgcolor=#c3c3c3></td>
    <td width="1" height="1" bgcolor=#d4d4d4></td>
    <td width="1" height="1" bgcolor=#dbdbdb></td>
    <td width="1" height="1" bgcolor=#dcdcdc></td>
    <td width="1" height="1" bgcolor=#dedede></td>
    <td width="1" height="1" bgcolor=#dbdbdb></td>
    <td width="1" height="1" bgcolor=#c2c2c2></td>
    <td width="1" height="1" bgcolor=#b2b2b2></td>
    <td width="1" height="1" bgcolor=#b5b5b5></td>
    <td width="1" height="1" bgcolor=#c3c3c3></td>
    <td width="1" height="1" bgcolor=#cfcfcf></td>
```

```
    <td width="1" height="1"
bgcolor=#d4d4d4></td>
    <td width="1" height="1"
bgcolor=#c6c6c6></td>
    <td width="1" height="1"
bgcolor=#c9c9c9></td>
    <td width="1" height="1"
bgcolor=#d4d4d4></td>
    <td width="1" height="1"
bgcolor=#d1d1d1></td>
    <td width="1" height="1"
bgcolor=#d4d4d4></td>
    <td width="1" height="1"
bgcolor=#c3c3c3></td>
    <td width="1" height="1"
bgcolor=#888888></td>
    <td width="1" height="1"
bgcolor=#444444></td>
    <td width="1" height="1"
bgcolor=#161616></td>
    <td width="1" height="1"
bgcolor=#000000></td>
    <td width="1" height="1"
bgcolor=#030303></td>
    <td width="1" height="1"
bgcolor=#0a0a0a></td>
    <td width="1" height="1"
bgcolor=#5e5e5e></td>
    <td width="1" height="1"
bgcolor=#c7c7c7></td>
    <td width="1" height="1"
bgcolor=#c9c9c9></td>
    <td width="1" height="1"
bgcolor=#cecece></td>
    <td width="1" height="1"
bgcolor=#d4d4d4></td>
    <td width="1" height="1"
bgcolor=#323232></td>
    <td width="1" height="1"
bgcolor=#1b1b1b></td>
    <td width="1" height="1"
bgcolor=#111111></td>
    <td width="1" height="1"
bgcolor=#222222></td>
    <td rowspan="1"
colspan="2" width="1"
height="1"
bgcolor=#383838></td>
    <td width="1" height="1"
bgcolor=#444444></td>
    <td width="1" height="1"
bgcolor=#3b3b3b></td>
    <td width="1" height="1"
bgcolor=#595959></td>
    <td width="1" height="1"
bgcolor=#555555></td>
  </tr>
  <tr>
    <td width="1" height="1"
bgcolor=#bbbbbb></td>
    <td width="1" height="1"
bgcolor=#adadad></td>
    <td width="1" height="1"
bgcolor=#9d9d9d></td>
    <td width="1" height="1"
bgcolor=#949494></td>
    <td width="1" height="1"
bgcolor=#a1a1a1></td>
    <td width="1" height="1"
bgcolor=#777777></td>
    <td width="1" height="1"
bgcolor=#464646></td>
    <td width="1" height="1"
bgcolor=#313131></td>
    <td width="1" height="1"
bgcolor=#515151></td>
    <td width="1" height="1"
bgcolor=#a3a3a3></td>
    <td width="1" height="1"
bgcolor=#777777></td>
    <td width="1" height="1"
bgcolor=#1d1d1d></td>
    <td width="1" height="1"
bgcolor=#272727></td>
    <td width="1" height="1"
bgcolor=#252525></td>
    <td width="1" height="1"
bgcolor=#1b1b1b></td>
    <td width="1" height="1"
bgcolor=#404040></td>
    <td width="1" height="1"
bgcolor=#7d7d7d></td>
    <td width="1" height="1"
bgcolor=#9d9d9d></td>
    <td width="1" height="1"
bgcolor=#9a9a9a></td>
    <td width="1" height="1"
bgcolor=#383838></td>
    <td width="1" height="1"
bgcolor=#232323></td>
    <td width="1" height="1"
bgcolor=#1d1d1d></td>
    <td width="1" height="1"
bgcolor=#343434></td>
    <td width="1" height="1"
bgcolor=#393939></td>
    <td width="1" height="1"
bgcolor=#262626></td>
    <td width="1" height="1"
bgcolor=#545454></td>
    <td width="1" height="1"
bgcolor=#717171></td>
    <td width="1" height="1"
bgcolor=#b1b1b1></td>
    <td width="1" height="1"
bgcolor=#d7d7d7></td>
    <td width="1" height="1"
bgcolor=#b5b5b5></td>
    <td width="1" height="1"
bgcolor=#d5d5d5></td>
    <td width="1" height="1"
bgcolor=#d8d8d8></td>
    <td width="1" height="1"
bgcolor=#dfdfdf></td>
    <td width="1" height="1"
bgcolor=#d7d7d7></td>
    <td width="1" height="1"
bgcolor=#d1d1d1></td>
    <td width="1" height="1"
bgcolor=#cdcdcd></td>
    <td width="1" height="1"
bgcolor=#d6d6d6></td>
    <td width="1" height="1"
bgcolor=#dadada></td>
    <td width="1" height="1"
bgcolor=#d1d1d1></td>
    <td width="1" height="1"
bgcolor=#d0d0d0></td>
    <td width="1" height="1"
bgcolor=#c8c8c8></td>
    <td width="1" height="1"
bgcolor=#d3d3d3></td>
    <td width="1" height="1"
bgcolor=#dbdbdb></td>
    <td width="1" height="1"
bgcolor=#d3d3d3></td>
    <td width="1" height="1"
bgcolor=#d6d6d6></td>
    <td width="1" height="1"
bgcolor=#b2b2b2></td>
    <td width="1" height="1"
bgcolor=#797979></td>
    <td width="1" height="1"
bgcolor=#454545></td>
    <td width="1" height="1"
bgcolor=#161616></td>
    <td width="1" height="1"
bgcolor=#0d0d0d></td>
    <td width="1" height="1"
bgcolor=#0b0b0b></td>
    <td width="1" height="1"
bgcolor=#020202></td>
    <td width="1" height="1"
bgcolor=#040404></td>
    <td width="1" height="1"
bgcolor=#050505></td>
    <td width="1" height="1"
bgcolor=#090909></td>
    <td width="1" height="1"
bgcolor=#4c4c4c></td>
    <td width="1" height="1"
bgcolor=#c8c8c8></td>
    <td rowspan="1"
colspan="2" width="1"
```

```
height="1"
bgcolor=#d1d1d1></td>
    <td width="1" height="1"
bgcolor=#d2d2d2></td>
    <td width="1" height="1"
bgcolor=#9c9c9c></td>
    <td width="1" height="1"
bgcolor=#363636></td>
    <td width="1" height="1"
bgcolor=#141414></td>
    <td width="1" height="1"
bgcolor=#161616></td>
    <td width="1" height="1"
bgcolor=#212121></td>
    <td width="1" height="1"
bgcolor=#414141></td>
    <td width="1" height="1"
bgcolor=#565656></td>
    <td width="1" height="1"
bgcolor=#7a7a7a></td>
    <td width="1" height="1"
bgcolor=#696969></td>
    <td width="1" height="1"
bgcolor=#6c6c6c></td>
    <td width="1" height="1"
bgcolor=#7c7c7c></td>
  </tr>
  <tr>
    <td rowspan="2"
colspan="1" width="1"
height="1"
bgcolor=#c0c0c0></td>
    <td width="1" height="1"
bgcolor=#b4b4b4></td>
    <td width="1" height="1"
bgcolor=#acacac></td>
    <td width="1" height="1"
bgcolor=#9c9c9c></td>
    <td width="1" height="1"
bgcolor=#a3a3a3></td>
    <td width="1" height="1"
bgcolor=#878787></td>
    <td width="1" height="1"
bgcolor=#606060></td>
    <td width="1" height="1"
bgcolor=#515151></td>
    <td width="1" height="1"
bgcolor=#4c4c4c></td>
    <td width="1" height="1"
bgcolor=#767676></td>
    <td width="1" height="1"
bgcolor=#717171></td>
    <td width="1" height="1"
bgcolor=#202020></td>
    <td width="1" height="1"
bgcolor=#2f2f2f></td>
    <td width="1" height="1"
bgcolor=#313131></td>
    <td width="1" height="1"
bgcolor=#212121></td>
    <td width="1" height="1"
bgcolor=#434343></td>
    <td width="1" height="1"
bgcolor=#5d5d5d></td>
    <td width="1" height="1"
bgcolor=#9c9c9c></td>
    <td width="1" height="1"
bgcolor=#aaaaaa></td>
    <td width="1" height="1"
bgcolor=#3b3b3b></td>
    <td width="1" height="1"
bgcolor=#171717></td>
    <td width="1" height="1"
bgcolor=#262626></td>
    <td width="1" height="1"
bgcolor=#242424></td>
    <td width="1" height="1"
bgcolor=#3d3d3d></td>
    <td width="1" height="1"
bgcolor=#515151></td>
    <td width="1" height="1"
bgcolor=#646464></td>
    <td width="1" height="1"
bgcolor=#959595></td>
    <td width="1" height="1"
bgcolor=#d9d9d9></td>
    <td width="1" height="1"
bgcolor=#c6c6c6></td>
    <td width="1" height="1"
bgcolor=#d9d9d9></td>
    <td width="1" height="1"
bgcolor=#d3d3d3></td>
    <td width="1" height="1"
bgcolor=#b9b9b9></td>
    <td width="1" height="1"
bgcolor=#cecece></td>
    <td width="1" height="1"
bgcolor=#dadada></td>
    <td width="1" height="1"
bgcolor=#d3d3d3></td>
    <td width="1" height="1"
bgcolor=#c3c3c3></td>
    <td width="1" height="1"
bgcolor=#c5c5c5></td>
    <td width="1" height="1"
bgcolor=#d2d2d2></td>
    <td width="1" height="1"
bgcolor=#e6e6e6></td>
    <td width="1" height="1"
bgcolor=#e1e1e1></td>
    <td width="1" height="1"
bgcolor=#dadada></td>
    <td width="1" height="1"
bgcolor=#d1d1d1></td>
    <td width="1" height="1"
bgcolor=#cacaca></td>
    <td width="1" height="1"
bgcolor=#bebebe></td>
    <td width="1" height="1"
bgcolor=#989898></td>
    <td width="1" height="1"
bgcolor=#656565></td>
    <td width="1" height="1"
bgcolor=#303030></td>
    <td width="1" height="1"
bgcolor=#141414></td>
    <td width="1" height="1"
bgcolor=#0c0c0c></td>
    <td width="1" height="1"
bgcolor=#010101></td>
    <td width="1" height="1"
bgcolor=#0c0c0c></td>
    <td width="1" height="1"
bgcolor=#080808></td>
    <td width="1" height="1"
bgcolor=#060606></td>
    <td rowspan="3"
colspan="1" width="1"
height="1"
bgcolor=#010101></td>
    <td width="1" height="1"
bgcolor=#0a0a0a></td>
    <td width="1" height="1"
bgcolor=#0c0c0c></td>
    <td width="1" height="1"
bgcolor=#323232></td>
    <td width="1" height="1"
bgcolor=#b7b7b7></td>
    <td width="1" height="1"
bgcolor=#cfcfcf></td>
    <td width="1" height="1"
bgcolor=#d3d3d3></td>
    <td width="1" height="1"
bgcolor=#cccccc></td>
    <td width="1" height="1"
bgcolor=#8e8e8e></td>
    <td width="1" height="1"
bgcolor=#2a2a2a></td>
    <td width="1" height="1"
bgcolor=#080808></td>
    <td width="1" height="1"
bgcolor=#0e0e0e></td>
    <td width="1" height="1"
bgcolor=#222222></td>
    <td width="1" height="1"
bgcolor=#3c3c3c></td>
    <td width="1" height="1"
bgcolor=#595959></td>
    <td width="1" height="1"
bgcolor=#7f7f7f></td>
    <td rowspan="2"
colspan="1" width="1"
height="1"
bgcolor=#646464></td>
```

```
    <td width="1" height="1"
bgcolor=#787878></td>
    <td width="1" height="1"
bgcolor=#adadad></td>
  </tr>
  <tr>
    <td rowspan="2"
colspan="1" width="1"
height="1"
bgcolor=#bababa></td>
    <td width="1" height="1"
bgcolor=#a5a5a5></td>
    <td width="1" height="1"
bgcolor=#838383></td>
    <td width="1" height="1"
bgcolor=#717171></td>
    <td width="1" height="1"
bgcolor=#696969></td>
    <td width="1" height="1"
bgcolor=#787878></td>
    <td width="1" height="1"
bgcolor=#6c6c6c></td>
    <td width="1" height="1"
bgcolor=#3e3e3e></td>
    <td width="1" height="1"
bgcolor=#777777></td>
    <td width="1" height="1"
bgcolor=#a9a9a9></td>
    <td width="1" height="1"
bgcolor=#424242></td>
    <td width="1" height="1"
bgcolor=#363636></td>
    <td rowspan="2"
colspan="1" width="1"
height="1"
bgcolor=#383838></td>
    <td width="1" height="1"
bgcolor=#494949></td>
    <td rowspan="2"
colspan="1" width="1"
height="1"
bgcolor=#323232></td>
    <td width="1" height="1"
bgcolor=#595959></td>
    <td width="1" height="1"
bgcolor=#7c7c7c></td>
    <td width="1" height="1"
bgcolor=#7f7f7f></td>
    <td width="1" height="1"
bgcolor=#373737></td>
    <td width="1" height="1"
bgcolor=#090909></td>
    <td width="1" height="1"
bgcolor=#141414></td>
    <td width="1" height="1"
bgcolor=#272727></td>
    <td width="1" height="1"
bgcolor=#3a3a3a></td>
    <td width="1" height="1"
bgcolor=#454545></td>
    <td width="1" height="1"
bgcolor=#7b7b7b></td>
    <td width="1" height="1"
bgcolor=#d0d0d0></td>
    <td width="1" height="1"
bgcolor=#e4e4e4></td>
    <td width="1" height="1"
bgcolor=#bdbdbd></td>
    <td width="1" height="1"
bgcolor=#c9c9c9></td>
    <td width="1" height="1"
bgcolor=#b5b5b5></td>
    <td width="1" height="1"
bgcolor=#9f9f9f></td>
    <td width="1" height="1"
bgcolor=#c5c5c5></td>
    <td width="1" height="1"
bgcolor=#d5d5d5></td>
    <td width="1" height="1"
bgcolor=#d2d2d2></td>
    <td width="1" height="1"
bgcolor=#b5b5b5></td>
    <td width="1" height="1"
bgcolor=#c9c9c9></td>
    <td width="1" height="1"
bgcolor=#d6d6d6></td>
    <td width="1" height="1"
bgcolor=#dbdbdb></td>
    <td width="1" height="1"
bgcolor=#d9d9d9></td>
    <td width="1" height="1"
bgcolor=#dbdbdb></td>
    <td width="1" height="1"
bgcolor=#dfdfdf></td>
    <td width="1" height="1"
bgcolor=#9e9e9e></td>
    <td width="1" height="1"
bgcolor=#3c3c3c></td>
    <td width="1" height="1"
bgcolor=#101010></td>
    <td width="1" height="1"
bgcolor=#131313></td>
    <td width="1" height="1"
bgcolor=#151515></td>
    <td width="1" height="1"
bgcolor=#1f1f1f></td>
    <td width="1" height="1"
bgcolor=#151515></td>
    <td width="1" height="1"
bgcolor=#040404></td>
    <td rowspan="3"
colspan="1" width="1"
height="1"
bgcolor=#050505></td>
    <td width="1" height="1"
bgcolor=#090909></td>
    <td rowspan="2"
colspan="1" width="1"
height="1"
bgcolor=#040404></td>
    <td rowspan="2"
colspan="1" width="1"
height="1"
bgcolor=#050505></td>
    <td width="1" height="1"
bgcolor=#010101></td>
    <td width="1" height="1"
bgcolor=#373737></td>
    <td width="1" height="1"
bgcolor=#b1b1b1></td>
    <td rowspan="2"
colspan="1" width="1"
height="1"
bgcolor=#c8c8c8></td>
    <td width="1" height="1"
bgcolor=#d5d5d5></td>
    <td width="1" height="1"
bgcolor=#d2d2d2></td>
    <td width="1" height="1"
bgcolor=#7b7b7b></td>
    <td width="1" height="1"
bgcolor=#0f0f0f></td>
    <td width="1" height="1"
bgcolor=#0a0a0a></td>
    <td rowspan="2"
colspan="1" width="1"
height="1"
bgcolor=#111111></td>
    <td width="1" height="1"
bgcolor=#171717></td>
    <td width="1" height="1"
bgcolor=#2c2c2c></td>
    <td width="1" height="1"
bgcolor=#5d5d5d></td>
    <td width="1" height="1"
bgcolor=#636363></td>
    <td width="1" height="1"
bgcolor=#747474></td>
    <td width="1" height="1"
bgcolor=#acacac></td>
  </tr>
  <tr>
    <td width="1" height="1"
bgcolor=#c4c4c4></td>
    <td width="1" height="1"
bgcolor=#a6a6a6></td>
    <td width="1" height="1"
bgcolor=#8d8d8d></td>
    <td width="1" height="1"
bgcolor=#686868></td>
    <td width="1" height="1"
bgcolor=#454545></td>
    <td width="1" height="1"
bgcolor=#616161></td>
```

```
    <td rowspan="2"
colspan="1" width="1"
height="1"
bgcolor=#767676></td>
    <td width="1" height="1"
bgcolor=#525252></td>
    <td width="1" height="1"
bgcolor=#828282></td>
    <td width="1" height="1"
bgcolor=#9d9d9d></td>
    <td rowspan="2"
colspan="1" width="1"
height="1"
bgcolor=#525252></td>
    <td width="1" height="1"
bgcolor=#2d2d2d></td>
    <td width="1" height="1"
bgcolor=#4b4b4b></td>
    <td width="1" height="1"
bgcolor=#303030></td>
    <td width="1" height="1"
bgcolor=#2f2f2f></td>
    <td width="1" height="1"
bgcolor=#3a3a3a></td>
    <td width="1" height="1"
bgcolor=#272727></td>
    <td width="1" height="1"
bgcolor=#1a1a1a></td>
    <td width="1" height="1"
bgcolor=#191919></td>
    <td width="1" height="1"
bgcolor=#1d1d1d></td>
    <td width="1" height="1"
bgcolor=#202020></td>
    <td width="1" height="1"
bgcolor=#252525></td>
    <td width="1" height="1"
bgcolor=#aeaeae></td>
    <td width="1" height="1"
bgcolor=#e9e9e9></td>
    <td width="1" height="1"
bgcolor=#d2d2d2></td>
    <td width="1" height="1"
bgcolor=#c1c1c1></td>
    <td width="1" height="1"
bgcolor=#b6b6b6></td>
    <td width="1" height="1"
bgcolor=#9d9d9d></td>
    <td width="1" height="1"
bgcolor=#a4a4a4></td>
    <td width="1" height="1"
bgcolor=#9c9c9c></td>
    <td width="1" height="1"
bgcolor=#a9a9a9></td>
    <td width="1" height="1"
bgcolor=#d1d1d1></td>
    <td rowspan="1"
colspan="2" width="1"
height="1"
bgcolor=#cccccc></td>
    <td width="1" height="1"
bgcolor=#dcdcdc></td>
    <td width="1" height="1"
bgcolor=#e1e1e1></td>
    <td width="1" height="1"
bgcolor=#e2e2e2></td>
    <td width="1" height="1"
bgcolor=#a4a4a4></td>
    <td width="1" height="1"
bgcolor=#4a4a4a></td>
    <td width="1" height="1"
bgcolor=#151515></td>
    <td width="1" height="1"
bgcolor=#0f0f0f></td>
    <td width="1" height="1"
bgcolor=#0b0b0b></td>
    <td width="1" height="1"
bgcolor=#1a1a1a></td>
    <td width="1" height="1"
bgcolor=#222222></td>
    <td width="1" height="1"
bgcolor=#121212></td>
    <td width="1" height="1"
bgcolor=#0a0a0a></td>
    <td width="1" height="1"
bgcolor=#0b0b0b></td>
    <td width="1" height="1"
bgcolor=#060606></td>
    <td width="1" height="1"
bgcolor=#000000></td>
    <td width="1" height="1"
bgcolor=#4a4a4a></td>
    <td width="1" height="1"
bgcolor=#acacac></td>
    <td width="1" height="1"
bgcolor=#d1d1d1></td>
    <td width="1" height="1"
bgcolor=#d5d5d5></td>
    <td width="1" height="1"
bgcolor=#888888></td>
    <td width="1" height="1"
bgcolor=#161616></td>
    <td width="1" height="1"
bgcolor=#0c0c0c></td>
    <td width="1" height="1"
bgcolor=#1b1b1b></td>
    <td width="1" height="1"
bgcolor=#303030></td>
    <td width="1" height="1"
bgcolor=#3f3f3f></td>
    <td width="1" height="1"
bgcolor=#616161></td>
    <td width="1" height="1"
bgcolor=#585858></td>
    <td width="1" height="1"
bgcolor=#3e3e3e></td>
    <td width="1" height="1"
bgcolor=#8a8a8a></td>
  </tr>
  <tr>
    <td width="1" height="1"
bgcolor=#bebebe></td>
    <td width="1" height="1"
bgcolor=#b7b7b7></td>
    <td width="1" height="1"
bgcolor=#aaaaaa></td>
    <td width="1" height="1"
bgcolor=#909090></td>
    <td width="1" height="1"
bgcolor=#888888></td>
    <td width="1" height="1"
bgcolor=#757575></td>
    <td width="1" height="1"
bgcolor=#696969></td>
    <td width="1" height="1"
bgcolor=#575757></td>
    <td width="1" height="1"
bgcolor=#909090></td>
    <td width="1" height="1"
bgcolor=#a3a3a3></td>
    <td width="1" height="1"
bgcolor=#414141></td>
    <td width="1" height="1"
bgcolor=#545454></td>
    <td width="1" height="1"
bgcolor=#333333></td>
    <td width="1" height="1"
bgcolor=#202020></td>
    <td rowspan="2"
colspan="1" width="1"
height="1"
bgcolor=#1f1f1f></td>
    <td width="1" height="1"
bgcolor=#161616></td>
    <td width="1" height="1"
bgcolor=#1d1d1d></td>
    <td width="1" height="1"
bgcolor=#1e1e1e></td>
    <td width="1" height="1"
bgcolor=#1b1b1b></td>
    <td width="1" height="1"
bgcolor=#1d1d1d></td>
    <td width="1" height="1"
bgcolor=#181818></td>
    <td width="1" height="1"
bgcolor=#111111></td>
    <td width="1" height="1"
bgcolor=#4d4d4d></td>
    <td width="1" height="1"
bgcolor=#dadada></td>
    <td width="1" height="1"
bgcolor=#d9d9d9></td>
    <td width="1" height="1"
bgcolor=#c5c5c5></td>
```

```
    <td width="1" height="1"
bgcolor=#b9b9b9></td>
    <td width="1" height="1"
bgcolor=#bfbfbf></td>
    <td width="1" height="1"
bgcolor=#cacaca></td>
    <td width="1" height="1"
bgcolor=#d4d4d4></td>
    <td width="1" height="1"
bgcolor=#cdcdcd></td>
    <td width="1" height="1"
bgcolor=#cfcfcf></td>
    <td width="1" height="1"
bgcolor=#d7d7d7></td>
    <td width="1" height="1"
bgcolor=#d0d0d0></td>
    <td width="1" height="1"
bgcolor=#d2d2d2></td>
    <td width="1" height="1"
bgcolor=#e4e4e4></td>
    <td width="1" height="1"
bgcolor=#aaaaaa></td>
    <td width="1" height="1"
bgcolor=#595959></td>
    <td width="1" height="1"
bgcolor=#0e0e0e></td>
    <td width="1" height="1"
bgcolor=#060606></td>
    <td width="1" height="1"
bgcolor=#0b0b0b></td>
    <td width="1" height="1"
bgcolor=#111111></td>
    <td width="1" height="1"
bgcolor=#101010></td>
    <td width="1" height="1"
bgcolor=#0c0c0c></td>
    <td width="1" height="1"
bgcolor=#0f0f0f></td>
    <td width="1" height="1"
bgcolor=#161616></td>
    <td rowspan="2"
colspan="1" width="1"
height="1"
bgcolor=#050505></td>
    <td width="1" height="1"
bgcolor=#080808></td>
    <td width="1" height="1"
bgcolor=#040404></td>
    <td width="1" height="1"
bgcolor=#050505></td>
    <td width="1" height="1"
bgcolor=#000000></td>
    <td width="1" height="1"
bgcolor=#161616></td>
    <td width="1" height="1"
bgcolor=#535353></td>
    <td width="1" height="1"
bgcolor=#646464></td>
    <td width="1" height="1"
bgcolor=#929292></td>
    <td width="1" height="1"
bgcolor=#bbbbbb></td>
    <td width="1" height="1"
bgcolor=#cecece></td>
    <td width="1" height="1"
bgcolor=#cbcbcb></td>
    <td width="1" height="1"
bgcolor=#8a8a8a></td>
    <td width="1" height="1"
bgcolor=#1c1c1c></td>
    <td width="1" height="1"
bgcolor=#0a0a0a></td>
    <td width="1" height="1"
bgcolor=#0f0f0f></td>
    <td width="1" height="1"
bgcolor=#141414></td>
    <td width="1" height="1"
bgcolor=#272727></td>
    <td width="1" height="1"
bgcolor=#3e3e3e></td>
    <td width="1" height="1"
bgcolor=#393939></td>
    <td width="1" height="1"
bgcolor=#3b3b3b></td>
    <td width="1" height="1"
bgcolor=#5d5d5d></td>
    <td width="1" height="1"
bgcolor=#4e4e4e></td>
  </tr>
  <tr>
    <td width="1" height="1"
bgcolor=#b4b4b4></td>
    <td width="1" height="1"
bgcolor=#a4a4a4></td>
    <td width="1" height="1"
bgcolor=#939393></td>
    <td width="1" height="1"
bgcolor=#858585></td>
    <td width="1" height="1"
bgcolor=#909090></td>
    <td width="1" height="1"
bgcolor=#939393></td>
    <td width="1" height="1"
bgcolor=#878787></td>
    <td width="1" height="1"
bgcolor=#787878></td>
    <td width="1" height="1"
bgcolor=#595959></td>
    <td width="1" height="1"
bgcolor=#959595></td>
    <td rowspan="2"
colspan="1" width="1"
height="1"
bgcolor=#c1c1c1></td>
    <td width="1" height="1"
bgcolor=#606060></td>
    <td width="1" height="1"
bgcolor=#4f4f4f></td>
    <td width="1" height="1"
bgcolor=#515151></td>
    <td width="1" height="1"
bgcolor=#2e2e2e></td>
    <td width="1" height="1"
bgcolor=#242424></td>
    <td width="1" height="1"
bgcolor=#1b1b1b></td>
    <td width="1" height="1"
bgcolor=#1c1c1c></td>
    <td width="1" height="1"
bgcolor=#2c2c2c></td>
    <td width="1" height="1"
bgcolor=#1d1d1d></td>
    <td width="1" height="1"
bgcolor=#161616></td>
    <td width="1" height="1"
bgcolor=#121212></td>
    <td width="1" height="1"
bgcolor=#2d2d2d></td>
    <td width="1" height="1"
bgcolor=#b8b8b8></td>
    <td width="1" height="1"
bgcolor=#d5d5d5></td>
    <td width="1" height="1"
bgcolor=#d4d4d4></td>
    <td rowspan="2"
colspan="1" width="1"
height="1"
bgcolor=#cbcbcb></td>
    <td width="1" height="1"
bgcolor=#c7c7c7></td>
    <td width="1" height="1"
bgcolor=#dcdcdc></td>
    <td width="1" height="1"
bgcolor=#d2d2d2></td>
    <td width="1" height="1"
bgcolor=#cccccc></td>
    <td width="1" height="1"
bgcolor=#e1e1e1></td>
    <td width="1" height="1"
bgcolor=#eaeaea></td>
    <td width="1" height="1"
bgcolor=#dddddd></td>
    <td width="1" height="1"
bgcolor=#cccccc></td>
    <td width="1" height="1"
bgcolor=#898989></td>
    <td width="1" height="1"
bgcolor=#434343></td>
    <td width="1" height="1"
bgcolor=#101010></td>
    <td width="1" height="1"
bgcolor=#030303></td>
    <td rowspan="2"
colspan="1" width="1"
```

```
height="1"
bgcolor=#0d0d0d></td>
    <td width="1" height="1"
bgcolor=#111111></td>
    <td rowspan="2"
colspan="1" width="1"
height="1"
bgcolor=#131313></td>
    <td width="1" height="1"
bgcolor=#0d0d0d></td>
    <td width="1" height="1"
bgcolor=#0e0e0e></td>
    <td rowspan="2"
colspan="1" width="1"
height="1"
bgcolor=#080808></td>
    <td width="1" height="1"
bgcolor=#040404></td>
    <td width="1" height="1"
bgcolor=#090909></td>
    <td width="1" height="1"
bgcolor=#030303></td>
    <td width="1" height="1"
bgcolor=#000000></td>
    <td width="1" height="1"
bgcolor=#020202></td>
    <td width="1" height="1"
bgcolor=#0f0f0f></td>
    <td width="1" height="1"
bgcolor=#333333></td>
    <td width="1" height="1"
bgcolor=#363636></td>
    <td width="1" height="1"
bgcolor=#b9b9b9></td>
    <td width="1" height="1"
bgcolor=#b8b8b8></td>
    <td width="1" height="1"
bgcolor=#a3a3a3></td>
    <td width="1" height="1"
bgcolor=#aaaaaa></td>
    <td width="1" height="1"
bgcolor=#c6c6c6></td>
    <td width="1" height="1"
bgcolor=#d5d5d5></td>
    <td width="1" height="1"
bgcolor=#8b8b8b></td>
    <td width="1" height="1"
bgcolor=#131313></td>
    <td width="1" height="1"
bgcolor=#0d0d0d></td>
    <td width="1" height="1"
bgcolor=#090909></td>
    <td width="1" height="1"
bgcolor=#181818></td>
    <td width="1" height="1"
bgcolor=#202020></td>
    <td width="1" height="1"
bgcolor=#2a2a2a></td>
    <td width="1" height="1"
bgcolor=#252525></td>
    <td width="1" height="1"
bgcolor=#3d3d3d></td>
    <td rowspan="1"
colspan="2" width="1"
height="1"
bgcolor=#6d6d6d></td>
  </tr>
  <tr>
    <td width="1" height="1"
bgcolor=#b6b6b6></td>
    <td width="1" height="1"
bgcolor=#9c9c9c></td>
    <td width="1" height="1"
bgcolor=#858585></td>
    <td width="1" height="1"
bgcolor=#8d8d8d></td>
    <td width="1" height="1"
bgcolor=#8a8a8a></td>
    <td width="1" height="1"
bgcolor=#747474></td>
    <td width="1" height="1"
bgcolor=#787878></td>
    <td width="1" height="1"
bgcolor=#747474></td>
    <td width="1" height="1"
bgcolor=#585858></td>
    <td width="1" height="1"
bgcolor=#949494></td>
    <td width="1" height="1"
bgcolor=#6b6b6b></td>
    <td width="1" height="1"
bgcolor=#353535></td>
    <td width="1" height="1"
bgcolor=#3c3c3c></td>
    <td width="1" height="1"
bgcolor=#242424></td>
    <td rowspan="2"
colspan="1" width="1"
height="1"
bgcolor=#171717></td>
    <td width="1" height="1"
bgcolor=#131313></td>
    <td width="1" height="1"
bgcolor=#161616></td>
    <td width="1" height="1"
bgcolor=#151515></td>
    <td width="1" height="1"
bgcolor=#191919></td>
    <td width="1" height="1"
bgcolor=#141414></td>
    <td width="1" height="1"
bgcolor=#040404></td>
    <td width="1" height="1"
bgcolor=#0d0d0d></td>
    <td width="1" height="1"
bgcolor=#747474></td>
    <td width="1" height="1"
bgcolor=#c8c8c8></td>
    <td width="1" height="1"
bgcolor=#b1b1b1></td>
    <td width="1" height="1"
bgcolor=#cdcdcd></td>
    <td width="1" height="1"
bgcolor=#cdcdcd></td>
    <td width="1" height="1"
bgcolor=#dbdbdb></td>
    <td width="1" height="1"
bgcolor=#bfbfbf></td>
    <td width="1" height="1"
bgcolor=#c2c2c2></td>
    <td width="1" height="1"
bgcolor=#cdcdcd></td>
    <td width="1" height="1"
bgcolor=#999999></td>
    <td width="1" height="1"
bgcolor=#515151></td>
    <td width="1" height="1"
bgcolor=#232323></td>
    <td width="1" height="1"
bgcolor=#050505></td>
    <td width="1" height="1"
bgcolor=#060606></td>
    <td width="1" height="1"
bgcolor=#0f0f0f></td>
    <td width="1" height="1"
bgcolor=#111111></td>
    <td width="1" height="1"
bgcolor=#0f0f0f></td>
    <td width="1" height="1"
bgcolor=#0b0b0b></td>
    <td width="1" height="1"
bgcolor=#090909></td>
    <td width="1" height="1"
bgcolor=#060606></td>
    <td width="1" height="1"
bgcolor=#010101></td>
    <td rowspan="1"
colspan="2" width="1"
height="1"
bgcolor=#040404></td>
    <td width="1" height="1"
bgcolor=#0d0d0d></td>
    <td width="1" height="1"
bgcolor=#050505></td>
    <td width="1" height="1"
bgcolor=#171717></td>
    <td width="1" height="1"
bgcolor=#a2a2a2></td>
    <td width="1" height="1"
bgcolor=#adadad></td>
    <td width="1" height="1"
bgcolor=#b2b2b2></td>
    <td width="1" height="1"
bgcolor=#cfcfcf></td>
```

```
    <td width="1" height="1"
bgcolor=#bebebe></td>
    <td width="1" height="1"
bgcolor=#a3a3a3></td>
    <td width="1" height="1"
bgcolor=#a7a7a7></td>
    <td width="1" height="1"
bgcolor=#d3d3d3></td>
    <td width="1" height="1"
bgcolor=#9c9c9c></td>
    <td width="1" height="1"
bgcolor=#1e1e1e></td>
    <td width="1" height="1"
bgcolor=#0e0e0e></td>
    <td width="1" height="1"
bgcolor=#0a0a0a></td>
    <td width="1" height="1"
bgcolor=#0c0c0c></td>
    <td width="1" height="1"
bgcolor=#1a1a1a></td>
    <td width="1" height="1"
bgcolor=#212121></td>
    <td width="1" height="1"
bgcolor=#202020></td>
    <td width="1" height="1"
bgcolor=#181818></td>
    <td width="1" height="1"
bgcolor=#5e5e5e></td>
    <td width="1" height="1"
bgcolor=#a0a0a0></td>
  </tr>
  <tr>
    <td width="1" height="1"
bgcolor=#b2b2b2></td>
    <td width="1" height="1"
bgcolor=#b7b7b7></td>
    <td width="1" height="1"
bgcolor=#919191></td>
    <td width="1" height="1"
bgcolor=#6e6e6e></td>
    <td width="1" height="1"
bgcolor=#757575></td>
    <td width="1" height="1"
bgcolor=#7d7d7d></td>
    <td width="1" height="1"
bgcolor=#747474></td>
    <td width="1" height="1"
bgcolor=#616161></td>
    <td width="1" height="1"
bgcolor=#555555></td>
    <td width="1" height="1"
bgcolor=#878787></td>
    <td width="1" height="1"
bgcolor=#bebebe></td>
    <td width="1" height="1"
bgcolor=#6e6e6e></td>
    <td width="1" height="1"
bgcolor=#383838></td>
    <td width="1" height="1"
bgcolor=#3b3b3b></td>
    <td width="1" height="1"
bgcolor=#232323></td>
    <td width="1" height="1"
bgcolor=#181818></td>
    <td width="1" height="1"
bgcolor=#282828></td>
    <td width="1" height="1"
bgcolor=#1d1d1d></td>
    <td width="1" height="1"
bgcolor=#141414></td>
    <td width="1" height="1"
bgcolor=#101010></td>
    <td width="1" height="1"
bgcolor=#050505></td>
    <td width="1" height="1"
bgcolor=#515151></td>
    <td width="1" height="1"
bgcolor=#c7c7c7></td>
    <td width="1" height="1"
bgcolor=#bababa></td>
    <td width="1" height="1"
bgcolor=#bcbcbc></td>
    <td width="1" height="1"
bgcolor=#b5b5b5></td>
    <td width="1" height="1"
bgcolor=#d0d0d0></td>
    <td width="1" height="1"
bgcolor=#d2d2d2></td>
    <td width="1" height="1"
bgcolor=#c6c6c6></td>
    <td width="1" height="1"
bgcolor=#979797></td>
    <td width="1" height="1"
bgcolor=#6a6a6a></td>
    <td width="1" height="1"
bgcolor=#292929></td>
    <td width="1" height="1"
bgcolor=#070707></td>
    <td width="1" height="1"
bgcolor=#000000></td>
    <td width="1" height="1"
bgcolor=#040404></td>
    <td width="1" height="1"
bgcolor=#141414></td>
    <td width="1" height="1"
bgcolor=#151515></td>
    <td width="1" height="1"
bgcolor=#070707></td>
    <td width="1" height="1"
bgcolor=#0d0d0d></td>
    <td width="1" height="1"
bgcolor=#090909></td>
    <td width="1" height="1"
bgcolor=#050505></td>
    <td width="1" height="1"
bgcolor=#080808></td>
    <td rowspan="2"
colspan="1" width="1"
height="1"
bgcolor=#050505></td>
    <td width="1" height="1"
bgcolor=#0a0a0a></td>
    <td width="1" height="1"
bgcolor=#060606></td>
    <td width="1" height="1"
bgcolor=#040404></td>
    <td width="1" height="1"
bgcolor=#060606></td>
    <td width="1" height="1"
bgcolor=#010101></td>
    <td width="1" height="1"
bgcolor=#030303></td>
    <td width="1" height="1"
bgcolor=#000000></td>
    <td width="1" height="1"
bgcolor=#080808></td>
    <td width="1" height="1"
bgcolor=#151515></td>
    <td width="1" height="1"
bgcolor=#5e5e5e></td>
    <td width="1" height="1"
bgcolor=#bbbbbb></td>
    <td width="1" height="1"
bgcolor=#c9c9c9></td>
    <td width="1" height="1"
bgcolor=#a1a1a1></td>
    <td width="1" height="1"
bgcolor=#c5c5c5></td>
    <td width="1" height="1"
bgcolor=#b7b7b7></td>
    <td width="1" height="1"
bgcolor=#9d9d9d></td>
    <td width="1" height="1"
bgcolor=#b6b6b6></td>
    <td width="1" height="1"
bgcolor=#898989></td>
    <td rowspan="2"
colspan="1" width="1"
height="1"
bgcolor=#1c1c1c></td>
    <td width="1" height="1"
bgcolor=#070707></td>
    <td width="1" height="1"
bgcolor=#0c0c0c></td>
    <td width="1" height="1"
bgcolor=#131313></td>
    <td width="1" height="1"
bgcolor=#1b1b1b></td>
    <td width="1" height="1"
bgcolor=#1f1f1f></td>
    <td width="1" height="1"
bgcolor=#141414></td>
    <td width="1" height="1"
bgcolor=#101010></td>
```

```
    <td width="1" height="1" bgcolor=#3d3d3d></td>
    <td width="1" height="1" bgcolor=#a5a5a5></td>
  </tr>
  <tr>
    <td width="1" height="1" bgcolor=#c1c1c1></td>
    <td width="1" height="1" bgcolor=#b4b4b4></td>
    <td width="1" height="1" bgcolor=#acacac></td>
    <td width="1" height="1" bgcolor=#7f7f7f></td>
    <td width="1" height="1" bgcolor=#727272></td>
    <td width="1" height="1" bgcolor=#6b6b6b></td>
    <td width="1" height="1" bgcolor=#535353></td>
    <td width="1" height="1" bgcolor=#595959></td>
    <td width="1" height="1" bgcolor=#616161></td>
    <td width="1" height="1" bgcolor=#7a7a7a></td>
    <td width="1" height="1" bgcolor=#aaaaaa></td>
    <td width="1" height="1" bgcolor=#737373></td>
    <td rowspan="2" colspan="1" width="1" height="1" bgcolor=#3d3d3d></td>
    <td width="1" height="1" bgcolor=#333333></td>
    <td width="1" height="1" bgcolor=#272727></td>
    <td width="1" height="1" bgcolor=#2d2d2d></td>
    <td width="1" height="1" bgcolor=#262626></td>
    <td width="1" height="1" bgcolor=#2f2f2f></td>
    <td width="1" height="1" bgcolor=#1c1c1c></td>
    <td rowspan="1" colspan="2" width="1" height="1" bgcolor=#1e1e1e></td>
    <td width="1" height="1" bgcolor=#1c1c1c></td>
    <td width="1" height="1" bgcolor=#b8b8b8></td>
    <td width="1" height="1" bgcolor=#f3f3f3></td>
    <td width="1" height="1" bgcolor=#e0e0e0></td>
    <td width="1" height="1" bgcolor=#d1d1d1></td>
    <td width="1" height="1" bgcolor=#d0d0d0></td>
    <td width="1" height="1" bgcolor=#cecece></td>
    <td width="1" height="1" bgcolor=#909090></td>
    <td width="1" height="1" bgcolor=#3e3e3e></td>
    <td width="1" height="1" bgcolor=#303030></td>
    <td width="1" height="1" bgcolor=#0d0d0d></td>
    <td width="1" height="1" bgcolor=#030303></td>
    <td width="1" height="1" bgcolor=#121212></td>
    <td width="1" height="1" bgcolor=#131313></td>
    <td width="1" height="1" bgcolor=#212121></td>
    <td rowspan="2" colspan="1" width="1" height="1" bgcolor=#2a2a2a></td>
    <td width="1" height="1" bgcolor=#1c1c1c></td>
    <td width="1" height="1" bgcolor=#040404></td>
    <td width="1" height="1" bgcolor=#151515></td>
    <td width="1" height="1" bgcolor=#1b1b1b></td>
    <td width="1" height="1" bgcolor=#0e0e0e></td>
    <td width="1" height="1" bgcolor=#060606></td>
    <td width="1" height="1" bgcolor=#080808></td>
    <td width="1" height="1" bgcolor=#070707></td>
    <td width="1" height="1" bgcolor=#060606></td>
    <td width="1" height="1" bgcolor=#0b0b0b></td>
    <td width="1" height="1" bgcolor=#030303></td>
    <td rowspan="3" colspan="1" width="1" height="1" bgcolor=#010101></td>
    <td width="1" height="1" bgcolor=#040404></td>
    <td width="1" height="1" bgcolor=#000000></td>
    <td width="1" height="1" bgcolor=#040404></td>
    <td width="1" height="1" bgcolor=#060606></td>
    <td width="1" height="1" bgcolor=#5a5a5a></td>
    <td width="1" height="1" bgcolor=#a0a0a0></td>
    <td width="1" height="1" bgcolor=#818181></td>
    <td width="1" height="1" bgcolor=#aeaeae></td>
    <td width="1" height="1" bgcolor=#ababab></td>
    <td width="1" height="1" bgcolor=#b5b5b5></td>
    <td width="1" height="1" bgcolor=#9c9c9c></td>
    <td width="1" height="1" bgcolor=#6d6d6d></td>
    <td width="1" height="1" bgcolor=#0e0e0e></td>
    <td width="1" height="1" bgcolor=#181818></td>
    <td width="1" height="1" bgcolor=#171717></td>
    <td width="1" height="1" bgcolor=#161616></td>
    <td width="1" height="1" bgcolor=#222222></td>
    <td width="1" height="1" bgcolor=#1e1e1e></td>
    <td width="1" height="1" bgcolor=#070707></td>
    <td width="1" height="1" bgcolor=#484848></td>
    <td width="1" height="1" bgcolor=#b4b4b4></td>
  </tr>
  <tr>
    <td width="1" height="1" bgcolor=#b2b2b2></td>
    <td width="1" height="1" bgcolor=#b0b0b0></td>
    <td width="1" height="1" bgcolor=#a1a1a1></td>
    <td width="1" height="1" bgcolor=#828282></td>
    <td width="1" height="1" bgcolor=#686868></td>
    <td rowspan="1" colspan="2" width="1" height="1" bgcolor=#5d5d5d></td>
    <td width="1" height="1" bgcolor=#767676></td>
    <td width="1" height="1" bgcolor=#6b6b6b></td>
    <td width="1" height="1" bgcolor=#797979></td>
```

```
    <td width="1" height="1"
bgcolor=#a8a8a8></td>
    <td width="1" height="1"
bgcolor=#848484></td>
    <td width="1" height="1"
bgcolor=#3a3a3a></td>
    <td width="1" height="1"
bgcolor=#373737></td>
    <td width="1" height="1"
bgcolor=#343434></td>
    <td rowspan="1"
colspan="2" width="1"
height="1"
bgcolor=#313131></td>
    <td width="1" height="1"
bgcolor=#272727></td>
    <td width="1" height="1"
bgcolor=#343434></td>
    <td width="1" height="1"
bgcolor=#1a1a1a></td>
    <td width="1" height="1"
bgcolor=#696969></td>
    <td width="1" height="1"
bgcolor=#f4f4f4></td>
    <td width="1" height="1"
bgcolor=#efefef></td>
    <td width="1" height="1"
bgcolor=#d8d8d8></td>
    <td width="1" height="1"
bgcolor=#a6a6a6></td>
    <td width="1" height="1"
bgcolor=#5b5b5b></td>
    <td width="1" height="1"
bgcolor=#292929></td>
    <td width="1" height="1"
bgcolor=#151515></td>
    <td width="1" height="1"
bgcolor=#242424></td>
    <td width="1" height="1"
bgcolor=#343434></td>
    <td width="1" height="1"
bgcolor=#303030></td>
    <td width="1" height="1"
bgcolor=#282828></td>
    <td width="1" height="1"
bgcolor=#131313></td>
    <td width="1" height="1"
bgcolor=#1e1e1e></td>
    <td width="1" height="1"
bgcolor=#353535></td>
    <td width="1" height="1"
bgcolor=#191919></td>
    <td width="1" height="1"
bgcolor=#0f0f0f></td>
    <td width="1" height="1"
bgcolor=#111111></td>
    <td width="1" height="1"
bgcolor=#141414></td>
    <td width="1" height="1"
bgcolor=#191919></td>
    <td width="1" height="1"
bgcolor=#121212></td>
    <td rowspan="1"
colspan="2" width="1"
height="1"
bgcolor=#040404></td>
    <td width="1" height="1"
bgcolor=#0f0f0f></td>
    <td width="1" height="1"
bgcolor=#0e0e0e></td>
    <td width="1" height="1"
bgcolor=#000000></td>
    <td width="1" height="1"
bgcolor=#020202></td>
    <td width="1" height="1"
bgcolor=#0d0d0d></td>
    <td width="1" height="1"
bgcolor=#242424></td>
    <td width="1" height="1"
bgcolor=#070707></td>
    <td width="1" height="1"
bgcolor=#020202></td>
    <td rowspan="2"
colspan="1" width="1"
height="1"
bgcolor=#0f0f0f></td>
    <td width="1" height="1"
bgcolor=#4c4c4c></td>
    <td width="1" height="1"
bgcolor=#878787></td>
    <td width="1" height="1"
bgcolor=#aaaaaa></td>
    <td width="1" height="1"
bgcolor=#868686></td>
    <td width="1" height="1"
bgcolor=#676767></td>
    <td width="1" height="1"
bgcolor=#a4a4a4></td>
    <td width="1" height="1"
bgcolor=#575757></td>
    <td width="1" height="1"
bgcolor=#0d0d0d></td>
    <td width="1" height="1"
bgcolor=#121212></td>
    <td width="1" height="1"
bgcolor=#171717></td>
    <td width="1" height="1"
bgcolor=#161616></td>
    <td width="1" height="1"
bgcolor=#191919></td>
    <td width="1" height="1"
bgcolor=#171717></td>
    <td width="1" height="1"
bgcolor=#323232></td>
    <td width="1" height="1"
bgcolor=#373737></td>
    <td width="1" height="1"
bgcolor=#464646></td>
    <td width="1" height="1"
bgcolor=#919191></td>
  </tr>
  <tr>
    <td width="1" height="1"
bgcolor=#949494></td>
    <td width="1" height="1"
bgcolor=#a5a5a5></td>
    <td width="1" height="1"
bgcolor=#6e6e6e></td>
    <td width="1" height="1"
bgcolor=#4e4e4e></td>
    <td width="1" height="1"
bgcolor=#424242></td>
    <td width="1" height="1"
bgcolor=#4f4f4f></td>
    <td width="1" height="1"
bgcolor=#676767></td>
    <td rowspan="1"
colspan="2" width="1"
height="1"
bgcolor=#626262></td>
    <td width="1" height="1"
bgcolor=#707070></td>
    <td width="1" height="1"
bgcolor=#aaaaaa></td>
    <td width="1" height="1"
bgcolor=#8d8d8d></td>
    <td width="1" height="1"
bgcolor=#565656></td>
    <td width="1" height="1"
bgcolor=#3e3e3e></td>
    <td width="1" height="1"
bgcolor=#292929></td>
    <td width="1" height="1"
bgcolor=#2b2b2b></td>
    <td width="1" height="1"
bgcolor=#2e2e2e></td>
    <td width="1" height="1"
bgcolor=#272727></td>
    <td width="1" height="1"
bgcolor=#212121></td>
    <td width="1" height="1"
bgcolor=#232323></td>
    <td width="1" height="1"
bgcolor=#1c1c1c></td>
    <td width="1" height="1"
bgcolor=#939393></td>
    <td width="1" height="1"
bgcolor=#bbbbbb></td>
    <td width="1" height="1"
bgcolor=#7f7f7f></td>
    <td width="1" height="1"
bgcolor=#3c3c3c></td>
    <td width="1" height="1"
bgcolor=#151515></td>
```

```
    <td width="1" height="1"
bgcolor=#000000></td>
    <td width="1" height="1"
bgcolor=#111111></td>
    <td width="1" height="1"
bgcolor=#1c1c1c></td>
    <td width="1" height="1"
bgcolor=#272727></td>
    <td width="1" height="1"
bgcolor=#212121></td>
    <td width="1" height="1"
bgcolor=#434343></td>
    <td width="1" height="1"
bgcolor=#414141></td>
    <td width="1" height="1"
bgcolor=#191919></td>
    <td width="1" height="1"
bgcolor=#1f1f1f></td>
    <td width="1" height="1"
bgcolor=#2d2d2d></td>
    <td width="1" height="1"
bgcolor=#222222></td>
    <td width="1" height="1"
bgcolor=#1d1d1d></td>
    <td width="1" height="1"
bgcolor=#232323></td>
    <td rowspan="2"
colspan="1" width="1"
height="1"
bgcolor=#161616></td>
    <td width="1" height="1"
bgcolor=#121212></td>
    <td width="1" height="1"
bgcolor=#202020></td>
    <td rowspan="2"
colspan="1" width="1"
height="1"
bgcolor=#161616></td>
    <td width="1" height="1"
bgcolor=#080808></td>
    <td rowspan="3"
colspan="1" width="1"
height="1"
bgcolor=#040404></td>
    <td width="1" height="1"
bgcolor=#040404></td>
    <td width="1" height="1"
bgcolor=#050505></td>
    <td width="1" height="1"
bgcolor=#020202></td>
    <td rowspan="3"
colspan="1" width="1"
height="1"
bgcolor=#000000></td>
    <td width="1" height="1"
bgcolor=#323232></td>
    <td width="1" height="1"
bgcolor=#a5a5a5></td>
    <td width="1" height="1"
bgcolor=#242424></td>
    <td width="1" height="1"
bgcolor=#000000></td>
    <td width="1" height="1"
bgcolor=#282828></td>
    <td width="1" height="1"
bgcolor=#646464></td>
    <td width="1" height="1"
bgcolor=#b1b1b1></td>
    <td width="1" height="1"
bgcolor=#b5b5b5></td>
    <td width="1" height="1"
bgcolor=#999999></td>
    <td width="1" height="1"
bgcolor=#bababa></td>
    <td width="1" height="1"
bgcolor=#5d5d5d></td>
    <td width="1" height="1"
bgcolor=#0b0b0b></td>
    <td width="1" height="1"
bgcolor=#070707></td>
    <td rowspan="2"
colspan="1" width="1"
height="1"
bgcolor=#1b1b1b></td>
    <td width="1" height="1"
bgcolor=#1a1a1a></td>
    <td width="1" height="1"
bgcolor=#202020></td>
    <td width="1" height="1"
bgcolor=#181818></td>
    <td width="1" height="1"
bgcolor=#2d2d2d></td>
    <td width="1" height="1"
bgcolor=#414141></td>
    <td width="1" height="1"
bgcolor=#444444></td>
    <td width="1" height="1"
bgcolor=#5f5f5f></td>
  </tr>
  <tr>
    <td width="1" height="1"
bgcolor=#6d6d6d></td>
    <td width="1" height="1"
bgcolor=#5b5b5b></td>
    <td width="1" height="1"
bgcolor=#555555></td>
    <td width="1" height="1"
bgcolor=#373737></td>
    <td width="1" height="1"
bgcolor=#1c1c1c></td>
    <td width="1" height="1"
bgcolor=#424242></td>
    <td width="1" height="1"
bgcolor=#626262></td>
    <td width="1" height="1"
bgcolor=#5f5f5f></td>
    <td width="1" height="1"
bgcolor=#767676></td>
    <td rowspan="2"
colspan="1" width="1"
height="1"
bgcolor=#9e9e9e></td>
    <td width="1" height="1"
bgcolor=#bdbdbd></td>
    <td width="1" height="1"
bgcolor=#a7a7a7></td>
    <td width="1" height="1"
bgcolor=#636363></td>
    <td width="1" height="1"
bgcolor=#333333></td>
    <td width="1" height="1"
bgcolor=#2e2e2e></td>
    <td width="1" height="1"
bgcolor=#2f2f2f></td>
    <td width="1" height="1"
bgcolor=#292929></td>
    <td width="1" height="1"
bgcolor=#1e1e1e></td>
    <td width="1" height="1"
bgcolor=#262626></td>
    <td width="1" height="1"
bgcolor=#2d2d2d></td>
    <td width="1" height="1"
bgcolor=#303030></td>
    <td width="1" height="1"
bgcolor=#414141></td>
    <td width="1" height="1"
bgcolor=#1c1c1c></td>
    <td width="1" height="1"
bgcolor=#070707></td>
    <td width="1" height="1"
bgcolor=#090909></td>
    <td width="1" height="1"
bgcolor=#141414></td>
    <td width="1" height="1"
bgcolor=#222222></td>
    <td width="1" height="1"
bgcolor=#2d2d2d></td>
    <td width="1" height="1"
bgcolor=#272727></td>
    <td width="1" height="1"
bgcolor=#2d2d2d></td>
    <td width="1" height="1"
bgcolor=#1c1c1c></td>
    <td width="1" height="1"
bgcolor=#252525></td>
    <td width="1" height="1"
bgcolor=#3b3b3b></td>
    <td rowspan="2"
colspan="1" width="1"
height="1"
bgcolor=#202020></td>
    <td rowspan="2"
colspan="1" width="1"
```

```
height="1"
bgcolor=#232323></td>
    <td width="1" height="1"
bgcolor=#252525></td>
    <td width="1" height="1"
bgcolor=#212121></td>
    <td width="1" height="1"
bgcolor=#121212></td>
    <td width="1" height="1"
bgcolor=#151515></td>
    <td width="1" height="1"
bgcolor=#0c0c0c></td>
    <td width="1" height="1"
bgcolor=#252525></td>
    <td width="1" height="1"
bgcolor=#050505></td>
    <td rowspan="2"
colspan="1" width="1"
height="1"
bgcolor=#020202></td>
    <td rowspan="2"
colspan="1" width="1"
height="1"
bgcolor=#000000></td>
    <td width="1" height="1"
bgcolor=#030303></td>
    <td width="1" height="1"
bgcolor=#020202></td>
    <td width="1" height="1"
bgcolor=#1d1d1d></td>
    <td width="1" height="1"
bgcolor=#b6b6b6></td>
    <td width="1" height="1"
bgcolor=#949494></td>
    <td width="1" height="1"
bgcolor=#3e3e3e></td>
    <td width="1" height="1"
bgcolor=#0d0d0d></td>
    <td width="1" height="1"
bgcolor=#4f4f4f></td>
    <td width="1" height="1"
bgcolor=#6c6c6c></td>
    <td width="1" height="1"
bgcolor=#c2c2c2></td>
    <td width="1" height="1"
bgcolor=#b8b8b8></td>
    <td width="1" height="1"
bgcolor=#a6a6a6></td>
    <td width="1" height="1"
bgcolor=#ababab></td>
    <td width="1" height="1"
bgcolor=#636363></td>
    <td width="1" height="1"
bgcolor=#070707></td>
    <td width="1" height="1"
bgcolor=#1b1b1b></td>
    <td rowspan="1"
colspan="2" width="1"
height="1"
bgcolor=#121212></td>
    <td width="1" height="1"
bgcolor=#1d1d1d></td>
    <td width="1" height="1"
bgcolor=#1e1e1e></td>
    <td width="1" height="1"
bgcolor=#343434></td>
    <td width="1" height="1"
bgcolor=#5b5b5b></td>
    <td width="1" height="1"
bgcolor=#595959></td>
  </tr>
  <tr>
    <td width="1" height="1"
bgcolor=#666666></td>
    <td width="1" height="1"
bgcolor=#545454></td>
    <td width="1" height="1"
bgcolor=#585858></td>
    <td width="1" height="1"
bgcolor=#3c3c3c></td>
    <td width="1" height="1"
bgcolor=#2a2a2a></td>
    <td width="1" height="1"
bgcolor=#303030></td>
    <td width="1" height="1"
bgcolor=#585858></td>
    <td width="1" height="1"
bgcolor=#848484></td>
    <td width="1" height="1"
bgcolor=#b8b8b8></td>
    <td width="1" height="1"
bgcolor=#8f8f8f></td>
    <td width="1" height="1"
bgcolor=#959595></td>
    <td width="1" height="1"
bgcolor=#2e2e2e></td>
    <td width="1" height="1"
bgcolor=#141414></td>
    <td width="1" height="1"
bgcolor=#242424></td>
    <td width="1" height="1"
bgcolor=#383838></td>
    <td width="1" height="1"
bgcolor=#2e2e2e></td>
    <td width="1" height="1"
bgcolor=#2b2b2b></td>
    <td width="1" height="1"
bgcolor=#242424></td>
    <td width="1" height="1"
bgcolor=#191919></td>
    <td width="1" height="1"
bgcolor=#1e1e1e></td>
    <td width="1" height="1"
bgcolor=#101010></td>
    <td width="1" height="1"
bgcolor=#161616></td>
    <td width="1" height="1"
bgcolor=#181818></td>
    <td width="1" height="1"
bgcolor=#151515></td>
    <td width="1" height="1"
bgcolor=#242424></td>
    <td width="1" height="1"
bgcolor=#313131></td>
    <td width="1" height="1"
bgcolor=#3a3a3a></td>
    <td width="1" height="1"
bgcolor=#383838></td>
    <td width="1" height="1"
bgcolor=#2a2a2a></td>
    <td width="1" height="1"
bgcolor=#181818></td>
    <td width="1" height="1"
bgcolor=#0e0e0e></td>
    <td width="1" height="1"
bgcolor=#191919></td>
    <td width="1" height="1"
bgcolor=#0d0d0d></td>
    <td width="1" height="1"
bgcolor=#101010></td>
    <td width="1" height="1"
bgcolor=#131313></td>
    <td width="1" height="1"
bgcolor=#161616></td>
    <td width="1" height="1"
bgcolor=#0c0c0c></td>
    <td width="1" height="1"
bgcolor=#010101></td>
    <td width="1" height="1"
bgcolor=#101010></td>
    <td width="1" height="1"
bgcolor=#040404></td>
    <td width="1" height="1"
bgcolor=#010101></td>
    <td width="1" height="1"
bgcolor=#000000></td>
    <td rowspan="4"
colspan="1" width="1"
height="1"
bgcolor=#000000></td>
    <td width="1" height="1"
bgcolor=#242424></td>
    <td width="1" height="1"
bgcolor=#a7a7a7></td>
    <td width="1" height="1"
bgcolor=#b6b6b6></td>
    <td width="1" height="1"
bgcolor=#848484></td>
    <td width="1" height="1"
bgcolor=#6c6c6c></td>
    <td width="1" height="1"
bgcolor=#2c2c2c></td>
    <td width="1" height="1"
bgcolor=#4e4e4e></td>
```

```
    <td width="1" height="1"
bgcolor=#9d9d9d></td>
    <td width="1" height="1"
bgcolor=#b2b2b2></td>
    <td rowspan="2"
colspan="1" width="1"
height="1"
bgcolor=#b6b6b6></td>
    <td width="1" height="1"
bgcolor=#c2c2c2></td>
    <td width="1" height="1"
bgcolor=#717171></td>
    <td width="1" height="1"
bgcolor=#0c0c0c></td>
    <td width="1" height="1"
bgcolor=#171717></td>
    <td width="1" height="1"
bgcolor=#121212></td>
    <td width="1" height="1"
bgcolor=#0d0d0d></td>
    <td width="1" height="1"
bgcolor=#111111></td>
    <td width="1" height="1"
bgcolor=#2c2c2c></td>
    <td width="1" height="1"
bgcolor=#323232></td>
    <td width="1" height="1"
bgcolor=#3a3a3a></td>
    <td width="1" height="1"
bgcolor=#535353></td>
    <td width="1" height="1"
bgcolor=#4e4e4e></td>
  </tr>
  <tr>
    <td width="1" height="1"
bgcolor=#8c8c8c></td>
    <td rowspan="1"
colspan="2" width="1"
height="1"
bgcolor=#8d8d8d></td>
    <td width="1" height="1"
bgcolor=#646464></td>
    <td width="1" height="1"
bgcolor=#4b4b4b></td>
    <td width="1" height="1"
bgcolor=#474747></td>
    <td width="1" height="1"
bgcolor=#828282></td>
    <td width="1" height="1"
bgcolor=#b8b8b8></td>
    <td width="1" height="1"
bgcolor=#777777></td>
    <td width="1" height="1"
bgcolor=#303030></td>
    <td width="1" height="1"
bgcolor=#7b7b7b></td>
    <td width="1" height="1"
bgcolor=#bfbfbf></td>
    <td width="1" height="1"
bgcolor=#3f3f3f></td>
    <td width="1" height="1"
bgcolor=#2b2b2b></td>
    <td width="1" height="1"
bgcolor=#3b3b3b></td>
    <td width="1" height="1"
bgcolor=#353535></td>
    <td width="1" height="1"
bgcolor=#373737></td>
    <td width="1" height="1"
bgcolor=#282828></td>
    <td width="1" height="1"
bgcolor=#1b1b1b></td>
    <td width="1" height="1"
bgcolor=#161616></td>
    <td width="1" height="1"
bgcolor=#181818></td>
    <td width="1" height="1"
bgcolor=#0f0f0f></td>
    <td rowspan="1"
colspan="2" width="1"
height="1"
bgcolor=#232323></td>
    <td width="1" height="1"
bgcolor=#212121></td>
    <td rowspan="2"
colspan="1" width="1"
height="1"
bgcolor=#2b2b2b></td>
    <td rowspan="1"
colspan="2" width="1"
height="1"
bgcolor=#2d2d2d></td>
    <td width="1" height="1"
bgcolor=#343434></td>
    <td width="1" height="1"
bgcolor=#191919></td>
    <td width="1" height="1"
bgcolor=#0f0f0f></td>
    <td width="1" height="1"
bgcolor=#0c0c0c></td>
    <td width="1" height="1"
bgcolor=#0b0b0b></td>
    <td width="1" height="1"
bgcolor=#1a1a1a></td>
    <td width="1" height="1"
bgcolor=#2b2b2b></td>
    <td width="1" height="1"
bgcolor=#1b1b1b></td>
    <td width="1" height="1"
bgcolor=#141414></td>
    <td width="1" height="1"
bgcolor=#121212></td>
    <td width="1" height="1"
bgcolor=#131313></td>
    <td width="1" height="1"
bgcolor=#070707></td>
    <td width="1" height="1"
bgcolor=#0c0c0c></td>
    <td width="1" height="1"
bgcolor=#0a0a0a></td>
    <td width="1" height="1"
bgcolor=#050505></td>
    <td width="1" height="1"
bgcolor=#0b0b0b></td>
    <td width="1" height="1"
bgcolor=#020202></td>
    <td width="1" height="1"
bgcolor=#000000></td>
    <td rowspan="1"
colspan="2" width="1"
height="1"
bgcolor=#010101></td>
    <td width="1" height="1"
bgcolor=#020202></td>
    <td width="1" height="1"
bgcolor=#2e2e2e></td>
    <td width="1" height="1"
bgcolor=#b8b8b8></td>
    <td width="1" height="1"
bgcolor=#bebebe></td>
    <td width="1" height="1"
bgcolor=#a0a0a0></td>
    <td width="1" height="1"
bgcolor=#b2b2b2></td>
    <td width="1" height="1"
bgcolor=#868686></td>
    <td width="1" height="1"
bgcolor=#545454></td>
    <td width="1" height="1"
bgcolor=#7d7d7d></td>
    <td width="1" height="1"
bgcolor=#9c9c9c></td>
    <td width="1" height="1"
bgcolor=#d6d6d6></td>
    <td width="1" height="1"
bgcolor=#707070></td>
    <td width="1" height="1"
bgcolor=#0e0e0e></td>
    <td width="1" height="1"
bgcolor=#141414></td>
    <td width="1" height="1"
bgcolor=#262626></td>
    <td width="1" height="1"
bgcolor=#191919></td>
    <td width="1" height="1"
bgcolor=#161616></td>
    <td width="1" height="1"
bgcolor=#323232></td>
    <td width="1" height="1"
bgcolor=#606060></td>
    <td width="1" height="1"
bgcolor=#686868></td>
    <td width="1" height="1"
bgcolor=#4a4a4a></td>
```

```
<td width="1" height="1"
bgcolor=#4b4b4b></td>
</tr>
<tr>
<td width="1" height="1"
bgcolor=#777777></td>
<td width="1" height="1"
bgcolor=#6a6a6a></td>
<td width="1" height="1"
bgcolor=#686868></td>
<td width="1" height="1"
bgcolor=#707070></td>
<td width="1" height="1"
bgcolor=#808080></td>
<td width="1" height="1"
bgcolor=#adadad></td>
<td width="1" height="1"
bgcolor=#bebebe></td>
<td width="1" height="1"
bgcolor=#555555></td>
<td width="1" height="1"
bgcolor=#191919></td>
<td width="1" height="1"
bgcolor=#1c1c1c></td>
<td width="1" height="1"
bgcolor=#8b8b8b></td>
<td width="1" height="1"
bgcolor=#cacaca></td>
<td width="1" height="1"
bgcolor=#636363></td>
<td width="1" height="1"
bgcolor=#2c2c2c></td>
<td width="1" height="1"
bgcolor=#353535></td>
<td width="1" height="1"
bgcolor=#343434></td>
<td width="1" height="1"
bgcolor=#2b2b2b></td>
<td width="1" height="1"
bgcolor=#1a1a1a></td>
<td rowspan="2"
colspan="1" width="1"
height="1"
bgcolor=#0d0d0d></td>
<td width="1" height="1"
bgcolor=#0b0b0b></td>
<td width="1" height="1"
bgcolor=#0a0a0a></td>
<td width="1" height="1"
bgcolor=#0d0d0d></td>
<td width="1" height="1"
bgcolor=#181818></td>
<td width="1" height="1"
bgcolor=#252525></td>
<td width="1" height="1"
bgcolor=#1e1e1e></td>
<td width="1" height="1"
bgcolor=#2e2e2e></td>
<td width="1" height="1"
bgcolor=#202020></td>
<td width="1" height="1"
bgcolor=#232323></td>
<td width="1" height="1"
bgcolor=#161616></td>
<td width="1" height="1"
bgcolor=#141414></td>
<td width="1" height="1"
bgcolor=#1f1f1f></td>
<td width="1" height="1"
bgcolor=#191919></td>
<td width="1" height="1"
bgcolor=#2f2f2f></td>
<td width="1" height="1"
bgcolor=#373737></td>
<td width="1" height="1"
bgcolor=#181818></td>
<td width="1" height="1"
bgcolor=#070707></td>
<td width="1" height="1"
bgcolor=#0a0a0a></td>
<td width="1" height="1"
bgcolor=#121212></td>
<td width="1" height="1"
bgcolor=#111111></td>
<td width="1" height="1"
bgcolor=#090909></td>
<td width="1" height="1"
bgcolor=#0d0d0d></td>
<td width="1" height="1"
bgcolor=#0c0c0c></td>
<td width="1" height="1"
bgcolor=#0a0a0a></td>
<td width="1" height="1"
bgcolor=#000000></td>
<td rowspan="2"
colspan="1" width="1"
height="1"
bgcolor=#040404></td>
<td width="1" height="1"
bgcolor=#070707></td>
<td width="1" height="1"
bgcolor=#040404></td>
<td width="1" height="1"
bgcolor=#0a0a0a></td>
<td width="1" height="1"
bgcolor=#2f2f2f></td>
<td width="1" height="1"
bgcolor=#8a8a8a></td>
<td width="1" height="1"
bgcolor=#848484></td>
<td width="1" height="1"
bgcolor=#9e9e9e></td>
<td width="1" height="1"
bgcolor=#989898></td>
<td width="1" height="1"
bgcolor=#aaaaaa></td>
<td width="1" height="1"
bgcolor=#b9b9b9></td>
<td width="1" height="1"
bgcolor=#9b9b9b></td>
<td width="1" height="1"
bgcolor=#888888></td>
<td width="1" height="1"
bgcolor=#a4a4a4></td>
<td width="1" height="1"
bgcolor=#bfbfbf></td>
<td width="1" height="1"
bgcolor=#646464></td>
<td width="1" height="1"
bgcolor=#1a1a1a></td>
<td width="1" height="1"
bgcolor=#181818></td>
<td width="1" height="1"
bgcolor=#212121></td>
<td width="1" height="1"
bgcolor=#262626></td>
<td width="1" height="1"
bgcolor=#343434></td>
<td width="1" height="1"
bgcolor=#525252></td>
<td width="1" height="1"
bgcolor=#686868></td>
<td width="1" height="1"
bgcolor=#5c5c5c></td>
<td width="1" height="1"
bgcolor=#3f3f3f></td>
<td width="1" height="1"
bgcolor=#464646></td>
</tr>
<tr>
<td width="1" height="1"
bgcolor=#9c9c9c></td>
<td width="1" height="1"
bgcolor=#6d6d6d></td>
<td width="1" height="1"
bgcolor=#696969></td>
<td width="1" height="1"
bgcolor=#878787></td>
<td width="1" height="1"
bgcolor=#b8b8b8></td>
<td width="1" height="1"
bgcolor=#bdbdbd></td>
<td width="1" height="1"
bgcolor=#686868></td>
<td width="1" height="1"
bgcolor=#1f1f1f></td>
<td width="1" height="1"
bgcolor=#272727></td>
<td width="1" height="1"
bgcolor=#1b1b1b></td>
<td width="1" height="1"
bgcolor=#737373></td>
<td width="1" height="1"
bgcolor=#b1b1b1></td>
```

```
    <td width="1" height="1" bgcolor=#555555></td>
    <td width="1" height="1" bgcolor=#1e1e1e></td>
    <td width="1" height="1" bgcolor=#191919></td>
    <td width="1" height="1" bgcolor=#1f1f1f></td>
    <td width="1" height="1" bgcolor=#353535></td>
    <td width="1" height="1" bgcolor=#252525></td>
    <td width="1" height="1" bgcolor=#111111></td>
    <td rowspan="2" colspan="1" width="1" height="1" bgcolor=#191919></td>
    <td width="1" height="1" bgcolor=#171717></td>
    <td width="1" height="1" bgcolor=#141414></td>
    <td width="1" height="1" bgcolor=#0b0b0b></td>
    <td width="1" height="1" bgcolor=#131313></td>
    <td width="1" height="1" bgcolor=#171717></td>
    <td width="1" height="1" bgcolor=#292929></td>
    <td width="1" height="1" bgcolor=#272727></td>
    <td rowspan="1" colspan="2" width="1" height="1" bgcolor=#2e2e2e></td>
    <td width="1" height="1" bgcolor=#2a2a2a></td>
    <td width="1" height="1" bgcolor=#3e3e3e></td>
    <td width="1" height="1" bgcolor=#454545></td>
    <td width="1" height="1" bgcolor=#4c4c4c></td>
    <td width="1" height="1" bgcolor=#383838></td>
    <td width="1" height="1" bgcolor=#191919></td>
    <td width="1" height="1" bgcolor=#151515></td>
    <td width="1" height="1" bgcolor=#121212></td>
    <td width="1" height="1" bgcolor=#0f0f0f></td>
    <td width="1" height="1" bgcolor=#1a1a1a></td>
    <td width="1" height="1" bgcolor=#101010></td>
    <td width="1" height="1" bgcolor=#0f0f0f></td>
    <td rowspan="2" colspan="1" width="1" height="1" bgcolor=#0b0b0b></td>
    <td width="1" height="1" bgcolor=#0f0f0f></td>
    <td width="1" height="1" bgcolor=#070707></td>
    <td width="1" height="1" bgcolor=#000000></td>
    <td width="1" height="1" bgcolor=#060606></td>
    <td width="1" height="1" bgcolor=#050505></td>
    <td width="1" height="1" bgcolor=#252525></td>
    <td width="1" height="1" bgcolor=#8d8d8d></td>
    <td rowspan="2" colspan="1" width="1" height="1" bgcolor=#818181></td>
    <td width="1" height="1" bgcolor=#969696></td>
    <td width="1" height="1" bgcolor=#acacac></td>
    <td width="1" height="1" bgcolor=#919191></td>
    <td width="1" height="1" bgcolor=#cacaca></td>
    <td width="1" height="1" bgcolor=#dfdfdf></td>
    <td width="1" height="1" bgcolor=#a4a4a4></td>
    <td width="1" height="1" bgcolor=#818181></td>
    <td width="1" height="1" bgcolor=#999999></td>
    <td width="1" height="1" bgcolor=#484848></td>
    <td width="1" height="1" bgcolor=#0a0a0a></td>
    <td width="1" height="1" bgcolor=#1d1d1d></td>
    <td width="1" height="1" bgcolor=#151515></td>
    <td width="1" height="1" bgcolor=#181818></td>
    <td width="1" height="1" bgcolor=#2d2d2d></td>
    <td width="1" height="1" bgcolor=#626262></td>
    <td width="1" height="1" bgcolor=#5d5d5d></td>
    <td width="1" height="1" bgcolor=#4c4c4c></td>
    <td width="1" height="1" bgcolor=#575757></td>
    <td width="1" height="1" bgcolor=#4c4c4c></td>
  </tr>
  <tr>
    <td rowspan="2" colspan="1" width="1" height="1" bgcolor=#818181></td>
    <td width="1" height="1" bgcolor=#515151></td>
    <td width="1" height="1" bgcolor=#7d7d7d></td>
    <td width="1" height="1" bgcolor=#b6b6b6></td>
    <td width="1" height="1" bgcolor=#acacac></td>
    <td width="1" height="1" bgcolor=#454545></td>
    <td rowspan="1" colspan="2" width="1" height="1" bgcolor=#3c3c3c></td>
    <td width="1" height="1" bgcolor=#2e2e2e></td>
    <td width="1" height="1" bgcolor=#121212></td>
    <td width="1" height="1" bgcolor=#4b4b4b></td>
    <td width="1" height="1" bgcolor=#a8a8a8></td>
    <td width="1" height="1" bgcolor=#464646></td>
    <td rowspan="1" colspan="2" width="1" height="1" bgcolor=#0f0f0f></td>
    <td width="1" height="1" bgcolor=#050505></td>
    <td width="1" height="1" bgcolor=#252525></td>
    <td width="1" height="1" bgcolor=#2b2b2b></td>
    <td width="1" height="1" bgcolor=#181818></td>
    <td width="1" height="1" bgcolor=#222222></td>
    <td width="1" height="1" bgcolor=#181818></td>
    <td width="1" height="1" bgcolor=#1e1e1e></td>
    <td width="1" height="1" bgcolor=#1d1d1d></td>
    <td width="1" height="1" bgcolor=#0a0a0a></td>
    <td width="1" height="1" bgcolor=#0e0e0e></td>
```

```
    <td width="1" height="1"
bgcolor=#191919></td>
    <td width="1" height="1"
bgcolor=#1d1d1d></td>
    <td width="1" height="1"
bgcolor=#353535></td>
    <td width="1" height="1"
bgcolor=#343434></td>
    <td width="1" height="1"
bgcolor=#232323></td>
    <td width="1" height="1"
bgcolor=#2a2a2a></td>
    <td width="1" height="1"
bgcolor=#424242></td>
    <td width="1" height="1"
bgcolor=#353535></td>
    <td rowspan="2"
colspan="1" width="1"
height="1"
bgcolor=#2a2a2a></td>
    <td width="1" height="1"
bgcolor=#262626></td>
    <td width="1" height="1"
bgcolor=#0c0c0c></td>
    <td width="1" height="1"
bgcolor=#060606></td>
    <td width="1" height="1"
bgcolor=#111111></td>
    <td rowspan="1"
colspan="2" width="1"
height="1"
bgcolor=#121212></td>
    <td width="1" height="1"
bgcolor=#0a0a0a></td>
    <td rowspan="2"
colspan="1" width="1"
height="1"
bgcolor=#050505></td>
    <td rowspan="2"
colspan="1" width="1"
height="1"
bgcolor=#020202></td>
    <td rowspan="2"
colspan="1" width="1"
height="1"
bgcolor=#050505></td>
    <td width="1" height="1"
bgcolor=#020202></td>
    <td width="1" height="1"
bgcolor=#040404></td>
    <td width="1" height="1"
bgcolor=#000000></td>
    <td width="1" height="1"
bgcolor=#020202></td>
    <td width="1" height="1"
bgcolor=#0d0d0d></td>
    <td width="1" height="1"
bgcolor=#737373></td>
    <td width="1" height="1"
bgcolor=#909090></td>
    <td width="1" height="1"
bgcolor=#8a8a8a></td>
    <td width="1" height="1"
bgcolor=#818181></td>
    <td width="1" height="1"
bgcolor=#999999></td>
    <td width="1" height="1"
bgcolor=#b6b6b6></td>
    <td width="1" height="1"
bgcolor=#5a5a5a></td>
    <td width="1" height="1"
bgcolor=#747474></td>
    <td width="1" height="1"
bgcolor=#b7b7b7></td>
    <td width="1" height="1"
bgcolor=#3b3b3b></td>
    <td width="1" height="1"
bgcolor=#111111></td>
    <td width="1" height="1"
bgcolor=#0d0d0d></td>
    <td width="1" height="1"
bgcolor=#101010></td>
    <td width="1" height="1"
bgcolor=#1e1e1e></td>
    <td width="1" height="1"
bgcolor=#303030></td>
    <td width="1" height="1"
bgcolor=#727272></td>
    <td width="1" height="1"
bgcolor=#545454></td>
    <td width="1" height="1"
bgcolor=#494949></td>
    <td width="1" height="1"
bgcolor=#5b5b5b></td>
    <td width="1" height="1"
bgcolor=#5c5c5c></td>
  </tr>
  <tr>
    <td width="1" height="1"
bgcolor=#6f6f6f></td>
    <td width="1" height="1"
bgcolor=#afafaf></td>
    <td width="1" height="1"
bgcolor=#949494></td>
    <td width="1" height="1"
bgcolor=#484848></td>
    <td width="1" height="1"
bgcolor=#212121></td>
    <td width="1" height="1"
bgcolor=#454545></td>
    <td width="1" height="1"
bgcolor=#4e4e4e></td>
    <td width="1" height="1"
bgcolor=#313131></td>
    <td width="1" height="1"
bgcolor=#1a1a1a></td>
    <td width="1" height="1"
bgcolor=#474747></td>
    <td width="1" height="1"
bgcolor=#8f8f8f></td>
    <td width="1" height="1"
bgcolor=#4d4d4d></td>
    <td width="1" height="1"
bgcolor=#222222></td>
    <td width="1" height="1"
bgcolor=#171717></td>
    <td width="1" height="1"
bgcolor=#1c1c1c></td>
    <td width="1" height="1"
bgcolor=#1b1b1b></td>
    <td width="1" height="1"
bgcolor=#272727></td>
    <td width="1" height="1"
bgcolor=#2a2a2a></td>
    <td width="1" height="1"
bgcolor=#232323></td>
    <td width="1" height="1"
bgcolor=#1f1f1f></td>
    <td width="1" height="1"
bgcolor=#1b1b1b></td>
    <td width="1" height="1"
bgcolor=#222222></td>
    <td width="1" height="1"
bgcolor=#262626></td>
    <td rowspan="1"
colspan="2" width="1"
height="1"
bgcolor=#1c1c1c></td>
    <td width="1" height="1"
bgcolor=#2a2a2a></td>
    <td width="1" height="1"
bgcolor=#1c1c1c></td>
    <td width="1" height="1"
bgcolor=#202020></td>
    <td width="1" height="1"
bgcolor=#252525></td>
    <td width="1" height="1"
bgcolor=#131313></td>
    <td width="1" height="1"
bgcolor=#111111></td>
    <td width="1" height="1"
bgcolor=#282828></td>
    <td width="1" height="1"
bgcolor=#252525></td>
    <td width="1" height="1"
bgcolor=#141414></td>
    <td width="1" height="1"
bgcolor=#040404></td>
    <td width="1" height="1"
bgcolor=#101010></td>
    <td width="1" height="1"
bgcolor=#080808></td>
    <td rowspan="2"
colspan="1" width="1"
```

```
height="1"
bgcolor=#0b0b0b></td>
    <td width="1" height="1"
bgcolor=#090909></td>
    <td width="1" height="1"
bgcolor=#070707></td>
    <td width="1" height="1"
bgcolor=#0a0a0a></td>
    <td width="1" height="1"
bgcolor=#040404></td>
    <td width="1" height="1"
bgcolor=#050505></td>
    <td width="1" height="1"
bgcolor=#040404></td>
    <td rowspan="2"
colspan="1" width="1"
height="1"
bgcolor=#000000></td>
    <td width="1" height="1"
bgcolor=#040404></td>
    <td width="1" height="1"
bgcolor=#515151></td>
    <td width="1" height="1"
bgcolor=#898989></td>
    <td width="1" height="1"
bgcolor=#a9a9a9></td>
    <td width="1" height="1"
bgcolor=#b2b2b2></td>
    <td width="1" height="1"
bgcolor=#969696></td>
    <td width="1" height="1"
bgcolor=#959595></td>
    <td rowspan="2"
colspan="1" width="1"
height="1"
bgcolor=#8e8e8e></td>
    <td width="1" height="1"
bgcolor=#8b8b8b></td>
    <td width="1" height="1"
bgcolor=#898989></td>
    <td width="1" height="1"
bgcolor=#adadad></td>
    <td width="1" height="1"
bgcolor=#3c3c3c></td>
    <td width="1" height="1"
bgcolor=#161616></td>
    <td width="1" height="1"
bgcolor=#1b1b1b></td>
    <td width="1" height="1"
bgcolor=#121212></td>
    <td width="1" height="1"
bgcolor=#252525></td>
    <td width="1" height="1"
bgcolor=#3b3b3b></td>
    <td width="1" height="1"
bgcolor=#6a6a6a></td>
    <td width="1" height="1"
bgcolor=#353535></td>
    <td width="1" height="1"
bgcolor=#303030></td>
    <td width="1" height="1"
bgcolor=#4b4b4b></td>
    <td width="1" height="1"
bgcolor=#515151></td>
  </tr>
  <tr>
    <td width="1" height="1"
bgcolor=#b6b6b6></td>
    <td width="1" height="1"
bgcolor=#a6a6a6></td>
    <td width="1" height="1"
bgcolor=#919191></td>
    <td width="1" height="1"
bgcolor=#565656></td>
    <td width="1" height="1"
bgcolor=#4d4d4d></td>
    <td width="1" height="1"
bgcolor=#4f4f4f></td>
    <td width="1" height="1"
bgcolor=#525252></td>
    <td width="1" height="1"
bgcolor=#363636></td>
    <td width="1" height="1"
bgcolor=#272727></td>
    <td width="1" height="1"
bgcolor=#1b1b1b></td>
    <td width="1" height="1"
bgcolor=#404040></td>
    <td width="1" height="1"
bgcolor=#7f7f7f></td>
    <td width="1" height="1"
bgcolor=#5a5a5a></td>
    <td width="1" height="1"
bgcolor=#2e2e2e></td>
    <td width="1" height="1"
bgcolor=#151515></td>
    <td width="1" height="1"
bgcolor=#1b1b1b></td>
    <td width="1" height="1"
bgcolor=#3c3c3c></td>
    <td width="1" height="1"
bgcolor=#434343></td>
    <td width="1" height="1"
bgcolor=#424242></td>
    <td width="1" height="1"
bgcolor=#2d2d2d></td>
    <td width="1" height="1"
bgcolor=#313131></td>
    <td width="1" height="1"
bgcolor=#242424></td>
    <td width="1" height="1"
bgcolor=#2d2d2d></td>
    <td width="1" height="1"
bgcolor=#2e2e2e></td>
    <td width="1" height="1"
bgcolor=#292929></td>
    <td width="1" height="1"
bgcolor=#272727></td>
    <td width="1" height="1"
bgcolor=#242424></td>
    <td width="1" height="1"
bgcolor=#1a1a1a></td>
    <td width="1" height="1"
bgcolor=#272727></td>
    <td width="1" height="1"
bgcolor=#2a2a2a></td>
    <td width="1" height="1"
bgcolor=#161616></td>
    <td width="1" height="1"
bgcolor=#121212></td>
    <td width="1" height="1"
bgcolor=#202020></td>
    <td width="1" height="1"
bgcolor=#1b1b1b></td>
    <td width="1" height="1"
bgcolor=#141414></td>
    <td width="1" height="1"
bgcolor=#0d0d0d></td>
    <td width="1" height="1"
bgcolor=#0f0f0f></td>
    <td width="1" height="1"
bgcolor=#121212></td>
    <td width="1" height="1"
bgcolor=#070707></td>
    <td rowspan="1"
colspan="3" width="1"
height="1"
bgcolor=#060606></td>
    <td width="1" height="1"
bgcolor=#040404></td>
    <td width="1" height="1"
bgcolor=#030303></td>
    <td width="1" height="1"
bgcolor=#060606></td>
    <td width="1" height="1"
bgcolor=#070707></td>
    <td width="1" height="1"
bgcolor=#030303></td>
    <td width="1" height="1"
bgcolor=#020202></td>
    <td width="1" height="1"
bgcolor=#090909></td>
    <td width="1" height="1"
bgcolor=#585858></td>
    <td width="1" height="1"
bgcolor=#939393></td>
    <td width="1" height="1"
bgcolor=#afafaf></td>
    <td width="1" height="1"
bgcolor=#c1c1c1></td>
    <td width="1" height="1"
bgcolor=#c2c2c2></td>
    <td width="1" height="1"
bgcolor=#bababa></td>
```

```
    <td width="1" height="1"
bgcolor=#aeaeae></td>
    <td width="1" height="1"
bgcolor=#cdcdcd></td>
    <td width="1" height="1"
bgcolor=#9f9f9f></td>
    <td rowspan="2"
colspan="1" width="1"
height="1"
bgcolor=#212121></td>
    <td width="1" height="1"
bgcolor=#141414></td>
    <td width="1" height="1"
bgcolor=#121212></td>
    <td width="1" height="1"
bgcolor=#212121></td>
    <td width="1" height="1"
bgcolor=#2b2b2b></td>
    <td width="1" height="1"
bgcolor=#3e3e3e></td>
    <td width="1" height="1"
bgcolor=#535353></td>
    <td width="1" height="1"
bgcolor=#363636></td>
    <td width="1" height="1"
bgcolor=#141414></td>
    <td width="1" height="1"
bgcolor=#2b2b2b></td>
    <td width="1" height="1"
bgcolor=#525252></td>
  </tr>
  <tr>
    <td width="1" height="1"
bgcolor=#888888></td>
    <td width="1" height="1"
bgcolor=#717171></td>
    <td width="1" height="1"
bgcolor=#696969></td>
    <td width="1" height="1"
bgcolor=#5a5a5a></td>
    <td rowspan="2"
colspan="1" width="1"
height="1"
bgcolor=#575757></td>
    <td width="1" height="1"
bgcolor=#474747></td>
    <td width="1" height="1"
bgcolor=#656565></td>
    <td width="1" height="1"
bgcolor=#505050></td>
    <td width="1" height="1"
bgcolor=#2a2a2a></td>
    <td width="1" height="1"
bgcolor=#121212></td>
    <td width="1" height="1"
bgcolor=#2f2f2f></td>
    <td width="1" height="1"
bgcolor=#868686></td>
    <td width="1" height="1"
bgcolor=#565656></td>
    <td width="1" height="1"
bgcolor=#1f1f1f></td>
    <td rowspan="2"
colspan="1" width="1"
height="1"
bgcolor=#212121></td>
    <td width="1" height="1"
bgcolor=#2a2a2a></td>
    <td width="1" height="1"
bgcolor=#3b3b3b></td>
    <td width="1" height="1"
bgcolor=#3c3c3c></td>
    <td width="1" height="1"
bgcolor=#2f2f2f></td>
    <td width="1" height="1"
bgcolor=#2e2e2e></td>
    <td width="1" height="1"
bgcolor=#474747></td>
    <td width="1" height="1"
bgcolor=#383838></td>
    <td width="1" height="1"
bgcolor=#3c3c3c></td>
    <td width="1" height="1"
bgcolor=#2a2a2a></td>
    <td width="1" height="1"
bgcolor=#141414></td>
    <td width="1" height="1"
bgcolor=#1b1b1b></td>
    <td width="1" height="1"
bgcolor=#252525></td>
    <td width="1" height="1"
bgcolor=#202020></td>
    <td rowspan="1"
colspan="2" width="1"
height="1"
bgcolor=#282828></td>
    <td width="1" height="1"
bgcolor=#141414></td>
    <td width="1" height="1"
bgcolor=#131313></td>
    <td width="1" height="1"
bgcolor=#181818></td>
    <td width="1" height="1"
bgcolor=#171717></td>
    <td width="1" height="1"
bgcolor=#1c1c1c></td>
    <td width="1" height="1"
bgcolor=#101010></td>
    <td width="1" height="1"
bgcolor=#171717></td>
    <td width="1" height="1"
bgcolor=#1f1f1f></td>
    <td width="1" height="1"
bgcolor=#0b0b0b></td>
    <td width="1" height="1"
bgcolor=#101010></td>
    <td width="1" height="1"
bgcolor=#161616></td>
    <td width="1" height="1"
bgcolor=#111111></td>
    <td width="1" height="1"
bgcolor=#0a0a0a></td>
    <td width="1" height="1"
bgcolor=#080808></td>
    <td rowspan="1"
colspan="2" width="1"
height="1"
bgcolor=#090909></td>
    <td width="1" height="1"
bgcolor=#080808></td>
    <td rowspan="1"
colspan="2" width="1"
height="1"
bgcolor=#000000></td>
    <td width="1" height="1"
bgcolor=#030303></td>
    <td width="1" height="1"
bgcolor=#050505></td>
    <td width="1" height="1"
bgcolor=#494949></td>
    <td width="1" height="1"
bgcolor=#9b9b9b></td>
    <td width="1" height="1"
bgcolor=#dddddd></td>
    <td width="1" height="1"
bgcolor=#dcdcdc></td>
    <td width="1" height="1"
bgcolor=#c1c1c1></td>
    <td width="1" height="1"
bgcolor=#b0b0b0></td>
    <td width="1" height="1"
bgcolor=#ababab></td>
    <td width="1" height="1"
bgcolor=#7f7f7f></td>
    <td width="1" height="1"
bgcolor=#ababab></td>
    <td width="1" height="1"
bgcolor=#a0a0a0></td>
    <td width="1" height="1"
bgcolor=#060606></td>
    <td width="1" height="1"
bgcolor=#151515></td>
    <td width="1" height="1"
bgcolor=#242424></td>
    <td width="1" height="1"
bgcolor=#303030></td>
    <td width="1" height="1"
bgcolor=#242424></td>
    <td rowspan="1"
colspan="2" width="1"
height="1"
bgcolor=#3a3a3a></td>
    <td width="1" height="1"
bgcolor=#1b1b1b></td>
```

```
    <td width="1" height="1" bgcolor=#1f1f1f></td>
    <td width="1" height="1" bgcolor=#919191></td>
  </tr>
  <tr>
    <td width="1" height="1" bgcolor=#636363></td>
    <td width="1" height="1" bgcolor=#454545></td>
    <td width="1" height="1" bgcolor=#6a6a6a></td>
    <td width="1" height="1" bgcolor=#6e6e6e></td>
    <td width="1" height="1" bgcolor=#292929></td>
    <td width="1" height="1" bgcolor=#4b4b4b></td>
    <td width="1" height="1" bgcolor=#525252></td>
    <td width="1" height="1" bgcolor=#5b5b5b></td>
    <td width="1" height="1" bgcolor=#454545></td>
    <td width="1" height="1" bgcolor=#272727></td>
    <td width="1" height="1" bgcolor=#6d6d6d></td>
    <td width="1" height="1" bgcolor=#424242></td>
    <td width="1" height="1" bgcolor=#101010></td>
    <td width="1" height="1" bgcolor=#252525></td>
    <td width="1" height="1" bgcolor=#232323></td>
    <td width="1" height="1" bgcolor=#282828></td>
    <td width="1" height="1" bgcolor=#1b1b1b></td>
    <td width="1" height="1" bgcolor=#1a1a1a></td>
    <td width="1" height="1" bgcolor=#262626></td>
    <td width="1" height="1" bgcolor=#222222></td>
    <td width="1" height="1" bgcolor=#262626></td>
    <td width="1" height="1" bgcolor=#1c1c1c></td>
    <td width="1" height="1" bgcolor=#161616></td>
    <td width="1" height="1" bgcolor=#191919></td>
    <td width="1" height="1" bgcolor=#2e2e2e></td>
    <td width="1" height="1" bgcolor=#212121></td>
    <td width="1" height="1" bgcolor=#161616></td>
    <td width="1" height="1" bgcolor=#272727></td>
    <td width="1" height="1" bgcolor=#232323></td>
    <td width="1" height="1" bgcolor=#1e1e1e></td>
    <td width="1" height="1" bgcolor=#1f1f1f></td>
    <td width="1" height="1" bgcolor=#2c2c2c></td>
    <td width="1" height="1" bgcolor=#383838></td>
    <td width="1" height="1" bgcolor=#2c2c2c></td>
    <td width="1" height="1" bgcolor=#262626></td>
    <td width="1" height="1" bgcolor=#212121></td>
    <td width="1" height="1" bgcolor=#141414></td>
    <td width="1" height="1" bgcolor=#181818></td>
    <td width="1" height="1" bgcolor=#1b1b1b></td>
    <td width="1" height="1" bgcolor=#121212></td>
    <td rowspan="1" colspan="2" width="1" height="1" bgcolor=#090909></td>
    <td rowspan="1" colspan="2" width="1" height="1" bgcolor=#0a0a0a></td>
    <td width="1" height="1" bgcolor=#090909></td>
    <td width="1" height="1" bgcolor=#050505></td>
    <td width="1" height="1" bgcolor=#040404></td>
    <td width="1" height="1" bgcolor=#000000></td>
    <td rowspan="3" colspan="1" width="1" height="1" bgcolor=#030303></td>
    <td width="1" height="1" bgcolor=#363636></td>
    <td width="1" height="1" bgcolor=#7c7c7c></td>
    <td width="1" height="1" bgcolor=#b0b0b0></td>
    <td width="1" height="1" bgcolor=#bbbbbb></td>
    <td width="1" height="1" bgcolor=#c9c9c9></td>
    <td width="1" height="1" bgcolor=#d3d3d3></td>
    <td width="1" height="1" bgcolor=#cacaca></td>
    <td width="1" height="1" bgcolor=#acacac></td>
    <td width="1" height="1" bgcolor=#a1a1a1></td>
    <td width="1" height="1" bgcolor=#848484></td>
    <td width="1" height="1" bgcolor=#161616></td>
    <td width="1" height="1" bgcolor=#090909></td>
    <td rowspan="1" colspan="2" width="1" height="1" bgcolor=#0d0d0d></td>
    <td width="1" height="1" bgcolor=#222222></td>
    <td width="1" height="1" bgcolor=#1f1f1f></td>
    <td width="1" height="1" bgcolor=#2d2d2d></td>
    <td width="1" height="1" bgcolor=#212121></td>
    <td width="1" height="1" bgcolor=#2b2b2b></td>
    <td width="1" height="1" bgcolor=#404040></td>
    <td width="1" height="1" bgcolor=#b3b3b3></td>
  </tr>
  <tr>
    <td width="1" height="1" bgcolor=#787878></td>
    <td width="1" height="1" bgcolor=#434343></td>
    <td width="1" height="1" bgcolor=#3b3b3b></td>
    <td width="1" height="1" bgcolor=#313131></td>
    <td width="1" height="1" bgcolor=#383838></td>
    <td width="1" height="1" bgcolor=#1a1a1a></td>
    <td width="1" height="1" bgcolor=#3e3e3e></td>
    <td width="1" height="1" bgcolor=#696969></td>
    <td width="1" height="1" bgcolor=#4f4f4f></td>
    <td width="1" height="1" bgcolor=#4d4d4d></td>
    <td width="1" height="1" bgcolor=#252525></td>
    <td width="1" height="1" bgcolor=#5e5e5e></td>
```

```
    <td width="1" height="1" bgcolor=#4c4c4c></td>
    <td width="1" height="1" bgcolor=#1e1e1e></td>
    <td width="1" height="1" bgcolor=#1c1c1c></td>
    <td width="1" height="1" bgcolor=#0d0d0d></td>
    <td width="1" height="1" bgcolor=#171717></td>
    <td rowspan="1" colspan="2" width="1" height="1" bgcolor=#181818></td>
    <td width="1" height="1" bgcolor=#0f0f0f></td>
    <td rowspan="2" colspan="1" width="1" height="1" bgcolor=#101010></td>
    <td rowspan="2" colspan="1" width="1" height="1" bgcolor=#202020></td>
    <td width="1" height="1" bgcolor=#1e1e1e></td>
    <td width="1" height="1" bgcolor=#212121></td>
    <td width="1" height="1" bgcolor=#121212></td>
    <td width="1" height="1" bgcolor=#1b1b1b></td>
    <td width="1" height="1" bgcolor=#1a1a1a></td>
    <td rowspan="2" colspan="1" width="1" height="1" bgcolor=#1e1e1e></td>
    <td width="1" height="1" bgcolor=#1e1e1e></td>
    <td width="1" height="1" bgcolor=#262626></td>
    <td width="1" height="1" bgcolor=#2c2c2c></td>
    <td width="1" height="1" bgcolor=#212121></td>
    <td width="1" height="1" bgcolor=#1e1e1e></td>
    <td width="1" height="1" bgcolor=#2b2b2b></td>
    <td width="1" height="1" bgcolor=#282828></td>
    <td width="1" height="1" bgcolor=#242424></td>
    <td width="1" height="1" bgcolor=#202020></td>
    <td width="1" height="1" bgcolor=#151515></td>
    <td width="1" height="1" bgcolor=#191919></td>
    <td width="1" height="1" bgcolor=#141414></td>
    <td width="1" height="1" bgcolor=#1a1a1a></td>
    <td width="1" height="1" bgcolor=#111111></td>
    <td width="1" height="1" bgcolor=#0a0a0a></td>
    <td width="1" height="1" bgcolor=#070707></td>
    <td width="1" height="1" bgcolor=#040404></td>
    <td rowspan="1" colspan="2" width="1" height="1" bgcolor=#010101></td>
    <td width="1" height="1" bgcolor=#020202></td>
    <td width="1" height="1" bgcolor=#000000></td>
    <td width="1" height="1" bgcolor=#030303></td>
    <td width="1" height="1" bgcolor=#2d2d2d></td>
    <td width="1" height="1" bgcolor=#6c6c6c></td>
    <td width="1" height="1" bgcolor=#acacac></td>
    <td width="1" height="1" bgcolor=#a4a4a4></td>
    <td width="1" height="1" bgcolor=#c2c2c2></td>
    <td width="1" height="1" bgcolor=#dedede></td>
    <td width="1" height="1" bgcolor=#b5b5b5></td>
    <td width="1" height="1" bgcolor=#bbbbbb></td>
    <td width="1" height="1" bgcolor=#b7b7b7></td>
    <td width="1" height="1" bgcolor=#9a9a9a></td>
    <td width="1" height="1" bgcolor=#232323></td>
    <td width="1" height="1" bgcolor=#070707></td>
    <td width="1" height="1" bgcolor=#151515></td>
    <td width="1" height="1" bgcolor=#262626></td>
    <td width="1" height="1" bgcolor=#313131></td>
    <td width="1" height="1" bgcolor=#2a2a2a></td>
    <td width="1" height="1" bgcolor=#363636></td>
    <td width="1" height="1" bgcolor=#2c2c2c></td>
    <td width="1" height="1" bgcolor=#343434></td>
    <td width="1" height="1" bgcolor=#595959></td>
    <td width="1" height="1" bgcolor=#c5c5c5></td>
  </tr>
  <tr>
    <td width="1" height="1" bgcolor=#757575></td>
    <td width="1" height="1" bgcolor=#5a5a5a></td>
    <td width="1" height="1" bgcolor=#444444></td>
    <td width="1" height="1" bgcolor=#2b2b2b></td>
    <td width="1" height="1" bgcolor=#212121></td>
    <td width="1" height="1" bgcolor=#252525></td>
    <td width="1" height="1" bgcolor=#464646></td>
    <td width="1" height="1" bgcolor=#424242></td>
    <td width="1" height="1" bgcolor=#292929></td>
    <td width="1" height="1" bgcolor=#1b1b1b></td>
    <td width="1" height="1" bgcolor=#1c1c1c></td>
    <td width="1" height="1" bgcolor=#4e4e4e></td>
    <td width="1" height="1" bgcolor=#494949></td>
    <td width="1" height="1" bgcolor=#2a2a2a></td>
    <td width="1" height="1" bgcolor=#303030></td>
    <td width="1" height="1" bgcolor=#2c2c2c></td>
    <td width="1" height="1" bgcolor=#232323></td>
    <td width="1" height="1" bgcolor=#1d1d1d></td>
    <td width="1" height="1" bgcolor=#272727></td>
    <td width="1" height="1" bgcolor=#191919></td>
    <td width="1" height="1" bgcolor=#272727></td>
    <td width="1" height="1" bgcolor=#363636></td>
    <td width="1" height="1" bgcolor=#161616></td>
    <td width="1" height="1" bgcolor=#252525></td>
```

```
    <td width="1" height="1"
bgcolor=#161616></td>
    <td width="1" height="1"
bgcolor=#272727></td>
    <td width="1" height="1"
bgcolor=#222222></td>
    <td width="1" height="1"
bgcolor=#242424></td>
    <td width="1" height="1"
bgcolor=#252525></td>
    <td width="1" height="1"
bgcolor=#262626></td>
    <td width="1" height="1"
bgcolor=#282828></td>
    <td width="1" height="1"
bgcolor=#252525></td>
    <td width="1" height="1"
bgcolor=#0f0f0f></td>
    <td width="1" height="1"
bgcolor=#111111></td>
    <td width="1" height="1"
bgcolor=#1b1b1b></td>
    <td width="1" height="1"
bgcolor=#171717></td>
    <td width="1" height="1"
bgcolor=#101010></td>
    <td width="1" height="1"
bgcolor=#111111></td>
    <td width="1" height="1"
bgcolor=#0d0d0d></td>
    <td width="1" height="1"
bgcolor=#0e0e0e></td>
    <td rowspan="2"
colspan="1" width="1"
height="1"
bgcolor=#090909></td>
    <td rowspan="2"
colspan="1" width="1"
height="1"
bgcolor=#030303></td>
    <td width="1" height="1"
bgcolor=#020202></td>
    <td width="1" height="1"
bgcolor=#010101></td>
    <td rowspan="2"
colspan="1" width="1"
height="1"
bgcolor=#060606></td>
    <td width="1" height="1"
bgcolor=#050505></td>
    <td width="1" height="1"
bgcolor=#000000></td>
    <td width="1" height="1"
bgcolor=#3d3d3d></td>
    <td width="1" height="1"
bgcolor=#777777></td>
    <td width="1" height="1"
bgcolor=#9f9f9f></td>
    <td width="1" height="1"
bgcolor=#888888></td>
    <td width="1" height="1"
bgcolor=#d7d7d7></td>
    <td width="1" height="1"
bgcolor=#d1d1d1></td>
    <td width="1" height="1"
bgcolor=#c0c0c0></td>
    <td width="1" height="1"
bgcolor=#bcbcbc></td>
    <td width="1" height="1"
bgcolor=#cfcfcf></td>
    <td width="1" height="1"
bgcolor=#c2c2c2></td>
    <td width="1" height="1"
bgcolor=#333333></td>
    <td width="1" height="1"
bgcolor=#0b0b0b></td>
    <td width="1" height="1"
bgcolor=#242424></td>
    <td width="1" height="1"
bgcolor=#4c4c4c></td>
    <td width="1" height="1"
bgcolor=#4f4f4f></td>
    <td width="1" height="1"
bgcolor=#1a1a1a></td>
    <td width="1" height="1"
bgcolor=#414141></td>
    <td width="1" height="1"
bgcolor=#4d4d4d></td>
    <td width="1" height="1"
bgcolor=#393939></td>
    <td width="1" height="1"
bgcolor=#484848></td>
    <td width="1" height="1"
bgcolor=#bcbcbc></td>
  </tr>
  <tr>
    <td width="1" height="1"
bgcolor=#5d5d5d></td>
    <td width="1" height="1"
bgcolor=#6b6b6b></td>
    <td width="1" height="1"
bgcolor=#777777></td>
    <td width="1" height="1"
bgcolor=#868686></td>
    <td width="1" height="1"
bgcolor=#6d6d6d></td>
    <td width="1" height="1"
bgcolor=#404040></td>
    <td width="1" height="1"
bgcolor=#252525></td>
    <td width="1" height="1"
bgcolor=#1a1a1a></td>
    <td width="1" height="1"
bgcolor=#181818></td>
    <td width="1" height="1"
bgcolor=#131313></td>
    <td width="1" height="1"
bgcolor=#1b1b1b></td>
    <td width="1" height="1"
bgcolor=#242424></td>
    <td width="1" height="1"
bgcolor=#454545></td>
    <td width="1" height="1"
bgcolor=#424242></td>
    <td width="1" height="1"
bgcolor=#3f3f3f></td>
    <td width="1" height="1"
bgcolor=#484848></td>
    <td width="1" height="1"
bgcolor=#343434></td>
    <td width="1" height="1"
bgcolor=#141414></td>
    <td width="1" height="1"
bgcolor=#121212></td>
    <td width="1" height="1"
bgcolor=#1e1e1e></td>
    <td rowspan="2"
colspan="1" width="1"
height="1"
bgcolor=#313131></td>
    <td width="1" height="1"
bgcolor=#363636></td>
    <td width="1" height="1"
bgcolor=#2b2b2b></td>
    <td width="1" height="1"
bgcolor=#1b1b1b></td>
    <td width="1" height="1"
bgcolor=#222222></td>
    <td width="1" height="1"
bgcolor=#282828></td>
    <td width="1" height="1"
bgcolor=#333333></td>
    <td width="1" height="1"
bgcolor=#2d2d2d></td>
    <td width="1" height="1"
bgcolor=#303030></td>
    <td width="1" height="1"
bgcolor=#353535></td>
    <td width="1" height="1"
bgcolor=#1a1a1a></td>
    <td width="1" height="1"
bgcolor=#1b1b1b></td>
    <td width="1" height="1"
bgcolor=#1d1d1d></td>
    <td width="1" height="1"
bgcolor=#1e1e1e></td>
    <td width="1" height="1"
bgcolor=#191919></td>
    <td width="1" height="1"
bgcolor=#0e0e0e></td>
    <td width="1" height="1"
bgcolor=#0c0c0c></td>
    <td width="1" height="1"
bgcolor=#050505></td>
```

```
    <td width="1" height="1" bgcolor=#090909></td>
    <td width="1" height="1" bgcolor=#0e0e0e></td>
    <td width="1" height="1" bgcolor=#0a0a0a></td>
    <td width="1" height="1" bgcolor=#090909></td>
    <td width="1" height="1" bgcolor=#0f0f0f></td>
    <td width="1" height="1" bgcolor=#040404></td>
    <td width="1" height="1" bgcolor=#020202></td>
    <td rowspan="1" colspan="2" width="1" height="1" bgcolor=#010101></td>
    <td width="1" height="1" bgcolor=#070707></td>
    <td width="1" height="1" bgcolor=#242424></td>
    <td width="1" height="1" bgcolor=#6d6d6d></td>
    <td width="1" height="1" bgcolor=#808080></td>
    <td width="1" height="1" bgcolor=#494949></td>
    <td width="1" height="1" bgcolor=#7d7d7d></td>
    <td width="1" height="1" bgcolor=#c2c2c2></td>
    <td width="1" height="1" bgcolor=#dedede></td>
    <td width="1" height="1" bgcolor=#d4d4d4></td>
    <td width="1" height="1" bgcolor=#d3d3d3></td>
    <td width="1" height="1" bgcolor=#c1c1c1></td>
    <td width="1" height="1" bgcolor=#454545></td>
    <td width="1" height="1" bgcolor=#3f3f3f></td>
    <td width="1" height="1" bgcolor=#333333></td>
    <td width="1" height="1" bgcolor=#242424></td>
    <td width="1" height="1" bgcolor=#323232></td>
    <td width="1" height="1" bgcolor=#191919></td>
    <td width="1" height="1" bgcolor=#444444></td>
    <td width="1" height="1" bgcolor=#5f5f5f></td>
    <td width="1" height="1" bgcolor=#4f4f4f></td>
    <td width="1" height="1" bgcolor=#626262></td>
    <td width="1" height="1" bgcolor=#838383></td>
  </tr>
  <tr>
    <td width="1" height="1" bgcolor=#545454></td>
    <td width="1" height="1" bgcolor=#6a6a6a></td>
    <td width="1" height="1" bgcolor=#757575></td>
    <td rowspan="2" colspan="1" width="1" height="1" bgcolor=#919191></td>
    <td width="1" height="1" bgcolor=#6a6a6a></td>
    <td rowspan="2" colspan="1" width="1" height="1" bgcolor=#545454></td>
    <td width="1" height="1" bgcolor=#696969></td>
    <td width="1" height="1" bgcolor=#454545></td>
    <td width="1" height="1" bgcolor=#252525></td>
    <td width="1" height="1" bgcolor=#242424></td>
    <td width="1" height="1" bgcolor=#191919></td>
    <td width="1" height="1" bgcolor=#2d2d2d></td>
    <td width="1" height="1" bgcolor=#575757></td>
    <td width="1" height="1" bgcolor=#454545></td>
    <td width="1" height="1" bgcolor=#333333></td>
    <td width="1" height="1" bgcolor=#2f2f2f></td>
    <td width="1" height="1" bgcolor=#424242></td>
    <td width="1" height="1" bgcolor=#1e1e1e></td>
    <td width="1" height="1" bgcolor=#242424></td>
    <td width="1" height="1" bgcolor=#232323></td>
    <td width="1" height="1" bgcolor=#3b3b3b></td>
    <td rowspan="2" colspan="1" width="1" height="1" bgcolor=#383838></td>
    <td width="1" height="1" bgcolor=#151515></td>
    <td width="1" height="1" bgcolor=#202020></td>
    <td width="1" height="1" bgcolor=#252525></td>
    <td width="1" height="1" bgcolor=#353535></td>
    <td width="1" height="1" bgcolor=#313131></td>
    <td width="1" height="1" bgcolor=#333333></td>
    <td width="1" height="1" bgcolor=#232323></td>
    <td width="1" height="1" bgcolor=#0f0f0f></td>
    <td width="1" height="1" bgcolor=#0e0e0e></td>
    <td width="1" height="1" bgcolor=#101010></td>
    <td width="1" height="1" bgcolor=#111111></td>
    <td width="1" height="1" bgcolor=#101010></td>
    <td width="1" height="1" bgcolor=#0a0a0a></td>
    <td width="1" height="1" bgcolor=#060606></td>
    <td rowspan="1" colspan="2" width="1" height="1" bgcolor=#080808></td>
    <td width="1" height="1" bgcolor=#030303></td>
    <td width="1" height="1" bgcolor=#151515></td>
    <td width="1" height="1" bgcolor=#0e0e0e></td>
    <td width="1" height="1" bgcolor=#090909></td>
    <td width="1" height="1" bgcolor=#0b0b0b></td>
    <td width="1" height="1" bgcolor=#070707></td>
    <td rowspan="1" colspan="2" width="1" height="1" bgcolor=#030303></td>
    <td width="1" height="1" bgcolor=#010101></td>
    <td width="1" height="1" bgcolor=#030303></td>
    <td width="1" height="1" bgcolor=#000000></td>
    <td width="1" height="1" bgcolor=#040404></td>
    <td width="1" height="1" bgcolor=#131313></td>
    <td width="1" height="1" bgcolor=#4c4c4c></td>
```

```
    <td width="1" height="1" bgcolor=#3f3f3f></td>
    <td width="1" height="1" bgcolor=#404040></td>
    <td width="1" height="1" bgcolor=#818181></td>
    <td width="1" height="1" bgcolor=#b5b5b5></td>
    <td width="1" height="1" bgcolor=#bebebe></td>
    <td width="1" height="1" bgcolor=#c5c5c5></td>
    <td width="1" height="1" bgcolor=#c8c8c8></td>
    <td width="1" height="1" bgcolor=#b2b2b2></td>
    <td width="1" height="1" bgcolor=#6e6e6e></td>
    <td width="1" height="1" bgcolor=#545454></td>
    <td rowspan="2" colspan="1" width="1" height="1" bgcolor=#4b4b4b></td>
    <td width="1" height="1" bgcolor=#454545></td>
    <td width="1" height="1" bgcolor=#434343></td>
    <td width="1" height="1" bgcolor=#3d3d3d></td>
    <td width="1" height="1" bgcolor=#4a4a4a></td>
    <td width="1" height="1" bgcolor=#6a6a6a></td>
    <td width="1" height="1" bgcolor=#8e8e8e></td>
    <td width="1" height="1" bgcolor=#a0a0a0></td>
    <td width="1" height="1" bgcolor=#989898></td>
  </tr>
  <tr>
    <td width="1" height="1" bgcolor=#3c3c3c></td>
    <td width="1" height="1" bgcolor=#414141></td>
    <td width="1" height="1" bgcolor=#9c9c9c></td>
    <td width="1" height="1" bgcolor=#626262></td>
    <td width="1" height="1" bgcolor=#676767></td>
    <td width="1" height="1" bgcolor=#717171></td>
    <td width="1" height="1" bgcolor=#434343></td>
    <td width="1" height="1" bgcolor=#2a2a2a></td>
    <td width="1" height="1" bgcolor=#2c2c2c></td>
    <td width="1" height="1" bgcolor=#555555></td>
    <td width="1" height="1" bgcolor=#6a6a6a></td>
    <td width="1" height="1" bgcolor=#565656></td>
    <td width="1" height="1" bgcolor=#353535></td>
    <td width="1" height="1" bgcolor=#333333></td>
    <td width="1" height="1" bgcolor=#474747></td>
    <td width="1" height="1" bgcolor=#333333></td>
    <td width="1" height="1" bgcolor=#323232></td>
    <td width="1" height="1" bgcolor=#363636></td>
    <td width="1" height="1" bgcolor=#3c3c3c></td>
    <td width="1" height="1" bgcolor=#3f3f3f></td>
    <td width="1" height="1" bgcolor=#383838></td>
    <td width="1" height="1" bgcolor=#343434></td>
    <td width="1" height="1" bgcolor=#282828></td>
    <td width="1" height="1" bgcolor=#2c2c2c></td>
    <td width="1" height="1" bgcolor=#3b3b3b></td>
    <td width="1" height="1" bgcolor=#2c2c2c></td>
    <td width="1" height="1" bgcolor=#323232></td>
    <td width="1" height="1" bgcolor=#393939></td>
    <td width="1" height="1" bgcolor=#2b2b2b></td>
    <td rowspan="1" colspan="2" width="1" height="1" bgcolor=#272727></td>
    <td width="1" height="1" bgcolor=#282828></td>
    <td width="1" height="1" bgcolor=#2d2d2d></td>
    <td width="1" height="1" bgcolor=#343434></td>
    <td width="1" height="1" bgcolor=#393939></td>
    <td width="1" height="1" bgcolor=#313131></td>
    <td width="1" height="1" bgcolor=#222222></td>
    <td width="1" height="1" bgcolor=#242424></td>
    <td width="1" height="1" bgcolor=#2a2a2a></td>
    <td width="1" height="1" bgcolor=#262626></td>
    <td width="1" height="1" bgcolor=#252525></td>
    <td width="1" height="1" bgcolor=#282828></td>
    <td width="1" height="1" bgcolor=#232323></td>
    <td width="1" height="1" bgcolor=#1b1b1b></td>
    <td width="1" height="1" bgcolor=#181818></td>
    <td width="1" height="1" bgcolor=#141414></td>
    <td width="1" height="1" bgcolor=#121212></td>
    <td width="1" height="1" bgcolor=#171717></td>
    <td width="1" height="1" bgcolor=#252525></td>
    <td width="1" height="1" bgcolor=#424242></td>
    <td width="1" height="1" bgcolor=#474747></td>
    <td width="1" height="1" bgcolor=#4c4c4c></td>
    <td width="1" height="1" bgcolor=#828282></td>
    <td width="1" height="1" bgcolor=#6c6c6c></td>
    <td width="1" height="1" bgcolor=#979797></td>
    <td width="1" height="1" bgcolor=#d0d0d0></td>
    <td width="1" height="1" bgcolor=#d4d4d4></td>
    <td width="1" height="1" bgcolor=#adadad></td>
    <td width="1" height="1" bgcolor=#858585></td>
    <td width="1" height="1" bgcolor=#585858></td>
    <td width="1" height="1" bgcolor=#7e7e7e></td>
    <td width="1" height="1" bgcolor=#979797></td>
    <td width="1" height="1" bgcolor=#b5b5b5></td>
    <td width="1" height="1" bgcolor=#939393></td>
    <td width="1" height="1" bgcolor=#878787></td>
    <td width="1" height="1" bgcolor=#b1b1b1></td>
```

```
    <td width="1" height="1"
bgcolor=#bababa></td>
    <td width="1" height="1"
bgcolor=#b2b2b2></td>
  </tr>
</table></body></html>
```

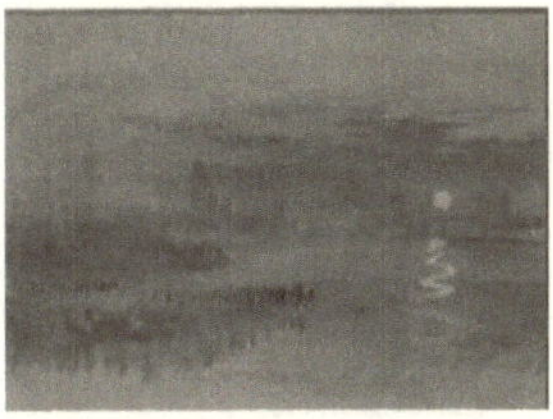

Turner's Sunrise

```
<html>
<head><title>Turner's Sunrise, written by Broose G. Dickinson</title></head>
<body>
<table border=0 cellpadding=0 cellspacing=0>
  <tr>
    <td width="1" height="1" bgcolor=#79786f></td>
    <td width="1" height="1" bgcolor=#75746c></td>
    <td width="1" height="1" bgcolor=#7a7971></td>
    <td width="1" height="1" bgcolor=#74746c></td>
    <td width="1" height="1" bgcolor=#7c7b74></td>
    <td width="1" height="1" bgcolor=#777670></td>
    <td width="1" height="1" bgcolor=#797870></td>
    <td width="1" height="1" bgcolor=#7b7a72></td>
    <td width="1" height="1" bgcolor=#76756d></td>
    <td width="1" height="1" bgcolor=#7a7971></td>
    <td width="1" height="1" bgcolor=#797871></td>
    <td width="1" height="1" bgcolor=#797770></td>
    <td width="1" height="1" bgcolor=#78776f></td>
    <td width="1" height="1" bgcolor=#76746b></td>
    <td width="1" height="1" bgcolor=#76756b></td>
    <td width="1" height="1" bgcolor=#79766d></td>
    <td width="1" height="1" bgcolor=#79776c></td>
    <td width="1" height="1" bgcolor=#787569></td>
    <td width="1" height="1" bgcolor=#78766a></td>
    <td width="1" height="1" bgcolor=#7b796e></td>
    <td width="1" height="1" bgcolor=#78766b></td>
    <td width="1" height="1" bgcolor=#747268></td>
    <td width="1" height="1" bgcolor=#7a7970></td>
    <td width="1" height="1" bgcolor=#77756b></td>
    <td width="1" height="1" bgcolor=#76756c></td>
    <td width="1" height="1" bgcolor=#737168></td>
    <td width="1" height="1" bgcolor=#7b796f></td>
    <td width="1" height="1" bgcolor=#77766d></td>
    <td width="1" height="1" bgcolor=#76766d></td>
    <td width="1" height="1" bgcolor=#78786d></td>
    <td width="1" height="1" bgcolor=#7a796f></td>
    <td width="1" height="1" bgcolor=#727266></td>
    <td width="1" height="1" bgcolor=#7a796d></td>
    <td width="1" height="1" bgcolor=#747367></td>
    <td width="1" height="1" bgcolor=#76766a></td>
    <td width="1" height="1" bgcolor=#757469></td>
    <td width="1" height="1" bgcolor=#737367></td>
    <td width="1" height="1" bgcolor=#727064></td>
    <td width="1" height="1" bgcolor=#737367></td>
    <td width="1" height="1" bgcolor=#727064></td>
    <td width="1" height="1" bgcolor=#717064></td>
    <td width="1" height="1" bgcolor=#757366></td>
    <td width="1" height="1" bgcolor=#717165></td>
    <td width="1" height="1" bgcolor=#707063></td>
    <td width="1" height="1" bgcolor=#737266></td>
    <td width="1" height="1" bgcolor=#727266></td>
    <td width="1" height="1" bgcolor=#6d6c61></td>
    <td width="1" height="1" bgcolor=#706f63></td>
    <td width="1" height="1" bgcolor=#6d6b60></td>
    <td width="1" height="1" bgcolor=#737065></td>
    <td width="1" height="1" bgcolor=#6f6d61></td>
    <td width="1" height="1" bgcolor=#6d6b5f></td>
    <td width="1" height="1" bgcolor=#727064></td>
    <td width="1" height="1" bgcolor=#6b695e></td>
    <td width="1" height="1" bgcolor=#706e62></td>
    <td width="1" height="1" bgcolor=#6e6d61></td>
    <td width="1" height="1" bgcolor=#6b695f></td>
    <td width="1" height="1" bgcolor=#6d6c61></td>
    <td width="1" height="1" bgcolor=#69685c></td>
    <td width="1" height="1" bgcolor=#6a695d></td>
    <td width="1" height="1" bgcolor=#69685c></td>
    <td width="1" height="1" bgcolor=#69695d></td>
    <td width="1" height="1" bgcolor=#68675d></td>
    <td width="1" height="1" bgcolor=#65665c></td>
    <td width="1" height="1" bgcolor=#686a62></td>
    <td width="1" height="1" bgcolor=#67675d></td>
    <td width="1" height="1" bgcolor=#65655a></td>
    <td width="1" height="1" bgcolor=#69685e></td>
    <td width="1" height="1" bgcolor=#64645a></td>
    <td width="1" height="1" bgcolor=#64655e></td>
    <td width="1" height="1" bgcolor=#5e625f></td>
    <td width="1" height="1" bgcolor=#646664></td>
  </tr>
  <tr>
    <td width="1" height="1" bgcolor=#aa9862></td>
    <td width="1" height="1" bgcolor=#a18b58></td>
    <td width="1" height="1" bgcolor=#a2915e></td>
```

```
    <td width="1" height="1"
bgcolor=#9e8f5d></td>
    <td width="1" height="1"
bgcolor=#a18e63></td>
    <td width="1" height="1"
bgcolor=#9e8d5f></td>
    <td width="1" height="1"
bgcolor=#a29061></td>
    <td width="1" height="1"
bgcolor=#9c8457></td>
    <td width="1" height="1"
bgcolor=#a18c5a></td>
    <td width="1" height="1"
bgcolor=#a38f59></td>
    <td width="1" height="1"
bgcolor=#a69064></td>
    <td width="1" height="1"
bgcolor=#a18b5b></td>
    <td width="1" height="1"
bgcolor=#a3915d></td>
    <td width="1" height="1"
bgcolor=#a48d59></td>
    <td width="1" height="1"
bgcolor=#a38c53></td>
    <td width="1" height="1"
bgcolor=#a48c57></td>
    <td width="1" height="1"
bgcolor=#a68e53></td>
    <td width="1" height="1"
bgcolor=#ab9053></td>
    <td width="1" height="1"
bgcolor=#a88f52></td>
    <td width="1" height="1"
bgcolor=#a68d50></td>
    <td width="1" height="1"
bgcolor=#a68d4b></td>
    <td width="1" height="1"
bgcolor=#9f894c></td>
    <td width="1" height="1"
bgcolor=#a6965e></td>
    <td width="1" height="1"
bgcolor=#a49458></td>
    <td width="1" height="1"
bgcolor=#a39764></td>
    <td width="1" height="1"
bgcolor=#a49665></td>
    <td width="1" height="1"
bgcolor=#aa975f></td>
    <td width="1" height="1"
bgcolor=#a69462></td>
    <td width="1" height="1"
bgcolor=#a89967></td>
    <td width="1" height="1"
bgcolor=#a79a5d></td>
    <td width="1" height="1"
bgcolor=#a79863></td>
    <td width="1" height="1"
bgcolor=#a69957></td>
    <td width="1" height="1"
bgcolor=#ac9950></td>
    <td width="1" height="1"
bgcolor=#a8984f></td>
    <td width="1" height="1"
bgcolor=#a4964f></td>
    <td width="1" height="1"
bgcolor=#aa9851></td>
    <td width="1" height="1"
bgcolor=#ab9650></td>
    <td width="1" height="1"
bgcolor=#a8944f></td>
    <td width="1" height="1"
bgcolor=#ab9651></td>
    <td width="1" height="1"
bgcolor=#a8954f></td>
    <td width="1" height="1"
bgcolor=#a6924a></td>
    <td width="1" height="1"
bgcolor=#a8934a></td>
    <td width="1" height="1"
bgcolor=#a69249></td>
    <td width="1" height="1"
bgcolor=#a49046></td>
    <td width="1" height="1"
bgcolor=#aa964a></td>
    <td width="1" height="1"
bgcolor=#a8944d></td>
    <td width="1" height="1"
bgcolor=#a58f4a></td>
    <td width="1" height="1"
bgcolor=#a68e44></td>
    <td width="1" height="1"
bgcolor=#a18c42></td>
    <td width="1" height="1"
bgcolor=#a28c46></td>
    <td width="1" height="1"
bgcolor=#a48c44></td>
    <td width="1" height="1"
bgcolor=#a4883e></td>
    <td width="1" height="1"
bgcolor=#a1863b></td>
    <td width="1" height="1"
bgcolor=#a08742></td>
    <td width="1" height="1"
bgcolor=#a38943></td>
    <td width="1" height="1"
bgcolor=#a08d48></td>
    <td width="1" height="1"
bgcolor=#9d874b></td>
    <td width="1" height="1"
bgcolor=#a28d4b></td>
    <td width="1" height="1"
bgcolor=#a28e46></td>
    <td width="1" height="1"
bgcolor=#a18f48></td>
    <td width="1" height="1"
bgcolor=#a3924d></td>
    <td width="1" height="1"
bgcolor=#a1914e></td>
    <td width="1" height="1"
bgcolor=#a3914d></td>
    <td width="1" height="1"
bgcolor=#9e934d></td>
    <td width="1" height="1"
bgcolor=#a0955c></td>
    <td width="1" height="1"
bgcolor=#9e9254></td>
    <td width="1" height="1"
bgcolor=#9e9153></td>
    <td width="1" height="1"
bgcolor=#a19455></td>
    <td width="1" height="1"
bgcolor=#9a904f></td>
    <td width="1" height="1"
bgcolor=#9d915d></td>
    <td width="1" height="1"
bgcolor=#9b9870></td>
    <td width="1" height="1"
bgcolor=#898671></td>
  </tr>
  <tr>
    <td width="1" height="1"
bgcolor=#a7945f></td>
    <td width="1" height="1"
bgcolor=#a28c5b></td>
    <td width="1" height="1"
bgcolor=#9e8c59></td>
    <td width="1" height="1"
bgcolor=#a28f5d></td>
    <td width="1" height="1"
bgcolor=#928154></td>
    <td width="1" height="1"
bgcolor=#9f8e5f></td>
    <td width="1" height="1"
bgcolor=#9c8655></td>
    <td width="1" height="1"
bgcolor=#a38f5d></td>
    <td width="1" height="1"
bgcolor=#a18d64></td>
    <td width="1" height="1"
bgcolor=#a08d5e></td>
    <td width="1" height="1"
bgcolor=#998654></td>
    <td width="1" height="1"
bgcolor=#a2925c></td>
    <td width="1" height="1"
bgcolor=#a5905a></td>
    <td width="1" height="1"
bgcolor=#a28e57></td>
    <td width="1" height="1"
bgcolor=#a68d56></td>
    <td width="1" height="1"
bgcolor=#a48e5c></td>
    <td width="1" height="1"
bgcolor=#a18f58></td>
```

```
    <td width="1" height="1" bgcolor=#a39153></td>
    <td width="1" height="1" bgcolor=#a59355></td>
    <td width="1" height="1" bgcolor=#a49054></td>
    <td width="1" height="1" bgcolor=#a38e52></td>
    <td width="1" height="1" bgcolor=#a08c4e></td>
    <td width="1" height="1" bgcolor=#a38f54></td>
    <td width="1" height="1" bgcolor=#9c844d></td>
    <td width="1" height="1" bgcolor=#a69464></td>
    <td width="1" height="1" bgcolor=#9e9461></td>
    <td width="1" height="1" bgcolor=#a29463></td>
    <td width="1" height="1" bgcolor=#a29767></td>
    <td width="1" height="1" bgcolor=#a39766></td>
    <td width="1" height="1" bgcolor=#a39765></td>
    <td width="1" height="1" bgcolor=#a49869></td>
    <td width="1" height="1" bgcolor=#a59a68></td>
    <td width="1" height="1" bgcolor=#a79859></td>
    <td width="1" height="1" bgcolor=#a39653></td>
    <td width="1" height="1" bgcolor=#a49554></td>
    <td width="1" height="1" bgcolor=#a79955></td>
    <td width="1" height="1" bgcolor=#a59753></td>
    <td width="1" height="1" bgcolor=#a59452></td>
    <td width="1" height="1" bgcolor=#a4904f></td>
    <td width="1" height="1" bgcolor=#a89654></td>
    <td width="1" height="1" bgcolor=#ae9d58></td>
    <td width="1" height="1" bgcolor=#a99550></td>
    <td width="1" height="1" bgcolor=#ac9955></td>
    <td width="1" height="1" bgcolor=#a99650></td>
    <td width="1" height="1" bgcolor=#aa984f></td>
    <td width="1" height="1" bgcolor=#a5934b></td>
    <td width="1" height="1" bgcolor=#a69246></td>
    <td width="1" height="1" bgcolor=#a38c42></td>
    <td width="1" height="1" bgcolor=#a08d43></td>
    <td width="1" height="1" bgcolor=#a08c47></td>
    <td width="1" height="1" bgcolor=#a38f47></td>
    <td width="1" height="1" bgcolor=#a48d43></td>
    <td width="1" height="1" bgcolor=#a38c3f></td>
    <td width="1" height="1" bgcolor=#9d8845></td>
    <td width="1" height="1" bgcolor=#a08c48></td>
    <td width="1" height="1" bgcolor=#9e8d50></td>
    <td width="1" height="1" bgcolor=#9a864c></td>
    <td width="1" height="1" bgcolor=#9f8b4b></td>
    <td width="1" height="1" bgcolor=#a5924d></td>
    <td width="1" height="1" bgcolor=#a1904a></td>
    <td width="1" height="1" bgcolor=#a0904c></td>
    <td width="1" height="1" bgcolor=#a1924f></td>
    <td width="1" height="1" bgcolor=#9c9350></td>
    <td width="1" height="1" bgcolor=#9d9750></td>
    <td width="1" height="1" bgcolor=#99914c></td>
    <td width="1" height="1" bgcolor=#9e914f></td>
    <td width="1" height="1" bgcolor=#9d9255></td>
    <td width="1" height="1" bgcolor=#9c9456></td>
    <td width="1" height="1" bgcolor=#9c9258></td>
    <td width="1" height="1" bgcolor=#9d8f54></td>
    <td width="1" height="1" bgcolor=#9c8a4f></td>
    <td width="1" height="1" bgcolor=#8c804c></td>
  </tr>
  <tr>
    <td width="1" height="1" bgcolor=#a48c59></td>
    <td width="1" height="1" bgcolor=#a28b58></td>
    <td width="1" height="1" bgcolor=#a18c5c></td>
    <td width="1" height="1" bgcolor=#9f8954></td>
    <td width="1" height="1" bgcolor=#9a865d></td>
    <td width="1" height="1" bgcolor=#9f8965></td>
    <td width="1" height="1" bgcolor=#9e875d></td>
    <td width="1" height="1" bgcolor=#a08c5c></td>
    <td width="1" height="1" bgcolor=#9e8f62></td>
    <td width="1" height="1" bgcolor=#9c8d60></td>
    <td width="1" height="1" bgcolor=#9e8f66></td>
    <td width="1" height="1" bgcolor=#a29464></td>
    <td width="1" height="1" bgcolor=#a28f5b></td>
    <td width="1" height="1" bgcolor=#a59356></td>
    <td width="1" height="1" bgcolor=#a58e51></td>
    <td width="1" height="1" bgcolor=#a28e55></td>
    <td width="1" height="1" bgcolor=#a5965c></td>
    <td width="1" height="1" bgcolor=#a4905b></td>
    <td width="1" height="1" bgcolor=#a1915c></td>
    <td width="1" height="1" bgcolor=#a1925e></td>
    <td width="1" height="1" bgcolor=#a19059></td>
    <td width="1" height="1" bgcolor=#a39158></td>
    <td width="1" height="1" bgcolor=#a29459></td>
    <td width="1" height="1" bgcolor=#a09057></td>
    <td width="1" height="1" bgcolor=#a4925c></td>
    <td width="1" height="1" bgcolor=#a48f52></td>
    <td width="1" height="1" bgcolor=#a59058></td>
    <td width="1" height="1" bgcolor=#9f905b></td>
    <td width="1" height="1" bgcolor=#a29660></td>
    <td width="1" height="1" bgcolor=#a09362></td>
    <td width="1" height="1" bgcolor=#a19463></td>
```

```
    <td width="1" height="1" bgcolor=#a39a67></td>
    <td width="1" height="1" bgcolor=#a79961></td>
    <td width="1" height="1" bgcolor=#a2965d></td>
    <td width="1" height="1" bgcolor=#a4975e></td>
    <td width="1" height="1" bgcolor=#a6975a></td>
    <td width="1" height="1" bgcolor=#a39655></td>
    <td width="1" height="1" bgcolor=#a49654></td>
    <td width="1" height="1" bgcolor=#a89658></td>
    <td width="1" height="1" bgcolor=#a89957></td>
    <td width="1" height="1" bgcolor=#aa9b58></td>
    <td width="1" height="1" bgcolor=#a59553></td>
    <td width="1" height="1" bgcolor=#a69656></td>
    <td width="1" height="1" bgcolor=#a79756></td>
    <td width="1" height="1" bgcolor=#a69754></td>
    <td width="1" height="1" bgcolor=#a59750></td>
    <td width="1" height="1" bgcolor=#a4944b></td>
    <td width="1" height="1" bgcolor=#a3914c></td>
    <td width="1" height="1" bgcolor=#a4914a></td>
    <td width="1" height="1" bgcolor=#a6944d></td>
    <td width="1" height="1" bgcolor=#a18f46></td>
    <td width="1" height="1" bgcolor=#a19044></td>
    <td width="1" height="1" bgcolor=#9d8d45></td>
    <td width="1" height="1" bgcolor=#9f8e4c></td>
    <td width="1" height="1" bgcolor=#a08d4f></td>
    <td width="1" height="1" bgcolor=#9f8f53></td>
    <td width="1" height="1" bgcolor=#a38f55></td>
    <td width="1" height="1" bgcolor=#9d8a4b></td>
    <td width="1" height="1" bgcolor=#9f8c49></td>
    <td width="1" height="1" bgcolor=#9f904a></td>
    <td width="1" height="1" bgcolor=#9d8e48></td>
    <td width="1" height="1" bgcolor=#a1924d></td>
    <td width="1" height="1" bgcolor=#a1964f></td>
    <td width="1" height="1" bgcolor=#9d9050></td>
    <td width="1" height="1" bgcolor=#9e924c></td>
    <td width="1" height="1" bgcolor=#9f9251></td>
    <td width="1" height="1" bgcolor=#9b9150></td>
    <td width="1" height="1" bgcolor=#9b9251></td>
    <td width="1" height="1" bgcolor=#9b8f54></td>
    <td width="1" height="1" bgcolor=#9b8f4b></td>
    <td width="1" height="1" bgcolor=#9b8944></td>
    <td width="1" height="1" bgcolor=#887a4e></td>
   </tr>
   <tr>
    <td width="1" height="1" bgcolor=#a68f5c></td>
    <td width="1" height="1" bgcolor=#a2905a></td>
    <td width="1" height="1" bgcolor=#968553></td>
    <td width="1" height="1" bgcolor=#a18c53></td>
    <td width="1" height="1" bgcolor=#9e8858></td>
    <td width="1" height="1" bgcolor=#9b8559></td>
    <td width="1" height="1" bgcolor=#9e885a></td>
    <td width="1" height="1" bgcolor=#9e8c5d></td>
    <td width="1" height="1" bgcolor=#988b5a></td>
    <td width="1" height="1" bgcolor=#9d8f5c></td>
    <td width="1" height="1" bgcolor=#a29462></td>
    <td width="1" height="1" bgcolor=#9e915d></td>
    <td width="1" height="1" bgcolor=#a79863></td>
    <td width="1" height="1" bgcolor=#a99562></td>
    <td width="1" height="1" bgcolor=#a4955a></td>
    <td width="1" height="1" bgcolor=#a2945b></td>
    <td width="1" height="1" bgcolor=#a3955e></td>
    <td width="1" height="1" bgcolor=#a38f55></td>
    <td width="1" height="1" bgcolor=#a69356></td>
    <td width="1" height="1" bgcolor=#a39054></td>
    <td width="1" height="1" bgcolor=#a19157></td>
    <td width="1" height="1" bgcolor=#a4955b></td>
    <td width="1" height="1" bgcolor=#9f9254></td>
    <td width="1" height="1" bgcolor=#a39657></td>
    <td width="1" height="1" bgcolor=#a49557></td>
    <td width="1" height="1" bgcolor=#a39357></td>
    <td width="1" height="1" bgcolor=#a29257></td>
    <td width="1" height="1" bgcolor=#a19055></td>
    <td width="1" height="1" bgcolor=#a1945f></td>
    <td width="1" height="1" bgcolor=#a29561></td>
    <td width="1" height="1" bgcolor=#9f915f></td>
    <td width="1" height="1" bgcolor=#9e9769></td>
    <td width="1" height="1" bgcolor=#a19868></td>
    <td width="1" height="1" bgcolor=#a09867></td>
    <td width="1" height="1" bgcolor=#a29967></td>
    <td width="1" height="1" bgcolor=#a1965e></td>
    <td width="1" height="1" bgcolor=#a3975b></td>
    <td width="1" height="1" bgcolor=#9f9552></td>
    <td width="1" height="1" bgcolor=#a39755></td>
    <td width="1" height="1" bgcolor=#a29655></td>
    <td width="1" height="1" bgcolor=#a89d5b></td>
    <td width="1" height="1" bgcolor=#a59a58></td>
    <td width="1" height="1" bgcolor=#9f9253></td>
    <td width="1" height="1" bgcolor=#a59959></td>
    <td width="1" height="1" bgcolor=#a49759></td>
```

```
    <td width="1" height="1" bgcolor=#a79751></td>
    <td width="1" height="1" bgcolor=#a89650></td>
    <td width="1" height="1" bgcolor=#a5934d></td>
    <td width="1" height="1" bgcolor=#a39348></td>
    <td width="1" height="1" bgcolor=#a59449></td>
    <td width="1" height="1" bgcolor=#a29143></td>
    <td width="1" height="1" bgcolor=#9f8e3f></td>
    <td width="1" height="1" bgcolor=#9f9047></td>
    <td width="1" height="1" bgcolor=#9c9150></td>
    <td width="1" height="1" bgcolor=#9d9256></td>
    <td width="1" height="1" bgcolor=#9c9153></td>
    <td width="1" height="1" bgcolor=#a19758></td>
    <td width="1" height="1" bgcolor=#9d9155></td>
    <td width="1" height="1" bgcolor=#9e9158></td>
    <td width="1" height="1" bgcolor=#9b9055></td>
    <td width="1" height="1" bgcolor=#988e4d></td>
    <td width="1" height="1" bgcolor=#9d904b></td>
    <td width="1" height="1" bgcolor=#9d9252></td>
    <td width="1" height="1" bgcolor=#9a8e52></td>
    <td width="1" height="1" bgcolor=#a19753></td>
    <td width="1" height="1" bgcolor=#999250></td>
    <td width="1" height="1" bgcolor=#9a9353></td>
    <td width="1" height="1" bgcolor=#999052></td>
    <td width="1" height="1" bgcolor=#978c52></td>
    <td width="1" height="1" bgcolor=#998b4a></td>
    <td width="1" height="1" bgcolor=#988945></td>
    <td width="1" height="1" bgcolor=#877b4b></td>
  </tr>
  <tr>
    <td width="1" height="1" bgcolor=#a6925e></td>
    <td width="1" height="1" bgcolor=#a69258></td>
    <td width="1" height="1" bgcolor=#a08b54></td>
    <td width="1" height="1" bgcolor=#a08a57></td>
    <td width="1" height="1" bgcolor=#9f895a></td>
    <td width="1" height="1" bgcolor=#a18c5d></td>
    <td width="1" height="1" bgcolor=#a48f58></td>
    <td width="1" height="1" bgcolor=#a2915b></td>
    <td width="1" height="1" bgcolor=#9e905a></td>
    <td width="1" height="1" bgcolor=#a3925c></td>
    <td width="1" height="1" bgcolor=#a3935c></td>
    <td width="1" height="1" bgcolor=#a69560></td>
    <td width="1" height="1" bgcolor=#a39457></td>
    <td width="1" height="1" bgcolor=#a4945f></td>
    <td width="1" height="1" bgcolor=#a1945b></td>
    <td width="1" height="1" bgcolor=#a4965c></td>
    <td width="1" height="1" bgcolor=#a5965a></td>
    <td width="1" height="1" bgcolor=#a89455></td>
    <td width="1" height="1" bgcolor=#a59151></td>
    <td width="1" height="1" bgcolor=#a79453></td>
    <td width="1" height="1" bgcolor=#a59557></td>
    <td width="1" height="1" bgcolor=#a39457></td>
    <td width="1" height="1" bgcolor=#a39451></td>
    <td width="1" height="1" bgcolor=#a79653></td>
    <td width="1" height="1" bgcolor=#a79350></td>
    <td width="1" height="1" bgcolor=#a59559></td>
    <td width="1" height="1" bgcolor=#a29358></td>
    <td width="1" height="1" bgcolor=#a5965b></td>
    <td width="1" height="1" bgcolor=#a3965d></td>
    <td width="1" height="1" bgcolor=#a0925b></td>
    <td width="1" height="1" bgcolor=#a0925d></td>
    <td width="1" height="1" bgcolor=#9c905e></td>
    <td width="1" height="1" bgcolor=#9d9564></td>
    <td width="1" height="1" bgcolor=#a29b6b></td>
    <td width="1" height="1" bgcolor=#9f9566></td>
    <td width="1" height="1" bgcolor=#a09664></td>
    <td width="1" height="1" bgcolor=#a09761></td>
    <td width="1" height="1" bgcolor=#a69b5c></td>
    <td width="1" height="1" bgcolor=#a79752></td>
    <td width="1" height="1" bgcolor=#a79552></td>
    <td width="1" height="1" bgcolor=#a69550></td>
    <td width="1" height="1" bgcolor=#a4944b></td>
    <td width="1" height="1" bgcolor=#a4924e></td>
    <td width="1" height="1" bgcolor=#a79551></td>
    <td width="1" height="1" bgcolor=#a79651></td>
    <td width="1" height="1" bgcolor=#a2914a></td>
    <td width="1" height="1" bgcolor=#a8954f></td>
    <td width="1" height="1" bgcolor=#a5914b></td>
    <td width="1" height="1" bgcolor=#a49246></td>
    <td width="1" height="1" bgcolor=#9f8e3f></td>
    <td width="1" height="1" bgcolor=#a39044></td>
    <td width="1" height="1" bgcolor=#a4934b></td>
    <td width="1" height="1" bgcolor=#a2934f></td>
    <td width="1" height="1" bgcolor=#a09456></td>
    <td width="1" height="1" bgcolor=#9f9458></td>
    <td width="1" height="1" bgcolor=#a29859></td>
    <td width="1" height="1" bgcolor=#9f9556></td>
    <td width="1" height="1" bgcolor=#9d9355></td>
    <td width="1" height="1" bgcolor=#9c9256></td>
```

```
    <td width="1" height="1"
bgcolor=#9c935a></td>
    <td width="1" height="1"
bgcolor=#988e50></td>
    <td width="1" height="1"
bgcolor=#9a8e4d></td>
    <td width="1" height="1"
bgcolor=#9d8f4e></td>
    <td width="1" height="1"
bgcolor=#a19251></td>
    <td width="1" height="1"
bgcolor=#9b8e4c></td>
    <td width="1" height="1"
bgcolor=#9b924e></td>
    <td width="1" height="1"
bgcolor=#998f4d></td>
    <td width="1" height="1"
bgcolor=#9a8f4f></td>
    <td width="1" height="1"
bgcolor=#9a8c51></td>
    <td width="1" height="1"
bgcolor=#9b8b4d></td>
    <td width="1" height="1"
bgcolor=#998847></td>
    <td width="1" height="1"
bgcolor=#8a7f49></td>
  </tr>
  <tr>
    <td width="1" height="1"
bgcolor=#a9935c></td>
    <td width="1" height="1"
bgcolor=#a48e54></td>
    <td width="1" height="1"
bgcolor=#a38d53></td>
    <td width="1" height="1"
bgcolor=#a28d53></td>
    <td width="1" height="1"
bgcolor=#a28d54></td>
    <td width="1" height="1"
bgcolor=#a48e56></td>
    <td width="1" height="1"
bgcolor=#a49157></td>
    <td width="1" height="1"
bgcolor=#9d8e54></td>
    <td width="1" height="1"
bgcolor=#a2955b></td>
    <td width="1" height="1"
bgcolor=#a19659></td>
    <td width="1" height="1"
bgcolor=#a29158></td>
    <td width="1" height="1"
bgcolor=#a39457></td>
    <td width="1" height="1"
bgcolor=#a39557></td>
    <td width="1" height="1"
bgcolor=#a09157></td>
    <td width="1" height="1"
bgcolor=#a29157></td>
    <td width="1" height="1"
bgcolor=#a5965b></td>
    <td width="1" height="1"
bgcolor=#a49759></td>
    <td width="1" height="1"
bgcolor=#a69a57></td>
    <td width="1" height="1"
bgcolor=#a59350></td>
    <td width="1" height="1"
bgcolor=#a8934f></td>
    <td width="1" height="1"
bgcolor=#a5914f></td>
    <td width="1" height="1"
bgcolor=#a5924f></td>
    <td width="1" height="1"
bgcolor=#a28f48></td>
    <td width="1" height="1"
bgcolor=#a28f49></td>
    <td width="1" height="1"
bgcolor=#a3914d></td>
    <td width="1" height="1"
bgcolor=#a79250></td>
    <td width="1" height="1"
bgcolor=#a59154></td>
    <td width="1" height="1"
bgcolor=#a39057></td>
    <td width="1" height="1"
bgcolor=#a0955c></td>
    <td width="1" height="1"
bgcolor=#9f9258></td>
    <td width="1" height="1"
bgcolor=#a29359></td>
    <td width="1" height="1"
bgcolor=#a3925b></td>
    <td width="1" height="1"
bgcolor=#a1975e></td>
    <td width="1" height="1"
bgcolor=#9c9159></td>
    <td width="1" height="1"
bgcolor=#a0915e></td>
    <td width="1" height="1"
bgcolor=#a1955c></td>
    <td width="1" height="1"
bgcolor=#a1955a></td>
    <td width="1" height="1"
bgcolor=#a29250></td>
    <td width="1" height="1"
bgcolor=#a38f47></td>
    <td width="1" height="1"
bgcolor=#a68f46></td>
    <td width="1" height="1"
bgcolor=#a9954a></td>
    <td width="1" height="1"
bgcolor=#a99448></td>
    <td width="1" height="1"
bgcolor=#a59144></td>
    <td width="1" height="1"
bgcolor=#a6924a></td>
    <td width="1" height="1"
bgcolor=#a69347></td>
    <td width="1" height="1"
bgcolor=#a58f44></td>
    <td width="1" height="1"
bgcolor=#a48d42></td>
    <td width="1" height="1"
bgcolor=#a28c40></td>
    <td width="1" height="1"
bgcolor=#a28b3e></td>
    <td width="1" height="1"
bgcolor=#a38c3e></td>
    <td width="1" height="1"
bgcolor=#a38d3c></td>
    <td width="1" height="1"
bgcolor=#a18c3b></td>
    <td width="1" height="1"
bgcolor=#a3903f></td>
    <td width="1" height="1"
bgcolor=#a08e46></td>
    <td width="1" height="1"
bgcolor=#9c8a45></td>
    <td width="1" height="1"
bgcolor=#9c8a44></td>
    <td rowspan="1"
colspan="2" width="1"
height="1"
bgcolor=#9e8c49></td>
    <td width="1" height="1"
bgcolor=#9e8c48></td>
    <td width="1" height="1"
bgcolor=#a08f4c></td>
    <td width="1" height="1"
bgcolor=#9b8d4a></td>
    <td width="1" height="1"
bgcolor=#9c8a47></td>
    <td width="1" height="1"
bgcolor=#9c8a45></td>
    <td width="1" height="1"
bgcolor=#9b8a43></td>
    <td width="1" height="1"
bgcolor=#9c8b44></td>
    <td rowspan="1"
colspan="2" width="1"
height="1"
bgcolor=#9c8b45></td>
    <td width="1" height="1"
bgcolor=#9b8b4c></td>
    <td width="1" height="1"
bgcolor=#958549></td>
    <td width="1" height="1"
bgcolor=#97874b></td>
    <td width="1" height="1"
bgcolor=#9a8546></td>
    <td width="1" height="1"
bgcolor=#8a7b49></td>
  </tr>
  <tr>
```

```
    <td width="1" height="1" bgcolor=#a48d58></td>
    <td width="1" height="1" bgcolor=#a48e57></td>
    <td width="1" height="1" bgcolor=#a28c53></td>
    <td width="1" height="1" bgcolor=#a18b52></td>
    <td width="1" height="1" bgcolor=#a18c53></td>
    <td width="1" height="1" bgcolor=#a69159></td>
    <td width="1" height="1" bgcolor=#a29259></td>
    <td width="1" height="1" bgcolor=#a8985d></td>
    <td width="1" height="1" bgcolor=#a69559></td>
    <td width="1" height="1" bgcolor=#a09250></td>
    <td width="1" height="1" bgcolor=#a39052></td>
    <td width="1" height="1" bgcolor=#a49452></td>
    <td width="1" height="1" bgcolor=#a39452></td>
    <td width="1" height="1" bgcolor=#a09150></td>
    <td width="1" height="1" bgcolor=#a2914d></td>
    <td width="1" height="1" bgcolor=#a6924e></td>
    <td width="1" height="1" bgcolor=#a8904c></td>
    <td width="1" height="1" bgcolor=#a68f48></td>
    <td width="1" height="1" bgcolor=#aa8e46></td>
    <td width="1" height="1" bgcolor=#a5863f></td>
    <td width="1" height="1" bgcolor=#a6853f></td>
    <td width="1" height="1" bgcolor=#a98940></td>
    <td width="1" height="1" bgcolor=#ad8d44></td>
    <td width="1" height="1" bgcolor=#aa8b43></td>
    <td width="1" height="1" bgcolor=#a78a42></td>
    <td width="1" height="1" bgcolor=#a68b43></td>
    <td width="1" height="1" bgcolor=#a68f48></td>
    <td width="1" height="1" bgcolor=#a18d4a></td>
    <td width="1" height="1" bgcolor=#a6924f></td>
    <td width="1" height="1" bgcolor=#a18d4a></td>
    <td width="1" height="1" bgcolor=#9f8a4a></td>
    <td width="1" height="1" bgcolor=#a0894a></td>
    <td width="1" height="1" bgcolor=#a39150></td>
    <td rowspan="1" colspan="2" width="1" height="1" bgcolor=#a18c4c></td>
    <td width="1" height="1" bgcolor=#9f8d4a></td>
    <td width="1" height="1" bgcolor=#a18f49></td>
    <td width="1" height="1" bgcolor=#a08c44></td>
    <td width="1" height="1" bgcolor=#a79145></td>
    <td width="1" height="1" bgcolor=#a99347></td>
    <td width="1" height="1" bgcolor=#a78f44></td>
    <td width="1" height="1" bgcolor=#a79146></td>
    <td width="1" height="1" bgcolor=#a89549></td>
    <td width="1" height="1" bgcolor=#a9964a></td>
    <td width="1" height="1" bgcolor=#a59346></td>
    <td width="1" height="1" bgcolor=#ac9744></td>
    <td width="1" height="1" bgcolor=#a5903e></td>
    <td width="1" height="1" bgcolor=#aa9543></td>
    <td width="1" height="1" bgcolor=#a6903d></td>
    <td width="1" height="1" bgcolor=#a48d39></td>
    <td width="1" height="1" bgcolor=#a58f39></td>
    <td width="1" height="1" bgcolor=#a48f3a></td>
    <td width="1" height="1" bgcolor=#a49042></td>
    <td rowspan="1" colspan="3" width="1" height="1" bgcolor=#a18e43></td>
    <td width="1" height="1" bgcolor=#9e8b3f></td>
    <td width="1" height="1" bgcolor=#a18e42></td>
    <td width="1" height="1" bgcolor=#9f8c3f></td>
    <td width="1" height="1" bgcolor=#a38a40></td>
    <td width="1" height="1" bgcolor=#a08c40></td>
    <td width="1" height="1" bgcolor=#a48c41></td>
    <td width="1" height="1" bgcolor=#9a823b></td>
    <td width="1" height="1" bgcolor=#9b833c></td>
    <td width="1" height="1" bgcolor=#9e853f></td>
    <td width="1" height="1" bgcolor=#9a823b></td>
    <td width="1" height="1" bgcolor=#9d843f></td>
    <td width="1" height="1" bgcolor=#99823f></td>
    <td width="1" height="1" bgcolor=#9a8341></td>
    <td width="1" height="1" bgcolor=#998340></td>
    <td width="1" height="1" bgcolor=#9b8342></td>
    <td width="1" height="1" bgcolor=#877644></td>
  </tr>
  <tr>
    <td width="1" height="1" bgcolor=#a79256></td>
    <td width="1" height="1" bgcolor=#a18c4e></td>
    <td width="1" height="1" bgcolor=#9f8a4c></td>
    <td width="1" height="1" bgcolor=#a18b54></td>
    <td width="1" height="1" bgcolor=#a28d54></td>
    <td width="1" height="1" bgcolor=#a28d53></td>
    <td width="1" height="1" bgcolor=#a59050></td>
    <td width="1" height="1" bgcolor=#a28b48></td>
    <td width="1" height="1" bgcolor=#a58645></td>
    <td width="1" height="1" bgcolor=#a18741></td>
    <td width="1" height="1" bgcolor=#a48744></td>
    <td width="1" height="1" bgcolor=#a58a47></td>
    <td width="1" height="1" bgcolor=#a48944></td>
    <td width="1" height="1" bgcolor=#a58c44></td>
    <td width="1" height="1" bgcolor=#a68741></td>
```

```
<td width="1" height="1" bgcolor=#a78942></td>
<td width="1" height="1" bgcolor=#a3863d></td>
<td width="1" height="1" bgcolor=#a7863f></td>
<td width="1" height="1" bgcolor=#a6853e></td>
<td width="1" height="1" bgcolor=#a7863d></td>
<td width="1" height="1" bgcolor=#a88740></td>
<td width="1" height="1" bgcolor=#a98840></td>
<td width="1" height="1" bgcolor=#a98942></td>
<td width="1" height="1" bgcolor=#a68741></td>
<td width="1" height="1" bgcolor=#a98b42></td>
<td width="1" height="1" bgcolor=#a6883f></td>
<td width="1" height="1" bgcolor=#a88c43></td>
<td width="1" height="1" bgcolor=#a38d43></td>
<td width="1" height="1" bgcolor=#aa8f45></td>
<td width="1" height="1" bgcolor=#a78e47></td>
<td width="1" height="1" bgcolor=#a38d4a></td>
<td width="1" height="1" bgcolor=#a9924c></td>
<td width="1" height="1" bgcolor=#a08942></td>
<td width="1" height="1" bgcolor=#a58843></td>
<td width="1" height="1" bgcolor=#a68a42></td>
<td width="1" height="1" bgcolor=#a58b43></td>
<td width="1" height="1" bgcolor=#a48b44></td>
<td width="1" height="1" bgcolor=#a78e47></td>
<td width="1" height="1" bgcolor=#a89148></td>
<td width="1" height="1" bgcolor=#a69247></td>
<td width="1" height="1" bgcolor=#ac8e46></td>
<td width="1" height="1" bgcolor=#aa9247></td>
<td width="1" height="1" bgcolor=#a7944c></td>
<td width="1" height="1" bgcolor=#ab9948></td>
<td width="1" height="1" bgcolor=#a79544></td>
<td width="1" height="1" bgcolor=#a69343></td>
<td width="1" height="1" bgcolor=#a89545></td>
<td width="1" height="1" bgcolor=#a59141></td>
<td width="1" height="1" bgcolor=#a68e3f></td>
<td width="1" height="1" bgcolor=#a58e3d></td>
<td width="1" height="1" bgcolor=#a7913f></td>
<td width="1" height="1" bgcolor=#a38c3d></td>
<td width="1" height="1" bgcolor=#a4903d></td>
<td width="1" height="1" bgcolor=#a08b3d></td>
<td width="1" height="1" bgcolor=#a28b40></td>
<td width="1" height="1" bgcolor=#a0893e></td>
<td width="1" height="1" bgcolor=#a18b3d></td>
<td width="1" height="1" bgcolor=#a48e40></td>
<td width="1" height="1" bgcolor=#a38d3f></td>
<td width="1" height="1" bgcolor=#a38b3b></td>
<td width="1" height="1" bgcolor=#a08d3c></td>
<td width="1" height="1" bgcolor=#a58c3d></td>
<td width="1" height="1" bgcolor=#a38d3c></td>
<td width="1" height="1" bgcolor=#a28b3f></td>
<td width="1" height="1" bgcolor=#9e863d></td>
<td width="1" height="1" bgcolor=#9f863c></td>
<td width="1" height="1" bgcolor=#a18840></td>
<td width="1" height="1" bgcolor=#9e8741></td>
<td width="1" height="1" bgcolor=#9a8340></td>
<td width="1" height="1" bgcolor=#99823f></td>
<td width="1" height="1" bgcolor=#a18643></td>
<td width="1" height="1" bgcolor=#8c7845></td>
</tr>
<tr>
<td width="1" height="1" bgcolor=#aa9159></td>
<td width="1" height="1" bgcolor=#a38d51></td>
<td width="1" height="1" bgcolor=#9f8b4c></td>
<td width="1" height="1" bgcolor=#a48c4c></td>
<td width="1" height="1" bgcolor=#a28d4e></td>
<td width="1" height="1" bgcolor=#a3884a></td>
<td width="1" height="1" bgcolor=#a18341></td>
<td width="1" height="1" bgcolor=#a17f3f></td>
<td width="1" height="1" bgcolor=#a5833f></td>
<td width="1" height="1" bgcolor=#a68440></td>
<td width="1" height="1" bgcolor=#a28240></td>
<td width="1" height="1" bgcolor=#a38444></td>
<td width="1" height="1" bgcolor=#a28341></td>
<td width="1" height="1" bgcolor=#aa8c46></td>
<td width="1" height="1" bgcolor=#a48744></td>
<td width="1" height="1" bgcolor=#a98b45></td>
<td width="1" height="1" bgcolor=#a88941></td>
<td width="1" height="1" bgcolor=#a78b41></td>
<td width="1" height="1" bgcolor=#a78940></td>
<td width="1" height="1" bgcolor=#a88940></td>
<td width="1" height="1" bgcolor=#aa8e43></td>
<td width="1" height="1" bgcolor=#a78b41></td>
<td width="1" height="1" bgcolor=#a68742></td>
<td width="1" height="1" bgcolor=#a38241></td>
<td width="1" height="1" bgcolor=#a78947></td>
<td width="1" height="1" bgcolor=#a58c44></td>
<td width="1" height="1" bgcolor=#a58d43></td>
<td width="1" height="1" bgcolor=#a68e46></td>
<td width="1" height="1" bgcolor=#a48c42></td>
```

```
    <td width="1" height="1"
bgcolor=#a89045></td>
    <td width="1" height="1"
bgcolor=#a99145></td>
    <td width="1" height="1"
bgcolor=#a89048></td>
    <td width="1" height="1"
bgcolor=#a38946></td>
    <td width="1" height="1"
bgcolor=#a28848></td>
    <td width="1" height="1"
bgcolor=#a38544></td>
    <td width="1" height="1"
bgcolor=#a08543></td>
    <td width="1" height="1"
bgcolor=#a28846></td>
    <td width="1" height="1"
bgcolor=#a68d49></td>
    <td width="1" height="1"
bgcolor=#a79348></td>
    <td width="1" height="1"
bgcolor=#a8954a></td>
    <td width="1" height="1"
bgcolor=#a89449></td>
    <td width="1" height="1"
bgcolor=#aa964e></td>
    <td width="1" height="1"
bgcolor=#a6934a></td>
    <td width="1" height="1"
bgcolor=#a99147></td>
    <td width="1" height="1"
bgcolor=#ae9447></td>
    <td width="1" height="1"
bgcolor=#a69042></td>
    <td width="1" height="1"
bgcolor=#a68f44></td>
    <td width="1" height="1"
bgcolor=#a78f45></td>
    <td width="1" height="1"
bgcolor=#a18739></td>
    <td width="1" height="1"
bgcolor=#a0893c></td>
    <td width="1" height="1"
bgcolor=#a0883d></td>
    <td width="1" height="1"
bgcolor=#a68c43></td>
    <td width="1" height="1"
bgcolor=#a0863d></td>
    <td width="1" height="1"
bgcolor=#a0863e></td>
    <td width="1" height="1"
bgcolor=#9c833a></td>
    <td width="1" height="1"
bgcolor=#9c823a></td>
    <td width="1" height="1"
bgcolor=#a1833c></td>
    <td width="1" height="1"
bgcolor=#9f823b></td>
    <td width="1" height="1"
bgcolor=#a68b41></td>
    <td width="1" height="1"
bgcolor=#a18b3b></td>
    <td width="1" height="1"
bgcolor=#a48c39></td>
    <td width="1" height="1"
bgcolor=#a88e39></td>
    <td width="1" height="1"
bgcolor=#9e8939></td>
    <td rowspan="1"
colspan="2" width="1"
height="1"
bgcolor=#a08a3e></td>
    <td width="1" height="1"
bgcolor=#9e883a></td>
    <td width="1" height="1"
bgcolor=#9e883e></td>
    <td width="1" height="1"
bgcolor=#9a8340></td>
    <td width="1" height="1"
bgcolor=#9c8541></td>
    <td width="1" height="1"
bgcolor=#9a833f></td>
    <td width="1" height="1"
bgcolor=#9c8945></td>
    <td width="1" height="1"
bgcolor=#8a7846></td>
  </tr>
  <tr>
    <td width="1" height="1"
bgcolor=#a68e56></td>
    <td width="1" height="1"
bgcolor=#a68d53></td>
    <td width="1" height="1"
bgcolor=#a2894b></td>
    <td width="1" height="1"
bgcolor=#a18849></td>
    <td width="1" height="1"
bgcolor=#9e8443></td>
    <td width="1" height="1"
bgcolor=#a38041></td>
    <td width="1" height="1"
bgcolor=#a68142></td>
    <td width="1" height="1"
bgcolor=#a28141></td>
    <td width="1" height="1"
bgcolor=#a88747></td>
    <td width="1" height="1"
bgcolor=#a38343></td>
    <td width="1" height="1"
bgcolor=#a38544></td>
    <td width="1" height="1"
bgcolor=#a1833f></td>
    <td width="1" height="1"
bgcolor=#a48543></td>
    <td width="1" height="1"
bgcolor=#a28244></td>
    <td width="1" height="1"
bgcolor=#a48640></td>
    <td width="1" height="1"
bgcolor=#a58940></td>
    <td width="1" height="1"
bgcolor=#a88d40></td>
    <td width="1" height="1"
bgcolor=#a98d43></td>
    <td width="1" height="1"
bgcolor=#a88b42></td>
    <td width="1" height="1"
bgcolor=#a98c42></td>
    <td width="1" height="1"
bgcolor=#ac9045></td>
    <td width="1" height="1"
bgcolor=#aa8e45></td>
    <td width="1" height="1"
bgcolor=#ac8d44></td>
    <td width="1" height="1"
bgcolor=#ab8b43></td>
    <td width="1" height="1"
bgcolor=#a88b41></td>
    <td rowspan="1"
colspan="2" width="1"
height="1"
bgcolor=#aa8e45></td>
    <td width="1" height="1"
bgcolor=#a88c45></td>
    <td width="1" height="1"
bgcolor=#a48b45></td>
    <td width="1" height="1"
bgcolor=#a48b44></td>
    <td width="1" height="1"
bgcolor=#a58c43></td>
    <td width="1" height="1"
bgcolor=#ac9549></td>
    <td width="1" height="1"
bgcolor=#ab944a></td>
    <td width="1" height="1"
bgcolor=#aa934a></td>
    <td width="1" height="1"
bgcolor=#a89247></td>
    <td width="1" height="1"
bgcolor=#a59044></td>
    <td width="1" height="1"
bgcolor=#a89045></td>
    <td width="1" height="1"
bgcolor=#a68e44></td>
    <td width="1" height="1"
bgcolor=#a68c49></td>
    <td width="1" height="1"
bgcolor=#aa8e47></td>
    <td width="1" height="1"
bgcolor=#ac8e49></td>
    <td width="1" height="1"
bgcolor=#a58744></td>
    <td width="1" height="1"
bgcolor=#a68941></td>
```

```
    <td width="1" height="1"
bgcolor=#a78940></td>
    <td width="1" height="1"
bgcolor=#aa893e></td>
    <td width="1" height="1"
bgcolor=#a88a3e></td>
    <td width="1" height="1"
bgcolor=#aa8b3f></td>
    <td width="1" height="1"
bgcolor=#a8893d></td>
    <td width="1" height="1"
bgcolor=#a7863a></td>
    <td width="1" height="1"
bgcolor=#a48439></td>
    <td width="1" height="1"
bgcolor=#a3833a></td>
    <td width="1" height="1"
bgcolor=#a7873a></td>
    <td width="1" height="1"
bgcolor=#a58438></td>
    <td width="1" height="1"
bgcolor=#a38334></td>
    <td width="1" height="1"
bgcolor=#a68639></td>
    <td width="1" height="1"
bgcolor=#a78639></td>
    <td width="1" height="1"
bgcolor=#a78839></td>
    <td width="1" height="1"
bgcolor=#a68938></td>
    <td width="1" height="1"
bgcolor=#a88c39></td>
    <td width="1" height="1"
bgcolor=#a68a3b></td>
    <td width="1" height="1"
bgcolor=#a58939></td>
    <td width="1" height="1"
bgcolor=#a58a3a></td>
    <td width="1" height="1"
bgcolor=#a18938></td>
    <td width="1" height="1"
bgcolor=#a48c3b></td>
    <td width="1" height="1"
bgcolor=#a28b3a></td>
    <td width="1" height="1"
bgcolor=#a38d3e></td>
    <td width="1" height="1"
bgcolor=#a0893f></td>
    <td width="1" height="1"
bgcolor=#9e8741></td>
    <td width="1" height="1"
bgcolor=#9d8541></td>
    <td width="1" height="1"
bgcolor=#9e8743></td>
    <td width="1" height="1"
bgcolor=#9a8440></td>
    <td width="1" height="1"
bgcolor=#8e7947></td>
  </tr>
  <tr>
    <td width="1" height="1"
bgcolor=#a48e55></td>
    <td width="1" height="1"
bgcolor=#a3894f></td>
    <td width="1" height="1"
bgcolor=#a18347></td>
    <td width="1" height="1"
bgcolor=#9e8244></td>
    <td width="1" height="1"
bgcolor=#9c7c3b></td>
    <td width="1" height="1"
bgcolor=#a17d3b></td>
    <td width="1" height="1"
bgcolor=#9e8240></td>
    <td width="1" height="1"
bgcolor=#a58745></td>
    <td width="1" height="1"
bgcolor=#a48444></td>
    <td width="1" height="1"
bgcolor=#a38542></td>
    <td width="1" height="1"
bgcolor=#a48942></td>
    <td width="1" height="1"
bgcolor=#a6893f></td>
    <td width="1" height="1"
bgcolor=#a28342></td>
    <td width="1" height="1"
bgcolor=#a4834e></td>
    <td width="1" height="1"
bgcolor=#a68546></td>
    <td width="1" height="1"
bgcolor=#a38743></td>
    <td width="1" height="1"
bgcolor=#a58f46></td>
    <td width="1" height="1"
bgcolor=#a58c41></td>
    <td width="1" height="1"
bgcolor=#a78b42></td>
    <td width="1" height="1"
bgcolor=#aa8e43></td>
    <td width="1" height="1"
bgcolor=#aa8f43></td>
    <td width="1" height="1"
bgcolor=#a78b41></td>
    <td width="1" height="1"
bgcolor=#a98a43></td>
    <td width="1" height="1"
bgcolor=#a78741></td>
    <td rowspan="1"
colspan="2" width="1"
height="1"
bgcolor=#a68941></td>
    <td width="1" height="1"
bgcolor=#ac8e46></td>
    <td width="1" height="1"
bgcolor=#a98c46></td>
    <td width="1" height="1"
bgcolor=#9e7a3b></td>
    <td width="1" height="1"
bgcolor=#aa8545></td>
    <td width="1" height="1"
bgcolor=#a4803e></td>
    <td width="1" height="1"
bgcolor=#a58641></td>
    <td width="1" height="1"
bgcolor=#a48641></td>
    <td width="1" height="1"
bgcolor=#a58841></td>
    <td width="1" height="1"
bgcolor=#a38b44></td>
    <td width="1" height="1"
bgcolor=#a28741></td>
    <td width="1" height="1"
bgcolor=#a48541></td>
    <td width="1" height="1"
bgcolor=#a4803f></td>
    <td width="1" height="1"
bgcolor=#a8823e></td>
    <td width="1" height="1"
bgcolor=#aa813f></td>
    <td width="1" height="1"
bgcolor=#a57b3c></td>
    <td width="1" height="1"
bgcolor=#a67d3f></td>
    <td width="1" height="1"
bgcolor=#ab823d></td>
    <td width="1" height="1"
bgcolor=#ab843c></td>
    <td width="1" height="1"
bgcolor=#a78136></td>
    <td width="1" height="1"
bgcolor=#a47e32></td>
    <td width="1" height="1"
bgcolor=#a67f31></td>
    <td width="1" height="1"
bgcolor=#aa8535></td>
    <td width="1" height="1"
bgcolor=#a78439></td>
    <td width="1" height="1"
bgcolor=#a48239></td>
    <td width="1" height="1"
bgcolor=#9e7c34></td>
    <td width="1" height="1"
bgcolor=#9b7a31></td>
    <td width="1" height="1"
bgcolor=#9c7a32></td>
    <td width="1" height="1"
bgcolor=#a18135></td>
    <td width="1" height="1"
bgcolor=#a78739></td>
    <td width="1" height="1"
bgcolor=#a08033></td>
    <td width="1" height="1"
bgcolor=#a98536></td>
```

```
    <td width="1" height="1"
bgcolor=#a48332></td>
    <td width="1" height="1"
bgcolor=#a0822e></td>
    <td width="1" height="1"
bgcolor=#a38033></td>
    <td width="1" height="1"
bgcolor=#a38437></td>
    <td width="1" height="1"
bgcolor=#a2843b></td>
    <td width="1" height="1"
bgcolor=#a0843a></td>
    <td width="1" height="1"
bgcolor=#a08537></td>
    <td width="1" height="1"
bgcolor=#a38939></td>
    <td width="1" height="1"
bgcolor=#a38d3c></td>
    <td width="1" height="1"
bgcolor=#9d853a></td>
    <td width="1" height="1"
bgcolor=#a18b41></td>
    <td width="1" height="1"
bgcolor=#a08a41></td>
    <td width="1" height="1"
bgcolor=#9e8744></td>
    <td width="1" height="1"
bgcolor=#a18845></td>
    <td width="1" height="1"
bgcolor=#8d7745></td>
  </tr>
  <tr>
    <td width="1" height="1"
bgcolor=#a38a51></td>
    <td width="1" height="1"
bgcolor=#a08148></td>
    <td width="1" height="1"
bgcolor=#a4813f></td>
    <td width="1" height="1"
bgcolor=#a17c3d></td>
    <td width="1" height="1"
bgcolor=#a58242></td>
    <td width="1" height="1"
bgcolor=#a18441></td>
    <td width="1" height="1"
bgcolor=#a08643></td>
    <td width="1" height="1"
bgcolor=#a28741></td>
    <td width="1" height="1"
bgcolor=#a38b43></td>
    <td width="1" height="1"
bgcolor=#a08542></td>
    <td width="1" height="1"
bgcolor=#a4813f></td>
    <td width="1" height="1"
bgcolor=#a27f3d></td>
    <td width="1" height="1"
bgcolor=#a48340></td>
    <td width="1" height="1"
bgcolor=#a68a43></td>
    <td width="1" height="1"
bgcolor=#a58747></td>
    <td width="1" height="1"
bgcolor=#a48745></td>
    <td width="1" height="1"
bgcolor=#a38743></td>
    <td width="1" height="1"
bgcolor=#aa8a45></td>
    <td rowspan="1"
colspan="2" width="1"
height="1"
bgcolor=#a98b46></td>
    <td width="1" height="1"
bgcolor=#a98b45></td>
    <td width="1" height="1"
bgcolor=#aa8941></td>
    <td width="1" height="1"
bgcolor=#ad8c3f></td>
    <td width="1" height="1"
bgcolor=#a7863c></td>
    <td width="1" height="1"
bgcolor=#aa8743></td>
    <td width="1" height="1"
bgcolor=#aa873f></td>
    <td width="1" height="1"
bgcolor=#ac8945></td>
    <td width="1" height="1"
bgcolor=#a57f3c></td>
    <td width="1" height="1"
bgcolor=#ad833e></td>
    <td width="1" height="1"
bgcolor=#ab803c></td>
    <td width="1" height="1"
bgcolor=#ad823e></td>
    <td width="1" height="1"
bgcolor=#a97d3e></td>
    <td width="1" height="1"
bgcolor=#a87a3a></td>
    <td width="1" height="1"
bgcolor=#a57339></td>
    <td width="1" height="1"
bgcolor=#a6753c></td>
    <td width="1" height="1"
bgcolor=#a26f39></td>
    <td rowspan="1"
colspan="2" width="1"
height="1"
bgcolor=#a66f39></td>
    <td width="1" height="1"
bgcolor=#a56837></td>
    <td width="1" height="1"
bgcolor=#a26a38></td>
    <td width="1" height="1"
bgcolor=#a4703a></td>
    <td width="1" height="1"
bgcolor=#a26f38></td>
    <td width="1" height="1"
bgcolor=#a8763c></td>
    <td width="1" height="1"
bgcolor=#a87d3c></td>
    <td width="1" height="1"
bgcolor=#a17b31></td>
    <td width="1" height="1"
bgcolor=#a27a33></td>
    <td width="1" height="1"
bgcolor=#9d742d></td>
    <td width="1" height="1"
bgcolor=#9e762e></td>
    <td width="1" height="1"
bgcolor=#9a732f></td>
    <td width="1" height="1"
bgcolor=#9a742f></td>
    <td width="1" height="1"
bgcolor=#9f7834></td>
    <td width="1" height="1"
bgcolor=#a67f37></td>
    <td width="1" height="1"
bgcolor=#a3813a></td>
    <td width="1" height="1"
bgcolor=#a7833a></td>
    <td width="1" height="1"
bgcolor=#a07b30></td>
    <td width="1" height="1"
bgcolor=#9f7e31></td>
    <td width="1" height="1"
bgcolor=#a07e34></td>
    <td width="1" height="1"
bgcolor=#9f7c2f></td>
    <td width="1" height="1"
bgcolor=#a17f2e></td>
    <td width="1" height="1"
bgcolor=#a17d29></td>
    <td width="1" height="1"
bgcolor=#9f8131></td>
    <td width="1" height="1"
bgcolor=#9e7d34></td>
    <td width="1" height="1"
bgcolor=#9e8030></td>
    <td width="1" height="1"
bgcolor=#a28039></td>
    <td width="1" height="1"
bgcolor=#9a7936></td>
    <td width="1" height="1"
bgcolor=#9a7b39></td>
    <td width="1" height="1"
bgcolor=#9e7f39></td>
    <td width="1" height="1"
bgcolor=#9e7e3c></td>
    <td width="1" height="1"
bgcolor=#9c7e40></td>
    <td width="1" height="1"
bgcolor=#9b813f></td>
    <td width="1" height="1"
bgcolor=#a1863f></td>
```

```
    <td width="1" height="1" bgcolor=#8e7947></td>
  </tr>
  <tr>
    <td width="1" height="1" bgcolor=#a6884e></td>
    <td width="1" height="1" bgcolor=#a07f45></td>
    <td width="1" height="1" bgcolor=#a48240></td>
    <td width="1" height="1" bgcolor=#a68440></td>
    <td width="1" height="1" bgcolor=#a68a42></td>
    <td width="1" height="1" bgcolor=#a28941></td>
    <td width="1" height="1" bgcolor=#a18440></td>
    <td width="1" height="1" bgcolor=#a2853f></td>
    <td width="1" height="1" bgcolor=#a0813a></td>
    <td width="1" height="1" bgcolor=#9f7c3d></td>
    <td width="1" height="1" bgcolor=#a47f3e></td>
    <td width="1" height="1" bgcolor=#a7823e></td>
    <td width="1" height="1" bgcolor=#a68540></td>
    <td width="1" height="1" bgcolor=#a68842></td>
    <td width="1" height="1" bgcolor=#a88540></td>
    <td width="1" height="1" bgcolor=#a47e3c></td>
    <td width="1" height="1" bgcolor=#a47b3a></td>
    <td width="1" height="1" bgcolor=#a97e3a></td>
    <td width="1" height="1" bgcolor=#a5803b></td>
    <td width="1" height="1" bgcolor=#a98840></td>
    <td width="1" height="1" bgcolor=#aa853a></td>
    <td width="1" height="1" bgcolor=#a7833a></td>
    <td width="1" height="1" bgcolor=#ab863d></td>
    <td width="1" height="1" bgcolor=#a88139></td>
    <td width="1" height="1" bgcolor=#a47c37></td>
    <td width="1" height="1" bgcolor=#a88138></td>
    <td width="1" height="1" bgcolor=#aa7f3d></td>
    <td width="1" height="1" bgcolor=#a97c39></td>
    <td width="1" height="1" bgcolor=#a67b37></td>
    <td width="1" height="1" bgcolor=#aa7e3b></td>
    <td width="1" height="1" bgcolor=#aa7f3b></td>
    <td width="1" height="1" bgcolor=#a97c3b></td>
    <td width="1" height="1" bgcolor=#ab783a></td>
    <td width="1" height="1" bgcolor=#a56d37></td>
    <td width="1" height="1" bgcolor=#a06a38></td>
    <td width="1" height="1" bgcolor=#9f6b3a></td>
    <td width="1" height="1" bgcolor=#9c6536></td>
    <td width="1" height="1" bgcolor=#a77141></td>
    <td width="1" height="1" bgcolor=#ac7941></td>
    <td width="1" height="1" bgcolor=#a97338></td>
    <td width="1" height="1" bgcolor=#a77336></td>
    <td width="1" height="1" bgcolor=#a97638></td>
    <td width="1" height="1" bgcolor=#a77435></td>
    <td width="1" height="1" bgcolor=#a97736></td>
    <td width="1" height="1" bgcolor=#a77732></td>
    <td width="1" height="1" bgcolor=#a77334></td>
    <td width="1" height="1" bgcolor=#a47031></td>
    <td width="1" height="1" bgcolor=#a06c2d></td>
    <td width="1" height="1" bgcolor=#996b31></td>
    <td width="1" height="1" bgcolor=#a07436></td>
    <td width="1" height="1" bgcolor=#a57a39></td>
    <td width="1" height="1" bgcolor=#aa843e></td>
    <td width="1" height="1" bgcolor=#a8833b></td>
    <td width="1" height="1" bgcolor=#9d7630></td>
    <td width="1" height="1" bgcolor=#9e742f></td>
    <td width="1" height="1" bgcolor=#9e6f2d></td>
    <td width="1" height="1" bgcolor=#a17935></td>
    <td width="1" height="1" bgcolor=#a37c33></td>
    <td width="1" height="1" bgcolor=#a47e31></td>
    <td width="1" height="1" bgcolor=#a07b35></td>
    <td width="1" height="1" bgcolor=#a28137></td>
    <td width="1" height="1" bgcolor=#a37b30></td>
    <td width="1" height="1" bgcolor=#9e7b34></td>
    <td width="1" height="1" bgcolor=#9e7935></td>
    <td width="1" height="1" bgcolor=#9f7936></td>
    <td width="1" height="1" bgcolor=#9f7c37></td>
    <td width="1" height="1" bgcolor=#a3813e></td>
    <td width="1" height="1" bgcolor=#a2813d></td>
    <td width="1" height="1" bgcolor=#a28341></td>
    <td width="1" height="1" bgcolor=#a08442></td>
    <td width="1" height="1" bgcolor=#a28741></td>
    <td width="1" height="1" bgcolor=#8f7a49></td>
  </tr>
  <tr>
    <td width="1" height="1" bgcolor=#a4874c></td>
    <td width="1" height="1" bgcolor=#9f8244></td>
    <td width="1" height="1" bgcolor=#a48842></td>
    <td width="1" height="1" bgcolor=#a28945></td>
    <td width="1" height="1" bgcolor=#a1833f></td>
    <td width="1" height="1" bgcolor=#a48340></td>
    <td width="1" height="1" bgcolor=#a0823d></td>
    <td width="1" height="1" bgcolor=#a3823c></td>
    <td width="1" height="1" bgcolor=#a6813c></td>
    <td width="1" height="1" bgcolor=#a27a3c></td>
    <td width="1" height="1" bgcolor=#a67e3e></td>
    <td width="1" height="1" bgcolor=#a7823c></td>
```

```
    <td width="1" height="1" bgcolor=#a4823a></td>
    <td width="1" height="1" bgcolor=#a4863e></td>
    <td width="1" height="1" bgcolor=#9f7d3b></td>
    <td width="1" height="1" bgcolor=#a27c3d></td>
    <td width="1" height="1" bgcolor=#a1773c></td>
    <td width="1" height="1" bgcolor=#a4793c></td>
    <td width="1" height="1" bgcolor=#9d7034></td>
    <td width="1" height="1" bgcolor=#9c6d32></td>
    <td width="1" height="1" bgcolor=#9f7237></td>
    <td width="1" height="1" bgcolor=#a47b3a></td>
    <td width="1" height="1" bgcolor=#a07534></td>
    <td width="1" height="1" bgcolor=#a07234></td>
    <td width="1" height="1" bgcolor=#a57736></td>
    <td width="1" height="1" bgcolor=#a37433></td>
    <td width="1" height="1" bgcolor=#9f6f34></td>
    <td width="1" height="1" bgcolor=#a06e32></td>
    <td width="1" height="1" bgcolor=#a7733a></td>
    <td width="1" height="1" bgcolor=#a57038></td>
    <td width="1" height="1" bgcolor=#a26d35></td>
    <td width="1" height="1" bgcolor=#a6723c></td>
    <td width="1" height="1" bgcolor=#a67936></td>
    <td width="1" height="1" bgcolor=#a67c3a></td>
    <td width="1" height="1" bgcolor=#a67d3c></td>
    <td width="1" height="1" bgcolor=#a48240></td>
    <td width="1" height="1" bgcolor=#a0783a></td>
    <td width="1" height="1" bgcolor=#a5773c></td>
    <td width="1" height="1" bgcolor=#a8753a></td>
    <td width="1" height="1" bgcolor=#a9733e></td>
    <td width="1" height="1" bgcolor=#a8723d></td>
    <td width="1" height="1" bgcolor=#aa763e></td>
    <td width="1" height="1" bgcolor=#a5743d></td>
    <td width="1" height="1" bgcolor=#a5723c></td>
    <td width="1" height="1" bgcolor=#a06d37></td>
    <td width="1" height="1" bgcolor=#955f30></td>
    <td width="1" height="1" bgcolor=#8f592a></td>
    <td width="1" height="1" bgcolor=#8c5729></td>
    <td width="1" height="1" bgcolor=#905c2e></td>
    <td width="1" height="1" bgcolor=#94602e></td>
    <td width="1" height="1" bgcolor=#98652f></td>
    <td width="1" height="1" bgcolor=#966431></td>
    <td width="1" height="1" bgcolor=#824d26></td>
    <td width="1" height="1" bgcolor=#895228></td>
    <td width="1" height="1" bgcolor=#945f2c></td>
    <td width="1" height="1" bgcolor=#9d6b2f></td>
    <td width="1" height="1" bgcolor=#986c31></td>
    <td width="1" height="1" bgcolor=#976d2f></td>
    <td width="1" height="1" bgcolor=#9b712f></td>
    <td width="1" height="1" bgcolor=#99742d></td>
    <td width="1" height="1" bgcolor=#9c7832></td>
    <td width="1" height="1" bgcolor=#a07633></td>
    <td width="1" height="1" bgcolor=#a07c32></td>
    <td width="1" height="1" bgcolor=#a07a31></td>
    <td width="1" height="1" bgcolor=#a37c33></td>
    <td width="1" height="1" bgcolor=#a18234></td>
    <td width="1" height="1" bgcolor=#9f8339></td>
    <td width="1" height="1" bgcolor=#a18338></td>
    <td width="1" height="1" bgcolor=#a4843f></td>
    <td width="1" height="1" bgcolor=#9e813f></td>
    <td width="1" height="1" bgcolor=#9b7e3b></td>
    <td width="1" height="1" bgcolor=#8e7849></td>
  </tr>
  <tr>
    <td width="1" height="1" bgcolor=#a4894a></td>
    <td width="1" height="1" bgcolor=#a58b49></td>
    <td width="1" height="1" bgcolor=#a18641></td>
    <td width="1" height="1" bgcolor=#a5853f></td>
    <td width="1" height="1" bgcolor=#a4843f></td>
    <td width="1" height="1" bgcolor=#a4853f></td>
    <td width="1" height="1" bgcolor=#a3833e></td>
    <td width="1" height="1" bgcolor=#a6813e></td>
    <td width="1" height="1" bgcolor=#a7803b></td>
    <td width="1" height="1" bgcolor=#a47d38></td>
    <td width="1" height="1" bgcolor=#a57e3a></td>
    <td width="1" height="1" bgcolor=#a17e3a></td>
    <td width="1" height="1" bgcolor=#a2833a></td>
    <td width="1" height="1" bgcolor=#a48641></td>
    <td width="1" height="1" bgcolor=#a28641></td>
    <td width="1" height="1" bgcolor=#a5863d></td>
    <td width="1" height="1" bgcolor=#aa893c></td>
    <td width="1" height="1" bgcolor=#aa843a></td>
    <td width="1" height="1" bgcolor=#ac843f></td>
    <td width="1" height="1" bgcolor=#a77d3b></td>
    <td width="1" height="1" bgcolor=#a6793a></td>
    <td width="1" height="1" bgcolor=#9e6c33></td>
    <td width="1" height="1" bgcolor=#9f6b33></td>
    <td width="1" height="1" bgcolor=#a46836></td>
    <td width="1" height="1" bgcolor=#a2642f></td>
    <td width="1" height="1" bgcolor=#a46a2d></td>
```

```
    <td width="1" height="1"
bgcolor=#a16431></td>
    <td width="1" height="1"
bgcolor=#a46e33></td>
    <td width="1" height="1"
bgcolor=#a36f37></td>
    <td width="1" height="1"
bgcolor=#a37137></td>
    <td width="1" height="1"
bgcolor=#a87038></td>
    <td width="1" height="1"
bgcolor=#a76d35></td>
    <td width="1" height="1"
bgcolor=#aa7237></td>
    <td width="1" height="1"
bgcolor=#a8703a></td>
    <td width="1" height="1"
bgcolor=#a7793d></td>
    <td width="1" height="1"
bgcolor=#a77b3b></td>
    <td width="1" height="1"
bgcolor=#ab783a></td>
    <td width="1" height="1"
bgcolor=#ac7939></td>
    <td width="1" height="1"
bgcolor=#aa7939></td>
    <td width="1" height="1"
bgcolor=#a87139></td>
    <td width="1" height="1"
bgcolor=#a87137></td>
    <td width="1" height="1"
bgcolor=#a77333></td>
    <td width="1" height="1"
bgcolor=#a87237></td>
    <td width="1" height="1"
bgcolor=#aa753b></td>
    <td width="1" height="1"
bgcolor=#a67037></td>
    <td width="1" height="1"
bgcolor=#a16b32></td>
    <td width="1" height="1"
bgcolor=#9d662f></td>
    <td width="1" height="1"
bgcolor=#99632e></td>
    <td width="1" height="1"
bgcolor=#996235></td>
    <td width="1" height="1"
bgcolor=#a05e38></td>
    <td width="1" height="1"
bgcolor=#9b5a32></td>
    <td width="1" height="1"
bgcolor=#985431></td>
    <td width="1" height="1"
bgcolor=#9c5536></td>
    <td width="1" height="1"
bgcolor=#9e5737></td>
    <td width="1" height="1"
bgcolor=#9b5332></td>
    <td width="1" height="1"
bgcolor=#994f2c></td>
    <td width="1" height="1"
bgcolor=#974c2b></td>
    <td width="1" height="1"
bgcolor=#954f2c></td>
    <td width="1" height="1"
bgcolor=#985c2b></td>
    <td width="1" height="1"
bgcolor=#986b31></td>
    <td width="1" height="1"
bgcolor=#9e7a35></td>
    <td width="1" height="1"
bgcolor=#a98732></td>
    <td width="1" height="1"
bgcolor=#a98b34></td>
    <td width="1" height="1"
bgcolor=#a28733></td>
    <td width="1" height="1"
bgcolor=#a98936></td>
    <td width="1" height="1"
bgcolor=#a68636></td>
    <td width="1" height="1"
bgcolor=#a58136></td>
    <td width="1" height="1"
bgcolor=#a7813b></td>
    <td width="1" height="1"
bgcolor=#a9823e></td>
    <td width="1" height="1"
bgcolor=#9f7a3a></td>
    <td width="1" height="1"
bgcolor=#9c7238></td>
    <td width="1" height="1"
bgcolor=#8a6d43></td>
  </tr>
  <tr>
    <td width="1" height="1"
bgcolor=#a88d4b></td>
    <td width="1" height="1"
bgcolor=#a68947></td>
    <td width="1" height="1"
bgcolor=#a18141></td>
    <td width="1" height="1"
bgcolor=#a4833d></td>
    <td width="1" height="1"
bgcolor=#a4823d></td>
    <td width="1" height="1"
bgcolor=#a6823f></td>
    <td width="1" height="1"
bgcolor=#a37c3d></td>
    <td width="1" height="1"
bgcolor=#a0783a></td>
    <td width="1" height="1"
bgcolor=#a47d3b></td>
    <td width="1" height="1"
bgcolor=#a47c3b></td>
    <td width="1" height="1"
bgcolor=#a1793a></td>
    <td width="1" height="1"
bgcolor=#9e7c3c></td>
    <td width="1" height="1"
bgcolor=#a2813a></td>
    <td width="1" height="1"
bgcolor=#a4823b></td>
    <td width="1" height="1"
bgcolor=#9f823c></td>
    <td width="1" height="1"
bgcolor=#a68440></td>
    <td width="1" height="1"
bgcolor=#a37e3f></td>
    <td width="1" height="1"
bgcolor=#a5813f></td>
    <td width="1" height="1"
bgcolor=#a1793a></td>
    <td width="1" height="1"
bgcolor=#a67e3f></td>
    <td width="1" height="1"
bgcolor=#ab8041></td>
    <td width="1" height="1"
bgcolor=#a97d3f></td>
    <td width="1" height="1"
bgcolor=#ad7f43></td>
    <td width="1" height="1"
bgcolor=#a66f38></td>
    <td width="1" height="1"
bgcolor=#a97038></td>
    <td width="1" height="1"
bgcolor=#a77738></td>
    <td width="1" height="1"
bgcolor=#a66c39></td>
    <td width="1" height="1"
bgcolor=#96552b></td>
    <td width="1" height="1"
bgcolor=#955529></td>
    <td width="1" height="1"
bgcolor=#9c5d33></td>
    <td width="1" height="1"
bgcolor=#944f29></td>
    <td width="1" height="1"
bgcolor=#915a32></td>
    <td width="1" height="1"
bgcolor=#985f35></td>
    <td width="1" height="1"
bgcolor=#915731></td>
    <td width="1" height="1"
bgcolor=#915a32></td>
    <td width="1" height="1"
bgcolor=#8f572d></td>
    <td width="1" height="1"
bgcolor=#976037></td>
    <td width="1" height="1"
bgcolor=#9b6234></td>
    <td width="1" height="1"
bgcolor=#a16a35></td>
    <td width="1" height="1"
bgcolor=#a16930></td>
```

```
    <td width="1" height="1" bgcolor=#9f672e></td>
    <td width="1" height="1" bgcolor=#9d672f></td>
    <td width="1" height="1" bgcolor=#9d662f></td>
    <td width="1" height="1" bgcolor=#a06930></td>
    <td width="1" height="1" bgcolor=#ab743a></td>
    <td width="1" height="1" bgcolor=#a96a37></td>
    <td width="1" height="1" bgcolor=#a66932></td>
    <td width="1" height="1" bgcolor=#a2662f></td>
    <td width="1" height="1" bgcolor=#a16330></td>
    <td width="1" height="1" bgcolor=#9f5a30></td>
    <td width="1" height="1" bgcolor=#9c582f></td>
    <td width="1" height="1" bgcolor=#9b522e></td>
    <td width="1" height="1" bgcolor=#9b4f2d></td>
    <td width="1" height="1" bgcolor=#984f2c></td>
    <td width="1" height="1" bgcolor=#964d2c></td>
    <td width="1" height="1" bgcolor=#994e2d></td>
    <td width="1" height="1" bgcolor=#9b5030></td>
    <td width="1" height="1" bgcolor=#985730></td>
    <td width="1" height="1" bgcolor=#a16a34></td>
    <td width="1" height="1" bgcolor=#9c7932></td>
    <td width="1" height="1" bgcolor=#a28438></td>
    <td width="1" height="1" bgcolor=#9c7830></td>
    <td width="1" height="1" bgcolor=#966b2c></td>
    <td width="1" height="1" bgcolor=#987033></td>
    <td width="1" height="1" bgcolor=#956a2c></td>
    <td width="1" height="1" bgcolor=#976e2e></td>
    <td width="1" height="1" bgcolor=#a57d3d></td>
    <td width="1" height="1" bgcolor=#a07338></td>
    <td width="1" height="1" bgcolor=#a07138></td>
    <td width="1" height="1" bgcolor=#9d6b3a></td>
    <td width="1" height="1" bgcolor=#915f31></td>
    <td width="1" height="1" bgcolor=#7f5d3d></td>
  </tr>
  <tr>
    <td width="1" height="1" bgcolor=#a9874d></td>
    <td width="1" height="1" bgcolor=#a68141></td>
    <td width="1" height="1" bgcolor=#a7803c></td>
    <td width="1" height="1" bgcolor=#a67e3d></td>
    <td width="1" height="1" bgcolor=#a47d3a></td>
    <td width="1" height="1" bgcolor=#a67e3c></td>
    <td width="1" height="1" bgcolor=#a67e3e></td>
    <td width="1" height="1" bgcolor=#a57f3e></td>
    <td width="1" height="1" bgcolor=#a47e3d></td>
    <td width="1" height="1" bgcolor=#a7823f></td>
    <td width="1" height="1" bgcolor=#a27b3f></td>
    <td width="1" height="1" bgcolor=#9b7a3c></td>
    <td width="1" height="1" bgcolor=#a5833d></td>
    <td width="1" height="1" bgcolor=#a7813c></td>
    <td width="1" height="1" bgcolor=#a47f39></td>
    <td width="1" height="1" bgcolor=#a47a3d></td>
    <td width="1" height="1" bgcolor=#a4763c></td>
    <td width="1" height="1" bgcolor=#a37238></td>
    <td width="1" height="1" bgcolor=#aa793c></td>
    <td width="1" height="1" bgcolor=#a57336></td>
    <td width="1" height="1" bgcolor=#a47337></td>
    <td width="1" height="1" bgcolor=#a37535></td>
    <td width="1" height="1" bgcolor=#a47635></td>
    <td width="1" height="1" bgcolor=#a67236></td>
    <td width="1" height="1" bgcolor=#a77137></td>
    <td width="1" height="1" bgcolor=#a87237></td>
    <td width="1" height="1" bgcolor=#aa7035></td>
    <td width="1" height="1" bgcolor=#a76c38></td>
    <td width="1" height="1" bgcolor=#a36633></td>
    <td width="1" height="1" bgcolor=#9c6132></td>
    <td width="1" height="1" bgcolor=#995a30></td>
    <td width="1" height="1" bgcolor=#9a5b33></td>
    <td width="1" height="1" bgcolor=#9c5b32></td>
    <td width="1" height="1" bgcolor=#a05d39></td>
    <td width="1" height="1" bgcolor=#9a5631></td>
    <td width="1" height="1" bgcolor=#9e5833></td>
    <td width="1" height="1" bgcolor=#995932></td>
    <td width="1" height="1" bgcolor=#a06033></td>
    <td width="1" height="1" bgcolor=#9b5b30></td>
    <td width="1" height="1" bgcolor=#9c5d30></td>
    <td width="1" height="1" bgcolor=#a16435></td>
    <td width="1" height="1" bgcolor=#9e6331></td>
    <td width="1" height="1" bgcolor=#9d6430></td>
    <td width="1" height="1" bgcolor=#9d6334></td>
    <td width="1" height="1" bgcolor=#985e32></td>
    <td width="1" height="1" bgcolor=#985d35></td>
    <td width="1" height="1" bgcolor=#995c33></td>
    <td width="1" height="1" bgcolor=#9e6137></td>
    <td width="1" height="1" bgcolor=#9c5d33></td>
    <td width="1" height="1" bgcolor=#9e5e34></td>
    <td width="1" height="1" bgcolor=#a16436></td>
    <td width="1" height="1" bgcolor=#a06336></td>
    <td width="1" height="1" bgcolor=#9e5e30></td>
    <td width="1" height="1" bgcolor=#9e6131></td>
```

```
    <td width="1" height="1" bgcolor=#9d5d31></td>
    <td width="1" height="1" bgcolor=#9c5a33></td>
    <td width="1" height="1" bgcolor=#9a5630></td>
    <td width="1" height="1" bgcolor=#9a5c34></td>
    <td width="1" height="1" bgcolor=#945a2c></td>
    <td width="1" height="1" bgcolor=#965d2c></td>
    <td width="1" height="1" bgcolor=#9a5d2d></td>
    <td width="1" height="1" bgcolor=#97562f></td>
    <td width="1" height="1" bgcolor=#935529></td>
    <td width="1" height="1" bgcolor=#8f5129></td>
    <td width="1" height="1" bgcolor=#96552c></td>
    <td width="1" height="1" bgcolor=#9b5d31></td>
    <td width="1" height="1" bgcolor=#965e2f></td>
    <td width="1" height="1" bgcolor=#945f30></td>
    <td width="1" height="1" bgcolor=#915930></td>
    <td width="1" height="1" bgcolor=#8e512e></td>
    <td width="1" height="1" bgcolor=#8f5332></td>
    <td width="1" height="1" bgcolor=#83563f></td>
  </tr>
  <tr>
    <td width="1" height="1" bgcolor=#a48045></td>
    <td width="1" height="1" bgcolor=#a58142></td>
    <td width="1" height="1" bgcolor=#a17f3a></td>
    <td width="1" height="1" bgcolor=#a68243></td>
    <td width="1" height="1" bgcolor=#a27f3e></td>
    <td width="1" height="1" bgcolor=#a4813c></td>
    <td width="1" height="1" bgcolor=#a27f3b></td>
    <td width="1" height="1" bgcolor=#a4833f></td>
    <td width="1" height="1" bgcolor=#a07d3b></td>
    <td width="1" height="1" bgcolor=#a27c3c></td>
    <td width="1" height="1" bgcolor=#9c763f></td>
    <td width="1" height="1" bgcolor=#966f37></td>
    <td width="1" height="1" bgcolor=#a17939></td>
    <td width="1" height="1" bgcolor=#a77d3b></td>
    <td width="1" height="1" bgcolor=#a47a36></td>
    <td width="1" height="1" bgcolor=#a5773b></td>
    <td width="1" height="1" bgcolor=#a47435></td>
    <td width="1" height="1" bgcolor=#a67437></td>
    <td width="1" height="1" bgcolor=#aa7738></td>
    <td width="1" height="1" bgcolor=#a57132></td>
    <td width="1" height="1" bgcolor=#a57138></td>
    <td width="1" height="1" bgcolor=#a67436></td>
    <td width="1" height="1" bgcolor=#a67437></td>
    <td width="1" height="1" bgcolor=#aa7539></td>
    <td width="1" height="1" bgcolor=#a97239></td>
    <td width="1" height="1" bgcolor=#a77238></td>
    <td width="1" height="1" bgcolor=#a97637></td>
    <td width="1" height="1" bgcolor=#a57137></td>
    <td width="1" height="1" bgcolor=#a36e33></td>
    <td width="1" height="1" bgcolor=#a87339></td>
    <td width="1" height="1" bgcolor=#a47037></td>
    <td width="1" height="1" bgcolor=#a36736></td>
    <td width="1" height="1" bgcolor=#a46635></td>
    <td width="1" height="1" bgcolor=#a36336></td>
    <td width="1" height="1" bgcolor=#a16234></td>
    <td width="1" height="1" bgcolor=#9f6130></td>
    <td width="1" height="1" bgcolor=#9e5f34></td>
    <td width="1" height="1" bgcolor=#995a31></td>
    <td width="1" height="1" bgcolor=#9c5d34></td>
    <td width="1" height="1" bgcolor=#9f6135></td>
    <td width="1" height="1" bgcolor=#9f6338></td>
    <td width="1" height="1" bgcolor=#9b6034></td>
    <td width="1" height="1" bgcolor=#995d31></td>
    <td width="1" height="1" bgcolor=#9d6034></td>
    <td width="1" height="1" bgcolor=#9a5e31></td>
    <td width="1" height="1" bgcolor=#9c5f33></td>
    <td width="1" height="1" bgcolor=#9a5b30></td>
    <td width="1" height="1" bgcolor=#99592e></td>
    <td width="1" height="1" bgcolor=#995831></td>
    <td width="1" height="1" bgcolor=#98562e></td>
    <td width="1" height="1" bgcolor=#975630></td>
    <td width="1" height="1" bgcolor=#9a5a32></td>
    <td width="1" height="1" bgcolor=#a05f35></td>
    <td width="1" height="1" bgcolor=#9e5a33></td>
    <td width="1" height="1" bgcolor=#96502c></td>
    <td width="1" height="1" bgcolor=#90552f></td>
    <td width="1" height="1" bgcolor=#945a32></td>
    <td width="1" height="1" bgcolor=#966134></td>
    <td width="1" height="1" bgcolor=#945b2c></td>
    <td width="1" height="1" bgcolor=#95582c></td>
    <td width="1" height="1" bgcolor=#98542c></td>
    <td width="1" height="1" bgcolor=#975c32></td>
    <td width="1" height="1" bgcolor=#93512d></td>
    <td width="1" height="1" bgcolor=#95512f></td>
    <td width="1" height="1" bgcolor=#94502e></td>
    <td width="1" height="1" bgcolor=#975832></td>
    <td width="1" height="1" bgcolor=#935835></td>
    <td width="1" height="1" bgcolor=#965c33></td>
```

```
    <td width="1" height="1"
bgcolor=#975a34></td>
    <td width="1" height="1"
bgcolor=#965436></td>
    <td width="1" height="1"
bgcolor=#945537></td>
    <td width="1" height="1"
bgcolor=#8a5741></td>
  </tr>
  <tr>
    <td width="1" height="1"
bgcolor=#a58549></td>
    <td width="1" height="1"
bgcolor=#a58444></td>
    <td width="1" height="1"
bgcolor=#a98944></td>
    <td width="1" height="1"
bgcolor=#a48142></td>
    <td width="1" height="1"
bgcolor=#a58242></td>
    <td width="1" height="1"
bgcolor=#a07e3c></td>
    <td width="1" height="1"
bgcolor=#a17f3e></td>
    <td width="1" height="1"
bgcolor=#9e7a3a></td>
    <td width="1" height="1"
bgcolor=#9f793a></td>
    <td width="1" height="1"
bgcolor=#a07a3b></td>
    <td width="1" height="1"
bgcolor=#98703b></td>
    <td width="1" height="1"
bgcolor=#936b38></td>
    <td width="1" height="1"
bgcolor=#a1793a></td>
    <td width="1" height="1"
bgcolor=#a47b37></td>
    <td width="1" height="1"
bgcolor=#a27835></td>
    <td width="1" height="1"
bgcolor=#a57b36></td>
    <td width="1" height="1"
bgcolor=#a3783a></td>
    <td width="1" height="1"
bgcolor=#a47738></td>
    <td width="1" height="1"
bgcolor=#a17434></td>
    <td width="1" height="1"
bgcolor=#a47636></td>
    <td width="1" height="1"
bgcolor=#a27237></td>
    <td width="1" height="1"
bgcolor=#a7763b></td>
    <td width="1" height="1"
bgcolor=#a47238></td>
    <td width="1" height="1"
bgcolor=#a27136></td>
    <td width="1" height="1"
bgcolor=#a06d35></td>
    <td width="1" height="1"
bgcolor=#8d592b></td>
    <td width="1" height="1"
bgcolor=#a16f3a></td>
    <td width="1" height="1"
bgcolor=#9e6c34></td>
    <td width="1" height="1"
bgcolor=#9c6e35></td>
    <td width="1" height="1"
bgcolor=#a37039></td>
    <td width="1" height="1"
bgcolor=#a46f35></td>
    <td width="1" height="1"
bgcolor=#a46838></td>
    <td width="1" height="1"
bgcolor=#a46638></td>
    <td width="1" height="1"
bgcolor=#a6683b></td>
    <td width="1" height="1"
bgcolor=#a06137></td>
    <td width="1" height="1"
bgcolor=#9d5e35></td>
    <td width="1" height="1"
bgcolor=#a06335></td>
    <td width="1" height="1"
bgcolor=#a16334></td>
    <td width="1" height="1"
bgcolor=#a16234></td>
    <td width="1" height="1"
bgcolor=#9e5e35></td>
    <td width="1" height="1"
bgcolor=#97592f></td>
    <td width="1" height="1"
bgcolor=#94582e></td>
    <td width="1" height="1"
bgcolor=#985b31></td>
    <td width="1" height="1"
bgcolor=#9e6237></td>
    <td width="1" height="1"
bgcolor=#a0643a></td>
    <td width="1" height="1"
bgcolor=#9f6135></td>
    <td width="1" height="1"
bgcolor=#9d6235></td>
    <td width="1" height="1"
bgcolor=#9c6133></td>
    <td width="1" height="1"
bgcolor=#9a5d33></td>
    <td width="1" height="1"
bgcolor=#9e603b></td>
    <td width="1" height="1"
bgcolor=#9a5f38></td>
    <td width="1" height="1"
bgcolor=#9b6339></td>
    <td width="1" height="1"
bgcolor=#915a32></td>
    <td width="1" height="1"
bgcolor=#8f5d35></td>
    <td width="1" height="1"
bgcolor=#985c38></td>
    <td width="1" height="1"
bgcolor=#9b5733></td>
    <td width="1" height="1"
bgcolor=#985434></td>
    <td width="1" height="1"
bgcolor=#965532></td>
    <td width="1" height="1"
bgcolor=#9c532e></td>
    <td width="1" height="1"
bgcolor=#98542d></td>
    <td width="1" height="1"
bgcolor=#93512d></td>
    <td width="1" height="1"
bgcolor=#935530></td>
    <td width="1" height="1"
bgcolor=#965630></td>
    <td width="1" height="1"
bgcolor=#955732></td>
    <td width="1" height="1"
bgcolor=#935432></td>
    <td width="1" height="1"
bgcolor=#905336></td>
    <td width="1" height="1"
bgcolor=#905439></td>
    <td width="1" height="1"
bgcolor=#925535></td>
    <td width="1" height="1"
bgcolor=#925334></td>
    <td width="1" height="1"
bgcolor=#945638></td>
    <td width="1" height="1"
bgcolor=#96583b></td>
    <td width="1" height="1"
bgcolor=#875c45></td>
  </tr>
  <tr>
    <td width="1" height="1"
bgcolor=#a5864a></td>
    <td width="1" height="1"
bgcolor=#a58646></td>
    <td width="1" height="1"
bgcolor=#a38641></td>
    <td width="1" height="1"
bgcolor=#a18442></td>
    <td width="1" height="1"
bgcolor=#a98c49></td>
    <td width="1" height="1"
bgcolor=#a48445></td>
    <td width="1" height="1"
bgcolor=#9f7e39></td>
    <td width="1" height="1"
bgcolor=#9d7b37></td>
    <td width="1" height="1"
bgcolor=#a07b3d></td>
```

```
    <td width="1" height="1"
bgcolor=#9e7839></td>
    <td width="1" height="1"
bgcolor=#9c743c></td>
    <td width="1" height="1"
bgcolor=#98713d></td>
    <td width="1" height="1"
bgcolor=#a27f41></td>
    <td width="1" height="1"
bgcolor=#a4863f></td>
    <td width="1" height="1"
bgcolor=#a2803c></td>
    <td width="1" height="1"
bgcolor=#a2803a></td>
    <td width="1" height="1"
bgcolor=#a27e3c></td>
    <td width="1" height="1"
bgcolor=#9f7936></td>
    <td width="1" height="1"
bgcolor=#a27c3a></td>
    <td width="1" height="1"
bgcolor=#9f7938></td>
    <td width="1" height="1"
bgcolor=#a07438></td>
    <td width="1" height="1"
bgcolor=#9f7136></td>
    <td width="1" height="1"
bgcolor=#a07138></td>
    <td width="1" height="1"
bgcolor=#a3733a></td>
    <td width="1" height="1"
bgcolor=#976634></td>
    <td width="1" height="1"
bgcolor=#855432></td>
    <td width="1" height="1"
bgcolor=#8e5b30></td>
    <td width="1" height="1"
bgcolor=#915a2c></td>
    <td width="1" height="1"
bgcolor=#955930></td>
    <td width="1" height="1"
bgcolor=#9a5a33></td>
    <td width="1" height="1"
bgcolor=#96522c></td>
    <td width="1" height="1"
bgcolor=#97522e></td>
    <td width="1" height="1"
bgcolor=#97502e></td>
    <td width="1" height="1"
bgcolor=#96502f></td>
    <td width="1" height="1"
bgcolor=#965433></td>
    <td width="1" height="1"
bgcolor=#914e30></td>
    <td width="1" height="1"
bgcolor=#945336></td>
    <td width="1" height="1"
bgcolor=#935638></td>
    <td width="1" height="1"
bgcolor=#8f5233></td>
    <td width="1" height="1"
bgcolor=#945131></td>
    <td width="1" height="1"
bgcolor=#965434></td>
    <td width="1" height="1"
bgcolor=#965937></td>
    <td width="1" height="1"
bgcolor=#966036></td>
    <td width="1" height="1"
bgcolor=#9c633b></td>
    <td width="1" height="1"
bgcolor=#9b623a></td>
    <td width="1" height="1"
bgcolor=#985d33></td>
    <td width="1" height="1"
bgcolor=#975e32></td>
    <td rowspan="1"
colspan="2" width="1"
height="1"
bgcolor=#9b6336></td>
    <td width="1" height="1"
bgcolor=#9a5d37></td>
    <td width="1" height="1"
bgcolor=#995b36></td>
    <td width="1" height="1"
bgcolor=#995d35></td>
    <td width="1" height="1"
bgcolor=#945932></td>
    <td width="1" height="1"
bgcolor=#915c33></td>
    <td width="1" height="1"
bgcolor=#975a34></td>
    <td width="1" height="1"
bgcolor=#9a5b34></td>
    <td width="1" height="1"
bgcolor=#96572e></td>
    <td width="1" height="1"
bgcolor=#965833></td>
    <td width="1" height="1"
bgcolor=#985931></td>
    <td width="1" height="1"
bgcolor=#985930></td>
    <td width="1" height="1"
bgcolor=#975a30></td>
    <td width="1" height="1"
bgcolor=#985b33></td>
    <td width="1" height="1"
bgcolor=#995c31></td>
    <td width="1" height="1"
bgcolor=#955a32></td>
    <td width="1" height="1"
bgcolor=#935631></td>
    <td width="1" height="1"
bgcolor=#905634></td>
    <td width="1" height="1"
bgcolor=#8d5433></td>
    <td width="1" height="1"
bgcolor=#895033></td>
    <td width="1" height="1"
bgcolor=#8a5136></td>
    <td width="1" height="1"
bgcolor=#8b5036></td>
    <td width="1" height="1"
bgcolor=#92563b></td>
    <td width="1" height="1"
bgcolor=#88604b></td>
  </tr>
  <tr>
    <td width="1" height="1"
bgcolor=#a9864f></td>
    <td width="1" height="1"
bgcolor=#a68447></td>
    <td width="1" height="1"
bgcolor=#a88544></td>
    <td width="1" height="1"
bgcolor=#9f7c3c></td>
    <td width="1" height="1"
bgcolor=#9d7a3c></td>
    <td width="1" height="1"
bgcolor=#96703b></td>
    <td width="1" height="1"
bgcolor=#9f7640></td>
    <td width="1" height="1"
bgcolor=#9c743f></td>
    <td width="1" height="1"
bgcolor=#9a723e></td>
    <td width="1" height="1"
bgcolor=#99723b></td>
    <td width="1" height="1"
bgcolor=#996e3d></td>
    <td width="1" height="1"
bgcolor=#946e40></td>
    <td width="1" height="1"
bgcolor=#98723f></td>
    <td width="1" height="1"
bgcolor=#a17a42></td>
    <td width="1" height="1"
bgcolor=#a47c3f></td>
    <td width="1" height="1"
bgcolor=#a3793d></td>
    <td width="1" height="1"
bgcolor=#a17639></td>
    <td width="1" height="1"
bgcolor=#a07239></td>
    <td width="1" height="1"
bgcolor=#9b6d35></td>
    <td width="1" height="1"
bgcolor=#986833></td>
    <td width="1" height="1"
bgcolor=#9c6936></td>
    <td width="1" height="1"
bgcolor=#9d6837></td>
    <td width="1" height="1"
bgcolor=#9b6638></td>
```

```
<td width="1" height="1" bgcolor=#9b6236></td>
<td width="1" height="1" bgcolor=#935b36></td>
<td width="1" height="1" bgcolor=#865132></td>
<td width="1" height="1" bgcolor=#8a522c></td>
<td width="1" height="1" bgcolor=#9d6137></td>
<td width="1" height="1" bgcolor=#93562f></td>
<td width="1" height="1" bgcolor=#9b5c36></td>
<td width="1" height="1" bgcolor=#9a5835></td>
<td width="1" height="1" bgcolor=#984e2f></td>
<td width="1" height="1" bgcolor=#974c2f></td>
<td width="1" height="1" bgcolor=#93472b></td>
<td width="1" height="1" bgcolor=#9a4a2f></td>
<td width="1" height="1" bgcolor=#9a4a31></td>
<td width="1" height="1" bgcolor=#994b31></td>
<td width="1" height="1" bgcolor=#9a5136></td>
<td width="1" height="1" bgcolor=#995739></td>
<td width="1" height="1" bgcolor=#995938></td>
<td width="1" height="1" bgcolor=#995a38></td>
<td width="1" height="1" bgcolor=#945935></td>
<td width="1" height="1" bgcolor=#925531></td>
<td width="1" height="1" bgcolor=#975936></td>
<td width="1" height="1" bgcolor=#955532></td>
<td width="1" height="1" bgcolor=#945632></td>
<td width="1" height="1" bgcolor=#975934></td>
<td width="1" height="1" bgcolor=#975933></td>
<td width="1" height="1" bgcolor=#995e35></td>
<td width="1" height="1" bgcolor=#985a33></td>
<td width="1" height="1" bgcolor=#985c37></td>
<td width="1" height="1" bgcolor=#976039></td>
<td width="1" height="1" bgcolor=#9a643c></td>
<td width="1" height="1" bgcolor=#9b633d></td>
<td width="1" height="1" bgcolor=#9c603c></td>
<td width="1" height="1" bgcolor=#9a5d3a></td>
<td width="1" height="1" bgcolor=#9d613b></td>
<td width="1" height="1" bgcolor=#975c37></td>
<td width="1" height="1" bgcolor=#995e36></td>
<td width="1" height="1" bgcolor=#9f6538></td>
<td width="1" height="1" bgcolor=#9c6437></td>
<td width="1" height="1" bgcolor=#965f31></td>
<td width="1" height="1" bgcolor=#986335></td>
<td width="1" height="1" bgcolor=#946135></td>
<td width="1" height="1" bgcolor=#99613a></td>
<td width="1" height="1" bgcolor=#945f37></td>
<td width="1" height="1" bgcolor=#935e3a></td>
<td rowspan="1" colspan="2" width="1" height="1" bgcolor=#925d3b></td>
<td width="1" height="1" bgcolor=#935f3d></td>
<td width="1" height="1" bgcolor=#94603f></td>
<td width="1" height="1" bgcolor=#845b45></td>
</tr>
<tr>
<td width="1" height="1" bgcolor=#a7804d></td>
<td width="1" height="1" bgcolor=#a68047></td>
<td width="1" height="1" bgcolor=#a57f42></td>
<td width="1" height="1" bgcolor=#a47b42></td>
<td width="1" height="1" bgcolor=#9b7641></td>
<td width="1" height="1" bgcolor=#997649></td>
<td width="1" height="1" bgcolor=#9b794f></td>
<td width="1" height="1" bgcolor=#9c7a51></td>
<td width="1" height="1" bgcolor=#9a764c></td>
<td width="1" height="1" bgcolor=#9a7649></td>
<td width="1" height="1" bgcolor=#9e794e></td>
<td width="1" height="1" bgcolor=#9a7244></td>
<td width="1" height="1" bgcolor=#a17b4a></td>
<td width="1" height="1" bgcolor=#a27f49></td>
<td width="1" height="1" bgcolor=#a48248></td>
<td width="1" height="1" bgcolor=#a68149></td>
<td width="1" height="1" bgcolor=#a77f48></td>
<td width="1" height="1" bgcolor=#a47e44></td>
<td width="1" height="1" bgcolor=#a17842></td>
<td width="1" height="1" bgcolor=#a0703e></td>
<td width="1" height="1" bgcolor=#a06b3c></td>
<td width="1" height="1" bgcolor=#9d683b></td>
<td width="1" height="1" bgcolor=#9d6639></td>
<td width="1" height="1" bgcolor=#a26739></td>
<td width="1" height="1" bgcolor=#975e36></td>
<td width="1" height="1" bgcolor=#8a552e></td>
<td width="1" height="1" bgcolor=#935b39></td>
<td width="1" height="1" bgcolor=#986137></td>
<td width="1" height="1" bgcolor=#9f683e></td>
<td width="1" height="1" bgcolor=#9d633b></td>
<td width="1" height="1" bgcolor=#9b5d39></td>
<td width="1" height="1" bgcolor=#985834></td>
<td width="1" height="1" bgcolor=#945432></td>
<td width="1" height="1" bgcolor=#945333></td>
<td width="1" height="1" bgcolor=#955437></td>
<td width="1" height="1" bgcolor=#965635></td>
<td width="1" height="1" bgcolor=#995937></td>
```

```
    <td width="1" height="1" bgcolor=#995535></td>
    <td width="1" height="1" bgcolor=#9d5937></td>
    <td width="1" height="1" bgcolor=#a05e3b></td>
    <td width="1" height="1" bgcolor=#9e5d39></td>
    <td width="1" height="1" bgcolor=#9e5b38></td>
    <td width="1" height="1" bgcolor=#9c5f38></td>
    <td width="1" height="1" bgcolor=#9c5e38></td>
    <td width="1" height="1" bgcolor=#985932></td>
    <td width="1" height="1" bgcolor=#995737></td>
    <td width="1" height="1" bgcolor=#965532></td>
    <td width="1" height="1" bgcolor=#985733></td>
    <td width="1" height="1" bgcolor=#9a5f38></td>
    <td width="1" height="1" bgcolor=#9a6037></td>
    <td width="1" height="1" bgcolor=#996236></td>
    <td width="1" height="1" bgcolor=#9a6637></td>
    <td width="1" height="1" bgcolor=#9f6b3c></td>
    <td width="1" height="1" bgcolor=#9c693d></td>
    <td width="1" height="1" bgcolor=#9a6d40></td>
    <td width="1" height="1" bgcolor=#9e6b40></td>
    <td width="1" height="1" bgcolor=#9f6940></td>
    <td width="1" height="1" bgcolor=#9a6635></td>
    <td width="1" height="1" bgcolor=#9b6736></td>
    <td width="1" height="1" bgcolor=#9b693a></td>
    <td width="1" height="1" bgcolor=#976736></td>
    <td width="1" height="1" bgcolor=#976737></td>
    <td width="1" height="1" bgcolor=#956b39></td>
    <td width="1" height="1" bgcolor=#91683a></td>
    <td width="1" height="1" bgcolor=#8f6236></td>
    <td width="1" height="1" bgcolor=#92643a></td>
    <td width="1" height="1" bgcolor=#93623a></td>
    <td width="1" height="1" bgcolor=#93613d></td>
    <td width="1" height="1" bgcolor=#92633f></td>
    <td width="1" height="1" bgcolor=#966c45></td>
    <td width="1" height="1" bgcolor=#9b7147></td>
    <td width="1" height="1" bgcolor=#8b6348></td>
  </tr>
  <tr>
    <td width="1" height="1" bgcolor=#a3794e></td>
    <td width="1" height="1" bgcolor=#9f7c49></td>
    <td width="1" height="1" bgcolor=#9d7e46></td>
    <td width="1" height="1" bgcolor=#9d774c></td>
    <td width="1" height="1" bgcolor=#987548></td>
    <td width="1" height="1" bgcolor=#987851></td>
    <td width="1" height="1" bgcolor=#99784f></td>
    <td width="1" height="1" bgcolor=#96744f></td>
    <td width="1" height="1" bgcolor=#977552></td>
    <td width="1" height="1" bgcolor=#9a7752></td>
    <td width="1" height="1" bgcolor=#94734d></td>
    <td width="1" height="1" bgcolor=#96754e></td>
    <td width="1" height="1" bgcolor=#9d7d53></td>
    <td width="1" height="1" bgcolor=#9f8154></td>
    <td width="1" height="1" bgcolor=#a4814f></td>
    <td width="1" height="1" bgcolor=#a27e50></td>
    <td width="1" height="1" bgcolor=#a17e4c></td>
    <td width="1" height="1" bgcolor=#a37d4a></td>
    <td width="1" height="1" bgcolor=#a37b49></td>
    <td width="1" height="1" bgcolor=#a07544></td>
    <td width="1" height="1" bgcolor=#9f6d41></td>
    <td width="1" height="1" bgcolor=#9e673f></td>
    <td width="1" height="1" bgcolor=#99643d></td>
    <td width="1" height="1" bgcolor=#9b643d></td>
    <td width="1" height="1" bgcolor=#98623f></td>
    <td width="1" height="1" bgcolor=#8e5a3d></td>
    <td width="1" height="1" bgcolor=#956142></td>
    <td width="1" height="1" bgcolor=#956040></td>
    <td width="1" height="1" bgcolor=#a9764e></td>
    <td width="1" height="1" bgcolor=#a36e49></td>
    <td width="1" height="1" bgcolor=#99653c></td>
    <td width="1" height="1" bgcolor=#9a623d></td>
    <td width="1" height="1" bgcolor=#945c3a></td>
    <td width="1" height="1" bgcolor=#996040></td>
    <td width="1" height="1" bgcolor=#986141></td>
    <td width="1" height="1" bgcolor=#976042></td>
    <td width="1" height="1" bgcolor=#966041></td>
    <td width="1" height="1" bgcolor=#9a623e></td>
    <td width="1" height="1" bgcolor=#9b623b></td>
    <td width="1" height="1" bgcolor=#9a6740></td>
    <td width="1" height="1" bgcolor=#99643e></td>
    <td width="1" height="1" bgcolor=#99653e></td>
    <td width="1" height="1" bgcolor=#9e613c></td>
    <td width="1" height="1" bgcolor=#9b5f39></td>
    <td width="1" height="1" bgcolor=#955e35></td>
    <td width="1" height="1" bgcolor=#985b30></td>
    <td width="1" height="1" bgcolor=#95582d></td>
    <td width="1" height="1" bgcolor=#96592e></td>
    <td width="1" height="1" bgcolor=#955c32></td>
    <td width="1" height="1" bgcolor=#945b31></td>
    <td width="1" height="1" bgcolor=#975c34></td>
```

```
    <td width="1" height="1"
bgcolor=#965a33></td>
    <td width="1" height="1"
bgcolor=#986237></td>
    <td width="1" height="1"
bgcolor=#946335></td>
    <td width="1" height="1"
bgcolor=#9a6c3d></td>
    <td width="1" height="1"
bgcolor=#9b6e3f></td>
    <td width="1" height="1"
bgcolor=#936938></td>
    <td width="1" height="1"
bgcolor=#ca9f48></td>
    <td width="1" height="1"
bgcolor=#bf943b></td>
    <td width="1" height="1"
bgcolor=#9c6e38></td>
    <td width="1" height="1"
bgcolor=#99733f></td>
    <td width="1" height="1"
bgcolor=#926d37></td>
    <td width="1" height="1"
bgcolor=#8f6a40></td>
    <td width="1" height="1"
bgcolor=#86643b></td>
    <td width="1" height="1"
bgcolor=#8e6b3e></td>
    <td width="1" height="1"
bgcolor=#8d6637></td>
    <td width="1" height="1"
bgcolor=#8e6440></td>
    <td width="1" height="1"
bgcolor=#946c41></td>
    <td width="1" height="1"
bgcolor=#9f744b></td>
    <td width="1" height="1"
bgcolor=#a37650></td>
    <td width="1" height="1"
bgcolor=#a87a57></td>
    <td width="1" height="1"
bgcolor=#8e6c51></td>
  </tr>
  <tr>
    <td width="1" height="1"
bgcolor=#9d764f></td>
    <td width="1" height="1"
bgcolor=#9a6d43></td>
    <td width="1" height="1"
bgcolor=#a06e42></td>
    <td width="1" height="1"
bgcolor=#9c6e47></td>
    <td width="1" height="1"
bgcolor=#996d43></td>
    <td width="1" height="1"
bgcolor=#97714f></td>
    <td width="1" height="1"
bgcolor=#967351></td>
    <td width="1" height="1"
bgcolor=#987553></td>
    <td width="1" height="1"
bgcolor=#957553></td>
    <td width="1" height="1"
bgcolor=#947351></td>
    <td width="1" height="1"
bgcolor=#97714f></td>
    <td width="1" height="1"
bgcolor=#9a7852></td>
    <td width="1" height="1"
bgcolor=#9e7c57></td>
    <td width="1" height="1"
bgcolor=#a07e58></td>
    <td width="1" height="1"
bgcolor=#9d7c55></td>
    <td width="1" height="1"
bgcolor=#9c7b57></td>
    <td width="1" height="1"
bgcolor=#9f7e57></td>
    <td width="1" height="1"
bgcolor=#a48053></td>
    <td width="1" height="1"
bgcolor=#a07a4d></td>
    <td width="1" height="1"
bgcolor=#a98457></td>
    <td width="1" height="1"
bgcolor=#a1774c></td>
    <td width="1" height="1"
bgcolor=#a07148></td>
    <td width="1" height="1"
bgcolor=#a0744b></td>
    <td width="1" height="1"
bgcolor=#a3764c></td>
    <td width="1" height="1"
bgcolor=#986c49></td>
    <td width="1" height="1"
bgcolor=#875e3f></td>
    <td width="1" height="1"
bgcolor=#8c6142></td>
    <td width="1" height="1"
bgcolor=#8a5d3e></td>
    <td width="1" height="1"
bgcolor=#9b6d48></td>
    <td width="1" height="1"
bgcolor=#946542></td>
    <td width="1" height="1"
bgcolor=#9a6940></td>
    <td width="1" height="1"
bgcolor=#97643e></td>
    <td width="1" height="1"
bgcolor=#96623e></td>
    <td width="1" height="1"
bgcolor=#95613f></td>
    <td width="1" height="1"
bgcolor=#996644></td>
    <td width="1" height="1"
bgcolor=#905d3e></td>
    <td width="1" height="1"
bgcolor=#8e5e40></td>
    <td width="1" height="1"
bgcolor=#966841></td>
    <td width="1" height="1"
bgcolor=#95643b></td>
    <td width="1" height="1"
bgcolor=#93673d></td>
    <td width="1" height="1"
bgcolor=#98663e></td>
    <td width="1" height="1"
bgcolor=#97613a></td>
    <td width="1" height="1"
bgcolor=#97623a></td>
    <td width="1" height="1"
bgcolor=#956138></td>
    <td width="1" height="1"
bgcolor=#956036></td>
    <td width="1" height="1"
bgcolor=#975e37></td>
    <td width="1" height="1"
bgcolor=#955c35></td>
    <td width="1" height="1"
bgcolor=#925932></td>
    <td width="1" height="1"
bgcolor=#915c34></td>
    <td width="1" height="1"
bgcolor=#946037></td>
    <td width="1" height="1"
bgcolor=#945f38></td>
    <td width="1" height="1"
bgcolor=#85542d></td>
    <td width="1" height="1"
bgcolor=#92633b></td>
    <td width="1" height="1"
bgcolor=#97663c></td>
    <td width="1" height="1"
bgcolor=#98683c></td>
    <td width="1" height="1"
bgcolor=#96683e></td>
    <td width="1" height="1"
bgcolor=#a67636></td>
    <td width="1" height="1"
bgcolor=#d09d40></td>
    <td width="1" height="1"
bgcolor=#d19e40></td>
    <td width="1" height="1"
bgcolor=#9a6e39></td>
    <td width="1" height="1"
bgcolor=#956f3d></td>
    <td width="1" height="1"
bgcolor=#916c38></td>
    <td width="1" height="1"
bgcolor=#836032></td>
    <td width="1" height="1"
bgcolor=#86693e></td>
    <td width="1" height="1"
bgcolor=#85663a></td>
```

```
    <td width="1" height="1"
bgcolor=#85643a></td>
    <td width="1" height="1"
bgcolor=#81603f></td>
    <td width="1" height="1"
bgcolor=#967549></td>
    <td width="1" height="1"
bgcolor=#9a774d></td>
    <td width="1" height="1"
bgcolor=#9b764e></td>
    <td width="1" height="1"
bgcolor=#9b7550></td>
    <td width="1" height="1"
bgcolor=#886b50></td>
  </tr>
  <tr>
    <td width="1" height="1"
bgcolor=#9c7455></td>
    <td width="1" height="1"
bgcolor=#986a48></td>
    <td width="1" height="1"
bgcolor=#9a6641></td>
    <td width="1" height="1"
bgcolor=#9c6d48></td>
    <td width="1" height="1"
bgcolor=#9c6d47></td>
    <td width="1" height="1"
bgcolor=#997050></td>
    <td width="1" height="1"
bgcolor=#966b4a></td>
    <td width="1" height="1"
bgcolor=#946a46></td>
    <td width="1" height="1"
bgcolor=#946745></td>
    <td width="1" height="1"
bgcolor=#916542></td>
    <td width="1" height="1"
bgcolor=#8f6842></td>
    <td width="1" height="1"
bgcolor=#8b693e></td>
    <td width="1" height="1"
bgcolor=#97764c></td>
    <td width="1" height="1"
bgcolor=#95724c></td>
    <td width="1" height="1"
bgcolor=#987655></td>
    <td width="1" height="1"
bgcolor=#926f52></td>
    <td width="1" height="1"
bgcolor=#8e6d4a></td>
    <td width="1" height="1"
bgcolor=#98704a></td>
    <td width="1" height="1"
bgcolor=#936a44></td>
    <td width="1" height="1"
bgcolor=#9c734d></td>
    <td width="1" height="1"
bgcolor=#986d48></td>
    <td width="1" height="1"
bgcolor=#9f6f48></td>
    <td width="1" height="1"
bgcolor=#986d44></td>
    <td width="1" height="1"
bgcolor=#976942></td>
    <td width="1" height="1"
bgcolor=#956a48></td>
    <td width="1" height="1"
bgcolor=#8a6147></td>
    <td width="1" height="1"
bgcolor=#8c6247></td>
    <td width="1" height="1"
bgcolor=#8d6144></td>
    <td width="1" height="1"
bgcolor=#8c6242></td>
    <td width="1" height="1"
bgcolor=#8f6342></td>
    <td width="1" height="1"
bgcolor=#9a6e44></td>
    <td width="1" height="1"
bgcolor=#986b42></td>
    <td width="1" height="1"
bgcolor=#966943></td>
    <td width="1" height="1"
bgcolor=#936641></td>
    <td width="1" height="1"
bgcolor=#956742></td>
    <td width="1" height="1"
bgcolor=#8a5d3d></td>
    <td width="1" height="1"
bgcolor=#8d5e40></td>
    <td width="1" height="1"
bgcolor=#996942></td>
    <td width="1" height="1"
bgcolor=#9a6a41></td>
    <td width="1" height="1"
bgcolor=#9a6840></td>
    <td width="1" height="1"
bgcolor=#96613a></td>
    <td width="1" height="1"
bgcolor=#96683f></td>
    <td width="1" height="1"
bgcolor=#93683c></td>
    <td width="1" height="1"
bgcolor=#96693d></td>
    <td width="1" height="1"
bgcolor=#96663a></td>
    <td width="1" height="1"
bgcolor=#9f6d3e></td>
    <td width="1" height="1"
bgcolor=#996739></td>
    <td width="1" height="1"
bgcolor=#9a693a></td>
    <td width="1" height="1"
bgcolor=#936333></td>
    <td width="1" height="1"
bgcolor=#976836></td>
    <td width="1" height="1"
bgcolor=#966638></td>
    <td width="1" height="1"
bgcolor=#926338></td>
    <td width="1" height="1"
bgcolor=#8f5f33></td>
    <td width="1" height="1"
bgcolor=#956339></td>
    <td width="1" height="1"
bgcolor=#95653a></td>
    <td width="1" height="1"
bgcolor=#92643a></td>
    <td width="1" height="1"
bgcolor=#9c703e></td>
    <td width="1" height="1"
bgcolor=#a57433></td>
    <td width="1" height="1"
bgcolor=#aa7a38></td>
    <td width="1" height="1"
bgcolor=#976935></td>
    <td width="1" height="1"
bgcolor=#946d3f></td>
    <td width="1" height="1"
bgcolor=#936d3c></td>
    <td width="1" height="1"
bgcolor=#8b6c40></td>
    <td width="1" height="1"
bgcolor=#856b45></td>
    <td width="1" height="1"
bgcolor=#856741></td>
    <td width="1" height="1"
bgcolor=#866541></td>
    <td width="1" height="1"
bgcolor=#805d45></td>
    <td width="1" height="1"
bgcolor=#957449></td>
    <td width="1" height="1"
bgcolor=#96744b></td>
    <td width="1" height="1"
bgcolor=#97714b></td>
    <td width="1" height="1"
bgcolor=#96734e></td>
    <td width="1" height="1"
bgcolor=#886f53></td>
  </tr>
  <tr>
    <td width="1" height="1"
bgcolor=#986a46></td>
    <td width="1" height="1"
bgcolor=#9b6543></td>
    <td width="1" height="1"
bgcolor=#996442></td>
    <td width="1" height="1"
bgcolor=#9f6547></td>
    <td width="1" height="1"
bgcolor=#9a6646></td>
    <td width="1" height="1"
bgcolor=#966343></td>
```

```
<td width="1" height="1" bgcolor=#9d6b48></td>
<td width="1" height="1" bgcolor=#986b42></td>
<td width="1" height="1" bgcolor=#976546></td>
<td width="1" height="1" bgcolor=#915f3f></td>
<td width="1" height="1" bgcolor=#93653f></td>
<td width="1" height="1" bgcolor=#94653f></td>
<td width="1" height="1" bgcolor=#966a43></td>
<td width="1" height="1" bgcolor=#946e45></td>
<td width="1" height="1" bgcolor=#926f4a></td>
<td width="1" height="1" bgcolor=#906a48></td>
<td width="1" height="1" bgcolor=#8d6647></td>
<td width="1" height="1" bgcolor=#8d603d></td>
<td width="1" height="1" bgcolor=#915e40></td>
<td width="1" height="1" bgcolor=#8c623f></td>
<td width="1" height="1" bgcolor=#8e6743></td>
<td width="1" height="1" bgcolor=#8e684a></td>
<td width="1" height="1" bgcolor=#8e6349></td>
<td width="1" height="1" bgcolor=#8a664a></td>
<td width="1" height="1" bgcolor=#866248></td>
<td width="1" height="1" bgcolor=#886545></td>
<td width="1" height="1" bgcolor=#876244></td>
<td width="1" height="1" bgcolor=#875e40></td>
<td width="1" height="1" bgcolor=#89654b></td>
<td width="1" height="1" bgcolor=#8b6245></td>
<td width="1" height="1" bgcolor=#88603e></td>
<td width="1" height="1" bgcolor=#865f3f></td>
<td width="1" height="1" bgcolor=#835a3a></td>
<td width="1" height="1" bgcolor=#875b3c></td>
<td width="1" height="1" bgcolor=#896040></td>
<td width="1" height="1" bgcolor=#825e3e></td>
<td width="1" height="1" bgcolor=#896648></td>
<td width="1" height="1" bgcolor=#97734e></td>
<td width="1" height="1" bgcolor=#936f48></td>
<td width="1" height="1" bgcolor=#97724c></td>
<td width="1" height="1" bgcolor=#916e4c></td>
<td width="1" height="1" bgcolor=#8d6c4a></td>
<td width="1" height="1" bgcolor=#936f50></td>
<td width="1" height="1" bgcolor=#906e48></td>
<td width="1" height="1" bgcolor=#96734f></td>
<td width="1" height="1" bgcolor=#916f4d></td>
<td width="1" height="1" bgcolor=#926f4d></td>
<td width="1" height="1" bgcolor=#89673e></td>
<td width="1" height="1" bgcolor=#8b6743></td>
<td width="1" height="1" bgcolor=#876446></td>
<td width="1" height="1" bgcolor=#876743></td>
<td width="1" height="1" bgcolor=#866543></td>
<td width="1" height="1" bgcolor=#825e3c></td>
<td width="1" height="1" bgcolor=#84613e></td>
<td width="1" height="1" bgcolor=#886544></td>
<td width="1" height="1" bgcolor=#896545></td>
<td width="1" height="1" bgcolor=#886343></td>
<td width="1" height="1" bgcolor=#8f6743></td>
<td width="1" height="1" bgcolor=#8d693d></td>
<td width="1" height="1" bgcolor=#88623f></td>
<td width="1" height="1" bgcolor=#876743></td>
<td width="1" height="1" bgcolor=#806240></td>
<td width="1" height="1" bgcolor=#7e6242></td>
<td width="1" height="1" bgcolor=#80664f></td>
<td width="1" height="1" bgcolor=#846650></td>
<td width="1" height="1" bgcolor=#81644e></td>
<td width="1" height="1" bgcolor=#7f6049></td>
<td width="1" height="1" bgcolor=#836448></td>
<td width="1" height="1" bgcolor=#88684f></td>
<td width="1" height="1" bgcolor=#88694d></td>
<td width="1" height="1" bgcolor=#856b4e></td>
<td width="1" height="1" bgcolor=#806a52></td>
</tr>
<tr>
<td width="1" height="1" bgcolor=#8e5640></td>
<td width="1" height="1" bgcolor=#91543c></td>
<td width="1" height="1" bgcolor=#955c40></td>
<td width="1" height="1" bgcolor=#975942></td>
<td width="1" height="1" bgcolor=#96563e></td>
<td width="1" height="1" bgcolor=#935139></td>
<td width="1" height="1" bgcolor=#965337></td>
<td width="1" height="1" bgcolor=#a66347></td>
<td width="1" height="1" bgcolor=#95503a></td>
<td width="1" height="1" bgcolor=#924e38></td>
<td width="1" height="1" bgcolor=#894931></td>
<td width="1" height="1" bgcolor=#905136></td>
<td width="1" height="1" bgcolor=#8c4f32></td>
<td width="1" height="1" bgcolor=#8b5033></td>
<td width="1" height="1" bgcolor=#8b5332></td>
<td width="1" height="1" bgcolor=#8d5232></td>
<td width="1" height="1" bgcolor=#945838></td>
<td width="1" height="1" bgcolor=#975a3d></td>
<td width="1" height="1" bgcolor=#945a3d></td>
<td width="1" height="1" bgcolor=#946948></td>
```

```
    <td width="1" height="1"
bgcolor=#8e6043></td>
    <td width="1" height="1"
bgcolor=#8f6145></td>
    <td width="1" height="1"
bgcolor=#90664a></td>
    <td width="1" height="1"
bgcolor=#906a4e></td>
    <td width="1" height="1"
bgcolor=#876146></td>
    <td width="1" height="1"
bgcolor=#896248></td>
    <td width="1" height="1"
bgcolor=#855f45></td>
    <td width="1" height="1"
bgcolor=#825c42></td>
    <td width="1" height="1"
bgcolor=#906d50></td>
    <td width="1" height="1"
bgcolor=#926a4e></td>
    <td width="1" height="1"
bgcolor=#866042></td>
    <td width="1" height="1"
bgcolor=#7f5841></td>
    <td width="1" height="1"
bgcolor=#7f5840></td>
    <td width="1" height="1"
bgcolor=#825c43></td>
    <td width="1" height="1"
bgcolor=#866146></td>
    <td width="1" height="1"
bgcolor=#856149></td>
    <td width="1" height="1"
bgcolor=#85634a></td>
    <td width="1" height="1"
bgcolor=#8d6e52></td>
    <td width="1" height="1"
bgcolor=#8e6f4f></td>
    <td width="1" height="1"
bgcolor=#977852></td>
    <td width="1" height="1"
bgcolor=#8a6a48></td>
    <td width="1" height="1"
bgcolor=#947552></td>
    <td width="1" height="1"
bgcolor=#937256></td>
    <td width="1" height="1"
bgcolor=#947450></td>
    <td width="1" height="1"
bgcolor=#967655></td>
    <td width="1" height="1"
bgcolor=#977954></td>
    <td width="1" height="1"
bgcolor=#8e6e50></td>
    <td width="1" height="1"
bgcolor=#876848></td>
    <td width="1" height="1"
bgcolor=#896b43></td>
    <td width="1" height="1"
bgcolor=#836544></td>
    <td width="1" height="1"
bgcolor=#82653f></td>
    <td width="1" height="1"
bgcolor=#886841></td>
    <td width="1" height="1"
bgcolor=#876740></td>
    <td width="1" height="1"
bgcolor=#82603e></td>
    <td width="1" height="1"
bgcolor=#8a6848></td>
    <td width="1" height="1"
bgcolor=#805c3e></td>
    <td width="1" height="1"
bgcolor=#876940></td>
    <td width="1" height="1"
bgcolor=#886743></td>
    <td width="1" height="1"
bgcolor=#896b49></td>
    <td width="1" height="1"
bgcolor=#856a48></td>
    <td width="1" height="1"
bgcolor=#83684e></td>
    <td width="1" height="1"
bgcolor=#7f634f></td>
    <td width="1" height="1"
bgcolor=#7c644f></td>
    <td width="1" height="1"
bgcolor=#7d644d></td>
    <td width="1" height="1"
bgcolor=#7e6045></td>
    <td width="1" height="1"
bgcolor=#7e5c44></td>
    <td width="1" height="1"
bgcolor=#78553c></td>
    <td width="1" height="1"
bgcolor=#775237></td>
    <td width="1" height="1"
bgcolor=#785237></td>
    <td width="1" height="1"
bgcolor=#7d5739></td>
    <td width="1" height="1"
bgcolor=#6c4a2f></td>
    <td width="1" height="1"
bgcolor=#795d46></td>
  </tr>
  <tr>
    <td width="1" height="1"
bgcolor=#96573d></td>
    <td width="1" height="1"
bgcolor=#8f4b39></td>
    <td width="1" height="1"
bgcolor=#8b4c3e></td>
    <td width="1" height="1"
bgcolor=#8d4b3a></td>
    <td width="1" height="1"
bgcolor=#884c39></td>
    <td width="1" height="1"
bgcolor=#8a513a></td>
    <td width="1" height="1"
bgcolor=#8f5135></td>
    <td width="1" height="1"
bgcolor=#95543c></td>
    <td width="1" height="1"
bgcolor=#91503d></td>
    <td width="1" height="1"
bgcolor=#8b4f39></td>
    <td width="1" height="1"
bgcolor=#804833></td>
    <td width="1" height="1"
bgcolor=#854932></td>
    <td width="1" height="1"
bgcolor=#854830></td>
    <td width="1" height="1"
bgcolor=#864630></td>
    <td width="1" height="1"
bgcolor=#8c4f35></td>
    <td width="1" height="1"
bgcolor=#925337></td>
    <td width="1" height="1"
bgcolor=#945436></td>
    <td width="1" height="1"
bgcolor=#905839></td>
    <td width="1" height="1"
bgcolor=#915236></td>
    <td width="1" height="1"
bgcolor=#8e5a3b></td>
    <td width="1" height="1"
bgcolor=#91573a></td>
    <td width="1" height="1"
bgcolor=#985b3e></td>
    <td width="1" height="1"
bgcolor=#986c4d></td>
    <td width="1" height="1"
bgcolor=#946b4f></td>
    <td width="1" height="1"
bgcolor=#956e54></td>
    <td width="1" height="1"
bgcolor=#936b4e></td>
    <td width="1" height="1"
bgcolor=#926c4c></td>
    <td width="1" height="1"
bgcolor=#987554></td>
    <td width="1" height="1"
bgcolor=#927052></td>
    <td width="1" height="1"
bgcolor=#926b50></td>
    <td width="1" height="1"
bgcolor=#8d684e></td>
    <td width="1" height="1"
bgcolor=#866148></td>
    <td width="1" height="1"
bgcolor=#88654c></td>
    <td width="1" height="1"
bgcolor=#88674d></td>
```

```
    <td width="1" height="1"
bgcolor=#917054></td>
    <td width="1" height="1"
bgcolor=#856349></td>
    <td width="1" height="1"
bgcolor=#916e55></td>
    <td width="1" height="1"
bgcolor=#916d58></td>
    <td width="1" height="1"
bgcolor=#8e6b51></td>
    <td width="1" height="1"
bgcolor=#8f704c></td>
    <td width="1" height="1"
bgcolor=#856448></td>
    <td width="1" height="1"
bgcolor=#8f694d></td>
    <td width="1" height="1"
bgcolor=#8d6a4d></td>
    <td width="1" height="1"
bgcolor=#906d49></td>
    <td width="1" height="1"
bgcolor=#92704e></td>
    <td width="1" height="1"
bgcolor=#8d6d50></td>
    <td width="1" height="1"
bgcolor=#866748></td>
    <td width="1" height="1"
bgcolor=#896b44></td>
    <td width="1" height="1"
bgcolor=#876844></td>
    <td width="1" height="1"
bgcolor=#8e7151></td>
    <td width="1" height="1"
bgcolor=#907250></td>
    <td width="1" height="1"
bgcolor=#8c6a43></td>
    <td width="1" height="1"
bgcolor=#8d6943></td>
    <td width="1" height="1"
bgcolor=#86603f></td>
    <td width="1" height="1"
bgcolor=#896543></td>
    <td width="1" height="1"
bgcolor=#815c3b></td>
    <td width="1" height="1"
bgcolor=#8f6944></td>
    <td width="1" height="1"
bgcolor=#895f3c></td>
    <td width="1" height="1"
bgcolor=#8b6440></td>
    <td width="1" height="1"
bgcolor=#896842></td>
    <td width="1" height="1"
bgcolor=#896540></td>
    <td width="1" height="1"
bgcolor=#8a6642></td>
    <td width="1" height="1"
bgcolor=#8f6e49></td>
    <td width="1" height="1"
bgcolor=#8a6641></td>
    <td width="1" height="1"
bgcolor=#8e643c></td>
    <td width="1" height="1"
bgcolor=#8f643e></td>
    <td width="1" height="1"
bgcolor=#8f623b></td>
    <td width="1" height="1"
bgcolor=#90663d></td>
    <td width="1" height="1"
bgcolor=#91693f></td>
    <td width="1" height="1"
bgcolor=#a17a4c></td>
    <td width="1" height="1"
bgcolor=#9e7e58></td>
    <td width="1" height="1"
bgcolor=#8d7354></td>
  </tr>
  <tr>
    <td width="1" height="1"
bgcolor=#91583e></td>
    <td width="1" height="1"
bgcolor=#8d523f></td>
    <td width="1" height="1"
bgcolor=#8b513a></td>
    <td width="1" height="1"
bgcolor=#884f3b></td>
    <td width="1" height="1"
bgcolor=#8a513b></td>
    <td width="1" height="1"
bgcolor=#844a34></td>
    <td width="1" height="1"
bgcolor=#814630></td>
    <td width="1" height="1"
bgcolor=#965c40></td>
    <td width="1" height="1"
bgcolor=#894f36></td>
    <td width="1" height="1"
bgcolor=#8a503a></td>
    <td width="1" height="1"
bgcolor=#804931></td>
    <td width="1" height="1"
bgcolor=#884f36></td>
    <td width="1" height="1"
bgcolor=#864b31></td>
    <td width="1" height="1"
bgcolor=#8a4d35></td>
    <td width="1" height="1"
bgcolor=#8d5537></td>
    <td width="1" height="1"
bgcolor=#8c5437></td>
    <td width="1" height="1"
bgcolor=#8e5738></td>
    <td width="1" height="1"
bgcolor=#8c5238></td>
    <td width="1" height="1"
bgcolor=#8c4f37></td>
    <td width="1" height="1"
bgcolor=#884937></td>
    <td width="1" height="1"
bgcolor=#8e4d35></td>
    <td width="1" height="1"
bgcolor=#8c4e35></td>
    <td width="1" height="1"
bgcolor=#90674e></td>
    <td width="1" height="1"
bgcolor=#8d6b59></td>
    <td width="1" height="1"
bgcolor=#8c6754></td>
    <td width="1" height="1"
bgcolor=#8f6a50></td>
    <td width="1" height="1"
bgcolor=#8e684f></td>
    <td width="1" height="1"
bgcolor=#916b54></td>
    <td width="1" height="1"
bgcolor=#957355></td>
    <td width="1" height="1"
bgcolor=#947255></td>
    <td width="1" height="1"
bgcolor=#916e55></td>
    <td width="1" height="1"
bgcolor=#947256></td>
    <td width="1" height="1"
bgcolor=#8e6e53></td>
    <td width="1" height="1"
bgcolor=#85664d></td>
    <td width="1" height="1"
bgcolor=#87674e></td>
    <td width="1" height="1"
bgcolor=#88654d></td>
    <td width="1" height="1"
bgcolor=#86654b></td>
    <td width="1" height="1"
bgcolor=#8d6f52></td>
    <td width="1" height="1"
bgcolor=#8f7356></td>
    <td width="1" height="1"
bgcolor=#876a4b></td>
    <td width="1" height="1"
bgcolor=#8b6c4d></td>
    <td width="1" height="1"
bgcolor=#906f51></td>
    <td width="1" height="1"
bgcolor=#906f52></td>
    <td width="1" height="1"
bgcolor=#957555></td>
    <td width="1" height="1"
bgcolor=#947653></td>
    <td width="1" height="1"
bgcolor=#8d7051></td>
    <td width="1" height="1"
bgcolor=#90704f></td>
    <td width="1" height="1"
bgcolor=#8d6c48></td>
```

```
    <td width="1" height="1"
bgcolor=#8b6b45></td>
    <td width="1" height="1"
bgcolor=#8b6d4c></td>
    <td width="1" height="1"
bgcolor=#8e7252></td>
    <td width="1" height="1"
bgcolor=#8d6e4e></td>
    <td width="1" height="1"
bgcolor=#886447></td>
    <td width="1" height="1"
bgcolor=#876040></td>
    <td width="1" height="1"
bgcolor=#896541></td>
    <td width="1" height="1"
bgcolor=#8c6244></td>
    <td width="1" height="1"
bgcolor=#a97d41></td>
    <td width="1" height="1"
bgcolor=#aa8040></td>
    <td width="1" height="1"
bgcolor=#875934></td>
    <td width="1" height="1"
bgcolor=#815a39></td>
    <td width="1" height="1"
bgcolor=#7e5936></td>
    <td width="1" height="1"
bgcolor=#795531></td>
    <td width="1" height="1"
bgcolor=#7c5430></td>
    <td width="1" height="1"
bgcolor=#7e552e></td>
    <td width="1" height="1"
bgcolor=#885b34></td>
    <td width="1" height="1"
bgcolor=#865c35></td>
    <td width="1" height="1"
bgcolor=#855a34></td>
    <td width="1" height="1"
bgcolor=#845834></td>
    <td width="1" height="1"
bgcolor=#89603a></td>
    <td width="1" height="1"
bgcolor=#8c623b></td>
    <td width="1" height="1"
bgcolor=#946941></td>
    <td width="1" height="1"
bgcolor=#856647></td>
  </tr>
  <tr>
    <td width="1" height="1"
bgcolor=#85543d></td>
    <td width="1" height="1"
bgcolor=#835040></td>
    <td width="1" height="1"
bgcolor=#804e3a></td>
    <td width="1" height="1"
bgcolor=#824d3b></td>
    <td width="1" height="1"
bgcolor=#7e4a36></td>
    <td width="1" height="1"
bgcolor=#74402a></td>
    <td width="1" height="1"
bgcolor=#7a432d></td>
    <td width="1" height="1"
bgcolor=#814c31></td>
    <td width="1" height="1"
bgcolor=#804d33></td>
    <td width="1" height="1"
bgcolor=#814d35></td>
    <td width="1" height="1"
bgcolor=#814b33></td>
    <td width="1" height="1"
bgcolor=#875134></td>
    <td width="1" height="1"
bgcolor=#854f32></td>
    <td width="1" height="1"
bgcolor=#8a5335></td>
    <td width="1" height="1"
bgcolor=#915c3b></td>
    <td width="1" height="1"
bgcolor=#8c5538></td>
    <td width="1" height="1"
bgcolor=#895337></td>
    <td width="1" height="1"
bgcolor=#8b5137></td>
    <td width="1" height="1"
bgcolor=#864d33></td>
    <td width="1" height="1"
bgcolor=#834a38></td>
    <td width="1" height="1"
bgcolor=#804833></td>
    <td width="1" height="1"
bgcolor=#7d4530></td>
    <td width="1" height="1"
bgcolor=#7f4e3a></td>
    <td width="1" height="1"
bgcolor=#794e3e></td>
    <td width="1" height="1"
bgcolor=#774d3b></td>
    <td width="1" height="1"
bgcolor=#744634></td>
    <td width="1" height="1"
bgcolor=#83563f></td>
    <td width="1" height="1"
bgcolor=#85573a></td>
    <td width="1" height="1"
bgcolor=#815c41></td>
    <td width="1" height="1"
bgcolor=#916e50></td>
    <td width="1" height="1"
bgcolor=#917050></td>
    <td width="1" height="1"
bgcolor=#8e6d50></td>
    <td width="1" height="1"
bgcolor=#8e7054></td>
    <td width="1" height="1"
bgcolor=#8a6c50></td>
    <td width="1" height="1"
bgcolor=#8d7054></td>
    <td width="1" height="1"
bgcolor=#917256></td>
    <td width="1" height="1"
bgcolor=#8e6f52></td>
    <td width="1" height="1"
bgcolor=#977a5a></td>
    <td width="1" height="1"
bgcolor=#967c5b></td>
    <td width="1" height="1"
bgcolor=#987e5b></td>
    <td width="1" height="1"
bgcolor=#967a57></td>
    <td width="1" height="1"
bgcolor=#987a58></td>
    <td width="1" height="1"
bgcolor=#947856></td>
    <td width="1" height="1"
bgcolor=#987857></td>
    <td width="1" height="1"
bgcolor=#9b7a58></td>
    <td width="1" height="1"
bgcolor=#95744b></td>
    <td width="1" height="1"
bgcolor=#997754></td>
    <td width="1" height="1"
bgcolor=#947353></td>
    <td width="1" height="1"
bgcolor=#957955></td>
    <td width="1" height="1"
bgcolor=#937754></td>
    <td width="1" height="1"
bgcolor=#937050></td>
    <td width="1" height="1"
bgcolor=#94714e></td>
    <td width="1" height="1"
bgcolor=#93714e></td>
    <td width="1" height="1"
bgcolor=#916c4a></td>
    <td width="1" height="1"
bgcolor=#917047></td>
    <td width="1" height="1"
bgcolor=#a07d55></td>
    <td width="1" height="1"
bgcolor=#c0934e></td>
    <td width="1" height="1"
bgcolor=#a57942></td>
    <td width="1" height="1"
bgcolor=#986d47></td>
    <td width="1" height="1"
bgcolor=#906a46></td>
    <td width="1" height="1"
bgcolor=#896441></td>
    <td width="1" height="1"
bgcolor=#815d3d></td>
```

```
    <td width="1" height="1"
bgcolor=#825b36></td>
    <td width="1" height="1"
bgcolor=#825933></td>
    <td width="1" height="1"
bgcolor=#895b33></td>
    <td width="1" height="1"
bgcolor=#8d5d37></td>
    <td width="1" height="1"
bgcolor=#8b5a33></td>
    <td width="1" height="1"
bgcolor=#8b5b35></td>
    <td width="1" height="1"
bgcolor=#8b6039></td>
    <td width="1" height="1"
bgcolor=#91653c></td>
    <td width="1" height="1"
bgcolor=#92663e></td>
    <td width="1" height="1"
bgcolor=#866546></td>
  </tr>
  <tr>
    <td width="1" height="1"
bgcolor=#80503d></td>
    <td width="1" height="1"
bgcolor=#7c4b3c></td>
    <td width="1" height="1"
bgcolor=#764636></td>
    <td width="1" height="1"
bgcolor=#784735></td>
    <td width="1" height="1"
bgcolor=#7b4a37></td>
    <td width="1" height="1"
bgcolor=#754430></td>
    <td width="1" height="1"
bgcolor=#7b4832></td>
    <td width="1" height="1"
bgcolor=#7e4c32></td>
    <td width="1" height="1"
bgcolor=#855036></td>
    <td width="1" height="1"
bgcolor=#845038></td>
    <td width="1" height="1"
bgcolor=#85553d></td>
    <td width="1" height="1"
bgcolor=#875736></td>
    <td width="1" height="1"
bgcolor=#835230></td>
    <td width="1" height="1"
bgcolor=#885636></td>
    <td width="1" height="1"
bgcolor=#8b5936></td>
    <td width="1" height="1"
bgcolor=#8a5839></td>
    <td width="1" height="1"
bgcolor=#865439></td>
    <td width="1" height="1"
bgcolor=#885632></td>
    <td width="1" height="1"
bgcolor=#885935></td>
    <td width="1" height="1"
bgcolor=#815235></td>
    <td width="1" height="1"
bgcolor=#825238></td>
    <td width="1" height="1"
bgcolor=#824f34></td>
    <td width="1" height="1"
bgcolor=#804d37></td>
    <td width="1" height="1"
bgcolor=#7b4f3c></td>
    <td width="1" height="1"
bgcolor=#805644></td>
    <td width="1" height="1"
bgcolor=#7d5038></td>
    <td width="1" height="1"
bgcolor=#83543c></td>
    <td width="1" height="1"
bgcolor=#87593d></td>
    <td width="1" height="1"
bgcolor=#825139></td>
    <td width="1" height="1"
bgcolor=#92684b></td>
    <td width="1" height="1"
bgcolor=#9f7b5a></td>
    <td width="1" height="1"
bgcolor=#927556></td>
    <td width="1" height="1"
bgcolor=#987c5e></td>
    <td width="1" height="1"
bgcolor=#977d5f></td>
    <td width="1" height="1"
bgcolor=#9b8062></td>
    <td width="1" height="1"
bgcolor=#9a7d60></td>
    <td width="1" height="1"
bgcolor=#9a7d5e></td>
    <td width="1" height="1"
bgcolor=#9a815e></td>
    <td width="1" height="1"
bgcolor=#99805d></td>
    <td width="1" height="1"
bgcolor=#9a805d></td>
    <td width="1" height="1"
bgcolor=#967b59></td>
    <td width="1" height="1"
bgcolor=#957755></td>
    <td width="1" height="1"
bgcolor=#957550></td>
    <td width="1" height="1"
bgcolor=#987550></td>
    <td width="1" height="1"
bgcolor=#9a744f></td>
    <td width="1" height="1"
bgcolor=#936e4b></td>
    <td width="1" height="1"
bgcolor=#92704b></td>
    <td width="1" height="1"
bgcolor=#8f6f49></td>
    <td width="1" height="1"
bgcolor=#947953></td>
    <td width="1" height="1"
bgcolor=#90764e></td>
    <td width="1" height="1"
bgcolor=#97734d></td>
    <td width="1" height="1"
bgcolor=#93704d></td>
    <td width="1" height="1"
bgcolor=#916f4b></td>
    <td width="1" height="1"
bgcolor=#967453></td>
    <td width="1" height="1"
bgcolor=#92744d></td>
    <td width="1" height="1"
bgcolor=#97754d></td>
    <td width="1" height="1"
bgcolor=#a8824c></td>
    <td width="1" height="1"
bgcolor=#b38f48></td>
    <td width="1" height="1"
bgcolor=#986f45></td>
    <td width="1" height="1"
bgcolor=#98724c></td>
    <td width="1" height="1"
bgcolor=#926e49></td>
    <td width="1" height="1"
bgcolor=#8b6547></td>
    <td width="1" height="1"
bgcolor=#876546></td>
    <td width="1" height="1"
bgcolor=#85623e></td>
    <td width="1" height="1"
bgcolor=#88603c></td>
    <td width="1" height="1"
bgcolor=#82603d></td>
    <td width="1" height="1"
bgcolor=#84603f></td>
    <td width="1" height="1"
bgcolor=#8a6340></td>
    <td width="1" height="1"
bgcolor=#8a6742></td>
    <td width="1" height="1"
bgcolor=#8c6740></td>
    <td width="1" height="1"
bgcolor=#956846></td>
    <td width="1" height="1"
bgcolor=#88674c></td>
  </tr>
  <tr>
    <td width="1" height="1"
bgcolor=#87583f></td>
    <td width="1" height="1"
bgcolor=#83543b></td>
    <td width="1" height="1"
bgcolor=#805138></td>
```

```
    <td width="1" height="1" bgcolor=#83543d></td>
    <td width="1" height="1" bgcolor=#815139></td>
    <td width="1" height="1" bgcolor=#805137></td>
    <td width="1" height="1" bgcolor=#7d4a2e></td>
    <td width="1" height="1" bgcolor=#804e34></td>
    <td width="1" height="1" bgcolor=#7f5233></td>
    <td width="1" height="1" bgcolor=#80553c></td>
    <td width="1" height="1" bgcolor=#805444></td>
    <td width="1" height="1" bgcolor=#835539></td>
    <td width="1" height="1" bgcolor=#835235></td>
    <td width="1" height="1" bgcolor=#835437></td>
    <td width="1" height="1" bgcolor=#865736></td>
    <td width="1" height="1" bgcolor=#835435></td>
    <td width="1" height="1" bgcolor=#88593c></td>
    <td width="1" height="1" bgcolor=#875a32></td>
    <td width="1" height="1" bgcolor=#8a5b38></td>
    <td width="1" height="1" bgcolor=#875937></td>
    <td width="1" height="1" bgcolor=#835637></td>
    <td width="1" height="1" bgcolor=#845336></td>
    <td width="1" height="1" bgcolor=#7e4c30></td>
    <td width="1" height="1" bgcolor=#7e5139></td>
    <td width="1" height="1" bgcolor=#784935></td>
    <td width="1" height="1" bgcolor=#794930></td>
    <td width="1" height="1" bgcolor=#7f4f34></td>
    <td width="1" height="1" bgcolor=#875639></td>
    <td width="1" height="1" bgcolor=#84583a></td>
    <td width="1" height="1" bgcolor=#906a4c></td>
    <td width="1" height="1" bgcolor=#947556></td>
    <td width="1" height="1" bgcolor=#95765a></td>
    <td width="1" height="1" bgcolor=#977b60></td>
    <td width="1" height="1" bgcolor=#987e63></td>
    <td width="1" height="1" bgcolor=#977f61></td>
    <td width="1" height="1" bgcolor=#967e65></td>
    <td width="1" height="1" bgcolor=#957b5e></td>
    <td width="1" height="1" bgcolor=#987a5d></td>
    <td width="1" height="1" bgcolor=#977759></td>
    <td width="1" height="1" bgcolor=#967758></td>
    <td width="1" height="1" bgcolor=#937355></td>
    <td width="1" height="1" bgcolor=#957355></td>
    <td width="1" height="1" bgcolor=#947755></td>
    <td width="1" height="1" bgcolor=#967857></td>
    <td width="1" height="1" bgcolor=#917250></td>
    <td width="1" height="1" bgcolor=#937352></td>
    <td width="1" height="1" bgcolor=#957552></td>
    <td width="1" height="1" bgcolor=#927350></td>
    <td width="1" height="1" bgcolor=#8f7552></td>
    <td width="1" height="1" bgcolor=#927652></td>
    <td width="1" height="1" bgcolor=#947852></td>
    <td width="1" height="1" bgcolor=#8f6e49></td>
    <td width="1" height="1" bgcolor=#8d6d49></td>
    <td width="1" height="1" bgcolor=#937953></td>
    <td width="1" height="1" bgcolor=#917a51></td>
    <td width="1" height="1" bgcolor=#957849></td>
    <td width="1" height="1" bgcolor=#a78741></td>
    <td width="1" height="1" bgcolor=#a98649></td>
    <td width="1" height="1" bgcolor=#b7954b></td>
    <td width="1" height="1" bgcolor=#a07a48></td>
    <td width="1" height="1" bgcolor=#99754e></td>
    <td width="1" height="1" bgcolor=#966f43></td>
    <td width="1" height="1" bgcolor=#8f6b4d></td>
    <td width="1" height="1" bgcolor=#8f6f4d></td>
    <td width="1" height="1" bgcolor=#906a47></td>
    <td width="1" height="1" bgcolor=#8d694b></td>
    <td width="1" height="1" bgcolor=#8d6d59></td>
    <td width="1" height="1" bgcolor=#8a6b52></td>
    <td width="1" height="1" bgcolor=#87694f></td>
    <td width="1" height="1" bgcolor=#8a6c51></td>
    <td width="1" height="1" bgcolor=#8a6d51></td>
    <td width="1" height="1" bgcolor=#7d6c55></td>
  </tr>
  <tr>
    <td width="1" height="1" bgcolor=#916444></td>
    <td width="1" height="1" bgcolor=#85573d></td>
    <td width="1" height="1" bgcolor=#875a39></td>
    <td width="1" height="1" bgcolor=#805939></td>
    <td width="1" height="1" bgcolor=#7e553a></td>
    <td width="1" height="1" bgcolor=#7d5539></td>
    <td width="1" height="1" bgcolor=#845938></td>
    <td width="1" height="1" bgcolor=#855b41></td>
    <td width="1" height="1" bgcolor=#815b47></td>
    <td width="1" height="1" bgcolor=#815d4a></td>
    <td width="1" height="1" bgcolor=#805a3e></td>
    <td width="1" height="1" bgcolor=#895d3c></td>
    <td width="1" height="1" bgcolor=#875738></td>
    <td width="1" height="1" bgcolor=#865939></td>
    <td width="1" height="1" bgcolor=#8b5c3a></td>
    <td width="1" height="1" bgcolor=#895a38></td>
    <td width="1" height="1" bgcolor=#8a5c39></td>
```

```
    <td width="1" height="1"
bgcolor=#8b5d39></td>
    <td width="1" height="1"
bgcolor=#8a5c37></td>
    <td width="1" height="1"
bgcolor=#8b5e37></td>
    <td width="1" height="1"
bgcolor=#8b5c37></td>
    <td width="1" height="1"
bgcolor=#91613e></td>
    <td width="1" height="1"
bgcolor=#8c5c3a></td>
    <td width="1" height="1"
bgcolor=#8e6342></td>
    <td width="1" height="1"
bgcolor=#90643f></td>
    <td width="1" height="1"
bgcolor=#976a41></td>
    <td width="1" height="1"
bgcolor=#956b43></td>
    <td width="1" height="1"
bgcolor=#9a734f></td>
    <td width="1" height="1"
bgcolor=#9b7a59></td>
    <td width="1" height="1"
bgcolor=#987a59></td>
    <td width="1" height="1"
bgcolor=#977d5c></td>
    <td width="1" height="1"
bgcolor=#987a5c></td>
    <td width="1" height="1"
bgcolor=#997e63></td>
    <td width="1" height="1"
bgcolor=#927961></td>
    <td width="1" height="1"
bgcolor=#947b62></td>
    <td width="1" height="1"
bgcolor=#957d63></td>
    <td width="1" height="1"
bgcolor=#967b5c></td>
    <td width="1" height="1"
bgcolor=#98775b></td>
    <td width="1" height="1"
bgcolor=#967457></td>
    <td width="1" height="1"
bgcolor=#967353></td>
    <td width="1" height="1"
bgcolor=#997756></td>
    <td width="1" height="1"
bgcolor=#937553></td>
    <td width="1" height="1"
bgcolor=#927552></td>
    <td width="1" height="1"
bgcolor=#937452></td>
    <td width="1" height="1"
bgcolor=#957353></td>
    <td width="1" height="1"
bgcolor=#91704f></td>
    <td width="1" height="1"
bgcolor=#977654></td>
    <td width="1" height="1"
bgcolor=#977653></td>
    <td width="1" height="1"
bgcolor=#957a55></td>
    <td width="1" height="1"
bgcolor=#947650></td>
    <td width="1" height="1"
bgcolor=#94754f></td>
    <td width="1" height="1"
bgcolor=#94704c></td>
    <td width="1" height="1"
bgcolor=#987550></td>
    <td width="1" height="1"
bgcolor=#967750></td>
    <td width="1" height="1"
bgcolor=#927750></td>
    <td width="1" height="1"
bgcolor=#957450></td>
    <td width="1" height="1"
bgcolor=#9c7653></td>
    <td width="1" height="1"
bgcolor=#9c7945></td>
    <td width="1" height="1"
bgcolor=#bb984d></td>
    <td width="1" height="1"
bgcolor=#b49544></td>
    <td width="1" height="1"
bgcolor=#916f44></td>
    <td width="1" height="1"
bgcolor=#936d41></td>
    <td width="1" height="1"
bgcolor=#946e4c></td>
    <td width="1" height="1"
bgcolor=#91704d></td>
    <td width="1" height="1"
bgcolor=#967551></td>
    <td width="1" height="1"
bgcolor=#8f744f></td>
    <td width="1" height="1"
bgcolor=#897051></td>
    <td width="1" height="1"
bgcolor=#88684e></td>
    <td width="1" height="1"
bgcolor=#8a6a51></td>
    <td width="1" height="1"
bgcolor=#876c54></td>
    <td width="1" height="1"
bgcolor=#8a6853></td>
    <td width="1" height="1"
bgcolor=#7a695c></td>
  </tr>
  <tr>
    <td width="1" height="1"
bgcolor=#8f6648></td>
    <td width="1" height="1"
bgcolor=#875d47></td>
    <td width="1" height="1"
bgcolor=#81583b></td>
    <td width="1" height="1"
bgcolor=#865c3f></td>
    <td width="1" height="1"
bgcolor=#876044></td>
    <td width="1" height="1"
bgcolor=#835f42></td>
    <td width="1" height="1"
bgcolor=#7c5639></td>
    <td width="1" height="1"
bgcolor=#835d3f></td>
    <td width="1" height="1"
bgcolor=#886143></td>
    <td width="1" height="1"
bgcolor=#825a44></td>
    <td width="1" height="1"
bgcolor=#835740></td>
    <td width="1" height="1"
bgcolor=#815433></td>
    <td width="1" height="1"
bgcolor=#855636></td>
    <td width="1" height="1"
bgcolor=#8a5d3a></td>
    <td width="1" height="1"
bgcolor=#845633></td>
    <td width="1" height="1"
bgcolor=#92643e></td>
    <td width="1" height="1"
bgcolor=#92653c></td>
    <td width="1" height="1"
bgcolor=#8d623c></td>
    <td width="1" height="1"
bgcolor=#95683a></td>
    <td width="1" height="1"
bgcolor=#97683b></td>
    <td width="1" height="1"
bgcolor=#97693e></td>
    <td width="1" height="1"
bgcolor=#91633b></td>
    <td width="1" height="1"
bgcolor=#9a6c40></td>
    <td width="1" height="1"
bgcolor=#966b3f></td>
    <td width="1" height="1"
bgcolor=#9a6f3e></td>
    <td width="1" height="1"
bgcolor=#a57846></td>
    <td width="1" height="1"
bgcolor=#a27742></td>
    <td width="1" height="1"
bgcolor=#a17745></td>
    <td width="1" height="1"
bgcolor=#9f7b53></td>
    <td width="1" height="1"
bgcolor=#997851></td>
    <td width="1" height="1"
bgcolor=#9e7f54></td>
```

```
    <td width="1" height="1"
bgcolor=#a1835a></td>
    <td width="1" height="1"
bgcolor=#987e5e></td>
    <td width="1" height="1"
bgcolor=#95795c></td>
    <td width="1" height="1"
bgcolor=#977558></td>
    <td width="1" height="1"
bgcolor=#927456></td>
    <td width="1" height="1"
bgcolor=#987556></td>
    <td width="1" height="1"
bgcolor=#997358></td>
    <td width="1" height="1"
bgcolor=#926c52></td>
    <td width="1" height="1"
bgcolor=#966c4c></td>
    <td width="1" height="1"
bgcolor=#936a4a></td>
    <td width="1" height="1"
bgcolor=#936d4c></td>
    <td width="1" height="1"
bgcolor=#946b4a></td>
    <td width="1" height="1"
bgcolor=#936a49></td>
    <td width="1" height="1"
bgcolor=#926646></td>
    <td width="1" height="1"
bgcolor=#956f4c></td>
    <td width="1" height="1"
bgcolor=#956e4b></td>
    <td width="1" height="1"
bgcolor=#956f4b></td>
    <td width="1" height="1"
bgcolor=#94704f></td>
    <td width="1" height="1"
bgcolor=#906a47></td>
    <td width="1" height="1"
bgcolor=#936b46></td>
    <td width="1" height="1"
bgcolor=#936943></td>
    <td width="1" height="1"
bgcolor=#946d46></td>
    <td width="1" height="1"
bgcolor=#936f47></td>
    <td width="1" height="1"
bgcolor=#947241></td>
    <td width="1" height="1"
bgcolor=#b8954c></td>
    <td width="1" height="1"
bgcolor=#c09d47></td>
    <td width="1" height="1"
bgcolor=#b28c49></td>
    <td width="1" height="1"
bgcolor=#997337></td>
    <td width="1" height="1"
bgcolor=#916b46></td>
    <td width="1" height="1"
bgcolor=#906844></td>
    <td width="1" height="1"
bgcolor=#956945></td>
    <td width="1" height="1"
bgcolor=#90643d></td>
    <td width="1" height="1"
bgcolor=#946b45></td>
    <td width="1" height="1"
bgcolor=#966a48></td>
    <td width="1" height="1"
bgcolor=#936a49></td>
    <td width="1" height="1"
bgcolor=#8e6845></td>
    <td width="1" height="1"
bgcolor=#8f6949></td>
    <td width="1" height="1"
bgcolor=#957254></td>
    <td width="1" height="1"
bgcolor=#8f6e53></td>
    <td width="1" height="1"
bgcolor=#906b4e></td>
    <td width="1" height="1"
bgcolor=#7b6351></td>
  </tr>
  <tr>
    <td width="1" height="1"
bgcolor=#986c46></td>
    <td width="1" height="1"
bgcolor=#845837></td>
    <td width="1" height="1"
bgcolor=#8a5f3c></td>
    <td width="1" height="1"
bgcolor=#7f5639></td>
    <td width="1" height="1"
bgcolor=#83593a></td>
    <td width="1" height="1"
bgcolor=#8a5e3d></td>
    <td width="1" height="1"
bgcolor=#875837></td>
    <td width="1" height="1"
bgcolor=#855431></td>
    <td width="1" height="1"
bgcolor=#8b5936></td>
    <td width="1" height="1"
bgcolor=#824f34></td>
    <td width="1" height="1"
bgcolor=#865134></td>
    <td width="1" height="1"
bgcolor=#90613f></td>
    <td width="1" height="1"
bgcolor=#7f5031></td>
    <td width="1" height="1"
bgcolor=#75452d></td>
    <td width="1" height="1"
bgcolor=#946642></td>
    <td width="1" height="1"
bgcolor=#986b43></td>
    <td width="1" height="1"
bgcolor=#986b40></td>
    <td width="1" height="1"
bgcolor=#9b6a44></td>
    <td width="1" height="1"
bgcolor=#996a3c></td>
    <td width="1" height="1"
bgcolor=#93663d></td>
    <td width="1" height="1"
bgcolor=#99653b></td>
    <td width="1" height="1"
bgcolor=#945f3c></td>
    <td width="1" height="1"
bgcolor=#9c683e></td>
    <td width="1" height="1"
bgcolor=#9c6a3e></td>
    <td width="1" height="1"
bgcolor=#9e6d3e></td>
    <td width="1" height="1"
bgcolor=#9d6d3f></td>
    <td width="1" height="1"
bgcolor=#a07042></td>
    <td width="1" height="1"
bgcolor=#9d6c44></td>
    <td width="1" height="1"
bgcolor=#9d6c42></td>
    <td width="1" height="1"
bgcolor=#95643e></td>
    <td width="1" height="1"
bgcolor=#926339></td>
    <td width="1" height="1"
bgcolor=#895734></td>
    <td width="1" height="1"
bgcolor=#885537></td>
    <td width="1" height="1"
bgcolor=#905839></td>
    <td width="1" height="1"
bgcolor=#82533a></td>
    <td width="1" height="1"
bgcolor=#865b43></td>
    <td width="1" height="1"
bgcolor=#7e513a></td>
    <td width="1" height="1"
bgcolor=#92644b></td>
    <td width="1" height="1"
bgcolor=#71432c></td>
    <td width="1" height="1"
bgcolor=#8b5e40></td>
    <td width="1" height="1"
bgcolor=#8f6242></td>
    <td width="1" height="1"
bgcolor=#916444></td>
    <td width="1" height="1"
bgcolor=#996848></td>
    <td width="1" height="1"
bgcolor=#956442></td>
    <td width="1" height="1"
bgcolor=#996644></td>
```

```
    <td width="1" height="1"
bgcolor=#956642></td>
    <td width="1" height="1"
bgcolor=#9a6b47></td>
    <td width="1" height="1"
bgcolor=#966843></td>
    <td width="1" height="1"
bgcolor=#936844></td>
    <td width="1" height="1"
bgcolor=#956942></td>
    <td width="1" height="1"
bgcolor=#966a42></td>
    <td width="1" height="1"
bgcolor=#986e46></td>
    <td width="1" height="1"
bgcolor=#9a6e47></td>
    <td width="1" height="1"
bgcolor=#996d45></td>
    <td width="1" height="1"
bgcolor=#936c46></td>
    <td width="1" height="1"
bgcolor=#9b7242></td>
    <td width="1" height="1"
bgcolor=#a57945></td>
    <td width="1" height="1"
bgcolor=#b99246></td>
    <td width="1" height="1"
bgcolor=#c8a348></td>
    <td width="1" height="1"
bgcolor=#a97b4b></td>
    <td width="1" height="1"
bgcolor=#925d3d></td>
    <td width="1" height="1"
bgcolor=#915b37></td>
    <td width="1" height="1"
bgcolor=#8f5d3a></td>
    <td width="1" height="1"
bgcolor=#8a5533></td>
    <td width="1" height="1"
bgcolor=#955f3e></td>
    <td width="1" height="1"
bgcolor=#975e40></td>
    <td width="1" height="1"
bgcolor=#925b3d></td>
    <td width="1" height="1"
bgcolor=#925c40></td>
    <td width="1" height="1"
bgcolor=#8f5c40></td>
    <td width="1" height="1"
bgcolor=#8c5b40></td>
    <td width="1" height="1"
bgcolor=#905a40></td>
    <td width="1" height="1"
bgcolor=#7f5646></td>
  </tr>
  <tr>
    <td width="1" height="1"
bgcolor=#945d3e></td>
    <td width="1" height="1"
bgcolor=#8c553b></td>
    <td width="1" height="1"
bgcolor=#8d563a></td>
    <td width="1" height="1"
bgcolor=#8c5738></td>
    <td width="1" height="1"
bgcolor=#8f5b3b></td>
    <td width="1" height="1"
bgcolor=#8e5c38></td>
    <td width="1" height="1"
bgcolor=#97673e></td>
    <td width="1" height="1"
bgcolor=#916437></td>
    <td width="1" height="1"
bgcolor=#986a3d></td>
    <td width="1" height="1"
bgcolor=#96673a></td>
    <td width="1" height="1"
bgcolor=#926536></td>
    <td width="1" height="1"
bgcolor=#9e743e></td>
    <td width="1" height="1"
bgcolor=#a07541></td>
    <td width="1" height="1"
bgcolor=#9c7140></td>
    <td width="1" height="1"
bgcolor=#a37840></td>
    <td width="1" height="1"
bgcolor=#9f743e></td>
    <td width="1" height="1"
bgcolor=#a0753f></td>
    <td width="1" height="1"
bgcolor=#9d6f3a></td>
    <td width="1" height="1"
bgcolor=#a1733e></td>
    <td width="1" height="1"
bgcolor=#905e33></td>
    <td width="1" height="1"
bgcolor=#9c6a3e></td>
    <td width="1" height="1"
bgcolor=#814e2b></td>
    <td width="1" height="1"
bgcolor=#936137></td>
    <td width="1" height="1"
bgcolor=#926235></td>
    <td width="1" height="1"
bgcolor=#926232></td>
    <td width="1" height="1"
bgcolor=#905e33></td>
    <td width="1" height="1"
bgcolor=#8e5c38></td>
    <td width="1" height="1"
bgcolor=#87562e></td>
    <td width="1" height="1"
bgcolor=#8c572e></td>
    <td width="1" height="1"
bgcolor=#875232></td>
    <td width="1" height="1"
bgcolor=#83502e></td>
    <td width="1" height="1"
bgcolor=#7f4e2b></td>
    <td width="1" height="1"
bgcolor=#7d4c2e></td>
    <td width="1" height="1"
bgcolor=#824d2b></td>
    <td width="1" height="1"
bgcolor=#784728></td>
    <td width="1" height="1"
bgcolor=#683a22></td>
    <td width="1" height="1"
bgcolor=#653824></td>
    <td width="1" height="1"
bgcolor=#6d3a1e></td>
    <td width="1" height="1"
bgcolor=#734028></td>
    <td width="1" height="1"
bgcolor=#7e5139></td>
    <td width="1" height="1"
bgcolor=#6c3e22></td>
    <td width="1" height="1"
bgcolor=#8e6140></td>
    <td width="1" height="1"
bgcolor=#91613f></td>
    <td width="1" height="1"
bgcolor=#946441></td>
    <td width="1" height="1"
bgcolor=#986640></td>
    <td width="1" height="1"
bgcolor=#966742></td>
    <td width="1" height="1"
bgcolor=#986944></td>
    <td width="1" height="1"
bgcolor=#966742></td>
    <td width="1" height="1"
bgcolor=#996d44></td>
    <td width="1" height="1"
bgcolor=#936a41></td>
    <td width="1" height="1"
bgcolor=#946840></td>
    <td width="1" height="1"
bgcolor=#976742></td>
    <td width="1" height="1"
bgcolor=#976c44></td>
    <td width="1" height="1"
bgcolor=#97724a></td>
    <td width="1" height="1"
bgcolor=#99784a></td>
    <td width="1" height="1"
bgcolor=#a17d4a></td>
    <td width="1" height="1"
bgcolor=#ab864a></td>
    <td width="1" height="1"
bgcolor=#ae8b45></td>
    <td width="1" height="1"
bgcolor=#a17c40></td>
```

```
    <td width="1" height="1" bgcolor=#926c3c></td>
    <td width="1" height="1" bgcolor=#916942></td>
    <td width="1" height="1" bgcolor=#916b41></td>
    <td width="1" height="1" bgcolor=#906540></td>
    <td width="1" height="1" bgcolor=#916540></td>
    <td width="1" height="1" bgcolor=#8a5e39></td>
    <td width="1" height="1" bgcolor=#895e3b></td>
    <td width="1" height="1" bgcolor=#906140></td>
    <td width="1" height="1" bgcolor=#8a5b3a></td>
    <td width="1" height="1" bgcolor=#8e5f3f></td>
    <td width="1" height="1" bgcolor=#8d6142></td>
    <td width="1" height="1" bgcolor=#8c5e41></td>
    <td width="1" height="1" bgcolor=#7f5c4a></td>
  </tr>
  <tr>
    <td width="1" height="1" bgcolor=#915c3c></td>
    <td width="1" height="1" bgcolor=#92563c></td>
    <td width="1" height="1" bgcolor=#905234></td>
    <td width="1" height="1" bgcolor=#945738></td>
    <td width="1" height="1" bgcolor=#965d38></td>
    <td width="1" height="1" bgcolor=#966039></td>
    <td width="1" height="1" bgcolor=#9a633a></td>
    <td width="1" height="1" bgcolor=#955f39></td>
    <td width="1" height="1" bgcolor=#975f3e></td>
    <td width="1" height="1" bgcolor=#9c633a></td>
    <td width="1" height="1" bgcolor=#9d693b></td>
    <td width="1" height="1" bgcolor=#976036></td>
    <td width="1" height="1" bgcolor=#a16d3e></td>
    <td width="1" height="1" bgcolor=#ad7946></td>
    <td width="1" height="1" bgcolor=#a57a48></td>
    <td width="1" height="1" bgcolor=#a37a45></td>
    <td width="1" height="1" bgcolor=#9d6d3f></td>
    <td width="1" height="1" bgcolor=#966839></td>
    <td width="1" height="1" bgcolor=#8f5e37></td>
    <td width="1" height="1" bgcolor=#9a6939></td>
    <td width="1" height="1" bgcolor=#936837></td>
    <td width="1" height="1" bgcolor=#906136></td>
    <td width="1" height="1" bgcolor=#905f38></td>
    <td width="1" height="1" bgcolor=#85552f></td>
    <td width="1" height="1" bgcolor=#946838></td>
    <td width="1" height="1" bgcolor=#956a38></td>
    <td width="1" height="1" bgcolor=#8e5f32></td>
    <td width="1" height="1" bgcolor=#936233></td>
    <td width="1" height="1" bgcolor=#926234></td>
    <td width="1" height="1" bgcolor=#8f5d33></td>
    <td width="1" height="1" bgcolor=#915e36></td>
    <td width="1" height="1" bgcolor=#854f2b></td>
    <td width="1" height="1" bgcolor=#7b4c2a></td>
    <td width="1" height="1" bgcolor=#7d512f></td>
    <td width="1" height="1" bgcolor=#7f5133></td>
    <td width="1" height="1" bgcolor=#7b4e32></td>
    <td width="1" height="1" bgcolor=#72452a></td>
    <td width="1" height="1" bgcolor=#8b5d3d></td>
    <td width="1" height="1" bgcolor=#7d5134></td>
    <td width="1" height="1" bgcolor=#7e5338></td>
    <td width="1" height="1" bgcolor=#8a5e3e></td>
    <td width="1" height="1" bgcolor=#8c613c></td>
    <td width="1" height="1" bgcolor=#8c6541></td>
    <td width="1" height="1" bgcolor=#8f6140></td>
    <td width="1" height="1" bgcolor=#8e6142></td>
    <td width="1" height="1" bgcolor=#8b5f3b></td>
    <td width="1" height="1" bgcolor=#916442></td>
    <td width="1" height="1" bgcolor=#916444></td>
    <td width="1" height="1" bgcolor=#8d6743></td>
    <td width="1" height="1" bgcolor=#916b46></td>
    <td width="1" height="1" bgcolor=#906742></td>
    <td width="1" height="1" bgcolor=#8f623c></td>
    <td width="1" height="1" bgcolor=#956a40></td>
    <td width="1" height="1" bgcolor=#946b43></td>
    <td width="1" height="1" bgcolor=#916f44></td>
    <td width="1" height="1" bgcolor=#937144></td>
    <td width="1" height="1" bgcolor=#916846></td>
    <td width="1" height="1" bgcolor=#906840></td>
    <td width="1" height="1" bgcolor=#956d3f></td>
    <td width="1" height="1" bgcolor=#926b40></td>
    <td width="1" height="1" bgcolor=#946c45></td>
    <td width="1" height="1" bgcolor=#916a3e></td>
    <td width="1" height="1" bgcolor=#937041></td>
    <td width="1" height="1" bgcolor=#8e6f41></td>
    <td width="1" height="1" bgcolor=#936b42></td>
    <td width="1" height="1" bgcolor=#916541></td>
    <td width="1" height="1" bgcolor=#92613f></td>
    <td width="1" height="1" bgcolor=#8f5e3b></td>
    <td width="1" height="1" bgcolor=#925b3e></td>
    <td width="1" height="1" bgcolor=#8b593d></td>
    <td width="1" height="1" bgcolor=#89593c></td>
    <td width="1" height="1" bgcolor=#7d5746></td>
  </tr>
  <tr>
```

```
<td width="1" height="1"
bgcolor=#8a593c></td>
<td width="1" height="1"
bgcolor=#8b583d></td>
<td width="1" height="1"
bgcolor=#885432></td>
<td width="1" height="1"
bgcolor=#8f5734></td>
<td width="1" height="1"
bgcolor=#8f5b33></td>
<td width="1" height="1"
bgcolor=#905c33></td>
<td width="1" height="1"
bgcolor=#925e35></td>
<td width="1" height="1"
bgcolor=#8c5832></td>
<td width="1" height="1"
bgcolor=#895633></td>
<td width="1" height="1"
bgcolor=#915e35></td>
<td width="1" height="1"
bgcolor=#8a4f2c></td>
<td width="1" height="1"
bgcolor=#89532e></td>
<td width="1" height="1"
bgcolor=#906037></td>
<td width="1" height="1"
bgcolor=#8c6335></td>
<td width="1" height="1"
bgcolor=#8d6438></td>
<td width="1" height="1"
bgcolor=#896136></td>
<td width="1" height="1"
bgcolor=#8a5d32></td>
<td width="1" height="1"
bgcolor=#8b5c38></td>
<td width="1" height="1"
bgcolor=#895836></td>
<td width="1" height="1"
bgcolor=#86552b></td>
<td width="1" height="1"
bgcolor=#8a5a31></td>
<td width="1" height="1"
bgcolor=#92613a></td>
<td width="1" height="1"
bgcolor=#8b5a31></td>
<td width="1" height="1"
bgcolor=#926235></td>
<td width="1" height="1"
bgcolor=#976935></td>
<td width="1" height="1"
bgcolor=#936a35></td>
<td width="1" height="1"
bgcolor=#8f6538></td>
<td width="1" height="1"
bgcolor=#8b6031></td>
<td width="1" height="1"
bgcolor=#895e34></td>
<td width="1" height="1"
bgcolor=#8a5d35></td>
<td width="1" height="1"
bgcolor=#845630></td>
<td width="1" height="1"
bgcolor=#85522b></td>
<td width="1" height="1"
bgcolor=#7f4f2b></td>
<td width="1" height="1"
bgcolor=#7b4f2b></td>
<td width="1" height="1"
bgcolor=#7f522d></td>
<td width="1" height="1"
bgcolor=#916440></td>
<td width="1" height="1"
bgcolor=#845634></td>
<td width="1" height="1"
bgcolor=#8e613e></td>
<td width="1" height="1"
bgcolor=#8e6948></td>
<td width="1" height="1"
bgcolor=#8c6746></td>
<td width="1" height="1"
bgcolor=#855f3c></td>
<td width="1" height="1"
bgcolor=#946e49></td>
<td width="1" height="1"
bgcolor=#8b6842></td>
<td width="1" height="1"
bgcolor=#926644></td>
<td width="1" height="1"
bgcolor=#8e6341></td>
<td width="1" height="1"
bgcolor=#8d5e40></td>
<td width="1" height="1"
bgcolor=#895b3d></td>
<td width="1" height="1"
bgcolor=#805235></td>
<td width="1" height="1"
bgcolor=#8f6340></td>
<td width="1" height="1"
bgcolor=#916541></td>
<td width="1" height="1"
bgcolor=#956c44></td>
<td width="1" height="1"
bgcolor=#8d643c></td>
<td width="1" height="1"
bgcolor=#976f46></td>
<td width="1" height="1"
bgcolor=#997245></td>
<td width="1" height="1"
bgcolor=#a38252></td>
<td width="1" height="1"
bgcolor=#a17f4e></td>
<td width="1" height="1"
bgcolor=#997c4f></td>
<td width="1" height="1"
bgcolor=#96784b></td>
<td width="1" height="1"
bgcolor=#95794b></td>
<td width="1" height="1"
bgcolor=#956f43></td>
<td width="1" height="1"
bgcolor=#926840></td>
<td width="1" height="1"
bgcolor=#91663d></td>
<td width="1" height="1"
bgcolor=#90663e></td>
<td width="1" height="1"
bgcolor=#8d643e></td>
<td width="1" height="1"
bgcolor=#8b603b></td>
<td width="1" height="1"
bgcolor=#90653e></td>
<td width="1" height="1"
bgcolor=#92643f></td>
<td width="1" height="1"
bgcolor=#91633f></td>
<td width="1" height="1"
bgcolor=#916042></td>
<td width="1" height="1"
bgcolor=#8b5b3f></td>
<td width="1" height="1"
bgcolor=#905b3f></td>
<td width="1" height="1"
bgcolor=#7f5746></td>
</tr>
<tr>
<td width="1" height="1"
bgcolor=#824d3a></td>
<td width="1" height="1"
bgcolor=#804c37></td>
<td width="1" height="1"
bgcolor=#804f2e></td>
<td width="1" height="1"
bgcolor=#8b5932></td>
<td width="1" height="1"
bgcolor=#8e5f34></td>
<td width="1" height="1"
bgcolor=#926439></td>
<td width="1" height="1"
bgcolor=#8a5b32></td>
<td width="1" height="1"
bgcolor=#8f613b></td>
<td width="1" height="1"
bgcolor=#825132></td>
<td width="1" height="1"
bgcolor=#8d663e></td>
<td width="1" height="1"
bgcolor=#8e6239></td>
<td width="1" height="1"
bgcolor=#825534></td>
<td width="1" height="1"
bgcolor=#825435></td>
<td width="1" height="1"
bgcolor=#7c4b2d></td>
```

```
    <td width="1" height="1" bgcolor=#7c5030></td>
    <td width="1" height="1" bgcolor=#814c35></td>
    <td width="1" height="1" bgcolor=#8d6039></td>
    <td width="1" height="1" bgcolor=#9a6f40></td>
    <td width="1" height="1" bgcolor=#81522f></td>
    <td width="1" height="1" bgcolor=#7e4c32></td>
    <td width="1" height="1" bgcolor=#7f5030></td>
    <td width="1" height="1" bgcolor=#855a35></td>
    <td width="1" height="1" bgcolor=#7b4f2c></td>
    <td width="1" height="1" bgcolor=#885f37></td>
    <td width="1" height="1" bgcolor=#865d34></td>
    <td width="1" height="1" bgcolor=#8d6534></td>
    <td width="1" height="1" bgcolor=#8f6a3e></td>
    <td width="1" height="1" bgcolor=#886537></td>
    <td width="1" height="1" bgcolor=#896638></td>
    <td width="1" height="1" bgcolor=#876135></td>
    <td width="1" height="1" bgcolor=#896238></td>
    <td width="1" height="1" bgcolor=#8c6739></td>
    <td width="1" height="1" bgcolor=#886439></td>
    <td width="1" height="1" bgcolor=#88653b></td>
    <td width="1" height="1" bgcolor=#8b673b></td>
    <td width="1" height="1" bgcolor=#89673d></td>
    <td width="1" height="1" bgcolor=#8a663c></td>
    <td width="1" height="1" bgcolor=#89623c></td>
    <td width="1" height="1" bgcolor=#855d3b></td>
    <td width="1" height="1" bgcolor=#85633d></td>
    <td width="1" height="1" bgcolor=#95734e></td>
    <td width="1" height="1" bgcolor=#8f6e4a></td>
    <td width="1" height="1" bgcolor=#906f4a></td>
    <td width="1" height="1" bgcolor=#956e49></td>
    <td width="1" height="1" bgcolor=#966f48></td>
    <td width="1" height="1" bgcolor=#956f48></td>
    <td width="1" height="1" bgcolor=#906a45></td>
    <td width="1" height="1" bgcolor=#916a47></td>
    <td width="1" height="1" bgcolor=#926642></td>
    <td width="1" height="1" bgcolor=#906941></td>
    <td width="1" height="1" bgcolor=#977448></td>
    <td width="1" height="1" bgcolor=#946e44></td>
    <td width="1" height="1" bgcolor=#946e46></td>
    <td width="1" height="1" bgcolor=#936d49></td>
    <td width="1" height="1" bgcolor=#93734c></td>
    <td width="1" height="1" bgcolor=#93744a></td>
    <td width="1" height="1" bgcolor=#98734b></td>
    <td width="1" height="1" bgcolor=#97784b></td>
    <td width="1" height="1" bgcolor=#9d834e></td>
    <td width="1" height="1" bgcolor=#9c834d></td>
    <td width="1" height="1" bgcolor=#9c7e45></td>
    <td width="1" height="1" bgcolor=#956f40></td>
    <td width="1" height="1" bgcolor=#8e653a></td>
    <td width="1" height="1" bgcolor=#90633a></td>
    <td width="1" height="1" bgcolor=#8e663f></td>
    <td width="1" height="1" bgcolor=#8e6240></td>
    <td width="1" height="1" bgcolor=#8e6342></td>
    <td width="1" height="1" bgcolor=#906644></td>
    <td width="1" height="1" bgcolor=#8e684a></td>
    <td width="1" height="1" bgcolor=#8d5e45></td>
    <td width="1" height="1" bgcolor=#8b5739></td>
    <td width="1" height="1" bgcolor=#815b47></td>
  </tr>
  <tr>
    <td width="1" height="1" bgcolor=#87523a></td>
    <td width="1" height="1" bgcolor=#7d4e32></td>
    <td width="1" height="1" bgcolor=#805336></td>
    <td width="1" height="1" bgcolor=#7f4f30></td>
    <td width="1" height="1" bgcolor=#8b5b37></td>
    <td width="1" height="1" bgcolor=#886136></td>
    <td width="1" height="1" bgcolor=#876137></td>
    <td width="1" height="1" bgcolor=#8c613a></td>
    <td width="1" height="1" bgcolor=#7d492a></td>
    <td width="1" height="1" bgcolor=#7b432c></td>
    <td width="1" height="1" bgcolor=#8c633d></td>
    <td width="1" height="1" bgcolor=#81502e></td>
    <td width="1" height="1" bgcolor=#804e30></td>
    <td width="1" height="1" bgcolor=#7c482f></td>
    <td width="1" height="1" bgcolor=#774630></td>
    <td width="1" height="1" bgcolor=#7f4f31></td>
    <td width="1" height="1" bgcolor=#8e5f3b></td>
    <td width="1" height="1" bgcolor=#936741></td>
    <td width="1" height="1" bgcolor=#825233></td>
    <td width="1" height="1" bgcolor=#814f32></td>
    <td width="1" height="1" bgcolor=#885435></td>
    <td width="1" height="1" bgcolor=#885a34></td>
    <td width="1" height="1" bgcolor=#8f5f3b></td>
    <td width="1" height="1" bgcolor=#895835></td>
    <td width="1" height="1" bgcolor=#8e6139></td>
    <td width="1" height="1" bgcolor=#8e683c></td>
    <td width="1" height="1" bgcolor=#926b3f></td>
    <td width="1" height="1" bgcolor=#8f653a></td>
```

```
    <td width="1" height="1"
bgcolor=#8d693d></td>
    <td width="1" height="1"
bgcolor=#8c643c></td>
    <td width="1" height="1"
bgcolor=#8e6440></td>
    <td width="1" height="1"
bgcolor=#8f673a></td>
    <td width="1" height="1"
bgcolor=#926c40></td>
    <td width="1" height="1"
bgcolor=#926d40></td>
    <td width="1" height="1"
bgcolor=#8b6a3c></td>
    <td width="1" height="1"
bgcolor=#946f42></td>
    <td width="1" height="1"
bgcolor=#94724a></td>
    <td width="1" height="1"
bgcolor=#8f6b45></td>
    <td width="1" height="1"
bgcolor=#8d633f></td>
    <td width="1" height="1"
bgcolor=#8b603b></td>
    <td width="1" height="1"
bgcolor=#94724d></td>
    <td width="1" height="1"
bgcolor=#97754a></td>
    <td width="1" height="1"
bgcolor=#94714e></td>
    <td width="1" height="1"
bgcolor=#95724e></td>
    <td width="1" height="1"
bgcolor=#95724f></td>
    <td width="1" height="1"
bgcolor=#997650></td>
    <td width="1" height="1"
bgcolor=#946d48></td>
    <td width="1" height="1"
bgcolor=#8d6b45></td>
    <td width="1" height="1"
bgcolor=#936e48></td>
    <td width="1" height="1"
bgcolor=#926a45></td>
    <td width="1" height="1"
bgcolor=#966b46></td>
    <td width="1" height="1"
bgcolor=#976a44></td>
    <td width="1" height="1"
bgcolor=#956a43></td>
    <td width="1" height="1"
bgcolor=#9a7149></td>
    <td width="1" height="1"
bgcolor=#987347></td>
    <td width="1" height="1"
bgcolor=#977748></td>
    <td width="1" height="1"
bgcolor=#917043></td>
    <td width="1" height="1"
bgcolor=#956e44></td>
    <td width="1" height="1"
bgcolor=#96774c></td>
    <td width="1" height="1"
bgcolor=#94774a></td>
    <td width="1" height="1"
bgcolor=#987246></td>
    <td width="1" height="1"
bgcolor=#967546></td>
    <td width="1" height="1"
bgcolor=#97734b></td>
    <td width="1" height="1"
bgcolor=#926e41></td>
    <td width="1" height="1"
bgcolor=#926c42></td>
    <td width="1" height="1"
bgcolor=#906740></td>
    <td width="1" height="1"
bgcolor=#916741></td>
    <td width="1" height="1"
bgcolor=#8d613f></td>
    <td width="1" height="1"
bgcolor=#8a5735></td>
    <td width="1" height="1"
bgcolor=#8e5738></td>
    <td width="1" height="1"
bgcolor=#8c593a></td>
    <td width="1" height="1"
bgcolor=#815744></td>
  </tr>
  <tr>
    <td width="1" height="1"
bgcolor=#8b5d3e></td>
    <td width="1" height="1"
bgcolor=#7b5132></td>
    <td width="1" height="1"
bgcolor=#7c4f33></td>
    <td width="1" height="1"
bgcolor=#7e4e2e></td>
    <td width="1" height="1"
bgcolor=#82542e></td>
    <td width="1" height="1"
bgcolor=#81592e></td>
    <td width="1" height="1"
bgcolor=#8b643b></td>
    <td width="1" height="1"
bgcolor=#8b653d></td>
    <td width="1" height="1"
bgcolor=#865f38></td>
    <td width="1" height="1"
bgcolor=#835031></td>
    <td width="1" height="1"
bgcolor=#7d482e></td>
    <td width="1" height="1"
bgcolor=#7e4b33></td>
    <td width="1" height="1"
bgcolor=#7c482d></td>
    <td width="1" height="1"
bgcolor=#84522f></td>
    <td width="1" height="1"
bgcolor=#7e4a2d></td>
    <td width="1" height="1"
bgcolor=#7b472b></td>
    <td width="1" height="1"
bgcolor=#7d492f></td>
    <td width="1" height="1"
bgcolor=#78482c></td>
    <td width="1" height="1"
bgcolor=#77442b></td>
    <td width="1" height="1"
bgcolor=#7f4b33></td>
    <td width="1" height="1"
bgcolor=#835132></td>
    <td width="1" height="1"
bgcolor=#7e4f2f></td>
    <td width="1" height="1"
bgcolor=#8c5d3b></td>
    <td width="1" height="1"
bgcolor=#90633f></td>
    <td width="1" height="1"
bgcolor=#8f663f></td>
    <td width="1" height="1"
bgcolor=#8f643d></td>
    <td width="1" height="1"
bgcolor=#8f693f></td>
    <td width="1" height="1"
bgcolor=#8e6e42></td>
    <td width="1" height="1"
bgcolor=#95714a></td>
    <td width="1" height="1"
bgcolor=#916a44></td>
    <td width="1" height="1"
bgcolor=#916741></td>
    <td width="1" height="1"
bgcolor=#906940></td>
    <td width="1" height="1"
bgcolor=#90683e></td>
    <td width="1" height="1"
bgcolor=#9f7d54></td>
    <td width="1" height="1"
bgcolor=#8f6e45></td>
    <td width="1" height="1"
bgcolor=#9d7c54></td>
    <td width="1" height="1"
bgcolor=#9b7e58></td>
    <td width="1" height="1"
bgcolor=#a2825c></td>
    <td width="1" height="1"
bgcolor=#9e7a55></td>
    <td width="1" height="1"
bgcolor=#9c754d></td>
    <td width="1" height="1"
bgcolor=#97744c></td>
    <td width="1" height="1"
bgcolor=#9a774b></td>
```

```
    <td width="1" height="1"
bgcolor=#987146></td>
    <td width="1" height="1"
bgcolor=#977146></td>
    <td width="1" height="1"
bgcolor=#997248></td>
    <td width="1" height="1"
bgcolor=#97714a></td>
    <td width="1" height="1"
bgcolor=#997049></td>
    <td width="1" height="1"
bgcolor=#916d45></td>
    <td width="1" height="1"
bgcolor=#937347></td>
    <td width="1" height="1"
bgcolor=#947244></td>
    <td width="1" height="1"
bgcolor=#967042></td>
    <td width="1" height="1"
bgcolor=#946b3f></td>
    <td width="1" height="1"
bgcolor=#987144></td>
    <td width="1" height="1"
bgcolor=#987647></td>
    <td width="1" height="1"
bgcolor=#9f7b4d></td>
    <td width="1" height="1"
bgcolor=#9a7042></td>
    <td width="1" height="1"
bgcolor=#9b703f></td>
    <td width="1" height="1"
bgcolor=#997241></td>
    <td width="1" height="1"
bgcolor=#9f7b4a></td>
    <td width="1" height="1"
bgcolor=#9b7643></td>
    <td width="1" height="1"
bgcolor=#977245></td>
    <td width="1" height="1"
bgcolor=#8f6942></td>
    <td width="1" height="1"
bgcolor=#8e6039></td>
    <td width="1" height="1"
bgcolor=#8f6339></td>
    <td width="1" height="1"
bgcolor=#8d613c></td>
    <td width="1" height="1"
bgcolor=#8f603e></td>
    <td width="1" height="1"
bgcolor=#8e5f3b></td>
    <td width="1" height="1"
bgcolor=#91623f></td>
    <td width="1" height="1"
bgcolor=#93623d></td>
    <td width="1" height="1"
bgcolor=#906040></td>
    <td width="1" height="1"
bgcolor=#906548></td>
    <td width="1" height="1"
bgcolor=#7f5b4a></td>
  </tr>
  <tr>
    <td width="1" height="1"
bgcolor=#91633f></td>
    <td width="1" height="1"
bgcolor=#7e4f2f></td>
    <td width="1" height="1"
bgcolor=#834f36></td>
    <td width="1" height="1"
bgcolor=#815433></td>
    <td width="1" height="1"
bgcolor=#825430></td>
    <td width="1" height="1"
bgcolor=#896438></td>
    <td width="1" height="1"
bgcolor=#88673c></td>
    <td width="1" height="1"
bgcolor=#865f37></td>
    <td width="1" height="1"
bgcolor=#855a3b></td>
    <td width="1" height="1"
bgcolor=#7e4d2e></td>
    <td width="1" height="1"
bgcolor=#7e482e></td>
    <td width="1" height="1"
bgcolor=#825739></td>
    <td width="1" height="1"
bgcolor=#8b6040></td>
    <td width="1" height="1"
bgcolor=#885d3c></td>
    <td width="1" height="1"
bgcolor=#826039></td>
    <td width="1" height="1"
bgcolor=#87653d></td>
    <td width="1" height="1"
bgcolor=#8c6a40></td>
    <td width="1" height="1"
bgcolor=#8e6c46></td>
    <td width="1" height="1"
bgcolor=#87653d></td>
    <td width="1" height="1"
bgcolor=#8e6a41></td>
    <td width="1" height="1"
bgcolor=#8e6941></td>
    <td width="1" height="1"
bgcolor=#8f6742></td>
    <td width="1" height="1"
bgcolor=#936e47></td>
    <td width="1" height="1"
bgcolor=#8f6e46></td>
    <td width="1" height="1"
bgcolor=#93764f></td>
    <td width="1" height="1"
bgcolor=#94744c></td>
    <td width="1" height="1"
bgcolor=#916e47></td>
    <td width="1" height="1"
bgcolor=#8f6b44></td>
    <td width="1" height="1"
bgcolor=#896f48></td>
    <td width="1" height="1"
bgcolor=#8e7048></td>
    <td width="1" height="1"
bgcolor=#856238></td>
    <td width="1" height="1"
bgcolor=#8d7248></td>
    <td width="1" height="1"
bgcolor=#8a6840></td>
    <td width="1" height="1"
bgcolor=#99855a></td>
    <td width="1" height="1"
bgcolor=#988960></td>
    <td width="1" height="1"
bgcolor=#977e59></td>
    <td width="1" height="1"
bgcolor=#9c805e></td>
    <td width="1" height="1"
bgcolor=#967953></td>
    <td width="1" height="1"
bgcolor=#9e8059></td>
    <td width="1" height="1"
bgcolor=#997c55></td>
    <td width="1" height="1"
bgcolor=#967b55></td>
    <td width="1" height="1"
bgcolor=#9c7c54></td>
    <td width="1" height="1"
bgcolor=#a07d54></td>
    <td width="1" height="1"
bgcolor=#9b7950></td>
    <td width="1" height="1"
bgcolor=#9d7a51></td>
    <td width="1" height="1"
bgcolor=#9d7c51></td>
    <td width="1" height="1"
bgcolor=#99744a></td>
    <td width="1" height="1"
bgcolor=#97764b></td>
    <td width="1" height="1"
bgcolor=#977345></td>
    <td width="1" height="1"
bgcolor=#916a44></td>
    <td width="1" height="1"
bgcolor=#956c48></td>
    <td width="1" height="1"
bgcolor=#966d45></td>
    <td width="1" height="1"
bgcolor=#966f46></td>
    <td width="1" height="1"
bgcolor=#967647></td>
    <td width="1" height="1"
bgcolor=#9b7c4a></td>
    <td width="1" height="1"
bgcolor=#9a7944></td>
```

```
    <td width="1" height="1"
bgcolor=#997a46></td>
    <td width="1" height="1"
bgcolor=#9c7d49></td>
    <td width="1" height="1"
bgcolor=#986a3d></td>
    <td width="1" height="1"
bgcolor=#99623b></td>
    <td width="1" height="1"
bgcolor=#96683d></td>
    <td width="1" height="1"
bgcolor=#916034></td>
    <td width="1" height="1"
bgcolor=#8d5f38></td>
    <td width="1" height="1"
bgcolor=#956c44></td>
    <td width="1" height="1"
bgcolor=#8c6240></td>
    <td width="1" height="1"
bgcolor=#8d5939></td>
    <td width="1" height="1"
bgcolor=#885332></td>
    <td width="1" height="1"
bgcolor=#8f5b3c></td>
    <td width="1" height="1"
bgcolor=#8e5d3e></td>
    <td width="1" height="1"
bgcolor=#8f644b></td>
    <td width="1" height="1"
bgcolor=#8d694f></td>
    <td width="1" height="1"
bgcolor=#846456></td>
  </tr>
  <tr>
    <td width="1" height="1"
bgcolor=#956c41></td>
    <td width="1" height="1"
bgcolor=#845f3b></td>
    <td width="1" height="1"
bgcolor=#845a37></td>
    <td width="1" height="1"
bgcolor=#89633c></td>
    <td width="1" height="1"
bgcolor=#836039></td>
    <td width="1" height="1"
bgcolor=#856340></td>
    <td width="1" height="1"
bgcolor=#8a6341></td>
    <td width="1" height="1"
bgcolor=#7e5f39></td>
    <td width="1" height="1"
bgcolor=#7d5334></td>
    <td width="1" height="1"
bgcolor=#86593a></td>
    <td width="1" height="1"
bgcolor=#88623d></td>
    <td width="1" height="1"
bgcolor=#87623d></td>
    <td width="1" height="1"
bgcolor=#8c7d57></td>
    <td width="1" height="1"
bgcolor=#896d47></td>
    <td width="1" height="1"
bgcolor=#8c6b45></td>
    <td width="1" height="1"
bgcolor=#886442></td>
    <td width="1" height="1"
bgcolor=#927447></td>
    <td width="1" height="1"
bgcolor=#90724b></td>
    <td width="1" height="1"
bgcolor=#8a6841></td>
    <td width="1" height="1"
bgcolor=#8a6b44></td>
    <td width="1" height="1"
bgcolor=#8b6e48></td>
    <td width="1" height="1"
bgcolor=#8d744b></td>
    <td width="1" height="1"
bgcolor=#8f6e4a></td>
    <td width="1" height="1"
bgcolor=#8d7148></td>
    <td width="1" height="1"
bgcolor=#8f7950></td>
    <td width="1" height="1"
bgcolor=#8a704d></td>
    <td width="1" height="1"
bgcolor=#846b41></td>
    <td width="1" height="1"
bgcolor=#866942></td>
    <td width="1" height="1"
bgcolor=#8f7a4f></td>
    <td width="1" height="1"
bgcolor=#8b7852></td>
    <td width="1" height="1"
bgcolor=#8f805d></td>
    <td width="1" height="1"
bgcolor=#90815e></td>
    <td width="1" height="1"
bgcolor=#998a67></td>
    <td width="1" height="1"
bgcolor=#968d67></td>
    <td width="1" height="1"
bgcolor=#938460></td>
    <td width="1" height="1"
bgcolor=#998563></td>
    <td width="1" height="1"
bgcolor=#95855f></td>
    <td width="1" height="1"
bgcolor=#968963></td>
    <td width="1" height="1"
bgcolor=#978864></td>
    <td width="1" height="1"
bgcolor=#9a8462></td>
    <td width="1" height="1"
bgcolor=#96835e></td>
    <td width="1" height="1"
bgcolor=#97865e></td>
    <td width="1" height="1"
bgcolor=#9b8561></td>
    <td width="1" height="1"
bgcolor=#9a835f></td>
    <td width="1" height="1"
bgcolor=#9d8861></td>
    <td width="1" height="1"
bgcolor=#9b8057></td>
    <td width="1" height="1"
bgcolor=#987e55></td>
    <td width="1" height="1"
bgcolor=#977f55></td>
    <td width="1" height="1"
bgcolor=#967a4c></td>
    <td width="1" height="1"
bgcolor=#957646></td>
    <td width="1" height="1"
bgcolor=#917648></td>
    <td width="1" height="1"
bgcolor=#967345></td>
    <td width="1" height="1"
bgcolor=#977142></td>
    <td width="1" height="1"
bgcolor=#957147></td>
    <td width="1" height="1"
bgcolor=#987649></td>
    <td width="1" height="1"
bgcolor=#997a45></td>
    <td width="1" height="1"
bgcolor=#977647></td>
    <td width="1" height="1"
bgcolor=#9b7a49></td>
    <td width="1" height="1"
bgcolor=#9d7a48></td>
    <td width="1" height="1"
bgcolor=#9e8044></td>
    <td width="1" height="1"
bgcolor=#966e3b></td>
    <td width="1" height="1"
bgcolor=#9b6c35></td>
    <td width="1" height="1"
bgcolor=#976b39></td>
    <td width="1" height="1"
bgcolor=#946938></td>
    <td width="1" height="1"
bgcolor=#976538></td>
    <td width="1" height="1"
bgcolor=#9e6e41></td>
    <td width="1" height="1"
bgcolor=#946b40></td>
    <td width="1" height="1"
bgcolor=#927149></td>
    <td width="1" height="1"
bgcolor=#8d7651></td>
    <td width="1" height="1"
bgcolor=#8d7759></td>
```

```
    <td width="1" height="1" bgcolor=#8e7456></td>
    <td width="1" height="1" bgcolor=#7d6650></td>
  </tr>
  <tr>
    <td width="1" height="1" bgcolor=#956c40></td>
    <td width="1" height="1" bgcolor=#855f3b></td>
    <td width="1" height="1" bgcolor=#8c6b46></td>
    <td width="1" height="1" bgcolor=#8b6f45></td>
    <td width="1" height="1" bgcolor=#876940></td>
    <td width="1" height="1" bgcolor=#8f714a></td>
    <td width="1" height="1" bgcolor=#8b7048></td>
    <td width="1" height="1" bgcolor=#896741></td>
    <td width="1" height="1" bgcolor=#87673e></td>
    <td width="1" height="1" bgcolor=#83623b></td>
    <td width="1" height="1" bgcolor=#8d744b></td>
    <td width="1" height="1" bgcolor=#87633d></td>
    <td width="1" height="1" bgcolor=#8f8363></td>
    <td width="1" height="1" bgcolor=#8a6845></td>
    <td width="1" height="1" bgcolor=#8c6d45></td>
    <td width="1" height="1" bgcolor=#8b643d></td>
    <td width="1" height="1" bgcolor=#8e734b></td>
    <td width="1" height="1" bgcolor=#917653></td>
    <td width="1" height="1" bgcolor=#82613c></td>
    <td width="1" height="1" bgcolor=#8b6f45></td>
    <td width="1" height="1" bgcolor=#8d784e></td>
    <td width="1" height="1" bgcolor=#8d7956></td>
    <td width="1" height="1" bgcolor=#8c734f></td>
    <td width="1" height="1" bgcolor=#8c6c44></td>
    <td width="1" height="1" bgcolor=#8d714e></td>
    <td width="1" height="1" bgcolor=#91775a></td>
    <td width="1" height="1" bgcolor=#896b46></td>
    <td width="1" height="1" bgcolor=#8a6d43></td>
    <td width="1" height="1" bgcolor=#958466></td>
    <td width="1" height="1" bgcolor=#968d6f></td>
    <td width="1" height="1" bgcolor=#939176></td>
    <td width="1" height="1" bgcolor=#969171></td>
    <td width="1" height="1" bgcolor=#9a9173></td>
    <td width="1" height="1" bgcolor=#918b6c></td>
    <td width="1" height="1" bgcolor=#968563></td>
    <td width="1" height="1" bgcolor=#978564></td>
    <td width="1" height="1" bgcolor=#948661></td>
    <td width="1" height="1" bgcolor=#938560></td>
    <td width="1" height="1" bgcolor=#968563></td>
    <td width="1" height="1" bgcolor=#958561></td>
    <td width="1" height="1" bgcolor=#958461></td>
    <td width="1" height="1" bgcolor=#998761></td>
    <td width="1" height="1" bgcolor=#998664></td>
    <td width="1" height="1" bgcolor=#998662></td>
    <td width="1" height="1" bgcolor=#978560></td>
    <td width="1" height="1" bgcolor=#968256></td>
    <td width="1" height="1" bgcolor=#978056></td>
    <td width="1" height="1" bgcolor=#997d55></td>
    <td width="1" height="1" bgcolor=#957d4e></td>
    <td width="1" height="1" bgcolor=#967e4d></td>
    <td width="1" height="1" bgcolor=#947945></td>
    <td width="1" height="1" bgcolor=#967545></td>
    <td width="1" height="1" bgcolor=#977743></td>
    <td width="1" height="1" bgcolor=#927741></td>
    <td width="1" height="1" bgcolor=#957947></td>
    <td width="1" height="1" bgcolor=#947546></td>
    <td width="1" height="1" bgcolor=#977746></td>
    <td width="1" height="1" bgcolor=#947541></td>
    <td width="1" height="1" bgcolor=#987944></td>
    <td width="1" height="1" bgcolor=#967340></td>
    <td width="1" height="1" bgcolor=#926d39></td>
    <td width="1" height="1" bgcolor=#99723f></td>
    <td width="1" height="1" bgcolor=#8f703c></td>
    <td width="1" height="1" bgcolor=#8f6b3a></td>
    <td width="1" height="1" bgcolor=#926f3e></td>
    <td width="1" height="1" bgcolor=#997c43></td>
    <td width="1" height="1" bgcolor=#967b45></td>
    <td width="1" height="1" bgcolor=#967f4b></td>
    <td width="1" height="1" bgcolor=#927c4d></td>
    <td width="1" height="1" bgcolor=#8a7151></td>
    <td width="1" height="1" bgcolor=#8e795b></td>
    <td width="1" height="1" bgcolor=#7e6a56></td>
  </tr>
  <tr>
    <td width="1" height="1" bgcolor=#9a7c47></td>
    <td width="1" height="1" bgcolor=#917346></td>
    <td width="1" height="1" bgcolor=#917e50></td>
    <td width="1" height="1" bgcolor=#9c865c></td>
    <td width="1" height="1" bgcolor=#957e54></td>
    <td width="1" height="1" bgcolor=#957e57></td>
    <td width="1" height="1" bgcolor=#938762></td>
    <td width="1" height="1" bgcolor=#86694a></td>
    <td width="1" height="1" bgcolor=#8a6e46></td>
    <td width="1" height="1" bgcolor=#8a6d48></td>
    <td width="1" height="1" bgcolor=#927b58></td>
```

```
    <td width="1" height="1"
bgcolor=#8f734d></td>
    <td width="1" height="1"
bgcolor=#98967a></td>
    <td width="1" height="1"
bgcolor=#917654></td>
    <td width="1" height="1"
bgcolor=#8f7953></td>
    <td width="1" height="1"
bgcolor=#896843></td>
    <td width="1" height="1"
bgcolor=#9c8b6c></td>
    <td width="1" height="1"
bgcolor=#8e805e></td>
    <td width="1" height="1"
bgcolor=#866640></td>
    <td width="1" height="1"
bgcolor=#8f6c44></td>
    <td width="1" height="1"
bgcolor=#958158></td>
    <td width="1" height="1"
bgcolor=#9b896b></td>
    <td width="1" height="1"
bgcolor=#907c61></td>
    <td width="1" height="1"
bgcolor=#967c5d></td>
    <td width="1" height="1"
bgcolor=#907958></td>
    <td width="1" height="1"
bgcolor=#938968></td>
    <td width="1" height="1"
bgcolor=#948060></td>
    <td width="1" height="1"
bgcolor=#9b8c6c></td>
    <td width="1" height="1"
bgcolor=#9c9374></td>
    <td width="1" height="1"
bgcolor=#9c9377></td>
    <td width="1" height="1"
bgcolor=#9c947b></td>
    <td width="1" height="1"
bgcolor=#9d9274></td>
    <td width="1" height="1"
bgcolor=#9c8c70></td>
    <td width="1" height="1"
bgcolor=#9c8c6f></td>
    <td width="1" height="1"
bgcolor=#988061></td>
    <td width="1" height="1"
bgcolor=#a08869></td>
    <td width="1" height="1"
bgcolor=#988663></td>
    <td width="1" height="1"
bgcolor=#998a67></td>
    <td width="1" height="1"
bgcolor=#998765></td>
    <td width="1" height="1"
bgcolor=#958160></td>
    <td width="1" height="1"
bgcolor=#9a8562></td>
    <td width="1" height="1"
bgcolor=#9c8261></td>
    <td width="1" height="1"
bgcolor=#967d58></td>
    <td width="1" height="1"
bgcolor=#987f59></td>
    <td width="1" height="1"
bgcolor=#99815a></td>
    <td width="1" height="1"
bgcolor=#997952></td>
    <td width="1" height="1"
bgcolor=#9a7e55></td>
    <td width="1" height="1"
bgcolor=#947c53></td>
    <td width="1" height="1"
bgcolor=#977f59></td>
    <td width="1" height="1"
bgcolor=#927e53></td>
    <td width="1" height="1"
bgcolor=#987d48></td>
    <td width="1" height="1"
bgcolor=#9a7b4b></td>
    <td width="1" height="1"
bgcolor=#977a4f></td>
    <td width="1" height="1"
bgcolor=#998156></td>
    <td width="1" height="1"
bgcolor=#977d50></td>
    <td width="1" height="1"
bgcolor=#947648></td>
    <td width="1" height="1"
bgcolor=#967549></td>
    <td width="1" height="1"
bgcolor=#97794b></td>
    <td width="1" height="1"
bgcolor=#95794a></td>
    <td width="1" height="1"
bgcolor=#977647></td>
    <td width="1" height="1"
bgcolor=#977c46></td>
    <td width="1" height="1"
bgcolor=#937847></td>
    <td width="1" height="1"
bgcolor=#987242></td>
    <td width="1" height="1"
bgcolor=#977646></td>
    <td width="1" height="1"
bgcolor=#937c4b></td>
    <td width="1" height="1"
bgcolor=#927b4a></td>
    <td width="1" height="1"
bgcolor=#947d4f></td>
    <td width="1" height="1"
bgcolor=#91794e></td>
    <td width="1" height="1"
bgcolor=#907049></td>
    <td width="1" height="1"
bgcolor=#927452></td>
    <td width="1" height="1"
bgcolor=#8f775b></td>
    <td width="1" height="1"
bgcolor=#7b6853></td>
  </tr>
  <tr>
    <td width="1" height="1"
bgcolor=#9c8b6c></td>
    <td width="1" height="1"
bgcolor=#98876b></td>
    <td width="1" height="1"
bgcolor=#96866e></td>
    <td width="1" height="1"
bgcolor=#998c71></td>
    <td width="1" height="1"
bgcolor=#998f71></td>
    <td width="1" height="1"
bgcolor=#978f7a></td>
    <td width="1" height="1"
bgcolor=#96948d></td>
    <td width="1" height="1"
bgcolor=#969484></td>
    <td width="1" height="1"
bgcolor=#948a77></td>
    <td width="1" height="1"
bgcolor=#928d79></td>
    <td width="1" height="1"
bgcolor=#969180></td>
    <td width="1" height="1"
bgcolor=#989482></td>
    <td width="1" height="1"
bgcolor=#9a9a90></td>
    <td width="1" height="1"
bgcolor=#928f7e></td>
    <td width="1" height="1"
bgcolor=#96927c></td>
    <td width="1" height="1"
bgcolor=#92886e></td>
    <td width="1" height="1"
bgcolor=#9b9a87></td>
    <td width="1" height="1"
bgcolor=#989580></td>
    <td width="1" height="1"
bgcolor=#8b734f></td>
    <td width="1" height="1"
bgcolor=#907955></td>
    <td width="1" height="1"
bgcolor=#988e70></td>
    <td width="1" height="1"
bgcolor=#989379></td>
    <td width="1" height="1"
bgcolor=#958d71></td>
    <td width="1" height="1"
bgcolor=#968d74></td>
    <td width="1" height="1"
bgcolor=#978c72></td>
```

```
<td width="1" height="1"
bgcolor=#928265></td>
<td width="1" height="1"
bgcolor=#988970></td>
<td width="1" height="1"
bgcolor=#998e70></td>
<td width="1" height="1"
bgcolor=#9d886f></td>
<td width="1" height="1"
bgcolor=#958368></td>
<td width="1" height="1"
bgcolor=#97876b></td>
<td width="1" height="1"
bgcolor=#9e8766></td>
<td width="1" height="1"
bgcolor=#977f60></td>
<td width="1" height="1"
bgcolor=#9b8263></td>
<td width="1" height="1"
bgcolor=#997e5d></td>
<td width="1" height="1"
bgcolor=#9d7a5c></td>
<td width="1" height="1"
bgcolor=#967757></td>
<td width="1" height="1"
bgcolor=#9b805c></td>
<td width="1" height="1"
bgcolor=#987a59></td>
<td width="1" height="1"
bgcolor=#987956></td>
<td width="1" height="1"
bgcolor=#9c7953></td>
<td width="1" height="1"
bgcolor=#9c7e59></td>
<td width="1" height="1"
bgcolor=#9c805b></td>
<td width="1" height="1"
bgcolor=#9d815c></td>
<td width="1" height="1"
bgcolor=#987c57></td>
<td width="1" height="1"
bgcolor=#9b7c53></td>
<td width="1" height="1"
bgcolor=#997e56></td>
<td width="1" height="1"
bgcolor=#9b835b></td>
<td width="1" height="1"
bgcolor=#957e5c></td>
<td width="1" height="1"
bgcolor=#947752></td>
<td width="1" height="1"
bgcolor=#987749></td>
<td width="1" height="1"
bgcolor=#96764c></td>
<td width="1" height="1"
bgcolor=#9a8258></td>
<td width="1" height="1"
bgcolor=#9a8159></td>
<td width="1" height="1"
bgcolor=#997d51></td>
<td width="1" height="1"
bgcolor=#9a7c4f></td>
<td width="1" height="1"
bgcolor=#987d51></td>
<td width="1" height="1"
bgcolor=#988153></td>
<td width="1" height="1"
bgcolor=#97794c></td>
<td width="1" height="1"
bgcolor=#987d4f></td>
<td width="1" height="1"
bgcolor=#957f50></td>
<td width="1" height="1"
bgcolor=#9a784d></td>
<td width="1" height="1"
bgcolor=#957c4c></td>
<td width="1" height="1"
bgcolor=#9a8757></td>
<td width="1" height="1"
bgcolor=#948354></td>
<td width="1" height="1"
bgcolor=#958659></td>
<td width="1" height="1"
bgcolor=#948458></td>
<td width="1" height="1"
bgcolor=#948054></td>
<td width="1" height="1"
bgcolor=#907e53></td>
<td width="1" height="1"
bgcolor=#918660></td>
<td width="1" height="1"
bgcolor=#8e755d></td>
<td width="1" height="1"
bgcolor=#81715e></td>
</tr>
<tr>
<td width="1" height="1"
bgcolor=#9b9585></td>
<td width="1" height="1"
bgcolor=#968d77></td>
<td width="1" height="1"
bgcolor=#968a70></td>
<td width="1" height="1"
bgcolor=#948a7c></td>
<td width="1" height="1"
bgcolor=#94927d></td>
<td width="1" height="1"
bgcolor=#938f81></td>
<td width="1" height="1"
bgcolor=#999286></td>
<td width="1" height="1"
bgcolor=#92918b></td>
<td width="1" height="1"
bgcolor=#96968c></td>
<td width="1" height="1"
bgcolor=#9a958f></td>
<td width="1" height="1"
bgcolor=#939184></td>
<td width="1" height="1"
bgcolor=#999989></td>
<td width="1" height="1"
bgcolor=#999286></td>
<td width="1" height="1"
bgcolor=#999986></td>
<td width="1" height="1"
bgcolor=#95938d></td>
<td width="1" height="1"
bgcolor=#9b968a></td>
<td width="1" height="1"
bgcolor=#9b9889></td>
<td width="1" height="1"
bgcolor=#939282></td>
<td width="1" height="1"
bgcolor=#8e8469></td>
<td width="1" height="1"
bgcolor=#949178></td>
<td width="1" height="1"
bgcolor=#979482></td>
<td width="1" height="1"
bgcolor=#969484></td>
<td width="1" height="1"
bgcolor=#969580></td>
<td width="1" height="1"
bgcolor=#999683></td>
<td width="1" height="1"
bgcolor=#97927b></td>
<td width="1" height="1"
bgcolor=#9c9178></td>
<td width="1" height="1"
bgcolor=#a29884></td>
<td width="1" height="1"
bgcolor=#939077></td>
<td width="1" height="1"
bgcolor=#9a927a></td>
<td width="1" height="1"
bgcolor=#9e957d></td>
<td width="1" height="1"
bgcolor=#998f77></td>
<td width="1" height="1"
bgcolor=#999579></td>
<td width="1" height="1"
bgcolor=#9b9577></td>
<td width="1" height="1"
bgcolor=#968e6e></td>
<td width="1" height="1"
bgcolor=#968665></td>
<td width="1" height="1"
bgcolor=#9b8667></td>
<td width="1" height="1"
bgcolor=#978565></td>
<td width="1" height="1"
bgcolor=#928866></td>
<td width="1" height="1"
bgcolor=#938869></td>
```

```
    <td width="1" height="1"
bgcolor=#948261></td>
    <td width="1" height="1"
bgcolor=#9a825d></td>
    <td width="1" height="1"
bgcolor=#95805c></td>
    <td width="1" height="1"
bgcolor=#967d59></td>
    <td width="1" height="1"
bgcolor=#987f5b></td>
    <td width="1" height="1"
bgcolor=#9b825e></td>
    <td width="1" height="1"
bgcolor=#977e5b></td>
    <td width="1" height="1"
bgcolor=#98815f></td>
    <td width="1" height="1"
bgcolor=#94815f></td>
    <td width="1" height="1"
bgcolor=#907a59></td>
    <td width="1" height="1"
bgcolor=#987a56></td>
    <td width="1" height="1"
bgcolor=#8f744d></td>
    <td width="1" height="1"
bgcolor=#927d54></td>
    <td width="1" height="1"
bgcolor=#94835c></td>
    <td width="1" height="1"
bgcolor=#937a55></td>
    <td width="1" height="1"
bgcolor=#977d54></td>
    <td width="1" height="1"
bgcolor=#967d57></td>
    <td width="1" height="1"
bgcolor=#9a865f></td>
    <td width="1" height="1"
bgcolor=#967e57></td>
    <td width="1" height="1"
bgcolor=#988259></td>
    <td width="1" height="1"
bgcolor=#96875b></td>
    <td width="1" height="1"
bgcolor=#918156></td>
    <td width="1" height="1"
bgcolor=#968358></td>
    <td width="1" height="1"
bgcolor=#938658></td>
    <td width="1" height="1"
bgcolor=#998d60></td>
    <td width="1" height="1"
bgcolor=#8e8457></td>
    <td width="1" height="1"
bgcolor=#928859></td>
    <td width="1" height="1"
bgcolor=#93885b></td>
    <td width="1" height="1"
bgcolor=#8f825f></td>
    <td width="1" height="1"
bgcolor=#8f8962></td>
    <td width="1" height="1"
bgcolor=#938a60></td>
    <td width="1" height="1"
bgcolor=#948560></td>
    <td width="1" height="1"
bgcolor=#7b7865></td>
  </tr>
  <tr>
    <td width="1" height="1"
bgcolor=#a0978b></td>
    <td width="1" height="1"
bgcolor=#9c9484></td>
    <td width="1" height="1"
bgcolor=#968d7c></td>
    <td width="1" height="1"
bgcolor=#988e80></td>
    <td width="1" height="1"
bgcolor=#969280></td>
    <td width="1" height="1"
bgcolor=#959385></td>
    <td width="1" height="1"
bgcolor=#969383></td>
    <td width="1" height="1"
bgcolor=#948f85></td>
    <td width="1" height="1"
bgcolor=#929182></td>
    <td width="1" height="1"
bgcolor=#938e85></td>
    <td width="1" height="1"
bgcolor=#969386></td>
    <td width="1" height="1"
bgcolor=#979189></td>
    <td width="1" height="1"
bgcolor=#939286></td>
    <td width="1" height="1"
bgcolor=#9d988d></td>
    <td width="1" height="1"
bgcolor=#96998a></td>
    <td width="1" height="1"
bgcolor=#939488></td>
    <td width="1" height="1"
bgcolor=#969185></td>
    <td width="1" height="1"
bgcolor=#98968c></td>
    <td width="1" height="1"
bgcolor=#9a9686></td>
    <td width="1" height="1"
bgcolor=#909283></td>
    <td width="1" height="1"
bgcolor=#939486></td>
    <td width="1" height="1"
bgcolor=#969489></td>
    <td width="1" height="1"
bgcolor=#919283></td>
    <td width="1" height="1"
bgcolor=#979686></td>
    <td width="1" height="1"
bgcolor=#95927e></td>
    <td width="1" height="1"
bgcolor=#91937d></td>
    <td width="1" height="1"
bgcolor=#989a86></td>
    <td width="1" height="1"
bgcolor=#979882></td>
    <td width="1" height="1"
bgcolor=#989a84></td>
    <td width="1" height="1"
bgcolor=#9a9b85></td>
    <td width="1" height="1"
bgcolor=#9d9b85></td>
    <td width="1" height="1"
bgcolor=#989783></td>
    <td width="1" height="1"
bgcolor=#96967f></td>
    <td width="1" height="1"
bgcolor=#97937a></td>
    <td width="1" height="1"
bgcolor=#969176></td>
    <td width="1" height="1"
bgcolor=#959378></td>
    <td width="1" height="1"
bgcolor=#938f76></td>
    <td width="1" height="1"
bgcolor=#949278></td>
    <td width="1" height="1"
bgcolor=#939074></td>
    <td width="1" height="1"
bgcolor=#938f70></td>
    <td width="1" height="1"
bgcolor=#958c6b></td>
    <td width="1" height="1"
bgcolor=#968368></td>
    <td width="1" height="1"
bgcolor=#99815f></td>
    <td width="1" height="1"
bgcolor=#978060></td>
    <td width="1" height="1"
bgcolor=#998364></td>
    <td width="1" height="1"
bgcolor=#988264></td>
    <td width="1" height="1"
bgcolor=#978466></td>
    <td width="1" height="1"
bgcolor=#958668></td>
    <td width="1" height="1"
bgcolor=#94805f></td>
    <td width="1" height="1"
bgcolor=#95835e></td>
    <td width="1" height="1"
bgcolor=#928660></td>
    <td width="1" height="1"
bgcolor=#958860></td>
    <td width="1" height="1"
bgcolor=#91815c></td>
```

```
    <td width="1" height="1"
bgcolor=#907d5a></td>
    <td width="1" height="1"
bgcolor=#91825e></td>
    <td width="1" height="1"
bgcolor=#938663></td>
    <td width="1" height="1"
bgcolor=#91855f></td>
    <td width="1" height="1"
bgcolor=#948561></td>
    <td width="1" height="1"
bgcolor=#958b64></td>
    <td width="1" height="1"
bgcolor=#93855e></td>
    <td width="1" height="1"
bgcolor=#928760></td>
    <td width="1" height="1"
bgcolor=#908a60></td>
    <td width="1" height="1"
bgcolor=#95885f></td>
    <td width="1" height="1"
bgcolor=#92895f></td>
    <td width="1" height="1"
bgcolor=#94895f></td>
    <td width="1" height="1"
bgcolor=#938759></td>
    <td width="1" height="1"
bgcolor=#94875b></td>
    <td width="1" height="1"
bgcolor=#8d805c></td>
    <td width="1" height="1"
bgcolor=#8e855c></td>
    <td width="1" height="1"
bgcolor=#958652></td>
    <td width="1" height="1"
bgcolor=#99824e></td>
    <td width="1" height="1"
bgcolor=#837b64></td>
  </tr>
  <tr>
    <td width="1" height="1"
bgcolor=#a29a8a></td>
    <td width="1" height="1"
bgcolor=#9d9583></td>
    <td width="1" height="1"
bgcolor=#9c9480></td>
    <td width="1" height="1"
bgcolor=#998e7b></td>
    <td width="1" height="1"
bgcolor=#9b9281></td>
    <td width="1" height="1"
bgcolor=#9a9482></td>
    <td width="1" height="1"
bgcolor=#949382></td>
    <td width="1" height="1"
bgcolor=#929283></td>
    <td width="1" height="1"
bgcolor=#959182></td>
    <td width="1" height="1"
bgcolor=#968f80></td>
    <td width="1" height="1"
bgcolor=#989281></td>
    <td width="1" height="1"
bgcolor=#959184></td>
    <td width="1" height="1"
bgcolor=#989488></td>
    <td width="1" height="1"
bgcolor=#999589></td>
    <td width="1" height="1"
bgcolor=#96968c></td>
    <td width="1" height="1"
bgcolor=#98968b></td>
    <td width="1" height="1"
bgcolor=#9a988b></td>
    <td width="1" height="1"
bgcolor=#94948b></td>
    <td width="1" height="1"
bgcolor=#96968b></td>
    <td width="1" height="1"
bgcolor=#979789></td>
    <td width="1" height="1"
bgcolor=#989787></td>
    <td width="1" height="1"
bgcolor=#989689></td>
    <td width="1" height="1"
bgcolor=#969587></td>
    <td width="1" height="1"
bgcolor=#9a9989></td>
    <td width="1" height="1"
bgcolor=#989583></td>
    <td width="1" height="1"
bgcolor=#969684></td>
    <td width="1" height="1"
bgcolor=#989985></td>
    <td width="1" height="1"
bgcolor=#9a9c86></td>
    <td width="1" height="1"
bgcolor=#959480></td>
    <td width="1" height="1"
bgcolor=#9b9a86></td>
    <td width="1" height="1"
bgcolor=#9c9b87></td>
    <td width="1" height="1"
bgcolor=#9a9986></td>
    <td width="1" height="1"
bgcolor=#949781></td>
    <td width="1" height="1"
bgcolor=#979680></td>
    <td width="1" height="1"
bgcolor=#989681></td>
    <td width="1" height="1"
bgcolor=#97927e></td>
    <td width="1" height="1"
bgcolor=#94917b></td>
    <td width="1" height="1"
bgcolor=#9a9881></td>
    <td width="1" height="1"
bgcolor=#99947f></td>
    <td width="1" height="1"
bgcolor=#979279></td>
    <td width="1" height="1"
bgcolor=#969178></td>
    <td width="1" height="1"
bgcolor=#98937a></td>
    <td width="1" height="1"
bgcolor=#9b8f72></td>
    <td width="1" height="1"
bgcolor=#978c70></td>
    <td width="1" height="1"
bgcolor=#978d72></td>
    <td width="1" height="1"
bgcolor=#998f71></td>
    <td width="1" height="1"
bgcolor=#978f72></td>
    <td width="1" height="1"
bgcolor=#9a9277></td>
    <td width="1" height="1"
bgcolor=#988d72></td>
    <td width="1" height="1"
bgcolor=#958b6e></td>
    <td width="1" height="1"
bgcolor=#9a9071></td>
    <td width="1" height="1"
bgcolor=#988b68></td>
    <td width="1" height="1"
bgcolor=#948563></td>
    <td width="1" height="1"
bgcolor=#938665></td>
    <td width="1" height="1"
bgcolor=#938768></td>
    <td width="1" height="1"
bgcolor=#91865f></td>
    <td width="1" height="1"
bgcolor=#968866></td>
    <td width="1" height="1"
bgcolor=#9d9469></td>
    <td width="1" height="1"
bgcolor=#938d6a></td>
    <td width="1" height="1"
bgcolor=#948b66></td>
    <td width="1" height="1"
bgcolor=#938968></td>
    <td width="1" height="1"
bgcolor=#948c67></td>
    <td width="1" height="1"
bgcolor=#908966></td>
    <td width="1" height="1"
bgcolor=#8f8b64></td>
    <td width="1" height="1"
bgcolor=#938b61></td>
    <td width="1" height="1"
bgcolor=#918861></td>
    <td width="1" height="1"
bgcolor=#8f8557></td>
```

```
    <td width="1" height="1" bgcolor=#93895c></td>
    <td width="1" height="1" bgcolor=#8e8355></td>
    <td width="1" height="1" bgcolor=#9f9158></td>
    <td width="1" height="1" bgcolor=#9b8c5e></td>
    <td width="1" height="1" bgcolor=#7d7963></td>
  </tr>
  <tr>
    <td width="1" height="1" bgcolor=#a09985></td>
    <td width="1" height="1" bgcolor=#9f9882></td>
    <td width="1" height="1" bgcolor=#9c947e></td>
    <td width="1" height="1" bgcolor=#979283></td>
    <td width="1" height="1" bgcolor=#989487></td>
    <td width="1" height="1" bgcolor=#979384></td>
    <td width="1" height="1" bgcolor=#959080></td>
    <td width="1" height="1" bgcolor=#928f82></td>
    <td width="1" height="1" bgcolor=#97938b></td>
    <td width="1" height="1" bgcolor=#98908b></td>
    <td width="1" height="1" bgcolor=#99918d></td>
    <td width="1" height="1" bgcolor=#9a9688></td>
    <td width="1" height="1" bgcolor=#9c998a></td>
    <td width="1" height="1" bgcolor=#9a9788></td>
    <td width="1" height="1" bgcolor=#9e9a91></td>
    <td width="1" height="1" bgcolor=#9a978c></td>
    <td width="1" height="1" bgcolor=#99978a></td>
    <td width="1" height="1" bgcolor=#99978d></td>
    <td rowspan="1" colspan="2" width="1" height="1" bgcolor=#9b998c></td>
    <td width="1" height="1" bgcolor=#999988></td>
    <td width="1" height="1" bgcolor=#9e9c8f></td>
    <td width="1" height="1" bgcolor=#9d9d90></td>
    <td width="1" height="1" bgcolor=#9a9b8b></td>
    <td width="1" height="1" bgcolor=#9f9e8d></td>
    <td width="1" height="1" bgcolor=#9a9b89></td>
    <td width="1" height="1" bgcolor=#9c9d8a></td>
    <td width="1" height="1" bgcolor=#9ea08a></td>
    <td width="1" height="1" bgcolor=#9c9b87></td>
    <td width="1" height="1" bgcolor=#9f9e8a></td>
    <td width="1" height="1" bgcolor=#9e9d89></td>
    <td width="1" height="1" bgcolor=#9a9c88></td>
    <td width="1" height="1" bgcolor=#979983></td>
    <td width="1" height="1" bgcolor=#9f9a85></td>
    <td width="1" height="1" bgcolor=#97987f></td>
    <td width="1" height="1" bgcolor=#9c9a83></td>
    <td width="1" height="1" bgcolor=#9a9982></td>
    <td width="1" height="1" bgcolor=#979780></td>
    <td width="1" height="1" bgcolor=#999782></td>
    <td width="1" height="1" bgcolor=#9a9680></td>
    <td width="1" height="1" bgcolor=#9d9b83></td>
    <td width="1" height="1" bgcolor=#989880></td>
    <td width="1" height="1" bgcolor=#97987f></td>
    <td width="1" height="1" bgcolor=#929177></td>
    <td width="1" height="1" bgcolor=#9b9a7e></td>
    <td width="1" height="1" bgcolor=#969678></td>
    <td width="1" height="1" bgcolor=#99957a></td>
    <td width="1" height="1" bgcolor=#948e76></td>
    <td width="1" height="1" bgcolor=#96907b></td>
    <td width="1" height="1" bgcolor=#968f79></td>
    <td width="1" height="1" bgcolor=#958d74></td>
    <td width="1" height="1" bgcolor=#988f71></td>
    <td width="1" height="1" bgcolor=#938a6a></td>
    <td width="1" height="1" bgcolor=#92876c></td>
    <td width="1" height="1" bgcolor=#978d6e></td>
    <td width="1" height="1" bgcolor=#918768></td>
    <td width="1" height="1" bgcolor=#8e866a></td>
    <td width="1" height="1" bgcolor=#99936e></td>
    <td width="1" height="1" bgcolor=#958f6f></td>
    <td width="1" height="1" bgcolor=#979171></td>
    <td width="1" height="1" bgcolor=#958f73></td>
    <td width="1" height="1" bgcolor=#918c6b></td>
    <td width="1" height="1" bgcolor=#938f71></td>
    <td width="1" height="1" bgcolor=#908b65></td>
    <td width="1" height="1" bgcolor=#91865b></td>
    <td width="1" height="1" bgcolor=#948a5a></td>
    <td width="1" height="1" bgcolor=#91845b></td>
    <td width="1" height="1" bgcolor=#95895b></td>
    <td width="1" height="1" bgcolor=#988e55></td>
    <td width="1" height="1" bgcolor=#9d9055></td>
    <td width="1" height="1" bgcolor=#91855f></td>
    <td width="1" height="1" bgcolor=#807b62></td>
  </tr>
</table></body></html>
```

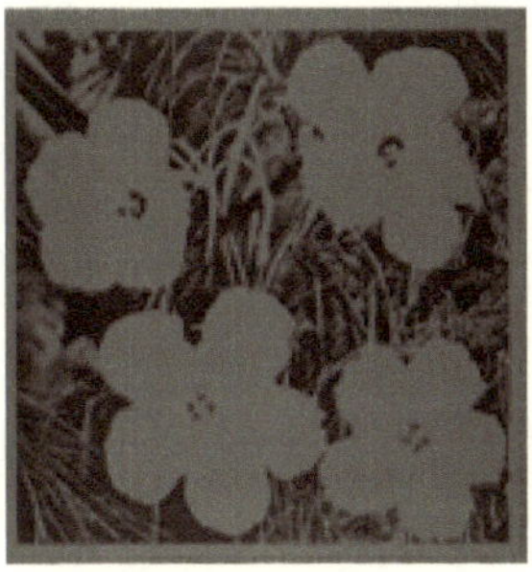

Sturtevant's Flowers

```
<html>

<head><title>Sturtevant's
Flowers, written by Broose G.
Dickinson</title></head>
<body>
<table border=0 cellpadding=0
cellspacing=0>
  <tr>
    <td width="1" height="1"
bgcolor=#70726e></td>
    <td width="1" height="1"
bgcolor=#737471></td>
    <td width="1" height="1"
bgcolor=#6f716d></td>
    <td rowspan="1"
colspan="2" width="1"
height="1"
bgcolor=#70716e></td>
    <td width="1" height="1"
bgcolor=#757673></td>
    <td width="1" height="1"
bgcolor=#757874></td>
    <td width="1" height="1"
bgcolor=#6e706d></td>
    <td width="1" height="1"
bgcolor=#70706d></td>
    <td width="1" height="1"
bgcolor=#71736f></td>
    <td width="1" height="1"
bgcolor=#747672></td>
    <td width="1" height="1"
bgcolor=#737472></td>
    <td width="1" height="1"
bgcolor=#6f716d></td>
    <td width="1" height="1"
bgcolor=#727470></td>
    <td width="1" height="1"
bgcolor=#737572></td>
    <td width="1" height="1"
bgcolor=#70726e></td>
    <td width="1" height="1"
bgcolor=#6f716d></td>
    <td width="1" height="1"
bgcolor=#727470></td>
    <td width="1" height="1"
bgcolor=#787976></td>
    <td width="1" height="1"
bgcolor=#71736f></td>
    <td width="1" height="1"
bgcolor=#71726f></td>
    <td width="1" height="1"
bgcolor=#6b6d6a></td>
    <td width="1" height="1"
bgcolor=#696b67></td>
    <td width="1" height="1"
bgcolor=#696a66></td>
    <td width="1" height="1"
bgcolor=#6c6d6a></td>
    <td width="1" height="1"
bgcolor=#6a6c68></td>
    <td width="1" height="1"
bgcolor=#70726f></td>
    <td width="1" height="1"
bgcolor=#656663></td>
    <td width="1" height="1"
bgcolor=#676865></td>
    <td width="1" height="1"
bgcolor=#70716e></td>
    <td width="1" height="1"
bgcolor=#686a66></td>
    <td rowspan="1"
colspan="2" width="1"
height="1"
bgcolor=#6c6d6a></td>
    <td width="1" height="1"
bgcolor=#6e706c></td>
    <td width="1" height="1"
bgcolor=#696b67></td>
    <td width="1" height="1"
bgcolor=#6b6d69></td>
    <td width="1" height="1"
bgcolor=#6a6b67></td>
    <td width="1" height="1"
bgcolor=#6e706c></td>
    <td width="1" height="1"
bgcolor=#70726f></td>
    <td width="1" height="1"
bgcolor=#696a66></td>
    <td width="1" height="1"
bgcolor=#676865></td>
    <td width="1" height="1"
bgcolor=#6c6d6a></td>
    <td width="1" height="1"
bgcolor=#6c6d69></td>
    <td width="1" height="1"
bgcolor=#6f706c></td>
    <td width="1" height="1"
bgcolor=#686a66></td>
    <td width="1" height="1"
bgcolor=#6b6d69></td>
    <td width="1" height="1"
bgcolor=#6c6e6a></td>
    <td width="1" height="1"
bgcolor=#6b6c69></td>
    <td width="1" height="1"
bgcolor=#676865></td>
    <td width="1" height="1"
bgcolor=#6b6d69></td>
    <td width="1" height="1"
bgcolor=#6f706d></td>
    <td width="1" height="1"
bgcolor=#6b6c69></td>
    <td width="1" height="1"
bgcolor=#696a67></td>
    <td width="1" height="1"
bgcolor=#626360></td>
    <td width="1" height="1"
bgcolor=#60625e></td>
    <td width="1" height="1"
bgcolor=#5f615d></td>
    <td width="1" height="1"
bgcolor=#626460></td>
    <td width="1" height="1"
bgcolor=#61635f></td>
    <td width="1" height="1"
bgcolor=#666764></td>
    <td width="1" height="1"
bgcolor=#5b5d5a></td>
    <td width="1" height="1"
bgcolor=#61625f></td>
    <td width="1" height="1"
bgcolor=#656663></td>
    <td width="1" height="1"
bgcolor=#61625f></td>
    <td width="1" height="1"
bgcolor=#616360></td>
    <td width="1" height="1"
bgcolor=#636561></td>
    <td width="1" height="1"
bgcolor=#656663></td>
    <td width="1" height="1"
bgcolor=#5f615d></td>
    <td width="1" height="1"
bgcolor=#626460></td>
    <td width="1" height="1"
bgcolor=#60625e></td>
    <td width="1" height="1"
bgcolor=#656663></td>
    <td width="1" height="1"
bgcolor=#666864></td>
    <td width="1" height="1"
bgcolor=#5b5e5c></td>
  </tr>
  <tr>
    <td width="1" height="1"
bgcolor=#556291></td>
    <td width="1" height="1"
bgcolor=#556589></td>
    <td width="1" height="1"
bgcolor=#57658b></td>
```

```
    <td width="1" height="1"
bgcolor=#586493></td>
    <td width="1" height="1"
bgcolor=#59678f></td>
    <td width="1" height="1"
bgcolor=#576890></td>
    <td width="1" height="1"
bgcolor=#5b6994></td>
    <td width="1" height="1"
bgcolor=#5c6890></td>
    <td width="1" height="1"
bgcolor=#596a93></td>
    <td width="1" height="1"
bgcolor=#5c6c94></td>
    <td width="1" height="1"
bgcolor=#5d6a96></td>
    <td width="1" height="1"
bgcolor=#5a6c92></td>
    <td width="1" height="1"
bgcolor=#5f6b93></td>
    <td width="1" height="1"
bgcolor=#5e6b97></td>
    <td width="1" height="1"
bgcolor=#5e6d96></td>
    <td width="1" height="1"
bgcolor=#5e6d92></td>
    <td width="1" height="1"
bgcolor=#5e6d98></td>
    <td width="1" height="1"
bgcolor=#5e6d97></td>
    <td width="1" height="1"
bgcolor=#5e6c96></td>
    <td width="1" height="1"
bgcolor=#5f6e94></td>
    <td width="1" height="1"
bgcolor=#5e6f95></td>
    <td width="1" height="1"
bgcolor=#5f6d97></td>
    <td width="1" height="1"
bgcolor=#616d9c></td>
    <td width="1" height="1"
bgcolor=#606d96></td>
    <td width="1" height="1"
bgcolor=#5e7096></td>
    <td width="1" height="1"
bgcolor=#606d98></td>
    <td width="1" height="1"
bgcolor=#626d97></td>
    <td width="1" height="1"
bgcolor=#616f99></td>
    <td width="1" height="1"
bgcolor=#626e99></td>
    <td width="1" height="1"
bgcolor=#5f7398></td>
    <td width="1" height="1"
bgcolor=#646d9c></td>
    <td width="1" height="1"
bgcolor=#607098></td>
    <td width="1" height="1"
bgcolor=#616e97></td>
    <td width="1" height="1"
bgcolor=#626f96></td>
    <td width="1" height="1"
bgcolor=#616d9b></td>
    <td width="1" height="1"
bgcolor=#627097></td>
    <td width="1" height="1"
bgcolor=#606e99></td>
    <td width="1" height="1"
bgcolor=#616e99></td>
    <td width="1" height="1"
bgcolor=#606e94></td>
    <td width="1" height="1"
bgcolor=#606f9c></td>
    <td width="1" height="1"
bgcolor=#617097></td>
    <td width="1" height="1"
bgcolor=#5f6d95></td>
    <td width="1" height="1"
bgcolor=#5f6c99></td>
    <td width="1" height="1"
bgcolor=#5e6c95></td>
    <td width="1" height="1"
bgcolor=#606f99></td>
    <td width="1" height="1"
bgcolor=#5f6b97></td>
    <td width="1" height="1"
bgcolor=#5e6a95></td>
    <td width="1" height="1"
bgcolor=#5d6b97></td>
    <td width="1" height="1"
bgcolor=#5f6d96></td>
    <td width="1" height="1"
bgcolor=#5c6995></td>
    <td width="1" height="1"
bgcolor=#5c6b90></td>
    <td width="1" height="1"
bgcolor=#5e6c97></td>
    <td width="1" height="1"
bgcolor=#5b6a91></td>
    <td width="1" height="1"
bgcolor=#5c6a91></td>
    <td width="1" height="1"
bgcolor=#5c6991></td>
    <td width="1" height="1"
bgcolor=#5b698f></td>
    <td width="1" height="1"
bgcolor=#5b6994></td>
    <td width="1" height="1"
bgcolor=#596a8f></td>
    <td width="1" height="1"
bgcolor=#586892></td>
    <td width="1" height="1"
bgcolor=#5b688f></td>
    <td width="1" height="1"
bgcolor=#58668b></td>
    <td width="1" height="1"
bgcolor=#57678c></td>
    <td width="1" height="1"
bgcolor=#57688d></td>
    <td width="1" height="1"
bgcolor=#576689></td>
    <td width="1" height="1"
bgcolor=#556490></td>
    <td rowspan="1"
colspan="2" width="1"
height="1"
bgcolor=#546289></td>
    <td width="1" height="1"
bgcolor=#53618b></td>
    <td width="1" height="1"
bgcolor=#526387></td>
    <td width="1" height="1"
bgcolor=#526089></td>
    <td width="1" height="1"
bgcolor=#505f8a></td>
    <td width="1" height="1"
bgcolor=#5e5f5c></td>
  </tr>
  <tr>
    <td width="1" height="1"
bgcolor=#56648c></td>
    <td width="1" height="1"
bgcolor=#596492></td>
    <td width="1" height="1"
bgcolor=#5c6a93></td>
    <td width="1" height="1"
bgcolor=#57668f></td>
    <td width="1" height="1"
bgcolor=#58658c></td>
    <td width="1" height="1"
bgcolor=#606b94></td>
    <td width="1" height="1"
bgcolor=#606c98></td>
    <td width="1" height="1"
bgcolor=#5f6e93></td>
    <td width="1" height="1"
bgcolor=#5f6b97></td>
    <td width="1" height="1"
bgcolor=#5d6891></td>
    <td width="1" height="1"
bgcolor=#5d6b92></td>
    <td width="1" height="1"
bgcolor=#5b6c92></td>
    <td width="1" height="1"
bgcolor=#636c9a></td>
    <td width="1" height="1"
bgcolor=#5b7296></td>
    <td width="1" height="1"
bgcolor=#626d96></td>
    <td width="1" height="1"
bgcolor=#616f99></td>
    <td width="1" height="1"
bgcolor=#617099></td>
```

```
<td width="1" height="1" bgcolor=#63719b></td>
<td width="1" height="1" bgcolor=#627099></td>
<td width="1" height="1" bgcolor=#656e9b></td>
<td width="1" height="1" bgcolor=#63709c></td>
<td width="1" height="1" bgcolor=#5f7096></td>
<td width="1" height="1" bgcolor=#627197></td>
<td width="1" height="1" bgcolor=#607098></td>
<td width="1" height="1" bgcolor=#64729b></td>
<td width="1" height="1" bgcolor=#61719a></td>
<td width="1" height="1" bgcolor=#5d6e95></td>
<td width="1" height="1" bgcolor=#606f97></td>
<td width="1" height="1" bgcolor=#64719c></td>
<td width="1" height="1" bgcolor=#63709b></td>
<td width="1" height="1" bgcolor=#646f93></td>
<td width="1" height="1" bgcolor=#61729b></td>
<td width="1" height="1" bgcolor=#63719b></td>
<td width="1" height="1" bgcolor=#616b96></td>
<td width="1" height="1" bgcolor=#646e9a></td>
<td width="1" height="1" bgcolor=#616e97></td>
<td width="1" height="1" bgcolor=#626f91></td>
<td width="1" height="1" bgcolor=#616f9b></td>
<td width="1" height="1" bgcolor=#617095></td>
<td width="1" height="1" bgcolor=#637197></td>
<td width="1" height="1" bgcolor=#5f6d9b></td>
<td width="1" height="1" bgcolor=#5f6c91></td>
<td width="1" height="1" bgcolor=#616f96></td>
<td width="1" height="1" bgcolor=#5d6d94></td>
<td width="1" height="1" bgcolor=#607197></td>
<td width="1" height="1" bgcolor=#5c6d92></td>
<td width="1" height="1" bgcolor=#5d6e95></td>
<td width="1" height="1" bgcolor=#5f6e94></td>
<td width="1" height="1" bgcolor=#5a6b90></td>
<td width="1" height="1" bgcolor=#5c6d94></td>
<td width="1" height="1" bgcolor=#5e6e9c></td>
<td width="1" height="1" bgcolor=#5c6d8f></td>
<td width="1" height="1" bgcolor=#5d6c91></td>
<td width="1" height="1" bgcolor=#5c6b90></td>
<td width="1" height="1" bgcolor=#5c6b93></td>
<td width="1" height="1" bgcolor=#5c6a90></td>
<td width="1" height="1" bgcolor=#5a6993></td>
<td width="1" height="1" bgcolor=#5a698c></td>
<td width="1" height="1" bgcolor=#5b6a8e></td>
<td width="1" height="1" bgcolor=#5a6a8f></td>
<td width="1" height="1" bgcolor=#57688e></td>
<td width="1" height="1" bgcolor=#586890></td>
<td width="1" height="1" bgcolor=#56678b></td>
<td width="1" height="1" bgcolor=#576790></td>
<td width="1" height="1" bgcolor=#59678a></td>
<td width="1" height="1" bgcolor=#55638b></td>
<td width="1" height="1" bgcolor=#55628e></td>
<td rowspan="1" colspan="2" width="1" height="1" bgcolor=#586489></td>
<td width="1" height="1" bgcolor=#536289></td>
<td width="1" height="1" bgcolor=#4e5d85></td>
<td width="1" height="1" bgcolor=#565754></td>
</tr>
<tr>
<td width="1" height="1" bgcolor=#51658d></td>
<td width="1" height="1" bgcolor=#485372></td>
<td width="1" height="1" bgcolor=#151a25></td>
<td width="1" height="1" bgcolor=#5b6992></td>
<td width="1" height="1" bgcolor=#596a92></td>
<td width="1" height="1" bgcolor=#232b3f></td>
<td width="1" height="1" bgcolor=#131113></td>
<td width="1" height="1" bgcolor=#131417></td>
<td width="1" height="1" bgcolor=#28303b></td>
<td width="1" height="1" bgcolor=#5e6e9a></td>
<td width="1" height="1" bgcolor=#475a76></td>
<td width="1" height="1" bgcolor=#59658b></td>
<td width="1" height="1" bgcolor=#1a1d25></td>
<td width="1" height="1" bgcolor=#141215></td>
<td width="1" height="1" bgcolor=#2b2e3e></td>
<td width="1" height="1" bgcolor=#303648></td>
<td width="1" height="1" bgcolor=#111212></td>
<td width="1" height="1" bgcolor=#202028></td>
<td rowspan="2" colspan="1" width="1" height="1" bgcolor=#171718></td>
<td width="1" height="1" bgcolor=#161716></td>
<td width="1" height="1" bgcolor=#212630></td>
<td width="1" height="1" bgcolor=#484b68></td>
<td width="1" height="1" bgcolor=#212831></td>
<td width="1" height="1" bgcolor=#3f4058></td>
<td width="1" height="1" bgcolor=#21202d></td>
<td width="1" height="1" bgcolor=#171718></td>
<td width="1" height="1" bgcolor=#494b6a></td>
<td width="1" height="1" bgcolor=#4a516d></td>
<td width="1" height="1" bgcolor=#272b31></td>
<td width="1" height="1" bgcolor=#222226></td>
```

```
<td width="1" height="1" bgcolor=#363e54></td>
<td width="1" height="1" bgcolor=#393f51></td>
<td width="1" height="1" bgcolor=#3c4563></td>
<td width="1" height="1" bgcolor=#657198></td>
<td width="1" height="1" bgcolor=#1f2831></td>
<td width="1" height="1" bgcolor=#535a7e></td>
<td width="1" height="1" bgcolor=#3f4b6a></td>
<td width="1" height="1" bgcolor=#4d5a7a></td>
<td width="1" height="1" bgcolor=#384057></td>
<td width="1" height="1" bgcolor=#1f1f26></td>
<td width="1" height="1" bgcolor=#2f3743></td>
<td width="1" height="1" bgcolor=#475070></td>
<td width="1" height="1" bgcolor=#191c21></td>
<td width="1" height="1" bgcolor=#302f42></td>
<td width="1" height="1" bgcolor=#29283a></td>
<td width="1" height="1" bgcolor=#35384a></td>
<td width="1" height="1" bgcolor=#1c1c25></td>
<td width="1" height="1" bgcolor=#151211></td>
<td width="1" height="1" bgcolor=#161618></td>
<td width="1" height="1" bgcolor=#17171b></td>
<td width="1" height="1" bgcolor=#262531></td>
<td width="1" height="1" bgcolor=#121212></td>
<td width="1" height="1" bgcolor=#141311></td>
<td width="1" height="1" bgcolor=#11100d></td>
<td width="1" height="1" bgcolor=#12110f></td>
<td width="1" height="1" bgcolor=#090a0e></td>
<td width="1" height="1" bgcolor=#292834></td>
<td width="1" height="1" bgcolor=#131317></td>
<td width="1" height="1" bgcolor=#0d0d12></td>
<td width="1" height="1" bgcolor=#0c0b0e></td>
<td width="1" height="1" bgcolor=#131212></td>
<td width="1" height="1" bgcolor=#0d0a0d></td>
<td width="1" height="1" bgcolor=#110f0d></td>
<td width="1" height="1" bgcolor=#101016></td>
<td width="1" height="1" bgcolor=#060b0a></td>
<td width="1" height="1" bgcolor=#3e4966></td>
<td width="1" height="1" bgcolor=#1b242c></td>
<td width="1" height="1" bgcolor=#0b0906></td>
<td width="1" height="1" bgcolor=#040507></td>
<td width="1" height="1" bgcolor=#3d485e></td>
<td width="1" height="1" bgcolor=#4e5d88></td>
<td width="1" height="1" bgcolor=#62635f></td>
</tr>
<tr>
<td width="1" height="1" bgcolor=#56628f></td>
<td width="1" height="1" bgcolor=#5a698d></td>
<td width="1" height="1" bgcolor=#353d58></td>
<td width="1" height="1" bgcolor=#363e57></td>
<td width="1" height="1" bgcolor=#5e6c96></td>
<td width="1" height="1" bgcolor=#3b435e></td>
<td width="1" height="1" bgcolor=#1a191e></td>
<td width="1" height="1" bgcolor=#0e0e11></td>
<td width="1" height="1" bgcolor=#151110></td>
<td width="1" height="1" bgcolor=#101414></td>
<td width="1" height="1" bgcolor=#424760></td>
<td width="1" height="1" bgcolor=#3e4a65></td>
<td width="1" height="1" bgcolor=#4d5a7b></td>
<td width="1" height="1" bgcolor=#100a0d></td>
<td width="1" height="1" bgcolor=#465475></td>
<td width="1" height="1" bgcolor=#3d4256></td>
<td width="1" height="1" bgcolor=#0e100d></td>
<td width="1" height="1" bgcolor=#353342></td>
<td width="1" height="1" bgcolor=#181920></td>
<td width="1" height="1" bgcolor=#3d4253></td>
<td width="1" height="1" bgcolor=#0c0f0b></td>
<td width="1" height="1" bgcolor=#323447></td>
<td width="1" height="1" bgcolor=#393c4f></td>
<td width="1" height="1" bgcolor=#151512></td>
<td width="1" height="1" bgcolor=#434b5e></td>
<td width="1" height="1" bgcolor=#252f3b></td>
<td width="1" height="1" bgcolor=#212027></td>
<td width="1" height="1" bgcolor=#171816></td>
<td width="1" height="1" bgcolor=#120f11></td>
<td width="1" height="1" bgcolor=#4f5172></td>
<td width="1" height="1" bgcolor=#161414></td>
<td width="1" height="1" bgcolor=#2a282f></td>
<td width="1" height="1" bgcolor=#373d4e></td>
<td width="1" height="1" bgcolor=#66719f></td>
<td width="1" height="1" bgcolor=#4f607e></td>
<td width="1" height="1" bgcolor=#656f9c></td>
<td width="1" height="1" bgcolor=#435373></td>
<td width="1" height="1" bgcolor=#455068></td>
<td width="1" height="1" bgcolor=#1d1a1b></td>
<td width="1" height="1" bgcolor=#111415></td>
<td width="1" height="1" bgcolor=#31303d></td>
<td width="1" height="1" bgcolor=#252835></td>
<td width="1" height="1" bgcolor=#4c597c></td>
<td width="1" height="1" bgcolor=#5c6689></td>
```

```
    <td width="1" height="1"
bgcolor=#54638c></td>
    <td width="1" height="1"
bgcolor=#4e5a74></td>
    <td width="1" height="1"
bgcolor=#16181d></td>
    <td width="1" height="1"
bgcolor=#181718></td>
    <td width="1" height="1"
bgcolor=#191a1e></td>
    <td width="1" height="1"
bgcolor=#10110f></td>
    <td width="1" height="1"
bgcolor=#232428></td>
    <td width="1" height="1"
bgcolor=#0f1012></td>
    <td width="1" height="1"
bgcolor=#10100e></td>
    <td width="1" height="1"
bgcolor=#0e0e0d></td>
    <td width="1" height="1"
bgcolor=#090b09></td>
    <td width="1" height="1"
bgcolor=#131217></td>
    <td width="1" height="1"
bgcolor=#0c0906></td>
    <td width="1" height="1"
bgcolor=#090707></td>
    <td width="1" height="1"
bgcolor=#0a0709></td>
    <td width="1" height="1"
bgcolor=#0d0f0a></td>
    <td width="1" height="1"
bgcolor=#19181c></td>
    <td width="1" height="1"
bgcolor=#090a08></td>
    <td width="1" height="1"
bgcolor=#363a4b></td>
    <td width="1" height="1"
bgcolor=#0c0b07></td>
    <td width="1" height="1"
bgcolor=#0b0f12></td>
    <td width="1" height="1"
bgcolor=#3f465f></td>
    <td width="1" height="1"
bgcolor=#000302></td>
    <td width="1" height="1"
bgcolor=#040308></td>
    <td width="1" height="1"
bgcolor=#3b455d></td>
    <td width="1" height="1"
bgcolor=#4e5e88></td>
    <td width="1" height="1"
bgcolor=#5d5d5b></td>
  </tr>
  <tr>
    <td width="1" height="1"
bgcolor=#57618c></td>
    <td width="1" height="1"
bgcolor=#495a7e></td>
    <td width="1" height="1"
bgcolor=#5b6c9b></td>
    <td width="1" height="1"
bgcolor=#292f3d></td>
    <td width="1" height="1"
bgcolor=#222837></td>
    <td width="1" height="1"
bgcolor=#323750></td>
    <td width="1" height="1"
bgcolor=#333c4d></td>
    <td width="1" height="1"
bgcolor=#14141b></td>
    <td width="1" height="1"
bgcolor=#100e0d></td>
    <td width="1" height="1"
bgcolor=#323547></td>
    <td width="1" height="1"
bgcolor=#3d4b67></td>
    <td width="1" height="1"
bgcolor=#151319></td>
    <td width="1" height="1"
bgcolor=#404c6b></td>
    <td width="1" height="1"
bgcolor=#292e38></td>
    <td width="1" height="1"
bgcolor=#120d11></td>
    <td width="1" height="1"
bgcolor=#24222e></td>
    <td width="1" height="1"
bgcolor=#242732></td>
    <td width="1" height="1"
bgcolor=#2b3140></td>
    <td width="1" height="1"
bgcolor=#17100f></td>
    <td width="1" height="1"
bgcolor=#111412></td>
    <td width="1" height="1"
bgcolor=#150e0b></td>
    <td width="1" height="1"
bgcolor=#33384d></td>
    <td width="1" height="1"
bgcolor=#1e1f21></td>
    <td width="1" height="1"
bgcolor=#2d2f3d></td>
    <td width="1" height="1"
bgcolor=#465270></td>
    <td width="1" height="1"
bgcolor=#2e3043></td>
    <td width="1" height="1"
bgcolor=#201f20></td>
    <td width="1" height="1"
bgcolor=#2c2a3b></td>
    <td width="1" height="1"
bgcolor=#333748></td>
    <td width="1" height="1"
bgcolor=#414760></td>
    <td width="1" height="1"
bgcolor=#565d7e></td>
    <td width="1" height="1"
bgcolor=#2f364a></td>
    <td width="1" height="1"
bgcolor=#1a1a1a></td>
    <td width="1" height="1"
bgcolor=#40405a></td>
    <td width="1" height="1"
bgcolor=#364057></td>
    <td width="1" height="1"
bgcolor=#50587b></td>
    <td width="1" height="1"
bgcolor=#626e98></td>
    <td width="1" height="1"
bgcolor=#23232d></td>
    <td width="1" height="1"
bgcolor=#384057></td>
    <td width="1" height="1"
bgcolor=#17151a></td>
    <td width="1" height="1"
bgcolor=#131613></td>
    <td width="1" height="1"
bgcolor=#4c5175></td>
    <td width="1" height="1"
bgcolor=#627195></td>
    <td width="1" height="1"
bgcolor=#5c6b93></td>
    <td width="1" height="1"
bgcolor=#5d6c92></td>
    <td width="1" height="1"
bgcolor=#5d6890></td>
    <td width="1" height="1"
bgcolor=#5c6892></td>
    <td width="1" height="1"
bgcolor=#606e96></td>
    <td width="1" height="1"
bgcolor=#212734></td>
    <td width="1" height="1"
bgcolor=#141110></td>
    <td width="1" height="1"
bgcolor=#141016></td>
    <td width="1" height="1"
bgcolor=#131011></td>
    <td width="1" height="1"
bgcolor=#0b0c0c></td>
    <td width="1" height="1"
bgcolor=#21222a></td>
    <td width="1" height="1"
bgcolor=#272a3c></td>
    <td width="1" height="1"
bgcolor=#546385></td>
    <td width="1" height="1"
bgcolor=#5e6d94></td>
    <td width="1" height="1"
bgcolor=#505c7f></td>
    <td width="1" height="1"
bgcolor=#47516e></td>
```

```
    <td width="1" height="1" bgcolor=#3c455f></td>
    <td width="1" height="1" bgcolor=#23262b></td>
    <td width="1" height="1" bgcolor=#06040a></td>
    <td width="1" height="1" bgcolor=#141518></td>
    <td width="1" height="1" bgcolor=#090908></td>
    <td width="1" height="1" bgcolor=#181721></td>
    <td width="1" height="1" bgcolor=#0d0d04></td>
    <td width="1" height="1" bgcolor=#12161a></td>
    <td width="1" height="1" bgcolor=#393c58></td>
    <td width="1" height="1" bgcolor=#020001></td>
    <td width="1" height="1" bgcolor=#343d55></td>
    <td width="1" height="1" bgcolor=#4d6085></td>
    <td width="1" height="1" bgcolor=#5c5d5a></td>
  </tr>
  <tr>
    <td width="1" height="1" bgcolor=#58638d></td>
    <td width="1" height="1" bgcolor=#2b3140></td>
    <td width="1" height="1" bgcolor=#343d4e></td>
    <td width="1" height="1" bgcolor=#5f709f></td>
    <td width="1" height="1" bgcolor=#20222d></td>
    <td width="1" height="1" bgcolor=#0d0f0a></td>
    <td width="1" height="1" bgcolor=#0f0d06></td>
    <td width="1" height="1" bgcolor=#100f0f></td>
    <td width="1" height="1" bgcolor=#131013></td>
    <td width="1" height="1" bgcolor=#333b50></td>
    <td width="1" height="1" bgcolor=#57688f></td>
    <td width="1" height="1" bgcolor=#546082></td>
    <td width="1" height="1" bgcolor=#5a688f></td>
    <td width="1" height="1" bgcolor=#0f0a0b></td>
    <td width="1" height="1" bgcolor=#13130e></td>
    <td width="1" height="1" bgcolor=#0b0c04></td>
    <td width="1" height="1" bgcolor=#495068></td>
    <td width="1" height="1" bgcolor=#0d0f0c></td>
    <td width="1" height="1" bgcolor=#131415></td>
    <td width="1" height="1" bgcolor=#15120e></td>
    <td width="1" height="1" bgcolor=#191c1e></td>
    <td width="1" height="1" bgcolor=#444c68></td>
    <td width="1" height="1" bgcolor=#120f0a></td>
    <td width="1" height="1" bgcolor=#485474></td>
    <td width="1" height="1" bgcolor=#4f5676></td>
    <td width="1" height="1" bgcolor=#1d1a1d></td>
    <td width="1" height="1" bgcolor=#151317></td>
    <td width="1" height="1" bgcolor=#16150c></td>
    <td width="1" height="1" bgcolor=#110c0b></td>
    <td width="1" height="1" bgcolor=#444964></td>
    <td width="1" height="1" bgcolor=#111011></td>
    <td width="1" height="1" bgcolor=#31343f></td>
    <td width="1" height="1" bgcolor=#3b3f57></td>
    <td width="1" height="1" bgcolor=#4b5775></td>
    <td width="1" height="1" bgcolor=#373f58></td>
    <td width="1" height="1" bgcolor=#4d5b74></td>
    <td width="1" height="1" bgcolor=#5b6892></td>
    <td width="1" height="1" bgcolor=#1f1d1c></td>
    <td width="1" height="1" bgcolor=#29293b></td>
    <td width="1" height="1" bgcolor=#130f0d></td>
    <td width="1" height="1" bgcolor=#3d4658></td>
    <td width="1" height="1" bgcolor=#5d6d98></td>
    <td width="1" height="1" bgcolor=#5e6896></td>
    <td width="1" height="1" bgcolor=#5d6a94></td>
    <td width="1" height="1" bgcolor=#5b6890></td>
    <td width="1" height="1" bgcolor=#5a6890></td>
    <td width="1" height="1" bgcolor=#5d6a92></td>
    <td width="1" height="1" bgcolor=#5d6892></td>
    <td width="1" height="1" bgcolor=#64759a></td>
    <td width="1" height="1" bgcolor=#1a1c24></td>
    <td width="1" height="1" bgcolor=#0f0f0f></td>
    <td width="1" height="1" bgcolor=#1b1e27></td>
    <td width="1" height="1" bgcolor=#576284></td>
    <td width="1" height="1" bgcolor=#5b6e92></td>
    <td width="1" height="1" bgcolor=#5b6a99></td>
    <td width="1" height="1" bgcolor=#58688d></td>
    <td width="1" height="1" bgcolor=#57668a></td>
    <td width="1" height="1" bgcolor=#56688d></td>
    <td width="1" height="1" bgcolor=#55678d></td>
    <td width="1" height="1" bgcolor=#54648c></td>
    <td width="1" height="1" bgcolor=#596c94></td>
    <td width="1" height="1" bgcolor=#4b5873></td>
    <td width="1" height="1" bgcolor=#07070d></td>
    <td width="1" height="1" bgcolor=#211f23></td>
    <td width="1" height="1" bgcolor=#101216></td>
    <td width="1" height="1" bgcolor=#21212f></td>
    <td width="1" height="1" bgcolor=#0d0d0c></td>
    <td width="1" height="1" bgcolor=#1a212b></td>
    <td width="1" height="1" bgcolor=#272b3b></td>
    <td width="1" height="1" bgcolor=#343a4c></td>
    <td width="1" height="1" bgcolor=#4c5e86></td>
    <td width="1" height="1" bgcolor=#61625f></td>
  </tr>
  <tr>
```

```
    <td width="1" height="1" bgcolor=#54658a></td>
    <td width="1" height="1" bgcolor=#2d354a></td>
    <td width="1" height="1" bgcolor=#050500></td>
    <td width="1" height="1" bgcolor=#353a4f></td>
    <td width="1" height="1" bgcolor=#616f9c></td>
    <td width="1" height="1" bgcolor=#191a1c></td>
    <td width="1" height="1" bgcolor=#100f14></td>
    <td width="1" height="1" bgcolor=#0e0e0a></td>
    <td width="1" height="1" bgcolor=#16151d></td>
    <td width="1" height="1" bgcolor=#566284></td>
    <td width="1" height="1" bgcolor=#5b6994></td>
    <td width="1" height="1" bgcolor=#596992></td>
    <td width="1" height="1" bgcolor=#565e81></td>
    <td width="1" height="1" bgcolor=#0f0d10></td>
    <td width="1" height="1" bgcolor=#14150e></td>
    <td width="1" height="1" bgcolor=#1c191d></td>
    <td width="1" height="1" bgcolor=#13141b></td>
    <td width="1" height="1" bgcolor=#17130f></td>
    <td width="1" height="1" bgcolor=#11130d></td>
    <td width="1" height="1" bgcolor=#17141e></td>
    <td width="1" height="1" bgcolor=#353e51></td>
    <td width="1" height="1" bgcolor=#262331></td>
    <td width="1" height="1" bgcolor=#13130b></td>
    <td width="1" height="1" bgcolor=#5e6b94></td>
    <td width="1" height="1" bgcolor=#151617></td>
    <td width="1" height="1" bgcolor=#191512></td>
    <td width="1" height="1" bgcolor=#1a1a1d></td>
    <td width="1" height="1" bgcolor=#333440></td>
    <td width="1" height="1" bgcolor=#312e44></td>
    <td width="1" height="1" bgcolor=#495771></td>
    <td width="1" height="1" bgcolor=#37384d></td>
    <td width="1" height="1" bgcolor=#313542></td>
    <td width="1" height="1" bgcolor=#404962></td>
    <td width="1" height="1" bgcolor=#393e51></td>
    <td width="1" height="1" bgcolor=#4d5a76></td>
    <td width="1" height="1" bgcolor=#313346></td>
    <td width="1" height="1" bgcolor=#69749d></td>
    <td width="1" height="1" bgcolor=#1e2027></td>
    <td width="1" height="1" bgcolor=#2c2836></td>
    <td width="1" height="1" bgcolor=#20242f></td>
    <td width="1" height="1" bgcolor=#66739c></td>
    <td width="1" height="1" bgcolor=#5b6992></td>
    <td width="1" height="1" bgcolor=#5f6995></td>
    <td width="1" height="1" bgcolor=#5c6c93></td>
    <td width="1" height="1" bgcolor=#5c6892></td>
    <td width="1" height="1" bgcolor=#5e6a93></td>
    <td width="1" height="1" bgcolor=#5b6890></td>
    <td width="1" height="1" bgcolor=#5b6a8f></td>
    <td width="1" height="1" bgcolor=#5d6793></td>
    <td width="1" height="1" bgcolor=#414e69></td>
    <td width="1" height="1" bgcolor=#060200></td>
    <td width="1" height="1" bgcolor=#59678d></td>
    <td width="1" height="1" bgcolor=#57698c></td>
    <td width="1" height="1" bgcolor=#5a678f></td>
    <td width="1" height="1" bgcolor=#5a668a></td>
    <td width="1" height="1" bgcolor=#586590></td>
    <td width="1" height="1" bgcolor=#586790></td>
    <td width="1" height="1" bgcolor=#596691></td>
    <td width="1" height="1" bgcolor=#58648f></td>
    <td width="1" height="1" bgcolor=#55658c></td>
    <td width="1" height="1" bgcolor=#59638c></td>
    <td width="1" height="1" bgcolor=#56678d></td>
    <td width="1" height="1" bgcolor=#394457></td>
    <td width="1" height="1" bgcolor=#050402></td>
    <td width="1" height="1" bgcolor=#24242e></td>
    <td width="1" height="1" bgcolor=#10151d></td>
    <td width="1" height="1" bgcolor=#17161f></td>
    <td width="1" height="1" bgcolor=#0a0806></td>
    <td width="1" height="1" bgcolor=#100f1c></td>
    <td width="1" height="1" bgcolor=#2e394d></td>
    <td width="1" height="1" bgcolor=#4d5e87></td>
    <td width="1" height="1" bgcolor=#5c5e5a></td>
  </tr>
  <tr>
    <td width="1" height="1" bgcolor=#56628c></td>
    <td width="1" height="1" bgcolor=#343850></td>
    <td width="1" height="1" bgcolor=#0c0d08></td>
    <td width="1" height="1" bgcolor=#060603></td>
    <td width="1" height="1" bgcolor=#2b3345></td>
    <td width="1" height="1" bgcolor=#606e99></td>
    <td width="1" height="1" bgcolor=#0d1113></td>
    <td width="1" height="1" bgcolor=#0e0b0c></td>
    <td width="1" height="1" bgcolor=#191b22></td>
    <td width="1" height="1" bgcolor=#54638d></td>
    <td width="1" height="1" bgcolor=#5c628b></td>
    <td width="1" height="1" bgcolor=#252c3f></td>
    <td width="1" height="1" bgcolor=#323947></td>
    <td width="1" height="1" bgcolor=#56658a></td>
```

```
    <td width="1" height="1"
bgcolor=#110b0f></td>
    <td width="1" height="1"
bgcolor=#383b50></td>
    <td width="1" height="1"
bgcolor=#151013></td>
    <td width="1" height="1"
bgcolor=#111113></td>
    <td width="1" height="1"
bgcolor=#0e0f0d></td>
    <td width="1" height="1"
bgcolor=#42435e></td>
    <td width="1" height="1"
bgcolor=#313947></td>
    <td width="1" height="1"
bgcolor=#101112></td>
    <td width="1" height="1"
bgcolor=#272638></td>
    <td width="1" height="1"
bgcolor=#393f53></td>
    <td width="1" height="1"
bgcolor=#191516></td>
    <td width="1" height="1"
bgcolor=#32384d></td>
    <td width="1" height="1"
bgcolor=#393d5b></td>
    <td width="1" height="1"
bgcolor=#2a3246></td>
    <td width="1" height="1"
bgcolor=#313949></td>
    <td width="1" height="1"
bgcolor=#46506e></td>
    <td width="1" height="1"
bgcolor=#424860></td>
    <td width="1" height="1"
bgcolor=#2b303d></td>
    <td width="1" height="1"
bgcolor=#211f2c></td>
    <td width="1" height="1"
bgcolor=#32374d></td>
    <td width="1" height="1"
bgcolor=#2a293a></td>
    <td width="1" height="1"
bgcolor=#161a22></td>
    <td width="1" height="1"
bgcolor=#545f82></td>
    <td width="1" height="1"
bgcolor=#4d567a></td>
    <td width="1" height="1"
bgcolor=#20202a></td>
    <td width="1" height="1"
bgcolor=#495371></td>
    <td width="1" height="1"
bgcolor=#5d6997></td>
    <td width="1" height="1"
bgcolor=#5d6b93></td>
    <td width="1" height="1"
bgcolor=#5c6a92></td>
    <td width="1" height="1"
bgcolor=#5c6993></td>
    <td rowspan="2"
colspan="1" width="1"
height="1"
bgcolor=#5d6993></td>
    <td width="1" height="1"
bgcolor=#596690></td>
    <td width="1" height="1"
bgcolor=#5c6994></td>
    <td width="1" height="1"
bgcolor=#596891></td>
    <td width="1" height="1"
bgcolor=#5e6993></td>
    <td width="1" height="1"
bgcolor=#5e6f97></td>
    <td width="1" height="1"
bgcolor=#2c334a></td>
    <td width="1" height="1"
bgcolor=#5d6c94></td>
    <td width="1" height="1"
bgcolor=#5b6991></td>
    <td width="1" height="1"
bgcolor=#586790></td>
    <td width="1" height="1"
bgcolor=#5b6a95></td>
    <td width="1" height="1"
bgcolor=#58698d></td>
    <td width="1" height="1"
bgcolor=#56678c></td>
    <td width="1" height="1"
bgcolor=#58668d></td>
    <td width="1" height="1"
bgcolor=#56658b></td>
    <td width="1" height="1"
bgcolor=#57678d></td>
    <td width="1" height="1"
bgcolor=#56638b></td>
    <td width="1" height="1"
bgcolor=#57658d></td>
    <td width="1" height="1"
bgcolor=#5c6690></td>
    <td width="1" height="1"
bgcolor=#111419></td>
    <td width="1" height="1"
bgcolor=#06050a></td>
    <td width="1" height="1"
bgcolor=#2b2e3a></td>
    <td width="1" height="1"
bgcolor=#161a24></td>
    <td width="1" height="1"
bgcolor=#0d0b11></td>
    <td width="1" height="1"
bgcolor=#070a06></td>
    <td width="1" height="1"
bgcolor=#333b54></td>
    <td width="1" height="1"
bgcolor=#4f5f84></td>
    <td width="1" height="1"
bgcolor=#585a56></td>
  </tr>
  <tr>
    <td width="1" height="1"
bgcolor=#54648f></td>
    <td width="1" height="1"
bgcolor=#2c3545></td>
    <td width="1" height="1"
bgcolor=#1f1b26></td>
    <td width="1" height="1"
bgcolor=#030b09></td>
    <td width="1" height="1"
bgcolor=#0d0806></td>
    <td width="1" height="1"
bgcolor=#1d242d></td>
    <td width="1" height="1"
bgcolor=#5a678d></td>
    <td width="1" height="1"
bgcolor=#0a0a08></td>
    <td width="1" height="1"
bgcolor=#0e0d0b></td>
    <td width="1" height="1"
bgcolor=#2f354a></td>
    <td width="1" height="1"
bgcolor=#283144></td>
    <td width="1" height="1"
bgcolor=#50597c></td>
    <td width="1" height="1"
bgcolor=#596489></td>
    <td width="1" height="1"
bgcolor=#272c42></td>
    <td width="1" height="1"
bgcolor=#3c4056></td>
    <td width="1" height="1"
bgcolor=#49547b></td>
    <td width="1" height="1"
bgcolor=#141616></td>
    <td rowspan="2"
colspan="1" width="1"
height="1"
bgcolor=#100d12></td>
    <td width="1" height="1"
bgcolor=#121110></td>
    <td width="1" height="1"
bgcolor=#0f0f11></td>
    <td width="1" height="1"
bgcolor=#383b4d></td>
    <td width="1" height="1"
bgcolor=#333448></td>
    <td width="1" height="1"
bgcolor=#21262e></td>
    <td width="1" height="1"
bgcolor=#2e3145></td>
    <td width="1" height="1"
bgcolor=#292e39></td>
    <td width="1" height="1"
bgcolor=#4e5979></td>
```

```
<td width="1" height="1" bgcolor=#485775></td>
<td width="1" height="1" bgcolor=#242832></td>
<td width="1" height="1" bgcolor=#3c4157></td>
<td width="1" height="1" bgcolor=#0d070a></td>
<td width="1" height="1" bgcolor=#252734></td>
<td width="1" height="1" bgcolor=#6675a2></td>
<td width="1" height="1" bgcolor=#556083></td>
<td width="1" height="1" bgcolor=#404a62></td>
<td width="1" height="1" bgcolor=#1b1724></td>
<td width="1" height="1" bgcolor=#63749d></td>
<td width="1" height="1" bgcolor=#313e4f></td>
<td width="1" height="1" bgcolor=#606a96></td>
<td width="1" height="1" bgcolor=#3f4861></td>
<td width="1" height="1" bgcolor=#5f6b94></td>
<td width="1" height="1" bgcolor=#5d6993></td>
<td rowspan="1" colspan="2" width="1" height="1" bgcolor=#5d6a94></td>
<td width="1" height="1" bgcolor=#5d6993></td>
<td width="1" height="1" bgcolor=#5c6993></td>
<td width="1" height="1" bgcolor=#5d6993></td>
<td rowspan="2" colspan="1" width="1" height="1" bgcolor=#5c6994></td>
<td width="1" height="1" bgcolor=#5c6892></td>
<td width="1" height="1" bgcolor=#5a698d></td>
<td width="1" height="1" bgcolor=#58678e></td>
<td width="1" height="1" bgcolor=#58688f></td>
<td width="1" height="1" bgcolor=#59688f></td>
<td width="1" height="1" bgcolor=#58678e></td>
<td width="1" height="1" bgcolor=#58678d></td>
<td rowspan="2" colspan="1" width="1" height="1" bgcolor=#57668d></td>
<td width="1" height="1" bgcolor=#57678d></td>
<td width="1" height="1" bgcolor=#55658b></td>
<td width="1" height="1" bgcolor=#56658c></td>
<td rowspan="2" colspan="1" width="1" height="1" bgcolor=#57668d></td>
<td width="1" height="1" bgcolor=#55638b></td>
<td width="1" height="1" bgcolor=#58658c></td>
<td width="1" height="1" bgcolor=#546789></td>
<td width="1" height="1" bgcolor=#3e4763></td>
<td width="1" height="1" bgcolor=#040500></td>
<td width="1" height="1" bgcolor=#151921></td>
<td width="1" height="1" bgcolor=#0a0a10></td>
<td width="1" height="1" bgcolor=#282838></td>
<td width="1" height="1" bgcolor=#000100></td>
<td width="1" height="1" bgcolor=#303749></td>
<td width="1" height="1" bgcolor=#4c5d89></td>
<td width="1" height="1" bgcolor=#61625f></td>
</tr>
<tr>
<td width="1" height="1" bgcolor=#556690></td>
<td width="1" height="1" bgcolor=#2f354b></td>
<td width="1" height="1" bgcolor=#060100></td>
<td width="1" height="1" bgcolor=#1f1e26></td>
<td width="1" height="1" bgcolor=#0e0f07></td>
<td width="1" height="1" bgcolor=#0d060e></td>
<td width="1" height="1" bgcolor=#0b130f></td>
<td width="1" height="1" bgcolor=#4e5777></td>
<td width="1" height="1" bgcolor=#121620></td>
<td width="1" height="1" bgcolor=#474e6d></td>
<td width="1" height="1" bgcolor=#5a6993></td>
<td width="1" height="1" bgcolor=#435073></td>
<td width="1" height="1" bgcolor=#2e3c4c></td>
<td width="1" height="1" bgcolor=#3f4865></td>
<td width="1" height="1" bgcolor=#4f5f83></td>
<td width="1" height="1" bgcolor=#2a303d></td>
<td width="1" height="1" bgcolor=#110f0d></td>
<td width="1" height="1" bgcolor=#0c0e0b></td>
<td width="1" height="1" bgcolor=#394054></td>
<td width="1" height="1" bgcolor=#191b21></td>
<td width="1" height="1" bgcolor=#3c4a66></td>
<td width="1" height="1" bgcolor=#2d303e></td>
<td width="1" height="1" bgcolor=#232535></td>
<td width="1" height="1" bgcolor=#3d415c></td>
<td width="1" height="1" bgcolor=#262838></td>
<td width="1" height="1" bgcolor=#271f29></td>
<td width="1" height="1" bgcolor=#1e1c23></td>
<td width="1" height="1" bgcolor=#39415a></td>
<td width="1" height="1" bgcolor=#252731></td>
<td width="1" height="1" bgcolor=#454b66></td>
<td width="1" height="1" bgcolor=#31374d></td>
<td width="1" height="1" bgcolor=#10080f></td>
<td width="1" height="1" bgcolor=#080807></td>
<td width="1" height="1" bgcolor=#546083></td>
<td width="1" height="1" bgcolor=#484e70></td>
<td width="1" height="1" bgcolor=#303546></td>
<td width="1" height="1" bgcolor=#2e354b></td>
<td width="1" height="1" bgcolor=#373d50></td>
```

```
    <td width="1" height="1"
bgcolor=#61709a></td>
    <td width="1" height="1"
bgcolor=#5d6a94></td>
    <td width="1" height="1"
bgcolor=#5e6b95></td>
    <td width="1" height="1"
bgcolor=#5d6993></td>
    <td rowspan="1"
colspan="2" width="1"
height="1"
bgcolor=#5d6a94></td>
    <td width="1" height="1"
bgcolor=#5d6993></td>
    <td rowspan="3"
colspan="1" width="1"
height="1"
bgcolor=#5b6892></td>
    <td width="1" height="1"
bgcolor=#5b6891></td>
    <td width="1" height="1"
bgcolor=#5c6991></td>
    <td width="1" height="1"
bgcolor=#5b6a91></td>
    <td width="1" height="1"
bgcolor=#58678f></td>
    <td width="1" height="1"
bgcolor=#58678e></td>
    <td rowspan="1"
colspan="2" width="1"
height="1"
bgcolor=#57668d></td>
    <td width="1" height="1"
bgcolor=#57668d></td>
    <td width="1" height="1"
bgcolor=#56658c></td>
    <td rowspan="2"
colspan="1" width="1"
height="1"
bgcolor=#57668d></td>
    <td width="1" height="1"
bgcolor=#56658b></td>
    <td width="1" height="1"
bgcolor=#546488></td>
    <td rowspan="2"
colspan="1" width="1"
height="1"
bgcolor=#546489></td>
    <td width="1" height="1"
bgcolor=#58668d></td>
    <td width="1" height="1"
bgcolor=#08050c></td>
    <td width="1" height="1"
bgcolor=#050504></td>
    <td width="1" height="1"
bgcolor=#14131c></td>
    <td width="1" height="1"
bgcolor=#070a0a></td>
    <td width="1" height="1"
bgcolor=#1d222f></td>
    <td width="1" height="1"
bgcolor=#495678></td>
    <td width="1" height="1"
bgcolor=#4e6081></td>
    <td width="1" height="1"
bgcolor=#5a5c58></td>
  </tr>
  <tr>
    <td width="1" height="1"
bgcolor=#54638b></td>
    <td width="1" height="1"
bgcolor=#57688e></td>
    <td width="1" height="1"
bgcolor=#111621></td>
    <td width="1" height="1"
bgcolor=#060500></td>
    <td width="1" height="1"
bgcolor=#191a21></td>
    <td width="1" height="1"
bgcolor=#0f1014></td>
    <td width="1" height="1"
bgcolor=#09060c></td>
    <td width="1" height="1"
bgcolor=#060807></td>
    <td width="1" height="1"
bgcolor=#404965></td>
    <td width="1" height="1"
bgcolor=#5c6c8e></td>
    <td width="1" height="1"
bgcolor=#4a597e></td>
    <td width="1" height="1"
bgcolor=#586185></td>
    <td width="1" height="1"
bgcolor=#4f5e86></td>
    <td width="1" height="1"
bgcolor=#434e70></td>
    <td width="1" height="1"
bgcolor=#464f6e></td>
    <td width="1" height="1"
bgcolor=#191a20></td>
    <td width="1" height="1"
bgcolor=#1f1c28></td>
    <td width="1" height="1"
bgcolor=#130f17></td>
    <td width="1" height="1"
bgcolor=#090905></td>
    <td width="1" height="1"
bgcolor=#201f2a></td>
    <td width="1" height="1"
bgcolor=#17151f></td>
    <td width="1" height="1"
bgcolor=#30384f></td>
    <td width="1" height="1"
bgcolor=#373b52></td>
    <td width="1" height="1"
bgcolor=#262b3e></td>
    <td width="1" height="1"
bgcolor=#1e1e24></td>
    <td width="1" height="1"
bgcolor=#161419></td>
    <td width="1" height="1"
bgcolor=#1c1e1b></td>
    <td width="1" height="1"
bgcolor=#181923></td>
    <td width="1" height="1"
bgcolor=#323144></td>
    <td width="1" height="1"
bgcolor=#242435></td>
    <td width="1" height="1"
bgcolor=#404b63></td>
    <td width="1" height="1"
bgcolor=#212532></td>
    <td width="1" height="1"
bgcolor=#312d42></td>
    <td width="1" height="1"
bgcolor=#1e1a29></td>
    <td width="1" height="1"
bgcolor=#6577a1></td>
    <td width="1" height="1"
bgcolor=#1b202a></td>
    <td width="1" height="1"
bgcolor=#434966></td>
    <td width="1" height="1"
bgcolor=#424a68></td>
    <td width="1" height="1"
bgcolor=#4a5073></td>
    <td width="1" height="1"
bgcolor=#5e6e94></td>
    <td rowspan="2"
colspan="2" width="1"
height="1"
bgcolor=#5d6993></td>
    <td width="1" height="1"
bgcolor=#5d6a94></td>
    <td width="1" height="1"
bgcolor=#5d6993></td>
    <td width="1" height="1"
bgcolor=#5c6993></td>
    <td width="1" height="1"
bgcolor=#5b6892></td>
    <td width="1" height="1"
bgcolor=#5b6892></td>
    <td width="1" height="1"
bgcolor=#5c6992></td>
    <td width="1" height="1"
bgcolor=#5a6891></td>
    <td width="1" height="1"
bgcolor=#596790></td>
    <td width="1" height="1"
bgcolor=#5a6992></td>
    <td rowspan="2"
colspan="1" width="1"
height="1"
bgcolor=#596891></td>
```

```
    <td width="1" height="1" bgcolor=#58678f></td>
    <td rowspan="2" colspan="1" width="1" height="1" bgcolor=#57668d></td>
    <td width="1" height="1" bgcolor=#57668f></td>
    <td rowspan="2" colspan="1" width="1" height="1" bgcolor=#56658f></td>
    <td width="1" height="1" bgcolor=#55648d></td>
    <td width="1" height="1" bgcolor=#57658d></td>
    <td width="1" height="1" bgcolor=#55658a></td>
    <td width="1" height="1" bgcolor=#556589></td>
    <td width="1" height="1" bgcolor=#59688c></td>
    <td width="1" height="1" bgcolor=#0a0e10></td>
    <td width="1" height="1" bgcolor=#080906></td>
    <td width="1" height="1" bgcolor=#181b23></td>
    <td width="1" height="1" bgcolor=#06090b></td>
    <td width="1" height="1" bgcolor=#20212c></td>
    <td width="1" height="1" bgcolor=#2f3c50></td>
    <td width="1" height="1" bgcolor=#4e5d89></td>
    <td width="1" height="1" bgcolor=#60625e></td>
  </tr>
  <tr>
    <td width="1" height="1" bgcolor=#55618a></td>
    <td width="1" height="1" bgcolor=#4d5f84></td>
    <td width="1" height="1" bgcolor=#5b6992></td>
    <td width="1" height="1" bgcolor=#0f141a></td>
    <td width="1" height="1" bgcolor=#09030d></td>
    <td width="1" height="1" bgcolor=#19191e></td>
    <td width="1" height="1" bgcolor=#13121c></td>
    <td width="1" height="1" bgcolor=#0a090c></td>
    <td width="1" height="1" bgcolor=#050206></td>
    <td width="1" height="1" bgcolor=#2f384d></td>
    <td width="1" height="1" bgcolor=#56668f></td>
    <td width="1" height="1" bgcolor=#596c90></td>
    <td width="1" height="1" bgcolor=#455270></td>
    <td width="1" height="1" bgcolor=#566685></td>
    <td width="1" height="1" bgcolor=#485574></td>
    <td width="1" height="1" bgcolor=#5e6c98></td>
    <td width="1" height="1" bgcolor=#616f99></td>
    <td width="1" height="1" bgcolor=#616e98></td>
    <td width="1" height="1" bgcolor=#616d97></td>
    <td width="1" height="1" bgcolor=#324055></td>
    <td width="1" height="1" bgcolor=#0b0307></td>
    <td width="1" height="1" bgcolor=#404b66></td>
    <td width="1" height="1" bgcolor=#15191c></td>
    <td width="1" height="1" bgcolor=#353a4f></td>
    <td width="1" height="1" bgcolor=#131117></td>
    <td width="1" height="1" bgcolor=#171416></td>
    <td width="1" height="1" bgcolor=#29293e></td>
    <td width="1" height="1" bgcolor=#393f5b></td>
    <td width="1" height="1" bgcolor=#353046></td>
    <td width="1" height="1" bgcolor=#445373></td>
    <td width="1" height="1" bgcolor=#35354d></td>
    <td width="1" height="1" bgcolor=#313449></td>
    <td width="1" height="1" bgcolor=#14171c></td>
    <td width="1" height="1" bgcolor=#3a4058></td>
    <td width="1" height="1" bgcolor=#56648c></td>
    <td width="1" height="1" bgcolor=#3c455f></td>
    <td width="1" height="1" bgcolor=#171620></td>
    <td width="1" height="1" bgcolor=#566486></td>
    <td width="1" height="1" bgcolor=#5c6d95></td>
    <td width="1" height="1" bgcolor=#5b6891></td>
    <td width="1" height="1" bgcolor=#5d6993></td>
    <td width="1" height="1" bgcolor=#5b6892></td>
    <td width="1" height="1" bgcolor=#5b6792></td>
    <td width="1" height="1" bgcolor=#5a6791></td>
    <td width="1" height="1" bgcolor=#5b6992></td>
    <td width="1" height="1" bgcolor=#5c6b94></td>
    <td width="1" height="1" bgcolor=#5b6a93></td>
    <td rowspan="5" colspan="1" width="1" height="1" bgcolor=#596891></td>
    <td rowspan="2" colspan="1" width="1" height="1" bgcolor=#586790></td>
    <td width="1" height="1" bgcolor=#57668f></td>
    <td width="1" height="1" bgcolor=#58678f></td>
    <td rowspan="2" colspan="1" width="1" height="1" bgcolor=#56658e></td>
    <td width="1" height="1" bgcolor=#586790></td>
    <td width="1" height="1" bgcolor=#57658e></td>
    <td width="1" height="1" bgcolor=#56658d></td>
    <td width="1" height="1" bgcolor=#54638c></td>
    <td width="1" height="1" bgcolor=#57668a></td>
    <td width="1" height="1" bgcolor=#313d5a></td>
    <td width="1" height="1" bgcolor=#404a66></td>
    <td width="1" height="1" bgcolor=#303a53></td>
    <td width="1" height="1" bgcolor=#353a59></td>
    <td width="1" height="1" bgcolor=#3e4763></td>
    <td width="1" height="1" bgcolor=#393f5e></td>
    <td width="1" height="1" bgcolor=#475171></td>
```

```
    <td width="1" height="1"
bgcolor=#505d8a></td>
    <td width="1" height="1"
bgcolor=#60625f></td>
  </tr>
  <tr>
    <td width="1" height="1"
bgcolor=#556589></td>
    <td width="1" height="1"
bgcolor=#435172></td>
    <td width="1" height="1"
bgcolor=#4a5779></td>
    <td width="1" height="1"
bgcolor=#5a6a92></td>
    <td width="1" height="1"
bgcolor=#14101a></td>
    <td width="1" height="1"
bgcolor=#09030b></td>
    <td width="1" height="1"
bgcolor=#14171a></td>
    <td width="1" height="1"
bgcolor=#0e0f13></td>
    <td width="1" height="1"
bgcolor=#0a0914></td>
    <td width="1" height="1"
bgcolor=#070500></td>
    <td width="1" height="1"
bgcolor=#454c6d></td>
    <td width="1" height="1"
bgcolor=#485a7b></td>
    <td width="1" height="1"
bgcolor=#556388></td>
    <td width="1" height="1"
bgcolor=#5d6992></td>
    <td width="1" height="1"
bgcolor=#5c6991></td>
    <td width="1" height="1"
bgcolor=#5d6a94></td>
    <td width="1" height="1"
bgcolor=#5d6993></td>
    <td rowspan="1"
colspan="2" width="1"
height="1"
bgcolor=#5b6a93></td>
    <td width="1" height="1"
bgcolor=#5f6a98></td>
    <td width="1" height="1"
bgcolor=#516385></td>
    <td width="1" height="1"
bgcolor=#262933></td>
    <td width="1" height="1"
bgcolor=#252238></td>
    <td width="1" height="1"
bgcolor=#0f1014></td>
    <td width="1" height="1"
bgcolor=#100d0e></td>
    <td width="1" height="1"
bgcolor=#272735></td>
    <td width="1" height="1"
bgcolor=#4a4f71></td>
    <td width="1" height="1"
bgcolor=#1d232d></td>
    <td width="1" height="1"
bgcolor=#181d24></td>
    <td width="1" height="1"
bgcolor=#606c92></td>
    <td width="1" height="1"
bgcolor=#1a1829></td>
    <td width="1" height="1"
bgcolor=#383b51></td>
    <td width="1" height="1"
bgcolor=#252233></td>
    <td width="1" height="1"
bgcolor=#556086></td>
    <td width="1" height="1"
bgcolor=#4b577b></td>
    <td width="1" height="1"
bgcolor=#4c5879></td>
    <td width="1" height="1"
bgcolor=#2b3141></td>
    <td width="1" height="1"
bgcolor=#565f85></td>
    <td width="1" height="1"
bgcolor=#1c202d></td>
    <td width="1" height="1"
bgcolor=#3c4a66></td>
    <td width="1" height="1"
bgcolor=#5f6a94></td>
    <td width="1" height="1"
bgcolor=#5b6c96></td>
    <td width="1" height="1"
bgcolor=#5e6894></td>
    <td width="1" height="1"
bgcolor=#5c6992></td>
    <td rowspan="1"
colspan="2" width="1"
height="1"
bgcolor=#5b6a93></td>
    <td width="1" height="1"
bgcolor=#5b6791></td>
    <td width="1" height="1"
bgcolor=#5c6993></td>
    <td width="1" height="1"
bgcolor=#5c6892></td>
    <td width="1" height="1"
bgcolor=#5b6892></td>
    <td width="1" height="1"
bgcolor=#596890></td>
    <td width="1" height="1"
bgcolor=#58678e></td>
    <td width="1" height="1"
bgcolor=#586790></td>
    <td width="1" height="1"
bgcolor=#57668f></td>
    <td width="1" height="1"
bgcolor=#56658c></td>
    <td width="1" height="1"
bgcolor=#55648d></td>
    <td width="1" height="1"
bgcolor=#56678d></td>
    <td width="1" height="1"
bgcolor=#56648a></td>
    <td width="1" height="1"
bgcolor=#536088></td>
    <td width="1" height="1"
bgcolor=#3e4d6c></td>
    <td width="1" height="1"
bgcolor=#42516d></td>
    <td width="1" height="1"
bgcolor=#4f5d7b></td>
    <td width="1" height="1"
bgcolor=#344160></td>
    <td width="1" height="1"
bgcolor=#353e53></td>
    <td width="1" height="1"
bgcolor=#35435b></td>
    <td width="1" height="1"
bgcolor=#120f1a></td>
    <td width="1" height="1"
bgcolor=#374159></td>
    <td width="1" height="1"
bgcolor=#4c5f8a></td>
    <td width="1" height="1"
bgcolor=#5b5d58></td>
  </tr>
  <tr>
    <td width="1" height="1"
bgcolor=#54638c></td>
    <td width="1" height="1"
bgcolor=#373f5c></td>
    <td width="1" height="1"
bgcolor=#2d3850></td>
    <td width="1" height="1"
bgcolor=#54618b></td>
    <td width="1" height="1"
bgcolor=#5a6c94></td>
    <td width="1" height="1"
bgcolor=#12101a></td>
    <td width="1" height="1"
bgcolor=#090902></td>
    <td width="1" height="1"
bgcolor=#101016></td>
    <td width="1" height="1"
bgcolor=#131316></td>
    <td width="1" height="1"
bgcolor=#0b0c0d></td>
    <td width="1" height="1"
bgcolor=#050502></td>
    <td width="1" height="1"
bgcolor=#323c4f></td>
    <td width="1" height="1"
bgcolor=#5f6c92></td>
    <td width="1" height="1"
bgcolor=#5b6890></td>
```

```
<td width="1" height="1" bgcolor=#5d6a91></td>
<td width="1" height="1" bgcolor=#5c6993></td>
<td width="1" height="1" bgcolor=#5c6a93></td>
<td width="1" height="1" bgcolor=#5a6891></td>
<td width="1" height="1" bgcolor=#5d6993></td>
<td width="1" height="1" bgcolor=#5e6a94></td>
<td width="1" height="1" bgcolor=#596b95></td>
<td width="1" height="1" bgcolor=#646f95></td>
<td width="1" height="1" bgcolor=#232b3b></td>
<td width="1" height="1" bgcolor=#0c0d08></td>
<td width="1" height="1" bgcolor=#100d0f></td>
<td width="1" height="1" bgcolor=#303147></td>
<td width="1" height="1" bgcolor=#303747></td>
<td width="1" height="1" bgcolor=#3f405a></td>
<td width="1" height="1" bgcolor=#313651></td>
<td width="1" height="1" bgcolor=#313448></td>
<td width="1" height="1" bgcolor=#363754></td>
<td width="1" height="1" bgcolor=#12111f></td>
<td width="1" height="1" bgcolor=#2d333c></td>
<td width="1" height="1" bgcolor=#63749d></td>
<td width="1" height="1" bgcolor=#455271></td>
<td width="1" height="1" bgcolor=#57648d></td>
<td width="1" height="1" bgcolor=#5f7195></td>
<td width="1" height="1" bgcolor=#586791></td>
<td width="1" height="1" bgcolor=#34394c></td>
<td width="1" height="1" bgcolor=#383c58></td>
<td width="1" height="1" bgcolor=#404760></td>
<td width="1" height="1" bgcolor=#5d6a95></td>
<td width="1" height="1" bgcolor=#5d698f></td>
<td width="1" height="1" bgcolor=#596a92></td>
<td width="1" height="1" bgcolor=#5b6992></td>
<td width="1" height="1" bgcolor=#5c6992></td>
<td width="1" height="1" bgcolor=#5b6892></td>
<td width="1" height="1" bgcolor=#5b6893></td>
<td width="1" height="1" bgcolor=#5a6791></td>
<td width="1" height="1" bgcolor=#5a6892></td>
<td width="1" height="1" bgcolor=#58678f></td>
<td rowspan="1" colspan="2" width="1" height="1" bgcolor=#57668d></td>
<td width="1" height="1" bgcolor=#58678e></td>
<td width="1" height="1" bgcolor=#58678f></td>
<td width="1" height="1" bgcolor=#55648b></td>
<td width="1" height="1" bgcolor=#57668e></td>
<td width="1" height="1" bgcolor=#56658d></td>
<td width="1" height="1" bgcolor=#57648e></td>
<td width="1" height="1" bgcolor=#4e5e80></td>
<td width="1" height="1" bgcolor=#3d4a6a></td>
<td width="1" height="1" bgcolor=#363f57></td>
<td width="1" height="1" bgcolor=#475677></td>
<td width="1" height="1" bgcolor=#35415a></td>
<td width="1" height="1" bgcolor=#1f2633></td>
<td width="1" height="1" bgcolor=#414d6d></td>
<td width="1" height="1" bgcolor=#546384></td>
<td width="1" height="1" bgcolor=#272734></td>
<td width="1" height="1" bgcolor=#36415c></td>
<td width="1" height="1" bgcolor=#4c5f87></td>
<td width="1" height="1" bgcolor=#5a5c58></td>
</tr>
<tr>
<td width="1" height="1" bgcolor=#53648d></td>
<td width="1" height="1" bgcolor=#2c334b></td>
<td width="1" height="1" bgcolor=#212532></td>
<td width="1" height="1" bgcolor=#4b5b7b></td>
<td width="1" height="1" bgcolor=#56638a></td>
<td width="1" height="1" bgcolor=#586a96></td>
<td width="1" height="1" bgcolor=#0d1213></td>
<td width="1" height="1" bgcolor=#070409></td>
<td width="1" height="1" bgcolor=#0e0c18></td>
<td width="1" height="1" bgcolor=#110c15></td>
<td width="1" height="1" bgcolor=#040402></td>
<td width="1" height="1" bgcolor=#404964></td>
<td width="1" height="1" bgcolor=#5b6992></td>
<td width="1" height="1" bgcolor=#5c6992></td>
<td width="1" height="1" bgcolor=#5b6890></td>
<td rowspan="1" colspan="2" width="1" height="1" bgcolor=#5b6993></td>
<td width="1" height="1" bgcolor=#5c6892></td>
<td width="1" height="1" bgcolor=#5c6993></td>
<td width="1" height="1" bgcolor=#5f6996></td>
<td width="1" height="1" bgcolor=#5d6b92></td>
<td width="1" height="1" bgcolor=#5e6a99></td>
<td width="1" height="1" bgcolor=#374057></td>
<td width="1" height="1" bgcolor=#0f090d></td>
<td width="1" height="1" bgcolor=#110d10></td>
<td width="1" height="1" bgcolor=#24242f></td>
<td width="1" height="1" bgcolor=#2a2b41></td>
<td width="1" height="1" bgcolor=#0a0a07></td>
<td width="1" height="1" bgcolor=#3e465f></td>
```

```
    <td width="1" height="1"
bgcolor=#15121b></td>
    <td width="1" height="1"
bgcolor=#4d5b7d></td>
    <td width="1" height="1"
bgcolor=#637098></td>
    <td width="1" height="1"
bgcolor=#606d9e></td>
    <td width="1" height="1"
bgcolor=#5f698a></td>
    <td width="1" height="1"
bgcolor=#455179></td>
    <td width="1" height="1"
bgcolor=#3c415d></td>
    <td width="1" height="1"
bgcolor=#2d354a></td>
    <td width="1" height="1"
bgcolor=#3a4462></td>
    <td width="1" height="1"
bgcolor=#383f52></td>
    <td width="1" height="1"
bgcolor=#252838></td>
    <td width="1" height="1"
bgcolor=#1d2327></td>
    <td width="1" height="1"
bgcolor=#455676></td>
    <td width="1" height="1"
bgcolor=#58638d></td>
    <td width="1" height="1"
bgcolor=#5f6c93></td>
    <td width="1" height="1"
bgcolor=#5c6891></td>
    <td width="1" height="1"
bgcolor=#5b6891></td>
    <td width="1" height="1"
bgcolor=#5c6892></td>
    <td width="1" height="1"
bgcolor=#5c6893></td>
    <td width="1" height="1"
bgcolor=#5b6892></td>
    <td width="1" height="1"
bgcolor=#596791></td>
    <td width="1" height="1"
bgcolor=#5a6991></td>
    <td width="1" height="1"
bgcolor=#58678e></td>
    <td width="1" height="1"
bgcolor=#57668d></td>
    <td width="1" height="1"
bgcolor=#59688f></td>
    <td width="1" height="1"
bgcolor=#58678d></td>
    <td width="1" height="1"
bgcolor=#57668d></td>
    <td width="1" height="1"
bgcolor=#55648b></td>
    <td width="1" height="1"
bgcolor=#55648c></td>
    <td width="1" height="1"
bgcolor=#55658a></td>
    <td width="1" height="1"
bgcolor=#56698a></td>
    <td width="1" height="1"
bgcolor=#4c587b></td>
    <td width="1" height="1"
bgcolor=#222838></td>
    <td width="1" height="1"
bgcolor=#222334></td>
    <td width="1" height="1"
bgcolor=#262a3b></td>
    <td width="1" height="1"
bgcolor=#262e44></td>
    <td width="1" height="1"
bgcolor=#38405a></td>
    <td width="1" height="1"
bgcolor=#1f2736></td>
    <td width="1" height="1"
bgcolor=#1a1e2d></td>
    <td width="1" height="1"
bgcolor=#303b54></td>
    <td width="1" height="1"
bgcolor=#4a5e85></td>
    <td width="1" height="1"
bgcolor=#5b5c59></td>
  </tr>
  <tr>
    <td width="1" height="1"
bgcolor=#53648a></td>
    <td width="1" height="1"
bgcolor=#2d3349></td>
    <td width="1" height="1"
bgcolor=#0b0a14></td>
    <td width="1" height="1"
bgcolor=#30394f></td>
    <td width="1" height="1"
bgcolor=#535e85></td>
    <td width="1" height="1"
bgcolor=#526385></td>
    <td width="1" height="1"
bgcolor=#58668e></td>
    <td width="1" height="1"
bgcolor=#0a1218></td>
    <td width="1" height="1"
bgcolor=#394257></td>
    <td width="1" height="1"
bgcolor=#3c465e></td>
    <td width="1" height="1"
bgcolor=#171b22></td>
    <td width="1" height="1"
bgcolor=#4b5673></td>
    <td width="1" height="1"
bgcolor=#5a6992></td>
    <td width="1" height="1"
bgcolor=#5b6a92></td>
    <td width="1" height="1"
bgcolor=#5c6b92></td>
    <td width="1" height="1"
bgcolor=#5c6893></td>
    <td width="1" height="1"
bgcolor=#5d6993></td>
    <td width="1" height="1"
bgcolor=#5c6993></td>
    <td width="1" height="1"
bgcolor=#5d6993></td>
    <td width="1" height="1"
bgcolor=#5b6a93></td>
    <td width="1" height="1"
bgcolor=#5d6a95></td>
    <td width="1" height="1"
bgcolor=#5d6991></td>
    <td width="1" height="1"
bgcolor=#4f5c7f></td>
    <td width="1" height="1"
bgcolor=#040505></td>
    <td width="1" height="1"
bgcolor=#1a1b22></td>
    <td width="1" height="1"
bgcolor=#343749></td>
    <td width="1" height="1"
bgcolor=#101019></td>
    <td width="1" height="1"
bgcolor=#171014></td>
    <td width="1" height="1"
bgcolor=#3e4764></td>
    <td width="1" height="1"
bgcolor=#5f6a90></td>
    <td width="1" height="1"
bgcolor=#3d495e></td>
    <td width="1" height="1"
bgcolor=#12111f></td>
    <td width="1" height="1"
bgcolor=#5e6d93></td>
    <td width="1" height="1"
bgcolor=#5d6d95></td>
    <td width="1" height="1"
bgcolor=#313954></td>
    <td width="1" height="1"
bgcolor=#18141a></td>
    <td width="1" height="1"
bgcolor=#2a2d3c></td>
    <td width="1" height="1"
bgcolor=#4a506a></td>
    <td width="1" height="1"
bgcolor=#56668c></td>
    <td width="1" height="1"
bgcolor=#222132></td>
    <td width="1" height="1"
bgcolor=#464967></td>
    <td width="1" height="1"
bgcolor=#5a6e97></td>
    <td width="1" height="1"
bgcolor=#363e53></td>
    <td width="1" height="1"
bgcolor=#2f374b></td>
```

```
    <td width="1" height="1"
bgcolor=#606d91></td>
    <td width="1" height="1"
bgcolor=#5c6994></td>
    <td width="1" height="1"
bgcolor=#5a6792></td>
    <td width="1" height="1"
bgcolor=#5b6891></td>
    <td width="1" height="1"
bgcolor=#5a6791></td>
    <td width="1" height="1"
bgcolor=#5a6892></td>
    <td width="1" height="1"
bgcolor=#58668f></td>
    <td width="1" height="1"
bgcolor=#5b6a93></td>
    <td width="1" height="1"
bgcolor=#596890></td>
    <td width="1" height="1"
bgcolor=#58688f></td>
    <td width="1" height="1"
bgcolor=#55648b></td>
    <td width="1" height="1"
bgcolor=#56658d></td>
    <td width="1" height="1"
bgcolor=#54638c></td>
    <td rowspan="2"
colspan="1" width="1"
height="1"
bgcolor=#56658c></td>
    <td width="1" height="1"
bgcolor=#56658c></td>
    <td width="1" height="1"
bgcolor=#55628d></td>
    <td width="1" height="1"
bgcolor=#536889></td>
    <td width="1" height="1"
bgcolor=#424d6e></td>
    <td width="1" height="1"
bgcolor=#050300></td>
    <td width="1" height="1"
bgcolor=#30354e></td>
    <td width="1" height="1"
bgcolor=#232c31></td>
    <td width="1" height="1"
bgcolor=#0e0a13></td>
    <td width="1" height="1"
bgcolor=#060501></td>
    <td width="1" height="1"
bgcolor=#232b38></td>
    <td width="1" height="1"
bgcolor=#2c3347></td>
    <td width="1" height="1"
bgcolor=#4b5e85></td>
    <td width="1" height="1"
bgcolor=#61625f></td>
  </tr>
  <tr>
    <td width="1" height="1"
bgcolor=#556489></td>
    <td width="1" height="1"
bgcolor=#2e364b></td>
    <td width="1" height="1"
bgcolor=#100e15></td>
    <td width="1" height="1"
bgcolor=#181a22></td>
    <td width="1" height="1"
bgcolor=#292a46></td>
    <td width="1" height="1"
bgcolor=#353f5c></td>
    <td width="1" height="1"
bgcolor=#56678a></td>
    <td width="1" height="1"
bgcolor=#5b6e96></td>
    <td width="1" height="1"
bgcolor=#54668c></td>
    <td width="1" height="1"
bgcolor=#57688e></td>
    <td width="1" height="1"
bgcolor=#5c6e96></td>
    <td width="1" height="1"
bgcolor=#5a6891></td>
    <td rowspan="2"
colspan="1" width="1"
height="1"
bgcolor=#5a688f></td>
    <td width="1" height="1"
bgcolor=#5a6992></td>
    <td width="1" height="1"
bgcolor=#5b6992></td>
    <td width="1" height="1"
bgcolor=#5b6894></td>
    <td width="1" height="1"
bgcolor=#5d6a95></td>
    <td width="1" height="1"
bgcolor=#5b6892></td>
    <td width="1" height="1"
bgcolor=#5b6993></td>
    <td width="1" height="1"
bgcolor=#596994></td>
    <td width="1" height="1"
bgcolor=#5c6a91></td>
    <td width="1" height="1"
bgcolor=#5c6a94></td>
    <td width="1" height="1"
bgcolor=#596392></td>
    <td width="1" height="1"
bgcolor=#505876></td>
    <td width="1" height="1"
bgcolor=#4a5a7d></td>
    <td width="1" height="1"
bgcolor=#121117></td>
    <td width="1" height="1"
bgcolor=#140f15></td>
    <td width="1" height="1"
bgcolor=#1a1f29></td>
    <td width="1" height="1"
bgcolor=#535c7f></td>
    <td width="1" height="1"
bgcolor=#4a5272></td>
    <td width="1" height="1"
bgcolor=#0d0a0b></td>
    <td width="1" height="1"
bgcolor=#2c2e47></td>
    <td width="1" height="1"
bgcolor=#5e7296></td>
    <td width="1" height="1"
bgcolor=#5d6b95></td>
    <td width="1" height="1"
bgcolor=#363b54></td>
    <td width="1" height="1"
bgcolor=#252638></td>
    <td width="1" height="1"
bgcolor=#5a688c></td>
    <td width="1" height="1"
bgcolor=#3d4967></td>
    <td width="1" height="1"
bgcolor=#505f84></td>
    <td width="1" height="1"
bgcolor=#262a36></td>
    <td width="1" height="1"
bgcolor=#4c5c7e></td>
    <td width="1" height="1"
bgcolor=#5e6b8f></td>
    <td width="1" height="1"
bgcolor=#4e5b85></td>
    <td width="1" height="1"
bgcolor=#38415f></td>
    <td width="1" height="1"
bgcolor=#5d6b91></td>
    <td width="1" height="1"
bgcolor=#596793></td>
    <td width="1" height="1"
bgcolor=#5b6792></td>
    <td width="1" height="1"
bgcolor=#5b6b96></td>
    <td width="1" height="1"
bgcolor=#5b6892></td>
    <td width="1" height="1"
bgcolor=#596690></td>
    <td width="1" height="1"
bgcolor=#59698f></td>
    <td width="1" height="1"
bgcolor=#5a6d94></td>
    <td width="1" height="1"
bgcolor=#2f2f4a></td>
    <td width="1" height="1"
bgcolor=#0a1314></td>
    <td width="1" height="1"
bgcolor=#4a4f71></td>
    <td width="1" height="1"
bgcolor=#566891></td>
    <td width="1" height="1"
bgcolor=#56658e></td>
```

```
    <td width="1" height="1" bgcolor=#57668e></td>
    <td width="1" height="1" bgcolor=#57668b></td>
    <td width="1" height="1" bgcolor=#54638a></td>
    <td width="1" height="1" bgcolor=#54648e></td>
    <td width="1" height="1" bgcolor=#586689></td>
    <td width="1" height="1" bgcolor=#111828></td>
    <td width="1" height="1" bgcolor=#181622></td>
    <td width="1" height="1" bgcolor=#1f242e></td>
    <td width="1" height="1" bgcolor=#010106></td>
    <td width="1" height="1" bgcolor=#060405></td>
    <td width="1" height="1" bgcolor=#000000></td>
    <td width="1" height="1" bgcolor=#4f5b82></td>
    <td width="1" height="1" bgcolor=#4e5d86></td>
    <td width="1" height="1" bgcolor=#60615d></td>
  </tr>
  <tr>
    <td width="1" height="1" bgcolor=#54638b></td>
    <td width="1" height="1" bgcolor=#2d344b></td>
    <td width="1" height="1" bgcolor=#111015></td>
    <td width="1" height="1" bgcolor=#15131d></td>
    <td width="1" height="1" bgcolor=#181b26></td>
    <td width="1" height="1" bgcolor=#58668c></td>
    <td width="1" height="1" bgcolor=#566691></td>
    <td width="1" height="1" bgcolor=#56658b></td>
    <td width="1" height="1" bgcolor=#586790></td>
    <td width="1" height="1" bgcolor=#596890></td>
    <td width="1" height="1" bgcolor=#596891></td>
    <td width="1" height="1" bgcolor=#59678f></td>
    <td width="1" height="1" bgcolor=#5b6a92></td>
    <td width="1" height="1" bgcolor=#5a6891></td>
    <td width="1" height="1" bgcolor=#5c6892></td>
    <td rowspan="1" colspan="2" width="1" height="1" bgcolor=#5d6993></td>
    <td width="1" height="1" bgcolor=#5c6a93></td>
    <td width="1" height="1" bgcolor=#5c6a90></td>
    <td width="1" height="1" bgcolor=#5e6b96></td>
    <td width="1" height="1" bgcolor=#596b92></td>
    <td width="1" height="1" bgcolor=#434e72></td>
    <td width="1" height="1" bgcolor=#000002></td>
    <td width="1" height="1" bgcolor=#515d7f></td>
    <td width="1" height="1" bgcolor=#586486></td>
    <td width="1" height="1" bgcolor=#0a0c19></td>
    <td width="1" height="1" bgcolor=#536182></td>
    <td width="1" height="1" bgcolor=#556489></td>
    <td width="1" height="1" bgcolor=#0d141d></td>
    <td width="1" height="1" bgcolor=#191821></td>
    <td width="1" height="1" bgcolor=#606f97></td>
    <td width="1" height="1" bgcolor=#606e95></td>
    <td width="1" height="1" bgcolor=#212336></td>
    <td width="1" height="1" bgcolor=#54668a></td>
    <td width="1" height="1" bgcolor=#424865></td>
    <td width="1" height="1" bgcolor=#3a4864></td>
    <td width="1" height="1" bgcolor=#616f99></td>
    <td width="1" height="1" bgcolor=#576586></td>
    <td width="1" height="1" bgcolor=#121620></td>
    <td width="1" height="1" bgcolor=#4c567c></td>
    <td width="1" height="1" bgcolor=#5c6896></td>
    <td width="1" height="1" bgcolor=#5b6a92></td>
    <td width="1" height="1" bgcolor=#5d6a94></td>
    <td width="1" height="1" bgcolor=#5a6893></td>
    <td width="1" height="1" bgcolor=#5d6a94></td>
    <td width="1" height="1" bgcolor=#5c6890></td>
    <td width="1" height="1" bgcolor=#5b6991></td>
    <td width="1" height="1" bgcolor=#5c6892></td>
    <td rowspan="3" colspan="1" width="1" height="1" bgcolor=#5b6790></td>
    <td width="1" height="1" bgcolor=#5a6990></td>
    <td width="1" height="1" bgcolor=#3e4963></td>
    <td width="1" height="1" bgcolor=#28313e></td>
    <td width="1" height="1" bgcolor=#5b6a8f></td>
    <td width="1" height="1" bgcolor=#0d161a></td>
    <td width="1" height="1" bgcolor=#57668c></td>
    <td width="1" height="1" bgcolor=#55648d></td>
    <td rowspan="3" colspan="1" width="1" height="1" bgcolor=#56658c></td>
    <td width="1" height="1" bgcolor=#57668d></td>
    <td rowspan="2" colspan="1" width="1" height="1" bgcolor=#56658d></td>
    <td width="1" height="1" bgcolor=#536289></td>
    <td width="1" height="1" bgcolor=#526088></td>
    <td width="1" height="1" bgcolor=#4f5e83></td>
    <td width="1" height="1" bgcolor=#4d5b7d></td>
    <td width="1" height="1" bgcolor=#000000></td>
    <td width="1" height="1" bgcolor=#212631></td>
    <td width="1" height="1" bgcolor=#000201></td>
    <td width="1" height="1" bgcolor=#020001></td>
    <td width="1" height="1" bgcolor=#171919></td>
    <td width="1" height="1" bgcolor=#313b5a></td>
```

```
    <td width="1" height="1" bgcolor=#516185></td>
    <td width="1" height="1" bgcolor=#535452></td>
  </tr>
  <tr>
    <td width="1" height="1" bgcolor=#54648c></td>
    <td width="1" height="1" bgcolor=#2c3349></td>
    <td width="1" height="1" bgcolor=#121118></td>
    <td width="1" height="1" bgcolor=#0d0813></td>
    <td width="1" height="1" bgcolor=#282e45></td>
    <td width="1" height="1" bgcolor=#556691></td>
    <td width="1" height="1" bgcolor=#546687></td>
    <td width="1" height="1" bgcolor=#57658f></td>
    <td rowspan="1" colspan="2" width="1" height="1" bgcolor=#56658e></td>
    <td width="1" height="1" bgcolor=#586790></td>
    <td width="1" height="1" bgcolor=#59668f></td>
    <td width="1" height="1" bgcolor=#58668e></td>
    <td width="1" height="1" bgcolor=#5b6a91></td>
    <td width="1" height="1" bgcolor=#5a6890></td>
    <td width="1" height="1" bgcolor=#5d6992></td>
    <td width="1" height="1" bgcolor=#5c6890></td>
    <td width="1" height="1" bgcolor=#5d6991></td>
    <td rowspan="2" colspan="1" width="1" height="1" bgcolor=#5c6a92></td>
    <td width="1" height="1" bgcolor=#5b6c93></td>
    <td width="1" height="1" bgcolor=#5c6995></td>
    <td width="1" height="1" bgcolor=#606e98></td>
    <td width="1" height="1" bgcolor=#42526d></td>
    <td width="1" height="1" bgcolor=#606b8f></td>
    <td width="1" height="1" bgcolor=#010007></td>
    <td width="1" height="1" bgcolor=#526284></td>
    <td width="1" height="1" bgcolor=#617195></td>
    <td width="1" height="1" bgcolor=#0f0e18></td>
    <td width="1" height="1" bgcolor=#56658c></td>
    <td width="1" height="1" bgcolor=#070000></td>
    <td width="1" height="1" bgcolor=#4d5979></td>
    <td width="1" height="1" bgcolor=#5c6c90></td>
    <td width="1" height="1" bgcolor=#4a5a7a></td>
    <td width="1" height="1" bgcolor=#181524></td>
    <td width="1" height="1" bgcolor=#5a638c></td>
    <td width="1" height="1" bgcolor=#46546f></td>
    <td width="1" height="1" bgcolor=#515e81></td>
    <td width="1" height="1" bgcolor=#4d5a7c></td>
    <td width="1" height="1" bgcolor=#535d80></td>
    <td width="1" height="1" bgcolor=#38415f></td>
    <td width="1" height="1" bgcolor=#4b5374></td>
    <td width="1" height="1" bgcolor=#59668f></td>
    <td width="1" height="1" bgcolor=#5d6a92></td>
    <td width="1" height="1" bgcolor=#5b6896></td>
    <td width="1" height="1" bgcolor=#5b6992></td>
    <td width="1" height="1" bgcolor=#5c6a92></td>
    <td width="1" height="1" bgcolor=#5d6b95></td>
    <td width="1" height="1" bgcolor=#596690></td>
    <td width="1" height="1" bgcolor=#5a678f></td>
    <td width="1" height="1" bgcolor=#5b6a91></td>
    <td width="1" height="1" bgcolor=#323c53></td>
    <td width="1" height="1" bgcolor=#1f2839></td>
    <td width="1" height="1" bgcolor=#536180></td>
    <td width="1" height="1" bgcolor=#5e6b99></td>
    <td width="1" height="1" bgcolor=#57688c></td>
    <td width="1" height="1" bgcolor=#55648c></td>
    <td rowspan="3" colspan="1" width="1" height="1" bgcolor=#56658c></td>
    <td width="1" height="1" bgcolor=#56648b></td>
    <td width="1" height="1" bgcolor=#536187></td>
    <td width="1" height="1" bgcolor=#54648c></td>
    <td width="1" height="1" bgcolor=#455678></td>
    <td width="1" height="1" bgcolor=#14131d></td>
    <td width="1" height="1" bgcolor=#0e0e1f></td>
    <td width="1" height="1" bgcolor=#030201></td>
    <td width="1" height="1" bgcolor=#010101></td>
    <td width="1" height="1" bgcolor=#272d3b></td>
    <td width="1" height="1" bgcolor=#47577b></td>
    <td width="1" height="1" bgcolor=#4a6082></td>
    <td width="1" height="1" bgcolor=#666764></td>
  </tr>
  <tr>
    <td width="1" height="1" bgcolor=#546389></td>
    <td width="1" height="1" bgcolor=#353c52></td>
    <td width="1" height="1" bgcolor=#0c0a13></td>
    <td width="1" height="1" bgcolor=#0a0f17></td>
    <td width="1" height="1" bgcolor=#59668b></td>
    <td width="1" height="1" bgcolor=#54658d></td>
    <td width="1" height="1" bgcolor=#58658e></td>
    <td width="1" height="1" bgcolor=#556490></td>
    <td width="1" height="1" bgcolor=#596891></td>
    <td width="1" height="1" bgcolor=#57668f></td>
    <td width="1" height="1" bgcolor=#57668e></td>
    <td width="1" height="1" bgcolor=#58678d></td>
```

```
    <td width="1" height="1" bgcolor=#59678f></td>
    <td width="1" height="1" bgcolor=#5a6990></td>
    <td width="1" height="1" bgcolor=#5c6991></td>
    <td rowspan="2" colspan="1" width="1" height="1" bgcolor=#5d6991></td>
    <td width="1" height="1" bgcolor=#5d6991></td>
    <td width="1" height="1" bgcolor=#5e6a92></td>
    <td width="1" height="1" bgcolor=#5e6c95></td>
    <td width="1" height="1" bgcolor=#5b6b8e></td>
    <td width="1" height="1" bgcolor=#5c6a9b></td>
    <td width="1" height="1" bgcolor=#2f384c></td>
    <td width="1" height="1" bgcolor=#1f262e></td>
    <td width="1" height="1" bgcolor=#5e6788></td>
    <td width="1" height="1" bgcolor=#333e55></td>
    <td width="1" height="1" bgcolor=#66729e></td>
    <td width="1" height="1" bgcolor=#1e1f2f></td>
    <td width="1" height="1" bgcolor=#48526c></td>
    <td width="1" height="1" bgcolor=#1e2632></td>
    <td width="1" height="1" bgcolor=#5b6a8c></td>
    <td width="1" height="1" bgcolor=#5a6c92></td>
    <td width="1" height="1" bgcolor=#4f5476></td>
    <td width="1" height="1" bgcolor=#657298></td>
    <td width="1" height="1" bgcolor=#3f4c69></td>
    <td width="1" height="1" bgcolor=#515d82></td>
    <td width="1" height="1" bgcolor=#2d3244></td>
    <td width="1" height="1" bgcolor=#3d455c></td>
    <td width="1" height="1" bgcolor=#26283c></td>
    <td width="1" height="1" bgcolor=#2f3244></td>
    <td width="1" height="1" bgcolor=#040803></td>
    <td width="1" height="1" bgcolor=#5d6e93></td>
    <td width="1" height="1" bgcolor=#5d6896></td>
    <td width="1" height="1" bgcolor=#5b6991></td>
    <td width="1" height="1" bgcolor=#5e6892></td>
    <td width="1" height="1" bgcolor=#5c6993></td>
    <td width="1" height="1" bgcolor=#596a93></td>
    <td width="1" height="1" bgcolor=#5b6890></td>
    <td width="1" height="1" bgcolor=#5d6a92></td>
    <td width="1" height="1" bgcolor=#59688f></td>
    <td width="1" height="1" bgcolor=#5a6a93></td>
    <td width="1" height="1" bgcolor=#52628c></td>
    <td width="1" height="1" bgcolor=#253545></td>
    <td width="1" height="1" bgcolor=#58688f></td>
    <td width="1" height="1" bgcolor=#59698d></td>
    <td rowspan="2" colspan="1" width="1" height="1" bgcolor=#55648b></td>
    <td width="1" height="1" bgcolor=#58678d></td>
    <td width="1" height="1" bgcolor=#54628b></td>
    <td width="1" height="1" bgcolor=#556389></td>
    <td width="1" height="1" bgcolor=#546489></td>
    <td width="1" height="1" bgcolor=#54628c></td>
    <td width="1" height="1" bgcolor=#394259></td>
    <td width="1" height="1" bgcolor=#040a0c></td>
    <td width="1" height="1" bgcolor=#010000></td>
    <td width="1" height="1" bgcolor=#4b5879></td>
    <td width="1" height="1" bgcolor=#272d43></td>
    <td width="1" height="1" bgcolor=#31364e></td>
    <td width="1" height="1" bgcolor=#4d5d8c></td>
    <td width="1" height="1" bgcolor=#5f615d></td>
  </tr>
  <tr>
    <td width="1" height="1" bgcolor=#536488></td>
    <td width="1" height="1" bgcolor=#303853></td>
    <td width="1" height="1" bgcolor=#030104></td>
    <td width="1" height="1" bgcolor=#4b5a7c></td>
    <td width="1" height="1" bgcolor=#54638b></td>
    <td width="1" height="1" bgcolor=#57668f></td>
    <td width="1" height="1" bgcolor=#57678f></td>
    <td rowspan="1" colspan="4" width="1" height="1" bgcolor=#58678e></td>
    <td width="1" height="1" bgcolor=#5a6890></td>
    <td rowspan="2" colspan="1" width="1" height="1" bgcolor=#5a678f></td>
    <td width="1" height="1" bgcolor=#59688f></td>
    <td width="1" height="1" bgcolor=#5b6a91></td>
    <td width="1" height="1" bgcolor=#5d6c90></td>
    <td width="1" height="1" bgcolor=#5b6b90></td>
    <td width="1" height="1" bgcolor=#5a6a91></td>
    <td width="1" height="1" bgcolor=#5b6a92></td>
    <td width="1" height="1" bgcolor=#5d6a95></td>
    <td width="1" height="1" bgcolor=#5e6994></td>
    <td width="1" height="1" bgcolor=#505c7f></td>
    <td width="1" height="1" bgcolor=#353c54></td>
    <td width="1" height="1" bgcolor=#34465a></td>
    <td width="1" height="1" bgcolor=#576085></td>
    <td width="1" height="1" bgcolor=#343e55></td>
    <td width="1" height="1" bgcolor=#61719c></td>
    <td width="1" height="1" bgcolor=#454f6e></td>
    <td width="1" height="1" bgcolor=#586385></td>
```

```
    <td width="1" height="1"
bgcolor=#323b4f></td>
    <td width="1" height="1"
bgcolor=#64709b></td>
    <td width="1" height="1"
bgcolor=#161921></td>
    <td width="1" height="1"
bgcolor=#302f42></td>
    <td width="1" height="1"
bgcolor=#5f6f95></td>
    <td width="1" height="1"
bgcolor=#556188></td>
    <td width="1" height="1"
bgcolor=#2e3951></td>
    <td width="1" height="1"
bgcolor=#404b6c></td>
    <td width="1" height="1"
bgcolor=#120f0c></td>
    <td width="1" height="1"
bgcolor=#10090a></td>
    <td width="1" height="1"
bgcolor=#151b29></td>
    <td width="1" height="1"
bgcolor=#606e9d></td>
    <td width="1" height="1"
bgcolor=#5c698f></td>
    <td width="1" height="1"
bgcolor=#5b6891></td>
    <td width="1" height="1"
bgcolor=#5a678f></td>
    <td width="1" height="1"
bgcolor=#5c6991></td>
    <td width="1" height="1"
bgcolor=#5a678f></td>
    <td width="1" height="1"
bgcolor=#5b6a91></td>
    <td width="1" height="1"
bgcolor=#58678e></td>
    <td width="1" height="1"
bgcolor=#5a6a90></td>
    <td width="1" height="1"
bgcolor=#58678e></td>
    <td width="1" height="1"
bgcolor=#58668d></td>
    <td width="1" height="1"
bgcolor=#596890></td>
    <td width="1" height="1"
bgcolor=#52618a></td>
    <td width="1" height="1"
bgcolor=#59688f></td>
    <td width="1" height="1"
bgcolor=#57668d></td>
    <td width="1" height="1"
bgcolor=#57668d></td>
    <td width="1" height="1"
bgcolor=#56658c></td>
    <td width="1" height="1"
bgcolor=#546489></td>
    <td width="1" height="1"
bgcolor=#556588></td>
    <td width="1" height="1"
bgcolor=#536388></td>
    <td width="1" height="1"
bgcolor=#55638b></td>
    <td width="1" height="1"
bgcolor=#4a597c></td>
    <td width="1" height="1"
bgcolor=#1f2333></td>
    <td width="1" height="1"
bgcolor=#2d3b4a></td>
    <td width="1" height="1"
bgcolor=#39425e></td>
    <td width="1" height="1"
bgcolor=#384159></td>
    <td width="1" height="1"
bgcolor=#36445c></td>
    <td width="1" height="1"
bgcolor=#4e6088></td>
    <td width="1" height="1"
bgcolor=#595a57></td>
  </tr>
  <tr>
    <td width="1" height="1"
bgcolor=#556388></td>
    <td width="1" height="1"
bgcolor=#2b3247></td>
    <td width="1" height="1"
bgcolor=#0a0a10></td>
    <td width="1" height="1"
bgcolor=#505e81></td>
    <td width="1" height="1"
bgcolor=#56658c></td>
    <td width="1" height="1"
bgcolor=#55648e></td>
    <td rowspan="1"
colspan="2" width="1"
height="1"
bgcolor=#57668d></td>
    <td rowspan="1"
colspan="3" width="1"
height="1"
bgcolor=#58678e></td>
    <td width="1" height="1"
bgcolor=#5b6990></td>
    <td width="1" height="1"
bgcolor=#5a6990></td>
    <td width="1" height="1"
bgcolor=#5a6890></td>
    <td width="1" height="1"
bgcolor=#5d6a92></td>
    <td width="1" height="1"
bgcolor=#5b6a92></td>
    <td width="1" height="1"
bgcolor=#5c6a92></td>
    <td width="1" height="1"
bgcolor=#5e6894></td>
    <td width="1" height="1"
bgcolor=#5f6a96></td>
    <td width="1" height="1"
bgcolor=#5d6a94></td>
    <td width="1" height="1"
bgcolor=#5b6891></td>
    <td width="1" height="1"
bgcolor=#5d6a91></td>
    <td width="1" height="1"
bgcolor=#5a6990></td>
    <td width="1" height="1"
bgcolor=#616b91></td>
    <td width="1" height="1"
bgcolor=#576e98></td>
    <td width="1" height="1"
bgcolor=#647098></td>
    <td width="1" height="1"
bgcolor=#596b91></td>
    <td width="1" height="1"
bgcolor=#66709f></td>
    <td width="1" height="1"
bgcolor=#0f131c></td>
    <td width="1" height="1"
bgcolor=#4b5673></td>
    <td width="1" height="1"
bgcolor=#566586></td>
    <td width="1" height="1"
bgcolor=#252534></td>
    <td width="1" height="1"
bgcolor=#272937></td>
    <td width="1" height="1"
bgcolor=#4c5c7c></td>
    <td width="1" height="1"
bgcolor=#5d6a93></td>
    <td width="1" height="1"
bgcolor=#373e52></td>
    <td width="1" height="1"
bgcolor=#0d1415></td>
    <td width="1" height="1"
bgcolor=#0a0a06></td>
    <td width="1" height="1"
bgcolor=#070d04></td>
    <td width="1" height="1"
bgcolor=#303b49></td>
    <td width="1" height="1"
bgcolor=#556788></td>
    <td width="1" height="1"
bgcolor=#5c6b91></td>
    <td width="1" height="1"
bgcolor=#5d6893></td>
    <td rowspan="1"
colspan="2" width="1"
height="1"
bgcolor=#5d6991></td>
    <td width="1" height="1"
bgcolor=#5c6991></td>
    <td width="1" height="1"
bgcolor=#5a6990></td>
```

```
    <td rowspan="1" colspan="2" width="1" height="1" bgcolor=#59688f></td>
    <td width="1" height="1" bgcolor=#5a6990></td>
    <td rowspan="2" colspan="1" width="1" height="1" bgcolor=#58678e></td>
    <td width="1" height="1" bgcolor=#58678e></td>
    <td width="1" height="1" bgcolor=#57668d></td>
    <td width="1" height="1" bgcolor=#56658c></td>
    <td width="1" height="1" bgcolor=#58678e></td>
    <td width="1" height="1" bgcolor=#57668d></td>
    <td rowspan="2" colspan="1" width="1" height="1" bgcolor=#56658c></td>
    <td width="1" height="1" bgcolor=#57668d></td>
    <td rowspan="2" colspan="1" width="1" height="1" bgcolor=#55648b></td>
    <td width="1" height="1" bgcolor=#56658c></td>
    <td rowspan="2" colspan="1" width="1" height="1" bgcolor=#546488></td>
    <td width="1" height="1" bgcolor=#536289></td>
    <td width="1" height="1" bgcolor=#54618a></td>
    <td width="1" height="1" bgcolor=#4e617f></td>
    <td width="1" height="1" bgcolor=#3f4c6f></td>
    <td width="1" height="1" bgcolor=#394263></td>
    <td width="1" height="1" bgcolor=#16171e></td>
    <td width="1" height="1" bgcolor=#121618></td>
    <td width="1" height="1" bgcolor=#3b4466></td>
    <td width="1" height="1" bgcolor=#506287></td>
    <td width="1" height="1" bgcolor=#626260></td>
  </tr>
  <tr>
    <td width="1" height="1" bgcolor=#54658c></td>
    <td width="1" height="1" bgcolor=#293347></td>
    <td width="1" height="1" bgcolor=#23273a></td>
    <td width="1" height="1" bgcolor=#566892></td>
    <td width="1" height="1" bgcolor=#57668d></td>
    <td width="1" height="1" bgcolor=#55648d></td>
    <td rowspan="1" colspan="2" width="1" height="1" bgcolor=#56658c></td>
    <td rowspan="1" colspan="3" width="1" height="1" bgcolor=#57668d></td>
    <td width="1" height="1" bgcolor=#596790></td>
    <td width="1" height="1" bgcolor=#5b6992></td>
    <td width="1" height="1" bgcolor=#5b6a93></td>
    <td width="1" height="1" bgcolor=#5a6892></td>
    <td width="1" height="1" bgcolor=#5d6992></td>
    <td width="1" height="1" bgcolor=#5b6892></td>
    <td width="1" height="1" bgcolor=#5e6c93></td>
    <td width="1" height="1" bgcolor=#59698e></td>
    <td width="1" height="1" bgcolor=#5d6a95></td>
    <td width="1" height="1" bgcolor=#5d6993></td>
    <td width="1" height="1" bgcolor=#5d6b92></td>
    <td width="1" height="1" bgcolor=#5c6a95></td>
    <td width="1" height="1" bgcolor=#5b6c97></td>
    <td width="1" height="1" bgcolor=#444c6b></td>
    <td width="1" height="1" bgcolor=#0e1012></td>
    <td width="1" height="1" bgcolor=#5b6a91></td>
    <td width="1" height="1" bgcolor=#606d97></td>
    <td width="1" height="1" bgcolor=#5d6d94></td>
    <td width="1" height="1" bgcolor=#040200></td>
    <td width="1" height="1" bgcolor=#5a6792></td>
    <td width="1" height="1" bgcolor=#464e71></td>
    <td width="1" height="1" bgcolor=#252530></td>
    <td width="1" height="1" bgcolor=#4a5276></td>
    <td width="1" height="1" bgcolor=#5b6e98></td>
    <td width="1" height="1" bgcolor=#62729a></td>
    <td width="1" height="1" bgcolor=#151822></td>
    <td width="1" height="1" bgcolor=#100b0a></td>
    <td width="1" height="1" bgcolor=#0d0815></td>
    <td width="1" height="1" bgcolor=#50516f></td>
    <td width="1" height="1" bgcolor=#373c54></td>
    <td width="1" height="1" bgcolor=#57618d></td>
    <td width="1" height="1" bgcolor=#5b6b90></td>
    <td width="1" height="1" bgcolor=#5d6a92></td>
    <td width="1" height="1" bgcolor=#5c6892></td>
    <td rowspan="2" colspan="1" width="1" height="1" bgcolor=#5b6890></td>
    <td width="1" height="1" bgcolor=#5a6890></td>
    <td width="1" height="1" bgcolor=#59688f></td>
    <td rowspan="1" colspan="2" width="1" height="1" bgcolor=#5a6990></td>
    <td width="1" height="1" bgcolor=#5b6a91></td>
    <td rowspan="2" colspan="1" width="1" height="1" bgcolor=#59688f></td>
    <td width="1" height="1" bgcolor=#58678e></td>
    <td rowspan="1" colspan="2" width="1" height="1" bgcolor=#57668d></td>
    <td width="1" height="1" bgcolor=#55648b></td>
    <td width="1" height="1" bgcolor=#56658c></td>
```

```
    <td width="1" height="1"
bgcolor=#55648c></td>
    <td width="1" height="1"
bgcolor=#54638a></td>
    <td width="1" height="1"
bgcolor=#53618b></td>
    <td width="1" height="1"
bgcolor=#55668b></td>
    <td width="1" height="1"
bgcolor=#3f4768></td>
    <td width="1" height="1"
bgcolor=#43506b></td>
    <td width="1" height="1"
bgcolor=#232739></td>
    <td width="1" height="1"
bgcolor=#2f374c></td>
    <td width="1" height="1"
bgcolor=#424e6a></td>
    <td width="1" height="1"
bgcolor=#4d5e86></td>
    <td rowspan="2"
colspan="1" width="1"
height="1"
bgcolor=#5d5f5b></td>
  </tr>
  <tr>
    <td width="1" height="1"
bgcolor=#55638e></td>
    <td width="1" height="1"
bgcolor=#2b3448></td>
    <td width="1" height="1"
bgcolor=#242438></td>
    <td width="1" height="1"
bgcolor=#58688f></td>
    <td rowspan="1"
colspan="2" width="1"
height="1"
bgcolor=#55648b></td>
    <td rowspan="1"
colspan="2" width="1"
height="1"
bgcolor=#57668d></td>
    <td rowspan="3"
colspan="1" width="1"
height="1"
bgcolor=#58678e></td>
    <td width="1" height="1"
bgcolor=#58678e></td>
    <td width="1" height="1"
bgcolor=#59688f></td>
    <td width="1" height="1"
bgcolor=#58678f></td>
    <td width="1" height="1"
bgcolor=#5b6a93></td>
    <td width="1" height="1"
bgcolor=#5a6992></td>
    <td width="1" height="1"
bgcolor=#5b6992></td>
    <td width="1" height="1"
bgcolor=#5d6a95></td>
    <td width="1" height="1"
bgcolor=#616c94></td>
    <td width="1" height="1"
bgcolor=#3a415e></td>
    <td width="1" height="1"
bgcolor=#5c6886></td>
    <td width="1" height="1"
bgcolor=#5a6891></td>
    <td width="1" height="1"
bgcolor=#5b6a91></td>
    <td width="1" height="1"
bgcolor=#5a6991></td>
    <td width="1" height="1"
bgcolor=#5c6992></td>
    <td width="1" height="1"
bgcolor=#5e6b91></td>
    <td width="1" height="1"
bgcolor=#5f6e96></td>
    <td width="1" height="1"
bgcolor=#475377></td>
    <td width="1" height="1"
bgcolor=#1d222e></td>
    <td width="1" height="1"
bgcolor=#13151b></td>
    <td width="1" height="1"
bgcolor=#687aa7></td>
    <td width="1" height="1"
bgcolor=#171927></td>
    <td width="1" height="1"
bgcolor=#65769b></td>
    <td width="1" height="1"
bgcolor=#14131a></td>
    <td width="1" height="1"
bgcolor=#2c3249></td>
    <td width="1" height="1"
bgcolor=#616e95></td>
    <td width="1" height="1"
bgcolor=#232940></td>
    <td width="1" height="1"
bgcolor=#404b65></td>
    <td width="1" height="1"
bgcolor=#303851></td>
    <td width="1" height="1"
bgcolor=#0b0c0d></td>
    <td width="1" height="1"
bgcolor=#1e202d></td>
    <td width="1" height="1"
bgcolor=#465776></td>
    <td width="1" height="1"
bgcolor=#495674></td>
    <td width="1" height="1"
bgcolor=#606e96></td>
    <td width="1" height="1"
bgcolor=#596990></td>
    <td width="1" height="1"
bgcolor=#5d6b92></td>
    <td width="1" height="1"
bgcolor=#5c6893></td>
    <td width="1" height="1"
bgcolor=#59678f></td>
    <td width="1" height="1"
bgcolor=#5a6990></td>
    <td rowspan="1"
colspan="3" width="1"
height="1"
bgcolor=#59688f></td>
    <td width="1" height="1"
bgcolor=#57668d></td>
    <td width="1" height="1"
bgcolor=#56658c></td>
    <td width="1" height="1"
bgcolor=#58678e></td>
    <td rowspan="1"
colspan="3" width="1"
height="1"
bgcolor=#57668d></td>
    <td width="1" height="1"
bgcolor=#58678e></td>
    <td width="1" height="1"
bgcolor=#57668d></td>
    <td width="1" height="1"
bgcolor=#56658c></td>
    <td rowspan="1"
colspan="2" width="1"
height="1"
bgcolor=#55648b></td>
    <td width="1" height="1"
bgcolor=#546484></td>
    <td width="1" height="1"
bgcolor=#54668b></td>
    <td width="1" height="1"
bgcolor=#263243></td>
    <td width="1" height="1"
bgcolor=#343d4e></td>
    <td width="1" height="1"
bgcolor=#02040c></td>
    <td width="1" height="1"
bgcolor=#303b4c></td>
    <td width="1" height="1"
bgcolor=#374665></td>
    <td width="1" height="1"
bgcolor=#516087></td>
  </tr>
  <tr>
    <td width="1" height="1"
bgcolor=#53628a></td>
    <td width="1" height="1"
bgcolor=#2c3148></td>
    <td width="1" height="1"
bgcolor=#08090e></td>
    <td width="1" height="1"
bgcolor=#454e71></td>
    <td width="1" height="1"
bgcolor=#57628b></td>
```

```
    <td width="1" height="1"
bgcolor=#53668c></td>
    <td width="1" height="1"
bgcolor=#5a6590></td>
    <td width="1" height="1"
bgcolor=#556789></td>
    <td width="1" height="1"
bgcolor=#57668d></td>
    <td width="1" height="1"
bgcolor=#596891></td>
    <td rowspan="3"
colspan="1" width="1"
height="1"
bgcolor=#586790></td>
    <td width="1" height="1"
bgcolor=#5b6991></td>
    <td width="1" height="1"
bgcolor=#5b6890></td>
    <td width="1" height="1"
bgcolor=#5b6891></td>
    <td width="1" height="1"
bgcolor=#5b6892></td>
    <td width="1" height="1"
bgcolor=#606c94></td>
    <td width="1" height="1"
bgcolor=#464e72></td>
    <td width="1" height="1"
bgcolor=#0d0f18></td>
    <td width="1" height="1"
bgcolor=#566383></td>
    <td width="1" height="1"
bgcolor=#5d6990></td>
    <td rowspan="2"
colspan="1" width="1"
height="1"
bgcolor=#5d6a92></td>
    <td width="1" height="1"
bgcolor=#5e6b93></td>
    <td width="1" height="1"
bgcolor=#5c6b93></td>
    <td width="1" height="1"
bgcolor=#5e6c92></td>
    <td width="1" height="1"
bgcolor=#374159></td>
    <td width="1" height="1"
bgcolor=#212531></td>
    <td width="1" height="1"
bgcolor=#010000></td>
    <td width="1" height="1"
bgcolor=#5f7092></td>
    <td width="1" height="1"
bgcolor=#303c55></td>
    <td width="1" height="1"
bgcolor=#5a6792></td>
    <td width="1" height="1"
bgcolor=#1c1b24></td>
    <td width="1" height="1"
bgcolor=#383d57></td>
    <td width="1" height="1"
bgcolor=#151b23></td>
    <td width="1" height="1"
bgcolor=#0a0403></td>
    <td width="1" height="1"
bgcolor=#333850></td>
    <td width="1" height="1"
bgcolor=#5b7093></td>
    <td width="1" height="1"
bgcolor=#414a65></td>
    <td width="1" height="1"
bgcolor=#3d4763></td>
    <td width="1" height="1"
bgcolor=#3e4e6f></td>
    <td width="1" height="1"
bgcolor=#353c51></td>
    <td width="1" height="1"
bgcolor=#596b98></td>
    <td width="1" height="1"
bgcolor=#57688a></td>
    <td width="1" height="1"
bgcolor=#5a698b></td>
    <td width="1" height="1"
bgcolor=#5c6791></td>
    <td width="1" height="1"
bgcolor=#586c91></td>
    <td width="1" height="1"
bgcolor=#5b6792></td>
    <td width="1" height="1"
bgcolor=#5b6a8e></td>
    <td width="1" height="1"
bgcolor=#5b6a93></td>
    <td width="1" height="1"
bgcolor=#59688e></td>
    <td width="1" height="1"
bgcolor=#5a698c></td>
    <td width="1" height="1"
bgcolor=#58668f></td>
    <td width="1" height="1"
bgcolor=#5b668f></td>
    <td width="1" height="1"
bgcolor=#58658d></td>
    <td width="1" height="1"
bgcolor=#586990></td>
    <td width="1" height="1"
bgcolor=#57648b></td>
    <td width="1" height="1"
bgcolor=#57668d></td>
    <td width="1" height="1"
bgcolor=#55648b></td>
    <td rowspan="2"
colspan="1" width="1"
height="1"
bgcolor=#56658c></td>
    <td width="1" height="1"
bgcolor=#56658d></td>
    <td width="1" height="1"
bgcolor=#485377></td>
    <td width="1" height="1"
bgcolor=#4c6081></td>
    <td width="1" height="1"
bgcolor=#58668b></td>
    <td width="1" height="1"
bgcolor=#50678d></td>
    <td width="1" height="1"
bgcolor=#526086></td>
    <td width="1" height="1"
bgcolor=#4a5a80></td>
    <td width="1" height="1"
bgcolor=#14181d></td>
    <td width="1" height="1"
bgcolor=#3a4467></td>
    <td width="1" height="1"
bgcolor=#282b38></td>
    <td width="1" height="1"
bgcolor=#1f2734></td>
    <td width="1" height="1"
bgcolor=#4f6089></td>
    <td width="1" height="1"
bgcolor=#5f5f5d></td>
  </tr>
  <tr>
    <td width="1" height="1"
bgcolor=#57658c></td>
    <td width="1" height="1"
bgcolor=#323a56></td>
    <td width="1" height="1"
bgcolor=#1e202f></td>
    <td width="1" height="1"
bgcolor=#1d1c30></td>
    <td width="1" height="1"
bgcolor=#586990></td>
    <td width="1" height="1"
bgcolor=#556688></td>
    <td width="1" height="1"
bgcolor=#57648f></td>
    <td width="1" height="1"
bgcolor=#56658c></td>
    <td rowspan="2"
colspan="1" width="1"
height="1"
bgcolor=#57668f></td>
    <td rowspan="2"
colspan="1" width="1"
height="1"
bgcolor=#586790></td>
    <td width="1" height="1"
bgcolor=#5a6991></td>
    <td width="1" height="1"
bgcolor=#5b6a91></td>
    <td width="1" height="1"
bgcolor=#5c6991></td>
    <td width="1" height="1"
bgcolor=#59638f></td>
    <td width="1" height="1"
bgcolor=#58658c></td>
```

```
<td width="1" height="1" bgcolor=#495a7e></td>
<td width="1" height="1" bgcolor=#2b3344></td>
<td width="1" height="1" bgcolor=#535e82></td>
<td width="1" height="1" bgcolor=#5b6a91></td>
<td width="1" height="1" bgcolor=#5d6a92></td>
<td width="1" height="1" bgcolor=#5b6c92></td>
<td width="1" height="1" bgcolor=#5c6a91></td>
<td width="1" height="1" bgcolor=#51597f></td>
<td width="1" height="1" bgcolor=#111412></td>
<td width="1" height="1" bgcolor=#050104></td>
<td width="1" height="1" bgcolor=#5c6d95></td>
<td width="1" height="1" bgcolor=#455070></td>
<td width="1" height="1" bgcolor=#3f4b69></td>
<td width="1" height="1" bgcolor=#030100></td>
<td width="1" height="1" bgcolor=#010500></td>
<td width="1" height="1" bgcolor=#050503></td>
<td width="1" height="1" bgcolor=#19161f></td>
<td width="1" height="1" bgcolor=#1d252c></td>
<td width="1" height="1" bgcolor=#5d7099></td>
<td width="1" height="1" bgcolor=#3b4562></td>
<td width="1" height="1" bgcolor=#414a6e></td>
<td width="1" height="1" bgcolor=#3c4762></td>
<td width="1" height="1" bgcolor=#46506c></td>
<td width="1" height="1" bgcolor=#272f43></td>
<td width="1" height="1" bgcolor=#616c92></td>
<td width="1" height="1" bgcolor=#5c6b93></td>
<td width="1" height="1" bgcolor=#5a6794></td>
<td width="1" height="1" bgcolor=#5d6791></td>
<td width="1" height="1" bgcolor=#586b91></td>
<td width="1" height="1" bgcolor=#5c6890></td>
<td width="1" height="1" bgcolor=#5a6790></td>
<td width="1" height="1" bgcolor=#58678f></td>
<td width="1" height="1" bgcolor=#59688e></td>
<td width="1" height="1" bgcolor=#576890></td>
<td width="1" height="1" bgcolor=#58678f></td>
<td rowspan="1" colspan="2" width="1" height="1" bgcolor=#56678d></td>
<td width="1" height="1" bgcolor=#59668f></td>
<td width="1" height="1" bgcolor=#58648c></td>
<td width="1" height="1" bgcolor=#57658d></td>
<td width="1" height="1" bgcolor=#566790></td>
<td width="1" height="1" bgcolor=#576489></td>
<td width="1" height="1" bgcolor=#576688></td>
<td width="1" height="1" bgcolor=#000308></td>
<td width="1" height="1" bgcolor=#0b0d17></td>
<td width="1" height="1" bgcolor=#424c64></td>
<td width="1" height="1" bgcolor=#425476></td>
<td width="1" height="1" bgcolor=#17171d></td>
<td width="1" height="1" bgcolor=#1c2028></td>
<td width="1" height="1" bgcolor=#060706></td>
<td width="1" height="1" bgcolor=#2d344c></td>
<td width="1" height="1" bgcolor=#4f6287></td>
<td width="1" height="1" bgcolor=#595a57></td>
</tr>
<tr>
<td width="1" height="1" bgcolor=#57658a></td>
<td width="1" height="1" bgcolor=#36425a></td>
<td width="1" height="1" bgcolor=#1c1f31></td>
<td width="1" height="1" bgcolor=#0d0c0f></td>
<td width="1" height="1" bgcolor=#546385></td>
<td width="1" height="1" bgcolor=#54628c></td>
<td width="1" height="1" bgcolor=#57668a></td>
<td width="1" height="1" bgcolor=#56648e></td>
<td rowspan="2" colspan="1" width="1" height="1" bgcolor=#57668f></td>
<td width="1" height="1" bgcolor=#59688f></td>
<td rowspan="2" colspan="1" width="1" height="1" bgcolor=#5a6990></td>
<td width="1" height="1" bgcolor=#5b6a91></td>
<td width="1" height="1" bgcolor=#4b5875></td>
<td width="1" height="1" bgcolor=#39455f></td>
<td width="1" height="1" bgcolor=#353b54></td>
<td width="1" height="1" bgcolor=#11161e></td>
<td width="1" height="1" bgcolor=#62729d></td>
<td width="1" height="1" bgcolor=#5c6a91></td>
<td width="1" height="1" bgcolor=#5b6a92></td>
<td width="1" height="1" bgcolor=#5d6b94></td>
<td width="1" height="1" bgcolor=#5c6c90></td>
<td width="1" height="1" bgcolor=#62719c></td>
<td width="1" height="1" bgcolor=#141f25></td>
<td width="1" height="1" bgcolor=#0b0b0b></td>
<td width="1" height="1" bgcolor=#0a0506></td>
<td width="1" height="1" bgcolor=#63739d></td>
<td width="1" height="1" bgcolor=#272e3e></td>
<td width="1" height="1" bgcolor=#2f3547></td>
<td width="1" height="1" bgcolor=#0c0708></td>
<td width="1" height="1" bgcolor=#07080a></td>
<td width="1" height="1" bgcolor=#0c0d11></td>
```

```
    <td width="1" height="1"
bgcolor=#6a749e></td>
    <td width="1" height="1"
bgcolor=#1a2433></td>
    <td width="1" height="1"
bgcolor=#5b678d></td>
    <td width="1" height="1"
bgcolor=#282b39></td>
    <td width="1" height="1"
bgcolor=#333853></td>
    <td width="1" height="1"
bgcolor=#343b4b></td>
    <td width="1" height="1"
bgcolor=#37435d></td>
    <td width="1" height="1"
bgcolor=#4c587c></td>
    <td width="1" height="1"
bgcolor=#617099></td>
    <td width="1" height="1"
bgcolor=#050808></td>
    <td width="1" height="1"
bgcolor=#516381></td>
    <td width="1" height="1"
bgcolor=#596b8d></td>
    <td width="1" height="1"
bgcolor=#5b6991></td>
    <td width="1" height="1"
bgcolor=#5b6891></td>
    <td width="1" height="1"
bgcolor=#5b688f></td>
    <td rowspan="1"
colspan="2" width="1"
height="1"
bgcolor=#59688f></td>
    <td width="1" height="1"
bgcolor=#5c6b8d></td>
    <td width="1" height="1"
bgcolor=#56678d></td>
    <td width="1" height="1"
bgcolor=#54678c></td>
    <td width="1" height="1"
bgcolor=#55668b></td>
    <td width="1" height="1"
bgcolor=#58678f></td>
    <td width="1" height="1"
bgcolor=#56668c></td>
    <td width="1" height="1"
bgcolor=#56638b></td>
    <td width="1" height="1"
bgcolor=#57648c></td>
    <td width="1" height="1"
bgcolor=#57668c></td>
    <td width="1" height="1"
bgcolor=#54648c></td>
    <td width="1" height="1"
bgcolor=#54648f></td>
    <td width="1" height="1"
bgcolor=#4b547b></td>
    <td width="1" height="1"
bgcolor=#0f0f19></td>
    <td width="1" height="1"
bgcolor=#1c2024></td>
    <td width="1" height="1"
bgcolor=#1f2329></td>
    <td width="1" height="1"
bgcolor=#0f0f1c></td>
    <td width="1" height="1"
bgcolor=#2b2d44></td>
    <td width="1" height="1"
bgcolor=#050708></td>
    <td width="1" height="1"
bgcolor=#2e354d></td>
    <td width="1" height="1"
bgcolor=#4d5f89></td>
    <td width="1" height="1"
bgcolor=#636460></td>
  </tr>
  <tr>
    <td width="1" height="1"
bgcolor=#546489></td>
    <td width="1" height="1"
bgcolor=#252e42></td>
    <td width="1" height="1"
bgcolor=#101116></td>
    <td width="1" height="1"
bgcolor=#1a1c2a></td>
    <td width="1" height="1"
bgcolor=#121420></td>
    <td width="1" height="1"
bgcolor=#5b6890></td>
    <td width="1" height="1"
bgcolor=#56688b></td>
    <td width="1" height="1"
bgcolor=#57668f></td>
    <td width="1" height="1"
bgcolor=#586790></td>
    <td rowspan="1"
colspan="2" width="1"
height="1"
bgcolor=#58678e></td>
    <td rowspan="2"
colspan="1" width="1"
height="1"
bgcolor=#5a6990></td>
    <td width="1" height="1"
bgcolor=#59688f></td>
    <td width="1" height="1"
bgcolor=#566a90></td>
    <td width="1" height="1"
bgcolor=#5e6b92></td>
    <td width="1" height="1"
bgcolor=#5a6a8f></td>
    <td width="1" height="1"
bgcolor=#5e6b92></td>
    <td width="1" height="1"
bgcolor=#5a6b8c></td>
    <td width="1" height="1"
bgcolor=#5c6b92></td>
    <td width="1" height="1"
bgcolor=#5d6991></td>
    <td width="1" height="1"
bgcolor=#5d6a91></td>
    <td width="1" height="1"
bgcolor=#5c6a92></td>
    <td width="1" height="1"
bgcolor=#5a6a91></td>
    <td width="1" height="1"
bgcolor=#414767></td>
    <td width="1" height="1"
bgcolor=#080a0e></td>
    <td width="1" height="1"
bgcolor=#23252b></td>
    <td width="1" height="1"
bgcolor=#616e9c></td>
    <td width="1" height="1"
bgcolor=#050202></td>
    <td width="1" height="1"
bgcolor=#060c0a></td>
    <td width="1" height="1"
bgcolor=#1d1b1f></td>
    <td width="1" height="1"
bgcolor=#0e0e14></td>
    <td width="1" height="1"
bgcolor=#262b2e></td>
    <td width="1" height="1"
bgcolor=#5f72a4></td>
    <td width="1" height="1"
bgcolor=#353c54></td>
    <td width="1" height="1"
bgcolor=#4e5a7b></td>
    <td width="1" height="1"
bgcolor=#1a1721></td>
    <td width="1" height="1"
bgcolor=#191a26></td>
    <td width="1" height="1"
bgcolor=#272c42></td>
    <td width="1" height="1"
bgcolor=#343d53></td>
    <td width="1" height="1"
bgcolor=#445170></td>
    <td width="1" height="1"
bgcolor=#262d41></td>
    <td width="1" height="1"
bgcolor=#393c4c></td>
    <td width="1" height="1"
bgcolor=#21233a></td>
    <td width="1" height="1"
bgcolor=#5d6b95></td>
    <td width="1" height="1"
bgcolor=#5c6b90></td>
    <td width="1" height="1"
bgcolor=#54668f></td>
    <td width="1" height="1"
bgcolor=#5b6a91></td>
```

```
    <td width="1" height="1"
bgcolor=#57668e></td>
    <td width="1" height="1"
bgcolor=#5c6991></td>
    <td width="1" height="1"
bgcolor=#414d69></td>
    <td width="1" height="1"
bgcolor=#515f7f></td>
    <td width="1" height="1"
bgcolor=#54668d></td>
    <td width="1" height="1"
bgcolor=#57678a></td>
    <td width="1" height="1"
bgcolor=#54668e></td>
    <td width="1" height="1"
bgcolor=#54658b></td>
    <td width="1" height="1"
bgcolor=#57668d></td>
    <td width="1" height="1"
bgcolor=#56658c></td>
    <td width="1" height="1"
bgcolor=#56638c></td>
    <td width="1" height="1"
bgcolor=#55668c></td>
    <td width="1" height="1"
bgcolor=#516285></td>
    <td width="1" height="1"
bgcolor=#495a73></td>
    <td width="1" height="1"
bgcolor=#11111b></td>
    <td width="1" height="1"
bgcolor=#1c2029></td>
    <td width="1" height="1"
bgcolor=#060309></td>
    <td width="1" height="1"
bgcolor=#050601></td>
    <td width="1" height="1"
bgcolor=#333c50></td>
    <td width="1" height="1"
bgcolor=#303751></td>
    <td width="1" height="1"
bgcolor=#2c364a></td>
    <td width="1" height="1"
bgcolor=#4e6387></td>
    <td width="1" height="1"
bgcolor=#575754></td>
  </tr>
  <tr>
    <td width="1" height="1"
bgcolor=#54638b></td>
    <td width="1" height="1"
bgcolor=#323a52></td>
    <td width="1" height="1"
bgcolor=#000000></td>
    <td width="1" height="1"
bgcolor=#0f111b></td>
    <td width="1" height="1"
bgcolor=#282c3b></td>
    <td width="1" height="1"
bgcolor=#516483></td>
    <td width="1" height="1"
bgcolor=#56678f></td>
    <td width="1" height="1"
bgcolor=#58668d></td>
    <td rowspan="1"
colspan="2" width="1"
height="1"
bgcolor=#58678e></td>
    <td rowspan="4"
colspan="1" width="1"
height="1"
bgcolor=#57668d></td>
    <td width="1" height="1"
bgcolor=#5a6990></td>
    <td rowspan="1"
colspan="2" width="1"
height="1"
bgcolor=#5b6a91></td>
    <td width="1" height="1"
bgcolor=#5b6991></td>
    <td width="1" height="1"
bgcolor=#59698f></td>
    <td width="1" height="1"
bgcolor=#5b6a90></td>
    <td width="1" height="1"
bgcolor=#5b6a91></td>
    <td width="1" height="1"
bgcolor=#5a6a90></td>
    <td width="1" height="1"
bgcolor=#5b6a91></td>
    <td rowspan="2"
colspan="1" width="1"
height="1"
bgcolor=#5a6990></td>
    <td width="1" height="1"
bgcolor=#5b6a91></td>
    <td width="1" height="1"
bgcolor=#5b6990></td>
    <td width="1" height="1"
bgcolor=#5d6c94></td>
    <td width="1" height="1"
bgcolor=#110f1a></td>
    <td width="1" height="1"
bgcolor=#1e2834></td>
    <td width="1" height="1"
bgcolor=#0d0d16></td>
    <td width="1" height="1"
bgcolor=#5c6d91></td>
    <td width="1" height="1"
bgcolor=#130f1a></td>
    <td width="1" height="1"
bgcolor=#181520></td>
    <td width="1" height="1"
bgcolor=#212630></td>
    <td width="1" height="1"
bgcolor=#1c1c2d></td>
    <td width="1" height="1"
bgcolor=#292939></td>
    <td width="1" height="1"
bgcolor=#4d5a7c></td>
    <td width="1" height="1"
bgcolor=#475977></td>
    <td width="1" height="1"
bgcolor=#3a4258></td>
    <td width="1" height="1"
bgcolor=#1c1923></td>
    <td width="1" height="1"
bgcolor=#181e24></td>
    <td width="1" height="1"
bgcolor=#333b59></td>
    <td width="1" height="1"
bgcolor=#3a485f></td>
    <td width="1" height="1"
bgcolor=#4d597a></td>
    <td width="1" height="1"
bgcolor=#333a4c></td>
    <td width="1" height="1"
bgcolor=#101518></td>
    <td width="1" height="1"
bgcolor=#050307></td>
    <td width="1" height="1"
bgcolor=#4d587a></td>
    <td width="1" height="1"
bgcolor=#465774></td>
    <td width="1" height="1"
bgcolor=#556089></td>
    <td width="1" height="1"
bgcolor=#2c354b></td>
    <td width="1" height="1"
bgcolor=#586b8f></td>
    <td width="1" height="1"
bgcolor=#22202e></td>
    <td width="1" height="1"
bgcolor=#29344d></td>
    <td width="1" height="1"
bgcolor=#586289></td>
    <td width="1" height="1"
bgcolor=#53678b></td>
    <td width="1" height="1"
bgcolor=#576692></td>
    <td width="1" height="1"
bgcolor=#55638a></td>
    <td width="1" height="1"
bgcolor=#56648c></td>
    <td rowspan="4"
colspan="1" width="1"
height="1"
bgcolor=#56658c></td>
    <td width="1" height="1"
bgcolor=#56648c></td>
    <td width="1" height="1"
bgcolor=#54648c></td>
    <td width="1" height="1"
bgcolor=#55638d></td>
```

```
    <td width="1" height="1"
bgcolor=#55628b></td>
    <td width="1" height="1"
bgcolor=#576487></td>
    <td width="1" height="1"
bgcolor=#39425b></td>
    <td width="1" height="1"
bgcolor=#000300></td>
    <td width="1" height="1"
bgcolor=#00000c></td>
    <td width="1" height="1"
bgcolor=#000000></td>
    <td width="1" height="1"
bgcolor=#1f1e2e></td>
    <td width="1" height="1"
bgcolor=#3b4963></td>
    <td width="1" height="1"
bgcolor=#2b3953></td>
    <td width="1" height="1"
bgcolor=#4e6189></td>
    <td width="1" height="1"
bgcolor=#5b5d59></td>
  </tr>
  <tr>
    <td width="1" height="1"
bgcolor=#56658d></td>
    <td width="1" height="1"
bgcolor=#363f5a></td>
    <td width="1" height="1"
bgcolor=#302f3c></td>
    <td width="1" height="1"
bgcolor=#0b1112></td>
    <td width="1" height="1"
bgcolor=#1a1c31></td>
    <td width="1" height="1"
bgcolor=#5b6c9a></td>
    <td width="1" height="1"
bgcolor=#57688e></td>
    <td width="1" height="1"
bgcolor=#586690></td>
    <td rowspan="2"
colspan="1" width="1"
height="1"
bgcolor=#586790></td>
    <td rowspan="2"
colspan="1" width="1"
height="1"
bgcolor=#596890></td>
    <td rowspan="2"
colspan="1" width="1"
height="1"
bgcolor=#59688f></td>
    <td width="1" height="1"
bgcolor=#58678e></td>
    <td rowspan="1"
colspan="2" width="1"
height="1"
bgcolor=#5a6990></td>
    <td rowspan="1"
colspan="2" width="1"
height="1"
bgcolor=#5b6a91></td>
    <td width="1" height="1"
bgcolor=#5c6a91></td>
    <td width="1" height="1"
bgcolor=#5c6b92></td>
    <td rowspan="2"
colspan="1" width="1"
height="1"
bgcolor=#5a6990></td>
    <td rowspan="3"
colspan="1" width="1"
height="1"
bgcolor=#5d6b92></td>
    <td rowspan="3"
colspan="1" width="1"
height="1"
bgcolor=#5d6b92></td>
    <td width="1" height="1"
bgcolor=#5a6991></td>
    <td width="1" height="1"
bgcolor=#5e6c91></td>
    <td width="1" height="1"
bgcolor=#010200></td>
    <td width="1" height="1"
bgcolor=#2a2c46></td>
    <td width="1" height="1"
bgcolor=#0f0f13></td>
    <td width="1" height="1"
bgcolor=#5b678c></td>
    <td width="1" height="1"
bgcolor=#111516></td>
    <td width="1" height="1"
bgcolor=#4a5371></td>
    <td width="1" height="1"
bgcolor=#37425d></td>
    <td width="1" height="1"
bgcolor=#25273b></td>
    <td width="1" height="1"
bgcolor=#404664></td>
    <td width="1" height="1"
bgcolor=#3b4c66></td>
    <td width="1" height="1"
bgcolor=#67739f></td>
    <td width="1" height="1"
bgcolor=#1f2530></td>
    <td width="1" height="1"
bgcolor=#0a0b0d></td>
    <td width="1" height="1"
bgcolor=#2b3349></td>
    <td width="1" height="1"
bgcolor=#59688e></td>
    <td width="1" height="1"
bgcolor=#5f6e95></td>
    <td width="1" height="1"
bgcolor=#16192c></td>
    <td width="1" height="1"
bgcolor=#424d62></td>
    <td width="1" height="1"
bgcolor=#050307></td>
    <td width="1" height="1"
bgcolor=#080500></td>
    <td width="1" height="1"
bgcolor=#34364d></td>
    <td width="1" height="1"
bgcolor=#0e0f1a></td>
    <td width="1" height="1"
bgcolor=#414d64></td>
    <td width="1" height="1"
bgcolor=#6173a3></td>
    <td width="1" height="1"
bgcolor=#090a0d></td>
    <td width="1" height="1"
bgcolor=#0f1015></td>
    <td width="1" height="1"
bgcolor=#02080f></td>
    <td width="1" height="1"
bgcolor=#566587></td>
    <td width="1" height="1"
bgcolor=#56668d></td>
    <td width="1" height="1"
bgcolor=#58658c></td>
    <td width="1" height="1"
bgcolor=#54668b></td>
    <td rowspan="2"
colspan="1" width="1"
height="1"
bgcolor=#57668d></td>
    <td width="1" height="1"
bgcolor=#56658c></td>
    <td width="1" height="1"
bgcolor=#55638c></td>
    <td width="1" height="1"
bgcolor=#56638a></td>
    <td width="1" height="1"
bgcolor=#556788></td>
    <td width="1" height="1"
bgcolor=#515f89></td>
    <td width="1" height="1"
bgcolor=#474d67></td>
    <td width="1" height="1"
bgcolor=#000001></td>
    <td width="1" height="1"
bgcolor=#030107></td>
    <td width="1" height="1"
bgcolor=#101015></td>
    <td width="1" height="1"
bgcolor=#040200></td>
    <td width="1" height="1"
bgcolor=#1f2734></td>
    <td width="1" height="1"
bgcolor=#424a6c></td>
    <td width="1" height="1"
bgcolor=#4e5f87></td>
```

```
    <td width="1" height="1"
bgcolor=#5f605d></td>
  </tr>
  <tr>
    <td width="1" height="1"
bgcolor=#55668d></td>
    <td width="1" height="1"
bgcolor=#313b52></td>
    <td width="1" height="1"
bgcolor=#03020a></td>
    <td width="1" height="1"
bgcolor=#13121d></td>
    <td width="1" height="1"
bgcolor=#242633></td>
    <td width="1" height="1"
bgcolor=#5a6e91></td>
    <td width="1" height="1"
bgcolor=#586792></td>
    <td width="1" height="1"
bgcolor=#57658d></td>
    <td width="1" height="1"
bgcolor=#5a6990></td>
    <td rowspan="1"
colspan="2" width="1"
height="1"
bgcolor=#5b6a91></td>
    <td width="1" height="1"
bgcolor=#5c6b92></td>
    <td width="1" height="1"
bgcolor=#5b6a91></td>
    <td width="1" height="1"
bgcolor=#5a6990></td>
    <td width="1" height="1"
bgcolor=#5b6a91></td>
    <td width="1" height="1"
bgcolor=#5d6c93></td>
    <td width="1" height="1"
bgcolor=#5b6a91></td>
    <td width="1" height="1"
bgcolor=#606b97></td>
    <td width="1" height="1"
bgcolor=#13171b></td>
    <td width="1" height="1"
bgcolor=#0d0e17></td>
    <td width="1" height="1"
bgcolor=#272933></td>
    <td width="1" height="1"
bgcolor=#465972></td>
    <td width="1" height="1"
bgcolor=#21213e></td>
    <td width="1" height="1"
bgcolor=#444e70></td>
    <td width="1" height="1"
bgcolor=#505f80></td>
    <td width="1" height="1"
bgcolor=#22253a></td>
    <td width="1" height="1"
bgcolor=#404c65></td>
    <td width="1" height="1"
bgcolor=#485373></td>
    <td width="1" height="1"
bgcolor=#60729c></td>
    <td width="1" height="1"
bgcolor=#1e212c></td>
    <td width="1" height="1"
bgcolor=#2b2f3e></td>
    <td width="1" height="1"
bgcolor=#575f89></td>
    <td width="1" height="1"
bgcolor=#3c4b64></td>
    <td width="1" height="1"
bgcolor=#3b445f></td>
    <td width="1" height="1"
bgcolor=#2f3442></td>
    <td width="1" height="1"
bgcolor=#333b55></td>
    <td width="1" height="1"
bgcolor=#474c61></td>
    <td width="1" height="1"
bgcolor=#434d67></td>
    <td width="1" height="1"
bgcolor=#4d5b7a></td>
    <td width="1" height="1"
bgcolor=#06070a></td>
    <td width="1" height="1"
bgcolor=#010b09></td>
    <td width="1" height="1"
bgcolor=#070c1d></td>
    <td width="1" height="1"
bgcolor=#5d678f></td>
    <td width="1" height="1"
bgcolor=#050308></td>
    <td width="1" height="1"
bgcolor=#010000></td>
    <td width="1" height="1"
bgcolor=#4a5477></td>
    <td width="1" height="1"
bgcolor=#52688b></td>
    <td width="1" height="1"
bgcolor=#596591></td>
    <td width="1" height="1"
bgcolor=#56668b></td>
    <td width="1" height="1"
bgcolor=#57668d></td>
    <td width="1" height="1"
bgcolor=#58678d></td>
    <td width="1" height="1"
bgcolor=#56648b></td>
    <td width="1" height="1"
bgcolor=#53648c></td>
    <td width="1" height="1"
bgcolor=#536184></td>
    <td width="1" height="1"
bgcolor=#0d151a></td>
    <td width="1" height="1"
bgcolor=#070707></td>
    <td width="1" height="1"
bgcolor=#0c0b16></td>
    <td width="1" height="1"
bgcolor=#272938></td>
    <td width="1" height="1"
bgcolor=#101217></td>
    <td width="1" height="1"
bgcolor=#444e70></td>
    <td width="1" height="1"
bgcolor=#1b2a34></td>
    <td width="1" height="1"
bgcolor=#50628c></td>
    <td rowspan="2"
colspan="1" width="1"
height="1"
bgcolor=#575855></td>
  </tr>
  <tr>
    <td width="1" height="1"
bgcolor=#55648b></td>
    <td width="1" height="1"
bgcolor=#2e3649></td>
    <td width="1" height="1"
bgcolor=#050409></td>
    <td width="1" height="1"
bgcolor=#050405></td>
    <td width="1" height="1"
bgcolor=#0e111d></td>
    <td width="1" height="1"
bgcolor=#5b6e97></td>
    <td width="1" height="1"
bgcolor=#56668b></td>
    <td width="1" height="1"
bgcolor=#57668c></td>
    <td width="1" height="1"
bgcolor=#57668d></td>
    <td width="1" height="1"
bgcolor=#58678e></td>
    <td width="1" height="1"
bgcolor=#58678d></td>
    <td rowspan="1"
colspan="2" width="1"
height="1"
bgcolor=#59688f></td>
    <td width="1" height="1"
bgcolor=#5a6990></td>
    <td width="1" height="1"
bgcolor=#5b6a91></td>
    <td width="1" height="1"
bgcolor=#5a6990></td>
    <td width="1" height="1"
bgcolor=#5c6b92></td>
    <td width="1" height="1"
bgcolor=#5d6b92></td>
    <td width="1" height="1"
bgcolor=#5b6990></td>
    <td width="1" height="1"
bgcolor=#5c6a91></td>
```

```
    <td width="1" height="1"
bgcolor=#5c6b8f></td>
    <td width="1" height="1"
bgcolor=#414c6c></td>
    <td width="1" height="1"
bgcolor=#303545></td>
    <td width="1" height="1"
bgcolor=#272639></td>
    <td width="1" height="1"
bgcolor=#2a3240></td>
    <td width="1" height="1"
bgcolor=#374058></td>
    <td width="1" height="1"
bgcolor=#131413></td>
    <td width="1" height="1"
bgcolor=#555e82></td>
    <td width="1" height="1"
bgcolor=#4a5475></td>
    <td width="1" height="1"
bgcolor=#2b2f3d></td>
    <td width="1" height="1"
bgcolor=#454f6d></td>
    <td width="1" height="1"
bgcolor=#242b39></td>
    <td width="1" height="1"
bgcolor=#627599></td>
    <td width="1" height="1"
bgcolor=#3a4164></td>
    <td width="1" height="1"
bgcolor=#2e394a></td>
    <td width="1" height="1"
bgcolor=#4c5779></td>
    <td width="1" height="1"
bgcolor=#34394d></td>
    <td width="1" height="1"
bgcolor=#384058></td>
    <td width="1" height="1"
bgcolor=#0e0d14></td>
    <td width="1" height="1"
bgcolor=#222527></td>
    <td width="1" height="1"
bgcolor=#2d334c></td>
    <td width="1" height="1"
bgcolor=#292f3e></td>
    <td width="1" height="1"
bgcolor=#020105></td>
    <td width="1" height="1"
bgcolor=#4f5971></td>
    <td width="1" height="1"
bgcolor=#020407></td>
    <td width="1" height="1"
bgcolor=#373e5e></td>
    <td width="1" height="1"
bgcolor=#1b2030></td>
    <td width="1" height="1"
bgcolor=#47536d></td>
    <td width="1" height="1"
bgcolor=#000000></td>
    <td width="1" height="1"
bgcolor=#0c0d11></td>
    <td width="1" height="1"
bgcolor=#5a668c></td>
    <td width="1" height="1"
bgcolor=#556a8a></td>
    <td width="1" height="1"
bgcolor=#56628c></td>
    <td width="1" height="1"
bgcolor=#57648c></td>
    <td width="1" height="1"
bgcolor=#56668b></td>
    <td width="1" height="1"
bgcolor=#55658a></td>
    <td width="1" height="1"
bgcolor=#536387></td>
    <td width="1" height="1"
bgcolor=#465676></td>
    <td width="1" height="1"
bgcolor=#3e4761></td>
    <td width="1" height="1"
bgcolor=#000002></td>
    <td width="1" height="1"
bgcolor=#000000></td>
    <td rowspan="2"
colspan="1" width="1"
height="1"
bgcolor=#000100></td>
    <td width="1" height="1"
bgcolor=#000000></td>
    <td width="1" height="1"
bgcolor=#272b39></td>
    <td width="1" height="1"
bgcolor=#404f6e></td>
    <td width="1" height="1"
bgcolor=#46566f></td>
    <td width="1" height="1"
bgcolor=#4d6087></td>
  </tr>
  <tr>
    <td width="1" height="1"
bgcolor=#566489></td>
    <td width="1" height="1"
bgcolor=#2f354b></td>
    <td width="1" height="1"
bgcolor=#141017></td>
    <td width="1" height="1"
bgcolor=#0c060f></td>
    <td width="1" height="1"
bgcolor=#0b0b11></td>
    <td width="1" height="1"
bgcolor=#5b6b97></td>
    <td width="1" height="1"
bgcolor=#586689></td>
    <td width="1" height="1"
bgcolor=#56678e></td>
    <td width="1" height="1"
bgcolor=#57658d></td>
    <td width="1" height="1"
bgcolor=#59668f></td>
    <td width="1" height="1"
bgcolor=#58688e></td>
    <td width="1" height="1"
bgcolor=#5a6990></td>
    <td width="1" height="1"
bgcolor=#5a698d></td>
    <td rowspan="2"
colspan="1" width="1"
height="1"
bgcolor=#5a6892></td>
    <td width="1" height="1"
bgcolor=#5b698e></td>
    <td width="1" height="1"
bgcolor=#5a6894></td>
    <td width="1" height="1"
bgcolor=#5d6a92></td>
    <td width="1" height="1"
bgcolor=#5b6990></td>
    <td width="1" height="1"
bgcolor=#5c6b91></td>
    <td width="1" height="1"
bgcolor=#5d6c93></td>
    <td width="1" height="1"
bgcolor=#5b6b8f></td>
    <td width="1" height="1"
bgcolor=#5c6b97></td>
    <td width="1" height="1"
bgcolor=#5c6c8f></td>
    <td width="1" height="1"
bgcolor=#596c98></td>
    <td width="1" height="1"
bgcolor=#494e72></td>
    <td width="1" height="1"
bgcolor=#242a3b></td>
    <td width="1" height="1"
bgcolor=#16161a></td>
    <td width="1" height="1"
bgcolor=#373c55></td>
    <td width="1" height="1"
bgcolor=#1b1f23></td>
    <td width="1" height="1"
bgcolor=#070102></td>
    <td width="1" height="1"
bgcolor=#505a7e></td>
    <td width="1" height="1"
bgcolor=#1b232a></td>
    <td width="1" height="1"
bgcolor=#30344f></td>
    <td width="1" height="1"
bgcolor=#333f50></td>
    <td width="1" height="1"
bgcolor=#242531></td>
    <td width="1" height="1"
bgcolor=#61729b></td>
    <td width="1" height="1"
bgcolor=#242e3c></td>
```

```
    <td width="1" height="1"
bgcolor=#616f98></td>
    <td width="1" height="1"
bgcolor=#3d4061></td>
    <td width="1" height="1"
bgcolor=#2a3643></td>
    <td width="1" height="1"
bgcolor=#0c0908></td>
    <td width="1" height="1"
bgcolor=#1a1b26></td>
    <td width="1" height="1"
bgcolor=#0c0c0c></td>
    <td width="1" height="1"
bgcolor=#383b51></td>
    <td width="1" height="1"
bgcolor=#505a7d></td>
    <td width="1" height="1"
bgcolor=#262634></td>
    <td width="1" height="1"
bgcolor=#242d3e></td>
    <td width="1" height="1"
bgcolor=#5b77a2></td>
    <td width="1" height="1"
bgcolor=#414362></td>
    <td width="1" height="1"
bgcolor=#070302></td>
    <td width="1" height="1"
bgcolor=#404e6a></td>
    <td width="1" height="1"
bgcolor=#191a24></td>
    <td width="1" height="1"
bgcolor=#1e1e29></td>
    <td width="1" height="1"
bgcolor=#050a13></td>
    <td width="1" height="1"
bgcolor=#566189></td>
    <td width="1" height="1"
bgcolor=#556b93></td>
    <td width="1" height="1"
bgcolor=#55628d></td>
    <td width="1" height="1"
bgcolor=#55688d></td>
    <td width="1" height="1"
bgcolor=#57668e></td>
    <td width="1" height="1"
bgcolor=#53668b></td>
    <td width="1" height="1"
bgcolor=#59678f></td>
    <td width="1" height="1"
bgcolor=#232c3b></td>
    <td width="1" height="1"
bgcolor=#2f3744></td>
    <td width="1" height="1"
bgcolor=#2b3044></td>
    <td width="1" height="1"
bgcolor=#010100></td>
    <td width="1" height="1"
bgcolor=#000104></td>
    <td width="1" height="1"
bgcolor=#09060c></td>
    <td width="1" height="1"
bgcolor=#000000></td>
    <td width="1" height="1"
bgcolor=#404b6f></td>
    <td width="1" height="1"
bgcolor=#465d82></td>
    <td width="1" height="1"
bgcolor=#676865></td>
  </tr>
  <tr>
    <td width="1" height="1"
bgcolor=#55638c></td>
    <td width="1" height="1"
bgcolor=#2e354f></td>
    <td width="1" height="1"
bgcolor=#191b26></td>
    <td width="1" height="1"
bgcolor=#12151e></td>
    <td width="1" height="1"
bgcolor=#06040a></td>
    <td width="1" height="1"
bgcolor=#3e4a61></td>
    <td width="1" height="1"
bgcolor=#586590></td>
    <td width="1" height="1"
bgcolor=#58668d></td>
    <td width="1" height="1"
bgcolor=#56658c></td>
    <td rowspan="2"
colspan="1" width="1"
height="1"
bgcolor=#58678e></td>
    <td width="1" height="1"
bgcolor=#5a6690></td>
    <td width="1" height="1"
bgcolor=#57668e></td>
    <td width="1" height="1"
bgcolor=#596c8f></td>
    <td width="1" height="1"
bgcolor=#5b698d></td>
    <td width="1" height="1"
bgcolor=#576a8e></td>
    <td width="1" height="1"
bgcolor=#5a6b91></td>
    <td width="1" height="1"
bgcolor=#5d6991></td>
    <td width="1" height="1"
bgcolor=#5b6891></td>
    <td width="1" height="1"
bgcolor=#5d6c95></td>
    <td width="1" height="1"
bgcolor=#5a698d></td>
    <td width="1" height="1"
bgcolor=#5d6a92></td>
    <td width="1" height="1"
bgcolor=#5e6e91></td>
    <td width="1" height="1"
bgcolor=#5e7293></td>
    <td width="1" height="1"
bgcolor=#414c6e></td>
    <td width="1" height="1"
bgcolor=#2b2b3c></td>
    <td width="1" height="1"
bgcolor=#070c12></td>
    <td width="1" height="1"
bgcolor=#110f16></td>
    <td width="1" height="1"
bgcolor=#303144></td>
    <td width="1" height="1"
bgcolor=#000505></td>
    <td width="1" height="1"
bgcolor=#354057></td>
    <td width="1" height="1"
bgcolor=#121217></td>
    <td width="1" height="1"
bgcolor=#4b5b78></td>
    <td width="1" height="1"
bgcolor=#13121b></td>
    <td width="1" height="1"
bgcolor=#1f2232></td>
    <td width="1" height="1"
bgcolor=#404a6a></td>
    <td width="1" height="1"
bgcolor=#3b465c></td>
    <td width="1" height="1"
bgcolor=#404e6a></td>
    <td width="1" height="1"
bgcolor=#50617b></td>
    <td width="1" height="1"
bgcolor=#3e4763></td>
    <td width="1" height="1"
bgcolor=#222635></td>
    <td width="1" height="1"
bgcolor=#090909></td>
    <td width="1" height="1"
bgcolor=#282c3b></td>
    <td width="1" height="1"
bgcolor=#0e0e0a></td>
    <td width="1" height="1"
bgcolor=#232e35></td>
    <td width="1" height="1"
bgcolor=#505e86></td>
    <td width="1" height="1"
bgcolor=#27303b></td>
    <td width="1" height="1"
bgcolor=#0f121e></td>
    <td width="1" height="1"
bgcolor=#435266></td>
    <td width="1" height="1"
bgcolor=#2d304b></td>
    <td width="1" height="1"
bgcolor=#090706></td>
    <td width="1" height="1"
bgcolor=#58698c></td>
```

```
    <td width="1" height="1"
bgcolor=#0c0e12></td>
    <td width="1" height="1"
bgcolor=#1e272c></td>
    <td width="1" height="1"
bgcolor=#0f1012></td>
    <td width="1" height="1"
bgcolor=#0d1218></td>
    <td width="1" height="1"
bgcolor=#58698e></td>
    <td width="1" height="1"
bgcolor=#57648d></td>
    <td width="1" height="1"
bgcolor=#59688b></td>
    <td width="1" height="1"
bgcolor=#535d81></td>
    <td width="1" height="1"
bgcolor=#353c5b></td>
    <td width="1" height="1"
bgcolor=#21252d></td>
    <td width="1" height="1"
bgcolor=#232235></td>
    <td width="1" height="1"
bgcolor=#0d0c09></td>
    <td width="1" height="1"
bgcolor=#1e222f></td>
    <td width="1" height="1"
bgcolor=#000000></td>
    <td width="1" height="1"
bgcolor=#010100></td>
    <td width="1" height="1"
bgcolor=#171a26></td>
    <td width="1" height="1"
bgcolor=#2e313d></td>
    <td width="1" height="1"
bgcolor=#26313e></td>
    <td width="1" height="1"
bgcolor=#4f6085></td>
    <td width="1" height="1"
bgcolor=#575855></td>
  </tr>
  <tr>
    <td width="1" height="1"
bgcolor=#566588></td>
    <td width="1" height="1"
bgcolor=#424c69></td>
    <td width="1" height="1"
bgcolor=#262b3f></td>
    <td width="1" height="1"
bgcolor=#32394c></td>
    <td width="1" height="1"
bgcolor=#2a273e></td>
    <td width="1" height="1"
bgcolor=#262b41></td>
    <td width="1" height="1"
bgcolor=#5a6f97></td>
    <td width="1" height="1"
bgcolor=#55678c></td>
    <td width="1" height="1"
bgcolor=#58678f></td>
    <td width="1" height="1"
bgcolor=#5b6990></td>
    <td width="1" height="1"
bgcolor=#5a6691></td>
    <td width="1" height="1"
bgcolor=#5b6990></td>
    <td width="1" height="1"
bgcolor=#5a688d></td>
    <td width="1" height="1"
bgcolor=#596b96></td>
    <td width="1" height="1"
bgcolor=#576990></td>
    <td width="1" height="1"
bgcolor=#596a94></td>
    <td width="1" height="1"
bgcolor=#5c6890></td>
    <td width="1" height="1"
bgcolor=#5c6b8e></td>
    <td width="1" height="1"
bgcolor=#5b6c92></td>
    <td width="1" height="1"
bgcolor=#5d6b91></td>
    <td width="1" height="1"
bgcolor=#5c6a91></td>
    <td width="1" height="1"
bgcolor=#5e6d98></td>
    <td width="1" height="1"
bgcolor=#5d648f></td>
    <td width="1" height="1"
bgcolor=#1a252f></td>
    <td width="1" height="1"
bgcolor=#110b12></td>
    <td width="1" height="1"
bgcolor=#272732></td>
    <td width="1" height="1"
bgcolor=#141615></td>
    <td width="1" height="1"
bgcolor=#2f3146></td>
    <td width="1" height="1"
bgcolor=#090a02></td>
    <td width="1" height="1"
bgcolor=#1d1d2d></td>
    <td width="1" height="1"
bgcolor=#232b40></td>
    <td width="1" height="1"
bgcolor=#49516b></td>
    <td width="1" height="1"
bgcolor=#0a0a0e></td>
    <td width="1" height="1"
bgcolor=#191a23></td>
    <td width="1" height="1"
bgcolor=#212a37></td>
    <td width="1" height="1"
bgcolor=#5d688b></td>
    <td width="1" height="1"
bgcolor=#3d445f></td>
    <td width="1" height="1"
bgcolor=#414765></td>
    <td width="1" height="1"
bgcolor=#121418></td>
    <td width="1" height="1"
bgcolor=#222533></td>
    <td width="1" height="1"
bgcolor=#0f0b10></td>
    <td width="1" height="1"
bgcolor=#08100f></td>
    <td width="1" height="1"
bgcolor=#0f0e10></td>
    <td width="1" height="1"
bgcolor=#070800></td>
    <td width="1" height="1"
bgcolor=#2c344e></td>
    <td width="1" height="1"
bgcolor=#454e64></td>
    <td width="1" height="1"
bgcolor=#2b2e41></td>
    <td width="1" height="1"
bgcolor=#07030b></td>
    <td width="1" height="1"
bgcolor=#20212a></td>
    <td width="1" height="1"
bgcolor=#18161c></td>
    <td width="1" height="1"
bgcolor=#343e54></td>
    <td width="1" height="1"
bgcolor=#465370></td>
    <td width="1" height="1"
bgcolor=#232635></td>
    <td width="1" height="1"
bgcolor=#2f3652></td>
    <td width="1" height="1"
bgcolor=#080a13></td>
    <td width="1" height="1"
bgcolor=#5a668a></td>
    <td width="1" height="1"
bgcolor=#40516b></td>
    <td width="1" height="1"
bgcolor=#0f121b></td>
    <td width="1" height="1"
bgcolor=#000101></td>
    <td width="1" height="1"
bgcolor=#020200></td>
    <td width="1" height="1"
bgcolor=#020300></td>
    <td width="1" height="1"
bgcolor=#03030a></td>
    <td width="1" height="1"
bgcolor=#050d0c></td>
    <td width="1" height="1"
bgcolor=#222532></td>
    <td width="1" height="1"
bgcolor=#1f2433></td>
    <td width="1" height="1"
bgcolor=#454766></td>
```

```
    <td width="1" height="1"
bgcolor=#11151e></td>
    <td width="1" height="1"
bgcolor=#070907></td>
    <td width="1" height="1"
bgcolor=#2e344b></td>
    <td width="1" height="1"
bgcolor=#516187></td>
    <td width="1" height="1"
bgcolor=#595b58></td>
  </tr>
  <tr>
    <td width="1" height="1"
bgcolor=#59688c></td>
    <td width="1" height="1"
bgcolor=#2a324c></td>
    <td width="1" height="1"
bgcolor=#1a1a2c></td>
    <td width="1" height="1"
bgcolor=#19182d></td>
    <td width="1" height="1"
bgcolor=#21253b></td>
    <td width="1" height="1"
bgcolor=#100e19></td>
    <td width="1" height="1"
bgcolor=#2e354d></td>
    <td width="1" height="1"
bgcolor=#626d92></td>
    <td width="1" height="1"
bgcolor=#5b688c></td>
    <td width="1" height="1"
bgcolor=#55658d></td>
    <td width="1" height="1"
bgcolor=#5b6a92></td>
    <td width="1" height="1"
bgcolor=#58678b></td>
    <td width="1" height="1"
bgcolor=#58678f></td>
    <td width="1" height="1"
bgcolor=#596a90></td>
    <td width="1" height="1"
bgcolor=#646e94></td>
    <td width="1" height="1"
bgcolor=#3c465d></td>
    <td width="1" height="1"
bgcolor=#626e95></td>
    <td width="1" height="1"
bgcolor=#5a6b95></td>
    <td width="1" height="1"
bgcolor=#5c6a91></td>
    <td width="1" height="1"
bgcolor=#5d6a93></td>
    <td width="1" height="1"
bgcolor=#5d6993></td>
    <td width="1" height="1"
bgcolor=#5f7194></td>
    <td width="1" height="1"
bgcolor=#657194></td>
    <td width="1" height="1"
bgcolor=#0e0f1c></td>
    <td width="1" height="1"
bgcolor=#0e0d07></td>
    <td width="1" height="1"
bgcolor=#2a2c40></td>
    <td width="1" height="1"
bgcolor=#0e0c14></td>
    <td width="1" height="1"
bgcolor=#333550></td>
    <td width="1" height="1"
bgcolor=#1c1f2a></td>
    <td width="1" height="1"
bgcolor=#0d0e17></td>
    <td width="1" height="1"
bgcolor=#090908></td>
    <td width="1" height="1"
bgcolor=#262f44></td>
    <td width="1" height="1"
bgcolor=#212536></td>
    <td width="1" height="1"
bgcolor=#222836></td>
    <td width="1" height="1"
bgcolor=#2a2e3f></td>
    <td width="1" height="1"
bgcolor=#374258></td>
    <td width="1" height="1"
bgcolor=#3e4460></td>
    <td width="1" height="1"
bgcolor=#3a4557></td>
    <td width="1" height="1"
bgcolor=#080903></td>
    <td width="1" height="1"
bgcolor=#0f0b0a></td>
    <td width="1" height="1"
bgcolor=#151614></td>
    <td width="1" height="1"
bgcolor=#16191e></td>
    <td width="1" height="1"
bgcolor=#21232e></td>
    <td width="1" height="1"
bgcolor=#272a38></td>
    <td width="1" height="1"
bgcolor=#383750></td>
    <td width="1" height="1"
bgcolor=#3e425d></td>
    <td width="1" height="1"
bgcolor=#202531></td>
    <td width="1" height="1"
bgcolor=#424e6e></td>
    <td width="1" height="1"
bgcolor=#323c50></td>
    <td width="1" height="1"
bgcolor=#15141c></td>
    <td width="1" height="1"
bgcolor=#39445a></td>
    <td width="1" height="1"
bgcolor=#1f2d39></td>
    <td width="1" height="1"
bgcolor=#32364f></td>
    <td width="1" height="1"
bgcolor=#030200></td>
    <td width="1" height="1"
bgcolor=#292637></td>
    <td width="1" height="1"
bgcolor=#1e2932></td>
    <td width="1" height="1"
bgcolor=#323c58></td>
    <td width="1" height="1"
bgcolor=#3f455d></td>
    <td width="1" height="1"
bgcolor=#060609></td>
    <td width="1" height="1"
bgcolor=#0b0a07></td>
    <td width="1" height="1"
bgcolor=#000000></td>
    <td width="1" height="1"
bgcolor=#05090d></td>
    <td width="1" height="1"
bgcolor=#3a394e></td>
    <td width="1" height="1"
bgcolor=#13151d></td>
    <td width="1" height="1"
bgcolor=#05070e></td>
    <td width="1" height="1"
bgcolor=#191d1f></td>
    <td width="1" height="1"
bgcolor=#06080c></td>
    <td width="1" height="1"
bgcolor=#16151d></td>
    <td width="1" height="1"
bgcolor=#2c2d43></td>
    <td width="1" height="1"
bgcolor=#222c3a></td>
    <td width="1" height="1"
bgcolor=#516189></td>
    <td width="1" height="1"
bgcolor=#5d5e5b></td>
  </tr>
  <tr>
    <td width="1" height="1"
bgcolor=#56658b></td>
    <td width="1" height="1"
bgcolor=#323b55></td>
    <td width="1" height="1"
bgcolor=#111320></td>
    <td width="1" height="1"
bgcolor=#222336></td>
    <td width="1" height="1"
bgcolor=#39405b></td>
    <td width="1" height="1"
bgcolor=#22273d></td>
    <td width="1" height="1"
bgcolor=#1e141f></td>
    <td width="1" height="1"
bgcolor=#090d0e></td>
```

```
    <td width="1" height="1"
bgcolor=#1a1b29></td>
    <td width="1" height="1"
bgcolor=#30344c></td>
    <td width="1" height="1"
bgcolor=#353f55></td>
    <td width="1" height="1"
bgcolor=#62719b></td>
    <td width="1" height="1"
bgcolor=#5e6e97></td>
    <td width="1" height="1"
bgcolor=#4b5473></td>
    <td width="1" height="1"
bgcolor=#0a0c15></td>
    <td width="1" height="1"
bgcolor=#060706></td>
    <td width="1" height="1"
bgcolor=#16191f></td>
    <td width="1" height="1"
bgcolor=#2a3146></td>
    <td width="1" height="1"
bgcolor=#414761></td>
    <td width="1" height="1"
bgcolor=#38394d></td>
    <td width="1" height="1"
bgcolor=#5d719b></td>
    <td width="1" height="1"
bgcolor=#1d1e2d></td>
    <td width="1" height="1"
bgcolor=#505983></td>
    <td width="1" height="1"
bgcolor=#070500></td>
    <td width="1" height="1"
bgcolor=#161b28></td>
    <td width="1" height="1"
bgcolor=#212430></td>
    <td width="1" height="1"
bgcolor=#0e0c11></td>
    <td width="1" height="1"
bgcolor=#212131></td>
    <td width="1" height="1"
bgcolor=#252026></td>
    <td width="1" height="1"
bgcolor=#151727></td>
    <td width="1" height="1"
bgcolor=#566386></td>
    <td width="1" height="1"
bgcolor=#5f7197></td>
    <td width="1" height="1"
bgcolor=#5e7197></td>
    <td width="1" height="1"
bgcolor=#536387></td>
    <td width="1" height="1"
bgcolor=#465477></td>
    <td width="1" height="1"
bgcolor=#435273></td>
    <td width="1" height="1"
bgcolor=#181923></td>
    <td width="1" height="1"
bgcolor=#4a5979></td>
    <td width="1" height="1"
bgcolor=#0e1315></td>
    <td width="1" height="1"
bgcolor=#16161a></td>
    <td width="1" height="1"
bgcolor=#3b3a4f></td>
    <td width="1" height="1"
bgcolor=#131a28></td>
    <td width="1" height="1"
bgcolor=#3d435c></td>
    <td width="1" height="1"
bgcolor=#35424f></td>
    <td width="1" height="1"
bgcolor=#04050a></td>
    <td width="1" height="1"
bgcolor=#030400></td>
    <td width="1" height="1"
bgcolor=#2d354c></td>
    <td width="1" height="1"
bgcolor=#3c495b></td>
    <td width="1" height="1"
bgcolor=#1b1b2e></td>
    <td width="1" height="1"
bgcolor=#2a2c44></td>
    <td width="1" height="1"
bgcolor=#495376></td>
    <td width="1" height="1"
bgcolor=#020003></td>
    <td width="1" height="1"
bgcolor=#46546c></td>
    <td width="1" height="1"
bgcolor=#08040a></td>
    <td width="1" height="1"
bgcolor=#1d1e28></td>
    <td width="1" height="1"
bgcolor=#2b3242></td>
    <td width="1" height="1"
bgcolor=#474f6f></td>
    <td width="1" height="1"
bgcolor=#000201></td>
    <td width="1" height="1"
bgcolor=#0d0c11></td>
    <td width="1" height="1"
bgcolor=#010307></td>
    <td width="1" height="1"
bgcolor=#303247></td>
    <td width="1" height="1"
bgcolor=#0d1615></td>
    <td width="1" height="1"
bgcolor=#040300></td>
    <td width="1" height="1"
bgcolor=#000301></td>
    <td width="1" height="1"
bgcolor=#040406></td>
    <td width="1" height="1"
bgcolor=#010000></td>
    <td width="1" height="1"
bgcolor=#091015></td>
    <td width="1" height="1"
bgcolor=#161e1d></td>
    <td width="1" height="1"
bgcolor=#1c1b2d></td>
    <td width="1" height="1"
bgcolor=#333e50></td>
    <td width="1" height="1"
bgcolor=#4b6186></td>
    <td width="1" height="1"
bgcolor=#5c5d5a></td>
  </tr>
  <tr>
    <td width="1" height="1"
bgcolor=#54628d></td>
    <td width="1" height="1"
bgcolor=#3f4663></td>
    <td width="1" height="1"
bgcolor=#24253b></td>
    <td width="1" height="1"
bgcolor=#363856></td>
    <td width="1" height="1"
bgcolor=#2d3648></td>
    <td width="1" height="1"
bgcolor=#1a1622></td>
    <td width="1" height="1"
bgcolor=#1d212e></td>
    <td width="1" height="1"
bgcolor=#1b1928></td>
    <td width="1" height="1"
bgcolor=#050308></td>
    <td width="1" height="1"
bgcolor=#0d070e></td>
    <td width="1" height="1"
bgcolor=#090706></td>
    <td width="1" height="1"
bgcolor=#020105></td>
    <td width="1" height="1"
bgcolor=#040201></td>
    <td width="1" height="1"
bgcolor=#0b0b06></td>
    <td width="1" height="1"
bgcolor=#110e0e></td>
    <td width="1" height="1"
bgcolor=#10090f></td>
    <td width="1" height="1"
bgcolor=#0d0813></td>
    <td width="1" height="1"
bgcolor=#1c1b29></td>
    <td width="1" height="1"
bgcolor=#0d0b13></td>
    <td width="1" height="1"
bgcolor=#0d1016></td>
    <td width="1" height="1"
bgcolor=#3d465e></td>
    <td width="1" height="1"
bgcolor=#525a78></td>
```

```
    <td width="1" height="1"
bgcolor=#334057></td>
    <td width="1" height="1"
bgcolor=#151415></td>
    <td width="1" height="1"
bgcolor=#1f1e2d></td>
    <td width="1" height="1"
bgcolor=#090c08></td>
    <td width="1" height="1"
bgcolor=#100f13></td>
    <td width="1" height="1"
bgcolor=#09080c></td>
    <td width="1" height="1"
bgcolor=#000101></td>
    <td width="1" height="1"
bgcolor=#576082></td>
    <td width="1" height="1"
bgcolor=#5d6d91></td>
    <td width="1" height="1"
bgcolor=#5c6a94></td>
    <td width="1" height="1"
bgcolor=#5c6b92></td>
    <td width="1" height="1"
bgcolor=#5d6d92></td>
    <td width="1" height="1"
bgcolor=#5d6c93></td>
    <td width="1" height="1"
bgcolor=#5f6e92></td>
    <td width="1" height="1"
bgcolor=#5b698c></td>
    <td width="1" height="1"
bgcolor=#16131d></td>
    <td width="1" height="1"
bgcolor=#100909></td>
    <td width="1" height="1"
bgcolor=#212835></td>
    <td width="1" height="1"
bgcolor=#535977></td>
    <td width="1" height="1"
bgcolor=#1a1f26></td>
    <td width="1" height="1"
bgcolor=#080809></td>
    <td width="1" height="1"
bgcolor=#3c4359></td>
    <td width="1" height="1"
bgcolor=#090607></td>
    <td width="1" height="1"
bgcolor=#1c1f2b></td>
    <td width="1" height="1"
bgcolor=#040705></td>
    <td width="1" height="1"
bgcolor=#333952></td>
    <td width="1" height="1"
bgcolor=#21212d></td>
    <td width="1" height="1"
bgcolor=#1b1e27></td>
    <td width="1" height="1"
bgcolor=#3c4a6d></td>
    <td width="1" height="1"
bgcolor=#212326></td>
    <td width="1" height="1"
bgcolor=#1b2024></td>
    <td width="1" height="1"
bgcolor=#242c39></td>
    <td width="1" height="1"
bgcolor=#111217></td>
    <td width="1" height="1"
bgcolor=#293547></td>
    <td width="1" height="1"
bgcolor=#506285></td>
    <td width="1" height="1"
bgcolor=#060409></td>
    <td width="1" height="1"
bgcolor=#131818></td>
    <td width="1" height="1"
bgcolor=#0e0f14></td>
    <td width="1" height="1"
bgcolor=#050e0e></td>
    <td width="1" height="1"
bgcolor=#333f50></td>
    <td width="1" height="1"
bgcolor=#020000></td>
    <td width="1" height="1"
bgcolor=#020201></td>
    <td width="1" height="1"
bgcolor=#050101></td>
    <td width="1" height="1"
bgcolor=#262d37></td>
    <td width="1" height="1"
bgcolor=#293547></td>
    <td width="1" height="1"
bgcolor=#202027></td>
    <td width="1" height="1"
bgcolor=#0e121b></td>
    <td width="1" height="1"
bgcolor=#384662></td>
    <td width="1" height="1"
bgcolor=#506288></td>
    <td width="1" height="1"
bgcolor=#595a57></td>
  </tr>
  <tr>
    <td width="1" height="1"
bgcolor=#576687></td>
    <td width="1" height="1"
bgcolor=#2e344c></td>
    <td width="1" height="1"
bgcolor=#222537></td>
    <td width="1" height="1"
bgcolor=#2d354c></td>
    <td width="1" height="1"
bgcolor=#404865></td>
    <td width="1" height="1"
bgcolor=#272b42></td>
    <td width="1" height="1"
bgcolor=#24263a></td>
    <td width="1" height="1"
bgcolor=#46506b></td>
    <td width="1" height="1"
bgcolor=#141a1e></td>
    <td width="1" height="1"
bgcolor=#030000></td>
    <td width="1" height="1"
bgcolor=#090606></td>
    <td width="1" height="1"
bgcolor=#0c070a></td>
    <td width="1" height="1"
bgcolor=#0d0d0e></td>
    <td width="1" height="1"
bgcolor=#090c0b></td>
    <td width="1" height="1"
bgcolor=#070b08></td>
    <td width="1" height="1"
bgcolor=#110f12></td>
    <td width="1" height="1"
bgcolor=#09090f></td>
    <td width="1" height="1"
bgcolor=#1f1d21></td>
    <td width="1" height="1"
bgcolor=#111015></td>
    <td width="1" height="1"
bgcolor=#474e68></td>
    <td width="1" height="1"
bgcolor=#000000></td>
    <td width="1" height="1"
bgcolor=#5c698f></td>
    <td width="1" height="1"
bgcolor=#232838></td>
    <td width="1" height="1"
bgcolor=#141619></td>
    <td width="1" height="1"
bgcolor=#0e0e04></td>
    <td width="1" height="1"
bgcolor=#0a070b></td>
    <td width="1" height="1"
bgcolor=#0d0e0a></td>
    <td width="1" height="1"
bgcolor=#050605></td>
    <td width="1" height="1"
bgcolor=#424962></td>
    <td width="1" height="1"
bgcolor=#5e7097></td>
    <td width="1" height="1"
bgcolor=#5e6e97></td>
    <td width="1" height="1"
bgcolor=#5d6a90></td>
    <td width="1" height="1"
bgcolor=#5f6b93></td>
    <td width="1" height="1"
bgcolor=#5c6b92></td>
    <td width="1" height="1"
bgcolor=#5d6c94></td>
    <td width="1" height="1"
bgcolor=#5f6c98></td>
```

```
<td width="1" height="1" bgcolor=#5b6c91></td>
<td width="1" height="1" bgcolor=#5f749a></td>
<td width="1" height="1" bgcolor=#1f2430></td>
<td width="1" height="1" bgcolor=#292c37></td>
<td width="1" height="1" bgcolor=#1f222c></td>
<td width="1" height="1" bgcolor=#101016></td>
<td width="1" height="1" bgcolor=#0a0608></td>
<td width="1" height="1" bgcolor=#4b5774></td>
<td width="1" height="1" bgcolor=#020300></td>
<td width="1" height="1" bgcolor=#414a64></td>
<td width="1" height="1" bgcolor=#09060b></td>
<td width="1" height="1" bgcolor=#3e485f></td>
<td width="1" height="1" bgcolor=#546994></td>
<td width="1" height="1" bgcolor=#464e6a></td>
<td width="1" height="1" bgcolor=#58638e></td>
<td width="1" height="1" bgcolor=#0c1115></td>
<td width="1" height="1" bgcolor=#293147></td>
<td width="1" height="1" bgcolor=#454e69></td>
<td width="1" height="1" bgcolor=#242b39></td>
<td width="1" height="1" bgcolor=#363e56></td>
<td width="1" height="1" bgcolor=#1e2135></td>
<td width="1" height="1" bgcolor=#0b0703></td>
<td width="1" height="1" bgcolor=#0c0d15></td>
<td width="1" height="1" bgcolor=#242735></td>
<td width="1" height="1" bgcolor=#2c313e></td>
<td width="1" height="1" bgcolor=#252c40></td>
<td width="1" height="1" bgcolor=#131515></td>
<td width="1" height="1" bgcolor=#030500></td>
<td width="1" height="1" bgcolor=#171a27></td>
<td width="1" height="1" bgcolor=#2b334e></td>
<td width="1" height="1" bgcolor=#394159></td>
<td width="1" height="1" bgcolor=#203142></td>
<td width="1" height="1" bgcolor=#424e6d></td>
<td width="1" height="1" bgcolor=#263147></td>
<td width="1" height="1" bgcolor=#4e6087></td>
<td width="1" height="1" bgcolor=#5a5b58></td>
</tr>
<tr>
<td width="1" height="1" bgcolor=#56648c></td>
<td width="1" height="1" bgcolor=#41496b></td>
<td width="1" height="1" bgcolor=#303954></td>
<td width="1" height="1" bgcolor=#3e4b65></td>
<td width="1" height="1" bgcolor=#4a597b></td>
<td width="1" height="1" bgcolor=#4e5c80></td>
<td width="1" height="1" bgcolor=#404964></td>
<td width="1" height="1" bgcolor=#34405b></td>
<td width="1" height="1" bgcolor=#1d202a></td>
<td width="1" height="1" bgcolor=#0a0508></td>
<td width="1" height="1" bgcolor=#090b05></td>
<td width="1" height="1" bgcolor=#060406></td>
<td width="1" height="1" bgcolor=#0d0a0a></td>
<td width="1" height="1" bgcolor=#0b0704></td>
<td width="1" height="1" bgcolor=#0d0a0f></td>
<td width="1" height="1" bgcolor=#0c060b></td>
<td width="1" height="1" bgcolor=#000500></td>
<td width="1" height="1" bgcolor=#20272c></td>
<td width="1" height="1" bgcolor=#484d6c></td>
<td width="1" height="1" bgcolor=#55688e></td>
<td width="1" height="1" bgcolor=#636f95></td>
<td width="1" height="1" bgcolor=#5f6f9b></td>
<td width="1" height="1" bgcolor=#282c3f></td>
<td width="1" height="1" bgcolor=#2c3147></td>
<td width="1" height="1" bgcolor=#09090a></td>
<td width="1" height="1" bgcolor=#0f0d0f></td>
<td width="1" height="1" bgcolor=#0f0d12></td>
<td width="1" height="1" bgcolor=#1b2028></td>
<td width="1" height="1" bgcolor=#64709c></td>
<td width="1" height="1" bgcolor=#5d6e92></td>
<td width="1" height="1" bgcolor=#5f6d94></td>
<td width="1" height="1" bgcolor=#5e6d93></td>
<td width="1" height="1" bgcolor=#5e6d94></td>
<td width="1" height="1" bgcolor=#5d6b92></td>
<td width="1" height="1" bgcolor=#5c6c93></td>
<td width="1" height="1" bgcolor=#606c92></td>
<td width="1" height="1" bgcolor=#5a6d8f></td>
<td width="1" height="1" bgcolor=#616992></td>
<td width="1" height="1" bgcolor=#627399></td>
<td width="1" height="1" bgcolor=#0b0c15></td>
<td width="1" height="1" bgcolor=#292f42></td>
<td width="1" height="1" bgcolor=#20222a></td>
<td width="1" height="1" bgcolor=#08030a></td>
<td width="1" height="1" bgcolor=#4c5473></td>
<td width="1" height="1" bgcolor=#030300></td>
<td width="1" height="1" bgcolor=#1f202b></td>
<td width="1" height="1" bgcolor=#16191f></td>
<td width="1" height="1" bgcolor=#121317></td>
<td width="1" height="1" bgcolor=#4e5777></td>
<td width="1" height="1" bgcolor=#130f19></td>
```

```
    <td width="1" height="1" bgcolor=#4a5975></td>
    <td width="1" height="1" bgcolor=#0f1417></td>
    <td width="1" height="1" bgcolor=#141519></td>
    <td width="1" height="1" bgcolor=#465069></td>
    <td width="1" height="1" bgcolor=#38455e></td>
    <td width="1" height="1" bgcolor=#343d50></td>
    <td width="1" height="1" bgcolor=#2a3034></td>
    <td width="1" height="1" bgcolor=#020002></td>
    <td width="1" height="1" bgcolor=#101419></td>
    <td width="1" height="1" bgcolor=#323e52></td>
    <td width="1" height="1" bgcolor=#373e56></td>
    <td width="1" height="1" bgcolor=#364052></td>
    <td width="1" height="1" bgcolor=#1d1e31></td>
    <td width="1" height="1" bgcolor=#1d2333></td>
    <td width="1" height="1" bgcolor=#3f465e></td>
    <td width="1" height="1" bgcolor=#1a2429></td>
    <td width="1" height="1" bgcolor=#1e2732></td>
    <td width="1" height="1" bgcolor=#0c1217></td>
    <td width="1" height="1" bgcolor=#060307></td>
    <td width="1" height="1" bgcolor=#2b3243></td>
    <td width="1" height="1" bgcolor=#4e6183></td>
    <td width="1" height="1" bgcolor=#575855></td>
  </tr>
  <tr>
    <td width="1" height="1" bgcolor=#56668a></td>
    <td width="1" height="1" bgcolor=#3e4868></td>
    <td width="1" height="1" bgcolor=#393f5a></td>
    <td width="1" height="1" bgcolor=#42506e></td>
    <td width="1" height="1" bgcolor=#3f5066></td>
    <td width="1" height="1" bgcolor=#343b58></td>
    <td width="1" height="1" bgcolor=#4f6280></td>
    <td width="1" height="1" bgcolor=#394059></td>
    <td width="1" height="1" bgcolor=#080b0f></td>
    <td width="1" height="1" bgcolor=#070507></td>
    <td width="1" height="1" bgcolor=#0a090a></td>
    <td width="1" height="1" bgcolor=#0d0605></td>
    <td width="1" height="1" bgcolor=#0d0907></td>
    <td width="1" height="1" bgcolor=#0c0e0e></td>
    <td width="1" height="1" bgcolor=#050206></td>
    <td width="1" height="1" bgcolor=#344157></td>
    <td width="1" height="1" bgcolor=#607093></td>
    <td width="1" height="1" bgcolor=#5c6c90></td>
    <td width="1" height="1" bgcolor=#5d6d91></td>
    <td width="1" height="1" bgcolor=#5c6c91></td>
    <td width="1" height="1" bgcolor=#5d6b93></td>
    <td width="1" height="1" bgcolor=#5d6d93></td>
    <td width="1" height="1" bgcolor=#5e6c94></td>
    <td width="1" height="1" bgcolor=#64739d></td>
    <td width="1" height="1" bgcolor=#222533></td>
    <td width="1" height="1" bgcolor=#10090f></td>
    <td width="1" height="1" bgcolor=#020a02></td>
    <td width="1" height="1" bgcolor=#434d6a></td>
    <td width="1" height="1" bgcolor=#5e6d94></td>
    <td width="1" height="1" bgcolor=#5d6b92></td>
    <td width="1" height="1" bgcolor=#5f6e95></td>
    <td width="1" height="1" bgcolor=#5f6d94></td>
    <td rowspan="1" colspan="2" width="1" height="1" bgcolor=#5e6b93></td>
    <td width="1" height="1" bgcolor=#5e6d94></td>
    <td width="1" height="1" bgcolor=#5d6c92></td>
    <td width="1" height="1" bgcolor=#5d6d94></td>
    <td width="1" height="1" bgcolor=#5e6c93></td>
    <td width="1" height="1" bgcolor=#5b6a90></td>
    <td width="1" height="1" bgcolor=#5f6b94></td>
    <td width="1" height="1" bgcolor=#373e56></td>
    <td width="1" height="1" bgcolor=#323949></td>
    <td width="1" height="1" bgcolor=#060201></td>
    <td width="1" height="1" bgcolor=#485173></td>
    <td width="1" height="1" bgcolor=#101012></td>
    <td width="1" height="1" bgcolor=#4b4f6e></td>
    <td width="1" height="1" bgcolor=#3b445a></td>
    <td width="1" height="1" bgcolor=#090f0a></td>
    <td width="1" height="1" bgcolor=#2e2f41></td>
    <td width="1" height="1" bgcolor=#181e26></td>
    <td width="1" height="1" bgcolor=#4b597e></td>
    <td width="1" height="1" bgcolor=#060502></td>
    <td width="1" height="1" bgcolor=#0d0804></td>
    <td width="1" height="1" bgcolor=#51658a></td>
    <td width="1" height="1" bgcolor=#384357></td>
    <td width="1" height="1" bgcolor=#0a0a0e></td>
    <td width="1" height="1" bgcolor=#1f2634></td>
    <td width="1" height="1" bgcolor=#020600></td>
    <td width="1" height="1" bgcolor=#3b405b></td>
    <td width="1" height="1" bgcolor=#3c4a65></td>
    <td width="1" height="1" bgcolor=#1e1f2a></td>
    <td width="1" height="1" bgcolor=#4f5c83></td>
    <td width="1" height="1" bgcolor=#4a5875></td>
    <td width="1" height="1" bgcolor=#384162></td>
```

```
    <td width="1" height="1"
bgcolor=#323a53></td>
    <td width="1" height="1"
bgcolor=#414c62></td>
    <td width="1" height="1"
bgcolor=#3f4f71></td>
    <td width="1" height="1"
bgcolor=#39465c></td>
    <td width="1" height="1"
bgcolor=#202d38></td>
    <td width="1" height="1"
bgcolor=#2c344b></td>
    <td width="1" height="1"
bgcolor=#516289></td>
    <td width="1" height="1"
bgcolor=#585956></td>
  </tr>
  <tr>
    <td width="1" height="1"
bgcolor=#57668e></td>
    <td width="1" height="1"
bgcolor=#343b55></td>
    <td width="1" height="1"
bgcolor=#252838></td>
    <td width="1" height="1"
bgcolor=#30374f></td>
    <td width="1" height="1"
bgcolor=#53678e></td>
    <td width="1" height="1"
bgcolor=#485170></td>
    <td width="1" height="1"
bgcolor=#262f48></td>
    <td width="1" height="1"
bgcolor=#5d6c97></td>
    <td width="1" height="1"
bgcolor=#16111b></td>
    <td width="1" height="1"
bgcolor=#030806></td>
    <td width="1" height="1"
bgcolor=#09050f></td>
    <td width="1" height="1"
bgcolor=#090d09></td>
    <td width="1" height="1"
bgcolor=#090d06></td>
    <td width="1" height="1"
bgcolor=#090705></td>
    <td width="1" height="1"
bgcolor=#56607b></td>
    <td width="1" height="1"
bgcolor=#596a93></td>
    <td width="1" height="1"
bgcolor=#5b6a91></td>
    <td width="1" height="1"
bgcolor=#5e6c93></td>
    <td width="1" height="1"
bgcolor=#5d6b92></td>
    <td width="1" height="1"
bgcolor=#5e6c93></td>
    <td width="1" height="1"
bgcolor=#5d6c93></td>
    <td rowspan="1"
colspan="2" width="1"
height="1"
bgcolor=#5d6b92></td>
    <td width="1" height="1"
bgcolor=#626f99></td>
    <td width="1" height="1"
bgcolor=#2f3847></td>
    <td width="1" height="1"
bgcolor=#262831></td>
    <td width="1" height="1"
bgcolor=#5c5f84></td>
    <td width="1" height="1"
bgcolor=#5e6c98></td>
    <td rowspan="2"
colspan="1" width="1"
height="1"
bgcolor=#5d6c93></td>
    <td width="1" height="1"
bgcolor=#5d6d94></td>
    <td width="1" height="1"
bgcolor=#5d6b92></td>
    <td width="1" height="1"
bgcolor=#5e6c94></td>
    <td width="1" height="1"
bgcolor=#5f6c94></td>
    <td width="1" height="1"
bgcolor=#5d6a92></td>
    <td width="1" height="1"
bgcolor=#5d6c93></td>
    <td width="1" height="1"
bgcolor=#5e6d94></td>
    <td width="1" height="1"
bgcolor=#5c6a91></td>
    <td rowspan="2"
colspan="1" width="1"
height="1"
bgcolor=#5e6d94></td>
    <td width="1" height="1"
bgcolor=#5d6b93></td>
    <td width="1" height="1"
bgcolor=#5d7093></td>
    <td width="1" height="1"
bgcolor=#454e77></td>
    <td width="1" height="1"
bgcolor=#526787></td>
    <td width="1" height="1"
bgcolor=#56607b></td>
    <td width="1" height="1"
bgcolor=#4f5b7e></td>
    <td width="1" height="1"
bgcolor=#1c1d26></td>
    <td width="1" height="1"
bgcolor=#1d2335></td>
    <td width="1" height="1"
bgcolor=#4a5471></td>
    <td width="1" height="1"
bgcolor=#0e0e16></td>
    <td width="1" height="1"
bgcolor=#272b3f></td>
    <td width="1" height="1"
bgcolor=#41495e></td>
    <td width="1" height="1"
bgcolor=#4b5b79></td>
    <td width="1" height="1"
bgcolor=#11121b></td>
    <td width="1" height="1"
bgcolor=#000205></td>
    <td width="1" height="1"
bgcolor=#4e5875></td>
    <td width="1" height="1"
bgcolor=#505b84></td>
    <td width="1" height="1"
bgcolor=#272c3c></td>
    <td width="1" height="1"
bgcolor=#4a5576></td>
    <td width="1" height="1"
bgcolor=#4a5674></td>
    <td width="1" height="1"
bgcolor=#465b6a></td>
    <td width="1" height="1"
bgcolor=#4c5b82></td>
    <td width="1" height="1"
bgcolor=#3b4660></td>
    <td width="1" height="1"
bgcolor=#394762></td>
    <td width="1" height="1"
bgcolor=#3b4159></td>
    <td width="1" height="1"
bgcolor=#38425f></td>
    <td width="1" height="1"
bgcolor=#293646></td>
    <td width="1" height="1"
bgcolor=#323f5e></td>
    <td width="1" height="1"
bgcolor=#3d4867></td>
    <td width="1" height="1"
bgcolor=#1f2333></td>
    <td width="1" height="1"
bgcolor=#10121f></td>
    <td width="1" height="1"
bgcolor=#334156></td>
    <td width="1" height="1"
bgcolor=#506284></td>
    <td width="1" height="1"
bgcolor=#5c5d5a></td>
  </tr>
  <tr>
    <td width="1" height="1"
bgcolor=#55658d></td>
    <td width="1" height="1"
bgcolor=#2f354d></td>
    <td width="1" height="1"
bgcolor=#23222c></td>
```

```
    <td width="1" height="1"
bgcolor=#282d42></td>
    <td width="1" height="1"
bgcolor=#505d7a></td>
    <td width="1" height="1"
bgcolor=#556890></td>
    <td width="1" height="1"
bgcolor=#56658b></td>
    <td width="1" height="1"
bgcolor=#485d77></td>
    <td width="1" height="1"
bgcolor=#0e0e16></td>
    <td width="1" height="1"
bgcolor=#010107></td>
    <td width="1" height="1"
bgcolor=#252c39></td>
    <td width="1" height="1"
bgcolor=#120d1a></td>
    <td width="1" height="1"
bgcolor=#0a0b09></td>
    <td width="1" height="1"
bgcolor=#2b2e41></td>
    <td width="1" height="1"
bgcolor=#5d7199></td>
    <td width="1" height="1"
bgcolor=#5b6990></td>
    <td width="1" height="1"
bgcolor=#5c6a91></td>
    <td width="1" height="1"
bgcolor=#5a6990></td>
    <td width="1" height="1"
bgcolor=#5d6c93></td>
    <td width="1" height="1"
bgcolor=#5d6b92></td>
    <td width="1" height="1"
bgcolor=#5e6d94></td>
    <td width="1" height="1"
bgcolor=#5c6a91></td>
    <td width="1" height="1"
bgcolor=#5d6b92></td>
    <td width="1" height="1"
bgcolor=#5f6d97></td>
    <td width="1" height="1"
bgcolor=#344557></td>
    <td width="1" height="1"
bgcolor=#110911></td>
    <td width="1" height="1"
bgcolor=#0b0b0b></td>
    <td width="1" height="1"
bgcolor=#5f7198></td>
    <td width="1" height="1"
bgcolor=#5f6e95></td>
    <td width="1" height="1"
bgcolor=#5d6b93></td>
    <td width="1" height="1"
bgcolor=#5e6b94></td>
    <td width="1" height="1"
bgcolor=#5f6d95></td>
    <td width="1" height="1"
bgcolor=#5d6c93></td>
    <td rowspan="2"
colspan="1" width="1"
height="1"
bgcolor=#5e6d94></td>
    <td width="1" height="1"
bgcolor=#5d6c93></td>
    <td width="1" height="1"
bgcolor=#5d6b92></td>
    <td width="1" height="1"
bgcolor=#5e6d93></td>
    <td width="1" height="1"
bgcolor=#414e67></td>
    <td width="1" height="1"
bgcolor=#3e405b></td>
    <td width="1" height="1"
bgcolor=#080704></td>
    <td width="1" height="1"
bgcolor=#060502></td>
    <td width="1" height="1"
bgcolor=#465062></td>
    <td width="1" height="1"
bgcolor=#060605></td>
    <td width="1" height="1"
bgcolor=#35344c></td>
    <td width="1" height="1"
bgcolor=#1f2335></td>
    <td width="1" height="1"
bgcolor=#0b0703></td>
    <td width="1" height="1"
bgcolor=#3c475d></td>
    <td width="1" height="1"
bgcolor=#0b0a12></td>
    <td width="1" height="1"
bgcolor=#5d6d94></td>
    <td width="1" height="1"
bgcolor=#151217></td>
    <td width="1" height="1"
bgcolor=#030300></td>
    <td width="1" height="1"
bgcolor=#485877></td>
    <td width="1" height="1"
bgcolor=#1a2023></td>
    <td width="1" height="1"
bgcolor=#171926></td>
    <td width="1" height="1"
bgcolor=#252d38></td>
    <td width="1" height="1"
bgcolor=#39425d></td>
    <td width="1" height="1"
bgcolor=#38455e></td>
    <td width="1" height="1"
bgcolor=#4b5479></td>
    <td width="1" height="1"
bgcolor=#060c13></td>
    <td width="1" height="1"
bgcolor=#5c6785></td>
    <td width="1" height="1"
bgcolor=#222e42></td>
    <td width="1" height="1"
bgcolor=#3c3d5b></td>
    <td width="1" height="1"
bgcolor=#1d2532></td>
    <td width="1" height="1"
bgcolor=#465070></td>
    <td width="1" height="1"
bgcolor=#232c3c></td>
    <td width="1" height="1"
bgcolor=#0d161c></td>
    <td width="1" height="1"
bgcolor=#0b100c></td>
    <td width="1" height="1"
bgcolor=#233041></td>
    <td width="1" height="1"
bgcolor=#51638b></td>
    <td width="1" height="1"
bgcolor=#5a5b58></td>
  </tr>
  <tr>
    <td width="1" height="1"
bgcolor=#566589></td>
    <td width="1" height="1"
bgcolor=#333752></td>
    <td width="1" height="1"
bgcolor=#262639></td>
    <td width="1" height="1"
bgcolor=#262a3e></td>
    <td width="1" height="1"
bgcolor=#1d2038></td>
    <td width="1" height="1"
bgcolor=#4c597c></td>
    <td width="1" height="1"
bgcolor=#5d6990></td>
    <td width="1" height="1"
bgcolor=#3a4461></td>
    <td width="1" height="1"
bgcolor=#050208></td>
    <td width="1" height="1"
bgcolor=#424e69></td>
    <td width="1" height="1"
bgcolor=#596a93></td>
    <td width="1" height="1"
bgcolor=#424c6d></td>
    <td width="1" height="1"
bgcolor=#101417></td>
    <td width="1" height="1"
bgcolor=#4b5673></td>
    <td width="1" height="1"
bgcolor=#5b6c95></td>
    <td width="1" height="1"
bgcolor=#5c6991></td>
    <td width="1" height="1"
bgcolor=#5e6b93></td>
    <td width="1" height="1"
bgcolor=#5b6a91></td>
```

```
    <td width="1" height="1" bgcolor=#5e6d94></td>
    <td width="1" height="1" bgcolor=#5b6a91></td>
    <td width="1" height="1" bgcolor=#5c6b92></td>
    <td width="1" height="1" bgcolor=#5d6b92></td>
    <td rowspan="2" colspan="1" width="1" height="1" bgcolor=#5d6c93></td>
    <td width="1" height="1" bgcolor=#5d6c91></td>
    <td width="1" height="1" bgcolor=#5f6f98></td>
    <td width="1" height="1" bgcolor=#2a2d3d></td>
    <td width="1" height="1" bgcolor=#282d3d></td>
    <td width="1" height="1" bgcolor=#616fa1></td>
    <td width="1" height="1" bgcolor=#5e6d94></td>
    <td width="1" height="1" bgcolor=#5d6c93></td>
    <td rowspan="2" colspan="1" width="1" height="1" bgcolor=#5d6c95></td>
    <td width="1" height="1" bgcolor=#5f6e97></td>
    <td width="1" height="1" bgcolor=#5e6d96></td>
    <td width="1" height="1" bgcolor=#5e6c94></td>
    <td width="1" height="1" bgcolor=#5e6d94></td>
    <td rowspan="1" colspan="2" width="1" height="1" bgcolor=#5d6c93></td>
    <td width="1" height="1" bgcolor=#5e6e92></td>
    <td width="1" height="1" bgcolor=#424f71></td>
    <td width="1" height="1" bgcolor=#111616></td>
    <td width="1" height="1" bgcolor=#0f0f08></td>
    <td width="1" height="1" bgcolor=#0b0f07></td>
    <td width="1" height="1" bgcolor=#1e1d26></td>
    <td width="1" height="1" bgcolor=#0f1013></td>
    <td width="1" height="1" bgcolor=#25292d></td>
    <td width="1" height="1" bgcolor=#2f3448></td>
    <td width="1" height="1" bgcolor=#18141f></td>
    <td width="1" height="1" bgcolor=#2e3447></td>
    <td width="1" height="1" bgcolor=#31394a></td>
    <td width="1" height="1" bgcolor=#5c6d8f></td>
    <td width="1" height="1" bgcolor=#1e2233></td>
    <td width="1" height="1" bgcolor=#050c08></td>
    <td width="1" height="1" bgcolor=#414b6a></td>
    <td width="1" height="1" bgcolor=#32354c></td>
    <td width="1" height="1" bgcolor=#374558></td>
    <td width="1" height="1" bgcolor=#435479></td>
    <td width="1" height="1" bgcolor=#353d50></td>
    <td width="1" height="1" bgcolor=#546385></td>
    <td width="1" height="1" bgcolor=#5b6690></td>
    <td width="1" height="1" bgcolor=#566587></td>
    <td width="1" height="1" bgcolor=#435273></td>
    <td width="1" height="1" bgcolor=#2c2a3c></td>
    <td width="1" height="1" bgcolor=#0a0c0e></td>
    <td width="1" height="1" bgcolor=#3f4866></td>
    <td width="1" height="1" bgcolor=#222e39></td>
    <td width="1" height="1" bgcolor=#42475e></td>
    <td width="1" height="1" bgcolor=#343e52></td>
    <td width="1" height="1" bgcolor=#191a21></td>
    <td width="1" height="1" bgcolor=#202a37></td>
    <td width="1" height="1" bgcolor=#52648c></td>
    <td rowspan="2" colspan="1" width="1" height="1" bgcolor=#585956></td>
  </tr>
  <tr>
    <td width="1" height="1" bgcolor=#56668a></td>
    <td width="1" height="1" bgcolor=#323a51></td>
    <td width="1" height="1" bgcolor=#232338></td>
    <td width="1" height="1" bgcolor=#3e4664></td>
    <td width="1" height="1" bgcolor=#333b4e></td>
    <td width="1" height="1" bgcolor=#3e4b6d></td>
    <td width="1" height="1" bgcolor=#586a8f></td>
    <td width="1" height="1" bgcolor=#464f6e></td>
    <td width="1" height="1" bgcolor=#35415b></td>
    <td width="1" height="1" bgcolor=#596890></td>
    <td width="1" height="1" bgcolor=#475674></td>
    <td width="1" height="1" bgcolor=#4e5f85></td>
    <td width="1" height="1" bgcolor=#344158></td>
    <td width="1" height="1" bgcolor=#616d96></td>
    <td width="1" height="1" bgcolor=#5c6d96></td>
    <td width="1" height="1" bgcolor=#5d6b91></td>
    <td width="1" height="1" bgcolor=#5d6b93></td>
    <td width="1" height="1" bgcolor=#5c6b92></td>
    <td width="1" height="1" bgcolor=#5d6b92></td>
    <td width="1" height="1" bgcolor=#5e6d94></td>
    <td width="1" height="1" bgcolor=#5d6b92></td>
    <td rowspan="2" colspan="1" width="1" height="1" bgcolor=#5e6d94></td>
    <td width="1" height="1" bgcolor=#5e6c94></td>
    <td rowspan="1" colspan="2" width="1" height="1" bgcolor=#5e6d94></td>
    <td width="1" height="1" bgcolor=#5c6b91></td>
    <td rowspan="1" colspan="2" width="1" height="1" bgcolor=#5d6c93></td>
    <td width="1" height="1" bgcolor=#5d6c94></td>
```

```
<td rowspan="1"
colspan="2" width="1"
height="1"
bgcolor=#5e6d95></td>
<td width="1" height="1"
bgcolor=#5e6d94></td>
<td width="1" height="1"
bgcolor=#5e6c93></td>
<td width="1" height="1"
bgcolor=#606c91></td>
<td width="1" height="1"
bgcolor=#5c6d95></td>
<td width="1" height="1"
bgcolor=#5e6c97></td>
<td width="1" height="1"
bgcolor=#5e6e95></td>
<td width="1" height="1"
bgcolor=#363e55></td>
<td width="1" height="1"
bgcolor=#36394f></td>
<td width="1" height="1"
bgcolor=#121116></td>
<td width="1" height="1"
bgcolor=#0e0e09></td>
<td width="1" height="1"
bgcolor=#1b2025></td>
<td width="1" height="1"
bgcolor=#0b0804></td>
<td width="1" height="1"
bgcolor=#373c4f></td>
<td width="1" height="1"
bgcolor=#2c2f3c></td>
<td width="1" height="1"
bgcolor=#010205></td>
<td width="1" height="1"
bgcolor=#3f485d></td>
<td width="1" height="1"
bgcolor=#5a6b8f></td>
<td width="1" height="1"
bgcolor=#5a6b91></td>
<td width="1" height="1"
bgcolor=#5c6a91></td>
<td width="1" height="1"
bgcolor=#5c6a95></td>
<td width="1" height="1"
bgcolor=#475575></td>
<td width="1" height="1"
bgcolor=#4f5e83></td>
<td width="1" height="1"
bgcolor=#566791></td>
<td width="1" height="1"
bgcolor=#566989></td>
<td width="1" height="1"
bgcolor=#515f83></td>
<td width="1" height="1"
bgcolor=#55638e></td>
<td width="1" height="1"
bgcolor=#53668a></td>
<td width="1" height="1"
bgcolor=#53648b></td>
<td width="1" height="1"
bgcolor=#56668d></td>
<td width="1" height="1"
bgcolor=#55658c></td>
<td width="1" height="1"
bgcolor=#3b4a65></td>
<td width="1" height="1"
bgcolor=#030406></td>
<td rowspan="2"
colspan="1" width="1"
height="1"
bgcolor=#000000></td>
<td width="1" height="1"
bgcolor=#22252c></td>
<td width="1" height="1"
bgcolor=#030007></td>
<td width="1" height="1"
bgcolor=#2b344b></td>
<td width="1" height="1"
bgcolor=#232e3d></td>
<td width="1" height="1"
bgcolor=#52608e></td>
</tr>
<tr>
<td width="1" height="1"
bgcolor=#57678c></td>
<td width="1" height="1"
bgcolor=#2f364e></td>
<td width="1" height="1"
bgcolor=#1a1828></td>
<td width="1" height="1"
bgcolor=#262a3b></td>
<td width="1" height="1"
bgcolor=#4d5879></td>
<td width="1" height="1"
bgcolor=#4a5e7e></td>
<td width="1" height="1"
bgcolor=#536086></td>
<td width="1" height="1"
bgcolor=#394662></td>
<td width="1" height="1"
bgcolor=#404f6f></td>
<td width="1" height="1"
bgcolor=#475976></td>
<td width="1" height="1"
bgcolor=#3a4869></td>
<td width="1" height="1"
bgcolor=#5e6d93></td>
<td width="1" height="1"
bgcolor=#4e5f7f></td>
<td width="1" height="1"
bgcolor=#5f6c95></td>
<td width="1" height="1"
bgcolor=#5e6c92></td>
<td width="1" height="1"
bgcolor=#5d6c92></td>
<td rowspan="3"
colspan="1" width="1"
height="1"
bgcolor=#5d6b92></td>
<td rowspan="3"
colspan="1" width="1"
height="1"
bgcolor=#5d6c93></td>
<td rowspan="2"
colspan="1" width="1"
height="1"
bgcolor=#5d6c93></td>
<td width="1" height="1"
bgcolor=#5c6b92></td>
<td width="1" height="1"
bgcolor=#5d6c93></td>
<td width="1" height="1"
bgcolor=#5d6b92></td>
<td rowspan="1"
colspan="2" width="1"
height="1"
bgcolor=#5f6e95></td>
<td width="1" height="1"
bgcolor=#5d6c93></td>
<td width="1" height="1"
bgcolor=#5e6d94></td>
<td rowspan="2"
colspan="1" width="1"
height="1"
bgcolor=#5f6e95></td>
<td width="1" height="1"
bgcolor=#606f96></td>
<td width="1" height="1"
bgcolor=#606f97></td>
<td width="1" height="1"
bgcolor=#5e6d96></td>
<td width="1" height="1"
bgcolor=#5f6e96></td>
<td width="1" height="1"
bgcolor=#5f6c94></td>
<td width="1" height="1"
bgcolor=#606d95></td>
<td width="1" height="1"
bgcolor=#5f6d94></td>
<td width="1" height="1"
bgcolor=#5c6e95></td>
<td width="1" height="1"
bgcolor=#616c93></td>
<td width="1" height="1"
bgcolor=#626e93></td>
<td width="1" height="1"
bgcolor=#5c739a></td>
<td width="1" height="1"
bgcolor=#282a35></td>
<td width="1" height="1"
bgcolor=#262830></td>
<td width="1" height="1"
bgcolor=#22222d></td>
```

```
    <td width="1" height="1" bgcolor=#110f14></td>
    <td width="1" height="1" bgcolor=#222732></td>
    <td width="1" height="1" bgcolor=#181523></td>
    <td width="1" height="1" bgcolor=#0f0b16></td>
    <td width="1" height="1" bgcolor=#292c39></td>
    <td width="1" height="1" bgcolor=#394760></td>
    <td width="1" height="1" bgcolor=#344259></td>
    <td width="1" height="1" bgcolor=#5d6e91></td>
    <td width="1" height="1" bgcolor=#596891></td>
    <td width="1" height="1" bgcolor=#5c6995></td>
    <td width="1" height="1" bgcolor=#5a678d></td>
    <td width="1" height="1" bgcolor=#5a6c97></td>
    <td width="1" height="1" bgcolor=#39455c></td>
    <td width="1" height="1" bgcolor=#1c2331></td>
    <td width="1" height="1" bgcolor=#525f88></td>
    <td width="1" height="1" bgcolor=#58678f></td>
    <td width="1" height="1" bgcolor=#57688d></td>
    <td width="1" height="1" bgcolor=#54678b></td>
    <td width="1" height="1" bgcolor=#57668d></td>
    <td width="1" height="1" bgcolor=#55648b></td>
    <td width="1" height="1" bgcolor=#546289></td>
    <td width="1" height="1" bgcolor=#58688d></td>
    <td width="1" height="1" bgcolor=#01040a></td>
    <td width="1" height="1" bgcolor=#272a36></td>
    <td width="1" height="1" bgcolor=#000200></td>
    <td width="1" height="1" bgcolor=#505e82></td>
    <td width="1" height="1" bgcolor=#36465f></td>
    <td width="1" height="1" bgcolor=#506188></td>
    <td width="1" height="1" bgcolor=#5e605c></td>
  </tr>
  <tr>
    <td width="1" height="1" bgcolor=#57678e></td>
    <td width="1" height="1" bgcolor=#333850></td>
    <td width="1" height="1" bgcolor=#14121d></td>
    <td width="1" height="1" bgcolor=#242034></td>
    <td width="1" height="1" bgcolor=#45516c></td>
    <td width="1" height="1" bgcolor=#4f5f82></td>
    <td width="1" height="1" bgcolor=#373d53></td>
    <td width="1" height="1" bgcolor=#26283a></td>
    <td width="1" height="1" bgcolor=#353648></td>
    <td width="1" height="1" bgcolor=#2d2f44></td>
    <td width="1" height="1" bgcolor=#2e3843></td>
    <td width="1" height="1" bgcolor=#3e496a></td>
    <td width="1" height="1" bgcolor=#5e6f95></td>
    <td width="1" height="1" bgcolor=#5d6d94></td>
    <td width="1" height="1" bgcolor=#5e6994></td>
    <td width="1" height="1" bgcolor=#5b6c94></td>
    <td width="1" height="1" bgcolor=#5e6c93></td>
    <td rowspan="2" colspan="1" width="1" height="1" bgcolor=#5d6b92></td>
    <td rowspan="1" colspan="3" width="1" height="1" bgcolor=#5d6c93></td>
    <td rowspan="1" colspan="3" width="1" height="1" bgcolor=#5f6e95></td>
    <td rowspan="2" colspan="2" width="1" height="1" bgcolor=#5e6d94></td>
    <td width="1" height="1" bgcolor=#5f6e97></td>
    <td width="1" height="1" bgcolor=#5f6d96></td>
    <td width="1" height="1" bgcolor=#616e96></td>
    <td width="1" height="1" bgcolor=#606d96></td>
    <td width="1" height="1" bgcolor=#5e6b95></td>
    <td width="1" height="1" bgcolor=#5f6f94></td>
    <td width="1" height="1" bgcolor=#5e6b97></td>
    <td width="1" height="1" bgcolor=#5f6e98></td>
    <td width="1" height="1" bgcolor=#58688a></td>
    <td width="1" height="1" bgcolor=#120e15></td>
    <td width="1" height="1" bgcolor=#0f100d></td>
    <td width="1" height="1" bgcolor=#1d1d2c></td>
    <td width="1" height="1" bgcolor=#1c1b21></td>
    <td width="1" height="1" bgcolor=#0f1210></td>
    <td width="1" height="1" bgcolor=#2a2c3f></td>
    <td width="1" height="1" bgcolor=#4d5a6f></td>
    <td width="1" height="1" bgcolor=#2f4059></td>
    <td width="1" height="1" bgcolor=#627096></td>
    <td width="1" height="1" bgcolor=#586a8d></td>
    <td width="1" height="1" bgcolor=#5b6990></td>
    <td width="1" height="1" bgcolor=#596994></td>
    <td width="1" height="1" bgcolor=#556990></td>
    <td width="1" height="1" bgcolor=#5a678e></td>
    <td width="1" height="1" bgcolor=#58688c></td>
    <td width="1" height="1" bgcolor=#5b6b90></td>
    <td width="1" height="1" bgcolor=#3c475c></td>
    <td width="1" height="1" bgcolor=#5b6a95></td>
    <td width="1" height="1" bgcolor=#58698b></td>
    <td width="1" height="1" bgcolor=#586590></td>
    <td width="1" height="1" bgcolor=#57668b></td>
    <td width="1" height="1" bgcolor=#55648b></td>
    <td width="1" height="1" bgcolor=#56658c></td>
```

```
    <td width="1" height="1" bgcolor=#55648b></td>
    <td width="1" height="1" bgcolor=#53648a></td>
    <td width="1" height="1" bgcolor=#576280></td>
    <td width="1" height="1" bgcolor=#171c21></td>
    <td width="1" height="1" bgcolor=#161a1c></td>
    <td width="1" height="1" bgcolor=#262635></td>
    <td width="1" height="1" bgcolor=#1d2a36></td>
    <td width="1" height="1" bgcolor=#4c577e></td>
    <td width="1" height="1" bgcolor=#4f6287></td>
    <td width="1" height="1" bgcolor=#5a5b58></td>
  </tr>
  <tr>
    <td width="1" height="1" bgcolor=#58678e></td>
    <td width="1" height="1" bgcolor=#32394f></td>
    <td width="1" height="1" bgcolor=#191720></td>
    <td width="1" height="1" bgcolor=#222233></td>
    <td width="1" height="1" bgcolor=#323c52></td>
    <td width="1" height="1" bgcolor=#454d6b></td>
    <td width="1" height="1" bgcolor=#2a2c43></td>
    <td width="1" height="1" bgcolor=#363752></td>
    <td width="1" height="1" bgcolor=#23253d></td>
    <td width="1" height="1" bgcolor=#19191f></td>
    <td width="1" height="1" bgcolor=#17101f></td>
    <td width="1" height="1" bgcolor=#0b0e08></td>
    <td width="1" height="1" bgcolor=#353a56></td>
    <td width="1" height="1" bgcolor=#636f96></td>
    <td width="1" height="1" bgcolor=#5c6b92></td>
    <td width="1" height="1" bgcolor=#5c6c90></td>
    <td rowspan="1" colspan="2" width="1" height="1" bgcolor=#5e6d94></td>
    <td rowspan="2" colspan="1" width="1" height="1" bgcolor=#5e6d94></td>
    <td rowspan="1" colspan="3" width="1" height="1" bgcolor=#5e6d94></td>
    <td width="1" height="1" bgcolor=#5d6c93></td>
    <td rowspan="1" colspan="2" width="1" height="1" bgcolor=#5e6d94></td>
    <td width="1" height="1" bgcolor=#5e6d96></td>
    <td width="1" height="1" bgcolor=#606e97></td>
    <td width="1" height="1" bgcolor=#5f6c94></td>
    <td width="1" height="1" bgcolor=#606d97></td>
    <td width="1" height="1" bgcolor=#606c97></td>
    <td width="1" height="1" bgcolor=#5e6b97></td>
    <td width="1" height="1" bgcolor=#5d6f90></td>
    <td width="1" height="1" bgcolor=#636d94></td>
    <td width="1" height="1" bgcolor=#2d364b></td>
    <td width="1" height="1" bgcolor=#17141a></td>
    <td width="1" height="1" bgcolor=#0f110d></td>
    <td width="1" height="1" bgcolor=#21202d></td>
    <td width="1" height="1" bgcolor=#151516></td>
    <td width="1" height="1" bgcolor=#31314b></td>
    <td width="1" height="1" bgcolor=#3f4f69></td>
    <td width="1" height="1" bgcolor=#2c3446></td>
    <td width="1" height="1" bgcolor=#3d4961></td>
    <td width="1" height="1" bgcolor=#5c6b94></td>
    <td width="1" height="1" bgcolor=#5c6b98></td>
    <td width="1" height="1" bgcolor=#5a6793></td>
    <td width="1" height="1" bgcolor=#5a698f></td>
    <td width="1" height="1" bgcolor=#576991></td>
    <td width="1" height="1" bgcolor=#58688e></td>
    <td width="1" height="1" bgcolor=#5a6892></td>
    <td width="1" height="1" bgcolor=#566b8b></td>
    <td width="1" height="1" bgcolor=#586894></td>
    <td width="1" height="1" bgcolor=#55668e></td>
    <td width="1" height="1" bgcolor=#5b6a8f></td>
    <td width="1" height="1" bgcolor=#58668e></td>
    <td width="1" height="1" bgcolor=#56678c></td>
    <td width="1" height="1" bgcolor=#56648c></td>
    <td width="1" height="1" bgcolor=#57648c></td>
    <td width="1" height="1" bgcolor=#55638b></td>
    <td width="1" height="1" bgcolor=#556589></td>
    <td width="1" height="1" bgcolor=#576691></td>
    <td width="1" height="1" bgcolor=#212d39></td>
    <td width="1" height="1" bgcolor=#1d1d2d></td>
    <td width="1" height="1" bgcolor=#000200></td>
    <td width="1" height="1" bgcolor=#464f69></td>
    <td width="1" height="1" bgcolor=#2f3851></td>
    <td width="1" height="1" bgcolor=#53658d></td>
    <td width="1" height="1" bgcolor=#4c4d4a></td>
  </tr>
  <tr>
    <td width="1" height="1" bgcolor=#5a678f></td>
    <td width="1" height="1" bgcolor=#364257></td>
    <td width="1" height="1" bgcolor=#171c20></td>
    <td width="1" height="1" bgcolor=#1c212d></td>
    <td width="1" height="1" bgcolor=#374053></td>
    <td width="1" height="1" bgcolor=#3a405b></td>
    <td width="1" height="1" bgcolor=#36354e></td>
    <td width="1" height="1" bgcolor=#313344></td>
```

```
    <td width="1" height="1"
bgcolor=#383f52></td>
    <td width="1" height="1"
bgcolor=#1d1c2a></td>
    <td width="1" height="1"
bgcolor=#1b2132></td>
    <td width="1" height="1"
bgcolor=#12151c></td>
    <td width="1" height="1"
bgcolor=#0f0c03></td>
    <td width="1" height="1"
bgcolor=#293440></td>
    <td width="1" height="1"
bgcolor=#64709a></td>
    <td width="1" height="1"
bgcolor=#5e6a92></td>
    <td rowspan="2"
colspan="1" width="1"
height="1"
bgcolor=#5d6d91></td>
    <td width="1" height="1"
bgcolor=#606e97></td>
    <td width="1" height="1"
bgcolor=#5d6c94></td>
    <td width="1" height="1"
bgcolor=#5d6f92></td>
    <td width="1" height="1"
bgcolor=#5e6d94></td>
    <td width="1" height="1"
bgcolor=#5d6c93></td>
    <td width="1" height="1"
bgcolor=#5e6d96></td>
    <td width="1" height="1"
bgcolor=#607094></td>
    <td width="1" height="1"
bgcolor=#5e6d97></td>
    <td width="1" height="1"
bgcolor=#5f6f91></td>
    <td width="1" height="1"
bgcolor=#606e96></td>
    <td width="1" height="1"
bgcolor=#5f6c96></td>
    <td width="1" height="1"
bgcolor=#5f6e97></td>
    <td rowspan="2"
colspan="1" width="1"
height="1"
bgcolor=#5e6d94></td>
    <td width="1" height="1"
bgcolor=#607096></td>
    <td width="1" height="1"
bgcolor=#5e6d96></td>
    <td width="1" height="1"
bgcolor=#5f6e97></td>
    <td width="1" height="1"
bgcolor=#606e96></td>
    <td width="1" height="1"
bgcolor=#626e99></td>
    <td width="1" height="1"
bgcolor=#5f7196></td>
    <td width="1" height="1"
bgcolor=#13141b></td>
    <td width="1" height="1"
bgcolor=#47536f></td>
    <td width="1" height="1"
bgcolor=#0c090b></td>
    <td width="1" height="1"
bgcolor=#0f1212></td>
    <td width="1" height="1"
bgcolor=#191718></td>
    <td width="1" height="1"
bgcolor=#130c0d></td>
    <td width="1" height="1"
bgcolor=#4c5f7b></td>
    <td width="1" height="1"
bgcolor=#1a1c27></td>
    <td width="1" height="1"
bgcolor=#060700></td>
    <td width="1" height="1"
bgcolor=#57658f></td>
    <td width="1" height="1"
bgcolor=#5a6d91></td>
    <td width="1" height="1"
bgcolor=#5c6a91></td>
    <td width="1" height="1"
bgcolor=#5b6a91></td>
    <td width="1" height="1"
bgcolor=#5c6b92></td>
    <td width="1" height="1"
bgcolor=#59688f></td>
    <td width="1" height="1"
bgcolor=#596990></td>
    <td width="1" height="1"
bgcolor=#57688e></td>
    <td width="1" height="1"
bgcolor=#586990></td>
    <td width="1" height="1"
bgcolor=#58698e></td>
    <td width="1" height="1"
bgcolor=#59688e></td>
    <td width="1" height="1"
bgcolor=#59688f></td>
    <td width="1" height="1"
bgcolor=#58678e></td>
    <td width="1" height="1"
bgcolor=#57668d></td>
    <td width="1" height="1"
bgcolor=#57658c></td>
    <td width="1" height="1"
bgcolor=#56658c></td>
    <td width="1" height="1"
bgcolor=#54638a></td>
    <td width="1" height="1"
bgcolor=#546489></td>
    <td width="1" height="1"
bgcolor=#536385></td>
    <td width="1" height="1"
bgcolor=#505f80></td>
    <td width="1" height="1"
bgcolor=#080f14></td>
    <td width="1" height="1"
bgcolor=#3c4656></td>
    <td width="1" height="1"
bgcolor=#252e42></td>
    <td width="1" height="1"
bgcolor=#343d55></td>
    <td width="1" height="1"
bgcolor=#4e618b></td>
    <td width="1" height="1"
bgcolor=#666864></td>
  </tr>
  <tr>
    <td width="1" height="1"
bgcolor=#56688e></td>
    <td width="1" height="1"
bgcolor=#32384f></td>
    <td width="1" height="1"
bgcolor=#100e1c></td>
    <td width="1" height="1"
bgcolor=#373b53></td>
    <td width="1" height="1"
bgcolor=#4b5474></td>
    <td width="1" height="1"
bgcolor=#394461></td>
    <td width="1" height="1"
bgcolor=#2e3751></td>
    <td width="1" height="1"
bgcolor=#3b415b></td>
    <td width="1" height="1"
bgcolor=#3a4c6d></td>
    <td width="1" height="1"
bgcolor=#475572></td>
    <td width="1" height="1"
bgcolor=#313950></td>
    <td width="1" height="1"
bgcolor=#323444></td>
    <td width="1" height="1"
bgcolor=#201f26></td>
    <td width="1" height="1"
bgcolor=#1f1c2a></td>
    <td width="1" height="1"
bgcolor=#405069></td>
    <td width="1" height="1"
bgcolor=#5d6f9c></td>
    <td width="1" height="1"
bgcolor=#5e6d91></td>
    <td width="1" height="1"
bgcolor=#5e6a95></td>
    <td width="1" height="1"
bgcolor=#606d96></td>
    <td width="1" height="1"
bgcolor=#5d6b92></td>
    <td width="1" height="1"
bgcolor=#5d6c93></td>
```

```
    <td width="1" height="1" bgcolor=#606f96></td>
    <td width="1" height="1" bgcolor=#5f6e93></td>
    <td width="1" height="1" bgcolor=#5f6e94></td>
    <td width="1" height="1" bgcolor=#606f97></td>
    <td width="1" height="1" bgcolor=#616f97></td>
    <td width="1" height="1" bgcolor=#617095></td>
    <td width="1" height="1" bgcolor=#5d6d92></td>
    <td width="1" height="1" bgcolor=#5f6f93></td>
    <td width="1" height="1" bgcolor=#5f6d94></td>
    <td width="1" height="1" bgcolor=#5e6d95></td>
    <td width="1" height="1" bgcolor=#5e6d94></td>
    <td width="1" height="1" bgcolor=#5f6d94></td>
    <td width="1" height="1" bgcolor=#606d94></td>
    <td width="1" height="1" bgcolor=#5d6e92></td>
    <td width="1" height="1" bgcolor=#656e99></td>
    <td width="1" height="1" bgcolor=#5d6d90></td>
    <td width="1" height="1" bgcolor=#3e4257></td>
    <td width="1" height="1" bgcolor=#0d0d0a></td>
    <td width="1" height="1" bgcolor=#232735></td>
    <td width="1" height="1" bgcolor=#181e22></td>
    <td width="1" height="1" bgcolor=#40405d></td>
    <td width="1" height="1" bgcolor=#090b09></td>
    <td width="1" height="1" bgcolor=#4c5671></td>
    <td width="1" height="1" bgcolor=#5f6e95></td>
    <td width="1" height="1" bgcolor=#5d6a90></td>
    <td rowspan="2" colspan="1" width="1" height="1" bgcolor=#5d6b92></td>
    <td width="1" height="1" bgcolor=#5c6a91></td>
    <td width="1" height="1" bgcolor=#5a6990></td>
    <td width="1" height="1" bgcolor=#5a6890></td>
    <td width="1" height="1" bgcolor=#5b6a91></td>
    <td rowspan="1" colspan="4" width="1" height="1" bgcolor=#59688f></td>
    <td width="1" height="1" bgcolor=#57668d></td>
    <td width="1" height="1" bgcolor=#56658c></td>
    <td width="1" height="1" bgcolor=#59688f></td>
    <td rowspan="2" colspan="2" width="1" height="1" bgcolor=#57668d></td>
    <td rowspan="3" colspan="1" width="1" height="1" bgcolor=#56658c></td>
    <td width="1" height="1" bgcolor=#55628b></td>
    <td width="1" height="1" bgcolor=#55658d></td>
    <td width="1" height="1" bgcolor=#55638a></td>
    <td width="1" height="1" bgcolor=#4c5879></td>
    <td width="1" height="1" bgcolor=#010004></td>
    <td width="1" height="1" bgcolor=#293240></td>
    <td width="1" height="1" bgcolor=#364058></td>
    <td width="1" height="1" bgcolor=#51638b></td>
    <td width="1" height="1" bgcolor=#575854></td>
  </tr>
  <tr>
    <td width="1" height="1" bgcolor=#5d668e></td>
    <td width="1" height="1" bgcolor=#394a6b></td>
    <td width="1" height="1" bgcolor=#3a465d></td>
    <td width="1" height="1" bgcolor=#2a283d></td>
    <td width="1" height="1" bgcolor=#33334e></td>
    <td width="1" height="1" bgcolor=#30334a></td>
    <td width="1" height="1" bgcolor=#2f354a></td>
    <td width="1" height="1" bgcolor=#3a4163></td>
    <td width="1" height="1" bgcolor=#3d435e></td>
    <td width="1" height="1" bgcolor=#242432></td>
    <td width="1" height="1" bgcolor=#1e1822></td>
    <td width="1" height="1" bgcolor=#0c0c10></td>
    <td width="1" height="1" bgcolor=#1d202c></td>
    <td width="1" height="1" bgcolor=#383c54></td>
    <td width="1" height="1" bgcolor=#1a181f></td>
    <td width="1" height="1" bgcolor=#2f3646></td>
    <td width="1" height="1" bgcolor=#686f9b></td>
    <td width="1" height="1" bgcolor=#5e6d98></td>
    <td width="1" height="1" bgcolor=#5a6e8e></td>
    <td width="1" height="1" bgcolor=#606d98></td>
    <td width="1" height="1" bgcolor=#606d95></td>
    <td width="1" height="1" bgcolor=#616e96></td>
    <td width="1" height="1" bgcolor=#5f6c97></td>
    <td width="1" height="1" bgcolor=#606c99></td>
    <td width="1" height="1" bgcolor=#627095></td>
    <td width="1" height="1" bgcolor=#5e6d97></td>
    <td width="1" height="1" bgcolor=#596886></td>
    <td width="1" height="1" bgcolor=#54618b></td>
    <td width="1" height="1" bgcolor=#5f6f97></td>
    <td width="1" height="1" bgcolor=#617096></td>
    <td width="1" height="1" bgcolor=#616f97></td>
    <td width="1" height="1" bgcolor=#606d95></td>
    <td width="1" height="1" bgcolor=#616e96></td>
    <td width="1" height="1" bgcolor=#606e95></td>
    <td width="1" height="1" bgcolor=#5f6e95></td>
    <td width="1" height="1" bgcolor=#616e97></td>
    <td width="1" height="1" bgcolor=#606c95></td>
```

```
    <td width="1" height="1" bgcolor=#607295></td>
    <td width="1" height="1" bgcolor=#606d95></td>
    <td width="1" height="1" bgcolor=#5d709a></td>
    <td width="1" height="1" bgcolor=#607094></td>
    <td width="1" height="1" bgcolor=#414861></td>
    <td width="1" height="1" bgcolor=#404460></td>
    <td width="1" height="1" bgcolor=#191c1d></td>
    <td width="1" height="1" bgcolor=#100e0a></td>
    <td width="1" height="1" bgcolor=#4a5674></td>
    <td width="1" height="1" bgcolor=#5c6e98></td>
    <td width="1" height="1" bgcolor=#5e6c92></td>
    <td width="1" height="1" bgcolor=#5e6d94></td>
    <td width="1" height="1" bgcolor=#5d6c93></td>
    <td width="1" height="1" bgcolor=#5b6990></td>
    <td width="1" height="1" bgcolor=#5b6890></td>
    <td width="1" height="1" bgcolor=#5a678f></td>
    <td rowspan="1" colspan="2" width="1" height="1" bgcolor=#5a6990></td>
    <td width="1" height="1" bgcolor=#57668d></td>
    <td rowspan="1" colspan="3" width="1" height="1" bgcolor=#58678e></td>
    <td width="1" height="1" bgcolor=#54668b></td>
    <td width="1" height="1" bgcolor=#53638c></td>
    <td width="1" height="1" bgcolor=#495b76></td>
    <td width="1" height="1" bgcolor=#0d0d14></td>
    <td width="1" height="1" bgcolor=#070200></td>
    <td width="1" height="1" bgcolor=#31374a></td>
    <td width="1" height="1" bgcolor=#353e5b></td>
    <td width="1" height="1" bgcolor=#526289></td>
    <td width="1" height="1" bgcolor=#5a5b59></td>
  </tr>
  <tr>
    <td width="1" height="1" bgcolor=#576794></td>
    <td width="1" height="1" bgcolor=#30354b></td>
    <td width="1" height="1" bgcolor=#131422></td>
    <td width="1" height="1" bgcolor=#4f5a7d></td>
    <td width="1" height="1" bgcolor=#3f4766></td>
    <td width="1" height="1" bgcolor=#373e58></td>
    <td width="1" height="1" bgcolor=#404c63></td>
    <td width="1" height="1" bgcolor=#242c38></td>
    <td width="1" height="1" bgcolor=#110b12></td>
    <td width="1" height="1" bgcolor=#0b0a0f></td>
    <td width="1" height="1" bgcolor=#17191d></td>
    <td width="1" height="1" bgcolor=#515c7a></td>
    <td width="1" height="1" bgcolor=#1c2235></td>
    <td width="1" height="1" bgcolor=#181212></td>
    <td width="1" height="1" bgcolor=#131418></td>
    <td width="1" height="1" bgcolor=#130e10></td>
    <td width="1" height="1" bgcolor=#060708></td>
    <td width="1" height="1" bgcolor=#444e6b></td>
    <td width="1" height="1" bgcolor=#616c99></td>
    <td width="1" height="1" bgcolor=#616f91></td>
    <td width="1" height="1" bgcolor=#5f6c94></td>
    <td width="1" height="1" bgcolor=#606d95></td>
    <td width="1" height="1" bgcolor=#616e96></td>
    <td width="1" height="1" bgcolor=#616f95></td>
    <td width="1" height="1" bgcolor=#616d96></td>
    <td width="1" height="1" bgcolor=#556282></td>
    <td width="1" height="1" bgcolor=#515e83></td>
    <td width="1" height="1" bgcolor=#596788></td>
    <td width="1" height="1" bgcolor=#59678a></td>
    <td width="1" height="1" bgcolor=#5e6d96></td>
    <td width="1" height="1" bgcolor=#617099></td>
    <td width="1" height="1" bgcolor=#606e97></td>
    <td width="1" height="1" bgcolor=#616e98></td>
    <td width="1" height="1" bgcolor=#616d97></td>
    <td width="1" height="1" bgcolor=#5f6f97></td>
    <td width="1" height="1" bgcolor=#606e93></td>
    <td width="1" height="1" bgcolor=#5e6d96></td>
    <td width="1" height="1" bgcolor=#626f95></td>
    <td width="1" height="1" bgcolor=#626e97></td>
    <td width="1" height="1" bgcolor=#606e8f></td>
    <td width="1" height="1" bgcolor=#606b9a></td>
    <td width="1" height="1" bgcolor=#607199></td>
    <td width="1" height="1" bgcolor=#596d9a></td>
    <td width="1" height="1" bgcolor=#121412></td>
    <td width="1" height="1" bgcolor=#151112></td>
    <td width="1" height="1" bgcolor=#2d3342></td>
    <td width="1" height="1" bgcolor=#60709b></td>
    <td width="1" height="1" bgcolor=#5b6b91></td>
    <td width="1" height="1" bgcolor=#5e6d94></td>
    <td width="1" height="1" bgcolor=#5d6c93></td>
    <td width="1" height="1" bgcolor=#5b6a91></td>
    <td width="1" height="1" bgcolor=#5c6b92></td>
    <td width="1" height="1" bgcolor=#5a6990></td>
    <td width="1" height="1" bgcolor=#59688f></td>
    <td width="1" height="1" bgcolor=#5c6991></td>
    <td width="1" height="1" bgcolor=#5a688f></td>
```

```
    <td rowspan="1" colspan="4" width="1" height="1" bgcolor=#59688f></td>
    <td width="1" height="1" bgcolor=#58678e></td>
    <td width="1" height="1" bgcolor=#57668d></td>
    <td width="1" height="1" bgcolor=#56648b></td>
    <td width="1" height="1" bgcolor=#59688a></td>
    <td width="1" height="1" bgcolor=#06050a></td>
    <td width="1" height="1" bgcolor=#060707></td>
    <td width="1" height="1" bgcolor=#0e0b15></td>
    <td width="1" height="1" bgcolor=#252b3a></td>
    <td width="1" height="1" bgcolor=#2e354c></td>
    <td width="1" height="1" bgcolor=#50638a></td>
    <td width="1" height="1" bgcolor=#5b5c59></td>
  </tr>
  <tr>
    <td width="1" height="1" bgcolor=#596790></td>
    <td width="1" height="1" bgcolor=#30384a></td>
    <td width="1" height="1" bgcolor=#0a0c06></td>
    <td width="1" height="1" bgcolor=#0b0911></td>
    <td width="1" height="1" bgcolor=#141a20></td>
    <td width="1" height="1" bgcolor=#445072></td>
    <td width="1" height="1" bgcolor=#3a4162></td>
    <td width="1" height="1" bgcolor=#1c2227></td>
    <td width="1" height="1" bgcolor=#211924></td>
    <td width="1" height="1" bgcolor=#282c38></td>
    <td width="1" height="1" bgcolor=#151521></td>
    <td width="1" height="1" bgcolor=#40485f></td>
    <td width="1" height="1" bgcolor=#16171c></td>
    <td width="1" height="1" bgcolor=#252730></td>
    <td width="1" height="1" bgcolor=#0e0c0c></td>
    <td width="1" height="1" bgcolor=#292f45></td>
    <td width="1" height="1" bgcolor=#596588></td>
    <td width="1" height="1" bgcolor=#5e6c94></td>
    <td width="1" height="1" bgcolor=#616f97></td>
    <td width="1" height="1" bgcolor=#606e96></td>
    <td width="1" height="1" bgcolor=#5e6d94></td>
    <td width="1" height="1" bgcolor=#5f6d94></td>
    <td rowspan="2" colspan="1" width="1" height="1" bgcolor=#606e95></td>
    <td width="1" height="1" bgcolor=#606d95></td>
    <td width="1" height="1" bgcolor=#64719a></td>
    <td width="1" height="1" bgcolor=#2c394e></td>
    <td width="1" height="1" bgcolor=#6a74a2></td>
    <td width="1" height="1" bgcolor=#5d6c89></td>
    <td width="1" height="1" bgcolor=#2f3b5a></td>
    <td width="1" height="1" bgcolor=#627097></td>
    <td width="1" height="1" bgcolor=#61709a></td>
    <td width="1" height="1" bgcolor=#616f98></td>
    <td width="1" height="1" bgcolor=#606d97></td>
    <td width="1" height="1" bgcolor=#626f99></td>
    <td rowspan="1" colspan="2" width="1" height="1" bgcolor=#616f98></td>
    <td width="1" height="1" bgcolor=#5e6d93></td>
    <td width="1" height="1" bgcolor=#616d96></td>
    <td width="1" height="1" bgcolor=#616f97></td>
    <td width="1" height="1" bgcolor=#606f98></td>
    <td width="1" height="1" bgcolor=#5e6e94></td>
    <td width="1" height="1" bgcolor=#606c94></td>
    <td width="1" height="1" bgcolor=#616e97></td>
    <td width="1" height="1" bgcolor=#515b7c></td>
    <td width="1" height="1" bgcolor=#141315></td>
    <td width="1" height="1" bgcolor=#252631></td>
    <td width="1" height="1" bgcolor=#627299></td>
    <td width="1" height="1" bgcolor=#5c6b94></td>
    <td width="1" height="1" bgcolor=#5e6d93></td>
    <td rowspan="1" colspan="2" width="1" height="1" bgcolor=#5d6b92></td>
    <td width="1" height="1" bgcolor=#5c6991></td>
    <td rowspan="2" colspan="1" width="1" height="1" bgcolor=#5c6b92></td>
    <td rowspan="1" colspan="2" width="1" height="1" bgcolor=#5a6990></td>
    <td width="1" height="1" bgcolor=#5c6993></td>
    <td width="1" height="1" bgcolor=#596691></td>
    <td width="1" height="1" bgcolor=#59668f></td>
    <td width="1" height="1" bgcolor=#5a6990></td>
    <td width="1" height="1" bgcolor=#58678d></td>
    <td width="1" height="1" bgcolor=#58668d></td>
    <td width="1" height="1" bgcolor=#54658c></td>
    <td width="1" height="1" bgcolor=#54658b></td>
    <td width="1" height="1" bgcolor=#58678f></td>
    <td width="1" height="1" bgcolor=#2c354b></td>
    <td width="1" height="1" bgcolor=#14191c></td>
    <td width="1" height="1" bgcolor=#000101></td>
    <td width="1" height="1" bgcolor=#0a080a></td>
    <td width="1" height="1" bgcolor=#202129></td>
    <td width="1" height="1" bgcolor=#282f47></td>
    <td width="1" height="1" bgcolor=#50648c></td>
```

```
    <td width="1" height="1"
bgcolor=#565754></td>
  </tr>
  <tr>
    <td width="1" height="1"
bgcolor=#5b6890></td>
    <td width="1" height="1"
bgcolor=#373e54></td>
    <td width="1" height="1"
bgcolor=#121218></td>
    <td width="1" height="1"
bgcolor=#1e1c23></td>
    <td width="1" height="1"
bgcolor=#120b13></td>
    <td width="1" height="1"
bgcolor=#211d29></td>
    <td width="1" height="1"
bgcolor=#2f3447></td>
    <td width="1" height="1"
bgcolor=#313648></td>
    <td width="1" height="1"
bgcolor=#0e0b13></td>
    <td width="1" height="1"
bgcolor=#14151b></td>
    <td width="1" height="1"
bgcolor=#131616></td>
    <td width="1" height="1"
bgcolor=#4a5772></td>
    <td width="1" height="1"
bgcolor=#16131a></td>
    <td width="1" height="1"
bgcolor=#121218></td>
    <td width="1" height="1"
bgcolor=#15191e></td>
    <td width="1" height="1"
bgcolor=#67749a></td>
    <td width="1" height="1"
bgcolor=#5f6e95></td>
    <td width="1" height="1"
bgcolor=#5d6c93></td>
    <td width="1" height="1"
bgcolor=#606e98></td>
    <td width="1" height="1"
bgcolor=#5f6e96></td>
    <td width="1" height="1"
bgcolor=#5e6d96></td>
    <td width="1" height="1"
bgcolor=#5f6e96></td>
    <td width="1" height="1"
bgcolor=#63709a></td>
    <td width="1" height="1"
bgcolor=#626f9a></td>
    <td width="1" height="1"
bgcolor=#576289></td>
    <td width="1" height="1"
bgcolor=#253645></td>
    <td width="1" height="1"
bgcolor=#627099></td>
    <td width="1" height="1"
bgcolor=#606d96></td>
    <td width="1" height="1"
bgcolor=#606f98></td>
    <td width="1" height="1"
bgcolor=#606d97></td>
    <td rowspan="1"
colspan="2" width="1"
height="1"
bgcolor=#616e98></td>
    <td width="1" height="1"
bgcolor=#606d97></td>
    <td rowspan="2"
colspan="1" width="1"
height="1"
bgcolor=#616e98></td>
    <td width="1" height="1"
bgcolor=#5e6c96></td>
    <td width="1" height="1"
bgcolor=#616f96></td>
    <td width="1" height="1"
bgcolor=#626f97></td>
    <td width="1" height="1"
bgcolor=#606e95></td>
    <td rowspan="2"
colspan="1" width="1"
height="1"
bgcolor=#5f6e96></td>
    <td width="1" height="1"
bgcolor=#5e6d94></td>
    <td rowspan="1"
colspan="2" width="1"
height="1"
bgcolor=#5f6c94></td>
    <td width="1" height="1"
bgcolor=#65739f></td>
    <td width="1" height="1"
bgcolor=#1d212a></td>
    <td width="1" height="1"
bgcolor=#36394b></td>
    <td width="1" height="1"
bgcolor=#54628b></td>
    <td width="1" height="1"
bgcolor=#616b94></td>
    <td width="1" height="1"
bgcolor=#5f6d94></td>
    <td width="1" height="1"
bgcolor=#5e6d94></td>
    <td width="1" height="1"
bgcolor=#5d6c93></td>
    <td width="1" height="1"
bgcolor=#5d6a92></td>
    <td width="1" height="1"
bgcolor=#5b6a91></td>
    <td rowspan="3"
colspan="1" width="1"
height="1"
bgcolor=#5a6990></td>
    <td width="1" height="1"
bgcolor=#58698d></td>
    <td width="1" height="1"
bgcolor=#586b8e></td>
    <td width="1" height="1"
bgcolor=#58688f></td>
    <td width="1" height="1"
bgcolor=#59688f></td>
    <td width="1" height="1"
bgcolor=#57658c></td>
    <td width="1" height="1"
bgcolor=#56658c></td>
    <td rowspan="1"
colspan="2" width="1"
height="1"
bgcolor=#54668c></td>
    <td width="1" height="1"
bgcolor=#52658b></td>
    <td width="1" height="1"
bgcolor=#55678f></td>
    <td width="1" height="1"
bgcolor=#536490></td>
    <td width="1" height="1"
bgcolor=#55668c></td>
    <td width="1" height="1"
bgcolor=#43506f></td>
    <td width="1" height="1"
bgcolor=#030402></td>
    <td width="1" height="1"
bgcolor=#343f5c></td>
    <td width="1" height="1"
bgcolor=#4e6488></td>
    <td width="1" height="1"
bgcolor=#575754></td>
  </tr>
  <tr>
    <td width="1" height="1"
bgcolor=#59668f></td>
    <td width="1" height="1"
bgcolor=#31394e></td>
    <td width="1" height="1"
bgcolor=#06060c></td>
    <td width="1" height="1"
bgcolor=#121115></td>
    <td width="1" height="1"
bgcolor=#2b3043></td>
    <td width="1" height="1"
bgcolor=#495173></td>
    <td width="1" height="1"
bgcolor=#10141e></td>
    <td width="1" height="1"
bgcolor=#1b1c26></td>
    <td width="1" height="1"
bgcolor=#454c63></td>
    <td width="1" height="1"
bgcolor=#09080b></td>
    <td width="1" height="1"
bgcolor=#262433></td>
```

```
<td width="1" height="1" bgcolor=#3c4861></td>
<td width="1" height="1" bgcolor=#19161b></td>
<td width="1" height="1" bgcolor=#100e10></td>
<td width="1" height="1" bgcolor=#424d60></td>
<td width="1" height="1" bgcolor=#606e99></td>
<td width="1" height="1" bgcolor=#5e6d95></td>
<td width="1" height="1" bgcolor=#5f6e95></td>
<td width="1" height="1" bgcolor=#5e6d95></td>
<td width="1" height="1" bgcolor=#606f98></td>
<td rowspan="1" colspan="2" width="1" height="1" bgcolor=#5e6d97></td>
<td width="1" height="1" bgcolor=#5f6d95></td>
<td width="1" height="1" bgcolor=#5f6e93></td>
<td width="1" height="1" bgcolor=#626f98></td>
<td width="1" height="1" bgcolor=#606d91></td>
<td width="1" height="1" bgcolor=#626d9e></td>
<td width="1" height="1" bgcolor=#617096></td>
<td width="1" height="1" bgcolor=#606f96></td>
<td width="1" height="1" bgcolor=#607094></td>
<td width="1" height="1" bgcolor=#626f98></td>
<td width="1" height="1" bgcolor=#626f9a></td>
<td rowspan="2" colspan="2" width="1" height="1" bgcolor=#626f99></td>
<td width="1" height="1" bgcolor=#606e98></td>
<td width="1" height="1" bgcolor=#626f98></td>
<td width="1" height="1" bgcolor=#616e96></td>
<td width="1" height="1" bgcolor=#616e97></td>
<td width="1" height="1" bgcolor=#606d95></td>
<td width="1" height="1" bgcolor=#606e96></td>
<td width="1" height="1" bgcolor=#5e6d95></td>
<td width="1" height="1" bgcolor=#3d445c></td>
<td width="1" height="1" bgcolor=#27292e></td>
<td width="1" height="1" bgcolor=#14181c></td>
<td width="1" height="1" bgcolor=#474e6f></td>
<td width="1" height="1" bgcolor=#4e5e78></td>
<td width="1" height="1" bgcolor=#5d6a92></td>
<td width="1" height="1" bgcolor=#5e6c94></td>
<td width="1" height="1" bgcolor=#5b6b90></td>
<td rowspan="2" colspan="1" width="1" height="1" bgcolor=#5c6b93></td>
<td width="1" height="1" bgcolor=#5d6c93></td>
<td rowspan="2" colspan="1" width="1" height="1" bgcolor=#5a6990></td>
<td width="1" height="1" bgcolor=#546187></td>
<td width="1" height="1" bgcolor=#4f5c82></td>
<td width="1" height="1" bgcolor=#5b6891></td>
<td width="1" height="1" bgcolor=#59668e></td>
<td width="1" height="1" bgcolor=#58678d></td>
<td width="1" height="1" bgcolor=#57668d></td>
<td width="1" height="1" bgcolor=#56668d></td>
<td width="1" height="1" bgcolor=#54668c></td>
<td width="1" height="1" bgcolor=#55658c></td>
<td width="1" height="1" bgcolor=#56648a></td>
<td width="1" height="1" bgcolor=#566489></td>
<td width="1" height="1" bgcolor=#55638b></td>
<td width="1" height="1" bgcolor=#566890></td>
<td width="1" height="1" bgcolor=#1a1c27></td>
<td width="1" height="1" bgcolor=#3c4661></td>
<td width="1" height="1" bgcolor=#4e6087></td>
<td width="1" height="1" bgcolor=#5a5c58></td>
</tr>
<tr>
<td width="1" height="1" bgcolor=#596890></td>
<td width="1" height="1" bgcolor=#2f364d></td>
<td width="1" height="1" bgcolor=#18181c></td>
<td width="1" height="1" bgcolor=#1a1618></td>
<td width="1" height="1" bgcolor=#1f1c2e></td>
<td width="1" height="1" bgcolor=#21242b></td>
<td width="1" height="1" bgcolor=#27273b></td>
<td width="1" height="1" bgcolor=#373744></td>
<td width="1" height="1" bgcolor=#0e100e></td>
<td width="1" height="1" bgcolor=#323a4d></td>
<td width="1" height="1" bgcolor=#495774></td>
<td width="1" height="1" bgcolor=#3f4660></td>
<td width="1" height="1" bgcolor=#171819></td>
<td width="1" height="1" bgcolor=#0d0c0c></td>
<td width="1" height="1" bgcolor=#495878></td>
<td width="1" height="1" bgcolor=#636e97></td>
<td width="1" height="1" bgcolor=#5f6c94></td>
<td width="1" height="1" bgcolor=#606d95></td>
<td width="1" height="1" bgcolor=#616e96></td>
<td width="1" height="1" bgcolor=#617096></td>
<td width="1" height="1" bgcolor=#5f6e95></td>
<td width="1" height="1" bgcolor=#606f95></td>
<td width="1" height="1" bgcolor=#606e96></td>
<td width="1" height="1" bgcolor=#616e99></td>
<td width="1" height="1" bgcolor=#63709b></td>
<td width="1" height="1" bgcolor=#616f98></td>
```

```
    <td width="1" height="1"
bgcolor=#606f94></td>
    <td width="1" height="1"
bgcolor=#64709a></td>
    <td rowspan="1"
colspan="2" width="1"
height="1"
bgcolor=#637097></td>
    <td rowspan="3"
colspan="1" width="1"
height="1"
bgcolor=#616e98></td>
    <td width="1" height="1"
bgcolor=#616e99></td>
    <td width="1" height="1"
bgcolor=#606d97></td>
    <td width="1" height="1"
bgcolor=#627098></td>
    <td rowspan="2"
colspan="1" width="1"
height="1"
bgcolor=#626f97></td>
    <td rowspan="1"
colspan="2" width="1"
height="1"
bgcolor=#626f97></td>
    <td width="1" height="1"
bgcolor=#627098></td>
    <td width="1" height="1"
bgcolor=#616e96></td>
    <td width="1" height="1"
bgcolor=#5e6d94></td>
    <td width="1" height="1"
bgcolor=#5f6e97></td>
    <td width="1" height="1"
bgcolor=#606f9a></td>
    <td width="1" height="1"
bgcolor=#272833></td>
    <td width="1" height="1"
bgcolor=#141519></td>
    <td width="1" height="1"
bgcolor=#4e526e></td>
    <td width="1" height="1"
bgcolor=#14192b></td>
    <td width="1" height="1"
bgcolor=#65729a></td>
    <td width="1" height="1"
bgcolor=#5d6c93></td>
    <td width="1" height="1"
bgcolor=#5d6b90></td>
    <td width="1" height="1"
bgcolor=#5c6b92></td>
    <td width="1" height="1"
bgcolor=#526080></td>
    <td width="1" height="1"
bgcolor=#3d4a65></td>
    <td width="1" height="1"
bgcolor=#5b688d></td>
    <td width="1" height="1"
bgcolor=#59688f></td>
    <td width="1" height="1"
bgcolor=#58678f></td>
    <td width="1" height="1"
bgcolor=#58678e></td>
    <td width="1" height="1"
bgcolor=#57648c></td>
    <td width="1" height="1"
bgcolor=#55658c></td>
    <td width="1" height="1"
bgcolor=#52648b></td>
    <td width="1" height="1"
bgcolor=#52648c></td>
    <td width="1" height="1"
bgcolor=#56658b></td>
    <td width="1" height="1"
bgcolor=#526187></td>
    <td width="1" height="1"
bgcolor=#546589></td>
    <td width="1" height="1"
bgcolor=#4c5678></td>
    <td width="1" height="1"
bgcolor=#27334a></td>
    <td width="1" height="1"
bgcolor=#506488></td>
    <td width="1" height="1"
bgcolor=#535351></td>
  </tr>
  <tr>
    <td width="1" height="1"
bgcolor=#586694></td>
    <td width="1" height="1"
bgcolor=#475169></td>
    <td width="1" height="1"
bgcolor=#1d212d></td>
    <td width="1" height="1"
bgcolor=#222431></td>
    <td width="1" height="1"
bgcolor=#1d2127></td>
    <td width="1" height="1"
bgcolor=#25273c></td>
    <td width="1" height="1"
bgcolor=#292c39></td>
    <td width="1" height="1"
bgcolor=#2f2e45></td>
    <td width="1" height="1"
bgcolor=#32354d></td>
    <td width="1" height="1"
bgcolor=#3c4154></td>
    <td width="1" height="1"
bgcolor=#4c5a7c></td>
    <td width="1" height="1"
bgcolor=#333e55></td>
    <td width="1" height="1"
bgcolor=#151015></td>
    <td width="1" height="1"
bgcolor=#1a1f21></td>
    <td width="1" height="1"
bgcolor=#63729b></td>
    <td width="1" height="1"
bgcolor=#606e96></td>
    <td width="1" height="1"
bgcolor=#606e94></td>
    <td width="1" height="1"
bgcolor=#616e96></td>
    <td width="1" height="1"
bgcolor=#606f97></td>
    <td width="1" height="1"
bgcolor=#5f6d95></td>
    <td width="1" height="1"
bgcolor=#616e96></td>
    <td width="1" height="1"
bgcolor=#606e95></td>
    <td width="1" height="1"
bgcolor=#616e96></td>
    <td width="1" height="1"
bgcolor=#616f98></td>
    <td width="1" height="1"
bgcolor=#626f98></td>
    <td width="1" height="1"
bgcolor=#606e96></td>
    <td width="1" height="1"
bgcolor=#606e97></td>
    <td width="1" height="1"
bgcolor=#626e9a></td>
    <td width="1" height="1"
bgcolor=#63709b></td>
    <td width="1" height="1"
bgcolor=#606f98></td>
    <td rowspan="5"
colspan="1" width="1"
height="1"
bgcolor=#616e98></td>
    <td rowspan="1"
colspan="4" width="1"
height="1"
bgcolor=#616e98></td>
    <td width="1" height="1"
bgcolor=#626f96></td>
    <td width="1" height="1"
bgcolor=#616e96></td>
    <td width="1" height="1"
bgcolor=#626f99></td>
    <td width="1" height="1"
bgcolor=#5f6d96></td>
    <td width="1" height="1"
bgcolor=#5f6d95></td>
    <td width="1" height="1"
bgcolor=#5f6c96></td>
    <td width="1" height="1"
bgcolor=#64709b></td>
    <td width="1" height="1"
bgcolor=#2b2e3d></td>
    <td width="1" height="1"
bgcolor=#1a1f1d></td>
```

```
    <td width="1" height="1" bgcolor=#454f71></td>
    <td width="1" height="1" bgcolor=#5e6a90></td>
    <td width="1" height="1" bgcolor=#5e6c94></td>
    <td width="1" height="1" bgcolor=#5d6d91></td>
    <td width="1" height="1" bgcolor=#5d6c92></td>
    <td rowspan="2" colspan="1" width="1" height="1" bgcolor=#5d6b92></td>
    <td width="1" height="1" bgcolor=#5d6b93></td>
    <td width="1" height="1" bgcolor=#5e6c92></td>
    <td width="1" height="1" bgcolor=#4f5e7f></td>
    <td width="1" height="1" bgcolor=#3a4968></td>
    <td width="1" height="1" bgcolor=#5d6e93></td>
    <td width="1" height="1" bgcolor=#3e4a6c></td>
    <td width="1" height="1" bgcolor=#546080></td>
    <td width="1" height="1" bgcolor=#586790></td>
    <td width="1" height="1" bgcolor=#57668d></td>
    <td width="1" height="1" bgcolor=#56658c></td>
    <td width="1" height="1" bgcolor=#56668b></td>
    <td width="1" height="1" bgcolor=#56678c></td>
    <td width="1" height="1" bgcolor=#55648a></td>
    <td rowspan="1" colspan="2" width="1" height="1" bgcolor=#54638a></td>
    <td width="1" height="1" bgcolor=#55648c></td>
    <td width="1" height="1" bgcolor=#54678b></td>
    <td width="1" height="1" bgcolor=#3d4966></td>
    <td width="1" height="1" bgcolor=#50618a></td>
    <td width="1" height="1" bgcolor=#5c5d59></td>
  </tr>
  <tr>
    <td width="1" height="1" bgcolor=#58688f></td>
    <td width="1" height="1" bgcolor=#313a4c></td>
    <td width="1" height="1" bgcolor=#232832></td>
    <td width="1" height="1" bgcolor=#1f2230></td>
    <td width="1" height="1" bgcolor=#22272e></td>
    <td width="1" height="1" bgcolor=#303743></td>
    <td width="1" height="1" bgcolor=#4b506e></td>
    <td width="1" height="1" bgcolor=#303244></td>
    <td width="1" height="1" bgcolor=#17201e></td>
    <td width="1" height="1" bgcolor=#0f0c17></td>
    <td width="1" height="1" bgcolor=#2e3344></td>
    <td width="1" height="1" bgcolor=#3c4355></td>
    <td width="1" height="1" bgcolor=#2c2b35></td>
    <td width="1" height="1" bgcolor=#303748></td>
    <td width="1" height="1" bgcolor=#607298></td>
    <td width="1" height="1" bgcolor=#616f96></td>
    <td width="1" height="1" bgcolor=#626f97></td>
    <td width="1" height="1" bgcolor=#637098></td>
    <td width="1" height="1" bgcolor=#616e98></td>
    <td width="1" height="1" bgcolor=#616f97></td>
    <td rowspan="3" colspan="1" width="1" height="1" bgcolor=#626f97></td>
    <td width="1" height="1" bgcolor=#616e96></td>
    <td width="1" height="1" bgcolor=#626f97></td>
    <td width="1" height="1" bgcolor=#626f98></td>
    <td width="1" height="1" bgcolor=#63709a></td>
    <td rowspan="3" colspan="2" width="1" height="1" bgcolor=#626f99></td>
    <td rowspan="2" colspan="1" width="1" height="1" bgcolor=#63709a></td>
    <td width="1" height="1" bgcolor=#627099></td>
    <td width="1" height="1" bgcolor=#616f98></td>
    <td rowspan="2" colspan="1" width="1" height="1" bgcolor=#63709a></td>
    <td rowspan="2" colspan="2" width="1" height="1" bgcolor=#626f99></td>
    <td width="1" height="1" bgcolor=#616e98></td>
    <td rowspan="2" colspan="1" width="1" height="1" bgcolor=#626f99></td>
    <td width="1" height="1" bgcolor=#64719a></td>
    <td width="1" height="1" bgcolor=#616e98></td>
    <td width="1" height="1" bgcolor=#616e99></td>
    <td width="1" height="1" bgcolor=#606c9b></td>
    <td width="1" height="1" bgcolor=#616e96></td>
    <td width="1" height="1" bgcolor=#606f94></td>
    <td width="1" height="1" bgcolor=#5d6f96></td>
    <td width="1" height="1" bgcolor=#58688c></td>
    <td width="1" height="1" bgcolor=#63709c></td>
    <td width="1" height="1" bgcolor=#5e6f9b></td>
    <td width="1" height="1" bgcolor=#5f6d92></td>
    <td width="1" height="1" bgcolor=#5f6d95></td>
    <td width="1" height="1" bgcolor=#5e6d94></td>
    <td width="1" height="1" bgcolor=#5e6c93></td>
    <td rowspan="2" colspan="1" width="1" height="1" bgcolor=#5d6c93></td>
    <td width="1" height="1" bgcolor=#5c6a93></td>
    <td width="1" height="1" bgcolor=#5d6b93></td>
    <td width="1" height="1" bgcolor=#5b698f></td>
    <td width="1" height="1" bgcolor=#384662></td>
```

```
    <td width="1" height="1" bgcolor=#424d6b></td>
    <td width="1" height="1" bgcolor=#515f84></td>
    <td width="1" height="1" bgcolor=#586a8f></td>
    <td rowspan="2" colspan="1" width="1" height="1" bgcolor=#59688f></td>
    <td rowspan="3" colspan="1" width="1" height="1" bgcolor=#57668d></td>
    <td width="1" height="1" bgcolor=#57668d></td>
    <td rowspan="1" colspan="3" width="1" height="1" bgcolor=#55648b></td>
    <td width="1" height="1" bgcolor=#56658c></td>
    <td width="1" height="1" bgcolor=#54628b></td>
    <td width="1" height="1" bgcolor=#506185></td>
    <td width="1" height="1" bgcolor=#34405e></td>
    <td width="1" height="1" bgcolor=#4f628b></td>
    <td width="1" height="1" bgcolor=#535451></td>
  </tr>
  <tr>
    <td width="1" height="1" bgcolor=#56678c></td>
    <td width="1" height="1" bgcolor=#434d69></td>
    <td width="1" height="1" bgcolor=#0e1215></td>
    <td width="1" height="1" bgcolor=#2c2b41></td>
    <td width="1" height="1" bgcolor=#262a38></td>
    <td width="1" height="1" bgcolor=#37384f></td>
    <td width="1" height="1" bgcolor=#14171e></td>
    <td width="1" height="1" bgcolor=#303446></td>
    <td width="1" height="1" bgcolor=#293043></td>
    <td width="1" height="1" bgcolor=#2f323c></td>
    <td width="1" height="1" bgcolor=#2b3645></td>
    <td width="1" height="1" bgcolor=#31364b></td>
    <td width="1" height="1" bgcolor=#16181b></td>
    <td width="1" height="1" bgcolor=#21232b></td>
    <td width="1" height="1" bgcolor=#6674a0></td>
    <td rowspan="1" colspan="2" width="1" height="1" bgcolor=#616e96></td>
    <td width="1" height="1" bgcolor=#626f97></td>
    <td rowspan="1" colspan="2" width="1" height="1" bgcolor=#616e96></td>
    <td rowspan="1" colspan="2" width="1" height="1" bgcolor=#626f98></td>
    <td rowspan="1" colspan="2" width="1" height="1" bgcolor=#626f99></td>
    <td rowspan="1" colspan="2" width="1" height="1" bgcolor=#617099></td>
    <td width="1" height="1" bgcolor=#5f6e97></td>
    <td width="1" height="1" bgcolor=#616e9a></td>
    <td width="1" height="1" bgcolor=#64719b></td>
    <td width="1" height="1" bgcolor=#63709a></td>
    <td width="1" height="1" bgcolor=#616e9c></td>
    <td width="1" height="1" bgcolor=#627094></td>
    <td width="1" height="1" bgcolor=#5f6d97></td>
    <td width="1" height="1" bgcolor=#5f6e95></td>
    <td width="1" height="1" bgcolor=#546184></td>
    <td width="1" height="1" bgcolor=#59658a></td>
    <td width="1" height="1" bgcolor=#5f6d93></td>
    <td width="1" height="1" bgcolor=#5f6c91></td>
    <td width="1" height="1" bgcolor=#5f6c96></td>
    <td width="1" height="1" bgcolor=#5f6d94></td>
    <td rowspan="2" colspan="1" width="1" height="1" bgcolor=#5d6c93></td>
    <td width="1" height="1" bgcolor=#5d6c92></td>
    <td width="1" height="1" bgcolor=#5d6c94></td>
    <td width="1" height="1" bgcolor=#5d6d91></td>
    <td width="1" height="1" bgcolor=#5a6a90></td>
    <td width="1" height="1" bgcolor=#5c6d94></td>
    <td width="1" height="1" bgcolor=#515d85></td>
    <td width="1" height="1" bgcolor=#5d6a8f></td>
    <td width="1" height="1" bgcolor=#596b8f></td>
    <td width="1" height="1" bgcolor=#5c6992></td>
    <td rowspan="1" colspan="2" width="1" height="1" bgcolor=#57668e></td>
    <td width="1" height="1" bgcolor=#56658c></td>
    <td width="1" height="1" bgcolor=#54638a></td>
    <td rowspan="2" colspan="1" width="1" height="1" bgcolor=#55648b></td>
    <td width="1" height="1" bgcolor=#536289></td>
    <td width="1" height="1" bgcolor=#4e5f84></td>
    <td width="1" height="1" bgcolor=#394763></td>
    <td width="1" height="1" bgcolor=#4e618a></td>
    <td width="1" height="1" bgcolor=#565755></td>
  </tr>
  <tr>
    <td width="1" height="1" bgcolor=#596891></td>
    <td width="1" height="1" bgcolor=#3b4665></td>
    <td width="1" height="1" bgcolor=#20262e></td>
    <td width="1" height="1" bgcolor=#202229></td>
    <td width="1" height="1" bgcolor=#1f1f29></td>
    <td width="1" height="1" bgcolor=#2d2e3d></td>
    <td width="1" height="1" bgcolor=#242a36></td>
```

```
    <td width="1" height="1"
bgcolor=#2f3040></td>
    <td width="1" height="1"
bgcolor=#181b22></td>
    <td width="1" height="1"
bgcolor=#252833></td>
    <td width="1" height="1"
bgcolor=#31394c></td>
    <td width="1" height="1"
bgcolor=#2f2c35></td>
    <td width="1" height="1"
bgcolor=#161a21></td>
    <td width="1" height="1"
bgcolor=#1b1a16></td>
    <td width="1" height="1"
bgcolor=#6674a2></td>
    <td width="1" height="1"
bgcolor=#626e93></td>
    <td rowspan="1"
colspan="2" width="1"
height="1"
bgcolor=#616e96></td>
    <td width="1" height="1"
bgcolor=#606d95></td>
    <td width="1" height="1"
bgcolor=#626f97></td>
    <td width="1" height="1"
bgcolor=#626f99></td>
    <td width="1" height="1"
bgcolor=#616e98></td>
    <td width="1" height="1"
bgcolor=#626f9a></td>
    <td width="1" height="1"
bgcolor=#626f99></td>
    <td rowspan="1"
colspan="4" width="1"
height="1"
bgcolor=#626f99></td>
    <td rowspan="2"
colspan="1" width="1"
height="1"
bgcolor=#626f99></td>
    <td width="1" height="1"
bgcolor=#616e98></td>
    <td rowspan="3"
colspan="1" width="1"
height="1"
bgcolor=#626f99></td>
    <td width="1" height="1"
bgcolor=#606d97></td>
    <td width="1" height="1"
bgcolor=#63709a></td>
    <td width="1" height="1"
bgcolor=#637098></td>
    <td width="1" height="1"
bgcolor=#616e98></td>
    <td rowspan="2"
colspan="1" width="1"
height="1"
bgcolor=#616f97></td>
    <td width="1" height="1"
bgcolor=#62709a></td>
    <td width="1" height="1"
bgcolor=#5e6e90></td>
    <td width="1" height="1"
bgcolor=#656f9a></td>
    <td width="1" height="1"
bgcolor=#424e6a></td>
    <td width="1" height="1"
bgcolor=#627197></td>
    <td width="1" height="1"
bgcolor=#5e6f96></td>
    <td width="1" height="1"
bgcolor=#606f96></td>
    <td width="1" height="1"
bgcolor=#5e6d96></td>
    <td width="1" height="1"
bgcolor=#606e96></td>
    <td rowspan="1"
colspan="2" width="1"
height="1"
bgcolor=#5e6d95></td>
    <td rowspan="2"
colspan="1" width="1"
height="1"
bgcolor=#5d6c94></td>
    <td rowspan="1"
colspan="2" width="1"
height="1"
bgcolor=#5d6c92></td>
    <td width="1" height="1"
bgcolor=#5a6991></td>
    <td width="1" height="1"
bgcolor=#5b6b93></td>
    <td width="1" height="1"
bgcolor=#5c6a93></td>
    <td width="1" height="1"
bgcolor=#5a6892></td>
    <td rowspan="2"
colspan="1" width="1"
height="1"
bgcolor=#596991></td>
    <td width="1" height="1"
bgcolor=#58678f></td>
    <td width="1" height="1"
bgcolor=#57668d></td>
    <td rowspan="1"
colspan="2" width="1"
height="1"
bgcolor=#57658c></td>
    <td width="1" height="1"
bgcolor=#55648b></td>
    <td width="1" height="1"
bgcolor=#54628a></td>
    <td width="1" height="1"
bgcolor=#546788></td>
    <td width="1" height="1"
bgcolor=#313e5a></td>
    <td width="1" height="1"
bgcolor=#50628b></td>
    <td width="1" height="1"
bgcolor=#565754></td>
  </tr>
  <tr>
    <td width="1" height="1"
bgcolor=#586890></td>
    <td width="1" height="1"
bgcolor=#363f55></td>
    <td width="1" height="1"
bgcolor=#30374b></td>
    <td width="1" height="1"
bgcolor=#262633></td>
    <td width="1" height="1"
bgcolor=#21282f></td>
    <td width="1" height="1"
bgcolor=#333d50></td>
    <td width="1" height="1"
bgcolor=#21202e></td>
    <td width="1" height="1"
bgcolor=#272f3d></td>
    <td width="1" height="1"
bgcolor=#373b4e></td>
    <td width="1" height="1"
bgcolor=#1c1e27></td>
    <td width="1" height="1"
bgcolor=#3c425a></td>
    <td width="1" height="1"
bgcolor=#171c24></td>
    <td width="1" height="1"
bgcolor=#191a1f></td>
    <td width="1" height="1"
bgcolor=#16191d></td>
    <td width="1" height="1"
bgcolor=#647297></td>
    <td width="1" height="1"
bgcolor=#627199></td>
    <td rowspan="1"
colspan="2" width="1"
height="1"
bgcolor=#617195></td>
    <td width="1" height="1"
bgcolor=#657199></td>
    <td width="1" height="1"
bgcolor=#616e99></td>
    <td width="1" height="1"
bgcolor=#626e99></td>
    <td width="1" height="1"
bgcolor=#626d98></td>
    <td width="1" height="1"
bgcolor=#636f99></td>
    <td width="1" height="1"
bgcolor=#607199></td>
    <td width="1" height="1"
bgcolor=#66709c></td>
```

```
    <td width="1" height="1"
bgcolor=#637093></td>
    <td width="1" height="1"
bgcolor=#626f9d></td>
    <td width="1" height="1"
bgcolor=#65729b></td>
    <td width="1" height="1"
bgcolor=#626f99></td>
    <td rowspan="3"
colspan="1" width="1"
height="1"
bgcolor=#63709a></td>
    <td width="1" height="1"
bgcolor=#63709a></td>
    <td width="1" height="1"
bgcolor=#626f99></td>
    <td width="1" height="1"
bgcolor=#59658f></td>
    <td width="1" height="1"
bgcolor=#5c688a></td>
    <td width="1" height="1"
bgcolor=#616f98></td>
    <td width="1" height="1"
bgcolor=#626d97></td>
    <td width="1" height="1"
bgcolor=#637097></td>
    <td width="1" height="1"
bgcolor=#637197></td>
    <td width="1" height="1"
bgcolor=#20222d></td>
    <td width="1" height="1"
bgcolor=#5d6a90></td>
    <td width="1" height="1"
bgcolor=#5f6c95></td>
    <td width="1" height="1"
bgcolor=#5e6b96></td>
    <td width="1" height="1"
bgcolor=#626d97></td>
    <td width="1" height="1"
bgcolor=#5e6b95></td>
    <td rowspan="1"
colspan="2" width="1"
height="1"
bgcolor=#5f6d96></td>
    <td width="1" height="1"
bgcolor=#5d6c94></td>
    <td width="1" height="1"
bgcolor=#5c6b93></td>
    <td width="1" height="1"
bgcolor=#5d6b95></td>
    <td width="1" height="1"
bgcolor=#5c6b95></td>
    <td width="1" height="1"
bgcolor=#5d6b93></td>
    <td width="1" height="1"
bgcolor=#5a6a91></td>
    <td rowspan="2"
colspan="1" width="1"
height="1"
bgcolor=#5b6a93></td>
    <td width="1" height="1"
bgcolor=#596892></td>
    <td rowspan="2"
colspan="1" width="1"
height="1"
bgcolor=#596891></td>
    <td width="1" height="1"
bgcolor=#58678e></td>
    <td width="1" height="1"
bgcolor=#59688f></td>
    <td width="1" height="1"
bgcolor=#57658d></td>
    <td width="1" height="1"
bgcolor=#556589></td>
    <td width="1" height="1"
bgcolor=#56668a></td>
    <td width="1" height="1"
bgcolor=#54658d></td>
    <td width="1" height="1"
bgcolor=#526386></td>
    <td width="1" height="1"
bgcolor=#3c4962></td>
    <td width="1" height="1"
bgcolor=#3b4763></td>
    <td width="1" height="1"
bgcolor=#54608b></td>
    <td width="1" height="1"
bgcolor=#4e504e></td>
  </tr>
  <tr>
    <td width="1" height="1"
bgcolor=#586991></td>
    <td width="1" height="1"
bgcolor=#343b4f></td>
    <td width="1" height="1"
bgcolor=#394257></td>
    <td width="1" height="1"
bgcolor=#151821></td>
    <td width="1" height="1"
bgcolor=#323648></td>
    <td width="1" height="1"
bgcolor=#1e1e2d></td>
    <td width="1" height="1"
bgcolor=#3e4a60></td>
    <td width="1" height="1"
bgcolor=#151016></td>
    <td width="1" height="1"
bgcolor=#272934></td>
    <td width="1" height="1"
bgcolor=#262b34></td>
    <td width="1" height="1"
bgcolor=#313348></td>
    <td width="1" height="1"
bgcolor=#2d3137></td>
    <td width="1" height="1"
bgcolor=#1c1d20></td>
    <td width="1" height="1"
bgcolor=#161819></td>
    <td width="1" height="1"
bgcolor=#586386></td>
    <td width="1" height="1"
bgcolor=#5d7092></td>
    <td width="1" height="1"
bgcolor=#636e99></td>
    <td width="1" height="1"
bgcolor=#626e9a></td>
    <td width="1" height="1"
bgcolor=#626f98></td>
    <td width="1" height="1"
bgcolor=#637197></td>
    <td width="1" height="1"
bgcolor=#616f97></td>
    <td width="1" height="1"
bgcolor=#616d9a></td>
    <td width="1" height="1"
bgcolor=#617195></td>
    <td width="1" height="1"
bgcolor=#6775a1></td>
    <td width="1" height="1"
bgcolor=#434866></td>
    <td width="1" height="1"
bgcolor=#6672a1></td>
    <td width="1" height="1"
bgcolor=#637198></td>
    <td width="1" height="1"
bgcolor=#63709b></td>
    <td rowspan="4"
colspan="1" width="1"
height="1"
bgcolor=#64719b></td>
    <td rowspan="1"
colspan="2" width="1"
height="1"
bgcolor=#626f99></td>
    <td rowspan="2"
colspan="1" width="1"
height="1"
bgcolor=#64719b></td>
    <td rowspan="3"
colspan="1" width="1"
height="1"
bgcolor=#63709a></td>
    <td width="1" height="1"
bgcolor=#657399></td>
    <td width="1" height="1"
bgcolor=#242a34></td>
    <td width="1" height="1"
bgcolor=#56607f></td>
    <td width="1" height="1"
bgcolor=#69759d></td>
    <td width="1" height="1"
bgcolor=#5d6591></td>
    <td width="1" height="1"
bgcolor=#3c485e></td>
```

```
    <td width="1" height="1" bgcolor=#151615></td>
    <td width="1" height="1" bgcolor=#1d1a1e></td>
    <td width="1" height="1" bgcolor=#5c6689></td>
    <td width="1" height="1" bgcolor=#626e9c></td>
    <td width="1" height="1" bgcolor=#616e9a></td>
    <td rowspan="1" colspan="2" width="1" height="1" bgcolor=#606d97></td>
    <td rowspan="1" colspan="2" width="1" height="1" bgcolor=#5f6c96></td>
    <td rowspan="1" colspan="2" width="1" height="1" bgcolor=#5e6d96></td>
    <td width="1" height="1" bgcolor=#5e6c95></td>
    <td width="1" height="1" bgcolor=#5c6b94></td>
    <td width="1" height="1" bgcolor=#5d6c95></td>
    <td width="1" height="1" bgcolor=#5c6b94></td>
    <td width="1" height="1" bgcolor=#5b6992></td>
    <td width="1" height="1" bgcolor=#5b6a93></td>
    <td width="1" height="1" bgcolor=#596891></td>
    <td width="1" height="1" bgcolor=#58678d></td>
    <td rowspan="2" colspan="1" width="1" height="1" bgcolor=#586790></td>
    <td width="1" height="1" bgcolor=#58668e></td>
    <td width="1" height="1" bgcolor=#56658c></td>
    <td width="1" height="1" bgcolor=#55658c></td>
    <td width="1" height="1" bgcolor=#54638c></td>
    <td width="1" height="1" bgcolor=#566894></td>
    <td width="1" height="1" bgcolor=#222430></td>
    <td width="1" height="1" bgcolor=#232c3b></td>
    <td width="1" height="1" bgcolor=#53658f></td>
    <td width="1" height="1" bgcolor=#535551></td>
  </tr>
  <tr>
    <td width="1" height="1" bgcolor=#5b698f></td>
    <td width="1" height="1" bgcolor=#3e455c></td>
    <td width="1" height="1" bgcolor=#141a1e></td>
    <td width="1" height="1" bgcolor=#383f56></td>
    <td width="1" height="1" bgcolor=#120f13></td>
    <td width="1" height="1" bgcolor=#323b4c></td>
    <td width="1" height="1" bgcolor=#1f1d2b></td>
    <td width="1" height="1" bgcolor=#536382></td>
    <td width="1" height="1" bgcolor=#1f202d></td>
    <td width="1" height="1" bgcolor=#1b1e21></td>
    <td width="1" height="1" bgcolor=#272d35></td>
    <td width="1" height="1" bgcolor=#131011></td>
    <td width="1" height="1" bgcolor=#28292f></td>
    <td width="1" height="1" bgcolor=#1b181e></td>
    <td width="1" height="1" bgcolor=#292f35></td>
    <td width="1" height="1" bgcolor=#6776a4></td>
    <td width="1" height="1" bgcolor=#607096></td>
    <td width="1" height="1" bgcolor=#616f96></td>
    <td width="1" height="1" bgcolor=#626f9a></td>
    <td width="1" height="1" bgcolor=#63709b></td>
    <td width="1" height="1" bgcolor=#626e99></td>
    <td width="1" height="1" bgcolor=#627196></td>
    <td width="1" height="1" bgcolor=#6774a2></td>
    <td width="1" height="1" bgcolor=#313a49></td>
    <td width="1" height="1" bgcolor=#2b2d33></td>
    <td width="1" height="1" bgcolor=#6a77a0></td>
    <td width="1" height="1" bgcolor=#616e99></td>
    <td width="1" height="1" bgcolor=#64719d></td>
    <td rowspan="1" colspan="2" width="1" height="1" bgcolor=#63709a></td>
    <td width="1" height="1" bgcolor=#64719b></td>
    <td width="1" height="1" bgcolor=#6673a1></td>
    <td width="1" height="1" bgcolor=#3a4055></td>
    <td width="1" height="1" bgcolor=#252734></td>
    <td width="1" height="1" bgcolor=#303442></td>
    <td width="1" height="1" bgcolor=#3f455e></td>
    <td width="1" height="1" bgcolor=#222226></td>
    <td width="1" height="1" bgcolor=#252832></td>
    <td width="1" height="1" bgcolor=#242327></td>
    <td width="1" height="1" bgcolor=#3e495f></td>
    <td width="1" height="1" bgcolor=#617099></td>
    <td width="1" height="1" bgcolor=#606d96></td>
    <td width="1" height="1" bgcolor=#626e9b></td>
    <td width="1" height="1" bgcolor=#606e98></td>
    <td rowspan="2" colspan="1" width="1" height="1" bgcolor=#606d97></td>
    <td width="1" height="1" bgcolor=#606d97></td>
    <td width="1" height="1" bgcolor=#5f6d96></td>
    <td width="1" height="1" bgcolor=#5d6c95></td>
    <td width="1" height="1" bgcolor=#5e6d95></td>
    <td rowspan="1" colspan="2" width="1" height="1" bgcolor=#5d6b94></td>
    <td rowspan="1" colspan="3" width="1" height="1" bgcolor=#5c6a93></td>
    <td width="1" height="1" bgcolor=#5c6b94></td>
    <td width="1" height="1" bgcolor=#5a6993></td>
```

```
    <td width="1" height="1"
bgcolor=#5b6992></td>
    <td width="1" height="1"
bgcolor=#5a6992></td>
    <td width="1" height="1"
bgcolor=#5a6793></td>
    <td width="1" height="1"
bgcolor=#465474></td>
    <td width="1" height="1"
bgcolor=#424d6c></td>
    <td width="1" height="1"
bgcolor=#36425b></td>
    <td width="1" height="1"
bgcolor=#414c66></td>
    <td width="1" height="1"
bgcolor=#0e121d></td>
    <td width="1" height="1"
bgcolor=#475473></td>
    <td width="1" height="1"
bgcolor=#4f6089></td>
    <td width="1" height="1"
bgcolor=#565854></td>
  </tr>
  <tr>
    <td width="1" height="1"
bgcolor=#5b6991></td>
    <td width="1" height="1"
bgcolor=#363f56></td>
    <td width="1" height="1"
bgcolor=#0c0c0b></td>
    <td width="1" height="1"
bgcolor=#454964></td>
    <td width="1" height="1"
bgcolor=#2e3343></td>
    <td width="1" height="1"
bgcolor=#2d3546></td>
    <td width="1" height="1"
bgcolor=#454d69></td>
    <td width="1" height="1"
bgcolor=#343648></td>
    <td width="1" height="1"
bgcolor=#4f5b7d></td>
    <td width="1" height="1"
bgcolor=#191c20></td>
    <td width="1" height="1"
bgcolor=#231f2a></td>
    <td width="1" height="1"
bgcolor=#2a3141></td>
    <td width="1" height="1"
bgcolor=#0e1114></td>
    <td width="1" height="1"
bgcolor=#202128></td>
    <td width="1" height="1"
bgcolor=#17191c></td>
    <td width="1" height="1"
bgcolor=#383c53></td>
    <td width="1" height="1"
bgcolor=#666f93></td>
    <td width="1" height="1"
bgcolor=#64719c></td>
    <td width="1" height="1"
bgcolor=#627099></td>
    <td width="1" height="1"
bgcolor=#647398></td>
    <td width="1" height="1"
bgcolor=#636e99></td>
    <td width="1" height="1"
bgcolor=#6572a1></td>
    <td width="1" height="1"
bgcolor=#444d65></td>
    <td width="1" height="1"
bgcolor=#191914></td>
    <td width="1" height="1"
bgcolor=#383850></td>
    <td width="1" height="1"
bgcolor=#6674a0></td>
    <td width="1" height="1"
bgcolor=#64709c></td>
    <td width="1" height="1"
bgcolor=#627099></td>
    <td rowspan="2"
colspan="1" width="1"
height="1"
bgcolor=#64719b></td>
    <td rowspan="1"
colspan="2" width="1"
height="1"
bgcolor=#64719b></td>
    <td width="1" height="1"
bgcolor=#626f99></td>
    <td rowspan="2"
colspan="1" width="1"
height="1"
bgcolor=#63709a></td>
    <td width="1" height="1"
bgcolor=#65729b></td>
    <td width="1" height="1"
bgcolor=#47526d></td>
    <td width="1" height="1"
bgcolor=#2e323c></td>
    <td width="1" height="1"
bgcolor=#302d3c></td>
    <td width="1" height="1"
bgcolor=#3c4562></td>
    <td width="1" height="1"
bgcolor=#3c4051></td>
    <td width="1" height="1"
bgcolor=#333b4a></td>
    <td width="1" height="1"
bgcolor=#1d1a1e></td>
    <td width="1" height="1"
bgcolor=#394159></td>
    <td width="1" height="1"
bgcolor=#637299></td>
    <td width="1" height="1"
bgcolor=#5f6f93></td>
    <td width="1" height="1"
bgcolor=#606a99></td>
    <td width="1" height="1"
bgcolor=#606f97></td>
    <td width="1" height="1"
bgcolor=#616e98></td>
    <td width="1" height="1"
bgcolor=#606d96></td>
    <td width="1" height="1"
bgcolor=#5f6c95></td>
    <td width="1" height="1"
bgcolor=#5f6d97></td>
    <td width="1" height="1"
bgcolor=#5c6b94></td>
    <td rowspan="1"
colspan="2" width="1"
height="1"
bgcolor=#5d6b94></td>
    <td width="1" height="1"
bgcolor=#5c6b94></td>
    <td width="1" height="1"
bgcolor=#5c6a93></td>
    <td width="1" height="1"
bgcolor=#5b6a93></td>
    <td width="1" height="1"
bgcolor=#5c6993></td>
    <td width="1" height="1"
bgcolor=#5b6892></td>
    <td width="1" height="1"
bgcolor=#59678f></td>
    <td width="1" height="1"
bgcolor=#576690></td>
    <td width="1" height="1"
bgcolor=#5d6a95></td>
    <td width="1" height="1"
bgcolor=#1b2535></td>
    <td width="1" height="1"
bgcolor=#282733></td>
    <td width="1" height="1"
bgcolor=#161719></td>
    <td width="1" height="1"
bgcolor=#12151e></td>
    <td width="1" height="1"
bgcolor=#0d1015></td>
    <td width="1" height="1"
bgcolor=#55648f></td>
    <td width="1" height="1"
bgcolor=#4f6285></td>
    <td width="1" height="1"
bgcolor=#4d4f4b></td>
  </tr>
  <tr>
    <td width="1" height="1"
bgcolor=#5c6992></td>
    <td width="1" height="1"
bgcolor=#3a435a></td>
    <td width="1" height="1"
bgcolor=#121015></td>
```

```
    <td width="1" height="1" bgcolor=#363b4d></td>
    <td width="1" height="1" bgcolor=#232838></td>
    <td width="1" height="1" bgcolor=#1d1c22></td>
    <td width="1" height="1" bgcolor=#2f3444></td>
    <td width="1" height="1" bgcolor=#292f3e></td>
    <td width="1" height="1" bgcolor=#45516a></td>
    <td width="1" height="1" bgcolor=#475070></td>
    <td width="1" height="1" bgcolor=#242d36></td>
    <td width="1" height="1" bgcolor=#272a32></td>
    <td width="1" height="1" bgcolor=#454a62></td>
    <td width="1" height="1" bgcolor=#2f3245></td>
    <td width="1" height="1" bgcolor=#2d2c3a></td>
    <td width="1" height="1" bgcolor=#1f1d21></td>
    <td width="1" height="1" bgcolor=#19191d></td>
    <td width="1" height="1" bgcolor=#485165></td>
    <td width="1" height="1" bgcolor=#606d95></td>
    <td width="1" height="1" bgcolor=#6775a5></td>
    <td width="1" height="1" bgcolor=#66779d></td>
    <td width="1" height="1" bgcolor=#484e6a></td>
    <td width="1" height="1" bgcolor=#151a15></td>
    <td width="1" height="1" bgcolor=#1f1e1d></td>
    <td width="1" height="1" bgcolor=#2d2f3c></td>
    <td width="1" height="1" bgcolor=#6675a2></td>
    <td width="1" height="1" bgcolor=#67709b></td>
    <td width="1" height="1" bgcolor=#63709a></td>
    <td width="1" height="1" bgcolor=#64719a></td>
    <td width="1" height="1" bgcolor=#647098></td>
    <td width="1" height="1" bgcolor=#64709c></td>
    <td width="1" height="1" bgcolor=#647297></td>
    <td width="1" height="1" bgcolor=#61739e></td>
    <td width="1" height="1" bgcolor=#3e4459></td>
    <td width="1" height="1" bgcolor=#444960></td>
    <td width="1" height="1" bgcolor=#2e2e38></td>
    <td width="1" height="1" bgcolor=#353a48></td>
    <td width="1" height="1" bgcolor=#2b2a33></td>
    <td width="1" height="1" bgcolor=#2c2d3a></td>
    <td width="1" height="1" bgcolor=#3f415b></td>
    <td width="1" height="1" bgcolor=#4f5b7d></td>
    <td width="1" height="1" bgcolor=#5d6b92></td>
    <td width="1" height="1" bgcolor=#5c6d98></td>
    <td width="1" height="1" bgcolor=#646d98></td>
    <td width="1" height="1" bgcolor=#5e6c95></td>
    <td width="1" height="1" bgcolor=#5f6b95></td>
    <td rowspan="2" colspan="1" width="1" height="1" bgcolor=#606d98></td>
    <td width="1" height="1" bgcolor=#606c96></td>
    <td width="1" height="1" bgcolor=#5f6d95></td>
    <td width="1" height="1" bgcolor=#606b9b></td>
    <td width="1" height="1" bgcolor=#5f6c94></td>
    <td width="1" height="1" bgcolor=#5f6c92></td>
    <td width="1" height="1" bgcolor=#5c6a96></td>
    <td width="1" height="1" bgcolor=#5d6b94></td>
    <td width="1" height="1" bgcolor=#5d6c95></td>
    <td rowspan="1" colspan="2" width="1" height="1" bgcolor=#5a6992></td>
    <td width="1" height="1" bgcolor=#5b6992></td>
    <td width="1" height="1" bgcolor=#5a6991></td>
    <td width="1" height="1" bgcolor=#596890></td>
    <td width="1" height="1" bgcolor=#576892></td>
    <td width="1" height="1" bgcolor=#3a4459></td>
    <td width="1" height="1" bgcolor=#231e2b></td>
    <td width="1" height="1" bgcolor=#161815></td>
    <td width="1" height="1" bgcolor=#343952></td>
    <td width="1" height="1" bgcolor=#080709></td>
    <td width="1" height="1" bgcolor=#475173></td>
    <td width="1" height="1" bgcolor=#4d6085></td>
    <td width="1" height="1" bgcolor=#595957></td>
  </tr>
  <tr>
    <td width="1" height="1" bgcolor=#5c6a90></td>
    <td width="1" height="1" bgcolor=#3c435c></td>
    <td rowspan="2" colspan="1" width="1" height="1" bgcolor=#121314></td>
    <td width="1" height="1" bgcolor=#1a1c26></td>
    <td width="1" height="1" bgcolor=#424861></td>
    <td width="1" height="1" bgcolor=#2d3343></td>
    <td width="1" height="1" bgcolor=#1c181a></td>
    <td width="1" height="1" bgcolor=#2a2d3e></td>
    <td width="1" height="1" bgcolor=#3c3b59></td>
    <td width="1" height="1" bgcolor=#3a4052></td>
    <td width="1" height="1" bgcolor=#484f6c></td>
    <td width="1" height="1" bgcolor=#2d3344></td>
    <td width="1" height="1" bgcolor=#1b1918></td>
    <td width="1" height="1" bgcolor=#343547></td>
    <td width="1" height="1" bgcolor=#3a4155></td>
    <td width="1" height="1" bgcolor=#2e323f></td>
    <td width="1" height="1" bgcolor=#25272b></td>
    <td width="1" height="1" bgcolor=#1e181f></td>
```

```
    <td width="1" height="1" bgcolor=#1b1b19></td>
    <td width="1" height="1" bgcolor=#2a2d3a></td>
    <td width="1" height="1" bgcolor=#434d61></td>
    <td width="1" height="1" bgcolor=#19171f></td>
    <td width="1" height="1" bgcolor=#221f24></td>
    <td width="1" height="1" bgcolor=#211d25></td>
    <td width="1" height="1" bgcolor=#171918></td>
    <td width="1" height="1" bgcolor=#5d678a></td>
    <td width="1" height="1" bgcolor=#607198></td>
    <td width="1" height="1" bgcolor=#63709b></td>
    <td width="1" height="1" bgcolor=#65729d></td>
    <td width="1" height="1" bgcolor=#63709a></td>
    <td width="1" height="1" bgcolor=#65729c></td>
    <td width="1" height="1" bgcolor=#63709c></td>
    <td width="1" height="1" bgcolor=#64719d></td>
    <td width="1" height="1" bgcolor=#65709d></td>
    <td width="1" height="1" bgcolor=#64709d></td>
    <td width="1" height="1" bgcolor=#6974a2></td>
    <td width="1" height="1" bgcolor=#2e3140></td>
    <td width="1" height="1" bgcolor=#3d4453></td>
    <td width="1" height="1" bgcolor=#2a2b36></td>
    <td width="1" height="1" bgcolor=#4e5471></td>
    <td width="1" height="1" bgcolor=#3e455d></td>
    <td width="1" height="1" bgcolor=#343747></td>
    <td width="1" height="1" bgcolor=#41455d></td>
    <td width="1" height="1" bgcolor=#373e4b></td>
    <td width="1" height="1" bgcolor=#252531></td>
    <td width="1" height="1" bgcolor=#5d6b90></td>
    <td width="1" height="1" bgcolor=#6575a4></td>
    <td width="1" height="1" bgcolor=#616d97></td>
    <td width="1" height="1" bgcolor=#5d6f97></td>
    <td width="1" height="1" bgcolor=#626f97></td>
    <td width="1" height="1" bgcolor=#606f96></td>
    <td width="1" height="1" bgcolor=#637197></td>
    <td width="1" height="1" bgcolor=#536387></td>
    <td width="1" height="1" bgcolor=#5c6d96></td>
    <td width="1" height="1" bgcolor=#5b6c91></td>
    <td rowspan="2" colspan="2" width="1" height="1" bgcolor=#5c6a93></td>
    <td width="1" height="1" bgcolor=#5b6a93></td>
    <td width="1" height="1" bgcolor=#5c6a93></td>
    <td rowspan="3" colspan="1" width="1" height="1" bgcolor=#5a6992></td>
    <td rowspan="2" colspan="1" width="1" height="1" bgcolor=#596891></td>
    <td width="1" height="1" bgcolor=#596891></td>
    <td width="1" height="1" bgcolor=#55668e></td>
    <td width="1" height="1" bgcolor=#475474></td>
    <td width="1" height="1" bgcolor=#1a1c21></td>
    <td width="1" height="1" bgcolor=#1c1b23></td>
    <td width="1" height="1" bgcolor=#313950></td>
    <td width="1" height="1" bgcolor=#1a1b1f></td>
    <td width="1" height="1" bgcolor=#38425b></td>
    <td width="1" height="1" bgcolor=#4f6288></td>
    <td width="1" height="1" bgcolor=#4e4f4c></td>
  </tr>
  <tr>
    <td width="1" height="1" bgcolor=#5c6b90></td>
    <td width="1" height="1" bgcolor=#3b435d></td>
    <td width="1" height="1" bgcolor=#100e0f></td>
    <td width="1" height="1" bgcolor=#4b5a78></td>
    <td width="1" height="1" bgcolor=#2a2a3e></td>
    <td width="1" height="1" bgcolor=#2b2e3b></td>
    <td width="1" height="1" bgcolor=#141519></td>
    <td width="1" height="1" bgcolor=#1d1e1e></td>
    <td width="1" height="1" bgcolor=#485473></td>
    <td width="1" height="1" bgcolor=#3a4459></td>
    <td width="1" height="1" bgcolor=#485675></td>
    <td width="1" height="1" bgcolor=#333c48></td>
    <td width="1" height="1" bgcolor=#171313></td>
    <td width="1" height="1" bgcolor=#242629></td>
    <td width="1" height="1" bgcolor=#4b4e6d></td>
    <td width="1" height="1" bgcolor=#2d3741></td>
    <td width="1" height="1" bgcolor=#323943></td>
    <td width="1" height="1" bgcolor=#1a1a1c></td>
    <td width="1" height="1" bgcolor=#1c1c1d></td>
    <td width="1" height="1" bgcolor=#484d68></td>
    <td width="1" height="1" bgcolor=#1a1d1a></td>
    <td width="1" height="1" bgcolor=#1e1d24></td>
    <td width="1" height="1" bgcolor=#1f201e></td>
    <td width="1" height="1" bgcolor=#212223></td>
    <td width="1" height="1" bgcolor=#2a2b3a></td>
    <td width="1" height="1" bgcolor=#6879a5></td>
    <td width="1" height="1" bgcolor=#64719a></td>
    <td width="1" height="1" bgcolor=#64719c></td>
    <td width="1" height="1" bgcolor=#64719d></td>
    <td width="1" height="1" bgcolor=#62709a></td>
    <td width="1" height="1" bgcolor=#647398></td>
```

```
    <td width="1" height="1"
bgcolor=#63709d></td>
    <td width="1" height="1"
bgcolor=#647398></td>
    <td width="1" height="1"
bgcolor=#61709c></td>
    <td width="1" height="1"
bgcolor=#5a698d></td>
    <td width="1" height="1"
bgcolor=#1f1f1d></td>
    <td width="1" height="1"
bgcolor=#393b50></td>
    <td width="1" height="1"
bgcolor=#495371></td>
    <td width="1" height="1"
bgcolor=#292c32></td>
    <td width="1" height="1"
bgcolor=#425166></td>
    <td width="1" height="1"
bgcolor=#282833></td>
    <td width="1" height="1"
bgcolor=#393c52></td>
    <td width="1" height="1"
bgcolor=#3f4759></td>
    <td width="1" height="1"
bgcolor=#302e42></td>
    <td width="1" height="1"
bgcolor=#414d65></td>
    <td width="1" height="1"
bgcolor=#232428></td>
    <td width="1" height="1"
bgcolor=#44526e></td>
    <td width="1" height="1"
bgcolor=#576289></td>
    <td width="1" height="1"
bgcolor=#4b536f></td>
    <td width="1" height="1"
bgcolor=#454e6c></td>
    <td width="1" height="1"
bgcolor=#445376></td>
    <td width="1" height="1"
bgcolor=#404c69></td>
    <td width="1" height="1"
bgcolor=#2f3341></td>
    <td width="1" height="1"
bgcolor=#616f96></td>
    <td width="1" height="1"
bgcolor=#5c6c93></td>
    <td width="1" height="1"
bgcolor=#5c6b94></td>
    <td width="1" height="1"
bgcolor=#5b6a93></td>
    <td width="1" height="1"
bgcolor=#586790></td>
    <td width="1" height="1"
bgcolor=#5c6b97></td>
    <td width="1" height="1"
bgcolor=#343d4f></td>
    <td width="1" height="1"
bgcolor=#242a34></td>
    <td width="1" height="1"
bgcolor=#1a1a24></td>
    <td width="1" height="1"
bgcolor=#3d485c></td>
    <td width="1" height="1"
bgcolor=#252632></td>
    <td width="1" height="1"
bgcolor=#293246></td>
    <td width="1" height="1"
bgcolor=#51658b></td>
    <td width="1" height="1"
bgcolor=#555753></td>
  </tr>
  <tr>
    <td width="1" height="1"
bgcolor=#5b6a90></td>
    <td width="1" height="1"
bgcolor=#3c445f></td>
    <td width="1" height="1"
bgcolor=#101211></td>
    <td width="1" height="1"
bgcolor=#120d12></td>
    <td width="1" height="1"
bgcolor=#5a6988></td>
    <td width="1" height="1"
bgcolor=#151416></td>
    <td width="1" height="1"
bgcolor=#383d51></td>
    <td width="1" height="1"
bgcolor=#252830></td>
    <td width="1" height="1"
bgcolor=#221e28></td>
    <td width="1" height="1"
bgcolor=#272e34></td>
    <td width="1" height="1"
bgcolor=#3a3e58></td>
    <td width="1" height="1"
bgcolor=#2f313a></td>
    <td width="1" height="1"
bgcolor=#3b455d></td>
    <td width="1" height="1"
bgcolor=#48506c></td>
    <td width="1" height="1"
bgcolor=#1c1b20></td>
    <td width="1" height="1"
bgcolor=#2c2933></td>
    <td width="1" height="1"
bgcolor=#3c3d4f></td>
    <td width="1" height="1"
bgcolor=#262630></td>
    <td width="1" height="1"
bgcolor=#2d2c35></td>
    <td width="1" height="1"
bgcolor=#2d303d></td>
    <td width="1" height="1"
bgcolor=#3d415b></td>
    <td width="1" height="1"
bgcolor=#1c1918></td>
    <td width="1" height="1"
bgcolor=#241e21></td>
    <td width="1" height="1"
bgcolor=#222025></td>
    <td width="1" height="1"
bgcolor=#212027></td>
    <td width="1" height="1"
bgcolor=#1d1e15></td>
    <td width="1" height="1"
bgcolor=#3a405a></td>
    <td width="1" height="1"
bgcolor=#6e7ca2></td>
    <td width="1" height="1"
bgcolor=#66739b></td>
    <td width="1" height="1"
bgcolor=#65729d></td>
    <td width="1" height="1"
bgcolor=#63739c></td>
    <td width="1" height="1"
bgcolor=#64739e></td>
    <td width="1" height="1"
bgcolor=#63729c></td>
    <td width="1" height="1"
bgcolor=#65749e></td>
    <td width="1" height="1"
bgcolor=#616c91></td>
    <td width="1" height="1"
bgcolor=#373b4b></td>
    <td width="1" height="1"
bgcolor=#49506d></td>
    <td width="1" height="1"
bgcolor=#48506b></td>
    <td width="1" height="1"
bgcolor=#474960></td>
    <td width="1" height="1"
bgcolor=#3c3e4c></td>
    <td width="1" height="1"
bgcolor=#444968></td>
    <td width="1" height="1"
bgcolor=#3d4257></td>
    <td width="1" height="1"
bgcolor=#201f22></td>
    <td width="1" height="1"
bgcolor=#394156></td>
    <td width="1" height="1"
bgcolor=#57678a></td>
    <td width="1" height="1"
bgcolor=#454c67></td>
    <td width="1" height="1"
bgcolor=#5e7399></td>
    <td width="1" height="1"
bgcolor=#3e4356></td>
    <td width="1" height="1"
bgcolor=#2e3242></td>
    <td width="1" height="1"
bgcolor=#232430></td>
```

```
    <td width="1" height="1"
bgcolor=#313246></td>
    <td width="1" height="1"
bgcolor=#4b5273></td>
    <td width="1" height="1"
bgcolor=#4b5675></td>
    <td width="1" height="1"
bgcolor=#1d1c24></td>
    <td width="1" height="1"
bgcolor=#5d6893></td>
    <td width="1" height="1"
bgcolor=#5e6c94></td>
    <td width="1" height="1"
bgcolor=#5d6c95></td>
    <td width="1" height="1"
bgcolor=#5b6992></td>
    <td width="1" height="1"
bgcolor=#5b6a93></td>
    <td width="1" height="1"
bgcolor=#5a6992></td>
    <td width="1" height="1"
bgcolor=#586790></td>
    <td width="1" height="1"
bgcolor=#5a6992></td>
    <td width="1" height="1"
bgcolor=#516088></td>
    <td width="1" height="1"
bgcolor=#1c2023></td>
    <td width="1" height="1"
bgcolor=#3f465f></td>
    <td width="1" height="1"
bgcolor=#151212></td>
    <td width="1" height="1"
bgcolor=#3e4765></td>
    <td width="1" height="1"
bgcolor=#1f1f2c></td>
    <td width="1" height="1"
bgcolor=#383f56></td>
    <td width="1" height="1"
bgcolor=#4f6489></td>
    <td width="1" height="1"
bgcolor=#565753></td>
  </tr>
  <tr>
    <td width="1" height="1"
bgcolor=#5b6a92></td>
    <td width="1" height="1"
bgcolor=#404661></td>
    <td width="1" height="1"
bgcolor=#131314></td>
    <td width="1" height="1"
bgcolor=#111310></td>
    <td width="1" height="1"
bgcolor=#4d5c7d></td>
    <td width="1" height="1"
bgcolor=#323a4c></td>
    <td width="1" height="1"
bgcolor=#19141c></td>
    <td width="1" height="1"
bgcolor=#3a3f53></td>
    <td width="1" height="1"
bgcolor=#22232b></td>
    <td width="1" height="1"
bgcolor=#333040></td>
    <td width="1" height="1"
bgcolor=#4d5674></td>
    <td width="1" height="1"
bgcolor=#1c1c28></td>
    <td width="1" height="1"
bgcolor=#1e1b1a></td>
    <td width="1" height="1"
bgcolor=#2b303c></td>
    <td width="1" height="1"
bgcolor=#525677></td>
    <td width="1" height="1"
bgcolor=#1c1e21></td>
    <td width="1" height="1"
bgcolor=#282934></td>
    <td width="1" height="1"
bgcolor=#3a3d51></td>
    <td width="1" height="1"
bgcolor=#282a36></td>
    <td width="1" height="1"
bgcolor=#212326></td>
    <td width="1" height="1"
bgcolor=#565f84></td>
    <td width="1" height="1"
bgcolor=#353642></td>
    <td width="1" height="1"
bgcolor=#1c2120></td>
    <td width="1" height="1"
bgcolor=#252124></td>
    <td width="1" height="1"
bgcolor=#222025></td>
    <td width="1" height="1"
bgcolor=#221f27></td>
    <td width="1" height="1"
bgcolor=#231f25></td>
    <td width="1" height="1"
bgcolor=#242c38></td>
    <td width="1" height="1"
bgcolor=#4f5a73></td>
    <td width="1" height="1"
bgcolor=#6a77a2></td>
    <td width="1" height="1"
bgcolor=#6777a4></td>
    <td width="1" height="1"
bgcolor=#64769f></td>
    <td width="1" height="1"
bgcolor=#697a9e></td>
    <td width="1" height="1"
bgcolor=#525879></td>
    <td width="1" height="1"
bgcolor=#1b1e21></td>
    <td width="1" height="1"
bgcolor=#323344></td>
    <td width="1" height="1"
bgcolor=#525474></td>
    <td width="1" height="1"
bgcolor=#1c221e></td>
    <td width="1" height="1"
bgcolor=#3d4156></td>
    <td width="1" height="1"
bgcolor=#343543></td>
    <td width="1" height="1"
bgcolor=#4a506d></td>
    <td width="1" height="1"
bgcolor=#4e597b></td>
    <td width="1" height="1"
bgcolor=#29272f></td>
    <td width="1" height="1"
bgcolor=#2c2d38></td>
    <td width="1" height="1"
bgcolor=#48516c></td>
    <td width="1" height="1"
bgcolor=#3f4459></td>
    <td width="1" height="1"
bgcolor=#333240></td>
    <td width="1" height="1"
bgcolor=#363648></td>
    <td width="1" height="1"
bgcolor=#282b35></td>
    <td width="1" height="1"
bgcolor=#27262a></td>
    <td width="1" height="1"
bgcolor=#232527></td>
    <td width="1" height="1"
bgcolor=#31394d></td>
    <td width="1" height="1"
bgcolor=#5e6c96></td>
    <td width="1" height="1"
bgcolor=#404b67></td>
    <td width="1" height="1"
bgcolor=#516185></td>
    <td width="1" height="1"
bgcolor=#616d99></td>
    <td width="1" height="1"
bgcolor=#5f6c97></td>
    <td width="1" height="1"
bgcolor=#5d6b93></td>
    <td width="1" height="1"
bgcolor=#5c6a93></td>
    <td width="1" height="1"
bgcolor=#5b6a93></td>
    <td width="1" height="1"
bgcolor=#58698f></td>
    <td width="1" height="1"
bgcolor=#586a8f></td>
    <td width="1" height="1"
bgcolor=#586690></td>
    <td width="1" height="1"
bgcolor=#4d5b7e></td>
    <td width="1" height="1"
bgcolor=#232533></td>
```

```
    <td width="1" height="1" bgcolor=#374156></td>
    <td width="1" height="1" bgcolor=#141214></td>
    <td width="1" height="1" bgcolor=#3a3f56></td>
    <td width="1" height="1" bgcolor=#0c0c11></td>
    <td width="1" height="1" bgcolor=#2f374b></td>
    <td width="1" height="1" bgcolor=#51658b></td>
    <td width="1" height="1" bgcolor=#50514e></td>
  </tr>
  <tr>
    <td width="1" height="1" bgcolor=#5b6b91></td>
    <td width="1" height="1" bgcolor=#414961></td>
    <td width="1" height="1" bgcolor=#121017></td>
    <td width="1" height="1" bgcolor=#141315></td>
    <td width="1" height="1" bgcolor=#46516a></td>
    <td width="1" height="1" bgcolor=#474e67></td>
    <td width="1" height="1" bgcolor=#201d26></td>
    <td width="1" height="1" bgcolor=#1f2629></td>
    <td width="1" height="1" bgcolor=#2c2e3a></td>
    <td width="1" height="1" bgcolor=#292933></td>
    <td width="1" height="1" bgcolor=#384251></td>
    <td width="1" height="1" bgcolor=#49546c></td>
    <td width="1" height="1" bgcolor=#202529></td>
    <td width="1" height="1" bgcolor=#221b20></td>
    <td width="1" height="1" bgcolor=#202528></td>
    <td width="1" height="1" bgcolor=#464f67></td>
    <td width="1" height="1" bgcolor=#212326></td>
    <td width="1" height="1" bgcolor=#1a1918></td>
    <td width="1" height="1" bgcolor=#282c32></td>
    <td width="1" height="1" bgcolor=#464d64></td>
    <td width="1" height="1" bgcolor=#424b63></td>
    <td width="1" height="1" bgcolor=#1b171b></td>
    <td width="1" height="1" bgcolor=#3b3e4c></td>
    <td width="1" height="1" bgcolor=#23202b></td>
    <td width="1" height="1" bgcolor=#1d1e1f></td>
    <td width="1" height="1" bgcolor=#1e1f21></td>
    <td width="1" height="1" bgcolor=#1e201f></td>
    <td width="1" height="1" bgcolor=#222022></td>
    <td width="1" height="1" bgcolor=#201c1d></td>
    <td width="1" height="1" bgcolor=#1a1b1e></td>
    <td width="1" height="1" bgcolor=#343746></td>
    <td width="1" height="1" bgcolor=#404564></td>
    <td width="1" height="1" bgcolor=#313744></td>
    <td width="1" height="1" bgcolor=#1e1a19></td>
    <td width="1" height="1" bgcolor=#232325></td>
    <td width="1" height="1" bgcolor=#555d7e></td>
    <td width="1" height="1" bgcolor=#333742></td>
    <td width="1" height="1" bgcolor=#353546></td>
    <td width="1" height="1" bgcolor=#282b41></td>
    <td width="1" height="1" bgcolor=#3e404f></td>
    <td width="1" height="1" bgcolor=#434c68></td>
    <td width="1" height="1" bgcolor=#48526f></td>
    <td width="1" height="1" bgcolor=#232226></td>
    <td width="1" height="1" bgcolor=#343542></td>
    <td width="1" height="1" bgcolor=#4c5b80></td>
    <td width="1" height="1" bgcolor=#231e23></td>
    <td width="1" height="1" bgcolor=#475873></td>
    <td width="1" height="1" bgcolor=#434b6a></td>
    <td width="1" height="1" bgcolor=#343a4d></td>
    <td width="1" height="1" bgcolor=#313442></td>
    <td width="1" height="1" bgcolor=#353b47></td>
    <td width="1" height="1" bgcolor=#293147></td>
    <td width="1" height="1" bgcolor=#22262c></td>
    <td width="1" height="1" bgcolor=#4f5a7a></td>
    <td width="1" height="1" bgcolor=#576d92></td>
    <td width="1" height="1" bgcolor=#42506b></td>
    <td width="1" height="1" bgcolor=#3f4e66></td>
    <td width="1" height="1" bgcolor=#5c6b93></td>
    <td width="1" height="1" bgcolor=#5b6994></td>
    <td width="1" height="1" bgcolor=#4f5b7d></td>
    <td width="1" height="1" bgcolor=#5c6891></td>
    <td width="1" height="1" bgcolor=#59668f></td>
    <td width="1" height="1" bgcolor=#556085></td>
    <td width="1" height="1" bgcolor=#3d4a65></td>
    <td width="1" height="1" bgcolor=#161a20></td>
    <td width="1" height="1" bgcolor=#464d6e></td>
    <td width="1" height="1" bgcolor=#171a1c></td>
    <td width="1" height="1" bgcolor=#151619></td>
    <td width="1" height="1" bgcolor=#100e12></td>
    <td width="1" height="1" bgcolor=#293343></td>
    <td width="1" height="1" bgcolor=#506585></td>
    <td width="1" height="1" bgcolor=#4f504d></td>
  </tr>
  <tr>
    <td width="1" height="1" bgcolor=#5d6b94></td>
    <td width="1" height="1" bgcolor=#566288></td>
    <td width="1" height="1" bgcolor=#4d5675></td>
    <td width="1" height="1" bgcolor=#4a5471></td>
    <td width="1" height="1" bgcolor=#545e84></td>
    <td width="1" height="1" bgcolor=#4b5876></td>
```

```
    <td width="1" height="1"
bgcolor=#4e5a78></td>
    <td width="1" height="1"
bgcolor=#495370></td>
    <td width="1" height="1"
bgcolor=#586287></td>
    <td width="1" height="1"
bgcolor=#50597a></td>
    <td width="1" height="1"
bgcolor=#4f5b7c></td>
    <td width="1" height="1"
bgcolor=#556084></td>
    <td width="1" height="1"
bgcolor=#586289></td>
    <td width="1" height="1"
bgcolor=#4e5a75></td>
    <td width="1" height="1"
bgcolor=#505877></td>
    <td width="1" height="1"
bgcolor=#4a546c></td>
    <td width="1" height="1"
bgcolor=#555e81></td>
    <td width="1" height="1"
bgcolor=#49526c></td>
    <td width="1" height="1"
bgcolor=#56607f></td>
    <td width="1" height="1"
bgcolor=#4c5875></td>
    <td width="1" height="1"
bgcolor=#5b6892></td>
    <td width="1" height="1"
bgcolor=#505676></td>
    <td width="1" height="1"
bgcolor=#4e5a72></td>
    <td width="1" height="1"
bgcolor=#515a79></td>
    <td width="1" height="1"
bgcolor=#505878></td>
    <td width="1" height="1"
bgcolor=#4f5778></td>
    <td width="1" height="1"
bgcolor=#515a78></td>
    <td rowspan="1"
colspan="2" width="1"
height="1"
bgcolor=#4e5874></td>
    <td width="1" height="1"
bgcolor=#515977></td>
    <td width="1" height="1"
bgcolor=#4e5873></td>
    <td width="1" height="1"
bgcolor=#5e6a8d></td>
    <td width="1" height="1"
bgcolor=#525e7c></td>
    <td width="1" height="1"
bgcolor=#4e5677></td>
    <td width="1" height="1"
bgcolor=#545f83></td>
    <td width="1" height="1"
bgcolor=#5d6990></td>
    <td width="1" height="1"
bgcolor=#4b5472></td>
    <td width="1" height="1"
bgcolor=#4d5776></td>
    <td width="1" height="1"
bgcolor=#596487></td>
    <td width="1" height="1"
bgcolor=#636d90></td>
    <td width="1" height="1"
bgcolor=#5c6990></td>
    <td width="1" height="1"
bgcolor=#5d688f></td>
    <td width="1" height="1"
bgcolor=#4c5672></td>
    <td width="1" height="1"
bgcolor=#596686></td>
    <td width="1" height="1"
bgcolor=#576085></td>
    <td width="1" height="1"
bgcolor=#556086></td>
    <td width="1" height="1"
bgcolor=#5c6a91></td>
    <td width="1" height="1"
bgcolor=#5b6b93></td>
    <td width="1" height="1"
bgcolor=#5f6c93></td>
    <td width="1" height="1"
bgcolor=#5a668f></td>
    <td width="1" height="1"
bgcolor=#505b7f></td>
    <td width="1" height="1"
bgcolor=#5c678e></td>
    <td width="1" height="1"
bgcolor=#5f6c94></td>
    <td width="1" height="1"
bgcolor=#5f6f94></td>
    <td width="1" height="1"
bgcolor=#5f6a96></td>
    <td width="1" height="1"
bgcolor=#535c81></td>
    <td width="1" height="1"
bgcolor=#465374></td>
    <td width="1" height="1"
bgcolor=#4f5f81></td>
    <td width="1" height="1"
bgcolor=#556384></td>
    <td width="1" height="1"
bgcolor=#46526f></td>
    <td width="1" height="1"
bgcolor=#4b587b></td>
    <td width="1" height="1"
bgcolor=#414f67></td>
    <td width="1" height="1"
bgcolor=#4b5677></td>
    <td width="1" height="1"
bgcolor=#4f5d83></td>
    <td width="1" height="1"
bgcolor=#46526c></td>
    <td width="1" height="1"
bgcolor=#475577></td>
    <td width="1" height="1"
bgcolor=#4a5373></td>
    <td width="1" height="1"
bgcolor=#434e69></td>
    <td width="1" height="1"
bgcolor=#434d68></td>
    <td width="1" height="1"
bgcolor=#4c5a7b></td>
    <td width="1" height="1"
bgcolor=#4f638b></td>
    <td rowspan="2"
colspan="1" width="1"
height="1"
bgcolor=#555653></td>
  </tr>
  <tr>
    <td width="1" height="1"
bgcolor=#5c6a92></td>
    <td width="1" height="1"
bgcolor=#5b6c94></td>
    <td width="1" height="1"
bgcolor=#5b6d95></td>
    <td width="1" height="1"
bgcolor=#5e7094></td>
    <td width="1" height="1"
bgcolor=#5f6f97></td>
    <td width="1" height="1"
bgcolor=#5d7097></td>
    <td width="1" height="1"
bgcolor=#5f719c></td>
    <td width="1" height="1"
bgcolor=#63729b></td>
    <td width="1" height="1"
bgcolor=#607296></td>
    <td width="1" height="1"
bgcolor=#61709d></td>
    <td width="1" height="1"
bgcolor=#63709f></td>
    <td width="1" height="1"
bgcolor=#627298></td>
    <td width="1" height="1"
bgcolor=#64739a></td>
    <td width="1" height="1"
bgcolor=#65749e></td>
    <td width="1" height="1"
bgcolor=#65769c></td>
    <td width="1" height="1"
bgcolor=#65759d></td>
    <td width="1" height="1"
bgcolor=#66779e></td>
    <td width="1" height="1"
bgcolor=#6373a2></td>
    <td width="1" height="1"
bgcolor=#66769d></td>
```

```
    <td width="1" height="1"
bgcolor=#6774a1></td>
    <td width="1" height="1"
bgcolor=#66769c></td>
    <td width="1" height="1"
bgcolor=#62779f></td>
    <td width="1" height="1"
bgcolor=#6476a3></td>
    <td width="1" height="1"
bgcolor=#6676a1></td>
    <td width="1" height="1"
bgcolor=#6777a3></td>
    <td width="1" height="1"
bgcolor=#6576a1></td>
    <td width="1" height="1"
bgcolor=#6576a0></td>
    <td width="1" height="1"
bgcolor=#6475a0></td>
    <td width="1" height="1"
bgcolor=#6677a1></td>
    <td width="1" height="1"
bgcolor=#66769e></td>
    <td width="1" height="1"
bgcolor=#6676a0></td>
    <td width="1" height="1"
bgcolor=#6573a0></td>
    <td width="1" height="1"
bgcolor=#6775a0></td>
    <td width="1" height="1"
bgcolor=#67789e></td>
    <td width="1" height="1"
bgcolor=#67759f></td>
    <td width="1" height="1"
bgcolor=#69769f></td>
    <td width="1" height="1"
bgcolor=#66769d></td>
    <td width="1" height="1"
bgcolor=#6877a3></td>
    <td width="1" height="1"
bgcolor=#66779c></td>
    <td width="1" height="1"
bgcolor=#6573a5></td>
    <td width="1" height="1"
bgcolor=#65769a></td>
    <td width="1" height="1"
bgcolor=#6473a0></td>
    <td width="1" height="1"
bgcolor=#64739f></td>
    <td width="1" height="1"
bgcolor=#6675a1></td>
    <td width="1" height="1"
bgcolor=#6472a0></td>
    <td width="1" height="1"
bgcolor=#62739a></td>
    <td width="1" height="1"
bgcolor=#6371a1></td>
    <td width="1" height="1"
bgcolor=#67719b></td>
    <td width="1" height="1"
bgcolor=#637299></td>
    <td width="1" height="1"
bgcolor=#61719e></td>
    <td width="1" height="1"
bgcolor=#607198></td>
    <td width="1" height="1"
bgcolor=#636f9f></td>
    <td width="1" height="1"
bgcolor=#5f7195></td>
    <td width="1" height="1"
bgcolor=#5f6f9b></td>
    <td width="1" height="1"
bgcolor=#606f98></td>
    <td width="1" height="1"
bgcolor=#5f709b></td>
    <td width="1" height="1"
bgcolor=#616d96></td>
    <td width="1" height="1"
bgcolor=#5f6e95></td>
    <td width="1" height="1"
bgcolor=#5e6e99></td>
    <td width="1" height="1"
bgcolor=#5e6c94></td>
    <td width="1" height="1"
bgcolor=#5e6d99></td>
    <td width="1" height="1"
bgcolor=#5b6a97></td>
    <td width="1" height="1"
bgcolor=#596997></td>
    <td width="1" height="1"
bgcolor=#57688d></td>
    <td width="1" height="1"
bgcolor=#556791></td>
    <td width="1" height="1"
bgcolor=#57688f></td>
    <td width="1" height="1"
bgcolor=#556691></td>
    <td width="1" height="1"
bgcolor=#55678f></td>
    <td width="1" height="1"
bgcolor=#51658d></td>
    <td width="1" height="1"
bgcolor=#50648b></td>
    <td width="1" height="1"
bgcolor=#4f648b></td>
  </tr>
  <tr>
    <td width="1" height="1"
bgcolor=#61625f></td>
    <td width="1" height="1"
bgcolor=#676865></td>
    <td width="1" height="1"
bgcolor=#5a5b59></td>
    <td width="1" height="1"
bgcolor=#5d5f5b></td>
    <td width="1" height="1"
bgcolor=#646662></td>
    <td width="1" height="1"
bgcolor=#696a67></td>
    <td width="1" height="1"
bgcolor=#5d5e5b></td>
    <td width="1" height="1"
bgcolor=#5f605d></td>
    <td width="1" height="1"
bgcolor=#60615d></td>
    <td rowspan="1"
colspan="2" width="1"
height="1"
bgcolor=#676965></td>
    <td width="1" height="1"
bgcolor=#5f615d></td>
    <td width="1" height="1"
bgcolor=#626460></td>
    <td width="1" height="1"
bgcolor=#61635f></td>
    <td width="1" height="1"
bgcolor=#666864></td>
    <td width="1" height="1"
bgcolor=#676965></td>
    <td width="1" height="1"
bgcolor=#5c5d5a></td>
    <td width="1" height="1"
bgcolor=#61625e></td>
    <td width="1" height="1"
bgcolor=#5e605c></td>
    <td width="1" height="1"
bgcolor=#62625f></td>
    <td width="1" height="1"
bgcolor=#5c5d5a></td>
    <td width="1" height="1"
bgcolor=#60615e></td>
    <td width="1" height="1"
bgcolor=#595b57></td>
    <td width="1" height="1"
bgcolor=#585a56></td>
    <td width="1" height="1"
bgcolor=#5c5d59></td>
    <td width="1" height="1"
bgcolor=#585956></td>
    <td width="1" height="1"
bgcolor=#575955></td>
    <td width="1" height="1"
bgcolor=#5f615d></td>
    <td width="1" height="1"
bgcolor=#5b5c59></td>
    <td width="1" height="1"
bgcolor=#61635f></td>
    <td width="1" height="1"
bgcolor=#595b58></td>
    <td width="1" height="1"
bgcolor=#575955></td>
    <td width="1" height="1"
bgcolor=#5f605c></td>
    <td width="1" height="1"
bgcolor=#616360></td>
```

```
    <td width="1" height="1"
bgcolor=#555653></td>
    <td width="1" height="1"
bgcolor=#585956></td>
    <td width="1" height="1"
bgcolor=#5e605c></td>
    <td width="1" height="1"
bgcolor=#646662></td>
    <td width="1" height="1"
bgcolor=#585a57></td>
    <td width="1" height="1"
bgcolor=#595b57></td>
    <td width="1" height="1"
bgcolor=#5b5c59></td>
    <td width="1" height="1"
bgcolor=#5f605d></td>
    <td width="1" height="1"
bgcolor=#626460></td>
    <td width="1" height="1"
bgcolor=#565854></td>
    <td width="1" height="1"
bgcolor=#5d5e5a></td>
    <td width="1" height="1"
bgcolor=#5c5d5a></td>
    <td width="1" height="1"
bgcolor=#60625d></td>
    <td width="1" height="1"
bgcolor=#61625f></td>
    <td width="1" height="1"
bgcolor=#575854></td>
    <td width="1" height="1"
bgcolor=#595b57></td>
    <td width="1" height="1"
bgcolor=#575855></td>
    <td width="1" height="1"
bgcolor=#5c5d5a></td>
    <td width="1" height="1"
bgcolor=#555653></td>
    <td width="1" height="1"
bgcolor=#5b5d59></td>
    <td width="1" height="1"
bgcolor=#555652></td>
    <td width="1" height="1"
bgcolor=#51524f></td>
    <td width="1" height="1"
bgcolor=#575956></td>
    <td width="1" height="1"
bgcolor=#525450></td>
    <td width="1" height="1"
bgcolor=#50514e></td>
    <td width="1" height="1"
bgcolor=#575955></td>
    <td width="1" height="1"
bgcolor=#515350></td>
    <td width="1" height="1"
bgcolor=#595b57></td>
    <td width="1" height="1"
bgcolor=#545552></td>
    <td width="1" height="1"
bgcolor=#4f504d></td>
    <td width="1" height="1"
bgcolor=#565755></td>
    <td width="1" height="1"
bgcolor=#595b57></td>
    <td width="1" height="1"
bgcolor=#4e4f4c></td>
    <td width="1" height="1"
bgcolor=#515350></td>
    <td width="1" height="1"
bgcolor=#555653></td>
    <td width="1" height="1"
bgcolor=#5d5d5a></td>
    <td width="1" height="1"
bgcolor=#50514e></td>
    <td width="1" height="1"
bgcolor=#515353></td>
  </tr>
</table></body></html>
```

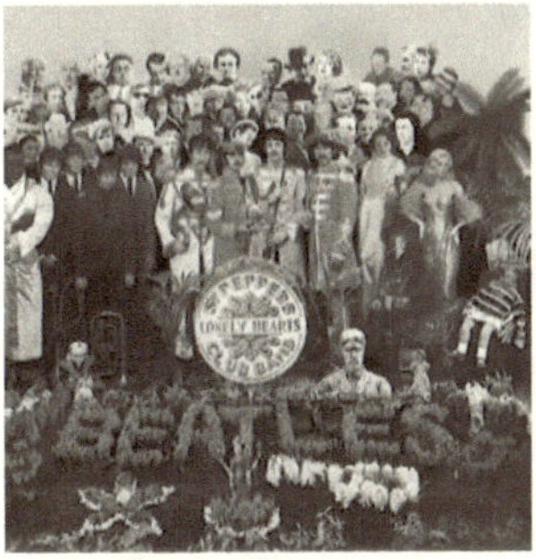


Sgt. Pepper's

```
<html>
<head><title>Sgt. Pepper's, written by Broose G. Dickinson</title></head>
<body>
<table border=0 cellpadding=0 cellspacing=0>
  <tr>
    <td width="1" height="1" bgcolor=#707271></td>
    <td width="1" height="1" bgcolor=#6f7170></td>
    <td width="1" height="1" bgcolor=#727473></td>
    <td width="1" height="1" bgcolor=#6f7170></td>
    <td width="1" height="1" bgcolor=#6e706f></td>
    <td width="1" height="1" bgcolor=#6c6e6d></td>
    <td width="1" height="1" bgcolor=#717372></td>
    <td width="1" height="1" bgcolor=#747676></td>
    <td width="1" height="1" bgcolor=#6d706f></td>
    <td width="1" height="1" bgcolor=#6f7170></td>
    <td width="1" height="1" bgcolor=#686a69></td>
    <td width="1" height="1" bgcolor=#717372></td>
    <td width="1" height="1" bgcolor=#6c6f6d></td>
    <td width="1" height="1" bgcolor=#6c6e6d></td>
    <td width="1" height="1" bgcolor=#696b6a></td>
    <td width="1" height="1" bgcolor=#6b6d6c></td>
    <td width="1" height="1" bgcolor=#6f7170></td>
    <td rowspan="1" colspan="2" width="1" height="1" bgcolor=#696b6a></td>
    <td width="1" height="1" bgcolor=#686a69></td>
    <td width="1" height="1" bgcolor=#6e706f></td>
    <td width="1" height="1" bgcolor=#6c6e6d></td>
    <td width="1" height="1" bgcolor=#6e7070></td>
    <td width="1" height="1" bgcolor=#6c6e6d></td>
    <td width="1" height="1" bgcolor=#6a6c6b></td>
    <td width="1" height="1" bgcolor=#6f7271></td>
    <td width="1" height="1" bgcolor=#747776></td>
    <td rowspan="1" colspan="2" width="1" height="1" bgcolor=#676968></td>
    <td width="1" height="1" bgcolor=#6f7170></td>
    <td width="1" height="1" bgcolor=#6b6d6c></td>
    <td width="1" height="1" bgcolor=#717473></td>
    <td width="1" height="1" bgcolor=#6c6e6e></td>
    <td width="1" height="1" bgcolor=#6f7170></td>
    <td width="1" height="1" bgcolor=#6d706f></td>
    <td width="1" height="1" bgcolor=#6e706f></td>
    <td width="1" height="1" bgcolor=#666867></td>
    <td width="1" height="1" bgcolor=#636664></td>
    <td width="1" height="1" bgcolor=#6b6d6c></td>
    <td width="1" height="1" bgcolor=#737574></td>
    <td width="1" height="1" bgcolor=#686a69></td>
    <td width="1" height="1" bgcolor=#656766></td>
    <td width="1" height="1" bgcolor=#646665></td>
    <td width="1" height="1" bgcolor=#6b6e6d></td>
    <td width="1" height="1" bgcolor=#626463></td>
    <td width="1" height="1" bgcolor=#646665></td>
    <td width="1" height="1" bgcolor=#626463></td>
    <td width="1" height="1" bgcolor=#676968></td>
    <td width="1" height="1" bgcolor=#646665></td>
    <td width="1" height="1" bgcolor=#606362></td>
    <td width="1" height="1" bgcolor=#5f6260></td>
    <td width="1" height="1" bgcolor=#616362></td>
    <td width="1" height="1" bgcolor=#626564></td>
    <td width="1" height="1" bgcolor=#656766></td>
    <td width="1" height="1" bgcolor=#646665></td>
    <td width="1" height="1" bgcolor=#636564></td>
    <td width="1" height="1" bgcolor=#626463></td>
    <td width="1" height="1" bgcolor=#6a6c6b></td>
    <td width="1" height="1" bgcolor=#6b6d6c></td>
    <td width="1" height="1" bgcolor=#5b5d5c></td>
    <td width="1" height="1" bgcolor=#626563></td>
    <td width="1" height="1" bgcolor=#646665></td>
    <td width="1" height="1" bgcolor=#606261></td>
    <td width="1" height="1" bgcolor=#626563></td>
    <td width="1" height="1" bgcolor=#696b6a></td>
    <td width="1" height="1" bgcolor=#666867></td>
    <td width="1" height="1" bgcolor=#616362></td>
    <td width="1" height="1" bgcolor=#656766></td>
    <td width="1" height="1" bgcolor=#5c5e5d></td>
    <td width="1" height="1" bgcolor=#5d5f5f></td>
    <td width="1" height="1" bgcolor=#626463></td>
    <td width="1" height="1" bgcolor=#646665></td>
  </tr>
  <tr>
    <td width="1" height="1" bgcolor=#7aa3a8></td>
    <td width="1" height="1" bgcolor=#80a8ae></td>
    <td width="1" height="1" bgcolor=#7ea8ae></td>
```

```
    <td width="1" height="1" bgcolor=#7da5ac></td>
    <td width="1" height="1" bgcolor=#7ba5ae></td>
    <td rowspan="1" colspan="2" width="1" height="1" bgcolor=#77a2ad></td>
    <td width="1" height="1" bgcolor=#77a1aa></td>
    <td width="1" height="1" bgcolor=#78a3ac></td>
    <td width="1" height="1" bgcolor=#7ba5ad></td>
    <td width="1" height="1" bgcolor=#79a4ab></td>
    <td width="1" height="1" bgcolor=#7da9b1></td>
    <td width="1" height="1" bgcolor=#78a3ab></td>
    <td width="1" height="1" bgcolor=#7aa6af></td>
    <td width="1" height="1" bgcolor=#7ba6b0></td>
    <td width="1" height="1" bgcolor=#7ea8b0></td>
    <td width="1" height="1" bgcolor=#7fa9b1></td>
    <td width="1" height="1" bgcolor=#7da8b1></td>
    <td width="1" height="1" bgcolor=#7ca7b0></td>
    <td width="1" height="1" bgcolor=#7ba7b2></td>
    <td width="1" height="1" bgcolor=#79a6af></td>
    <td width="1" height="1" bgcolor=#78a4ae></td>
    <td width="1" height="1" bgcolor=#7ba5b0></td>
    <td width="1" height="1" bgcolor=#789fa9></td>
    <td width="1" height="1" bgcolor=#7fa4ab></td>
    <td width="1" height="1" bgcolor=#81a6ae></td>
    <td width="1" height="1" bgcolor=#81a9b2></td>
    <td width="1" height="1" bgcolor=#7aa1ab></td>
    <td width="1" height="1" bgcolor=#7ca4ad></td>
    <td width="1" height="1" bgcolor=#7ca6af></td>
    <td width="1" height="1" bgcolor=#7ba2ad></td>
    <td width="1" height="1" bgcolor=#6f9aa5></td>
    <td width="1" height="1" bgcolor=#769eaa></td>
    <td width="1" height="1" bgcolor=#79a7b0></td>
    <td width="1" height="1" bgcolor=#73a1ab></td>
    <td width="1" height="1" bgcolor=#77a3ab></td>
    <td width="1" height="1" bgcolor=#77a0aa></td>
    <td width="1" height="1" bgcolor=#78a1ac></td>
    <td width="1" height="1" bgcolor=#7aa3ae></td>
    <td width="1" height="1" bgcolor=#7ca4ae></td>
    <td width="1" height="1" bgcolor=#7ba2ac></td>
    <td width="1" height="1" bgcolor=#779fa9></td>
    <td width="1" height="1" bgcolor=#769fab></td>
    <td width="1" height="1" bgcolor=#75a1ad></td>
    <td width="1" height="1" bgcolor=#719da9></td>
    <td width="1" height="1" bgcolor=#75a0ac></td>
    <td width="1" height="1" bgcolor=#74a0ac></td>
    <td width="1" height="1" bgcolor=#75a0ac></td>
    <td width="1" height="1" bgcolor=#75a1ad></td>
    <td width="1" height="1" bgcolor=#75a0ac></td>
    <td width="1" height="1" bgcolor=#719da9></td>
    <td width="1" height="1" bgcolor=#759fab></td>
    <td width="1" height="1" bgcolor=#76a2ad></td>
    <td width="1" height="1" bgcolor=#74a0aa></td>
    <td width="1" height="1" bgcolor=#78a1ad></td>
    <td width="1" height="1" bgcolor=#6f99a1></td>
    <td width="1" height="1" bgcolor=#759da5></td>
    <td rowspan="1" colspan="2" width="1" height="1" bgcolor=#789fa8></td>
    <td width="1" height="1" bgcolor=#7699a2></td>
    <td width="1" height="1" bgcolor=#7a9da6></td>
    <td width="1" height="1" bgcolor=#7b9ea6></td>
    <td width="1" height="1" bgcolor=#799ca3></td>
    <td width="1" height="1" bgcolor=#72959c></td>
    <td width="1" height="1" bgcolor=#7799a1></td>
    <td width="1" height="1" bgcolor=#7b9ba3></td>
    <td width="1" height="1" bgcolor=#7a9aa1></td>
    <td width="1" height="1" bgcolor=#7b99a0></td>
    <td width="1" height="1" bgcolor=#79989e></td>
    <td width="1" height="1" bgcolor=#79999f></td>
    <td width="1" height="1" bgcolor=#78969d></td>
    <td width="1" height="1" bgcolor=#7a959b></td>
  </tr>
  <tr>
    <td width="1" height="1" bgcolor=#87d6e3></td>
    <td width="1" height="1" bgcolor=#8bd9e6></td>
    <td width="1" height="1" bgcolor=#8fdeec></td>
    <td width="1" height="1" bgcolor=#91dfee></td>
    <td width="1" height="1" bgcolor=#8bdbed></td>
    <td width="1" height="1" bgcolor=#85daef></td>
    <td width="1" height="1" bgcolor=#83daed></td>
    <td width="1" height="1" bgcolor=#87def1></td>
    <td width="1" height="1" bgcolor=#88dcef></td>
    <td width="1" height="1" bgcolor=#89daec></td>
    <td width="1" height="1" bgcolor=#85d9ec></td>
    <td width="1" height="1" bgcolor=#87dbeb></td>
    <td width="1" height="1" bgcolor=#88dced></td>
    <td width="1" height="1" bgcolor=#8ddff1></td>
    <td width="1" height="1" bgcolor=#8fdef1></td>
    <td width="1" height="1" bgcolor=#8eddf3></td>
    <td width="1" height="1" bgcolor=#8eddf2></td>
```

```
<td width="1" height="1" bgcolor=#90dff3></td>
<td width="1" height="1" bgcolor=#8cddf2></td>
<td width="1" height="1" bgcolor=#86d9ee></td>
<td width="1" height="1" bgcolor=#86d9f0></td>
<td width="1" height="1" bgcolor=#8bdcf2></td>
<td width="1" height="1" bgcolor=#8edbf5></td>
<td width="1" height="1" bgcolor=#91dff0></td>
<td width="1" height="1" bgcolor=#9ce2f2></td>
<td width="1" height="1" bgcolor=#97e0f4></td>
<td width="1" height="1" bgcolor=#93e0f4></td>
<td width="1" height="1" bgcolor=#95e0f3></td>
<td width="1" height="1" bgcolor=#93e0f4></td>
<td width="1" height="1" bgcolor=#8eddf0></td>
<td width="1" height="1" bgcolor=#8eddf2></td>
<td width="1" height="1" bgcolor=#88dbf0></td>
<td width="1" height="1" bgcolor=#89dbef></td>
<td width="1" height="1" bgcolor=#83d9ef></td>
<td width="1" height="1" bgcolor=#87d7eb></td>
<td width="1" height="1" bgcolor=#83ddef></td>
<td width="1" height="1" bgcolor=#87daf0></td>
<td width="1" height="1" bgcolor=#8cddf2></td>
<td width="1" height="1" bgcolor=#89def2></td>
<td width="1" height="1" bgcolor=#8edbf2></td>
<td width="1" height="1" bgcolor=#91dcf4></td>
<td width="1" height="1" bgcolor=#86d8ee></td>
<td width="1" height="1" bgcolor=#7cd6ee></td>
<td width="1" height="1" bgcolor=#7dd6f0></td>
<td width="1" height="1" bgcolor=#74cfe8></td>
<td width="1" height="1" bgcolor=#7bd7f0></td>
<td width="1" height="1" bgcolor=#7bd6ef></td>
<td width="1" height="1" bgcolor=#81d7f1></td>
<td width="1" height="1" bgcolor=#85daf5></td>
<td width="1" height="1" bgcolor=#7cd6f0></td>
<td width="1" height="1" bgcolor=#82daf5></td>
<td width="1" height="1" bgcolor=#80d8ef></td>
<td width="1" height="1" bgcolor=#85daf2></td>
<td width="1" height="1" bgcolor=#81d9ef></td>
<td width="1" height="1" bgcolor=#8bdbf0></td>
<td width="1" height="1" bgcolor=#8edbf5></td>
<td width="1" height="1" bgcolor=#91dcf3></td>
<td width="1" height="1" bgcolor=#95ddf6></td>
<td width="1" height="1" bgcolor=#93def3></td>
<td width="1" height="1" bgcolor=#98e2f7></td>
<td width="1" height="1" bgcolor=#94def1></td>
<td width="1" height="1" bgcolor=#98e1f4></td>
<td width="1" height="1" bgcolor=#9ae3f4></td>
<td width="1" height="1" bgcolor=#9be0f5></td>
<td width="1" height="1" bgcolor=#9fe3f5></td>
<td width="1" height="1" bgcolor=#a5e6f9></td>
<td width="1" height="1" bgcolor=#a7e6f8></td>
<td width="1" height="1" bgcolor=#a4e3f6></td>
<td width="1" height="1" bgcolor=#a3e2f4></td>
<td width="1" height="1" bgcolor=#a0e3f5></td>
<td width="1" height="1" bgcolor=#9de2f1></td>
<td width="1" height="1" bgcolor=#a7e7f5></td>
</tr>
<tr>
<td width="1" height="1" bgcolor=#8cdbe6></td>
<td width="1" height="1" bgcolor=#8fdeec></td>
<td width="1" height="1" bgcolor=#90dfee></td>
<td width="1" height="1" bgcolor=#8fdeec></td>
<td width="1" height="1" bgcolor=#8fdfec></td>
<td width="1" height="1" bgcolor=#8edded></td>
<td width="1" height="1" bgcolor=#8addf1></td>
<td width="1" height="1" bgcolor=#87daef></td>
<td width="1" height="1" bgcolor=#85dbef></td>
<td width="1" height="1" bgcolor=#8addf2></td>
<td width="1" height="1" bgcolor=#8adbef></td>
<td width="1" height="1" bgcolor=#8cdff4></td>
<td width="1" height="1" bgcolor=#8adff0></td>
<td width="1" height="1" bgcolor=#8fdcf2></td>
<td width="1" height="1" bgcolor=#92e1f5></td>
<td width="1" height="1" bgcolor=#99e3f6></td>
<td width="1" height="1" bgcolor=#98e4f6></td>
<td width="1" height="1" bgcolor=#96e3f6></td>
<td width="1" height="1" bgcolor=#96e4f7></td>
<td width="1" height="1" bgcolor=#8adef2></td>
<td width="1" height="1" bgcolor=#8ddef2></td>
<td width="1" height="1" bgcolor=#91dff4></td>
<td width="1" height="1" bgcolor=#8fdbf3></td>
<td width="1" height="1" bgcolor=#96e3f5></td>
<td width="1" height="1" bgcolor=#a0e4f5></td>
<td width="1" height="1" bgcolor=#9be3f4></td>
<td width="1" height="1" bgcolor=#94e0f4></td>
<td width="1" height="1" bgcolor=#95e2f6></td>
<td width="1" height="1" bgcolor=#97e1f7></td>
<td width="1" height="1" bgcolor=#96e0f2></td>
<td width="1" height="1" bgcolor=#99e1f7></td>
```

```
    <td width="1" height="1"
bgcolor=#92e0f5></td>
    <td width="1" height="1"
bgcolor=#8edef5></td>
    <td width="1" height="1"
bgcolor=#8dddf3></td>
    <td width="1" height="1"
bgcolor=#93e0f8></td>
    <td width="1" height="1"
bgcolor=#8edef3></td>
    <td width="1" height="1"
bgcolor=#87def0></td>
    <td width="1" height="1"
bgcolor=#93e0f5></td>
    <td width="1" height="1"
bgcolor=#8fddf5></td>
    <td width="1" height="1"
bgcolor=#8eddf3></td>
    <td width="1" height="1"
bgcolor=#88daf0></td>
    <td width="1" height="1"
bgcolor=#84dbf5></td>
    <td width="1" height="1"
bgcolor=#7dd5ef></td>
    <td width="1" height="1"
bgcolor=#79d8f2></td>
    <td width="1" height="1"
bgcolor=#70d3ec></td>
    <td width="1" height="1"
bgcolor=#74d8f1></td>
    <td width="1" height="1"
bgcolor=#7cd9f4></td>
    <td width="1" height="1"
bgcolor=#7ad7f1></td>
    <td width="1" height="1"
bgcolor=#7ddbf5></td>
    <td width="1" height="1"
bgcolor=#7bd9f3></td>
    <td width="1" height="1"
bgcolor=#81dbf5></td>
    <td width="1" height="1"
bgcolor=#87dbf5></td>
    <td width="1" height="1"
bgcolor=#84d9f2></td>
    <td width="1" height="1"
bgcolor=#83ddf6></td>
    <td width="1" height="1"
bgcolor=#89dcf3></td>
    <td width="1" height="1"
bgcolor=#93def8></td>
    <td width="1" height="1"
bgcolor=#93e0f7></td>
    <td width="1" height="1"
bgcolor=#9ae0f7></td>
    <td width="1" height="1"
bgcolor=#99e2f9></td>
    <td width="1" height="1"
bgcolor=#9ae0f7></td>
    <td width="1" height="1"
bgcolor=#9fe3f7></td>
    <td width="1" height="1"
bgcolor=#9ae2f6></td>
    <td width="1" height="1"
bgcolor=#9de5f8></td>
    <td width="1" height="1"
bgcolor=#a1e5f7></td>
    <td width="1" height="1"
bgcolor=#a1e3f5></td>
    <td width="1" height="1"
bgcolor=#a6e7fa></td>
    <td width="1" height="1"
bgcolor=#a9e7fa></td>
    <td width="1" height="1"
bgcolor=#a5e6f8></td>
    <td width="1" height="1"
bgcolor=#a4e4f8></td>
    <td width="1" height="1"
bgcolor=#a5e6f9></td>
    <td width="1" height="1"
bgcolor=#a3e4f5></td>
    <td width="1" height="1"
bgcolor=#ace6f7></td>
  </tr>
  <tr>
    <td width="1" height="1"
bgcolor=#8cdae9></td>
    <td width="1" height="1"
bgcolor=#8eddea></td>
    <td width="1" height="1"
bgcolor=#91e0ee></td>
    <td width="1" height="1"
bgcolor=#94e0f4></td>
    <td width="1" height="1"
bgcolor=#97def1></td>
    <td width="1" height="1"
bgcolor=#99e1f2></td>
    <td width="1" height="1"
bgcolor=#93def2></td>
    <td width="1" height="1"
bgcolor=#8fdef1></td>
    <td width="1" height="1"
bgcolor=#87e1f5></td>
    <td width="1" height="1"
bgcolor=#90def2></td>
    <td width="1" height="1"
bgcolor=#8edbee></td>
    <td width="1" height="1"
bgcolor=#8ee1f3></td>
    <td width="1" height="1"
bgcolor=#91dff5></td>
    <td width="1" height="1"
bgcolor=#8de1f5></td>
    <td width="1" height="1"
bgcolor=#98e0f0></td>
    <td width="1" height="1"
bgcolor=#97e4f7></td>
    <td width="1" height="1"
bgcolor=#97e1f3></td>
    <td width="1" height="1"
bgcolor=#95def1></td>
    <td width="1" height="1"
bgcolor=#91e1f4></td>
    <td width="1" height="1"
bgcolor=#8adef4></td>
    <td width="1" height="1"
bgcolor=#8dddf1></td>
    <td width="1" height="1"
bgcolor=#90dbf7></td>
    <td width="1" height="1"
bgcolor=#8ee0e9></td>
    <td width="1" height="1"
bgcolor=#9bdcf8></td>
    <td width="1" height="1"
bgcolor=#96e6f0></td>
    <td width="1" height="1"
bgcolor=#9ee1f7></td>
    <td width="1" height="1"
bgcolor=#95e4f5></td>
    <td width="1" height="1"
bgcolor=#99e2f2></td>
    <td width="1" height="1"
bgcolor=#9de5f3></td>
    <td width="1" height="1"
bgcolor=#9be2f7></td>
    <td width="1" height="1"
bgcolor=#99e3f3></td>
    <td width="1" height="1"
bgcolor=#98e3f7></td>
    <td width="1" height="1"
bgcolor=#93e2f5></td>
    <td width="1" height="1"
bgcolor=#8ddff7></td>
    <td width="1" height="1"
bgcolor=#94dbf4></td>
    <td width="1" height="1"
bgcolor=#8fdff3></td>
    <td width="1" height="1"
bgcolor=#87ddf2></td>
    <td width="1" height="1"
bgcolor=#92e0fa></td>
    <td width="1" height="1"
bgcolor=#8de1f2></td>
    <td width="1" height="1"
bgcolor=#89dff4></td>
    <td width="1" height="1"
bgcolor=#8fd8f5></td>
    <td width="1" height="1"
bgcolor=#80d6f2></td>
    <td width="1" height="1"
bgcolor=#72ddf3></td>
    <td width="1" height="1"
bgcolor=#78d6f5></td>
    <td width="1" height="1"
bgcolor=#74d1f0></td>
```

```
    <td width="1" height="1"
bgcolor=#70d2f1></td>
    <td width="1" height="1"
bgcolor=#73d4f3></td>
    <td width="1" height="1"
bgcolor=#75d5f3></td>
    <td width="1" height="1"
bgcolor=#74d6f2></td>
    <td width="1" height="1"
bgcolor=#72d6f4></td>
    <td width="1" height="1"
bgcolor=#76d4f3></td>
    <td width="1" height="1"
bgcolor=#80d6f4></td>
    <td width="1" height="1"
bgcolor=#78d8f3></td>
    <td width="1" height="1"
bgcolor=#82d9f0></td>
    <td width="1" height="1"
bgcolor=#8ddefa></td>
    <td width="1" height="1"
bgcolor=#95e0f5></td>
    <td width="1" height="1"
bgcolor=#9cdff6></td>
    <td width="1" height="1"
bgcolor=#98e2f2></td>
    <td width="1" height="1"
bgcolor=#97e4f5></td>
    <td width="1" height="1"
bgcolor=#9be1fc></td>
    <td width="1" height="1"
bgcolor=#9de3f3></td>
    <td width="1" height="1"
bgcolor=#a0e5f4></td>
    <td width="1" height="1"
bgcolor=#a0e5f5></td>
    <td width="1" height="1"
bgcolor=#a0e4f7></td>
    <td width="1" height="1"
bgcolor=#a3e4f5></td>
    <td width="1" height="1"
bgcolor=#a9e6f8></td>
    <td width="1" height="1"
bgcolor=#abe7f9></td>
    <td width="1" height="1"
bgcolor=#aae8f9></td>
    <td width="1" height="1"
bgcolor=#a2e2f3></td>
    <td width="1" height="1"
bgcolor=#a4e6f7></td>
    <td width="1" height="1"
bgcolor=#a2e3f4></td>
    <td width="1" height="1"
bgcolor=#aceaf8></td>
  </tr>
  <tr>
    <td width="1" height="1"
bgcolor=#8cdbe6></td>
    <td width="1" height="1"
bgcolor=#8bddee></td>
    <td width="1" height="1"
bgcolor=#8edcef></td>
    <td width="1" height="1"
bgcolor=#8fddef></td>
    <td width="1" height="1"
bgcolor=#8cdef3></td>
    <td width="1" height="1"
bgcolor=#8dddef></td>
    <td width="1" height="1"
bgcolor=#8bdeed></td>
    <td width="1" height="1"
bgcolor=#8bdbf2></td>
    <td width="1" height="1"
bgcolor=#87dbef></td>
    <td width="1" height="1"
bgcolor=#8bdef5></td>
    <td width="1" height="1"
bgcolor=#87e0f3></td>
    <td width="1" height="1"
bgcolor=#94e0ee></td>
    <td width="1" height="1"
bgcolor=#91dff2></td>
    <td width="1" height="1"
bgcolor=#94e2f6></td>
    <td width="1" height="1"
bgcolor=#89dff4></td>
    <td width="1" height="1"
bgcolor=#98e1f4></td>
    <td width="1" height="1"
bgcolor=#94dff5></td>
    <td width="1" height="1"
bgcolor=#8de1f6></td>
    <td width="1" height="1"
bgcolor=#91def1></td>
    <td width="1" height="1"
bgcolor=#8adcf1></td>
    <td width="1" height="1"
bgcolor=#87deef></td>
    <td width="1" height="1"
bgcolor=#8edbf1></td>
    <td width="1" height="1"
bgcolor=#88dffc></td>
    <td width="1" height="1"
bgcolor=#93e5f5></td>
    <td width="1" height="1"
bgcolor=#96ddfb></td>
    <td width="1" height="1"
bgcolor=#a1e6f2></td>
    <td width="1" height="1"
bgcolor=#a1e3ef></td>
    <td width="1" height="1"
bgcolor=#95e2f8></td>
    <td width="1" height="1"
bgcolor=#9ce4f7></td>
    <td width="1" height="1"
bgcolor=#99e9f7></td>
    <td width="1" height="1"
bgcolor=#9be7fb></td>
    <td width="1" height="1"
bgcolor=#9eeafe></td>
    <td width="1" height="1"
bgcolor=#95ddfa></td>
    <td width="1" height="1"
bgcolor=#8bdcea></td>
    <td width="1" height="1"
bgcolor=#81dff7></td>
    <td width="1" height="1"
bgcolor=#8adef3></td>
    <td width="1" height="1"
bgcolor=#85def1></td>
    <td width="1" height="1"
bgcolor=#89d9f4></td>
    <td width="1" height="1"
bgcolor=#89def7></td>
    <td width="1" height="1"
bgcolor=#86ddf6></td>
    <td width="1" height="1"
bgcolor=#7be1fe></td>
    <td width="1" height="1"
bgcolor=#89d7e6></td>
    <td width="1" height="1"
bgcolor=#79d9f5></td>
    <td width="1" height="1"
bgcolor=#70d5ef></td>
    <td width="1" height="1"
bgcolor=#69d5f2></td>
    <td width="1" height="1"
bgcolor=#6bd7f8></td>
    <td width="1" height="1"
bgcolor=#6cd6f0></td>
    <td width="1" height="1"
bgcolor=#68d4f2></td>
    <td width="1" height="1"
bgcolor=#68d3f3></td>
    <td width="1" height="1"
bgcolor=#65d4f0></td>
    <td width="1" height="1"
bgcolor=#6ad2ed></td>
    <td width="1" height="1"
bgcolor=#6ed8f5></td>
    <td width="1" height="1"
bgcolor=#7cdbf9></td>
    <td width="1" height="1"
bgcolor=#7cdff9></td>
    <td width="1" height="1"
bgcolor=#94def4></td>
    <td width="1" height="1"
bgcolor=#90e2f8></td>
    <td width="1" height="1"
bgcolor=#9fe1ee></td>
    <td width="1" height="1"
bgcolor=#abe0f5></td>
    <td width="1" height="1"
bgcolor=#c0e1de></td>
```

```
    <td width="1" height="1"
bgcolor=#aed8d3></td>
    <td width="1" height="1"
bgcolor=#99e5f6></td>
    <td width="1" height="1"
bgcolor=#9fe3f8></td>
    <td width="1" height="1"
bgcolor=#9fe5f6></td>
    <td width="1" height="1"
bgcolor=#a2e7f9></td>
    <td width="1" height="1"
bgcolor=#a6e9fa></td>
    <td width="1" height="1"
bgcolor=#a7e5f8></td>
    <td width="1" height="1"
bgcolor=#aaeafc></td>
    <td width="1" height="1"
bgcolor=#abebfd></td>
    <td width="1" height="1"
bgcolor=#a6e9f9></td>
    <td width="1" height="1"
bgcolor=#a3e5f7></td>
    <td width="1" height="1"
bgcolor=#aaeafc></td>
    <td width="1" height="1"
bgcolor=#aee9fb></td>
  </tr>
  <tr>
    <td width="1" height="1"
bgcolor=#8ad8eb></td>
    <td width="1" height="1"
bgcolor=#91dce3></td>
    <td width="1" height="1"
bgcolor=#b4dcd0></td>
    <td width="1" height="1"
bgcolor=#b3dddf></td>
    <td width="1" height="1"
bgcolor=#8fd9ef></td>
    <td width="1" height="1"
bgcolor=#87dcf1></td>
    <td width="1" height="1"
bgcolor=#86dbed></td>
    <td width="1" height="1"
bgcolor=#b5d9d1></td>
    <td width="1" height="1"
bgcolor=#abdcdb></td>
    <td width="1" height="1"
bgcolor=#81dfec></td>
    <td width="1" height="1"
bgcolor=#91deee></td>
    <td width="1" height="1"
bgcolor=#99cbcd></td>
    <td width="1" height="1"
bgcolor=#e0e6c5></td>
    <td width="1" height="1"
bgcolor=#8d9986></td>
    <td width="1" height="1"
bgcolor=#98d7e5></td>
    <td width="1" height="1"
bgcolor=#68a9bb></td>
    <td width="1" height="1"
bgcolor=#81cde2></td>
    <td width="1" height="1"
bgcolor=#8fdcf4></td>
    <td width="1" height="1"
bgcolor=#84dcf4></td>
    <td width="1" height="1"
bgcolor=#8acee1></td>
    <td width="1" height="1"
bgcolor=#67929c></td>
    <td width="1" height="1"
bgcolor=#78bdc2></td>
    <td width="1" height="1"
bgcolor=#dee16b></td>
    <td width="1" height="1"
bgcolor=#e5d05a></td>
    <td width="1" height="1"
bgcolor=#cbe396></td>
    <td width="1" height="1"
bgcolor=#ace8ed></td>
    <td width="1" height="1"
bgcolor=#aae4ef></td>
    <td width="1" height="1"
bgcolor=#bae4e8></td>
    <td width="1" height="1"
bgcolor=#94e3f6></td>
    <td width="1" height="1"
bgcolor=#658483></td>
    <td width="1" height="1"
bgcolor=#746f5e></td>
    <td width="1" height="1"
bgcolor=#677b78></td>
    <td width="1" height="1"
bgcolor=#8fdcee></td>
    <td width="1" height="1"
bgcolor=#87def6></td>
    <td width="1" height="1"
bgcolor=#88dbf8></td>
    <td width="1" height="1"
bgcolor=#7fd8f0></td>
    <td width="1" height="1"
bgcolor=#82dbf6></td>
    <td width="1" height="1"
bgcolor=#88dff6></td>
    <td width="1" height="1"
bgcolor=#82dffb></td>
    <td width="1" height="1"
bgcolor=#779d9d></td>
    <td width="1" height="1"
bgcolor=#3e5659></td>
    <td width="1" height="1"
bgcolor=#863d35></td>
    <td width="1" height="1"
bgcolor=#83ddf1></td>
    <td width="1" height="1"
bgcolor=#80d7e8></td>
    <td width="1" height="1"
bgcolor=#a0c19f></td>
    <td width="1" height="1"
bgcolor=#99c1aa></td>
    <td width="1" height="1"
bgcolor=#77d4eb></td>
    <td width="1" height="1"
bgcolor=#69d2ef></td>
    <td width="1" height="1"
bgcolor=#6bd3f5></td>
    <td width="1" height="1"
bgcolor=#6dd4f7></td>
    <td width="1" height="1"
bgcolor=#67d8f9></td>
    <td width="1" height="1"
bgcolor=#71a1aa></td>
    <td width="1" height="1"
bgcolor=#725e6e></td>
    <td width="1" height="1"
bgcolor=#87b4d3></td>
    <td width="1" height="1"
bgcolor=#85defa></td>
    <td width="1" height="1"
bgcolor=#8ccdd0></td>
    <td width="1" height="1"
bgcolor=#dfdebc></td>
    <td width="1" height="1"
bgcolor=#c7ba94></td>
    <td width="1" height="1"
bgcolor=#7f816b></td>
    <td width="1" height="1"
bgcolor=#958976></td>
    <td width="1" height="1"
bgcolor=#a6d0d3></td>
    <td width="1" height="1"
bgcolor=#a0e5f7></td>
    <td width="1" height="1"
bgcolor=#a1e5f9></td>
    <td width="1" height="1"
bgcolor=#a3e6f9></td>
    <td width="1" height="1"
bgcolor=#9fe5f7></td>
    <td width="1" height="1"
bgcolor=#a2e5f9></td>
    <td width="1" height="1"
bgcolor=#aae8f3></td>
    <td width="1" height="1"
bgcolor=#abeafc></td>
    <td width="1" height="1"
bgcolor=#a8e9fb></td>
    <td width="1" height="1"
bgcolor=#a4e5f6></td>
    <td width="1" height="1"
bgcolor=#a8e8f9></td>
    <td width="1" height="1"
bgcolor=#adeafc></td>
  </tr>
  <tr>
```

```
<td width="1" height="1" bgcolor=#83daec></td>
<td width="1" height="1" bgcolor=#a1bd9f></td>
<td width="1" height="1" bgcolor=#837253></td>
<td width="1" height="1" bgcolor=#c1b189></td>
<td width="1" height="1" bgcolor=#c3d6ca></td>
<td width="1" height="1" bgcolor=#7bd9f9></td>
<td width="1" height="1" bgcolor=#a5d4c0></td>
<td width="1" height="1" bgcolor=#e3b981></td>
<td width="1" height="1" bgcolor=#e1be87></td>
<td width="1" height="1" bgcolor=#8dd8ef></td>
<td width="1" height="1" bgcolor=#90d7d5></td>
<td width="1" height="1" bgcolor=#dcce8e></td>
<td width="1" height="1" bgcolor=#efe0ad></td>
<td width="1" height="1" bgcolor=#c2b587></td>
<td width="1" height="1" bgcolor=#4c4b3f></td>
<td width="1" height="1" bgcolor=#cea479></td>
<td width="1" height="1" bgcolor=#a6957f></td>
<td width="1" height="1" bgcolor=#7ad4e9></td>
<td width="1" height="1" bgcolor=#74dcf1></td>
<td width="1" height="1" bgcolor=#525249></td>
<td width="1" height="1" bgcolor=#5e3c34></td>
<td width="1" height="1" bgcolor=#71692e></td>
<td width="1" height="1" bgcolor=#d8cc66></td>
<td width="1" height="1" bgcolor=#e6d488></td>
<td width="1" height="1" bgcolor=#c1a470></td>
<td width="1" height="1" bgcolor=#dbdb7e></td>
<td width="1" height="1" bgcolor=#aa9163></td>
<td width="1" height="1" bgcolor=#e6c79c></td>
<td width="1" height="1" bgcolor=#d8d2bc></td>
<td width="1" height="1" bgcolor=#9f8c7b></td>
<td width="1" height="1" bgcolor=#f1dfcd></td>
<td width="1" height="1" bgcolor=#fdf3ca></td>
<td width="1" height="1" bgcolor=#4e7b89></td>
<td width="1" height="1" bgcolor=#75daf3></td>
<td width="1" height="1" bgcolor=#79d9f4></td>
<td width="1" height="1" bgcolor=#6bdbf8></td>
<td width="1" height="1" bgcolor=#72aab8></td>
<td width="1" height="1" bgcolor=#6d929f></td>
<td width="1" height="1" bgcolor=#8ed9f3></td>
<td width="1" height="1" bgcolor=#729088></td>
<td width="1" height="1" bgcolor=#4b3425></td>
<td width="1" height="1" bgcolor=#8d9388></td>
<td width="1" height="1" bgcolor=#adb9a1></td>
<td width="1" height="1" bgcolor=#c2d7b1></td>
<td width="1" height="1" bgcolor=#e3dec3></td>
<td width="1" height="1" bgcolor=#999178></td>
<td width="1" height="1" bgcolor=#789b8e></td>
<td width="1" height="1" bgcolor=#68d5f7></td>
<td width="1" height="1" bgcolor=#68d4f3></td>
<td width="1" height="1" bgcolor=#6bd2ea></td>
<td width="1" height="1" bgcolor=#77d4fc></td>
<td width="1" height="1" bgcolor=#c6bb7e></td>
<td width="1" height="1" bgcolor=#ceb37b></td>
<td width="1" height="1" bgcolor=#6a8082></td>
<td width="1" height="1" bgcolor=#7eddfd></td>
<td width="1" height="1" bgcolor=#a4ccc0></td>
<td width="1" height="1" bgcolor=#d5cfa6></td>
<td width="1" height="1" bgcolor=#d0d4b8></td>
<td width="1" height="1" bgcolor=#c4c2a8></td>
<td width="1" height="1" bgcolor=#827860></td>
<td width="1" height="1" bgcolor=#9baea9></td>
<td width="1" height="1" bgcolor=#a9e9f8></td>
<td width="1" height="1" bgcolor=#a9e6f8></td>
<td width="1" height="1" bgcolor=#9de6f3></td>
<td width="1" height="1" bgcolor=#9fe4f8></td>
<td width="1" height="1" bgcolor=#a0e5f9></td>
<td width="1" height="1" bgcolor=#a3e6f8></td>
<td width="1" height="1" bgcolor=#a8e9fb></td>
<td width="1" height="1" bgcolor=#a9e8fa></td>
<td width="1" height="1" bgcolor=#a9e8f6></td>
<td width="1" height="1" bgcolor=#a9e8fb></td>
<td width="1" height="1" bgcolor=#afebf5></td>
</tr>
<tr>
<td width="1" height="1" bgcolor=#86d9e9></td>
<td width="1" height="1" bgcolor=#a4b495></td>
<td width="1" height="1" bgcolor=#7f7357></td>
<td width="1" height="1" bgcolor=#97906e></td>
<td width="1" height="1" bgcolor=#b3c0a7></td>
<td width="1" height="1" bgcolor=#7fdbec></td>
<td width="1" height="1" bgcolor=#bccba4></td>
<td width="1" height="1" bgcolor=#b2a16d></td>
<td width="1" height="1" bgcolor=#a38b64></td>
<td width="1" height="1" bgcolor=#7abbc6></td>
<td width="1" height="1" bgcolor=#9ae3e0></td>
<td width="1" height="1" bgcolor=#c8bf78></td>
<td width="1" height="1" bgcolor=#d1c491></td>
<td width="1" height="1" bgcolor=#b29372></td>
```

```
    <td width="1" height="1"
bgcolor=#6e5343></td>
    <td width="1" height="1"
bgcolor=#91825f></td>
    <td width="1" height="1"
bgcolor=#b8a486></td>
    <td width="1" height="1"
bgcolor=#99d7e7></td>
    <td width="1" height="1"
bgcolor=#84d6f4></td>
    <td width="1" height="1"
bgcolor=#505632></td>
    <td width="1" height="1"
bgcolor=#f6d293></td>
    <td width="1" height="1"
bgcolor=#baa244></td>
    <td width="1" height="1"
bgcolor=#a69266></td>
    <td width="1" height="1"
bgcolor=#c5b17e></td>
    <td width="1" height="1"
bgcolor=#c1ac72></td>
    <td width="1" height="1"
bgcolor=#8b7e62></td>
    <td width="1" height="1"
bgcolor=#9d886b></td>
    <td width="1" height="1"
bgcolor=#9c895c></td>
    <td width="1" height="1"
bgcolor=#b6baaa></td>
    <td width="1" height="1"
bgcolor=#97967b></td>
    <td width="1" height="1"
bgcolor=#caa596></td>
    <td width="1" height="1"
bgcolor=#dcd2a1></td>
    <td width="1" height="1"
bgcolor=#62acc9></td>
    <td width="1" height="1"
bgcolor=#69d4eb></td>
    <td width="1" height="1"
bgcolor=#65d4f3></td>
    <td width="1" height="1"
bgcolor=#76ccd8></td>
    <td width="1" height="1"
bgcolor=#f0d2ab></td>
    <td width="1" height="1"
bgcolor=#a98660></td>
    <td width="1" height="1"
bgcolor=#577f88></td>
    <td width="1" height="1"
bgcolor=#555c46></td>
    <td width="1" height="1"
bgcolor=#312e29></td>
    <td width="1" height="1"
bgcolor=#504031></td>
    <td width="1" height="1"
bgcolor=#b8986e></td>
    <td width="1" height="1"
bgcolor=#c1cab2></td>
    <td width="1" height="1"
bgcolor=#d3d9bd></td>
    <td width="1" height="1"
bgcolor=#c2ba9c></td>
    <td width="1" height="1"
bgcolor=#716645></td>
    <td width="1" height="1"
bgcolor=#8cdaed></td>
    <td width="1" height="1"
bgcolor=#68d2f7></td>
    <td width="1" height="1"
bgcolor=#6ad0f6></td>
    <td width="1" height="1"
bgcolor=#6bdbfb></td>
    <td width="1" height="1"
bgcolor=#d3aa6e></td>
    <td width="1" height="1"
bgcolor=#dcae77></td>
    <td width="1" height="1"
bgcolor=#9ba792></td>
    <td width="1" height="1"
bgcolor=#86e1fc></td>
    <td width="1" height="1"
bgcolor=#acbaae></td>
    <td width="1" height="1"
bgcolor=#b7bd8b></td>
    <td width="1" height="1"
bgcolor=#dfdac3></td>
    <td width="1" height="1"
bgcolor=#cfd1a7></td>
    <td width="1" height="1"
bgcolor=#694e3d></td>
    <td width="1" height="1"
bgcolor=#92cadb></td>
    <td width="1" height="1"
bgcolor=#a4f0fc></td>
    <td width="1" height="1"
bgcolor=#a5e9ff></td>
    <td width="1" height="1"
bgcolor=#a6e5f5></td>
    <td width="1" height="1"
bgcolor=#a2e5f5></td>
    <td width="1" height="1"
bgcolor=#a4e6f6></td>
    <td width="1" height="1"
bgcolor=#a4e7f8></td>
    <td width="1" height="1"
bgcolor=#a4e6f5></td>
    <td width="1" height="1"
bgcolor=#a6e7f8></td>
    <td width="1" height="1"
bgcolor=#a9eaf7></td>
    <td width="1" height="1"
bgcolor=#aee7fc></td>
    <td width="1" height="1"
bgcolor=#b8f0f7></td>
  </tr>
  <tr>
    <td width="1" height="1"
bgcolor=#85dcee></td>
    <td width="1" height="1"
bgcolor=#717361></td>
    <td width="1" height="1"
bgcolor=#706e5c></td>
    <td width="1" height="1"
bgcolor=#908c6b></td>
    <td width="1" height="1"
bgcolor=#bec4ab></td>
    <td width="1" height="1"
bgcolor=#84ddf5></td>
    <td width="1" height="1"
bgcolor=#9ecdc0></td>
    <td width="1" height="1"
bgcolor=#ceac72></td>
    <td width="1" height="1"
bgcolor=#a59760></td>
    <td width="1" height="1"
bgcolor=#535651></td>
    <td width="1" height="1"
bgcolor=#38474d></td>
    <td width="1" height="1"
bgcolor=#cea56d></td>
    <td width="1" height="1"
bgcolor=#e5cf88></td>
    <td width="1" height="1"
bgcolor=#7d674e></td>
    <td width="1" height="1"
bgcolor=#6f654e></td>
    <td width="1" height="1"
bgcolor=#ac8d69></td>
    <td width="1" height="1"
bgcolor=#f5e6b4></td>
    <td width="1" height="1"
bgcolor=#8edcf4></td>
    <td width="1" height="1"
bgcolor=#86e2ef></td>
    <td width="1" height="1"
bgcolor=#9cc096></td>
    <td width="1" height="1"
bgcolor=#8c7351></td>
    <td width="1" height="1"
bgcolor=#e6cd92></td>
    <td width="1" height="1"
bgcolor=#bca783></td>
    <td width="1" height="1"
bgcolor=#a49761></td>
    <td width="1" height="1"
bgcolor=#c9ba71></td>
    <td width="1" height="1"
bgcolor=#625547></td>
    <td width="1" height="1"
bgcolor=#665843></td>
    <td width="1" height="1"
bgcolor=#99785d></td>
```

```
<td width="1" height="1" bgcolor=#8bcfe3></td>
<td width="1" height="1" bgcolor=#90d5d2></td>
<td width="1" height="1" bgcolor=#988268></td>
<td width="1" height="1" bgcolor=#f6ebd8></td>
<td width="1" height="1" bgcolor=#5dd5f8></td>
<td width="1" height="1" bgcolor=#69d1eb></td>
<td width="1" height="1" bgcolor=#5fd0ef></td>
<td width="1" height="1" bgcolor=#6bc3c3></td>
<td width="1" height="1" bgcolor=#968061></td>
<td width="1" height="1" bgcolor=#6f5442></td>
<td width="1" height="1" bgcolor=#71919b></td>
<td width="1" height="1" bgcolor=#85cbda></td>
<td width="1" height="1" bgcolor=#b99d6d></td>
<td width="1" height="1" bgcolor=#9f8a64></td>
<td width="1" height="1" bgcolor=#cbb79b></td>
<td width="1" height="1" bgcolor=#b1d3c1></td>
<td width="1" height="1" bgcolor=#c9c9aa></td>
<td width="1" height="1" bgcolor=#c3b28a></td>
<td width="1" height="1" bgcolor=#535445></td>
<td width="1" height="1" bgcolor=#efdcaa></td>
<td width="1" height="1" bgcolor=#74d8f5></td>
<td width="1" height="1" bgcolor=#76d5f3></td>
<td width="1" height="1" bgcolor=#73d9d4></td>
<td width="1" height="1" bgcolor=#857d50></td>
<td width="1" height="1" bgcolor=#b99560></td>
<td width="1" height="1" bgcolor=#6f5245></td>
<td width="1" height="1" bgcolor=#61bb88></td>
<td width="1" height="1" bgcolor=#8bb19d></td>
<td width="1" height="1" bgcolor=#b4b390></td>
<td width="1" height="1" bgcolor=#c9c49c></td>
<td width="1" height="1" bgcolor=#d4caa2></td>
<td width="1" height="1" bgcolor=#69625e></td>
<td width="1" height="1" bgcolor=#a3e1f0></td>
<td width="1" height="1" bgcolor=#caa154></td>
<td width="1" height="1" bgcolor=#bf5930></td>
<td width="1" height="1" bgcolor=#a6e2e3></td>
<td width="1" height="1" bgcolor=#a0e3f5></td>
<td width="1" height="1" bgcolor=#a0e4f7></td>
<td width="1" height="1" bgcolor=#9ee2f4></td>
<td width="1" height="1" bgcolor=#a4e6f9></td>
<td width="1" height="1" bgcolor=#a1e4f4></td>
<td width="1" height="1" bgcolor=#abecf7></td>
<td width="1" height="1" bgcolor=#87d2a0></td>
<td width="1" height="1" bgcolor=#6fc187></td>
</tr>
<tr>
<td width="1" height="1" bgcolor=#80cfd7></td>
<td width="1" height="1" bgcolor=#9bb095></td>
<td width="1" height="1" bgcolor=#8b9d7a></td>
<td width="1" height="1" bgcolor=#8e8f73></td>
<td width="1" height="1" bgcolor=#afcab7></td>
<td width="1" height="1" bgcolor=#7ea498></td>
<td width="1" height="1" bgcolor=#93aa8d></td>
<td width="1" height="1" bgcolor=#b3b187></td>
<td width="1" height="1" bgcolor=#8e8a68></td>
<td width="1" height="1" bgcolor=#382d25></td>
<td width="1" height="1" bgcolor=#262311></td>
<td width="1" height="1" bgcolor=#291f19></td>
<td width="1" height="1" bgcolor=#64523e></td>
<td width="1" height="1" bgcolor=#7a6a4d></td>
<td width="1" height="1" bgcolor=#8c834b></td>
<td width="1" height="1" bgcolor=#8a7b5c></td>
<td width="1" height="1" bgcolor=#c4b97e></td>
<td width="1" height="1" bgcolor=#c4d2a8></td>
<td width="1" height="1" bgcolor=#a3b699></td>
<td width="1" height="1" bgcolor=#969557></td>
<td width="1" height="1" bgcolor=#67583d></td>
<td width="1" height="1" bgcolor=#a8946d></td>
<td width="1" height="1" bgcolor=#959d63></td>
<td width="1" height="1" bgcolor=#c0bb8b></td>
<td width="1" height="1" bgcolor=#958d6c></td>
<td width="1" height="1" bgcolor=#352b1d></td>
<td width="1" height="1" bgcolor=#36291f></td>
<td width="1" height="1" bgcolor=#70634b></td>
<td width="1" height="1" bgcolor=#403729></td>
<td width="1" height="1" bgcolor=#6a8c7d></td>
<td width="1" height="1" bgcolor=#2b2519></td>
<td width="1" height="1" bgcolor=#909c85></td>
<td width="1" height="1" bgcolor=#9bc4bc></td>
<td width="1" height="1" bgcolor=#a2d7d1></td>
<td width="1" height="1" bgcolor=#92c8bf></td>
<td width="1" height="1" bgcolor=#7ccac8></td>
<td width="1" height="1" bgcolor=#8e7554></td>
<td width="1" height="1" bgcolor=#4d3f2f></td>
<td width="1" height="1" bgcolor=#99d0d7></td>
<td width="1" height="1" bgcolor=#678080></td>
<td width="1" height="1" bgcolor=#876e4b></td>
<td width="1" height="1" bgcolor=#524d37></td>
```

```
    <td width="1" height="1"
bgcolor=#9e7643></td>
    <td width="1" height="1"
bgcolor=#bfccb7></td>
    <td width="1" height="1"
bgcolor=#d0c5a4></td>
    <td width="1" height="1"
bgcolor=#cdd4ba></td>
    <td width="1" height="1"
bgcolor=#dee292></td>
    <td width="1" height="1"
bgcolor=#e3d768></td>
    <td width="1" height="1"
bgcolor=#d2dbc0></td>
    <td width="1" height="1"
bgcolor=#9dd2d4></td>
    <td width="1" height="1"
bgcolor=#728d68></td>
    <td width="1" height="1"
bgcolor=#5c7e56></td>
    <td width="1" height="1"
bgcolor=#5a4336></td>
    <td width="1" height="1"
bgcolor=#5f5843></td>
    <td width="1" height="1"
bgcolor=#5f9f62></td>
    <td width="1" height="1"
bgcolor=#568155></td>
    <td width="1" height="1"
bgcolor=#614b3a></td>
    <td width="1" height="1"
bgcolor=#67614a></td>
    <td width="1" height="1"
bgcolor=#7d7153></td>
    <td width="1" height="1"
bgcolor=#6b5045></td>
    <td width="1" height="1"
bgcolor=#b68834></td>
    <td width="1" height="1"
bgcolor=#e35231></td>
    <td width="1" height="1"
bgcolor=#f0a935></td>
    <td width="1" height="1"
bgcolor=#919aa3></td>
    <td width="1" height="1"
bgcolor=#97e2fa></td>
    <td width="1" height="1"
bgcolor=#96e0f1></td>
    <td width="1" height="1"
bgcolor=#93e1f0></td>
    <td width="1" height="1"
bgcolor=#9ae1f3></td>
    <td width="1" height="1"
bgcolor=#9ee2fb></td>
    <td width="1" height="1"
bgcolor=#73cc7e></td>
    <td width="1" height="1"
bgcolor=#549f3e></td>
    <td width="1" height="1"
bgcolor=#55bc64></td>
  </tr>
  <tr>
    <td width="1" height="1"
bgcolor=#85c2c2></td>
    <td width="1" height="1"
bgcolor=#a4a982></td>
    <td width="1" height="1"
bgcolor=#b1b694></td>
    <td width="1" height="1"
bgcolor=#656c56></td>
    <td width="1" height="1"
bgcolor=#6e886f></td>
    <td width="1" height="1"
bgcolor=#ccd2af></td>
    <td width="1" height="1"
bgcolor=#d2d4ac></td>
    <td width="1" height="1"
bgcolor=#718c74></td>
    <td width="1" height="1"
bgcolor=#dec482></td>
    <td width="1" height="1"
bgcolor=#4d371d></td>
    <td width="1" height="1"
bgcolor=#271e1a></td>
    <td width="1" height="1"
bgcolor=#87633e></td>
    <td width="1" height="1"
bgcolor=#c9895a></td>
    <td width="1" height="1"
bgcolor=#738332></td>
    <td width="1" height="1"
bgcolor=#f4e8a3></td>
    <td width="1" height="1"
bgcolor=#c1ce9f></td>
    <td width="1" height="1"
bgcolor=#d3d58c></td>
    <td width="1" height="1"
bgcolor=#ada38f></td>
    <td width="1" height="1"
bgcolor=#dad9bd></td>
    <td width="1" height="1"
bgcolor=#c3bc8a></td>
    <td width="1" height="1"
bgcolor=#fbedd5></td>
    <td width="1" height="1"
bgcolor=#736a49></td>
    <td width="1" height="1"
bgcolor=#332926></td>
    <td width="1" height="1"
bgcolor=#3d312b></td>
    <td width="1" height="1"
bgcolor=#372f20></td>
    <td width="1" height="1"
bgcolor=#6f6046></td>
    <td width="1" height="1"
bgcolor=#a79569></td>
    <td width="1" height="1"
bgcolor=#bfb451></td>
    <td width="1" height="1"
bgcolor=#d4cc56></td>
    <td width="1" height="1"
bgcolor=#f3e361></td>
    <td width="1" height="1"
bgcolor=#d6d9a0></td>
    <td width="1" height="1"
bgcolor=#c1cca0></td>
    <td width="1" height="1"
bgcolor=#8e9b78></td>
    <td width="1" height="1"
bgcolor=#9aa68a></td>
    <td width="1" height="1"
bgcolor=#e4e7d2></td>
    <td width="1" height="1"
bgcolor=#b9bda4></td>
    <td width="1" height="1"
bgcolor=#908865></td>
    <td width="1" height="1"
bgcolor=#706d54></td>
    <td width="1" height="1"
bgcolor=#584734></td>
    <td width="1" height="1"
bgcolor=#341d17></td>
    <td width="1" height="1"
bgcolor=#231610></td>
    <td width="1" height="1"
bgcolor=#2d160d></td>
    <td width="1" height="1"
bgcolor=#2b2b28></td>
    <td width="1" height="1"
bgcolor=#decb8e></td>
    <td width="1" height="1"
bgcolor=#a28667></td>
    <td width="1" height="1"
bgcolor=#c5caad></td>
    <td width="1" height="1"
bgcolor=#c4af00></td>
    <td width="1" height="1"
bgcolor=#a2940f></td>
    <td width="1" height="1"
bgcolor=#a2a150></td>
    <td width="1" height="1"
bgcolor=#e8e8d0></td>
    <td width="1" height="1"
bgcolor=#fff6e5></td>
    <td width="1" height="1"
bgcolor=#cec7a2></td>
    <td width="1" height="1"
bgcolor=#c8c086></td>
    <td width="1" height="1"
bgcolor=#fbe1a9></td>
    <td width="1" height="1"
bgcolor=#51372b></td>
    <td width="1" height="1"
bgcolor=#986a4c></td>
```

```
    <td width="1" height="1" bgcolor=#d0a564></td>
    <td width="1" height="1" bgcolor=#422121></td>
    <td width="1" height="1" bgcolor=#ccc697></td>
    <td width="1" height="1" bgcolor=#e1bd96></td>
    <td width="1" height="1" bgcolor=#b67757></td>
    <td width="1" height="1" bgcolor=#dc9625></td>
    <td width="1" height="1" bgcolor=#964624></td>
    <td width="1" height="1" bgcolor=#5ba646></td>
    <td width="1" height="1" bgcolor=#5fb675></td>
    <td width="1" height="1" bgcolor=#81dadc></td>
    <td width="1" height="1" bgcolor=#92dbf7></td>
    <td width="1" height="1" bgcolor=#90def7></td>
    <td width="1" height="1" bgcolor=#79cc98></td>
    <td width="1" height="1" bgcolor=#4d9937></td>
    <td width="1" height="1" bgcolor=#47b246></td>
    <td width="1" height="1" bgcolor=#4fac44></td>
  </tr>
  <tr>
    <td width="1" height="1" bgcolor=#a1c2a6></td>
    <td width="1" height="1" bgcolor=#b1c19a></td>
    <td width="1" height="1" bgcolor=#cbca9c></td>
    <td width="1" height="1" bgcolor=#adae8c></td>
    <td width="1" height="1" bgcolor=#7d836e></td>
    <td width="1" height="1" bgcolor=#c3d3ad></td>
    <td width="1" height="1" bgcolor=#a7a980></td>
    <td width="1" height="1" bgcolor=#b19867></td>
    <td width="1" height="1" bgcolor=#d9b972></td>
    <td width="1" height="1" bgcolor=#39311f></td>
    <td width="1" height="1" bgcolor=#3e2c22></td>
    <td width="1" height="1" bgcolor=#b58952></td>
    <td width="1" height="1" bgcolor=#b67e45></td>
    <td width="1" height="1" bgcolor=#ac9a4a></td>
    <td width="1" height="1" bgcolor=#c9cdb1></td>
    <td width="1" height="1" bgcolor=#99b588></td>
    <td width="1" height="1" bgcolor=#c7d675></td>
    <td width="1" height="1" bgcolor=#a59574></td>
    <td width="1" height="1" bgcolor=#b4b092></td>
    <td width="1" height="1" bgcolor=#594a37></td>
    <td width="1" height="1" bgcolor=#737558></td>
    <td width="1" height="1" bgcolor=#715d3f></td>
    <td width="1" height="1" bgcolor=#4b452b></td>
    <td width="1" height="1" bgcolor=#b8986c></td>
    <td width="1" height="1" bgcolor=#9a8754></td>
    <td width="1" height="1" bgcolor=#eed997></td>
    <td width="1" height="1" bgcolor=#eacf71></td>
    <td width="1" height="1" bgcolor=#a99d48></td>
    <td width="1" height="1" bgcolor=#8f8344></td>
    <td width="1" height="1" bgcolor=#9c9655></td>
    <td width="1" height="1" bgcolor=#8a8a68></td>
    <td width="1" height="1" bgcolor=#868b6c></td>
    <td width="1" height="1" bgcolor=#f3f5d7></td>
    <td width="1" height="1" bgcolor=#dfe0bc></td>
    <td width="1" height="1" bgcolor=#b7ba9d></td>
    <td width="1" height="1" bgcolor=#666e57></td>
    <td width="1" height="1" bgcolor=#71674a></td>
    <td width="1" height="1" bgcolor=#e0a068></td>
    <td width="1" height="1" bgcolor=#eb9350></td>
    <td width="1" height="1" bgcolor=#42291b></td>
    <td width="1" height="1" bgcolor=#2e190f></td>
    <td width="1" height="1" bgcolor=#2e1c1b></td>
    <td width="1" height="1" bgcolor=#3b2b22></td>
    <td width="1" height="1" bgcolor=#cbc8a1></td>
    <td width="1" height="1" bgcolor=#b49973></td>
    <td width="1" height="1" bgcolor=#b5ba63></td>
    <td width="1" height="1" bgcolor=#cbc387></td>
    <td width="1" height="1" bgcolor=#d9ca84></td>
    <td width="1" height="1" bgcolor=#a4996d></td>
    <td width="1" height="1" bgcolor=#9a9982></td>
    <td width="1" height="1" bgcolor=#cad0ac></td>
    <td width="1" height="1" bgcolor=#dfbf95></td>
    <td width="1" height="1" bgcolor=#d8c38b></td>
    <td width="1" height="1" bgcolor=#dec889></td>
    <td width="1" height="1" bgcolor=#a98e61></td>
    <td width="1" height="1" bgcolor=#a46f50></td>
    <td width="1" height="1" bgcolor=#c27c50></td>
    <td width="1" height="1" bgcolor=#60472e></td>
    <td width="1" height="1" bgcolor=#685544></td>
    <td width="1" height="1" bgcolor=#9a6b4e></td>
    <td width="1" height="1" bgcolor=#776649></td>
    <td width="1" height="1" bgcolor=#b97044></td>
    <td width="1" height="1" bgcolor=#765f55></td>
    <td width="1" height="1" bgcolor=#55b35a></td>
    <td width="1" height="1" bgcolor=#4b8f29></td>
    <td width="1" height="1" bgcolor=#53a63d></td>
    <td width="1" height="1" bgcolor=#6ac7af></td>
    <td width="1" height="1" bgcolor=#7fdac3></td>
    <td width="1" height="1" bgcolor=#4da242></td>
    <td width="1" height="1" bgcolor=#4d9131></td>
```

```
    <td width="1" height="1" bgcolor=#4b9a37></td>
    <td width="1" height="1" bgcolor=#44bd4e></td>
  </tr>
  <tr>
    <td width="1" height="1" bgcolor=#9da586></td>
    <td width="1" height="1" bgcolor=#c7c89b></td>
    <td width="1" height="1" bgcolor=#a29f7f></td>
    <td width="1" height="1" bgcolor=#687249></td>
    <td width="1" height="1" bgcolor=#7b8e5f></td>
    <td width="1" height="1" bgcolor=#c2c9a7></td>
    <td width="1" height="1" bgcolor=#85956f></td>
    <td width="1" height="1" bgcolor=#867f55></td>
    <td width="1" height="1" bgcolor=#dbba7d></td>
    <td width="1" height="1" bgcolor=#362a24></td>
    <td width="1" height="1" bgcolor=#463825></td>
    <td width="1" height="1" bgcolor=#9e8047></td>
    <td width="1" height="1" bgcolor=#ca8d50></td>
    <td width="1" height="1" bgcolor=#584234></td>
    <td width="1" height="1" bgcolor=#7c8d6f></td>
    <td width="1" height="1" bgcolor=#a9a78a></td>
    <td width="1" height="1" bgcolor=#859d55></td>
    <td width="1" height="1" bgcolor=#e2deb7></td>
    <td width="1" height="1" bgcolor=#a49f71></td>
    <td width="1" height="1" bgcolor=#382a25></td>
    <td width="1" height="1" bgcolor=#7e6e4f></td>
    <td width="1" height="1" bgcolor=#c4b065></td>
    <td width="1" height="1" bgcolor=#64583e></td>
    <td width="1" height="1" bgcolor=#b69259></td>
    <td width="1" height="1" bgcolor=#8a7843></td>
    <td width="1" height="1" bgcolor=#f0df98></td>
    <td width="1" height="1" bgcolor=#e5c787></td>
    <td width="1" height="1" bgcolor=#533b1c></td>
    <td width="1" height="1" bgcolor=#716038></td>
    <td width="1" height="1" bgcolor=#d5c782></td>
    <td width="1" height="1" bgcolor=#4b4022></td>
    <td width="1" height="1" bgcolor=#727865></td>
    <td width="1" height="1" bgcolor=#c2c99b></td>
    <td width="1" height="1" bgcolor=#d2d4aa></td>
    <td width="1" height="1" bgcolor=#f0eed0></td>
    <td width="1" height="1" bgcolor=#a2a77e></td>
    <td width="1" height="1" bgcolor=#826a52></td>
    <td width="1" height="1" bgcolor=#a29663></td>
    <td width="1" height="1" bgcolor=#bc9166></td>
    <td width="1" height="1" bgcolor=#67453b></td>
    <td width="1" height="1" bgcolor=#ad9e77></td>
    <td width="1" height="1" bgcolor=#cdbb84></td>
    <td width="1" height="1" bgcolor=#9b865c></td>
    <td width="1" height="1" bgcolor=#bdb478></td>
    <td width="1" height="1" bgcolor=#cbb67c></td>
    <td width="1" height="1" bgcolor=#897955></td>
    <td width="1" height="1" bgcolor=#d7ae7e></td>
    <td width="1" height="1" bgcolor=#dbac77></td>
    <td width="1" height="1" bgcolor=#dab188></td>
    <td width="1" height="1" bgcolor=#554f3c></td>
    <td width="1" height="1" bgcolor=#928c71></td>
    <td width="1" height="1" bgcolor=#c3b48a></td>
    <td width="1" height="1" bgcolor=#977e5d></td>
    <td width="1" height="1" bgcolor=#c2af71></td>
    <td width="1" height="1" bgcolor=#af936b></td>
    <td width="1" height="1" bgcolor=#432d1f></td>
    <td width="1" height="1" bgcolor=#876748></td>
    <td width="1" height="1" bgcolor=#c5a565></td>
    <td width="1" height="1" bgcolor=#93733c></td>
    <td width="1" height="1" bgcolor=#7b6852></td>
    <td width="1" height="1" bgcolor=#3e2e1e></td>
    <td width="1" height="1" bgcolor=#cd8f55></td>
    <td width="1" height="1" bgcolor=#c98145></td>
    <td width="1" height="1" bgcolor=#517e71></td>
    <td width="1" height="1" bgcolor=#51b659></td>
    <td width="1" height="1" bgcolor=#55942e></td>
    <td width="1" height="1" bgcolor=#489e40></td>
    <td width="1" height="1" bgcolor=#4fb85c></td>
    <td width="1" height="1" bgcolor=#517830></td>
    <td width="1" height="1" bgcolor=#4a8333></td>
    <td width="1" height="1" bgcolor=#4d8c35></td>
    <td width="1" height="1" bgcolor=#4b6624></td>
  </tr>
  <tr>
    <td width="1" height="1" bgcolor=#b9b489></td>
    <td width="1" height="1" bgcolor=#a7a57f></td>
    <td width="1" height="1" bgcolor=#434330></td>
    <td width="1" height="1" bgcolor=#637439></td>
    <td width="1" height="1" bgcolor=#7f8f43></td>
    <td width="1" height="1" bgcolor=#9aa18a></td>
    <td width="1" height="1" bgcolor=#b5a980></td>
    <td width="1" height="1" bgcolor=#474335></td>
    <td width="1" height="1" bgcolor=#d4c67f></td>
    <td width="1" height="1" bgcolor=#1d0f06></td>
    <td width="1" height="1" bgcolor=#2b241c></td>
```

```
    <td width="1" height="1" bgcolor=#2d1f1b></td>
    <td width="1" height="1" bgcolor=#a15732></td>
    <td width="1" height="1" bgcolor=#424038></td>
    <td width="1" height="1" bgcolor=#a3b68d></td>
    <td width="1" height="1" bgcolor=#ccd5b5></td>
    <td width="1" height="1" bgcolor=#545838></td>
    <td width="1" height="1" bgcolor=#d8dab8></td>
    <td width="1" height="1" bgcolor=#b7a97c></td>
    <td width="1" height="1" bgcolor=#553e28></td>
    <td width="1" height="1" bgcolor=#7c6949></td>
    <td width="1" height="1" bgcolor=#d2c58a></td>
    <td width="1" height="1" bgcolor=#442d15></td>
    <td width="1" height="1" bgcolor=#c48e59></td>
    <td width="1" height="1" bgcolor=#855531></td>
    <td width="1" height="1" bgcolor=#dac28f></td>
    <td width="1" height="1" bgcolor=#dbd095></td>
    <td width="1" height="1" bgcolor=#66583f></td>
    <td width="1" height="1" bgcolor=#574231></td>
    <td width="1" height="1" bgcolor=#83612f></td>
    <td width="1" height="1" bgcolor=#cf934c></td>
    <td width="1" height="1" bgcolor=#684829></td>
    <td width="1" height="1" bgcolor=#919470></td>
    <td width="1" height="1" bgcolor=#e9dcac></td>
    <td width="1" height="1" bgcolor=#64675b></td>
    <td width="1" height="1" bgcolor=#847a5b></td>
    <td width="1" height="1" bgcolor=#ac9555></td>
    <td width="1" height="1" bgcolor=#bb925d></td>
    <td width="1" height="1" bgcolor=#d38e61></td>
    <td width="1" height="1" bgcolor=#795537></td>
    <td width="1" height="1" bgcolor=#776b53></td>
    <td width="1" height="1" bgcolor=#bfab74></td>
    <td width="1" height="1" bgcolor=#caa869></td>
    <td width="1" height="1" bgcolor=#e9c878></td>
    <td width="1" height="1" bgcolor=#e0c861></td>
    <td width="1" height="1" bgcolor=#937c4a></td>
    <td width="1" height="1" bgcolor=#c4ac7f></td>
    <td width="1" height="1" bgcolor=#bca57b></td>
    <td width="1" height="1" bgcolor=#635534></td>
    <td width="1" height="1" bgcolor=#8f8c75></td>
    <td width="1" height="1" bgcolor=#d1d9b4></td>
    <td width="1" height="1" bgcolor=#d8c995></td>
    <td width="1" height="1" bgcolor=#d2be7a></td>
    <td width="1" height="1" bgcolor=#bcad86></td>
    <td width="1" height="1" bgcolor=#452e1e></td>
    <td width="1" height="1" bgcolor=#412f25></td>
    <td width="1" height="1" bgcolor=#948464></td>
    <td width="1" height="1" bgcolor=#dc9e53></td>
    <td width="1" height="1" bgcolor=#dea758></td>
    <td width="1" height="1" bgcolor=#b6a26f></td>
    <td width="1" height="1" bgcolor=#392629></td>
    <td width="1" height="1" bgcolor=#5c4a29></td>
    <td width="1" height="1" bgcolor=#654a34></td>
    <td width="1" height="1" bgcolor=#3c3339></td>
    <td width="1" height="1" bgcolor=#64c4bb></td>
    <td width="1" height="1" bgcolor=#46b650></td>
    <td width="1" height="1" bgcolor=#488326></td>
    <td width="1" height="1" bgcolor=#4e8234></td>
    <td width="1" height="1" bgcolor=#4e6027></td>
    <td width="1" height="1" bgcolor=#486427></td>
    <td width="1" height="1" bgcolor=#41521e></td>
    <td width="1" height="1" bgcolor=#505225></td>
  </tr>
  <tr>
    <td width="1" height="1" bgcolor=#aeb48e></td>
    <td width="1" height="1" bgcolor=#889573></td>
    <td width="1" height="1" bgcolor=#595f47></td>
    <td width="1" height="1" bgcolor=#70673c></td>
    <td width="1" height="1" bgcolor=#746f4e></td>
    <td width="1" height="1" bgcolor=#ced9b2></td>
    <td width="1" height="1" bgcolor=#dde6c4></td>
    <td width="1" height="1" bgcolor=#a49d71></td>
    <td width="1" height="1" bgcolor=#727551></td>
    <td width="1" height="1" bgcolor=#503b51></td>
    <td width="1" height="1" bgcolor=#604663></td>
    <td width="1" height="1" bgcolor=#695f50></td>
    <td width="1" height="1" bgcolor=#d8be9c></td>
    <td width="1" height="1" bgcolor=#aba073></td>
    <td width="1" height="1" bgcolor=#aabf98></td>
    <td width="1" height="1" bgcolor=#c5d4a7></td>
    <td width="1" height="1" bgcolor=#615b4b></td>
    <td width="1" height="1" bgcolor=#e6e9c0></td>
    <td width="1" height="1" bgcolor=#dedda8></td>
    <td width="1" height="1" bgcolor=#ccba92></td>
    <td width="1" height="1" bgcolor=#614b39></td>
    <td width="1" height="1" bgcolor=#d3b47e></td>
    <td width="1" height="1" bgcolor=#81796a></td>
    <td width="1" height="1" bgcolor=#8c7544></td>
    <td width="1" height="1" bgcolor=#765636></td>
```

```
    <td width="1" height="1"
bgcolor=#7c6245></td>
    <td width="1" height="1"
bgcolor=#594c3d></td>
    <td width="1" height="1"
bgcolor=#392e23></td>
    <td width="1" height="1"
bgcolor=#6c5948></td>
    <td width="1" height="1"
bgcolor=#523527></td>
    <td width="1" height="1"
bgcolor=#9f7237></td>
    <td width="1" height="1"
bgcolor=#a8713e></td>
    <td width="1" height="1"
bgcolor=#524e38></td>
    <td width="1" height="1"
bgcolor=#958d66></td>
    <td width="1" height="1"
bgcolor=#473e29></td>
    <td width="1" height="1"
bgcolor=#493026></td>
    <td width="1" height="1"
bgcolor=#887147></td>
    <td width="1" height="1"
bgcolor=#bf8f50></td>
    <td width="1" height="1"
bgcolor=#dab17c></td>
    <td width="1" height="1"
bgcolor=#976e43></td>
    <td width="1" height="1"
bgcolor=#bb864f></td>
    <td width="1" height="1"
bgcolor=#7e5e3d></td>
    <td width="1" height="1"
bgcolor=#67442c></td>
    <td width="1" height="1"
bgcolor=#cba256></td>
    <td width="1" height="1"
bgcolor=#e2b757></td>
    <td width="1" height="1"
bgcolor=#9e7a4c></td>
    <td width="1" height="1"
bgcolor=#85886b></td>
    <td width="1" height="1"
bgcolor=#b6c0a0></td>
    <td width="1" height="1"
bgcolor=#b1a47f></td>
    <td width="1" height="1"
bgcolor=#352014></td>
    <td width="1" height="1"
bgcolor=#a9a788></td>
    <td width="1" height="1"
bgcolor=#c3b482></td>
    <td width="1" height="1"
bgcolor=#c89f5f></td>
    <td width="1" height="1"
bgcolor=#ccb88a></td>
    <td width="1" height="1"
bgcolor=#4b372a></td>
    <td width="1" height="1"
bgcolor=#635649></td>
    <td width="1" height="1"
bgcolor=#3f2f24></td>
    <td width="1" height="1"
bgcolor=#966234></td>
    <td width="1" height="1"
bgcolor=#e6ac63></td>
    <td width="1" height="1"
bgcolor=#b4a07d></td>
    <td width="1" height="1"
bgcolor=#322216></td>
    <td width="1" height="1"
bgcolor=#484839></td>
    <td width="1" height="1"
bgcolor=#4f452c></td>
    <td width="1" height="1"
bgcolor=#494020></td>
    <td width="1" height="1"
bgcolor=#486b38></td>
    <td width="1" height="1"
bgcolor=#5a984a></td>
    <td width="1" height="1"
bgcolor=#4c7f2b></td>
    <td width="1" height="1"
bgcolor=#44461b></td>
    <td width="1" height="1"
bgcolor=#454c21></td>
    <td width="1" height="1"
bgcolor=#46501a></td>
    <td width="1" height="1"
bgcolor=#475124></td>
    <td width="1" height="1"
bgcolor=#475623></td>
  </tr>
  <tr>
    <td width="1" height="1"
bgcolor=#81bcb6></td>
    <td width="1" height="1"
bgcolor=#7db7b7></td>
    <td width="1" height="1"
bgcolor=#91cac7></td>
    <td width="1" height="1"
bgcolor=#9baa8a></td>
    <td width="1" height="1"
bgcolor=#b7a392></td>
    <td width="1" height="1"
bgcolor=#c2c096></td>
    <td width="1" height="1"
bgcolor=#cad0a2></td>
    <td width="1" height="1"
bgcolor=#b9bc80></td>
    <td width="1" height="1"
bgcolor=#82766f></td>
    <td width="1" height="1"
bgcolor=#baa768></td>
    <td width="1" height="1"
bgcolor=#c5bc5f></td>
    <td width="1" height="1"
bgcolor=#e8deb7></td>
    <td width="1" height="1"
bgcolor=#b2bb5b></td>
    <td width="1" height="1"
bgcolor=#878143></td>
    <td width="1" height="1"
bgcolor=#96a180></td>
    <td width="1" height="1"
bgcolor=#c7c495></td>
    <td width="1" height="1"
bgcolor=#9d9a7e></td>
    <td width="1" height="1"
bgcolor=#e2e7bd></td>
    <td width="1" height="1"
bgcolor=#f7edc8></td>
    <td width="1" height="1"
bgcolor=#f8edc7></td>
    <td width="1" height="1"
bgcolor=#a1916a></td>
    <td width="1" height="1"
bgcolor=#7a3e1d></td>
    <td width="1" height="1"
bgcolor=#4d2c22></td>
    <td width="1" height="1"
bgcolor=#6e6244></td>
    <td width="1" height="1"
bgcolor=#43391d></td>
    <td width="1" height="1"
bgcolor=#d58440></td>
    <td width="1" height="1"
bgcolor=#c38545></td>
    <td width="1" height="1"
bgcolor=#412f24></td>
    <td width="1" height="1"
bgcolor=#5c4e2f></td>
    <td width="1" height="1"
bgcolor=#7c6744></td>
    <td width="1" height="1"
bgcolor=#975f41></td>
    <td width="1" height="1"
bgcolor=#856b46></td>
    <td width="1" height="1"
bgcolor=#968e73></td>
    <td width="1" height="1"
bgcolor=#666747></td>
    <td width="1" height="1"
bgcolor=#bba98a></td>
    <td width="1" height="1"
bgcolor=#171203></td>
    <td width="1" height="1"
bgcolor=#cab28b></td>
    <td width="1" height="1"
bgcolor=#ab9471></td>
    <td width="1" height="1"
bgcolor=#e5c990></td>
```

```
    <td width="1" height="1"
bgcolor=#ac6a42></td>
    <td width="1" height="1"
bgcolor=#af7244></td>
    <td width="1" height="1"
bgcolor=#b89656></td>
    <td width="1" height="1"
bgcolor=#381e13></td>
    <td width="1" height="1"
bgcolor=#c7a364></td>
    <td width="1" height="1"
bgcolor=#e1c565></td>
    <td width="1" height="1"
bgcolor=#623b29></td>
    <td width="1" height="1"
bgcolor=#c4cf9a></td>
    <td width="1" height="1"
bgcolor=#e7e5b0></td>
    <td width="1" height="1"
bgcolor=#f5ebbc></td>
    <td width="1" height="1"
bgcolor=#857147></td>
    <td width="1" height="1"
bgcolor=#ebcd71></td>
    <td width="1" height="1"
bgcolor=#f5d484></td>
    <td width="1" height="1"
bgcolor=#ab7f4f></td>
    <td width="1" height="1"
bgcolor=#7c6045></td>
    <td width="1" height="1"
bgcolor=#9fa08c></td>
    <td width="1" height="1"
bgcolor=#f7f0d3></td>
    <td width="1" height="1"
bgcolor=#c7ae90></td>
    <td width="1" height="1"
bgcolor=#220f0a></td>
    <td width="1" height="1"
bgcolor=#aa9771></td>
    <td width="1" height="1"
bgcolor=#4a3a1b></td>
    <td width="1" height="1"
bgcolor=#444d2e></td>
    <td width="1" height="1"
bgcolor=#576430></td>
    <td width="1" height="1"
bgcolor=#53632f></td>
    <td width="1" height="1"
bgcolor=#494e27></td>
    <td width="1" height="1"
bgcolor=#424624></td>
    <td width="1" height="1"
bgcolor=#404422></td>
    <td width="1" height="1"
bgcolor=#41441f></td>
    <td width="1" height="1"
bgcolor=#404621></td>
    <td width="1" height="1"
bgcolor=#434920></td>
    <td width="1" height="1"
bgcolor=#465723></td>
    <td width="1" height="1"
bgcolor=#45541e></td>
    <td width="1" height="1"
bgcolor=#485521></td>
  </tr>
  <tr>
    <td width="1" height="1"
bgcolor=#8dc0aa></td>
    <td width="1" height="1"
bgcolor=#84917d></td>
    <td width="1" height="1"
bgcolor=#49483a></td>
    <td width="1" height="1"
bgcolor=#73a196></td>
    <td width="1" height="1"
bgcolor=#78795e></td>
    <td width="1" height="1"
bgcolor=#cdbd7a></td>
    <td width="1" height="1"
bgcolor=#bba67b></td>
    <td width="1" height="1"
bgcolor=#94895d></td>
    <td width="1" height="1"
bgcolor=#917576></td>
    <td width="1" height="1"
bgcolor=#c3592b></td>
    <td width="1" height="1"
bgcolor=#936e5e></td>
    <td width="1" height="1"
bgcolor=#a6a562></td>
    <td width="1" height="1"
bgcolor=#9a9065></td>
    <td width="1" height="1"
bgcolor=#a59e7b></td>
    <td width="1" height="1"
bgcolor=#7a6d56></td>
    <td width="1" height="1"
bgcolor=#dad5a7></td>
    <td width="1" height="1"
bgcolor=#e9dfa1></td>
    <td width="1" height="1"
bgcolor=#d2c9a6></td>
    <td width="1" height="1"
bgcolor=#e9e1c2></td>
    <td width="1" height="1"
bgcolor=#fcf3d7></td>
    <td width="1" height="1"
bgcolor=#816e4a></td>
    <td width="1" height="1"
bgcolor=#b6a689></td>
    <td width="1" height="1"
bgcolor=#dbdbb7></td>
    <td width="1" height="1"
bgcolor=#9a8b6b></td>
    <td width="1" height="1"
bgcolor=#7c5a33></td>
    <td width="1" height="1"
bgcolor=#c57d50></td>
    <td width="1" height="1"
bgcolor=#8b6944></td>
    <td width="1" height="1"
bgcolor=#57432e></td>
    <td width="1" height="1"
bgcolor=#825b34></td>
    <td width="1" height="1"
bgcolor=#c1a772></td>
    <td width="1" height="1"
bgcolor=#35190d></td>
    <td width="1" height="1"
bgcolor=#676747></td>
    <td width="1" height="1"
bgcolor=#877d59></td>
    <td width="1" height="1"
bgcolor=#e2dec1></td>
    <td width="1" height="1"
bgcolor=#b7a97b></td>
    <td width="1" height="1"
bgcolor=#271007></td>
    <td width="1" height="1"
bgcolor=#2c1510></td>
    <td width="1" height="1"
bgcolor=#2a120c></td>
    <td width="1" height="1"
bgcolor=#5c3e29></td>
    <td width="1" height="1"
bgcolor=#9d5b3a></td>
    <td width="1" height="1"
bgcolor=#8e5b3b></td>
    <td width="1" height="1"
bgcolor=#886f3f></td>
    <td width="1" height="1"
bgcolor=#331f1f></td>
    <td width="1" height="1"
bgcolor=#a86734></td>
    <td width="1" height="1"
bgcolor=#e4a355></td>
    <td width="1" height="1"
bgcolor=#b1b54c></td>
    <td width="1" height="1"
bgcolor=#b1dc02></td>
    <td width="1" height="1"
bgcolor=#b3d509></td>
    <td width="1" height="1"
bgcolor=#d5ccb1></td>
    <td width="1" height="1"
bgcolor=#978449></td>
    <td width="1" height="1"
bgcolor=#b8a573></td>
    <td width="1" height="1"
bgcolor=#ad9751></td>
    <td width="1" height="1"
bgcolor=#4c3323></td>
```

```
    <td width="1" height="1"
bgcolor=#574330></td>
    <td width="1" height="1"
bgcolor=#8f8074></td>
    <td width="1" height="1"
bgcolor=#e5dfca></td>
    <td width="1" height="1"
bgcolor=#fcefd4></td>
    <td width="1" height="1"
bgcolor=#2b1a0d></td>
    <td width="1" height="1"
bgcolor=#2c1b12></td>
    <td width="1" height="1"
bgcolor=#526e34></td>
    <td width="1" height="1"
bgcolor=#5a7c37></td>
    <td width="1" height="1"
bgcolor=#586535></td>
    <td width="1" height="1"
bgcolor=#4d4d2f></td>
    <td width="1" height="1"
bgcolor=#42392b></td>
    <td width="1" height="1"
bgcolor=#3e372a></td>
    <td width="1" height="1"
bgcolor=#45482b></td>
    <td width="1" height="1"
bgcolor=#444a24></td>
    <td width="1" height="1"
bgcolor=#464923></td>
    <td width="1" height="1"
bgcolor=#424622></td>
    <td width="1" height="1"
bgcolor=#404d22></td>
    <td width="1" height="1"
bgcolor=#475221></td>
    <td width="1" height="1"
bgcolor=#49541b></td>
  </tr>
  <tr>
    <td width="1" height="1"
bgcolor=#596657></td>
    <td width="1" height="1"
bgcolor=#5a3d37></td>
    <td width="1" height="1"
bgcolor=#ba6c48></td>
    <td width="1" height="1"
bgcolor=#899082></td>
    <td width="1" height="1"
bgcolor=#be819f></td>
    <td width="1" height="1"
bgcolor=#af9e6e></td>
    <td width="1" height="1"
bgcolor=#c6ba7a></td>
    <td width="1" height="1"
bgcolor=#776950></td>
    <td width="1" height="1"
bgcolor=#604a42></td>
    <td width="1" height="1"
bgcolor=#b67d3a></td>
    <td width="1" height="1"
bgcolor=#c16c3d></td>
    <td width="1" height="1"
bgcolor=#885842></td>
    <td width="1" height="1"
bgcolor=#e0d9a7></td>
    <td width="1" height="1"
bgcolor=#ccc89b></td>
    <td width="1" height="1"
bgcolor=#604c2b></td>
    <td width="1" height="1"
bgcolor=#342f21></td>
    <td width="1" height="1"
bgcolor=#bfb890></td>
    <td width="1" height="1"
bgcolor=#594e27></td>
    <td width="1" height="1"
bgcolor=#8f824d></td>
    <td width="1" height="1"
bgcolor=#7f744a></td>
    <td width="1" height="1"
bgcolor=#f0e7b3></td>
    <td width="1" height="1"
bgcolor=#e7d8a9></td>
    <td width="1" height="1"
bgcolor=#e5dec1></td>
    <td width="1" height="1"
bgcolor=#837f5c></td>
    <td width="1" height="1"
bgcolor=#5c452e></td>
    <td width="1" height="1"
bgcolor=#42220f></td>
    <td width="1" height="1"
bgcolor=#3b241b></td>
    <td width="1" height="1"
bgcolor=#391c0f></td>
    <td width="1" height="1"
bgcolor=#6d4c2f></td>
    <td width="1" height="1"
bgcolor=#a96d59></td>
    <td width="1" height="1"
bgcolor=#572528></td>
    <td width="1" height="1"
bgcolor=#d59f9b></td>
    <td width="1" height="1"
bgcolor=#f6d7c6></td>
    <td width="1" height="1"
bgcolor=#c1bc90></td>
    <td width="1" height="1"
bgcolor=#5c4224></td>
    <td width="1" height="1"
bgcolor=#240d09></td>
    <td width="1" height="1"
bgcolor=#876e40></td>
    <td width="1" height="1"
bgcolor=#926546></td>
    <td width="1" height="1"
bgcolor=#351c0a></td>
    <td width="1" height="1"
bgcolor=#5a352c></td>
    <td width="1" height="1"
bgcolor=#70533b></td>
    <td width="1" height="1"
bgcolor=#6a4326></td>
    <td width="1" height="1"
bgcolor=#d72823></td>
    <td width="1" height="1"
bgcolor=#b41f18></td>
    <td width="1" height="1"
bgcolor=#c21911></td>
    <td width="1" height="1"
bgcolor=#c77c38></td>
    <td width="1" height="1"
bgcolor=#a6903b></td>
    <td width="1" height="1"
bgcolor=#68c30c></td>
    <td width="1" height="1"
bgcolor=#949c49></td>
    <td width="1" height="1"
bgcolor=#60432e></td>
    <td width="1" height="1"
bgcolor=#c1b078></td>
    <td width="1" height="1"
bgcolor=#5e3e33></td>
    <td width="1" height="1"
bgcolor=#d4a065></td>
    <td width="1" height="1"
bgcolor=#6b462a></td>
    <td width="1" height="1"
bgcolor=#6b5e4d></td>
    <td width="1" height="1"
bgcolor=#e8e0bd></td>
    <td width="1" height="1"
bgcolor=#dfd7b7></td>
    <td width="1" height="1"
bgcolor=#321c15></td>
    <td width="1" height="1"
bgcolor=#281412></td>
    <td width="1" height="1"
bgcolor=#4f612f></td>
    <td width="1" height="1"
bgcolor=#4a442b></td>
    <td width="1" height="1"
bgcolor=#34281b></td>
    <td width="1" height="1"
bgcolor=#33211e></td>
    <td width="1" height="1"
bgcolor=#33221c></td>
    <td width="1" height="1"
bgcolor=#434322></td>
    <td width="1" height="1"
bgcolor=#4a5821></td>
    <td width="1" height="1"
bgcolor=#48511e></td>
```

```
    <td width="1" height="1"
bgcolor=#4e5225></td>
    <td width="1" height="1"
bgcolor=#42431c></td>
    <td width="1" height="1"
bgcolor=#495324></td>
    <td width="1" height="1"
bgcolor=#4f6627></td>
    <td width="1" height="1"
bgcolor=#455a21></td>
  </tr>
  <tr>
    <td width="1" height="1"
bgcolor=#362d1e></td>
    <td width="1" height="1"
bgcolor=#8f655d></td>
    <td width="1" height="1"
bgcolor=#a46046></td>
    <td width="1" height="1"
bgcolor=#7b7052></td>
    <td width="1" height="1"
bgcolor=#533744></td>
    <td width="1" height="1"
bgcolor=#3a3022></td>
    <td width="1" height="1"
bgcolor=#584f39></td>
    <td width="1" height="1"
bgcolor=#332619></td>
    <td width="1" height="1"
bgcolor=#413222></td>
    <td width="1" height="1"
bgcolor=#4a3526></td>
    <td width="1" height="1"
bgcolor=#b3643f></td>
    <td width="1" height="1"
bgcolor=#a65638></td>
    <td width="1" height="1"
bgcolor=#808061></td>
    <td width="1" height="1"
bgcolor=#8c7e5a></td>
    <td width="1" height="1"
bgcolor=#362419></td>
    <td width="1" height="1"
bgcolor=#51432f></td>
    <td width="1" height="1"
bgcolor=#362518></td>
    <td width="1" height="1"
bgcolor=#584332></td>
    <td width="1" height="1"
bgcolor=#a28f5a></td>
    <td width="1" height="1"
bgcolor=#e6cd85></td>
    <td width="1" height="1"
bgcolor=#544a34></td>
    <td width="1" height="1"
bgcolor=#ebe7ce></td>
    <td width="1" height="1"
bgcolor=#afb189></td>
    <td width="1" height="1"
bgcolor=#89785b></td>
    <td width="1" height="1"
bgcolor=#3e302d></td>
    <td width="1" height="1"
bgcolor=#44210b></td>
    <td width="1" height="1"
bgcolor=#73482b></td>
    <td width="1" height="1"
bgcolor=#8d5c3a></td>
    <td width="1" height="1"
bgcolor=#342011></td>
    <td width="1" height="1"
bgcolor=#7b4629></td>
    <td width="1" height="1"
bgcolor=#dd6140></td>
    <td width="1" height="1"
bgcolor=#b8632c></td>
    <td width="1" height="1"
bgcolor=#9b5421></td>
    <td width="1" height="1"
bgcolor=#946933></td>
    <td width="1" height="1"
bgcolor=#150600></td>
    <td width="1" height="1"
bgcolor=#271a14></td>
    <td width="1" height="1"
bgcolor=#c7905a></td>
    <td width="1" height="1"
bgcolor=#e2ad66></td>
    <td width="1" height="1"
bgcolor=#a66b42></td>
    <td width="1" height="1"
bgcolor=#754230></td>
    <td width="1" height="1"
bgcolor=#7a6048></td>
    <td width="1" height="1"
bgcolor=#ad2412></td>
    <td width="1" height="1"
bgcolor=#642519></td>
    <td width="1" height="1"
bgcolor=#80573e></td>
    <td width="1" height="1"
bgcolor=#693d1f></td>
    <td width="1" height="1"
bgcolor=#5f1b10></td>
    <td width="1" height="1"
bgcolor=#b2131e></td>
    <td width="1" height="1"
bgcolor=#aa7d12></td>
    <td width="1" height="1"
bgcolor=#bab26f></td>
    <td width="1" height="1"
bgcolor=#4b2e1d></td>
    <td width="1" height="1"
bgcolor=#452913></td>
    <td width="1" height="1"
bgcolor=#645242></td>
    <td width="1" height="1"
bgcolor=#cf9060></td>
    <td width="1" height="1"
bgcolor=#c5a560></td>
    <td width="1" height="1"
bgcolor=#452e27></td>
    <td width="1" height="1"
bgcolor=#dad9b6></td>
    <td width="1" height="1"
bgcolor=#e7dbb6></td>
    <td width="1" height="1"
bgcolor=#28150a></td>
    <td width="1" height="1"
bgcolor=#281511></td>
    <td width="1" height="1"
bgcolor=#301c18></td>
    <td width="1" height="1"
bgcolor=#2e1d1c></td>
    <td width="1" height="1"
bgcolor=#2c1b17></td>
    <td width="1" height="1"
bgcolor=#35271d></td>
    <td width="1" height="1"
bgcolor=#4c4a20></td>
    <td width="1" height="1"
bgcolor=#444d1c></td>
    <td width="1" height="1"
bgcolor=#587333></td>
    <td width="1" height="1"
bgcolor=#4f5523></td>
    <td width="1" height="1"
bgcolor=#4f5824></td>
    <td width="1" height="1"
bgcolor=#44481c></td>
    <td width="1" height="1"
bgcolor=#485120></td>
    <td width="1" height="1"
bgcolor=#537724></td>
    <td width="1" height="1"
bgcolor=#508b2e></td>
  </tr>
  <tr>
    <td width="1" height="1"
bgcolor=#5e5231></td>
    <td width="1" height="1"
bgcolor=#826a55></td>
    <td width="1" height="1"
bgcolor=#90634b></td>
    <td width="1" height="1"
bgcolor=#635849></td>
    <td width="1" height="1"
bgcolor=#372618></td>
    <td width="1" height="1"
bgcolor=#443528></td>
    <td width="1" height="1"
bgcolor=#45342d></td>
    <td width="1" height="1"
bgcolor=#523924></td>
```

```
<td width="1" height="1" bgcolor=#966a3f></td>
<td width="1" height="1" bgcolor=#846330></td>
<td width="1" height="1" bgcolor=#8c512d></td>
<td width="1" height="1" bgcolor=#9e7750></td>
<td width="1" height="1" bgcolor=#402c20></td>
<td width="1" height="1" bgcolor=#2d1911></td>
<td width="1" height="1" bgcolor=#382920></td>
<td width="1" height="1" bgcolor=#3c2a20></td>
<td width="1" height="1" bgcolor=#3d251e></td>
<td width="1" height="1" bgcolor=#3d271c></td>
<td width="1" height="1" bgcolor=#836d45></td>
<td width="1" height="1" bgcolor=#927846></td>
<td width="1" height="1" bgcolor=#34251a></td>
<td width="1" height="1" bgcolor=#a49f86></td>
<td width="1" height="1" bgcolor=#9c9168></td>
<td width="1" height="1" bgcolor=#524221></td>
<td width="1" height="1" bgcolor=#120007></td>
<td width="1" height="1" bgcolor=#a27142></td>
<td width="1" height="1" bgcolor=#e2a261></td>
<td width="1" height="1" bgcolor=#cf8847></td>
<td width="1" height="1" bgcolor=#6a4849></td>
<td width="1" height="1" bgcolor=#362319></td>
<td width="1" height="1" bgcolor=#7d5127></td>
<td width="1" height="1" bgcolor=#94563b></td>
<td width="1" height="1" bgcolor=#7d512b></td>
<td width="1" height="1" bgcolor=#f8f4d6></td>
<td width="1" height="1" bgcolor=#af9e74></td>
<td width="1" height="1" bgcolor=#190d03></td>
<td width="1" height="1" bgcolor=#c2834c></td>
<td width="1" height="1" bgcolor=#a67f4b></td>
<td width="1" height="1" bgcolor=#824b20></td>
<td width="1" height="1" bgcolor=#6d3f31></td>
<td width="1" height="1" bgcolor=#79372e></td>
<td width="1" height="1" bgcolor=#adaa8e></td>
<td width="1" height="1" bgcolor=#331308></td>
<td width="1" height="1" bgcolor=#dc754d></td>
<td width="1" height="1" bgcolor=#d49f4a></td>
<td width="1" height="1" bgcolor=#944e22></td>
<td width="1" height="1" bgcolor=#676d59></td>
<td width="1" height="1" bgcolor=#6c714b></td>
<td width="1" height="1" bgcolor=#b2753f></td>
<td width="1" height="1" bgcolor=#c98344></td>
<td width="1" height="1" bgcolor=#240f18></td>
<td width="1" height="1" bgcolor=#8d6c42></td>
<td width="1" height="1" bgcolor=#9f7654></td>
<td width="1" height="1" bgcolor=#c8a847></td>
<td width="1" height="1" bgcolor=#3d231b></td>
<td width="1" height="1" bgcolor=#6a5f55></td>
<td width="1" height="1" bgcolor=#917962></td>
<td width="1" height="1" bgcolor=#281413></td>
<td width="1" height="1" bgcolor=#1f130c></td>
<td width="1" height="1" bgcolor=#5d5236></td>
<td width="1" height="1" bgcolor=#d3c97a></td>
<td width="1" height="1" bgcolor=#bca26c></td>
<td width="1" height="1" bgcolor=#463d22></td>
<td width="1" height="1" bgcolor=#40461f></td>
<td width="1" height="1" bgcolor=#52652d></td>
<td width="1" height="1" bgcolor=#414926></td>
<td width="1" height="1" bgcolor=#505921></td>
<td width="1" height="1" bgcolor=#4a5223></td>
<td width="1" height="1" bgcolor=#464c1e></td>
<td width="1" height="1" bgcolor=#555721></td>
<td width="1" height="1" bgcolor=#476c25></td>
<td width="1" height="1" bgcolor=#579f37></td>
</tr>
<tr>
<td width="1" height="1" bgcolor=#534425></td>
<td width="1" height="1" bgcolor=#635655></td>
<td width="1" height="1" bgcolor=#514443></td>
<td width="1" height="1" bgcolor=#40311f></td>
<td width="1" height="1" bgcolor=#a17054></td>
<td width="1" height="1" bgcolor=#ae8a52></td>
<td width="1" height="1" bgcolor=#6a4d33></td>
<td width="1" height="1" bgcolor=#4a3423></td>
<td width="1" height="1" bgcolor=#d5844e></td>
<td width="1" height="1" bgcolor=#b97148></td>
<td width="1" height="1" bgcolor=#575321></td>
<td width="1" height="1" bgcolor=#a99f39></td>
<td width="1" height="1" bgcolor=#512e1d></td>
<td width="1" height="1" bgcolor=#52382b></td>
<td width="1" height="1" bgcolor=#48372a></td>
<td width="1" height="1" bgcolor=#673923></td>
<td width="1" height="1" bgcolor=#9b6c3a></td>
<td width="1" height="1" bgcolor=#814b27></td>
<td width="1" height="1" bgcolor=#595139></td>
<td width="1" height="1" bgcolor=#4c3c31></td>
<td width="1" height="1" bgcolor=#6c684b></td>
<td width="1" height="1" bgcolor=#a39f65></td>
```

```
    <td width="1" height="1"
bgcolor=#c1b481></td>
    <td width="1" height="1"
bgcolor=#998e6a></td>
    <td width="1" height="1"
bgcolor=#231710></td>
    <td width="1" height="1"
bgcolor=#af6238></td>
    <td width="1" height="1"
bgcolor=#bc7a33></td>
    <td width="1" height="1"
bgcolor=#b66c3c></td>
    <td width="1" height="1"
bgcolor=#9a5a8d></td>
    <td width="1" height="1"
bgcolor=#311d13></td>
    <td width="1" height="1"
bgcolor=#7b4b26></td>
    <td width="1" height="1"
bgcolor=#d79046></td>
    <td width="1" height="1"
bgcolor=#ad7941></td>
    <td width="1" height="1"
bgcolor=#ebe4c3></td>
    <td width="1" height="1"
bgcolor=#d2c396></td>
    <td width="1" height="1"
bgcolor=#634631></td>
    <td width="1" height="1"
bgcolor=#a6b07c></td>
    <td width="1" height="1"
bgcolor=#b17a42></td>
    <td width="1" height="1"
bgcolor=#9b805c></td>
    <td width="1" height="1"
bgcolor=#482c17></td>
    <td width="1" height="1"
bgcolor=#4e2d18></td>
    <td width="1" height="1"
bgcolor=#56351f></td>
    <td width="1" height="1"
bgcolor=#3a1c18></td>
    <td width="1" height="1"
bgcolor=#6a4428></td>
    <td width="1" height="1"
bgcolor=#b16b31></td>
    <td width="1" height="1"
bgcolor=#ae7a4c></td>
    <td width="1" height="1"
bgcolor=#ced9b3></td>
    <td width="1" height="1"
bgcolor=#d9dbaf></td>
    <td width="1" height="1"
bgcolor=#c27a42></td>
    <td width="1" height="1"
bgcolor=#bd663b></td>
    <td width="1" height="1"
bgcolor=#988637></td>
    <td width="1" height="1"
bgcolor=#a4ae6d></td>
    <td width="1" height="1"
bgcolor=#a7c7be></td>
    <td width="1" height="1"
bgcolor=#eaea18></td>
    <td width="1" height="1"
bgcolor=#b7c242></td>
    <td width="1" height="1"
bgcolor=#645026></td>
    <td width="1" height="1"
bgcolor=#574737></td>
    <td width="1" height="1"
bgcolor=#534932></td>
    <td width="1" height="1"
bgcolor=#49362c></td>
    <td width="1" height="1"
bgcolor=#a68e51></td>
    <td width="1" height="1"
bgcolor=#d4a350></td>
    <td width="1" height="1"
bgcolor=#edb966></td>
    <td width="1" height="1"
bgcolor=#745e32></td>
    <td width="1" height="1"
bgcolor=#494e29></td>
    <td width="1" height="1"
bgcolor=#414823></td>
    <td width="1" height="1"
bgcolor=#39271b></td>
    <td width="1" height="1"
bgcolor=#546a2c></td>
    <td width="1" height="1"
bgcolor=#494826></td>
    <td width="1" height="1"
bgcolor=#423e1e></td>
    <td width="1" height="1"
bgcolor=#494f20></td>
    <td width="1" height="1"
bgcolor=#4e4b18></td>
    <td width="1" height="1"
bgcolor=#579c41></td>
  </tr>
  <tr>
    <td width="1" height="1"
bgcolor=#53421e></td>
    <td width="1" height="1"
bgcolor=#655d40></td>
    <td width="1" height="1"
bgcolor=#191911></td>
    <td width="1" height="1"
bgcolor=#3d342d></td>
    <td width="1" height="1"
bgcolor=#ae7440></td>
    <td width="1" height="1"
bgcolor=#c6844d></td>
    <td width="1" height="1"
bgcolor=#815f3b></td>
    <td width="1" height="1"
bgcolor=#645539></td>
    <td width="1" height="1"
bgcolor=#955b31></td>
    <td width="1" height="1"
bgcolor=#896434></td>
    <td width="1" height="1"
bgcolor=#372a1c></td>
    <td width="1" height="1"
bgcolor=#3f2b1d></td>
    <td width="1" height="1"
bgcolor=#43291b></td>
    <td width="1" height="1"
bgcolor=#6b4c22></td>
    <td width="1" height="1"
bgcolor=#67422e></td>
    <td width="1" height="1"
bgcolor=#835434></td>
    <td width="1" height="1"
bgcolor=#c46b3d></td>
    <td width="1" height="1"
bgcolor=#8e4726></td>
    <td width="1" height="1"
bgcolor=#4e493a></td>
    <td width="1" height="1"
bgcolor=#463620></td>
    <td width="1" height="1"
bgcolor=#858763></td>
    <td width="1" height="1"
bgcolor=#bb7c21></td>
    <td width="1" height="1"
bgcolor=#c39249></td>
    <td width="1" height="1"
bgcolor=#746027></td>
    <td width="1" height="1"
bgcolor=#99c60c></td>
    <td width="1" height="1"
bgcolor=#f1a713></td>
    <td width="1" height="1"
bgcolor=#cb643c></td>
    <td width="1" height="1"
bgcolor=#513217></td>
    <td width="1" height="1"
bgcolor=#87598a></td>
    <td width="1" height="1"
bgcolor=#211004></td>
    <td width="1" height="1"
bgcolor=#f5655c></td>
    <td width="1" height="1"
bgcolor=#b96f3f></td>
    <td width="1" height="1"
bgcolor=#bdac95></td>
    <td width="1" height="1"
bgcolor=#e2cda4></td>
    <td width="1" height="1"
bgcolor=#99bfaa></td>
    <td width="1" height="1"
bgcolor=#82c6bb></td>
```

```
    <td width="1" height="1" bgcolor=#81c8ca></td>
    <td width="1" height="1" bgcolor=#c4a679></td>
    <td width="1" height="1" bgcolor=#667554></td>
    <td width="1" height="1" bgcolor=#69a29e></td>
    <td width="1" height="1" bgcolor=#a0a887></td>
    <td width="1" height="1" bgcolor=#67402b></td>
    <td width="1" height="1" bgcolor=#705036></td>
    <td width="1" height="1" bgcolor=#7b6a1f></td>
    <td width="1" height="1" bgcolor=#b57d4f></td>
    <td width="1" height="1" bgcolor=#e77932></td>
    <td width="1" height="1" bgcolor=#dd7447></td>
    <td width="1" height="1" bgcolor=#926e2f></td>
    <td width="1" height="1" bgcolor=#c1a128></td>
    <td width="1" height="1" bgcolor=#895f35></td>
    <td width="1" height="1" bgcolor=#bac539></td>
    <td width="1" height="1" bgcolor=#87c6ac></td>
    <td width="1" height="1" bgcolor=#99d2cc></td>
    <td width="1" height="1" bgcolor=#c2c839></td>
    <td width="1" height="1" bgcolor=#dce13d></td>
    <td width="1" height="1" bgcolor=#d6c540></td>
    <td width="1" height="1" bgcolor=#7c592b></td>
    <td width="1" height="1" bgcolor=#a4662a></td>
    <td width="1" height="1" bgcolor=#836a42></td>
    <td width="1" height="1" bgcolor=#ab8846></td>
    <td width="1" height="1" bgcolor=#d79b4d></td>
    <td width="1" height="1" bgcolor=#d18d4a></td>
    <td width="1" height="1" bgcolor=#715b39></td>
    <td width="1" height="1" bgcolor=#362d0f></td>
    <td width="1" height="1" bgcolor=#2f2118></td>
    <td width="1" height="1" bgcolor=#372f1e></td>
    <td width="1" height="1" bgcolor=#4d5923></td>
    <td width="1" height="1" bgcolor=#44401e></td>
    <td width="1" height="1" bgcolor=#383718></td>
    <td width="1" height="1" bgcolor=#565e2b></td>
    <td width="1" height="1" bgcolor=#4b4d20></td>
    <td width="1" height="1" bgcolor=#485e1e></td>
  </tr>
  <tr>
    <td width="1" height="1" bgcolor=#7e7e5b></td>
    <td width="1" height="1" bgcolor=#d2bb71></td>
    <td width="1" height="1" bgcolor=#c49840></td>
    <td width="1" height="1" bgcolor=#43452b></td>
    <td width="1" height="1" bgcolor=#bfa26e></td>
    <td width="1" height="1" bgcolor=#af8a5b></td>
    <td width="1" height="1" bgcolor=#3d2d23></td>
    <td width="1" height="1" bgcolor=#626740></td>
    <td width="1" height="1" bgcolor=#a5955e></td>
    <td width="1" height="1" bgcolor=#a09563></td>
    <td width="1" height="1" bgcolor=#3c2d20></td>
    <td width="1" height="1" bgcolor=#4a3421></td>
    <td width="1" height="1" bgcolor=#a96433></td>
    <td width="1" height="1" bgcolor=#d78c3c></td>
    <td width="1" height="1" bgcolor=#97572c></td>
    <td width="1" height="1" bgcolor=#918d5a></td>
    <td width="1" height="1" bgcolor=#794f28></td>
    <td width="1" height="1" bgcolor=#897449></td>
    <td width="1" height="1" bgcolor=#3f321d></td>
    <td width="1" height="1" bgcolor=#b3b481></td>
    <td width="1" height="1" bgcolor=#5e4c24></td>
    <td width="1" height="1" bgcolor=#bf6228></td>
    <td width="1" height="1" bgcolor=#f0521f></td>
    <td width="1" height="1" bgcolor=#c1dc13></td>
    <td width="1" height="1" bgcolor=#ecdb0d></td>
    <td width="1" height="1" bgcolor=#e8c014></td>
    <td width="1" height="1" bgcolor=#da3d12></td>
    <td width="1" height="1" bgcolor=#b2c822></td>
    <td width="1" height="1" bgcolor=#8b3b22></td>
    <td width="1" height="1" bgcolor=#ba554f></td>
    <td width="1" height="1" bgcolor=#fb6849></td>
    <td width="1" height="1" bgcolor=#e67a3f></td>
    <td width="1" height="1" bgcolor=#897855></td>
    <td width="1" height="1" bgcolor=#ba6855></td>
    <td width="1" height="1" bgcolor=#9eb4bd></td>
    <td width="1" height="1" bgcolor=#bce7d9></td>
    <td width="1" height="1" bgcolor=#bae4e6></td>
    <td width="1" height="1" bgcolor=#dfe281></td>
    <td width="1" height="1" bgcolor=#7b7269></td>
    <td width="1" height="1" bgcolor=#bdead9></td>
    <td width="1" height="1" bgcolor=#95d7c8></td>
    <td width="1" height="1" bgcolor=#878f60></td>
    <td width="1" height="1" bgcolor=#9f7c45></td>
    <td width="1" height="1" bgcolor=#e0c396></td>
    <td width="1" height="1" bgcolor=#f4c89f></td>
    <td width="1" height="1" bgcolor=#efccb0></td>
    <td width="1" height="1" bgcolor=#f0d599></td>
    <td width="1" height="1" bgcolor=#edcd9a></td>
    <td width="1" height="1" bgcolor=#b8923a></td>
    <td width="1" height="1" bgcolor=#585f22></td>
```

```
    <td width="1" height="1"
bgcolor=#95bd6c></td>
    <td width="1" height="1"
bgcolor=#80c9b5></td>
    <td width="1" height="1"
bgcolor=#8fd3bd></td>
    <td width="1" height="1"
bgcolor=#cad94e></td>
    <td width="1" height="1"
bgcolor=#c3b235></td>
    <td width="1" height="1"
bgcolor=#bd9225></td>
    <td width="1" height="1"
bgcolor=#d06219></td>
    <td width="1" height="1"
bgcolor=#864427></td>
    <td width="1" height="1"
bgcolor=#8e6b3c></td>
    <td width="1" height="1"
bgcolor=#b78f50></td>
    <td width="1" height="1"
bgcolor=#d58c47></td>
    <td width="1" height="1"
bgcolor=#be7640></td>
    <td width="1" height="1"
bgcolor=#866a47></td>
    <td width="1" height="1"
bgcolor=#443423></td>
    <td width="1" height="1"
bgcolor=#4f482c></td>
    <td width="1" height="1"
bgcolor=#3e3b1c></td>
    <td width="1" height="1"
bgcolor=#4f592c></td>
    <td width="1" height="1"
bgcolor=#413f1d></td>
    <td width="1" height="1"
bgcolor=#383714></td>
    <td width="1" height="1"
bgcolor=#5d7335></td>
    <td width="1" height="1"
bgcolor=#495f2b></td>
    <td width="1" height="1"
bgcolor=#544f23></td>
  </tr>
  <tr>
    <td width="1" height="1"
bgcolor=#ececb8></td>
    <td width="1" height="1"
bgcolor=#d0b565></td>
    <td width="1" height="1"
bgcolor=#e2c46b></td>
    <td width="1" height="1"
bgcolor=#e6dda2></td>
    <td width="1" height="1"
bgcolor=#d1c992></td>
    <td width="1" height="1"
bgcolor=#7b764a></td>
    <td width="1" height="1"
bgcolor=#382713></td>
    <td width="1" height="1"
bgcolor=#3c2c2a></td>
    <td width="1" height="1"
bgcolor=#6c5e3c></td>
    <td width="1" height="1"
bgcolor=#726347></td>
    <td width="1" height="1"
bgcolor=#432e1b></td>
    <td width="1" height="1"
bgcolor=#3b2d1d></td>
    <td width="1" height="1"
bgcolor=#7a4725></td>
    <td width="1" height="1"
bgcolor=#986235></td>
    <td width="1" height="1"
bgcolor=#4d2f19></td>
    <td width="1" height="1"
bgcolor=#51442d></td>
    <td width="1" height="1"
bgcolor=#695c39></td>
    <td width="1" height="1"
bgcolor=#846f41></td>
    <td width="1" height="1"
bgcolor=#594635></td>
    <td width="1" height="1"
bgcolor=#67633a></td>
    <td width="1" height="1"
bgcolor=#141307></td>
    <td width="1" height="1"
bgcolor=#b55c17></td>
    <td width="1" height="1"
bgcolor=#dbdd16></td>
    <td width="1" height="1"
bgcolor=#f3ee21></td>
    <td width="1" height="1"
bgcolor=#865c1b></td>
    <td width="1" height="1"
bgcolor=#ddd43d></td>
    <td width="1" height="1"
bgcolor=#ea6b18></td>
    <td width="1" height="1"
bgcolor=#dbcf1b></td>
    <td width="1" height="1"
bgcolor=#e6ae35></td>
    <td width="1" height="1"
bgcolor=#eb5c66></td>
    <td width="1" height="1"
bgcolor=#f0606d></td>
    <td width="1" height="1"
bgcolor=#f27052></td>
    <td width="1" height="1"
bgcolor=#a54c35></td>
    <td width="1" height="1"
bgcolor=#bc8d99></td>
    <td width="1" height="1"
bgcolor=#886c7a></td>
    <td width="1" height="1"
bgcolor=#d3d8d7></td>
    <td width="1" height="1"
bgcolor=#d3ceb6></td>
    <td width="1" height="1"
bgcolor=#d5ad83></td>
    <td width="1" height="1"
bgcolor=#986047></td>
    <td width="1" height="1"
bgcolor=#c2d7b8></td>
    <td width="1" height="1"
bgcolor=#67bfcd></td>
    <td width="1" height="1"
bgcolor=#6bb5a5></td>
    <td width="1" height="1"
bgcolor=#d47d32></td>
    <td width="1" height="1"
bgcolor=#eb8d37></td>
    <td width="1" height="1"
bgcolor=#cf5733></td>
    <td width="1" height="1"
bgcolor=#f07a3e></td>
    <td width="1" height="1"
bgcolor=#f25e33></td>
    <td width="1" height="1"
bgcolor=#f18a4b></td>
    <td width="1" height="1"
bgcolor=#cc8855></td>
    <td width="1" height="1"
bgcolor=#75941c></td>
    <td width="1" height="1"
bgcolor=#7cbd91></td>
    <td width="1" height="1"
bgcolor=#7ac19f></td>
    <td width="1" height="1"
bgcolor=#7cc3b3></td>
    <td width="1" height="1"
bgcolor=#d5da4c></td>
    <td width="1" height="1"
bgcolor=#60421e></td>
    <td width="1" height="1"
bgcolor=#a4882a></td>
    <td width="1" height="1"
bgcolor=#774533></td>
    <td width="1" height="1"
bgcolor=#a57744></td>
    <td width="1" height="1"
bgcolor=#9d6840></td>
    <td width="1" height="1"
bgcolor=#896445></td>
    <td width="1" height="1"
bgcolor=#d4904f></td>
    <td width="1" height="1"
bgcolor=#d5a258></td>
    <td width="1" height="1"
bgcolor=#d1ab54></td>
    <td width="1" height="1"
bgcolor=#685b33></td>
```

```
    <td width="1" height="1"
bgcolor=#4d5127></td>
    <td width="1" height="1"
bgcolor=#5a5d2d></td>
    <td width="1" height="1"
bgcolor=#445221></td>
    <td width="1" height="1"
bgcolor=#434722></td>
    <td width="1" height="1"
bgcolor=#393717></td>
    <td width="1" height="1"
bgcolor=#3d5419></td>
    <td width="1" height="1"
bgcolor=#4e7630></td>
    <td width="1" height="1"
bgcolor=#4d5930></td>
  </tr>
  <tr>
    <td width="1" height="1"
bgcolor=#f4f7ce></td>
    <td width="1" height="1"
bgcolor=#e2c784></td>
    <td width="1" height="1"
bgcolor=#f5f4c6></td>
    <td width="1" height="1"
bgcolor=#f0ebbf></td>
    <td width="1" height="1"
bgcolor=#f9f4c2></td>
    <td width="1" height="1"
bgcolor=#75653f></td>
    <td width="1" height="1"
bgcolor=#332a1f></td>
    <td width="1" height="1"
bgcolor=#3b2d23></td>
    <td width="1" height="1"
bgcolor=#342313></td>
    <td width="1" height="1"
bgcolor=#7c5838></td>
    <td width="1" height="1"
bgcolor=#4f3520></td>
    <td width="1" height="1"
bgcolor=#452b20></td>
    <td width="1" height="1"
bgcolor=#321e14></td>
    <td width="1" height="1"
bgcolor=#321c13></td>
    <td width="1" height="1"
bgcolor=#3b281a></td>
    <td width="1" height="1"
bgcolor=#3b271d></td>
    <td width="1" height="1"
bgcolor=#473522></td>
    <td width="1" height="1"
bgcolor=#57482c></td>
    <td width="1" height="1"
bgcolor=#4b3c2a></td>
    <td width="1" height="1"
bgcolor=#584b2d></td>
    <td width="1" height="1"
bgcolor=#2d1a14></td>
    <td width="1" height="1"
bgcolor=#d8a011></td>
    <td width="1" height="1"
bgcolor=#d2ec0d></td>
    <td width="1" height="1"
bgcolor=#b46e1b></td>
    <td width="1" height="1"
bgcolor=#8d500b></td>
    <td width="1" height="1"
bgcolor=#825813></td>
    <td width="1" height="1"
bgcolor=#a5862c></td>
    <td width="1" height="1"
bgcolor=#83655b></td>
    <td width="1" height="1"
bgcolor=#d04f83></td>
    <td width="1" height="1"
bgcolor=#d6467e></td>
    <td width="1" height="1"
bgcolor=#f64a89></td>
    <td width="1" height="1"
bgcolor=#fa3a88></td>
    <td width="1" height="1"
bgcolor=#b1876d></td>
    <td width="1" height="1"
bgcolor=#969db3></td>
    <td width="1" height="1"
bgcolor=#a94a49></td>
    <td width="1" height="1"
bgcolor=#72e7f2></td>
    <td width="1" height="1"
bgcolor=#a15853></td>
    <td width="1" height="1"
bgcolor=#f8d079></td>
    <td width="1" height="1"
bgcolor=#c1ab63></td>
    <td width="1" height="1"
bgcolor=#81ddf1></td>
    <td width="1" height="1"
bgcolor=#62b9d2></td>
    <td width="1" height="1"
bgcolor=#7aaa92></td>
    <td width="1" height="1"
bgcolor=#c97a2e></td>
    <td width="1" height="1"
bgcolor=#cc8449></td>
    <td width="1" height="1"
bgcolor=#e29642></td>
    <td width="1" height="1"
bgcolor=#f15728></td>
    <td width="1" height="1"
bgcolor=#f94525></td>
    <td width="1" height="1"
bgcolor=#fa511d></td>
    <td width="1" height="1"
bgcolor=#fc7239></td>
    <td width="1" height="1"
bgcolor=#759a29></td>
    <td width="1" height="1"
bgcolor=#77ac88></td>
    <td width="1" height="1"
bgcolor=#81b5a1></td>
    <td width="1" height="1"
bgcolor=#92b7a6></td>
    <td width="1" height="1"
bgcolor=#c1c034></td>
    <td width="1" height="1"
bgcolor=#765927></td>
    <td width="1" height="1"
bgcolor=#a89b35></td>
    <td width="1" height="1"
bgcolor=#b0843f></td>
    <td width="1" height="1"
bgcolor=#d69445></td>
    <td width="1" height="1"
bgcolor=#e89a4e></td>
    <td width="1" height="1"
bgcolor=#d3ab52></td>
    <td width="1" height="1"
bgcolor=#f1be5f></td>
    <td width="1" height="1"
bgcolor=#f5ca62></td>
    <td width="1" height="1"
bgcolor=#f5c251></td>
    <td width="1" height="1"
bgcolor=#f7d478></td>
    <td width="1" height="1"
bgcolor=#554d1a></td>
    <td width="1" height="1"
bgcolor=#616e2d></td>
    <td width="1" height="1"
bgcolor=#4c5724></td>
    <td width="1" height="1"
bgcolor=#434725></td>
    <td width="1" height="1"
bgcolor=#3f421c></td>
    <td width="1" height="1"
bgcolor=#4c5b29></td>
    <td width="1" height="1"
bgcolor=#516c29></td>
    <td width="1" height="1"
bgcolor=#475521></td>
  </tr>
  <tr>
    <td width="1" height="1"
bgcolor=#d9bd4a></td>
    <td width="1" height="1"
bgcolor=#f3ecc9></td>
    <td width="1" height="1"
bgcolor=#f3edc8></td>
    <td width="1" height="1"
bgcolor=#ede9b0></td>
    <td width="1" height="1"
bgcolor=#f6f4c4></td>
```

```
    <td width="1" height="1" bgcolor=#a79470></td>
    <td width="1" height="1" bgcolor=#2e231c></td>
    <td width="1" height="1" bgcolor=#32231a></td>
    <td width="1" height="1" bgcolor=#322215></td>
    <td width="1" height="1" bgcolor=#412617></td>
    <td width="1" height="1" bgcolor=#3c2d23></td>
    <td width="1" height="1" bgcolor=#3c2217></td>
    <td width="1" height="1" bgcolor=#372317></td>
    <td width="1" height="1" bgcolor=#2d1c13></td>
    <td width="1" height="1" bgcolor=#3a251c></td>
    <td width="1" height="1" bgcolor=#382715></td>
    <td width="1" height="1" bgcolor=#3a2a1d></td>
    <td width="1" height="1" bgcolor=#3a2a19></td>
    <td width="1" height="1" bgcolor=#453623></td>
    <td width="1" height="1" bgcolor=#483521></td>
    <td width="1" height="1" bgcolor=#533b1d></td>
    <td width="1" height="1" bgcolor=#b5a90e></td>
    <td width="1" height="1" bgcolor=#a5db0c></td>
    <td width="1" height="1" bgcolor=#aac50c></td>
    <td width="1" height="1" bgcolor=#442410></td>
    <td width="1" height="1" bgcolor=#cba639></td>
    <td width="1" height="1" bgcolor=#e3cb0d></td>
    <td width="1" height="1" bgcolor=#836649></td>
    <td width="1" height="1" bgcolor=#de3b86></td>
    <td width="1" height="1" bgcolor=#ab7994></td>
    <td width="1" height="1" bgcolor=#fb376f></td>
    <td width="1" height="1" bgcolor=#f85e76></td>
    <td width="1" height="1" bgcolor=#697c67></td>
    <td width="1" height="1" bgcolor=#7dced7></td>
    <td width="1" height="1" bgcolor=#5a6159></td>
    <td width="1" height="1" bgcolor=#99847f></td>
    <td width="1" height="1" bgcolor=#ccac66></td>
    <td width="1" height="1" bgcolor=#ae803a></td>
    <td width="1" height="1" bgcolor=#bfb3a2></td>
    <td width="1" height="1" bgcolor=#90beac></td>
    <td width="1" height="1" bgcolor=#61c4d7></td>
    <td width="1" height="1" bgcolor=#60583e></td>
    <td width="1" height="1" bgcolor=#7d6c1d></td>
    <td width="1" height="1" bgcolor=#eec9a2></td>
    <td width="1" height="1" bgcolor=#e1a891></td>
    <td width="1" height="1" bgcolor=#ef3e18></td>
    <td rowspan="2" colspan="1" width="1" height="1" bgcolor=#f63315></td>
    <td width="1" height="1" bgcolor=#f6591b></td>
    <td width="1" height="1" bgcolor=#ff662a></td>
    <td width="1" height="1" bgcolor=#6d9228></td>
    <td width="1" height="1" bgcolor=#96c295></td>
    <td width="1" height="1" bgcolor=#9ac9ad></td>
    <td width="1" height="1" bgcolor=#a5bf6b></td>
    <td width="1" height="1" bgcolor=#8d7f2e></td>
    <td width="1" height="1" bgcolor=#946d31></td>
    <td width="1" height="1" bgcolor=#8d6a42></td>
    <td width="1" height="1" bgcolor=#c2863b></td>
    <td width="1" height="1" bgcolor=#ca823d></td>
    <td width="1" height="1" bgcolor=#98773b></td>
    <td width="1" height="1" bgcolor=#e7ca61></td>
    <td width="1" height="1" bgcolor=#e7be56></td>
    <td width="1" height="1" bgcolor=#f2cb55></td>
    <td width="1" height="1" bgcolor=#c3833c></td>
    <td width="1" height="1" bgcolor=#ddaa54></td>
    <td width="1" height="1" bgcolor=#ae8a4e></td>
    <td width="1" height="1" bgcolor=#5c5718></td>
    <td width="1" height="1" bgcolor=#424423></td>
    <td width="1" height="1" bgcolor=#444f1e></td>
    <td width="1" height="1" bgcolor=#414d20></td>
    <td width="1" height="1" bgcolor=#474c1f></td>
    <td width="1" height="1" bgcolor=#435919></td>
    <td width="1" height="1" bgcolor=#4d5f22></td>
  </tr>
  <tr>
    <td width="1" height="1" bgcolor=#ecdd9b></td>
    <td width="1" height="1" bgcolor=#ebd97f></td>
    <td width="1" height="1" bgcolor=#e2c976></td>
    <td width="1" height="1" bgcolor=#e7dcad></td>
    <td width="1" height="1" bgcolor=#ecebbd></td>
    <td width="1" height="1" bgcolor=#998f63></td>
    <td width="1" height="1" bgcolor=#2a1c16></td>
    <td width="1" height="1" bgcolor=#2c1e15></td>
    <td width="1" height="1" bgcolor=#2f1e15></td>
    <td width="1" height="1" bgcolor=#342416></td>
    <td width="1" height="1" bgcolor=#362014></td>
    <td width="1" height="1" bgcolor=#361f11></td>
    <td width="1" height="1" bgcolor=#321c13></td>
    <td width="1" height="1" bgcolor=#2d1913></td>
    <td width="1" height="1" bgcolor=#312013></td>
    <td width="1" height="1" bgcolor=#352014></td>
    <td width="1" height="1" bgcolor=#331f0e></td>
    <td width="1" height="1" bgcolor=#2f190d></td>
```

```
    <td width="1" height="1" bgcolor=#3b2d1a></td>
    <td width="1" height="1" bgcolor=#422d1a></td>
    <td width="1" height="1" bgcolor=#ae9e26></td>
    <td width="1" height="1" bgcolor=#bdb70e></td>
    <td width="1" height="1" bgcolor=#91c910></td>
    <td width="1" height="1" bgcolor=#b1c40b></td>
    <td width="1" height="1" bgcolor=#5c3a14></td>
    <td width="1" height="1" bgcolor=#56320a></td>
    <td width="1" height="1" bgcolor=#7c510b></td>
    <td width="1" height="1" bgcolor=#764e3a></td>
    <td width="1" height="1" bgcolor=#f92986></td>
    <td width="1" height="1" bgcolor=#db435a></td>
    <td width="1" height="1" bgcolor=#ad5c78></td>
    <td width="1" height="1" bgcolor=#957c8a></td>
    <td width="1" height="1" bgcolor=#c46731></td>
    <td width="1" height="1" bgcolor=#7bb4bf></td>
    <td width="1" height="1" bgcolor=#d7e0a7></td>
    <td width="1" height="1" bgcolor=#5fc0d2></td>
    <td width="1" height="1" bgcolor=#6a5d3f></td>
    <td width="1" height="1" bgcolor=#644629></td>
    <td width="1" height="1" bgcolor=#aece9b></td>
    <td width="1" height="1" bgcolor=#68bab4></td>
    <td width="1" height="1" bgcolor=#58b8c2></td>
    <td width="1" height="1" bgcolor=#685034></td>
    <td width="1" height="1" bgcolor=#a77646></td>
    <td width="1" height="1" bgcolor=#e9cfb7></td>
    <td width="1" height="1" bgcolor=#e3885a></td>
    <td width="1" height="1" bgcolor=#fc270a></td>
    <td width="1" height="1" bgcolor=#fa5b2b></td>
    <td width="1" height="1" bgcolor=#ff5715></td>
    <td width="1" height="1" bgcolor=#80a623></td>
    <td width="1" height="1" bgcolor=#dee537></td>
    <td width="1" height="1" bgcolor=#e5e142></td>
    <td width="1" height="1" bgcolor=#c3b426></td>
    <td width="1" height="1" bgcolor=#7f553e></td>
    <td width="1" height="1" bgcolor=#634135></td>
    <td width="1" height="1" bgcolor=#a77a40></td>
    <td width="1" height="1" bgcolor=#c3833e></td>
    <td width="1" height="1" bgcolor=#a96c36></td>
    <td width="1" height="1" bgcolor=#77622a></td>
    <td width="1" height="1" bgcolor=#c1c555></td>
    <td width="1" height="1" bgcolor=#878031></td>
    <td width="1" height="1" bgcolor=#c7c152></td>
    <td width="1" height="1" bgcolor=#7b572a></td>
    <td width="1" height="1" bgcolor=#a47a3a></td>
    <td width="1" height="1" bgcolor=#b79145></td>
    <td width="1" height="1" bgcolor=#a49a37></td>
    <td width="1" height="1" bgcolor=#514f20></td>
    <td width="1" height="1" bgcolor=#40501c></td>
    <td width="1" height="1" bgcolor=#3c481c></td>
    <td width="1" height="1" bgcolor=#41441b></td>
    <td width="1" height="1" bgcolor=#46491f></td>
    <td width="1" height="1" bgcolor=#4a581c></td>
  </tr>
  <tr>
    <td width="1" height="1" bgcolor=#d2d2a8></td>
    <td width="1" height="1" bgcolor=#6c613d></td>
    <td width="1" height="1" bgcolor=#5d5331></td>
    <td width="1" height="1" bgcolor=#f3f1d6></td>
    <td width="1" height="1" bgcolor=#efeec6></td>
    <td width="1" height="1" bgcolor=#8d825f></td>
    <td width="1" height="1" bgcolor=#251c11></td>
    <td width="1" height="1" bgcolor=#27180e></td>
    <td width="1" height="1" bgcolor=#291a12></td>
    <td width="1" height="1" bgcolor=#2f1d14></td>
    <td width="1" height="1" bgcolor=#2c1b0e></td>
    <td width="1" height="1" bgcolor=#331e12></td>
    <td width="1" height="1" bgcolor=#301a13></td>
    <td width="1" height="1" bgcolor=#2a150e></td>
    <td width="1" height="1" bgcolor=#341f14></td>
    <td width="1" height="1" bgcolor=#2f1a10></td>
    <td width="1" height="1" bgcolor=#321e11></td>
    <td width="1" height="1" bgcolor=#2b1406></td>
    <td width="1" height="1" bgcolor=#331f14></td>
    <td width="1" height="1" bgcolor=#402d1e></td>
    <td width="1" height="1" bgcolor=#beea0c></td>
    <td width="1" height="1" bgcolor=#b5e00d></td>
    <td width="1" height="1" bgcolor=#878714></td>
    <td width="1" height="1" bgcolor=#5a3d0c></td>
    <td width="1" height="1" bgcolor=#7e581c></td>
    <td width="1" height="1" bgcolor=#a8a213></td>
    <td width="1" height="1" bgcolor=#953914></td>
    <td width="1" height="1" bgcolor=#a77f21></td>
    <td width="1" height="1" bgcolor=#edc120></td>
    <td width="1" height="1" bgcolor=#c99534></td>
    <td width="1" height="1" bgcolor=#d25829></td>
    <td width="1" height="1" bgcolor=#cc5764></td>
    <td width="1" height="1" bgcolor=#f15b69></td>
```

```
    <td width="1" height="1"
bgcolor=#448670></td>
    <td width="1" height="1"
bgcolor=#5c8782></td>
    <td width="1" height="1"
bgcolor=#8b9c8b></td>
    <td width="1" height="1"
bgcolor=#8ca58d></td>
    <td width="1" height="1"
bgcolor=#7f7549></td>
    <td width="1" height="1"
bgcolor=#82bfaf></td>
    <td width="1" height="1"
bgcolor=#62c1c9></td>
    <td width="1" height="1"
bgcolor=#61c4d0></td>
    <td width="1" height="1"
bgcolor=#ad9e48></td>
    <td width="1" height="1"
bgcolor=#be5520></td>
    <td width="1" height="1"
bgcolor=#ef9161></td>
    <td width="1" height="1"
bgcolor=#eb5126></td>
    <td width="1" height="1"
bgcolor=#f93311></td>
    <td width="1" height="1"
bgcolor=#e23821></td>
    <td width="1" height="1"
bgcolor=#f05c1b></td>
    <td width="1" height="1"
bgcolor=#ef3c17></td>
    <td width="1" height="1"
bgcolor=#afcd1e></td>
    <td width="1" height="1"
bgcolor=#c7cb18></td>
    <td width="1" height="1"
bgcolor=#ded830></td>
    <td width="1" height="1"
bgcolor=#bdad1d></td>
    <td width="1" height="1"
bgcolor=#5d3c2e></td>
    <td width="1" height="1"
bgcolor=#513726></td>
    <td width="1" height="1"
bgcolor=#9e7d47></td>
    <td width="1" height="1"
bgcolor=#ab742d></td>
    <td width="1" height="1"
bgcolor=#b57937></td>
    <td width="1" height="1"
bgcolor=#714d22></td>
    <td width="1" height="1"
bgcolor=#918e3b></td>
    <td width="1" height="1"
bgcolor=#b7b84f></td>
    <td width="1" height="1"
bgcolor=#83883e></td>
    <td width="1" height="1"
bgcolor=#4b3717></td>
    <td width="1" height="1"
bgcolor=#82612c></td>
    <td width="1" height="1"
bgcolor=#b98e47></td>
    <td width="1" height="1"
bgcolor=#bcae45></td>
    <td width="1" height="1"
bgcolor=#938931></td>
    <td width="1" height="1"
bgcolor=#3a3b12></td>
    <td width="1" height="1"
bgcolor=#40471b></td>
    <td width="1" height="1"
bgcolor=#4a6427></td>
    <td width="1" height="1"
bgcolor=#53792c></td>
    <td width="1" height="1"
bgcolor=#5a782d></td>
  </tr>
  <tr>
    <td width="1" height="1"
bgcolor=#534923></td>
    <td width="1" height="1"
bgcolor=#372c14></td>
    <td width="1" height="1"
bgcolor=#8e8769></td>
    <td width="1" height="1"
bgcolor=#e7e7b3></td>
    <td width="1" height="1"
bgcolor=#d5d59c></td>
    <td width="1" height="1"
bgcolor=#373117></td>
    <td width="1" height="1"
bgcolor=#1f160d></td>
    <td width="1" height="1"
bgcolor=#21140b></td>
    <td width="1" height="1"
bgcolor=#21150e></td>
    <td width="1" height="1"
bgcolor=#27180f></td>
    <td width="1" height="1"
bgcolor=#28170f></td>
    <td width="1" height="1"
bgcolor=#2a1c0f></td>
    <td width="1" height="1"
bgcolor=#2a1811></td>
    <td width="1" height="1"
bgcolor=#2e1b13></td>
    <td width="1" height="1"
bgcolor=#2d1b12></td>
    <td width="1" height="1"
bgcolor=#29170f></td>
    <td width="1" height="1"
bgcolor=#2f1d11></td>
    <td width="1" height="1"
bgcolor=#281108></td>
    <td width="1" height="1"
bgcolor=#311c0b></td>
    <td width="1" height="1"
bgcolor=#3f2b1a></td>
    <td width="1" height="1"
bgcolor=#d0eb10></td>
    <td width="1" height="1"
bgcolor=#bce404></td>
    <td width="1" height="1"
bgcolor=#574811></td>
    <td width="1" height="1"
bgcolor=#9aa70e></td>
    <td width="1" height="1"
bgcolor=#cbc411></td>
    <td width="1" height="1"
bgcolor=#c6d915></td>
    <td width="1" height="1"
bgcolor=#b13d0b></td>
    <td width="1" height="1"
bgcolor=#d42a5b></td>
    <td width="1" height="1"
bgcolor=#ed4b59></td>
    <td width="1" height="1"
bgcolor=#ed216a></td>
    <td width="1" height="1"
bgcolor=#ac5f20></td>
    <td width="1" height="1"
bgcolor=#c14755></td>
    <td width="1" height="1"
bgcolor=#d74b44></td>
    <td width="1" height="1"
bgcolor=#ae7d4b></td>
    <td width="1" height="1"
bgcolor=#706335></td>
    <td width="1" height="1"
bgcolor=#9f7521></td>
    <td width="1" height="1"
bgcolor=#7c6e2b></td>
    <td width="1" height="1"
bgcolor=#a6996f></td>
    <td width="1" height="1"
bgcolor=#c2c3a0></td>
    <td width="1" height="1"
bgcolor=#70c8df></td>
    <td width="1" height="1"
bgcolor=#76b768></td>
    <td width="1" height="1"
bgcolor=#cb6f3f></td>
    <td width="1" height="1"
bgcolor=#7a552b></td>
    <td width="1" height="1"
bgcolor=#dbb580></td>
    <td width="1" height="1"
bgcolor=#e16133></td>
    <td width="1" height="1"
bgcolor=#ea5421></td>
    <td width="1" height="1"
bgcolor=#d5371c></td>
```

```
    <td width="1" height="1"
bgcolor=#f39957></td>
    <td width="1" height="1"
bgcolor=#da4124></td>
    <td width="1" height="1"
bgcolor=#c7d317></td>
    <td width="1" height="1"
bgcolor=#b4c121></td>
    <td width="1" height="1"
bgcolor=#dcd825></td>
    <td width="1" height="1"
bgcolor=#9d8127></td>
    <td width="1" height="1"
bgcolor=#674a34></td>
    <td width="1" height="1"
bgcolor=#4c3128></td>
    <td width="1" height="1"
bgcolor=#462b1a></td>
    <td width="1" height="1"
bgcolor=#a48d53></td>
    <td width="1" height="1"
bgcolor=#b39c6b></td>
    <td width="1" height="1"
bgcolor=#67451a></td>
    <td width="1" height="1"
bgcolor=#847b30></td>
    <td width="1" height="1"
bgcolor=#d3d654></td>
    <td width="1" height="1"
bgcolor=#8d8733></td>
    <td width="1" height="1"
bgcolor=#462e19></td>
    <td width="1" height="1"
bgcolor=#6f582e></td>
    <td width="1" height="1"
bgcolor=#a18a43></td>
    <td width="1" height="1"
bgcolor=#ad9f50></td>
    <td width="1" height="1"
bgcolor=#7f7c30></td>
    <td width="1" height="1"
bgcolor=#3f4617></td>
    <td width="1" height="1"
bgcolor=#3e411a></td>
    <td width="1" height="1"
bgcolor=#444d21></td>
    <td width="1" height="1"
bgcolor=#4f792b></td>
    <td width="1" height="1"
bgcolor=#527427></td>
  </tr>
  <tr>
    <td width="1" height="1"
bgcolor=#aea46f></td>
    <td width="1" height="1"
bgcolor=#d1c6a1></td>
    <td width="1" height="1"
bgcolor=#e2e9af></td>
    <td width="1" height="1"
bgcolor=#e3e1a5></td>
    <td width="1" height="1"
bgcolor=#9d9b66></td>
    <td width="1" height="1"
bgcolor=#1c1404></td>
    <td width="1" height="1"
bgcolor=#1f1610></td>
    <td width="1" height="1"
bgcolor=#221609></td>
    <td width="1" height="1"
bgcolor=#24140d></td>
    <td width="1" height="1"
bgcolor=#24170f></td>
    <td width="1" height="1"
bgcolor=#24160e></td>
    <td width="1" height="1"
bgcolor=#28170e></td>
    <td width="1" height="1"
bgcolor=#28160f></td>
    <td width="1" height="1"
bgcolor=#29170f></td>
    <td width="1" height="1"
bgcolor=#27140e></td>
    <td width="1" height="1"
bgcolor=#25110c></td>
    <td width="1" height="1"
bgcolor=#2a1710></td>
    <td width="1" height="1"
bgcolor=#231006></td>
    <td width="1" height="1"
bgcolor=#30180d></td>
    <td width="1" height="1"
bgcolor=#3a251a></td>
    <td width="1" height="1"
bgcolor=#738a0f></td>
    <td width="1" height="1"
bgcolor=#e2f002></td>
    <td width="1" height="1"
bgcolor=#6d4e16></td>
    <td width="1" height="1"
bgcolor=#63451b></td>
    <td width="1" height="1"
bgcolor=#9bab1a></td>
    <td width="1" height="1"
bgcolor=#a06809></td>
    <td width="1" height="1"
bgcolor=#ba6413></td>
    <td width="1" height="1"
bgcolor=#b96d49></td>
    <td width="1" height="1"
bgcolor=#ef337e></td>
    <td width="1" height="1"
bgcolor=#eb6459></td>
    <td width="1" height="1"
bgcolor=#e09b43></td>
    <td width="1" height="1"
bgcolor=#ea506c></td>
    <td width="1" height="1"
bgcolor=#df8f48></td>
    <td width="1" height="1"
bgcolor=#9a622c></td>
    <td width="1" height="1"
bgcolor=#5d9797></td>
    <td width="1" height="1"
bgcolor=#78985e></td>
    <td width="1" height="1"
bgcolor=#7c602c></td>
    <td width="1" height="1"
bgcolor=#ba9669></td>
    <td width="1" height="1"
bgcolor=#6aa2ab></td>
    <td width="1" height="1"
bgcolor=#b2e0dd></td>
    <td width="1" height="1"
bgcolor=#9d7b56></td>
    <td width="1" height="1"
bgcolor=#8e7826></td>
    <td width="1" height="1"
bgcolor=#b44123></td>
    <td width="1" height="1"
bgcolor=#f1572b></td>
    <td width="1" height="1"
bgcolor=#f94819></td>
    <td width="1" height="1"
bgcolor=#f84114></td>
    <td width="1" height="1"
bgcolor=#ed9255></td>
    <td width="1" height="1"
bgcolor=#eeb98e></td>
    <td width="1" height="1"
bgcolor=#812711></td>
    <td width="1" height="1"
bgcolor=#c1cd1b></td>
    <td width="1" height="1"
bgcolor=#b7c22d></td>
    <td width="1" height="1"
bgcolor=#dddd27></td>
    <td width="1" height="1"
bgcolor=#8d6436></td>
    <td width="1" height="1"
bgcolor=#59422d></td>
    <td width="1" height="1"
bgcolor=#533628></td>
    <td width="1" height="1"
bgcolor=#5a3e2c></td>
    <td width="1" height="1"
bgcolor=#5a412d></td>
    <td width="1" height="1"
bgcolor=#8c8566></td>
    <td width="1" height="1"
bgcolor=#b39b61></td>
    <td width="1" height="1"
bgcolor=#a49f34></td>
    <td width="1" height="1"
bgcolor=#e4e456></td>
```

```
    <td width="1" height="1" bgcolor=#9a982c></td>
    <td width="1" height="1" bgcolor=#6e7042></td>
    <td width="1" height="1" bgcolor=#aca477></td>
    <td width="1" height="1" bgcolor=#695921></td>
    <td width="1" height="1" bgcolor=#51491a></td>
    <td width="1" height="1" bgcolor=#484b23></td>
    <td width="1" height="1" bgcolor=#42531d></td>
    <td width="1" height="1" bgcolor=#485427></td>
    <td width="1" height="1" bgcolor=#629036></td>
    <td width="1" height="1" bgcolor=#5b9234></td>
    <td width="1" height="1" bgcolor=#5a7e27></td>
  </tr>
  <tr>
    <td width="1" height="1" bgcolor=#e6d38c></td>
    <td width="1" height="1" bgcolor=#e5e4b3></td>
    <td width="1" height="1" bgcolor=#d8dc9f></td>
    <td width="1" height="1" bgcolor=#b6b47d></td>
    <td width="1" height="1" bgcolor=#2d2411></td>
    <td width="1" height="1" bgcolor=#251c12></td>
    <td width="1" height="1" bgcolor=#20160f></td>
    <td width="1" height="1" bgcolor=#23150e></td>
    <td width="1" height="1" bgcolor=#1f130b></td>
    <td width="1" height="1" bgcolor=#20130b></td>
    <td width="1" height="1" bgcolor=#21130c></td>
    <td width="1" height="1" bgcolor=#20110a></td>
    <td width="1" height="1" bgcolor=#23120b></td>
    <td width="1" height="1" bgcolor=#22110b></td>
    <td width="1" height="1" bgcolor=#24130e></td>
    <td width="1" height="1" bgcolor=#200e0a></td>
    <td width="1" height="1" bgcolor=#26110d></td>
    <td width="1" height="1" bgcolor=#1d0c04></td>
    <td width="1" height="1" bgcolor=#2e1910></td>
    <td width="1" height="1" bgcolor=#402719></td>
    <td width="1" height="1" bgcolor=#1e1504></td>
    <td width="1" height="1" bgcolor=#dcfd0e></td>
    <td width="1" height="1" bgcolor=#cac512></td>
    <td width="1" height="1" bgcolor=#95b419></td>
    <td width="1" height="1" bgcolor=#8e7015></td>
    <td width="1" height="1" bgcolor=#d0e00a></td>
    <td width="1" height="1" bgcolor=#914912></td>
    <td width="1" height="1" bgcolor=#8b6911></td>
    <td width="1" height="1" bgcolor=#b76d4f></td>
    <td width="1" height="1" bgcolor=#e24650></td>
    <td width="1" height="1" bgcolor=#a86622></td>
    <td width="1" height="1" bgcolor=#af2b4c></td>
    <td width="1" height="1" bgcolor=#af3241></td>
    <td width="1" height="1" bgcolor=#883025></td>
    <td width="1" height="1" bgcolor=#5cada4></td>
    <td width="1" height="1" bgcolor=#62b9bf></td>
    <td width="1" height="1" bgcolor=#9c5d30></td>
    <td width="1" height="1" bgcolor=#f0b05c></td>
    <td width="1" height="1" bgcolor=#f89f55></td>
    <td width="1" height="1" bgcolor=#9ce3f8></td>
    <td width="1" height="1" bgcolor=#513b1c></td>
    <td width="1" height="1" bgcolor=#130001></td>
    <td width="1" height="1" bgcolor=#c33312></td>
    <td width="1" height="1" bgcolor=#ed4b1f></td>
    <td width="1" height="1" bgcolor=#f4380b></td>
    <td width="1" height="1" bgcolor=#f94512></td>
    <td width="1" height="1" bgcolor=#e65f3f></td>
    <td width="1" height="1" bgcolor=#f18d52></td>
    <td width="1" height="1" bgcolor=#370409></td>
    <td width="1" height="1" bgcolor=#a6bc1a></td>
    <td width="1" height="1" bgcolor=#cbdb27></td>
    <td width="1" height="1" bgcolor=#e5e22f></td>
    <td width="1" height="1" bgcolor=#64412a></td>
    <td width="1" height="1" bgcolor=#503924></td>
    <td width="1" height="1" bgcolor=#5c5239></td>
    <td width="1" height="1" bgcolor=#6e4e36></td>
    <td width="1" height="1" bgcolor=#573926></td>
    <td width="1" height="1" bgcolor=#695645></td>
    <td width="1" height="1" bgcolor=#8f7d33></td>
    <td width="1" height="1" bgcolor=#8f8521></td>
    <td width="1" height="1" bgcolor=#e4e23f></td>
    <td width="1" height="1" bgcolor=#a09d33></td>
    <td width="1" height="1" bgcolor=#dadca0></td>
    <td width="1" height="1" bgcolor=#423618></td>
    <td width="1" height="1" bgcolor=#312a1a></td>
    <td width="1" height="1" bgcolor=#2c2309></td>
    <td width="1" height="1" bgcolor=#404122></td>
    <td width="1" height="1" bgcolor=#424623></td>
    <td width="1" height="1" bgcolor=#4e822b></td>
    <td width="1" height="1" bgcolor=#516d33></td>
    <td width="1" height="1" bgcolor=#65752f></td>
    <td width="1" height="1" bgcolor=#537e26></td>
  </tr>
  <tr>
    <td width="1" height="1" bgcolor=#c39f4d></td>
    <td width="1" height="1" bgcolor=#e8e9b3></td>
```

```
<td width="1" height="1" bgcolor=#c8c483></td>
<td width="1" height="1" bgcolor=#312715></td>
<td width="1" height="1" bgcolor=#291d17></td>
<td width="1" height="1" bgcolor=#25170d></td>
<td width="1" height="1" bgcolor=#22180e></td>
<td width="1" height="1" bgcolor=#1c1208></td>
<td width="1" height="1" bgcolor=#23180f></td>
<td width="1" height="1" bgcolor=#1b1106></td>
<td width="1" height="1" bgcolor=#1b1005></td>
<td width="1" height="1" bgcolor=#1e1108></td>
<td width="1" height="1" bgcolor=#1d100a></td>
<td width="1" height="1" bgcolor=#1e110b></td>
<td width="1" height="1" bgcolor=#1f120d></td>
<td width="1" height="1" bgcolor=#1e0c0b></td>
<td width="1" height="1" bgcolor=#2b1813></td>
<td width="1" height="1" bgcolor=#1d0d09></td>
<td width="1" height="1" bgcolor=#301c0f></td>
<td width="1" height="1" bgcolor=#3e261c></td>
<td width="1" height="1" bgcolor=#090200></td>
<td width="1" height="1" bgcolor=#cec411></td>
<td width="1" height="1" bgcolor=#ca391b></td>
<td width="1" height="1" bgcolor=#f1a65a></td>
<td width="1" height="1" bgcolor=#874b1f></td>
<td width="1" height="1" bgcolor=#daf607></td>
<td width="1" height="1" bgcolor=#b2701f></td>
<td width="1" height="1" bgcolor=#bec510></td>
<td width="1" height="1" bgcolor=#f06278></td>
<td width="1" height="1" bgcolor=#f52f8d></td>
<td width="1" height="1" bgcolor=#e13167></td>
<td width="1" height="1" bgcolor=#d52c5c></td>
<td width="1" height="1" bgcolor=#d23947></td>
<td width="1" height="1" bgcolor=#754b52></td>
<td width="1" height="1" bgcolor=#61b2a1></td>
<td width="1" height="1" bgcolor=#5fc0c2></td>
<td width="1" height="1" bgcolor=#9c5a2f></td>
<td width="1" height="1" bgcolor=#b5693a></td>
<td width="1" height="1" bgcolor=#4b592d></td>
<td width="1" height="1" bgcolor=#65aaaa></td>
<td width="1" height="1" bgcolor=#4e5940></td>
<td width="1" height="1" bgcolor=#0e0404></td>
<td width="1" height="1" bgcolor=#cd3419></td>
<td width="1" height="1" bgcolor=#f15a32></td>
<td width="1" height="1" bgcolor=#f83b16></td>
<td width="1" height="1" bgcolor=#eb5828></td>
<td width="1" height="1" bgcolor=#f28240></td>
<td width="1" height="1" bgcolor=#f57d52></td>
<td width="1" height="1" bgcolor=#261006></td>
<td width="1" height="1" bgcolor=#99a716></td>
<td width="1" height="1" bgcolor=#d0d522></td>
<td width="1" height="1" bgcolor=#d3cd30></td>
<td width="1" height="1" bgcolor=#6e613f></td>
<td width="1" height="1" bgcolor=#50362e></td>
<td width="1" height="1" bgcolor=#b5ad74></td>
<td width="1" height="1" bgcolor=#947445></td>
<td width="1" height="1" bgcolor=#61452a></td>
<td width="1" height="1" bgcolor=#674b39></td>
<td width="1" height="1" bgcolor=#6e5323></td>
<td width="1" height="1" bgcolor=#756a2b></td>
<td width="1" height="1" bgcolor=#b5ae3c></td>
<td width="1" height="1" bgcolor=#979731></td>
<td width="1" height="1" bgcolor=#94974c></td>
<td width="1" height="1" bgcolor=#706446></td>
<td width="1" height="1" bgcolor=#2c240a></td>
<td width="1" height="1" bgcolor=#362d16></td>
<td width="1" height="1" bgcolor=#32250e></td>
<td width="1" height="1" bgcolor=#2e3e1c></td>
<td width="1" height="1" bgcolor=#8d895c></td>
<td width="1" height="1" bgcolor=#92a54e></td>
<td width="1" height="1" bgcolor=#465b1c></td>
<td width="1" height="1" bgcolor=#6b8133></td>
</tr>
<tr>
<td width="1" height="1" bgcolor=#797937></td>
<td width="1" height="1" bgcolor=#e1ce92></td>
<td width="1" height="1" bgcolor=#ab691f></td>
<td width="1" height="1" bgcolor=#504930></td>
<td width="1" height="1" bgcolor=#3a2a1a></td>
<td width="1" height="1" bgcolor=#4f3f29></td>
<td width="1" height="1" bgcolor=#211509></td>
<td width="1" height="1" bgcolor=#110a04></td>
<td width="1" height="1" bgcolor=#1b120a></td>
<td width="1" height="1" bgcolor=#1d120b></td>
<td width="1" height="1" bgcolor=#1d0d0b></td>
<td width="1" height="1" bgcolor=#150a05></td>
<td width="1" height="1" bgcolor=#160804></td>
<td width="1" height="1" bgcolor=#190e09></td>
<td width="1" height="1" bgcolor=#1d0e0a></td>
<td width="1" height="1" bgcolor=#180a05></td>
```

```
    <td width="1" height="1"
bgcolor=#24130f></td>
    <td width="1" height="1"
bgcolor=#1d0501></td>
    <td width="1" height="1"
bgcolor=#27160d></td>
    <td width="1" height="1"
bgcolor=#431f15></td>
    <td width="1" height="1"
bgcolor=#0c000e></td>
    <td width="1" height="1"
bgcolor=#ae2212></td>
    <td width="1" height="1"
bgcolor=#69270e></td>
    <td width="1" height="1"
bgcolor=#ab6438></td>
    <td width="1" height="1"
bgcolor=#aa8f20></td>
    <td width="1" height="1"
bgcolor=#d4e900></td>
    <td width="1" height="1"
bgcolor=#ba700d></td>
    <td width="1" height="1"
bgcolor=#cee600></td>
    <td width="1" height="1"
bgcolor=#e04e73></td>
    <td width="1" height="1"
bgcolor=#f32987></td>
    <td width="1" height="1"
bgcolor=#fd257d></td>
    <td width="1" height="1"
bgcolor=#ef2a72></td>
    <td width="1" height="1"
bgcolor=#ba2d2e></td>
    <td width="1" height="1"
bgcolor=#637d75></td>
    <td width="1" height="1"
bgcolor=#4f9f89></td>
    <td width="1" height="1"
bgcolor=#5a927e></td>
    <td width="1" height="1"
bgcolor=#543217></td>
    <td width="1" height="1"
bgcolor=#3e2a1e></td>
    <td width="1" height="1"
bgcolor=#65bdac></td>
    <td width="1" height="1"
bgcolor=#56c2d2></td>
    <td width="1" height="1"
bgcolor=#65a49b></td>
    <td width="1" height="1"
bgcolor=#130901></td>
    <td width="1" height="1"
bgcolor=#c93216></td>
    <td width="1" height="1"
bgcolor=#e85d3b></td>
    <td width="1" height="1"
bgcolor=#f73b14></td>
    <td width="1" height="1"
bgcolor=#d96a22></td>
    <td width="1" height="1"
bgcolor=#ee4223></td>
    <td width="1" height="1"
bgcolor=#ee662a></td>
    <td width="1" height="1"
bgcolor=#552410></td>
    <td width="1" height="1"
bgcolor=#a4b214></td>
    <td width="1" height="1"
bgcolor=#d7d527></td>
    <td width="1" height="1"
bgcolor=#c8c41c></td>
    <td width="1" height="1"
bgcolor=#829e70></td>
    <td width="1" height="1"
bgcolor=#513d32></td>
    <td width="1" height="1"
bgcolor=#b0ab72></td>
    <td width="1" height="1"
bgcolor=#846940></td>
    <td width="1" height="1"
bgcolor=#4e3227></td>
    <td width="1" height="1"
bgcolor=#50351f></td>
    <td width="1" height="1"
bgcolor=#6c5928></td>
    <td width="1" height="1"
bgcolor=#80712e></td>
    <td width="1" height="1"
bgcolor=#a29d38></td>
    <td width="1" height="1"
bgcolor=#bdb140></td>
    <td width="1" height="1"
bgcolor=#9a9037></td>
    <td width="1" height="1"
bgcolor=#544329></td>
    <td width="1" height="1"
bgcolor=#291e14></td>
    <td width="1" height="1"
bgcolor=#36361b></td>
    <td width="1" height="1"
bgcolor=#1b0d05></td>
    <td width="1" height="1"
bgcolor=#c8c475></td>
    <td width="1" height="1"
bgcolor=#d6c675></td>
    <td width="1" height="1"
bgcolor=#c0b163></td>
    <td width="1" height="1"
bgcolor=#81914a></td>
    <td width="1" height="1"
bgcolor=#536724></td>
  </tr>
  <tr>
    <td width="1" height="1"
bgcolor=#6d7630></td>
    <td width="1" height="1"
bgcolor=#6d6b15></td>
    <td width="1" height="1"
bgcolor=#ac7127></td>
    <td width="1" height="1"
bgcolor=#6c633d></td>
    <td width="1" height="1"
bgcolor=#6b402e></td>
    <td width="1" height="1"
bgcolor=#705436></td>
    <td width="1" height="1"
bgcolor=#1c1009></td>
    <td width="1" height="1"
bgcolor=#130401></td>
    <td width="1" height="1"
bgcolor=#170904></td>
    <td width="1" height="1"
bgcolor=#1c1005></td>
    <td width="1" height="1"
bgcolor=#1a0904></td>
    <td width="1" height="1"
bgcolor=#140803></td>
    <td width="1" height="1"
bgcolor=#241210></td>
    <td width="1" height="1"
bgcolor=#1e0a07></td>
    <td width="1" height="1"
bgcolor=#1d0d09></td>
    <td width="1" height="1"
bgcolor=#1b0902></td>
    <td width="1" height="1"
bgcolor=#23120d></td>
    <td width="1" height="1"
bgcolor=#190b06></td>
    <td width="1" height="1"
bgcolor=#3c170a></td>
    <td width="1" height="1"
bgcolor=#6d3825></td>
    <td width="1" height="1"
bgcolor=#080001></td>
    <td width="1" height="1"
bgcolor=#180505></td>
    <td width="1" height="1"
bgcolor=#9da514></td>
    <td width="1" height="1"
bgcolor=#cae70b></td>
    <td width="1" height="1"
bgcolor=#e6eb05></td>
    <td width="1" height="1"
bgcolor=#ebf401></td>
    <td width="1" height="1"
bgcolor=#6a3306></td>
    <td width="1" height="1"
bgcolor=#cff90c></td>
    <td width="1" height="1"
bgcolor=#d9416d></td>
    <td width="1" height="1"
bgcolor=#f72279></td>
```

```
    <td width="1" height="1" bgcolor=#f83283></td>
    <td width="1" height="1" bgcolor=#ec5d70></td>
    <td width="1" height="1" bgcolor=#b9956e></td>
    <td width="1" height="1" bgcolor=#af9f7a></td>
    <td width="1" height="1" bgcolor=#a3ad7d></td>
    <td width="1" height="1" bgcolor=#7f8155></td>
    <td width="1" height="1" bgcolor=#746c43></td>
    <td width="1" height="1" bgcolor=#1f0a00></td>
    <td width="1" height="1" bgcolor=#70bfbd></td>
    <td width="1" height="1" bgcolor=#63bdca></td>
    <td width="1" height="1" bgcolor=#679b6d></td>
    <td width="1" height="1" bgcolor=#1a1106></td>
    <td width="1" height="1" bgcolor=#eb4526></td>
    <td width="1" height="1" bgcolor=#c5511b></td>
    <td width="1" height="1" bgcolor=#e24d13></td>
    <td width="1" height="1" bgcolor=#b6b326></td>
    <td width="1" height="1" bgcolor=#b1be11></td>
    <td width="1" height="1" bgcolor=#cd3e21></td>
    <td width="1" height="1" bgcolor=#9c451b></td>
    <td width="1" height="1" bgcolor=#aaba29></td>
    <td width="1" height="1" bgcolor=#acac29></td>
    <td width="1" height="1" bgcolor=#b3bc28></td>
    <td width="1" height="1" bgcolor=#6d8b64></td>
    <td width="1" height="1" bgcolor=#4a3127></td>
    <td width="1" height="1" bgcolor=#9e8f64></td>
    <td width="1" height="1" bgcolor=#543f25></td>
    <td width="1" height="1" bgcolor=#483026></td>
    <td width="1" height="1" bgcolor=#4b3127></td>
    <td width="1" height="1" bgcolor=#725e28></td>
    <td width="1" height="1" bgcolor=#887832></td>
    <td width="1" height="1" bgcolor=#968735></td>
    <td width="1" height="1" bgcolor=#b8af4e></td>
    <td width="1" height="1" bgcolor=#b4ac3e></td>
    <td width="1" height="1" bgcolor=#56431f></td>
    <td width="1" height="1" bgcolor=#24130f></td>
    <td width="1" height="1" bgcolor=#291c0e></td>
    <td width="1" height="1" bgcolor=#1b0807></td>
    <td width="1" height="1" bgcolor=#958546></td>
    <td width="1" height="1" bgcolor=#bdb461></td>
    <td width="1" height="1" bgcolor=#d2b86f></td>
    <td width="1" height="1" bgcolor=#8e8b44></td>
    <td width="1" height="1" bgcolor=#707e39></td>
  </tr>
  <tr>
    <td width="1" height="1" bgcolor=#919f58></td>
    <td width="1" height="1" bgcolor=#868b3c></td>
    <td width="1" height="1" bgcolor=#c6c586></td>
    <td width="1" height="1" bgcolor=#71653b></td>
    <td width="1" height="1" bgcolor=#271912></td>
    <td width="1" height="1" bgcolor=#271b12></td>
    <td width="1" height="1" bgcolor=#1a100b></td>
    <td width="1" height="1" bgcolor=#140d08></td>
    <td width="1" height="1" bgcolor=#170903></td>
    <td width="1" height="1" bgcolor=#1c1207></td>
    <td width="1" height="1" bgcolor=#1c0c03></td>
    <td width="1" height="1" bgcolor=#160702></td>
    <td width="1" height="1" bgcolor=#170803></td>
    <td width="1" height="1" bgcolor=#0f0200></td>
    <td width="1" height="1" bgcolor=#190803></td>
    <td width="1" height="1" bgcolor=#1e0a02></td>
    <td width="1" height="1" bgcolor=#24100e></td>
    <td width="1" height="1" bgcolor=#1a0a08></td>
    <td width="1" height="1" bgcolor=#371609></td>
    <td width="1" height="1" bgcolor=#59261b></td>
    <td width="1" height="1" bgcolor=#080104></td>
    <td width="1" height="1" bgcolor=#020001></td>
    <td width="1" height="1" bgcolor=#aebd10></td>
    <td width="1" height="1" bgcolor=#e4e604></td>
    <td width="1" height="1" bgcolor=#d7e204></td>
    <td width="1" height="1" bgcolor=#e3f009></td>
    <td width="1" height="1" bgcolor=#622905></td>
    <td width="1" height="1" bgcolor=#d3e70a></td>
    <td width="1" height="1" bgcolor=#c64957></td>
    <td width="1" height="1" bgcolor=#e77b76></td>
    <td width="1" height="1" bgcolor=#d2b256></td>
    <td width="1" height="1" bgcolor=#d67f3a></td>
    <td width="1" height="1" bgcolor=#7c551c></td>
    <td width="1" height="1" bgcolor=#a67e3a></td>
    <td width="1" height="1" bgcolor=#b98749></td>
    <td width="1" height="1" bgcolor=#a3742b></td>
    <td width="1" height="1" bgcolor=#a28d5d></td>
    <td width="1" height="1" bgcolor=#947456></td>
    <td width="1" height="1" bgcolor=#71b1ad></td>
    <td width="1" height="1" bgcolor=#57adb7></td>
    <td width="1" height="1" bgcolor=#5d9c46></td>
    <td width="1" height="1" bgcolor=#30281a></td>
    <td width="1" height="1" bgcolor=#de2a16></td>
    <td width="1" height="1" bgcolor=#908f3f></td>
```

```
    <td width="1" height="1"
bgcolor=#b67d22></td>
    <td width="1" height="1"
bgcolor=#824a2e></td>
    <td width="1" height="1"
bgcolor=#763e28></td>
    <td width="1" height="1"
bgcolor=#f5301f></td>
    <td width="1" height="1"
bgcolor=#e74824></td>
    <td width="1" height="1"
bgcolor=#788a30></td>
    <td width="1" height="1"
bgcolor=#9fa438></td>
    <td width="1" height="1"
bgcolor=#a4ac28></td>
    <td width="1" height="1"
bgcolor=#586a45></td>
    <td width="1" height="1"
bgcolor=#482b22></td>
    <td width="1" height="1"
bgcolor=#433021></td>
    <td width="1" height="1"
bgcolor=#463629></td>
    <td width="1" height="1"
bgcolor=#473425></td>
    <td width="1" height="1"
bgcolor=#422c1d></td>
    <td width="1" height="1"
bgcolor=#5b4d25></td>
    <td width="1" height="1"
bgcolor=#7a712d></td>
    <td width="1" height="1"
bgcolor=#7c6b2c></td>
    <td width="1" height="1"
bgcolor=#c2ae49></td>
    <td width="1" height="1"
bgcolor=#aea53c></td>
    <td width="1" height="1"
bgcolor=#463921></td>
    <td width="1" height="1"
bgcolor=#20190f></td>
    <td width="1" height="1"
bgcolor=#211407></td>
    <td width="1" height="1"
bgcolor=#1c100f></td>
    <td width="1" height="1"
bgcolor=#665230></td>
    <td width="1" height="1"
bgcolor=#9d8047></td>
    <td width="1" height="1"
bgcolor=#937441></td>
    <td width="1" height="1"
bgcolor=#7f6e40></td>
    <td width="1" height="1"
bgcolor=#758539></td>
  </tr>
  <tr>
    <td width="1" height="1"
bgcolor=#839e36></td>
    <td width="1" height="1"
bgcolor=#afb276></td>
    <td width="1" height="1"
bgcolor=#a4a666></td>
    <td width="1" height="1"
bgcolor=#939152></td>
    <td width="1" height="1"
bgcolor=#140a0a></td>
    <td width="1" height="1"
bgcolor=#170d0c></td>
    <td width="1" height="1"
bgcolor=#170e0d></td>
    <td width="1" height="1"
bgcolor=#1a0d08></td>
    <td width="1" height="1"
bgcolor=#191005></td>
    <td width="1" height="1"
bgcolor=#3e1d10></td>
    <td width="1" height="1"
bgcolor=#120800></td>
    <td width="1" height="1"
bgcolor=#150904></td>
    <td width="1" height="1"
bgcolor=#0d0100></td>
    <td width="1" height="1"
bgcolor=#130707></td>
    <td width="1" height="1"
bgcolor=#100503></td>
    <td width="1" height="1"
bgcolor=#220b08></td>
    <td width="1" height="1"
bgcolor=#6d4426></td>
    <td width="1" height="1"
bgcolor=#200b09></td>
    <td width="1" height="1"
bgcolor=#362a19></td>
    <td width="1" height="1"
bgcolor=#3b2a15></td>
    <td width="1" height="1"
bgcolor=#30210c></td>
    <td width="1" height="1"
bgcolor=#4b4821></td>
    <td width="1" height="1"
bgcolor=#7e8614></td>
    <td width="1" height="1"
bgcolor=#c7db15></td>
    <td width="1" height="1"
bgcolor=#c7cd1a></td>
    <td width="1" height="1"
bgcolor=#adbb1b></td>
    <td width="1" height="1"
bgcolor=#6a400b></td>
    <td width="1" height="1"
bgcolor=#a2b218></td>
    <td width="1" height="1"
bgcolor=#898551></td>
    <td width="1" height="1"
bgcolor=#b29645></td>
    <td width="1" height="1"
bgcolor=#a58350></td>
    <td width="1" height="1"
bgcolor=#a68a72></td>
    <td width="1" height="1"
bgcolor=#bcac88></td>
    <td width="1" height="1"
bgcolor=#b4a27c></td>
    <td width="1" height="1"
bgcolor=#bfbe92></td>
    <td width="1" height="1"
bgcolor=#aa997e></td>
    <td width="1" height="1"
bgcolor=#937a4a></td>
    <td width="1" height="1"
bgcolor=#9c9745></td>
    <td width="1" height="1"
bgcolor=#a99b57></td>
    <td width="1" height="1"
bgcolor=#56958a></td>
    <td width="1" height="1"
bgcolor=#5ba553></td>
    <td width="1" height="1"
bgcolor=#33321c></td>
    <td width="1" height="1"
bgcolor=#d93529></td>
    <td width="1" height="1"
bgcolor=#86ba43></td>
    <td width="1" height="1"
bgcolor=#83791f></td>
    <td width="1" height="1"
bgcolor=#c42a1d></td>
    <td width="1" height="1"
bgcolor=#a74d14></td>
    <td width="1" height="1"
bgcolor=#af8117></td>
    <td width="1" height="1"
bgcolor=#b59527></td>
    <td width="1" height="1"
bgcolor=#818b25></td>
    <td width="1" height="1"
bgcolor=#6a6718></td>
    <td width="1" height="1"
bgcolor=#a09628></td>
    <td width="1" height="1"
bgcolor=#51442c></td>
    <td width="1" height="1"
bgcolor=#433623></td>
    <td width="1" height="1"
bgcolor=#544232></td>
    <td width="1" height="1"
bgcolor=#423123></td>
    <td width="1" height="1"
bgcolor=#463422></td>
    <td width="1" height="1"
bgcolor=#3f2b20></td>
```

```
    <td width="1" height="1"
bgcolor=#4d3d21></td>
    <td width="1" height="1"
bgcolor=#605629></td>
    <td width="1" height="1"
bgcolor=#755f23></td>
    <td width="1" height="1"
bgcolor=#b7a93d></td>
    <td width="1" height="1"
bgcolor=#a0933a></td>
    <td width="1" height="1"
bgcolor=#332311></td>
    <td width="1" height="1"
bgcolor=#1b1108></td>
    <td width="1" height="1"
bgcolor=#1b0d04></td>
    <td width="1" height="1"
bgcolor=#1e100c></td>
    <td width="1" height="1"
bgcolor=#58412a></td>
    <td width="1" height="1"
bgcolor=#74532e></td>
    <td width="1" height="1"
bgcolor=#665431></td>
    <td width="1" height="1"
bgcolor=#b28f48></td>
    <td width="1" height="1"
bgcolor=#796931></td>
  </tr>
  <tr>
    <td width="1" height="1"
bgcolor=#969e64></td>
    <td width="1" height="1"
bgcolor=#848f3d></td>
    <td width="1" height="1"
bgcolor=#bfc37e></td>
    <td width="1" height="1"
bgcolor=#a59f64></td>
    <td width="1" height="1"
bgcolor=#140a06></td>
    <td width="1" height="1"
bgcolor=#20140d></td>
    <td width="1" height="1"
bgcolor=#120e06></td>
    <td width="1" height="1"
bgcolor=#291911></td>
    <td width="1" height="1"
bgcolor=#362015></td>
    <td width="1" height="1"
bgcolor=#ae652f></td>
    <td width="1" height="1"
bgcolor=#1f1512></td>
    <td width="1" height="1"
bgcolor=#0c0001></td>
    <td width="1" height="1"
bgcolor=#0d0000></td>
    <td width="1" height="1"
bgcolor=#0e0201></td>
    <td width="1" height="1"
bgcolor=#110003></td>
    <td width="1" height="1"
bgcolor=#1b0c07></td>
    <td width="1" height="1"
bgcolor=#965124></td>
    <td width="1" height="1"
bgcolor=#180204></td>
    <td width="1" height="1"
bgcolor=#250f06></td>
    <td width="1" height="1"
bgcolor=#1b1004></td>
    <td width="1" height="1"
bgcolor=#4c5119></td>
    <td width="1" height="1"
bgcolor=#5c6623></td>
    <td width="1" height="1"
bgcolor=#585e11></td>
    <td width="1" height="1"
bgcolor=#a0ad22></td>
    <td width="1" height="1"
bgcolor=#76841e></td>
    <td width="1" height="1"
bgcolor=#6b8c1e></td>
    <td width="1" height="1"
bgcolor=#5b591c></td>
    <td width="1" height="1"
bgcolor=#6c6c27></td>
    <td width="1" height="1"
bgcolor=#81713e></td>
    <td width="1" height="1"
bgcolor=#a7a582></td>
    <td width="1" height="1"
bgcolor=#e8e4b0></td>
    <td width="1" height="1"
bgcolor=#bf823b></td>
    <td width="1" height="1"
bgcolor=#e2d362></td>
    <td width="1" height="1"
bgcolor=#cb8916></td>
    <td width="1" height="1"
bgcolor=#d7ca61></td>
    <td width="1" height="1"
bgcolor=#b38832></td>
    <td width="1" height="1"
bgcolor=#eee2bc></td>
    <td width="1" height="1"
bgcolor=#b7b68b></td>
    <td width="1" height="1"
bgcolor=#979c46></td>
    <td width="1" height="1"
bgcolor=#a0a26a></td>
    <td width="1" height="1"
bgcolor=#464740></td>
    <td width="1" height="1"
bgcolor=#5a6337></td>
    <td width="1" height="1"
bgcolor=#d33827></td>
    <td width="1" height="1"
bgcolor=#95bb44></td>
    <td width="1" height="1"
bgcolor=#4f5418></td>
    <td width="1" height="1"
bgcolor=#db4d12></td>
    <td width="1" height="1"
bgcolor=#8d9a21></td>
    <td width="1" height="1"
bgcolor=#ee2e0d></td>
    <td width="1" height="1"
bgcolor=#f02c12></td>
    <td width="1" height="1"
bgcolor=#624a1c></td>
    <td width="1" height="1"
bgcolor=#afa921></td>
    <td width="1" height="1"
bgcolor=#887a2c></td>
    <td width="1" height="1"
bgcolor=#544732></td>
    <td width="1" height="1"
bgcolor=#49412c></td>
    <td width="1" height="1"
bgcolor=#646048></td>
    <td width="1" height="1"
bgcolor=#483c28></td>
    <td width="1" height="1"
bgcolor=#403121></td>
    <td width="1" height="1"
bgcolor=#392617></td>
    <td width="1" height="1"
bgcolor=#4b3628></td>
    <td width="1" height="1"
bgcolor=#50421f></td>
    <td width="1" height="1"
bgcolor=#6b5f24></td>
    <td width="1" height="1"
bgcolor=#b7a640></td>
    <td width="1" height="1"
bgcolor=#7b6429></td>
    <td width="1" height="1"
bgcolor=#200d06></td>
    <td width="1" height="1"
bgcolor=#1d1106></td>
    <td width="1" height="1"
bgcolor=#190e04></td>
    <td width="1" height="1"
bgcolor=#41261b></td>
    <td width="1" height="1"
bgcolor=#512f1d></td>
    <td width="1" height="1"
bgcolor=#4c2a1a></td>
    <td width="1" height="1"
bgcolor=#705540></td>
    <td width="1" height="1"
bgcolor=#d88a35></td>
    <td width="1" height="1"
bgcolor=#985541></td>
```

```
  </tr>
  <tr>
    <td width="1" height="1" bgcolor=#717231></td>
    <td width="1" height="1" bgcolor=#9aa265></td>
    <td width="1" height="1" bgcolor=#b6b969></td>
    <td width="1" height="1" bgcolor=#a2a05f></td>
    <td width="1" height="1" bgcolor=#190f07></td>
    <td width="1" height="1" bgcolor=#433229></td>
    <td width="1" height="1" bgcolor=#1f110b></td>
    <td width="1" height="1" bgcolor=#180c09></td>
    <td width="1" height="1" bgcolor=#160b06></td>
    <td width="1" height="1" bgcolor=#321615></td>
    <td width="1" height="1" bgcolor=#0c0101></td>
    <td width="1" height="1" bgcolor=#0e0201></td>
    <td width="1" height="1" bgcolor=#0e0301></td>
    <td width="1" height="1" bgcolor=#0c0200></td>
    <td width="1" height="1" bgcolor=#110103></td>
    <td width="1" height="1" bgcolor=#160800></td>
    <td width="1" height="1" bgcolor=#1c0710></td>
    <td width="1" height="1" bgcolor=#1c0c01></td>
    <td width="1" height="1" bgcolor=#21120c></td>
    <td width="1" height="1" bgcolor=#352214></td>
    <td width="1" height="1" bgcolor=#392018></td>
    <td width="1" height="1" bgcolor=#422d13></td>
    <td width="1" height="1" bgcolor=#696c17></td>
    <td width="1" height="1" bgcolor=#626c1d></td>
    <td width="1" height="1" bgcolor=#5a6c1a></td>
    <td width="1" height="1" bgcolor=#93aa13></td>
    <td width="1" height="1" bgcolor=#795523></td>
    <td width="1" height="1" bgcolor=#a27952></td>
    <td width="1" height="1" bgcolor=#dcd3b4></td>
    <td width="1" height="1" bgcolor=#ab821a></td>
    <td width="1" height="1" bgcolor=#e5d175></td>
    <td width="1" height="1" bgcolor=#d08e22></td>
    <td width="1" height="1" bgcolor=#e2ca81></td>
    <td width="1" height="1" bgcolor=#dfdcba></td>
    <td width="1" height="1" bgcolor=#d8c249></td>
    <td width="1" height="1" bgcolor=#e3e59e></td>
    <td width="1" height="1" bgcolor=#be930d></td>
    <td width="1" height="1" bgcolor=#b3936f></td>
    <td width="1" height="1" bgcolor=#ced09b></td>
    <td width="1" height="1" bgcolor=#869135></td>
    <td width="1" height="1" bgcolor=#6b7337></td>
    <td width="1" height="1" bgcolor=#5b6215></td>
    <td width="1" height="1" bgcolor=#6f722a></td>
    <td width="1" height="1" bgcolor=#79a634></td>
    <td width="1" height="1" bgcolor=#516a23></td>
    <td width="1" height="1" bgcolor=#6c872a></td>
    <td width="1" height="1" bgcolor=#e2230c></td>
    <td width="1" height="1" bgcolor=#913626></td>
    <td width="1" height="1" bgcolor=#cc4128></td>
    <td width="1" height="1" bgcolor=#655526></td>
    <td width="1" height="1" bgcolor=#896f22></td>
    <td width="1" height="1" bgcolor=#726028></td>
    <td width="1" height="1" bgcolor=#534631></td>
    <td width="1" height="1" bgcolor=#534b38></td>
    <td width="1" height="1" bgcolor=#443f21></td>
    <td width="1" height="1" bgcolor=#4a4329></td>
    <td width="1" height="1" bgcolor=#372819></td>
    <td width="1" height="1" bgcolor=#402d1f></td>
    <td width="1" height="1" bgcolor=#473424></td>
    <td width="1" height="1" bgcolor=#493721></td>
    <td width="1" height="1" bgcolor=#5a4b24></td>
    <td width="1" height="1" bgcolor=#aba132></td>
    <td width="1" height="1" bgcolor=#60491d></td>
    <td width="1" height="1" bgcolor=#1a1207></td>
    <td width="1" height="1" bgcolor=#1b1308></td>
    <td width="1" height="1" bgcolor=#1c1106></td>
    <td width="1" height="1" bgcolor=#4a301b></td>
    <td width="1" height="1" bgcolor=#806149></td>
    <td width="1" height="1" bgcolor=#a3956b></td>
    <td width="1" height="1" bgcolor=#82542c></td>
    <td width="1" height="1" bgcolor=#b26148></td>
    <td width="1" height="1" bgcolor=#5d3a1d></td>
  </tr>
  <tr>
    <td width="1" height="1" bgcolor=#a2ab5e></td>
    <td width="1" height="1" bgcolor=#85883f></td>
    <td width="1" height="1" bgcolor=#bfbf75></td>
    <td width="1" height="1" bgcolor=#9f9663></td>
    <td width="1" height="1" bgcolor=#1b120a></td>
    <td width="1" height="1" bgcolor=#2a1a17></td>
    <td width="1" height="1" bgcolor=#291a16></td>
    <td width="1" height="1" bgcolor=#0c0300></td>
    <td width="1" height="1" bgcolor=#110603></td>
    <td width="1" height="1" bgcolor=#2d1811></td>
    <td width="1" height="1" bgcolor=#0a0100></td>
    <td width="1" height="1" bgcolor=#0c0100></td>
    <td width="1" height="1" bgcolor=#100103></td>
```

```
    <td width="1" height="1"
bgcolor=#0f0004></td>
    <td width="1" height="1"
bgcolor=#100000></td>
    <td width="1" height="1"
bgcolor=#120102></td>
    <td width="1" height="1"
bgcolor=#110200></td>
    <td width="1" height="1"
bgcolor=#1d0b09></td>
    <td width="1" height="1"
bgcolor=#26100e></td>
    <td width="1" height="1"
bgcolor=#2f1c09></td>
    <td width="1" height="1"
bgcolor=#424119></td>
    <td width="1" height="1"
bgcolor=#5e4f1e></td>
    <td width="1" height="1"
bgcolor=#52271c></td>
    <td width="1" height="1"
bgcolor=#683f17></td>
    <td width="1" height="1"
bgcolor=#ad2816></td>
    <td width="1" height="1"
bgcolor=#4d210e></td>
    <td width="1" height="1"
bgcolor=#776a27></td>
    <td width="1" height="1"
bgcolor=#d0c2a2></td>
    <td width="1" height="1"
bgcolor=#be9b4e></td>
    <td width="1" height="1"
bgcolor=#f0e55f></td>
    <td width="1" height="1"
bgcolor=#ebe6ad></td>
    <td width="1" height="1"
bgcolor=#e8e98e></td>
    <td width="1" height="1"
bgcolor=#edebca></td>
    <td width="1" height="1"
bgcolor=#a9b81b></td>
    <td width="1" height="1"
bgcolor=#f2ebd9></td>
    <td width="1" height="1"
bgcolor=#d1ce78></td>
    <td width="1" height="1"
bgcolor=#bf9557></td>
    <td width="1" height="1"
bgcolor=#e0c94b></td>
    <td width="1" height="1"
bgcolor=#a8762b></td>
    <td width="1" height="1"
bgcolor=#c8c8af></td>
    <td width="1" height="1"
bgcolor=#715e31></td>
    <td width="1" height="1"
bgcolor=#2c250f></td>
    <td width="1" height="1"
bgcolor=#4b441f></td>
    <td width="1" height="1"
bgcolor=#54160f></td>
    <td width="1" height="1"
bgcolor=#52742b></td>
    <td width="1" height="1"
bgcolor=#872017></td>
    <td width="1" height="1"
bgcolor=#7f5629></td>
    <td width="1" height="1"
bgcolor=#524818></td>
    <td width="1" height="1"
bgcolor=#3f2018></td>
    <td width="1" height="1"
bgcolor=#5c4f23></td>
    <td width="1" height="1"
bgcolor=#7b6022></td>
    <td width="1" height="1"
bgcolor=#524f20></td>
    <td width="1" height="1"
bgcolor=#685e41></td>
    <td width="1" height="1"
bgcolor=#433e24></td>
    <td width="1" height="1"
bgcolor=#46402b></td>
    <td width="1" height="1"
bgcolor=#3f331d></td>
    <td width="1" height="1"
bgcolor=#403023></td>
    <td width="1" height="1"
bgcolor=#493723></td>
    <td width="1" height="1"
bgcolor=#453324></td>
    <td width="1" height="1"
bgcolor=#42311b></td>
    <td width="1" height="1"
bgcolor=#59411e></td>
    <td width="1" height="1"
bgcolor=#a08f37></td>
    <td width="1" height="1"
bgcolor=#5f451e></td>
    <td width="1" height="1"
bgcolor=#191005></td>
    <td width="1" height="1"
bgcolor=#200701></td>
    <td width="1" height="1"
bgcolor=#211107></td>
    <td width="1" height="1"
bgcolor=#a4674e></td>
    <td width="1" height="1"
bgcolor=#94705f></td>
    <td width="1" height="1"
bgcolor=#7a6849></td>
    <td width="1" height="1"
bgcolor=#b8ac8e></td>
    <td width="1" height="1"
bgcolor=#90704e></td>
    <td width="1" height="1"
bgcolor=#8e6a52></td>
  </tr>
  <tr>
    <td width="1" height="1"
bgcolor=#959b4a></td>
    <td width="1" height="1"
bgcolor=#aeb170></td>
    <td width="1" height="1"
bgcolor=#a29f56></td>
    <td width="1" height="1"
bgcolor=#a19a63></td>
    <td width="1" height="1"
bgcolor=#0c0706></td>
    <td width="1" height="1"
bgcolor=#271412></td>
    <td width="1" height="1"
bgcolor=#2c181b></td>
    <td width="1" height="1"
bgcolor=#0d0401></td>
    <td width="1" height="1"
bgcolor=#0f0104></td>
    <td width="1" height="1"
bgcolor=#2a1410></td>
    <td width="1" height="1"
bgcolor=#0a0201></td>
    <td width="1" height="1"
bgcolor=#100100></td>
    <td width="1" height="1"
bgcolor=#090000></td>
    <td width="1" height="1"
bgcolor=#090002></td>
    <td width="1" height="1"
bgcolor=#140604></td>
    <td width="1" height="1"
bgcolor=#190404></td>
    <td width="1" height="1"
bgcolor=#160201></td>
    <td width="1" height="1"
bgcolor=#1b0504></td>
    <td width="1" height="1"
bgcolor=#230e09></td>
    <td width="1" height="1"
bgcolor=#45401f></td>
    <td width="1" height="1"
bgcolor=#332b0c></td>
    <td width="1" height="1"
bgcolor=#3b3d11></td>
    <td width="1" height="1"
bgcolor=#3d350f></td>
    <td width="1" height="1"
bgcolor=#565a13></td>
    <td width="1" height="1"
bgcolor=#3c320d></td>
    <td width="1" height="1"
bgcolor=#311c0e></td>
    <td width="1" height="1"
bgcolor=#b0aa85></td>
```

```
    <td width="1" height="1" bgcolor=#b98641></td>
    <td width="1" height="1" bgcolor=#c99e67></td>
    <td width="1" height="1" bgcolor=#f5f6d4></td>
    <td width="1" height="1" bgcolor=#e8d772></td>
    <td width="1" height="1" bgcolor=#98aa16></td>
    <td width="1" height="1" bgcolor=#aeb33b></td>
    <td width="1" height="1" bgcolor=#7e8433></td>
    <td width="1" height="1" bgcolor=#a6b81b></td>
    <td width="1" height="1" bgcolor=#9aa010></td>
    <td width="1" height="1" bgcolor=#dbc299></td>
    <td width="1" height="1" bgcolor=#d5be6a></td>
    <td width="1" height="1" bgcolor=#cdc476></td>
    <td width="1" height="1" bgcolor=#e8e1b7></td>
    <td width="1" height="1" bgcolor=#beb886></td>
    <td width="1" height="1" bgcolor=#45381c></td>
    <td width="1" height="1" bgcolor=#5b4e10></td>
    <td width="1" height="1" bgcolor=#521a20></td>
    <td width="1" height="1" bgcolor=#74371b></td>
    <td width="1" height="1" bgcolor=#965726></td>
    <td width="1" height="1" bgcolor=#8b8424></td>
    <td width="1" height="1" bgcolor=#533d2b></td>
    <td width="1" height="1" bgcolor=#413e20></td>
    <td width="1" height="1" bgcolor=#5f5312></td>
    <td width="1" height="1" bgcolor=#71622d></td>
    <td width="1" height="1" bgcolor=#787550></td>
    <td width="1" height="1" bgcolor=#57522c></td>
    <td width="1" height="1" bgcolor=#93955d></td>
    <td width="1" height="1" bgcolor=#6d6b47></td>
    <td width="1" height="1" bgcolor=#8d7952></td>
    <td width="1" height="1" bgcolor=#3b2916></td>
    <td width="1" height="1" bgcolor=#36241b></td>
    <td width="1" height="1" bgcolor=#3a281b></td>
    <td width="1" height="1" bgcolor=#39261b></td>
    <td width="1" height="1" bgcolor=#533a1d></td>
    <td width="1" height="1" bgcolor=#6c521f></td>
    <td width="1" height="1" bgcolor=#5f4120></td>
    <td width="1" height="1" bgcolor=#4d372c></td>
    <td width="1" height="1" bgcolor=#3a3d30></td>
    <td width="1" height="1" bgcolor=#89684f></td>
    <td width="1" height="1" bgcolor=#a05952></td>
    <td width="1" height="1" bgcolor=#6e2f21></td>
    <td width="1" height="1" bgcolor=#b8957b></td>
    <td width="1" height="1" bgcolor=#855c4b></td>
    <td width="1" height="1" bgcolor=#746c55></td>
    <td width="1" height="1" bgcolor=#896f53></td>
  </tr>
  <tr>
    <td width="1" height="1" bgcolor=#ab9c5f></td>
    <td width="1" height="1" bgcolor=#acab55></td>
    <td width="1" height="1" bgcolor=#bbb764></td>
    <td width="1" height="1" bgcolor=#9c945d></td>
    <td width="1" height="1" bgcolor=#0c0704></td>
    <td width="1" height="1" bgcolor=#2c1810></td>
    <td width="1" height="1" bgcolor=#291a12></td>
    <td width="1" height="1" bgcolor=#0e0603></td>
    <td width="1" height="1" bgcolor=#110700></td>
    <td width="1" height="1" bgcolor=#2c1b15></td>
    <td width="1" height="1" bgcolor=#0e0100></td>
    <td width="1" height="1" bgcolor=#1d0d06></td>
    <td width="1" height="1" bgcolor=#5b4926></td>
    <td width="1" height="1" bgcolor=#65552b></td>
    <td width="1" height="1" bgcolor=#44331c></td>
    <td width="1" height="1" bgcolor=#140000></td>
    <td width="1" height="1" bgcolor=#1b0904></td>
    <td width="1" height="1" bgcolor=#241109></td>
    <td width="1" height="1" bgcolor=#261606></td>
    <td width="1" height="1" bgcolor=#3c3c12></td>
    <td width="1" height="1" bgcolor=#4c4925></td>
    <td width="1" height="1" bgcolor=#382713></td>
    <td width="1" height="1" bgcolor=#5a5b14></td>
    <td width="1" height="1" bgcolor=#547222></td>
    <td width="1" height="1" bgcolor=#424016></td>
    <td width="1" height="1" bgcolor=#54431f></td>
    <td width="1" height="1" bgcolor=#d1d0b3></td>
    <td width="1" height="1" bgcolor=#d09d0e></td>
    <td width="1" height="1" bgcolor=#ddc749></td>
    <td width="1" height="1" bgcolor=#d9de44></td>
    <td width="1" height="1" bgcolor=#a3bc39></td>
    <td width="1" height="1" bgcolor=#b2b172></td>
    <td width="1" height="1" bgcolor=#b5c240></td>
    <td width="1" height="1" bgcolor=#956e1b></td>
    <td width="1" height="1" bgcolor=#a0b151></td>
    <td width="1" height="1" bgcolor=#9fa051></td>
    <td width="1" height="1" bgcolor=#8a8a15></td>
    <td width="1" height="1" bgcolor=#c7bc86></td>
    <td width="1" height="1" bgcolor=#a59303></td>
    <td width="1" height="1" bgcolor=#945f1b></td>
    <td width="1" height="1" bgcolor=#c8d0bb></td>
```

```
<td width="1" height="1" bgcolor=#5b471f></td>
<td width="1" height="1" bgcolor=#443d1e></td>
<td width="1" height="1" bgcolor=#411e14></td>
<td width="1" height="1" bgcolor=#6e2c16></td>
<td width="1" height="1" bgcolor=#9a672e></td>
<td width="1" height="1" bgcolor=#8a8b25></td>
<td width="1" height="1" bgcolor=#883121></td>
<td width="1" height="1" bgcolor=#352e1a></td>
<td width="1" height="1" bgcolor=#625525></td>
<td width="1" height="1" bgcolor=#564022></td>
<td width="1" height="1" bgcolor=#5b5834></td>
<td width="1" height="1" bgcolor=#463e22></td>
<td width="1" height="1" bgcolor=#646133></td>
<td width="1" height="1" bgcolor=#4f412e></td>
<td width="1" height="1" bgcolor=#5f452d></td>
<td width="1" height="1" bgcolor=#3f261e></td>
<td width="1" height="1" bgcolor=#35281a></td>
<td width="1" height="1" bgcolor=#39281c></td>
<td width="1" height="1" bgcolor=#3c291a></td>
<td width="1" height="1" bgcolor=#4d341c></td>
<td width="1" height="1" bgcolor=#735927></td>
<td width="1" height="1" bgcolor=#847127></td>
<td width="1" height="1" bgcolor=#4c3a1f></td>
<td width="1" height="1" bgcolor=#d35f3b></td>
<td width="1" height="1" bgcolor=#92776f></td>
<td width="1" height="1" bgcolor=#753219></td>
<td width="1" height="1" bgcolor=#cc9b88></td>
<td width="1" height="1" bgcolor=#a45447></td>
<td width="1" height="1" bgcolor=#8a5b47></td>
<td width="1" height="1" bgcolor=#885347></td>
<td width="1" height="1" bgcolor=#5f3023></td>
</tr>
<tr>
<td width="1" height="1" bgcolor=#aaa062></td>
<td width="1" height="1" bgcolor=#b0b057></td>
<td width="1" height="1" bgcolor=#c5bd6f></td>
<td width="1" height="1" bgcolor=#8f884f></td>
<td width="1" height="1" bgcolor=#0b0301></td>
<td width="1" height="1" bgcolor=#2b1813></td>
<td width="1" height="1" bgcolor=#2b1d15></td>
<td width="1" height="1" bgcolor=#0e0004></td>
<td width="1" height="1" bgcolor=#20150f></td>
<td width="1" height="1" bgcolor=#1d0b0a></td>
<td width="1" height="1" bgcolor=#130603></td>
<td width="1" height="1" bgcolor=#281911></td>
<td width="1" height="1" bgcolor=#180806></td>
<td width="1" height="1" bgcolor=#0b0000></td>
<td width="1" height="1" bgcolor=#1d0f08></td>
<td width="1" height="1" bgcolor=#2f160f></td>
<td width="1" height="1" bgcolor=#0f0202></td>
<td width="1" height="1" bgcolor=#1d0b08></td>
<td width="1" height="1" bgcolor=#160203></td>
<td width="1" height="1" bgcolor=#2a1f0e></td>
<td width="1" height="1" bgcolor=#3b4117></td>
<td width="1" height="1" bgcolor=#443f1b></td>
<td width="1" height="1" bgcolor=#3d3a0d></td>
<td width="1" height="1" bgcolor=#486612></td>
<td width="1" height="1" bgcolor=#4b410e></td>
<td width="1" height="1" bgcolor=#887649></td>
<td width="1" height="1" bgcolor=#e7ecbd></td>
<td width="1" height="1" bgcolor=#fbefc2></td>
<td width="1" height="1" bgcolor=#f8f1c6></td>
<td width="1" height="1" bgcolor=#dbc697></td>
<td width="1" height="1" bgcolor=#dcb895></td>
<td width="1" height="1" bgcolor=#ca9264></td>
<td width="1" height="1" bgcolor=#cd9d7e></td>
<td width="1" height="1" bgcolor=#e4ad8d></td>
<td width="1" height="1" bgcolor=#d0a284></td>
<td width="1" height="1" bgcolor=#d09365></td>
<td width="1" height="1" bgcolor=#d7a88e></td>
<td width="1" height="1" bgcolor=#d5b087></td>
<td width="1" height="1" bgcolor=#f8eeca></td>
<td width="1" height="1" bgcolor=#f5eec5></td>
<td width="1" height="1" bgcolor=#e0dfb8></td>
<td width="1" height="1" bgcolor=#846839></td>
<td width="1" height="1" bgcolor=#382a13></td>
<td width="1" height="1" bgcolor=#452617></td>
<td width="1" height="1" bgcolor=#452518></td>
<td width="1" height="1" bgcolor=#b13414></td>
<td width="1" height="1" bgcolor=#e54618></td>
<td width="1" height="1" bgcolor=#a83724></td>
<td width="1" height="1" bgcolor=#312a1d></td>
<td width="1" height="1" bgcolor=#574b21></td>
<td width="1" height="1" bgcolor=#3a2f18></td>
<td width="1" height="1" bgcolor=#3c2b1c></td>
<td width="1" height="1" bgcolor=#352013></td>
<td width="1" height="1" bgcolor=#362b1a></td>
<td width="1" height="1" bgcolor=#3a2b1d></td>
```

```
    <td width="1" height="1"
bgcolor=#3b281b></td>
    <td width="1" height="1"
bgcolor=#322a17></td>
    <td width="1" height="1"
bgcolor=#37241a></td>
    <td width="1" height="1"
bgcolor=#4b362c></td>
    <td width="1" height="1"
bgcolor=#583c34></td>
    <td width="1" height="1"
bgcolor=#6d4928></td>
    <td width="1" height="1"
bgcolor=#7f5731></td>
    <td width="1" height="1"
bgcolor=#583823></td>
    <td width="1" height="1"
bgcolor=#674f2c></td>
    <td width="1" height="1"
bgcolor=#d3bc90></td>
    <td width="1" height="1"
bgcolor=#f8f9dc></td>
    <td width="1" height="1"
bgcolor=#e9d5ae></td>
    <td width="1" height="1"
bgcolor=#c25245></td>
    <td width="1" height="1"
bgcolor=#7c4d3f></td>
    <td width="1" height="1"
bgcolor=#90654c></td>
    <td width="1" height="1"
bgcolor=#958f7b></td>
    <td width="1" height="1"
bgcolor=#a37357></td>
  </tr>
  <tr>
    <td width="1" height="1"
bgcolor=#a5965f></td>
    <td width="1" height="1"
bgcolor=#b5b358></td>
    <td width="1" height="1"
bgcolor=#c0b761></td>
    <td width="1" height="1"
bgcolor=#8e844b></td>
    <td width="1" height="1"
bgcolor=#1a100b></td>
    <td width="1" height="1"
bgcolor=#29170d></td>
    <td width="1" height="1"
bgcolor=#2d1d1a></td>
    <td width="1" height="1"
bgcolor=#2c1c17></td>
    <td width="1" height="1"
bgcolor=#170805></td>
    <td width="1" height="1"
bgcolor=#190d0b></td>
    <td width="1" height="1"
bgcolor=#1c0a03></td>
    <td width="1" height="1"
bgcolor=#2e1507></td>
    <td width="1" height="1"
bgcolor=#29190c></td>
    <td width="1" height="1"
bgcolor=#301c19></td>
    <td width="1" height="1"
bgcolor=#291307></td>
    <td width="1" height="1"
bgcolor=#381c17></td>
    <td width="1" height="1"
bgcolor=#160807></td>
    <td width="1" height="1"
bgcolor=#160103></td>
    <td width="1" height="1"
bgcolor=#1d0709></td>
    <td width="1" height="1"
bgcolor=#1d0706></td>
    <td width="1" height="1"
bgcolor=#2b270c></td>
    <td width="1" height="1"
bgcolor=#353717></td>
    <td width="1" height="1"
bgcolor=#393610></td>
    <td width="1" height="1"
bgcolor=#5e9917></td>
    <td width="1" height="1"
bgcolor=#4c4b11></td>
    <td width="1" height="1"
bgcolor=#817b4b></td>
    <td width="1" height="1"
bgcolor=#b4ab4f></td>
    <td width="1" height="1"
bgcolor=#c0c67b></td>
    <td width="1" height="1"
bgcolor=#c5ca59></td>
    <td width="1" height="1"
bgcolor=#cfd271></td>
    <td width="1" height="1"
bgcolor=#dbdf8d></td>
    <td width="1" height="1"
bgcolor=#f5f2c9></td>
    <td width="1" height="1"
bgcolor=#b3bb6a></td>
    <td width="1" height="1"
bgcolor=#fdfed1></td>
    <td width="1" height="1"
bgcolor=#a2a64f></td>
    <td width="1" height="1"
bgcolor=#96a758></td>
    <td width="1" height="1"
bgcolor=#d8db81></td>
    <td width="1" height="1"
bgcolor=#b9c07c></td>
    <td width="1" height="1"
bgcolor=#bbc28a></td>
    <td width="1" height="1"
bgcolor=#c2bf93></td>
    <td width="1" height="1"
bgcolor=#afbf88></td>
    <td width="1" height="1"
bgcolor=#927741></td>
    <td width="1" height="1"
bgcolor=#34270b></td>
    <td width="1" height="1"
bgcolor=#442c1a></td>
    <td width="1" height="1"
bgcolor=#442315></td>
    <td width="1" height="1"
bgcolor=#c43d25></td>
    <td width="1" height="1"
bgcolor=#846c21></td>
    <td width="1" height="1"
bgcolor=#9e351d></td>
    <td width="1" height="1"
bgcolor=#27190f></td>
    <td width="1" height="1"
bgcolor=#3c331f></td>
    <td width="1" height="1"
bgcolor=#382c1b></td>
    <td width="1" height="1"
bgcolor=#31271d></td>
    <td width="1" height="1"
bgcolor=#35271f></td>
    <td rowspan="1"
colspan="2" width="1"
height="1"
bgcolor=#31251a></td>
    <td width="1" height="1"
bgcolor=#412c20></td>
    <td width="1" height="1"
bgcolor=#8e3b39></td>
    <td width="1" height="1"
bgcolor=#43321e></td>
    <td width="1" height="1"
bgcolor=#5a4731></td>
    <td width="1" height="1"
bgcolor=#60492c></td>
    <td width="1" height="1"
bgcolor=#7c4a2d></td>
    <td width="1" height="1"
bgcolor=#894730></td>
    <td width="1" height="1"
bgcolor=#55391e></td>
    <td width="1" height="1"
bgcolor=#412f22></td>
    <td width="1" height="1"
bgcolor=#f8de84></td>
    <td width="1" height="1"
bgcolor=#927d48></td>
    <td width="1" height="1"
bgcolor=#917e69></td>
    <td width="1" height="1"
bgcolor=#f5f3c5></td>
    <td width="1" height="1"
bgcolor=#fff7d3></td>
```

```
    <td width="1" height="1"
bgcolor=#b3b398></td>
    <td width="1" height="1"
bgcolor=#9f976c></td>
    <td width="1" height="1"
bgcolor=#6b5144></td>
  </tr>
  <tr>
    <td width="1" height="1"
bgcolor=#a79857></td>
    <td width="1" height="1"
bgcolor=#b1af54></td>
    <td width="1" height="1"
bgcolor=#b3ac57></td>
    <td width="1" height="1"
bgcolor=#857b48></td>
    <td width="1" height="1"
bgcolor=#120906></td>
    <td width="1" height="1"
bgcolor=#221008></td>
    <td width="1" height="1"
bgcolor=#21110a></td>
    <td width="1" height="1"
bgcolor=#18070b></td>
    <td width="1" height="1"
bgcolor=#0c080a></td>
    <td width="1" height="1"
bgcolor=#140b0e></td>
    <td width="1" height="1"
bgcolor=#221309></td>
    <td width="1" height="1"
bgcolor=#30160a></td>
    <td width="1" height="1"
bgcolor=#1f0b07></td>
    <td width="1" height="1"
bgcolor=#2d1d11></td>
    <td width="1" height="1"
bgcolor=#392111></td>
    <td width="1" height="1"
bgcolor=#361910></td>
    <td width="1" height="1"
bgcolor=#170506></td>
    <td width="1" height="1"
bgcolor=#190401></td>
    <td width="1" height="1"
bgcolor=#1d0702></td>
    <td width="1" height="1"
bgcolor=#1e0907></td>
    <td width="1" height="1"
bgcolor=#240809></td>
    <td width="1" height="1"
bgcolor=#2b1d0a></td>
    <td width="1" height="1"
bgcolor=#322e0c></td>
    <td width="1" height="1"
bgcolor=#4d9112></td>
    <td width="1" height="1"
bgcolor=#362b07></td>
    <td width="1" height="1"
bgcolor=#746237></td>
    <td width="1" height="1"
bgcolor=#d3d483></td>
    <td width="1" height="1"
bgcolor=#d0cf79></td>
    <td width="1" height="1"
bgcolor=#e1e1a0></td>
    <td width="1" height="1"
bgcolor=#cbc877></td>
    <td width="1" height="1"
bgcolor=#d9cf9d></td>
    <td width="1" height="1"
bgcolor=#d5cda0></td>
    <td width="1" height="1"
bgcolor=#ddcc8c></td>
    <td width="1" height="1"
bgcolor=#eeddb6></td>
    <td width="1" height="1"
bgcolor=#d0bd80></td>
    <td width="1" height="1"
bgcolor=#c2af7d></td>
    <td width="1" height="1"
bgcolor=#d6c989></td>
    <td width="1" height="1"
bgcolor=#c0b383></td>
    <td width="1" height="1"
bgcolor=#dedfa7></td>
    <td width="1" height="1"
bgcolor=#dfdfa7></td>
    <td width="1" height="1"
bgcolor=#d0d2a1></td>
    <td width="1" height="1"
bgcolor=#a98748></td>
    <td width="1" height="1"
bgcolor=#312408></td>
    <td width="1" height="1"
bgcolor=#351d0f></td>
    <td width="1" height="1"
bgcolor=#4b7326></td>
    <td width="1" height="1"
bgcolor=#9e5717></td>
    <td width="1" height="1"
bgcolor=#bd4e3d></td>
    <td width="1" height="1"
bgcolor=#e8d4bb></td>
    <td width="1" height="1"
bgcolor=#d9d8ca></td>
    <td width="1" height="1"
bgcolor=#4a402c></td>
    <td width="1" height="1"
bgcolor=#39281c></td>
    <td width="1" height="1"
bgcolor=#3a2d1e></td>
    <td width="1" height="1"
bgcolor=#412d24></td>
    <td width="1" height="1"
bgcolor=#3e2b1e></td>
    <td width="1" height="1"
bgcolor=#633330></td>
    <td width="1" height="1"
bgcolor=#652d29></td>
    <td width="1" height="1"
bgcolor=#563224></td>
    <td width="1" height="1"
bgcolor=#4f382f></td>
    <td width="1" height="1"
bgcolor=#6c3b20></td>
    <td width="1" height="1"
bgcolor=#745628></td>
    <td width="1" height="1"
bgcolor=#5f3626></td>
    <td width="1" height="1"
bgcolor=#7d3e1b></td>
    <td width="1" height="1"
bgcolor=#4b3323></td>
    <td width="1" height="1"
bgcolor=#8f743e></td>
    <td width="1" height="1"
bgcolor=#eec762></td>
    <td width="1" height="1"
bgcolor=#4b302b></td>
    <td width="1" height="1"
bgcolor=#897e52></td>
    <td width="1" height="1"
bgcolor=#ffe986></td>
    <td width="1" height="1"
bgcolor=#cab68a></td>
    <td width="1" height="1"
bgcolor=#a28248></td>
    <td width="1" height="1"
bgcolor=#bd864b></td>
    <td width="1" height="1"
bgcolor=#54402e></td>
  </tr>
  <tr>
    <td width="1" height="1"
bgcolor=#99894b></td>
    <td width="1" height="1"
bgcolor=#bab553></td>
    <td width="1" height="1"
bgcolor=#b4a851></td>
    <td width="1" height="1"
bgcolor=#84763e></td>
    <td width="1" height="1"
bgcolor=#0e0505></td>
    <td width="1" height="1"
bgcolor=#1c100a></td>
    <td width="1" height="1"
bgcolor=#261010></td>
    <td width="1" height="1"
bgcolor=#1a0f08></td>
    <td width="1" height="1"
bgcolor=#6e7757></td>
    <td width="1" height="1"
bgcolor=#625d47></td>
```

```
    <td width="1" height="1"
bgcolor=#190c02></td>
    <td width="1" height="1"
bgcolor=#2d1c12></td>
    <td width="1" height="1"
bgcolor=#2b1709></td>
    <td width="1" height="1"
bgcolor=#301911></td>
    <td width="1" height="1"
bgcolor=#30130d></td>
    <td width="1" height="1"
bgcolor=#391e11></td>
    <td width="1" height="1"
bgcolor=#140609></td>
    <td width="1" height="1"
bgcolor=#180505></td>
    <td width="1" height="1"
bgcolor=#1e0805></td>
    <td width="1" height="1"
bgcolor=#1c0404></td>
    <td width="1" height="1"
bgcolor=#240911></td>
    <td width="1" height="1"
bgcolor=#2f190f></td>
    <td width="1" height="1"
bgcolor=#373508></td>
    <td width="1" height="1"
bgcolor=#5bb507></td>
    <td width="1" height="1"
bgcolor=#404d20></td>
    <td width="1" height="1"
bgcolor=#48301c></td>
    <td width="1" height="1"
bgcolor=#dfe3b8></td>
    <td width="1" height="1"
bgcolor=#f3efba></td>
    <td width="1" height="1"
bgcolor=#f1f2b8></td>
    <td width="1" height="1"
bgcolor=#cbbd63></td>
    <td width="1" height="1"
bgcolor=#cabb5f></td>
    <td width="1" height="1"
bgcolor=#b37725></td>
    <td width="1" height="1"
bgcolor=#9c7769></td>
    <td width="1" height="1"
bgcolor=#bf7149></td>
    <td width="1" height="1"
bgcolor=#917466></td>
    <td width="1" height="1"
bgcolor=#a4872e></td>
    <td width="1" height="1"
bgcolor=#a3aa4f></td>
    <td width="1" height="1"
bgcolor=#bfc187></td>
    <td width="1" height="1"
bgcolor=#e2e0a0></td>
    <td width="1" height="1"
bgcolor=#d3cca4></td>
    <td width="1" height="1"
bgcolor=#cdd7aa></td>
    <td width="1" height="1"
bgcolor=#694b24></td>
    <td width="1" height="1"
bgcolor=#3a2911></td>
    <td width="1" height="1"
bgcolor=#472c16></td>
    <td width="1" height="1"
bgcolor=#423b12></td>
    <td width="1" height="1"
bgcolor=#882b07></td>
    <td width="1" height="1"
bgcolor=#a89e78></td>
    <td width="1" height="1"
bgcolor=#c6c18c></td>
    <td width="1" height="1"
bgcolor=#ada979></td>
    <td width="1" height="1"
bgcolor=#a1a176></td>
    <td width="1" height="1"
bgcolor=#361f13></td>
    <td width="1" height="1"
bgcolor=#372a1c></td>
    <td width="1" height="1"
bgcolor=#522521></td>
    <td width="1" height="1"
bgcolor=#6a372e></td>
    <td width="1" height="1"
bgcolor=#372c1d></td>
    <td width="1" height="1"
bgcolor=#462f27></td>
    <td width="1" height="1"
bgcolor=#422f23></td>
    <td width="1" height="1"
bgcolor=#98433f></td>
    <td width="1" height="1"
bgcolor=#764723></td>
    <td width="1" height="1"
bgcolor=#6f482c></td>
    <td width="1" height="1"
bgcolor=#79371d></td>
    <td width="1" height="1"
bgcolor=#8e5124></td>
    <td width="1" height="1"
bgcolor=#361811></td>
    <td width="1" height="1"
bgcolor=#9f753c></td>
    <td width="1" height="1"
bgcolor=#cda453></td>
    <td width="1" height="1"
bgcolor=#291912></td>
    <td width="1" height="1"
bgcolor=#cda356></td>
    <td width="1" height="1"
bgcolor=#b69653></td>
    <td width="1" height="1"
bgcolor=#4d392a></td>
    <td width="1" height="1"
bgcolor=#ab9463></td>
    <td width="1" height="1"
bgcolor=#905633></td>
    <td width="1" height="1"
bgcolor=#7b2926></td>
  </tr>
  <tr>
    <td width="1" height="1"
bgcolor=#a19c4e></td>
    <td width="1" height="1"
bgcolor=#baaf4d></td>
    <td width="1" height="1"
bgcolor=#c0b65d></td>
    <td width="1" height="1"
bgcolor=#928549></td>
    <td width="1" height="1"
bgcolor=#1d1418></td>
    <td width="1" height="1"
bgcolor=#1f1507></td>
    <td width="1" height="1"
bgcolor=#281b0f></td>
    <td width="1" height="1"
bgcolor=#35311f></td>
    <td width="1" height="1"
bgcolor=#e2e7c9></td>
    <td width="1" height="1"
bgcolor=#d1cda4></td>
    <td width="1" height="1"
bgcolor=#211702></td>
    <td width="1" height="1"
bgcolor=#382114></td>
    <td width="1" height="1"
bgcolor=#341f0d></td>
    <td width="1" height="1"
bgcolor=#392014></td>
    <td width="1" height="1"
bgcolor=#2b150b></td>
    <td width="1" height="1"
bgcolor=#2e1509></td>
    <td width="1" height="1"
bgcolor=#110403></td>
    <td width="1" height="1"
bgcolor=#1c0605></td>
    <td width="1" height="1"
bgcolor=#1d0807></td>
    <td width="1" height="1"
bgcolor=#1f0909></td>
    <td width="1" height="1"
bgcolor=#210805></td>
    <td width="1" height="1"
bgcolor=#2c110c></td>
    <td width="1" height="1"
bgcolor=#3b330f></td>
    <td width="1" height="1"
bgcolor=#84cb11></td>
```

```
    <td width="1" height="1" bgcolor=#5d931a></td>
    <td width="1" height="1" bgcolor=#2c1304></td>
    <td width="1" height="1" bgcolor=#c7bfa3></td>
    <td width="1" height="1" bgcolor=#daaf41></td>
    <td width="1" height="1" bgcolor=#a87b3a></td>
    <td width="1" height="1" bgcolor=#e4df9e></td>
    <td width="1" height="1" bgcolor=#c59656></td>
    <td width="1" height="1" bgcolor=#b7a56e></td>
    <td width="1" height="1" bgcolor=#c1bf08></td>
    <td width="1" height="1" bgcolor=#6d6326></td>
    <td width="1" height="1" bgcolor=#abab0e></td>
    <td width="1" height="1" bgcolor=#96805b></td>
    <td width="1" height="1" bgcolor=#c1b179></td>
    <td width="1" height="1" bgcolor=#d0a58e></td>
    <td width="1" height="1" bgcolor=#af8f29></td>
    <td width="1" height="1" bgcolor=#9b7f25></td>
    <td width="1" height="1" bgcolor=#e2d8b1></td>
    <td width="1" height="1" bgcolor=#36250c></td>
    <td width="1" height="1" bgcolor=#2f210f></td>
    <td width="1" height="1" bgcolor=#411703></td>
    <td width="1" height="1" bgcolor=#3f2f19></td>
    <td width="1" height="1" bgcolor=#9b321c></td>
    <td width="1" height="1" bgcolor=#6e6035></td>
    <td width="1" height="1" bgcolor=#bcbc76></td>
    <td width="1" height="1" bgcolor=#bbbb6e></td>
    <td width="1" height="1" bgcolor=#969660></td>
    <td width="1" height="1" bgcolor=#371f19></td>
    <td width="1" height="1" bgcolor=#38291b></td>
    <td width="1" height="1" bgcolor=#33281c></td>
    <td width="1" height="1" bgcolor=#562d23></td>
    <td width="1" height="1" bgcolor=#322822></td>
    <td width="1" height="1" bgcolor=#3e311a></td>
    <td width="1" height="1" bgcolor=#3e2b1f></td>
    <td width="1" height="1" bgcolor=#4c231d></td>
    <td width="1" height="1" bgcolor=#6d3b2f></td>
    <td width="1" height="1" bgcolor=#432f1a></td>
    <td width="1" height="1" bgcolor=#563c24></td>
    <td width="1" height="1" bgcolor=#5c3d17></td>
    <td width="1" height="1" bgcolor=#241314></td>
    <td width="1" height="1" bgcolor=#cac2a1></td>
    <td width="1" height="1" bgcolor=#79603c></td>
    <td width="1" height="1" bgcolor=#2e2413></td>
    <td width="1" height="1" bgcolor=#dfbe5c></td>
    <td width="1" height="1" bgcolor=#71513b></td>
    <td width="1" height="1" bgcolor=#352115></td>
    <td width="1" height="1" bgcolor=#6f5a3b></td>
    <td width="1" height="1" bgcolor=#482220></td>
    <td width="1" height="1" bgcolor=#c1995c></td>
  </tr>
  <tr>
    <td width="1" height="1" bgcolor=#9c9d45></td>
    <td width="1" height="1" bgcolor=#a09e50></td>
    <td width="1" height="1" bgcolor=#92904b></td>
    <td width="1" height="1" bgcolor=#544a2e></td>
    <td width="1" height="1" bgcolor=#1e1315></td>
    <td width="1" height="1" bgcolor=#251a13></td>
    <td width="1" height="1" bgcolor=#2f170b></td>
    <td width="1" height="1" bgcolor=#987348></td>
    <td width="1" height="1" bgcolor=#b87b42></td>
    <td width="1" height="1" bgcolor=#a76f36></td>
    <td width="1" height="1" bgcolor=#452a29></td>
    <td width="1" height="1" bgcolor=#231610></td>
    <td width="1" height="1" bgcolor=#301d14></td>
    <td width="1" height="1" bgcolor=#220b04></td>
    <td width="1" height="1" bgcolor=#231209></td>
    <td width="1" height="1" bgcolor=#32180f></td>
    <td width="1" height="1" bgcolor=#210e0e></td>
    <td width="1" height="1" bgcolor=#1e0704></td>
    <td width="1" height="1" bgcolor=#230d0e></td>
    <td width="1" height="1" bgcolor=#1d0503></td>
    <td width="1" height="1" bgcolor=#230905></td>
    <td width="1" height="1" bgcolor=#280c00></td>
    <td width="1" height="1" bgcolor=#392d0f></td>
    <td width="1" height="1" bgcolor=#6e901a></td>
    <td width="1" height="1" bgcolor=#76b90f></td>
    <td width="1" height="1" bgcolor=#302106></td>
    <td width="1" height="1" bgcolor=#968a60></td>
    <td width="1" height="1" bgcolor=#b89869></td>
    <td width="1" height="1" bgcolor=#f2dc74></td>
    <td width="1" height="1" bgcolor=#ceb980></td>
    <td width="1" height="1" bgcolor=#cdd268></td>
    <td width="1" height="1" bgcolor=#a19c03></td>
    <td width="1" height="1" bgcolor=#ae876f></td>
    <td width="1" height="1" bgcolor=#899629></td>
    <td width="1" height="1" bgcolor=#a09062></td>
    <td width="1" height="1" bgcolor=#868a03></td>
    <td width="1" height="1" bgcolor=#ab9570></td>
    <td width="1" height="1" bgcolor=#cac550></td>
```

```
<td width="1" height="1" bgcolor=#a68834></td>
<td width="1" height="1" bgcolor=#d5cea9></td>
<td width="1" height="1" bgcolor=#b3a259></td>
<td width="1" height="1" bgcolor=#261b08></td>
<td width="1" height="1" bgcolor=#2b1c10></td>
<td width="1" height="1" bgcolor=#2f130d></td>
<td width="1" height="1" bgcolor=#351b04></td>
<td width="1" height="1" bgcolor=#bb2010></td>
<td width="1" height="1" bgcolor=#cc8254></td>
<td width="1" height="1" bgcolor=#676931></td>
<td width="1" height="1" bgcolor=#8e9259></td>
<td width="1" height="1" bgcolor=#8d835e></td>
<td width="1" height="1" bgcolor=#2b1710></td>
<td width="1" height="1" bgcolor=#31211a></td>
<td width="1" height="1" bgcolor=#2f2018></td>
<td width="1" height="1" bgcolor=#312316></td>
<td width="1" height="1" bgcolor=#443125></td>
<td width="1" height="1" bgcolor=#584f3f></td>
<td width="1" height="1" bgcolor=#6d6f47></td>
<td width="1" height="1" bgcolor=#7b7147></td>
<td width="1" height="1" bgcolor=#4c3d2e></td>
<td width="1" height="1" bgcolor=#3d251c></td>
<td width="1" height="1" bgcolor=#482c16></td>
<td width="1" height="1" bgcolor=#754921></td>
<td width="1" height="1" bgcolor=#90674c></td>
<td width="1" height="1" bgcolor=#ffecc8></td>
<td width="1" height="1" bgcolor=#453a27></td>
<td width="1" height="1" bgcolor=#363022></td>
<td width="1" height="1" bgcolor=#fffff0></td>
<td width="1" height="1" bgcolor=#4a2f20></td>
<td width="1" height="1" bgcolor=#3d271c></td>
<td width="1" height="1" bgcolor=#462623></td>
<td width="1" height="1" bgcolor=#2f1d13></td>
<td width="1" height="1" bgcolor=#3b2516></td>
</tr>
<tr>
<td width="1" height="1" bgcolor=#0d0805></td>
<td width="1" height="1" bgcolor=#050200></td>
<td width="1" height="1" bgcolor=#070003></td>
<td width="1" height="1" bgcolor=#110903></td>
<td width="1" height="1" bgcolor=#0f0502></td>
<td width="1" height="1" bgcolor=#1a1108></td>
<td width="1" height="1" bgcolor=#655a75></td>
<td width="1" height="1" bgcolor=#716f7f></td>
<td width="1" height="1" bgcolor=#5d492c></td>
<td width="1" height="1" bgcolor=#573b34></td>
<td width="1" height="1" bgcolor=#63535d></td>
<td width="1" height="1" bgcolor=#120406></td>
<td width="1" height="1" bgcolor=#140702></td>
<td width="1" height="1" bgcolor=#200c08></td>
<td width="1" height="1" bgcolor=#290d0c></td>
<td width="1" height="1" bgcolor=#2f130c></td>
<td width="1" height="1" bgcolor=#150405></td>
<td width="1" height="1" bgcolor=#170101></td>
<td width="1" height="1" bgcolor=#220a05></td>
<td width="1" height="1" bgcolor=#1f0902></td>
<td width="1" height="1" bgcolor=#2d140e></td>
<td width="1" height="1" bgcolor=#311211></td>
<td width="1" height="1" bgcolor=#33160c></td>
<td width="1" height="1" bgcolor=#230c01></td>
<td width="1" height="1" bgcolor=#191211></td>
<td width="1" height="1" bgcolor=#250a03></td>
<td width="1" height="1" bgcolor=#4d2a0c></td>
<td width="1" height="1" bgcolor=#d3c8a9></td>
<td width="1" height="1" bgcolor=#9d7638></td>
<td width="1" height="1" bgcolor=#f5f9bb></td>
<td width="1" height="1" bgcolor=#d2a138></td>
<td width="1" height="1" bgcolor=#d8b688></td>
<td width="1" height="1" bgcolor=#e5e7b5></td>
<td width="1" height="1" bgcolor=#bfae68></td>
<td width="1" height="1" bgcolor=#e7dea0></td>
<td width="1" height="1" bgcolor=#f4e8bf></td>
<td width="1" height="1" bgcolor=#c6ad38></td>
<td width="1" height="1" bgcolor=#b49450></td>
<td width="1" height="1" bgcolor=#ebe8c1></td>
<td width="1" height="1" bgcolor=#e0e39b></td>
<td width="1" height="1" bgcolor=#4d3018></td>
<td width="1" height="1" bgcolor=#412107></td>
<td width="1" height="1" bgcolor=#411514></td>
<td width="1" height="1" bgcolor=#412210></td>
<td width="1" height="1" bgcolor=#473013></td>
<td width="1" height="1" bgcolor=#483415></td>
<td width="1" height="1" bgcolor=#5d411b></td>
<td width="1" height="1" bgcolor=#b1b466></td>
<td width="1" height="1" bgcolor=#8f9175></td>
<td width="1" height="1" bgcolor=#524631></td>
<td width="1" height="1" bgcolor=#180e0b></td>
<td width="1" height="1" bgcolor=#251617></td>
```

```
    <td width="1" height="1" bgcolor=#322218></td>
    <td width="1" height="1" bgcolor=#362518></td>
    <td width="1" height="1" bgcolor=#3d3124></td>
    <td width="1" height="1" bgcolor=#5c552b></td>
    <td width="1" height="1" bgcolor=#737d4e></td>
    <td width="1" height="1" bgcolor=#a86226></td>
    <td width="1" height="1" bgcolor=#48361d></td>
    <td width="1" height="1" bgcolor=#2b221c></td>
    <td width="1" height="1" bgcolor=#3c2a1f></td>
    <td width="1" height="1" bgcolor=#6b4524></td>
    <td width="1" height="1" bgcolor=#6f2121></td>
    <td width="1" height="1" bgcolor=#b41a14></td>
    <td width="1" height="1" bgcolor=#322117></td>
    <td width="1" height="1" bgcolor=#482b22></td>
    <td width="1" height="1" bgcolor=#e6caae></td>
    <td width="1" height="1" bgcolor=#382115></td>
    <td width="1" height="1" bgcolor=#3e2216></td>
    <td width="1" height="1" bgcolor=#3d2417></td>
    <td width="1" height="1" bgcolor=#321c17></td>
    <td width="1" height="1" bgcolor=#2f1813></td>
  </tr>
  <tr>
    <td width="1" height="1" bgcolor=#1a1711></td>
    <td width="1" height="1" bgcolor=#382626></td>
    <td width="1" height="1" bgcolor=#261610></td>
    <td width="1" height="1" bgcolor=#221416></td>
    <td width="1" height="1" bgcolor=#0f0701></td>
    <td width="1" height="1" bgcolor=#4b3d19></td>
    <td width="1" height="1" bgcolor=#2e2014></td>
    <td width="1" height="1" bgcolor=#454453></td>
    <td width="1" height="1" bgcolor=#504240></td>
    <td width="1" height="1" bgcolor=#463135></td>
    <td width="1" height="1" bgcolor=#2b1616></td>
    <td width="1" height="1" bgcolor=#291411></td>
    <td width="1" height="1" bgcolor=#2a190d></td>
    <td width="1" height="1" bgcolor=#27170e></td>
    <td width="1" height="1" bgcolor=#230803></td>
    <td width="1" height="1" bgcolor=#32130b></td>
    <td width="1" height="1" bgcolor=#0f0202></td>
    <td width="1" height="1" bgcolor=#200702></td>
    <td width="1" height="1" bgcolor=#250c06></td>
    <td width="1" height="1" bgcolor=#260c05></td>
    <td width="1" height="1" bgcolor=#331b0c></td>
    <td width="1" height="1" bgcolor=#321609></td>
    <td width="1" height="1" bgcolor=#33170b></td>
    <td width="1" height="1" bgcolor=#3b1f15></td>
    <td width="1" height="1" bgcolor=#231002></td>
    <td width="1" height="1" bgcolor=#190807></td>
    <td width="1" height="1" bgcolor=#29120b></td>
    <td width="1" height="1" bgcolor=#2d210e></td>
    <td width="1" height="1" bgcolor=#d2c7a1></td>
    <td width="1" height="1" bgcolor=#d8d6b0></td>
    <td width="1" height="1" bgcolor=#d3913f></td>
    <td width="1" height="1" bgcolor=#d0ae57></td>
    <td width="1" height="1" bgcolor=#d8a613></td>
    <td width="1" height="1" bgcolor=#f7edd2></td>
    <td width="1" height="1" bgcolor=#b57f04></td>
    <td width="1" height="1" bgcolor=#b79855></td>
    <td width="1" height="1" bgcolor=#b09757></td>
    <td width="1" height="1" bgcolor=#d1bb97></td>
    <td width="1" height="1" bgcolor=#e0d1a7></td>
    <td width="1" height="1" bgcolor=#553623></td>
    <td width="1" height="1" bgcolor=#30270c></td>
    <td width="1" height="1" bgcolor=#352311></td>
    <td width="1" height="1" bgcolor=#3c2b10></td>
    <td width="1" height="1" bgcolor=#3e2b12></td>
    <td width="1" height="1" bgcolor=#362a0d></td>
    <td width="1" height="1" bgcolor=#4f511a></td>
    <td width="1" height="1" bgcolor=#5d5428></td>
    <td width="1" height="1" bgcolor=#a59c59></td>
    <td width="1" height="1" bgcolor=#8e9368></td>
    <td width="1" height="1" bgcolor=#82825a></td>
    <td width="1" height="1" bgcolor=#0d0300></td>
    <td width="1" height="1" bgcolor=#1f0e0f></td>
    <td width="1" height="1" bgcolor=#302014></td>
    <td width="1" height="1" bgcolor=#3c2b21></td>
    <td width="1" height="1" bgcolor=#41382a></td>
    <td width="1" height="1" bgcolor=#55534a></td>
    <td width="1" height="1" bgcolor=#8d8f3a></td>
    <td width="1" height="1" bgcolor=#aaa542></td>
    <td width="1" height="1" bgcolor=#98a262></td>
    <td width="1" height="1" bgcolor=#2d2112></td>
    <td width="1" height="1" bgcolor=#462722></td>
    <td width="1" height="1" bgcolor=#773c1c></td>
    <td width="1" height="1" bgcolor=#362d15></td>
    <td width="1" height="1" bgcolor=#331f13></td>
    <td width="1" height="1" bgcolor=#36251e></td>
    <td width="1" height="1" bgcolor=#402012></td>
```

```
    <td width="1" height="1" bgcolor=#d25048></td>
    <td width="1" height="1" bgcolor=#371412></td>
    <td width="1" height="1" bgcolor=#342219></td>
    <td width="1" height="1" bgcolor=#3f251c></td>
    <td width="1" height="1" bgcolor=#2f1b13></td>
    <td width="1" height="1" bgcolor=#321611></td>
  </tr>
  <tr>
    <td width="1" height="1" bgcolor=#170e0a></td>
    <td width="1" height="1" bgcolor=#2f2121></td>
    <td width="1" height="1" bgcolor=#382724></td>
    <td width="1" height="1" bgcolor=#42261e></td>
    <td width="1" height="1" bgcolor=#25170d></td>
    <td width="1" height="1" bgcolor=#48341e></td>
    <td width="1" height="1" bgcolor=#291f12></td>
    <td width="1" height="1" bgcolor=#6d533d></td>
    <td width="1" height="1" bgcolor=#5a524c></td>
    <td width="1" height="1" bgcolor=#9b865f></td>
    <td width="1" height="1" bgcolor=#8e7f54></td>
    <td width="1" height="1" bgcolor=#55200e></td>
    <td width="1" height="1" bgcolor=#210f05></td>
    <td width="1" height="1" bgcolor=#1b110a></td>
    <td width="1" height="1" bgcolor=#3c1609></td>
    <td width="1" height="1" bgcolor=#91792d></td>
    <td width="1" height="1" bgcolor=#321713></td>
    <td width="1" height="1" bgcolor=#271002></td>
    <td width="1" height="1" bgcolor=#2b0e0d></td>
    <td width="1" height="1" bgcolor=#270e04></td>
    <td width="1" height="1" bgcolor=#2b130b></td>
    <td width="1" height="1" bgcolor=#240800></td>
    <td width="1" height="1" bgcolor=#28180f></td>
    <td width="1" height="1" bgcolor=#423d0c></td>
    <td width="1" height="1" bgcolor=#2e0e06></td>
    <td width="1" height="1" bgcolor=#3a2d0d></td>
    <td width="1" height="1" bgcolor=#2d1e0e></td>
    <td width="1" height="1" bgcolor=#361f09></td>
    <td width="1" height="1" bgcolor=#525723></td>
    <td width="1" height="1" bgcolor=#8f874b></td>
    <td width="1" height="1" bgcolor=#cdc49a></td>
    <td width="1" height="1" bgcolor=#dec8a1></td>
    <td width="1" height="1" bgcolor=#aa7733></td>
    <td width="1" height="1" bgcolor=#dde2a4></td>
    <td width="1" height="1" bgcolor=#c5a663></td>
    <td width="1" height="1" bgcolor=#afae81></td>
    <td width="1" height="1" bgcolor=#d4d091></td>
    <td width="1" height="1" bgcolor=#8b8e55></td>
    <td width="1" height="1" bgcolor=#463314></td>
    <td width="1" height="1" bgcolor=#392911></td>
    <td width="1" height="1" bgcolor=#37200f></td>
    <td width="1" height="1" bgcolor=#372512></td>
    <td width="1" height="1" bgcolor=#321b0a></td>
    <td width="1" height="1" bgcolor=#341711></td>
    <td width="1" height="1" bgcolor=#7e7b50></td>
    <td width="1" height="1" bgcolor=#b4b470></td>
    <td width="1" height="1" bgcolor=#d3c284></td>
    <td width="1" height="1" bgcolor=#6e6438></td>
    <td width="1" height="1" bgcolor=#6e6a51></td>
    <td width="1" height="1" bgcolor=#dcd9a8></td>
    <td width="1" height="1" bgcolor=#d8d6b1></td>
    <td width="1" height="1" bgcolor=#6e6864></td>
    <td width="1" height="1" bgcolor=#2b1f13></td>
    <td width="1" height="1" bgcolor=#302117></td>
    <td width="1" height="1" bgcolor=#362b1b></td>
    <td width="1" height="1" bgcolor=#4c4632></td>
    <td width="1" height="1" bgcolor=#5d4a21></td>
    <td width="1" height="1" bgcolor=#aec53d></td>
    <td width="1" height="1" bgcolor=#616a39></td>
    <td width="1" height="1" bgcolor=#36221b></td>
    <td width="1" height="1" bgcolor=#382c19></td>
    <td width="1" height="1" bgcolor=#322416></td>
    <td width="1" height="1" bgcolor=#332313></td>
    <td width="1" height="1" bgcolor=#2c2311></td>
    <td width="1" height="1" bgcolor=#321f18></td>
    <td width="1" height="1" bgcolor=#2c1b1c></td>
    <td width="1" height="1" bgcolor=#271b0f></td>
    <td width="1" height="1" bgcolor=#2f1813></td>
    <td width="1" height="1" bgcolor=#443c23></td>
    <td width="1" height="1" bgcolor=#2c371b></td>
    <td width="1" height="1" bgcolor=#270f04></td>
    <td width="1" height="1" bgcolor=#2c1d11></td>
  </tr>
  <tr>
    <td width="1" height="1" bgcolor=#101612></td>
    <td width="1" height="1" bgcolor=#221a18></td>
    <td width="1" height="1" bgcolor=#695040></td>
    <td width="1" height="1" bgcolor=#5b3d38></td>
    <td width="1" height="1" bgcolor=#341814></td>
    <td width="1" height="1" bgcolor=#701917></td>
    <td width="1" height="1" bgcolor=#9c332b></td>
```

```
<td width="1" height="1" bgcolor=#76413f></td>
<td width="1" height="1" bgcolor=#865650></td>
<td width="1" height="1" bgcolor=#75a96c></td>
<td width="1" height="1" bgcolor=#94814d></td>
<td width="1" height="1" bgcolor=#c61115></td>
<td width="1" height="1" bgcolor=#842216></td>
<td width="1" height="1" bgcolor=#2a1803></td>
<td width="1" height="1" bgcolor=#3d2711></td>
<td width="1" height="1" bgcolor=#54401a></td>
<td width="1" height="1" bgcolor=#321a02></td>
<td width="1" height="1" bgcolor=#2d1315></td>
<td width="1" height="1" bgcolor=#2a110c></td>
<td width="1" height="1" bgcolor=#42310d></td>
<td width="1" height="1" bgcolor=#3c2711></td>
<td width="1" height="1" bgcolor=#362415></td>
<td width="1" height="1" bgcolor=#352f12></td>
<td width="1" height="1" bgcolor=#3e4219></td>
<td width="1" height="1" bgcolor=#4a301a></td>
<td width="1" height="1" bgcolor=#372709></td>
<td width="1" height="1" bgcolor=#2a220b></td>
<td width="1" height="1" bgcolor=#34230c></td>
<td width="1" height="1" bgcolor=#3d351a></td>
<td width="1" height="1" bgcolor=#3e4917></td>
<td width="1" height="1" bgcolor=#618020></td>
<td width="1" height="1" bgcolor=#837558></td>
<td width="1" height="1" bgcolor=#afad6e></td>
<td width="1" height="1" bgcolor=#908b55></td>
<td width="1" height="1" bgcolor=#89844c></td>
<td width="1" height="1" bgcolor=#6d6b34></td>
<td width="1" height="1" bgcolor=#494515></td>
<td width="1" height="1" bgcolor=#403d13></td>
<td width="1" height="1" bgcolor=#4f5921></td>
<td width="1" height="1" bgcolor=#4d5111></td>
<td width="1" height="1" bgcolor=#6f8b24></td>
<td width="1" height="1" bgcolor=#6f8d21></td>
<td width="1" height="1" bgcolor=#565e1f></td>
<td width="1" height="1" bgcolor=#8c9354></td>
<td width="1" height="1" bgcolor=#c2b98b></td>
<td width="1" height="1" bgcolor=#b6b35d></td>
<td width="1" height="1" bgcolor=#cdc496></td>
<td width="1" height="1" bgcolor=#98945a></td>
<td width="1" height="1" bgcolor=#7b8353></td>
<td width="1" height="1" bgcolor=#e9e6cc></td>
<td width="1" height="1" bgcolor=#dfd9a0></td>
<td width="1" height="1" bgcolor=#e7e5a5></td>
<td width="1" height="1" bgcolor=#d8d69f></td>
<td width="1" height="1" bgcolor=#3b2e1b></td>
<td width="1" height="1" bgcolor=#4b3628></td>
<td width="1" height="1" bgcolor=#4d412a></td>
<td width="1" height="1" bgcolor=#676b34></td>
<td width="1" height="1" bgcolor=#a1cf3b></td>
<td width="1" height="1" bgcolor=#88aa52></td>
<td width="1" height="1" bgcolor=#352f21></td>
<td width="1" height="1" bgcolor=#3d3629></td>
<td width="1" height="1" bgcolor=#4e473c></td>
<td width="1" height="1" bgcolor=#42342e></td>
<td width="1" height="1" bgcolor=#311b16></td>
<td width="1" height="1" bgcolor=#342b11></td>
<td width="1" height="1" bgcolor=#3b361e></td>
<td width="1" height="1" bgcolor=#301e1f></td>
<td width="1" height="1" bgcolor=#e06454></td>
<td width="1" height="1" bgcolor=#6e5f36></td>
<td width="1" height="1" bgcolor=#984745></td>
<td width="1" height="1" bgcolor=#88393e></td>
<td width="1" height="1" bgcolor=#30130b></td>
</tr>
<tr>
<td width="1" height="1" bgcolor=#4c302d></td>
<td width="1" height="1" bgcolor=#81614b></td>
<td width="1" height="1" bgcolor=#6d4749></td>
<td width="1" height="1" bgcolor=#625e20></td>
<td width="1" height="1" bgcolor=#aca419></td>
<td width="1" height="1" bgcolor=#563035></td>
<td width="1" height="1" bgcolor=#71474f></td>
<td width="1" height="1" bgcolor=#533237></td>
<td width="1" height="1" bgcolor=#7a7d52></td>
<td width="1" height="1" bgcolor=#97d499></td>
<td width="1" height="1" bgcolor=#90b57c></td>
<td width="1" height="1" bgcolor=#210905></td>
<td width="1" height="1" bgcolor=#463112></td>
<td width="1" height="1" bgcolor=#75813e></td>
<td width="1" height="1" bgcolor=#585825></td>
<td width="1" height="1" bgcolor=#50471c></td>
<td width="1" height="1" bgcolor=#372711></td>
<td width="1" height="1" bgcolor=#2f1906></td>
<td width="1" height="1" bgcolor=#3e3617></td>
<td width="1" height="1" bgcolor=#544f1c></td>
<td width="1" height="1" bgcolor=#1a0d06></td>
```

```
    <td width="1" height="1" bgcolor=#524f16></td>
    <td width="1" height="1" bgcolor=#647023></td>
    <td width="1" height="1" bgcolor=#63791d></td>
    <td width="1" height="1" bgcolor=#3f2a12></td>
    <td width="1" height="1" bgcolor=#443610></td>
    <td width="1" height="1" bgcolor=#5e6220></td>
    <td width="1" height="1" bgcolor=#666728></td>
    <td width="1" height="1" bgcolor=#4e4221></td>
    <td width="1" height="1" bgcolor=#64662f></td>
    <td width="1" height="1" bgcolor=#799249></td>
    <td width="1" height="1" bgcolor=#789338></td>
    <td width="1" height="1" bgcolor=#373617></td>
    <td width="1" height="1" bgcolor=#808f50></td>
    <td width="1" height="1" bgcolor=#42611b></td>
    <td width="1" height="1" bgcolor=#587918></td>
    <td width="1" height="1" bgcolor=#424a19></td>
    <td width="1" height="1" bgcolor=#697126></td>
    <td width="1" height="1" bgcolor=#6d8735></td>
    <td width="1" height="1" bgcolor=#8a9d4b></td>
    <td width="1" height="1" bgcolor=#7d9f31></td>
    <td width="1" height="1" bgcolor=#5a7116></td>
    <td width="1" height="1" bgcolor=#9da65e></td>
    <td width="1" height="1" bgcolor=#7c873a></td>
    <td width="1" height="1" bgcolor=#41440e></td>
    <td width="1" height="1" bgcolor=#a9b064></td>
    <td width="1" height="1" bgcolor=#b6b677></td>
    <td width="1" height="1" bgcolor=#b5be84></td>
    <td width="1" height="1" bgcolor=#a5b16c></td>
    <td width="1" height="1" bgcolor=#c1cb84></td>
    <td width="1" height="1" bgcolor=#e5e6a5></td>
    <td width="1" height="1" bgcolor=#69703c></td>
    <td width="1" height="1" bgcolor=#dde296></td>
    <td width="1" height="1" bgcolor=#665c44></td>
    <td width="1" height="1" bgcolor=#454427></td>
    <td width="1" height="1" bgcolor=#5d6840></td>
    <td width="1" height="1" bgcolor=#99b25f></td>
    <td width="1" height="1" bgcolor=#9cbc52></td>
    <td width="1" height="1" bgcolor=#85a53a></td>
    <td width="1" height="1" bgcolor=#6c6863></td>
    <td width="1" height="1" bgcolor=#62584b></td>
    <td width="1" height="1" bgcolor=#695c5c></td>
    <td width="1" height="1" bgcolor=#7e7371></td>
    <td width="1" height="1" bgcolor=#2f2819></td>
    <td width="1" height="1" bgcolor=#e0e751></td>
    <td width="1" height="1" bgcolor=#e4e83e></td>
    <td width="1" height="1" bgcolor=#a69c2e></td>
    <td width="1" height="1" bgcolor=#831a19></td>
    <td width="1" height="1" bgcolor=#f6594a></td>
    <td width="1" height="1" bgcolor=#e2433a></td>
    <td width="1" height="1" bgcolor=#963434></td>
    <td width="1" height="1" bgcolor=#342719></td>
  </tr>
  <tr>
    <td width="1" height="1" bgcolor=#ae6f50></td>
    <td width="1" height="1" bgcolor=#dfd618></td>
    <td width="1" height="1" bgcolor=#c2b41a></td>
    <td width="1" height="1" bgcolor=#666826></td>
    <td width="1" height="1" bgcolor=#7d6639></td>
    <td width="1" height="1" bgcolor=#5b4057></td>
    <td width="1" height="1" bgcolor=#694d5d></td>
    <td width="1" height="1" bgcolor=#54393c></td>
    <td width="1" height="1" bgcolor=#75985b></td>
    <td width="1" height="1" bgcolor=#5e730e></td>
    <td width="1" height="1" bgcolor=#728534></td>
    <td width="1" height="1" bgcolor=#5c5a1d></td>
    <td width="1" height="1" bgcolor=#4e5428></td>
    <td width="1" height="1" bgcolor=#3b2d08></td>
    <td width="1" height="1" bgcolor=#3f320f></td>
    <td width="1" height="1" bgcolor=#464b1b></td>
    <td width="1" height="1" bgcolor=#3e3e13></td>
    <td width="1" height="1" bgcolor=#6c6929></td>
    <td width="1" height="1" bgcolor=#4c461c></td>
    <td width="1" height="1" bgcolor=#616826></td>
    <td width="1" height="1" bgcolor=#473d1a></td>
    <td width="1" height="1" bgcolor=#58581f></td>
    <td width="1" height="1" bgcolor=#3c3f13></td>
    <td width="1" height="1" bgcolor=#535c1e></td>
    <td width="1" height="1" bgcolor=#695b32></td>
    <td width="1" height="1" bgcolor=#333108></td>
    <td width="1" height="1" bgcolor=#6e7331></td>
    <td width="1" height="1" bgcolor=#5d6921></td>
    <td width="1" height="1" bgcolor=#4e3a1b></td>
    <td width="1" height="1" bgcolor=#3d371c></td>
    <td width="1" height="1" bgcolor=#756f28></td>
    <td width="1" height="1" bgcolor=#707a3d></td>
    <td width="1" height="1" bgcolor=#494419></td>
    <td width="1" height="1" bgcolor=#829556></td>
    <td width="1" height="1" bgcolor=#708240></td>
```

```
    <td width="1" height="1" bgcolor=#6d733a></td>
    <td width="1" height="1" bgcolor=#464d22></td>
    <td width="1" height="1" bgcolor=#688127></td>
    <td width="1" height="1" bgcolor=#60732c></td>
    <td width="1" height="1" bgcolor=#57621d></td>
    <td width="1" height="1" bgcolor=#597525></td>
    <td width="1" height="1" bgcolor=#685d2d></td>
    <td width="1" height="1" bgcolor=#807941></td>
    <td width="1" height="1" bgcolor=#817937></td>
    <td width="1" height="1" bgcolor=#6d7f3f></td>
    <td width="1" height="1" bgcolor=#6c783c></td>
    <td width="1" height="1" bgcolor=#879041></td>
    <td width="1" height="1" bgcolor=#759240></td>
    <td width="1" height="1" bgcolor=#5d722d></td>
    <td width="1" height="1" bgcolor=#6f823b></td>
    <td width="1" height="1" bgcolor=#819f51></td>
    <td width="1" height="1" bgcolor=#789847></td>
    <td width="1" height="1" bgcolor=#7f9a3b></td>
    <td width="1" height="1" bgcolor=#6a762d></td>
    <td width="1" height="1" bgcolor=#658040></td>
    <td width="1" height="1" bgcolor=#6b7b29></td>
    <td width="1" height="1" bgcolor=#5b5221></td>
    <td width="1" height="1" bgcolor=#687a3a></td>
    <td width="1" height="1" bgcolor=#b4c36f></td>
    <td width="1" height="1" bgcolor=#312919></td>
    <td width="1" height="1" bgcolor=#4a3630></td>
    <td width="1" height="1" bgcolor=#5d4945></td>
    <td width="1" height="1" bgcolor=#736864></td>
    <td width="1" height="1" bgcolor=#9f8986></td>
    <td width="1" height="1" bgcolor=#d6c984></td>
    <td width="1" height="1" bgcolor=#f5ef94></td>
    <td width="1" height="1" bgcolor=#fdfd31></td>
    <td width="1" height="1" bgcolor=#9e7e2f></td>
    <td width="1" height="1" bgcolor=#992519></td>
    <td width="1" height="1" bgcolor=#c38839></td>
    <td width="1" height="1" bgcolor=#984e31></td>
    <td width="1" height="1" bgcolor=#424c2a></td>
  </tr>
  <tr>
    <td width="1" height="1" bgcolor=#a5ae40></td>
    <td width="1" height="1" bgcolor=#a19819></td>
    <td width="1" height="1" bgcolor=#534c39></td>
    <td width="1" height="1" bgcolor=#6a5460></td>
    <td width="1" height="1" bgcolor=#68515f></td>
    <td width="1" height="1" bgcolor=#634b55></td>
    <td width="1" height="1" bgcolor=#4f4143></td>
    <td width="1" height="1" bgcolor=#23120a></td>
    <td width="1" height="1" bgcolor=#696f25></td>
    <td width="1" height="1" bgcolor=#4d5219></td>
    <td width="1" height="1" bgcolor=#5e6f22></td>
    <td width="1" height="1" bgcolor=#78532c></td>
    <td width="1" height="1" bgcolor=#603614></td>
    <td width="1" height="1" bgcolor=#6b4c26></td>
    <td width="1" height="1" bgcolor=#403719></td>
    <td width="1" height="1" bgcolor=#45331c></td>
    <td width="1" height="1" bgcolor=#743f24></td>
    <td width="1" height="1" bgcolor=#443207></td>
    <td width="1" height="1" bgcolor=#723f21></td>
    <td width="1" height="1" bgcolor=#4f3a1b></td>
    <td width="1" height="1" bgcolor=#382111></td>
    <td width="1" height="1" bgcolor=#4e261b></td>
    <td width="1" height="1" bgcolor=#362c0d></td>
    <td width="1" height="1" bgcolor=#351510></td>
    <td width="1" height="1" bgcolor=#5b391c></td>
    <td width="1" height="1" bgcolor=#c65832></td>
    <td width="1" height="1" bgcolor=#b45435></td>
    <td width="1" height="1" bgcolor=#bf3e2e></td>
    <td width="1" height="1" bgcolor=#2a1000></td>
    <td width="1" height="1" bgcolor=#622a16></td>
    <td width="1" height="1" bgcolor=#55371e></td>
    <td width="1" height="1" bgcolor=#483811></td>
    <td width="1" height="1" bgcolor=#684824></td>
    <td width="1" height="1" bgcolor=#7b4b2e></td>
    <td width="1" height="1" bgcolor=#4f3a1a></td>
    <td width="1" height="1" bgcolor=#6c371f></td>
    <td width="1" height="1" bgcolor=#6a3725></td>
    <td width="1" height="1" bgcolor=#ce3829></td>
    <td width="1" height="1" bgcolor=#af5041></td>
    <td width="1" height="1" bgcolor=#31321a></td>
    <td width="1" height="1" bgcolor=#422914></td>
    <td width="1" height="1" bgcolor=#6b7224></td>
    <td width="1" height="1" bgcolor=#37190b></td>
    <td width="1" height="1" bgcolor=#332300></td>
    <td width="1" height="1" bgcolor=#3a3214></td>
    <td width="1" height="1" bgcolor=#493a1d></td>
    <td width="1" height="1" bgcolor=#4f5024></td>
    <td width="1" height="1" bgcolor=#4c1f18></td>
    <td width="1" height="1" bgcolor=#494c22></td>
```

```
    <td width="1" height="1"
bgcolor=#675e33></td>
    <td width="1" height="1"
bgcolor=#6a5534></td>
    <td width="1" height="1"
bgcolor=#4b361d></td>
    <td width="1" height="1"
bgcolor=#767e41></td>
    <td width="1" height="1"
bgcolor=#76854a></td>
    <td width="1" height="1"
bgcolor=#85983f></td>
    <td width="1" height="1"
bgcolor=#3f2914></td>
    <td width="1" height="1"
bgcolor=#4e5520></td>
    <td width="1" height="1"
bgcolor=#797c38></td>
    <td width="1" height="1"
bgcolor=#625e33></td>
    <td width="1" height="1"
bgcolor=#674727></td>
    <td width="1" height="1"
bgcolor=#3c2a1b></td>
    <td width="1" height="1"
bgcolor=#544335></td>
    <td width="1" height="1"
bgcolor=#4d3531></td>
    <td width="1" height="1"
bgcolor=#4a3a2b></td>
    <td width="1" height="1"
bgcolor=#978b4c></td>
    <td width="1" height="1"
bgcolor=#ece250></td>
    <td width="1" height="1"
bgcolor=#a1935b></td>
    <td width="1" height="1"
bgcolor=#8f9038></td>
    <td width="1" height="1"
bgcolor=#aaa072></td>
    <td width="1" height="1"
bgcolor=#d0c524></td>
    <td width="1" height="1"
bgcolor=#aa9475></td>
    <td width="1" height="1"
bgcolor=#83ac26></td>
  </tr>
  <tr>
    <td width="1" height="1"
bgcolor=#605f65></td>
    <td width="1" height="1"
bgcolor=#60505b></td>
    <td width="1" height="1"
bgcolor=#664a5e></td>
    <td width="1" height="1"
bgcolor=#6a4c66></td>
    <td width="1" height="1"
bgcolor=#533d4e></td>
    <td width="1" height="1"
bgcolor=#594144></td>
    <td width="1" height="1"
bgcolor=#33291f></td>
    <td width="1" height="1"
bgcolor=#6b331c></td>
    <td width="1" height="1"
bgcolor=#c2442f></td>
    <td width="1" height="1"
bgcolor=#c93829></td>
    <td width="1" height="1"
bgcolor=#c14528></td>
    <td width="1" height="1"
bgcolor=#d13624></td>
    <td width="1" height="1"
bgcolor=#db2c24></td>
    <td width="1" height="1"
bgcolor=#eb4435></td>
    <td width="1" height="1"
bgcolor=#782f1e></td>
    <td width="1" height="1"
bgcolor=#392014></td>
    <td width="1" height="1"
bgcolor=#d23b35></td>
    <td width="1" height="1"
bgcolor=#c13830></td>
    <td width="1" height="1"
bgcolor=#c52c30></td>
    <td width="1" height="1"
bgcolor=#d1352e></td>
    <td width="1" height="1"
bgcolor=#ae3c2d></td>
    <td width="1" height="1"
bgcolor=#cb3729></td>
    <td width="1" height="1"
bgcolor=#49130e></td>
    <td width="1" height="1"
bgcolor=#2c0e05></td>
    <td width="1" height="1"
bgcolor=#e64c41></td>
    <td width="1" height="1"
bgcolor=#a73429></td>
    <td width="1" height="1"
bgcolor=#7c0f0e></td>
    <td width="1" height="1"
bgcolor=#de3a28></td>
    <td width="1" height="1"
bgcolor=#a23731></td>
    <td width="1" height="1"
bgcolor=#df2f32></td>
    <td width="1" height="1"
bgcolor=#f04338></td>
    <td width="1" height="1"
bgcolor=#e34c41></td>
    <td width="1" height="1"
bgcolor=#c83221></td>
    <td width="1" height="1"
bgcolor=#ed3d37></td>
    <td width="1" height="1"
bgcolor=#c93a30></td>
    <td width="1" height="1"
bgcolor=#ae2421></td>
    <td width="1" height="1"
bgcolor=#6d1f16></td>
    <td width="1" height="1"
bgcolor=#ae3b1f></td>
    <td width="1" height="1"
bgcolor=#d33f38></td>
    <td width="1" height="1"
bgcolor=#1f1c0f></td>
    <td width="1" height="1"
bgcolor=#311e06></td>
    <td width="1" height="1"
bgcolor=#44320f></td>
    <td width="1" height="1"
bgcolor=#4e4e35></td>
    <td width="1" height="1"
bgcolor=#2e190b></td>
    <td width="1" height="1"
bgcolor=#2d1a09></td>
    <td width="1" height="1"
bgcolor=#381e11></td>
    <td width="1" height="1"
bgcolor=#7c211f></td>
    <td width="1" height="1"
bgcolor=#db4b46></td>
    <td width="1" height="1"
bgcolor=#d85b4f></td>
    <td width="1" height="1"
bgcolor=#d54335></td>
    <td width="1" height="1"
bgcolor=#ec403b></td>
    <td width="1" height="1"
bgcolor=#cf5646></td>
    <td width="1" height="1"
bgcolor=#d9423e></td>
    <td width="1" height="1"
bgcolor=#c55a4f></td>
    <td width="1" height="1"
bgcolor=#191d12></td>
    <td width="1" height="1"
bgcolor=#9a4436></td>
    <td width="1" height="1"
bgcolor=#d53f3c></td>
    <td width="1" height="1"
bgcolor=#e66953></td>
    <td width="1" height="1"
bgcolor=#df6646></td>
    <td width="1" height="1"
bgcolor=#e7483a></td>
    <td width="1" height="1"
bgcolor=#bf4d3a></td>
    <td width="1" height="1"
bgcolor=#723f29></td>
    <td width="1" height="1"
bgcolor=#3d2a1b></td>
```

```
    <td width="1" height="1"
bgcolor=#3f2e1b></td>
    <td width="1" height="1"
bgcolor=#50461d></td>
    <td width="1" height="1"
bgcolor=#b2b648></td>
    <td width="1" height="1"
bgcolor=#4b4a33></td>
    <td width="1" height="1"
bgcolor=#5e5757></td>
    <td width="1" height="1"
bgcolor=#5a5964></td>
    <td width="1" height="1"
bgcolor=#493545></td>
    <td width="1" height="1"
bgcolor=#3f4536></td>
    <td width="1" height="1"
bgcolor=#6b7e3f></td>
  </tr>
  <tr>
    <td width="1" height="1"
bgcolor=#5f5967></td>
    <td width="1" height="1"
bgcolor=#533c3d></td>
    <td width="1" height="1"
bgcolor=#933838></td>
    <td width="1" height="1"
bgcolor=#514451></td>
    <td width="1" height="1"
bgcolor=#2a1f17></td>
    <td width="1" height="1"
bgcolor=#3a2921></td>
    <td width="1" height="1"
bgcolor=#352512></td>
    <td width="1" height="1"
bgcolor=#ab4b3a></td>
    <td width="1" height="1"
bgcolor=#bf3a30></td>
    <td width="1" height="1"
bgcolor=#200a00></td>
    <td width="1" height="1"
bgcolor=#401011></td>
    <td width="1" height="1"
bgcolor=#3a1209></td>
    <td width="1" height="1"
bgcolor=#81251a></td>
    <td width="1" height="1"
bgcolor=#d83828></td>
    <td width="1" height="1"
bgcolor=#b93f2c></td>
    <td width="1" height="1"
bgcolor=#9d3630></td>
    <td width="1" height="1"
bgcolor=#d63d30></td>
    <td width="1" height="1"
bgcolor=#832524></td>
    <td width="1" height="1"
bgcolor=#501015></td>
    <td width="1" height="1"
bgcolor=#74141d></td>
    <td width="1" height="1"
bgcolor=#5e120f></td>
    <td width="1" height="1"
bgcolor=#941b1f></td>
    <td width="1" height="1"
bgcolor=#7d1e1a></td>
    <td width="1" height="1"
bgcolor=#5c1e16></td>
    <td width="1" height="1"
bgcolor=#cc2b28></td>
    <td width="1" height="1"
bgcolor=#4e220a></td>
    <td width="1" height="1"
bgcolor=#24220d></td>
    <td width="1" height="1"
bgcolor=#df4437></td>
    <td width="1" height="1"
bgcolor=#c84737></td>
    <td width="1" height="1"
bgcolor=#541011></td>
    <td width="1" height="1"
bgcolor=#a41e1b></td>
    <td width="1" height="1"
bgcolor=#a7161a></td>
    <td width="1" height="1"
bgcolor=#dd3936></td>
    <td width="1" height="1"
bgcolor=#ca3c2c></td>
    <td width="1" height="1"
bgcolor=#4c0f0d></td>
    <td width="1" height="1"
bgcolor=#3a0d04></td>
    <td width="1" height="1"
bgcolor=#2c1509></td>
    <td width="1" height="1"
bgcolor=#be3432></td>
    <td width="1" height="1"
bgcolor=#df4e3e></td>
    <td width="1" height="1"
bgcolor=#662816></td>
    <td width="1" height="1"
bgcolor=#402111></td>
    <td width="1" height="1"
bgcolor=#4b2312></td>
    <td width="1" height="1"
bgcolor=#683912></td>
    <td width="1" height="1"
bgcolor=#542d1b></td>
    <td width="1" height="1"
bgcolor=#381a0d></td>
    <td width="1" height="1"
bgcolor=#412415></td>
    <td width="1" height="1"
bgcolor=#853125></td>
    <td width="1" height="1"
bgcolor=#f15b53></td>
    <td width="1" height="1"
bgcolor=#9f302d></td>
    <td width="1" height="1"
bgcolor=#781d18></td>
    <td width="1" height="1"
bgcolor=#731717></td>
    <td width="1" height="1"
bgcolor=#761a1b></td>
    <td width="1" height="1"
bgcolor=#8f2725></td>
    <td width="1" height="1"
bgcolor=#611b13></td>
    <td width="1" height="1"
bgcolor=#1e1f0f></td>
    <td width="1" height="1"
bgcolor=#d85846></td>
    <td width="1" height="1"
bgcolor=#e85347></td>
    <td width="1" height="1"
bgcolor=#ab3728></td>
    <td width="1" height="1"
bgcolor=#532215></td>
    <td width="1" height="1"
bgcolor=#5f2510></td>
    <td width="1" height="1"
bgcolor=#c53f2c></td>
    <td width="1" height="1"
bgcolor=#5c2919></td>
    <td width="1" height="1"
bgcolor=#301f15></td>
    <td width="1" height="1"
bgcolor=#392a19></td>
    <td width="1" height="1"
bgcolor=#373215></td>
    <td width="1" height="1"
bgcolor=#a7a250></td>
    <td width="1" height="1"
bgcolor=#646c45></td>
    <td width="1" height="1"
bgcolor=#472e21></td>
    <td width="1" height="1"
bgcolor=#32281d></td>
    <td width="1" height="1"
bgcolor=#311f17></td>
    <td width="1" height="1"
bgcolor=#281913></td>
    <td width="1" height="1"
bgcolor=#4c4339></td>
  </tr>
  <tr>
    <td width="1" height="1"
bgcolor=#443d3e></td>
    <td width="1" height="1"
bgcolor=#414132></td>
    <td width="1" height="1"
bgcolor=#7b5c32></td>
    <td width="1" height="1"
bgcolor=#2f1e15></td>
```

```
    <td width="1" height="1"
bgcolor=#352617></td>
    <td width="1" height="1"
bgcolor=#402916></td>
    <td width="1" height="1"
bgcolor=#783b1f></td>
    <td width="1" height="1"
bgcolor=#db4234></td>
    <td width="1" height="1"
bgcolor=#b43723></td>
    <td width="1" height="1"
bgcolor=#b93328></td>
    <td width="1" height="1"
bgcolor=#a12b22></td>
    <td width="1" height="1"
bgcolor=#602214></td>
    <td width="1" height="1"
bgcolor=#9a2a1d></td>
    <td width="1" height="1"
bgcolor=#9e251f></td>
    <td width="1" height="1"
bgcolor=#4b1414></td>
    <td width="1" height="1"
bgcolor=#94322a></td>
    <td width="1" height="1"
bgcolor=#d33627></td>
    <td width="1" height="1"
bgcolor=#8c3726></td>
    <td width="1" height="1"
bgcolor=#a94733></td>
    <td width="1" height="1"
bgcolor=#8d211a></td>
    <td width="1" height="1"
bgcolor=#6a2519></td>
    <td width="1" height="1"
bgcolor=#300e0c></td>
    <td width="1" height="1"
bgcolor=#3b1304></td>
    <td width="1" height="1"
bgcolor=#c04e34></td>
    <td width="1" height="1"
bgcolor=#d84432></td>
    <td width="1" height="1"
bgcolor=#2d1810></td>
    <td width="1" height="1"
bgcolor=#39191a></td>
    <td width="1" height="1"
bgcolor=#7e2014></td>
    <td width="1" height="1"
bgcolor=#de3330></td>
    <td width="1" height="1"
bgcolor=#1b0c04></td>
    <td width="1" height="1"
bgcolor=#290c0c></td>
    <td width="1" height="1"
bgcolor=#3b1209></td>
    <td width="1" height="1"
bgcolor=#df7155></td>
    <td width="1" height="1"
bgcolor=#cd463e></td>
    <td width="1" height="1"
bgcolor=#1e0e05></td>
    <td width="1" height="1"
bgcolor=#270f08></td>
    <td width="1" height="1"
bgcolor=#3f1e13></td>
    <td width="1" height="1"
bgcolor=#b22f28></td>
    <td width="1" height="1"
bgcolor=#ed5e4c></td>
    <td width="1" height="1"
bgcolor=#52290f></td>
    <td width="1" height="1"
bgcolor=#543314></td>
    <td width="1" height="1"
bgcolor=#7b3c13></td>
    <td width="1" height="1"
bgcolor=#1f190f></td>
    <td width="1" height="1"
bgcolor=#492d19></td>
    <td width="1" height="1"
bgcolor=#6d3f23></td>
    <td width="1" height="1"
bgcolor=#6d3f20></td>
    <td width="1" height="1"
bgcolor=#b33830></td>
    <td width="1" height="1"
bgcolor=#ed564b></td>
    <td width="1" height="1"
bgcolor=#d14d4b></td>
    <td width="1" height="1"
bgcolor=#8e4a45></td>
    <td width="1" height="1"
bgcolor=#884139></td>
    <td width="1" height="1"
bgcolor=#8c4f3d></td>
    <td width="1" height="1"
bgcolor=#8d4139></td>
    <td width="1" height="1"
bgcolor=#1a160c></td>
    <td width="1" height="1"
bgcolor=#26180c></td>
    <td width="1" height="1"
bgcolor=#663517></td>
    <td width="1" height="1"
bgcolor=#d5312b></td>
    <td width="1" height="1"
bgcolor=#b72d25></td>
    <td width="1" height="1"
bgcolor=#c54944></td>
    <td width="1" height="1"
bgcolor=#934d39></td>
    <td width="1" height="1"
bgcolor=#3d2b13></td>
    <td width="1" height="1"
bgcolor=#20130d></td>
    <td width="1" height="1"
bgcolor=#372012></td>
    <td width="1" height="1"
bgcolor=#382415></td>
    <td width="1" height="1"
bgcolor=#372e0e></td>
    <td width="1" height="1"
bgcolor=#4e432c></td>
    <td width="1" height="1"
bgcolor=#605938></td>
    <td width="1" height="1"
bgcolor=#34241c></td>
    <td width="1" height="1"
bgcolor=#35231a></td>
    <td width="1" height="1"
bgcolor=#29200b></td>
    <td width="1" height="1"
bgcolor=#302015></td>
    <td width="1" height="1"
bgcolor=#331f18></td>
  </tr>
  <tr>
    <td width="1" height="1"
bgcolor=#392716></td>
    <td width="1" height="1"
bgcolor=#553123></td>
    <td width="1" height="1"
bgcolor=#f21f27></td>
    <td width="1" height="1"
bgcolor=#4b2614></td>
    <td width="1" height="1"
bgcolor=#3e1f11></td>
    <td width="1" height="1"
bgcolor=#31230a></td>
    <td width="1" height="1"
bgcolor=#c4352b></td>
    <td width="1" height="1"
bgcolor=#ae3e23></td>
    <td width="1" height="1"
bgcolor=#8c3324></td>
    <td width="1" height="1"
bgcolor=#792017></td>
    <td width="1" height="1"
bgcolor=#b02c26></td>
    <td width="1" height="1"
bgcolor=#a82f23></td>
    <td width="1" height="1"
bgcolor=#e4492e></td>
    <td width="1" height="1"
bgcolor=#803321></td>
    <td width="1" height="1"
bgcolor=#461717></td>
    <td width="1" height="1"
bgcolor=#b84421></td>
    <td width="1" height="1"
bgcolor=#9b231d></td>
    <td width="1" height="1"
bgcolor=#731d14></td>
```

```
    <td width="1" height="1"
bgcolor=#98171f></td>
    <td width="1" height="1"
bgcolor=#b2151d></td>
    <td width="1" height="1"
bgcolor=#8c1814></td>
    <td width="1" height="1"
bgcolor=#371a0d></td>
    <td width="1" height="1"
bgcolor=#1a0b05></td>
    <td width="1" height="1"
bgcolor=#e64c40></td>
    <td width="1" height="1"
bgcolor=#cf3237></td>
    <td width="1" height="1"
bgcolor=#9a241f></td>
    <td width="1" height="1"
bgcolor=#c43a2e></td>
    <td width="1" height="1"
bgcolor=#c6322f></td>
    <td width="1" height="1"
bgcolor=#c52627></td>
    <td width="1" height="1"
bgcolor=#70221a></td>
    <td width="1" height="1"
bgcolor=#210e0a></td>
    <td width="1" height="1"
bgcolor=#6d4c27></td>
    <td width="1" height="1"
bgcolor=#e25a48></td>
    <td width="1" height="1"
bgcolor=#c54b38></td>
    <td width="1" height="1"
bgcolor=#1f1003></td>
    <td width="1" height="1"
bgcolor=#261202></td>
    <td width="1" height="1"
bgcolor=#361611></td>
    <td width="1" height="1"
bgcolor=#6c321a></td>
    <td width="1" height="1"
bgcolor=#eb3f35></td>
    <td width="1" height="1"
bgcolor=#93302b></td>
    <td width="1" height="1"
bgcolor=#281107></td>
    <td width="1" height="1"
bgcolor=#37201a></td>
    <td width="1" height="1"
bgcolor=#422b12></td>
    <td width="1" height="1"
bgcolor=#321f19></td>
    <td width="1" height="1"
bgcolor=#3a2313></td>
    <td width="1" height="1"
bgcolor=#241200></td>
    <td width="1" height="1"
bgcolor=#993322></td>
    <td width="1" height="1"
bgcolor=#da6052></td>
    <td width="1" height="1"
bgcolor=#91382d></td>
    <td width="1" height="1"
bgcolor=#461b06></td>
    <td width="1" height="1"
bgcolor=#6f3d23></td>
    <td width="1" height="1"
bgcolor=#7e2f1e></td>
    <td width="1" height="1"
bgcolor=#ad2a25></td>
    <td width="1" height="1"
bgcolor=#250f0b></td>
    <td width="1" height="1"
bgcolor=#2f2714></td>
    <td width="1" height="1"
bgcolor=#281f12></td>
    <td width="1" height="1"
bgcolor=#6e221d></td>
    <td width="1" height="1"
bgcolor=#4d1f15></td>
    <td width="1" height="1"
bgcolor=#902721></td>
    <td width="1" height="1"
bgcolor=#dc3d33></td>
    <td width="1" height="1"
bgcolor=#dc5849></td>
    <td width="1" height="1"
bgcolor=#712d20></td>
    <td width="1" height="1"
bgcolor=#2c1a10></td>
    <td width="1" height="1"
bgcolor=#39210f></td>
    <td width="1" height="1"
bgcolor=#4e3f32></td>
    <td width="1" height="1"
bgcolor=#77814a></td>
    <td width="1" height="1"
bgcolor=#7f2f22></td>
    <td width="1" height="1"
bgcolor=#4f2511></td>
    <td width="1" height="1"
bgcolor=#2d1c11></td>
    <td width="1" height="1"
bgcolor=#28160d></td>
    <td width="1" height="1"
bgcolor=#322010></td>
    <td width="1" height="1"
bgcolor=#3f251b></td>
  </tr>
  <tr>
    <td width="1" height="1"
bgcolor=#d93137></td>
    <td width="1" height="1"
bgcolor=#6f2f26></td>
    <td width="1" height="1"
bgcolor=#47291c></td>
    <td width="1" height="1"
bgcolor=#2e2115></td>
    <td width="1" height="1"
bgcolor=#392710></td>
    <td width="1" height="1"
bgcolor=#6d4128></td>
    <td width="1" height="1"
bgcolor=#c03929></td>
    <td width="1" height="1"
bgcolor=#ce543a></td>
    <td width="1" height="1"
bgcolor=#953f24></td>
    <td width="1" height="1"
bgcolor=#461719></td>
    <td width="1" height="1"
bgcolor=#2e130a></td>
    <td width="1" height="1"
bgcolor=#a83826></td>
    <td width="1" height="1"
bgcolor=#c53a2b></td>
    <td width="1" height="1"
bgcolor=#8a2320></td>
    <td width="1" height="1"
bgcolor=#902a21></td>
    <td width="1" height="1"
bgcolor=#c2352c></td>
    <td width="1" height="1"
bgcolor=#440d0e></td>
    <td width="1" height="1"
bgcolor=#1b1003></td>
    <td width="1" height="1"
bgcolor=#1c0002></td>
    <td width="1" height="1"
bgcolor=#120000></td>
    <td width="1" height="1"
bgcolor=#422a14></td>
    <td width="1" height="1"
bgcolor=#210b02></td>
    <td width="1" height="1"
bgcolor=#452d18></td>
    <td width="1" height="1"
bgcolor=#ef3b35></td>
    <td width="1" height="1"
bgcolor=#854727></td>
    <td width="1" height="1"
bgcolor=#79121c></td>
    <td width="1" height="1"
bgcolor=#881415></td>
    <td width="1" height="1"
bgcolor=#ab2923></td>
    <td width="1" height="1"
bgcolor=#d3362d></td>
    <td width="1" height="1"
bgcolor=#7d331d></td>
    <td width="1" height="1"
bgcolor=#2f2011></td>
    <td width="1" height="1"
bgcolor=#be9133></td>
```

```
    <td width="1" height="1" bgcolor=#b6523b></td>
    <td width="1" height="1" bgcolor=#c84134></td>
    <td width="1" height="1" bgcolor=#772e2b></td>
    <td width="1" height="1" bgcolor=#381903></td>
    <td width="1" height="1" bgcolor=#473316></td>
    <td width="1" height="1" bgcolor=#573e19></td>
    <td width="1" height="1" bgcolor=#cd3f35></td>
    <td width="1" height="1" bgcolor=#d34f41></td>
    <td width="1" height="1" bgcolor=#b74b33></td>
    <td width="1" height="1" bgcolor=#b94835></td>
    <td width="1" height="1" bgcolor=#a74b34></td>
    <td width="1" height="1" bgcolor=#985a3a></td>
    <td width="1" height="1" bgcolor=#a7372e></td>
    <td width="1" height="1" bgcolor=#85302f></td>
    <td width="1" height="1" bgcolor=#6b2118></td>
    <td width="1" height="1" bgcolor=#bf3222></td>
    <td width="1" height="1" bgcolor=#bb5545></td>
    <td width="1" height="1" bgcolor=#45241a></td>
    <td width="1" height="1" bgcolor=#845443></td>
    <td width="1" height="1" bgcolor=#392110></td>
    <td width="1" height="1" bgcolor=#512921></td>
    <td width="1" height="1" bgcolor=#301706></td>
    <td width="1" height="1" bgcolor=#261f11></td>
    <td width="1" height="1" bgcolor=#8b3033></td>
    <td width="1" height="1" bgcolor=#6b5427></td>
    <td width="1" height="1" bgcolor=#3f2b11></td>
    <td width="1" height="1" bgcolor=#443c1c></td>
    <td width="1" height="1" bgcolor=#9c2816></td>
    <td width="1" height="1" bgcolor=#c84338></td>
    <td width="1" height="1" bgcolor=#c95638></td>
    <td width="1" height="1" bgcolor=#53341f></td>
    <td width="1" height="1" bgcolor=#29190a></td>
    <td width="1" height="1" bgcolor=#302712></td>
    <td width="1" height="1" bgcolor=#cf171e></td>
    <td width="1" height="1" bgcolor=#da1a11></td>
    <td width="1" height="1" bgcolor=#d01a24></td>
    <td width="1" height="1" bgcolor=#861e1b></td>
    <td width="1" height="1" bgcolor=#7b331f></td>
    <td width="1" height="1" bgcolor=#832225></td>
    <td width="1" height="1" bgcolor=#231204></td>
  </tr>
  <tr>
    <td width="1" height="1" bgcolor=#512921></td>
    <td width="1" height="1" bgcolor=#693523></td>
    <td width="1" height="1" bgcolor=#753c18></td>
    <td width="1" height="1" bgcolor=#452017></td>
    <td width="1" height="1" bgcolor=#3a280f></td>
    <td width="1" height="1" bgcolor=#653219></td>
    <td width="1" height="1" bgcolor=#ae352a></td>
    <td width="1" height="1" bgcolor=#7f2515></td>
    <td width="1" height="1" bgcolor=#b1261a></td>
    <td width="1" height="1" bgcolor=#b83a26></td>
    <td width="1" height="1" bgcolor=#a62f23></td>
    <td width="1" height="1" bgcolor=#831d14></td>
    <td width="1" height="1" bgcolor=#9a2518></td>
    <td width="1" height="1" bgcolor=#1b0711></td>
    <td width="1" height="1" bgcolor=#831f16></td>
    <td width="1" height="1" bgcolor=#b3301c></td>
    <td width="1" height="1" bgcolor=#6e2415></td>
    <td width="1" height="1" bgcolor=#7a1f1b></td>
    <td width="1" height="1" bgcolor=#6c3017></td>
    <td width="1" height="1" bgcolor=#8a2c1b></td>
    <td width="1" height="1" bgcolor=#66211e></td>
    <td width="1" height="1" bgcolor=#29160a></td>
    <td width="1" height="1" bgcolor=#71160d></td>
    <td width="1" height="1" bgcolor=#b42c25></td>
    <td width="1" height="1" bgcolor=#46120e></td>
    <td width="1" height="1" bgcolor=#180e02></td>
    <td width="1" height="1" bgcolor=#350e0a></td>
    <td width="1" height="1" bgcolor=#991c1a></td>
    <td width="1" height="1" bgcolor=#bf4032></td>
    <td width="1" height="1" bgcolor=#cc4034></td>
    <td width="1" height="1" bgcolor=#220b01></td>
    <td width="1" height="1" bgcolor=#e3b771></td>
    <td width="1" height="1" bgcolor=#7c2f19></td>
    <td width="1" height="1" bgcolor=#8b3d24></td>
    <td width="1" height="1" bgcolor=#7e2617></td>
    <td width="1" height="1" bgcolor=#3a1302></td>
    <td width="1" height="1" bgcolor=#2e1004></td>
    <td width="1" height="1" bgcolor=#32180a></td>
    <td width="1" height="1" bgcolor=#c0242d></td>
    <td width="1" height="1" bgcolor=#902618></td>
    <td width="1" height="1" bgcolor=#73350e></td>
    <td width="1" height="1" bgcolor=#c43329></td>
    <td width="1" height="1" bgcolor=#c83124></td>
    <td width="1" height="1" bgcolor=#cb4b39></td>
    <td width="1" height="1" bgcolor=#9d2c21></td>
    <td width="1" height="1" bgcolor=#651c15></td>
```

```
    <td width="1" height="1"
bgcolor=#371d0b></td>
    <td width="1" height="1"
bgcolor=#b92b25></td>
    <td width="1" height="1"
bgcolor=#e2322d></td>
    <td width="1" height="1"
bgcolor=#b13832></td>
    <td width="1" height="1"
bgcolor=#96321e></td>
    <td width="1" height="1"
bgcolor=#bf3935></td>
    <td width="1" height="1"
bgcolor=#d9392c></td>
    <td width="1" height="1"
bgcolor=#c84539></td>
    <td width="1" height="1"
bgcolor=#732b23></td>
    <td width="1" height="1"
bgcolor=#86201d></td>
    <td width="1" height="1"
bgcolor=#c34f37></td>
    <td width="1" height="1"
bgcolor=#694321></td>
    <td width="1" height="1"
bgcolor=#2e250f></td>
    <td width="1" height="1"
bgcolor=#6d2f22></td>
    <td width="1" height="1"
bgcolor=#8d3622></td>
    <td width="1" height="1"
bgcolor=#a92a2e></td>
    <td width="1" height="1"
bgcolor=#95391e></td>
    <td width="1" height="1"
bgcolor=#5f2f18></td>
    <td width="1" height="1"
bgcolor=#be2624></td>
    <td width="1" height="1"
bgcolor=#74290d></td>
    <td width="1" height="1"
bgcolor=#5c1916></td>
    <td width="1" height="1"
bgcolor=#4f220f></td>
    <td width="1" height="1"
bgcolor=#b31914></td>
    <td width="1" height="1"
bgcolor=#982420></td>
    <td width="1" height="1"
bgcolor=#860e17></td>
    <td width="1" height="1"
bgcolor=#3d1b0d></td>
  </tr>
  <tr>
    <td width="1" height="1"
bgcolor=#943c28></td>
    <td width="1" height="1"
bgcolor=#65261f></td>
    <td width="1" height="1"
bgcolor=#b7232a></td>
    <td width="1" height="1"
bgcolor=#71271b></td>
    <td width="1" height="1"
bgcolor=#331813></td>
    <td width="1" height="1"
bgcolor=#1f130b></td>
    <td width="1" height="1"
bgcolor=#1f1108></td>
    <td width="1" height="1"
bgcolor=#2a210c></td>
    <td width="1" height="1"
bgcolor=#3a0c10></td>
    <td width="1" height="1"
bgcolor=#5b1c14></td>
    <td width="1" height="1"
bgcolor=#4e1917></td>
    <td width="1" height="1"
bgcolor=#3b1a10></td>
    <td width="1" height="1"
bgcolor=#35140a></td>
    <td width="1" height="1"
bgcolor=#373915></td>
    <td width="1" height="1"
bgcolor=#a02e26></td>
    <td width="1" height="1"
bgcolor=#8e2511></td>
    <td width="1" height="1"
bgcolor=#94261a></td>
    <td width="1" height="1"
bgcolor=#9a251a></td>
    <td width="1" height="1"
bgcolor=#992829></td>
    <td width="1" height="1"
bgcolor=#8d1811></td>
    <td width="1" height="1"
bgcolor=#a52a1d></td>
    <td width="1" height="1"
bgcolor=#3a391c></td>
    <td width="1" height="1"
bgcolor=#671615></td>
    <td width="1" height="1"
bgcolor=#531f10></td>
    <td width="1" height="1"
bgcolor=#240e09></td>
    <td width="1" height="1"
bgcolor=#1c0105></td>
    <td width="1" height="1"
bgcolor=#2c1809></td>
    <td width="1" height="1"
bgcolor=#36140a></td>
    <td width="1" height="1"
bgcolor=#8d1e14></td>
    <td width="1" height="1"
bgcolor=#47200e></td>
    <td width="1" height="1"
bgcolor=#280b04></td>
    <td width="1" height="1"
bgcolor=#a48637></td>
    <td width="1" height="1"
bgcolor=#bc3e1b></td>
    <td width="1" height="1"
bgcolor=#873227></td>
    <td width="1" height="1"
bgcolor=#786438></td>
    <td width="1" height="1"
bgcolor=#331604></td>
    <td width="1" height="1"
bgcolor=#8b8463></td>
    <td width="1" height="1"
bgcolor=#9f9e60></td>
    <td width="1" height="1"
bgcolor=#897b3f></td>
    <td width="1" height="1"
bgcolor=#5b5326></td>
    <td width="1" height="1"
bgcolor=#483c13></td>
    <td width="1" height="1"
bgcolor=#4f3017></td>
    <td width="1" height="1"
bgcolor=#480f06></td>
    <td width="1" height="1"
bgcolor=#4b0d07></td>
    <td width="1" height="1"
bgcolor=#3d1f10></td>
    <td width="1" height="1"
bgcolor=#2f1507></td>
    <td width="1" height="1"
bgcolor=#35140d></td>
    <td width="1" height="1"
bgcolor=#7f1d19></td>
    <td width="1" height="1"
bgcolor=#ba2423></td>
    <td width="1" height="1"
bgcolor=#531612></td>
    <td width="1" height="1"
bgcolor=#491f12></td>
    <td width="1" height="1"
bgcolor=#621f18></td>
    <td width="1" height="1"
bgcolor=#661f16></td>
    <td width="1" height="1"
bgcolor=#8b261f></td>
    <td width="1" height="1"
bgcolor=#4b1315></td>
    <td width="1" height="1"
bgcolor=#351d0d></td>
    <td width="1" height="1"
bgcolor=#851814></td>
    <td width="1" height="1"
bgcolor=#d5392d></td>
    <td width="1" height="1"
bgcolor=#c15545></td>
    <td width="1" height="1"
bgcolor=#8d3126></td>
```

```
    <td width="1" height="1" bgcolor=#c2382f></td>
    <td width="1" height="1" bgcolor=#712315></td>
    <td width="1" height="1" bgcolor=#d01c1b></td>
    <td width="1" height="1" bgcolor=#d8151b></td>
    <td width="1" height="1" bgcolor=#c51619></td>
    <td width="1" height="1" bgcolor=#831d1a></td>
    <td width="1" height="1" bgcolor=#3c2814></td>
    <td width="1" height="1" bgcolor=#5c2212></td>
    <td width="1" height="1" bgcolor=#b01f1e></td>
    <td width="1" height="1" bgcolor=#b21d22></td>
    <td width="1" height="1" bgcolor=#722316></td>
    <td width="1" height="1" bgcolor=#6e2a1f></td>
  </tr>
  <tr>
    <td width="1" height="1" bgcolor=#3f1b12></td>
    <td width="1" height="1" bgcolor=#292b1f></td>
    <td width="1" height="1" bgcolor=#b9211c></td>
    <td width="1" height="1" bgcolor=#261404></td>
    <td width="1" height="1" bgcolor=#1d0f09></td>
    <td width="1" height="1" bgcolor=#100b03></td>
    <td width="1" height="1" bgcolor=#18180e></td>
    <td width="1" height="1" bgcolor=#1e160c></td>
    <td width="1" height="1" bgcolor=#100601></td>
    <td width="1" height="1" bgcolor=#241a07></td>
    <td width="1" height="1" bgcolor=#1d1108></td>
    <td width="1" height="1" bgcolor=#2c220c></td>
    <td width="1" height="1" bgcolor=#221a0b></td>
    <td width="1" height="1" bgcolor=#0f0900></td>
    <td width="1" height="1" bgcolor=#4c130f></td>
    <td width="1" height="1" bgcolor=#2b0405></td>
    <td width="1" height="1" bgcolor=#3f170f></td>
    <td width="1" height="1" bgcolor=#2d0e08></td>
    <td width="1" height="1" bgcolor=#4c140b></td>
    <td width="1" height="1" bgcolor=#2f1111></td>
    <td width="1" height="1" bgcolor=#380606></td>
    <td width="1" height="1" bgcolor=#130003></td>
    <td width="1" height="1" bgcolor=#1f0f06></td>
    <td width="1" height="1" bgcolor=#3c1d0e></td>
    <td width="1" height="1" bgcolor=#190500></td>
    <td width="1" height="1" bgcolor=#220a01></td>
    <td width="1" height="1" bgcolor=#301106></td>
    <td width="1" height="1" bgcolor=#35170e></td>
    <td width="1" height="1" bgcolor=#270e04></td>
    <td width="1" height="1" bgcolor=#836739></td>
    <td width="1" height="1" bgcolor=#8f2d00></td>
    <td width="1" height="1" bgcolor=#83201c></td>
    <td width="1" height="1" bgcolor=#751a0e></td>
    <td width="1" height="1" bgcolor=#6d3624></td>
    <td width="1" height="1" bgcolor=#3f1a0a></td>
    <td width="1" height="1" bgcolor=#3e270d></td>
    <td width="1" height="1" bgcolor=#a39b63></td>
    <td width="1" height="1" bgcolor=#c9ca48></td>
    <td width="1" height="1" bgcolor=#eae655></td>
    <td width="1" height="1" bgcolor=#ebf483></td>
    <td width="1" height="1" bgcolor=#4a5526></td>
    <td width="1" height="1" bgcolor=#dee471></td>
    <td width="1" height="1" bgcolor=#aeba55></td>
    <td width="1" height="1" bgcolor=#8b9b4d></td>
    <td width="1" height="1" bgcolor=#5a5d2f></td>
    <td width="1" height="1" bgcolor=#595d3a></td>
    <td width="1" height="1" bgcolor=#2a1c09></td>
    <td width="1" height="1" bgcolor=#484422></td>
    <td width="1" height="1" bgcolor=#b0884b></td>
    <td width="1" height="1" bgcolor=#7c873b></td>
    <td width="1" height="1" bgcolor=#a59954></td>
    <td width="1" height="1" bgcolor=#423e1b></td>
    <td width="1" height="1" bgcolor=#564c36></td>
    <td width="1" height="1" bgcolor=#2e1d06></td>
    <td width="1" height="1" bgcolor=#392418></td>
    <td width="1" height="1" bgcolor=#291f0d></td>
    <td width="1" height="1" bgcolor=#391f0d></td>
    <td width="1" height="1" bgcolor=#872b1f></td>
    <td width="1" height="1" bgcolor=#812d1e></td>
    <td width="1" height="1" bgcolor=#982c1d></td>
    <td width="1" height="1" bgcolor=#602211></td>
    <td width="1" height="1" bgcolor=#9e221e></td>
    <td width="1" height="1" bgcolor=#632013></td>
    <td width="1" height="1" bgcolor=#413616></td>
    <td width="1" height="1" bgcolor=#bc221d></td>
    <td width="1" height="1" bgcolor=#7d2819></td>
    <td width="1" height="1" bgcolor=#532e12></td>
    <td width="1" height="1" bgcolor=#aa201c></td>
    <td width="1" height="1" bgcolor=#aa1f1f></td>
    <td width="1" height="1" bgcolor=#471a10></td>
    <td width="1" height="1" bgcolor=#551f19></td>
    <td width="1" height="1" bgcolor=#642015></td>
  </tr>
  <tr>
    <td width="1" height="1" bgcolor=#982914></td>
```

```
    <td width="1" height="1"
bgcolor=#af3123></td>
    <td width="1" height="1"
bgcolor=#84171a></td>
    <td width="1" height="1"
bgcolor=#141005></td>
    <td width="1" height="1"
bgcolor=#1b0f05></td>
    <td width="1" height="1"
bgcolor=#1a0f05></td>
    <td width="1" height="1"
bgcolor=#100803></td>
    <td width="1" height="1"
bgcolor=#201609></td>
    <td width="1" height="1"
bgcolor=#25180a></td>
    <td width="1" height="1"
bgcolor=#2b1d09></td>
    <td width="1" height="1"
bgcolor=#1f1504></td>
    <td width="1" height="1"
bgcolor=#2b200e></td>
    <td width="1" height="1"
bgcolor=#180802></td>
    <td width="1" height="1"
bgcolor=#321f11></td>
    <td width="1" height="1"
bgcolor=#3e3d18></td>
    <td width="1" height="1"
bgcolor=#3a2a20></td>
    <td width="1" height="1"
bgcolor=#180c08></td>
    <td width="1" height="1"
bgcolor=#1b0b0b></td>
    <td width="1" height="1"
bgcolor=#150c03></td>
    <td width="1" height="1"
bgcolor=#2b0b0b></td>
    <td width="1" height="1"
bgcolor=#1a0805></td>
    <td width="1" height="1"
bgcolor=#210d03></td>
    <td width="1" height="1"
bgcolor=#2b1009></td>
    <td width="1" height="1"
bgcolor=#281c0d></td>
    <td width="1" height="1"
bgcolor=#251109></td>
    <td width="1" height="1"
bgcolor=#2f1107></td>
    <td width="1" height="1"
bgcolor=#371107></td>
    <td width="1" height="1"
bgcolor=#36160b></td>
    <td width="1" height="1"
bgcolor=#2d100a></td>
    <td width="1" height="1"
bgcolor=#2e0f07></td>
    <td width="1" height="1"
bgcolor=#a47040></td>
    <td width="1" height="1"
bgcolor=#a5651a></td>
    <td width="1" height="1"
bgcolor=#703c1b></td>
    <td width="1" height="1"
bgcolor=#5c2a17></td>
    <td width="1" height="1"
bgcolor=#2b1b04></td>
    <td width="1" height="1"
bgcolor=#5b4a17></td>
    <td width="1" height="1"
bgcolor=#cdd026></td>
    <td width="1" height="1"
bgcolor=#908d37></td>
    <td width="1" height="1"
bgcolor=#dfdb55></td>
    <td width="1" height="1"
bgcolor=#efe346></td>
    <td width="1" height="1"
bgcolor=#818530></td>
    <td width="1" height="1"
bgcolor=#e3df4c></td>
    <td width="1" height="1"
bgcolor=#e8dd44></td>
    <td width="1" height="1"
bgcolor=#c3c54a></td>
    <td width="1" height="1"
bgcolor=#dbdd6c></td>
    <td width="1" height="1"
bgcolor=#f7f347></td>
    <td width="1" height="1"
bgcolor=#88a35f></td>
    <td width="1" height="1"
bgcolor=#aaba45></td>
    <td width="1" height="1"
bgcolor=#e3d853></td>
    <td width="1" height="1"
bgcolor=#afb845></td>
    <td width="1" height="1"
bgcolor=#ddd233></td>
    <td width="1" height="1"
bgcolor=#939f33></td>
    <td width="1" height="1"
bgcolor=#d4d85a></td>
    <td width="1" height="1"
bgcolor=#8a8244></td>
    <td width="1" height="1"
bgcolor=#e5e36f></td>
    <td width="1" height="1"
bgcolor=#c5c370></td>
    <td width="1" height="1"
bgcolor=#b3b375></td>
    <td width="1" height="1"
bgcolor=#281609></td>
    <td width="1" height="1"
bgcolor=#2e1306></td>
    <td width="1" height="1"
bgcolor=#2b0f05></td>
    <td width="1" height="1"
bgcolor=#1b1005></td>
    <td width="1" height="1"
bgcolor=#421f0e></td>
    <td width="1" height="1"
bgcolor=#423115></td>
    <td width="1" height="1"
bgcolor=#492a12></td>
    <td width="1" height="1"
bgcolor=#a61815></td>
    <td width="1" height="1"
bgcolor=#822514></td>
    <td width="1" height="1"
bgcolor=#b7171b></td>
    <td width="1" height="1"
bgcolor=#8a1913></td>
    <td width="1" height="1"
bgcolor=#552214></td>
    <td width="1" height="1"
bgcolor=#3c2217></td>
    <td width="1" height="1"
bgcolor=#3b2112></td>
    <td width="1" height="1"
bgcolor=#331c0c></td>
  </tr>
  <tr>
    <td width="1" height="1"
bgcolor=#591410></td>
    <td width="1" height="1"
bgcolor=#3f1a12></td>
    <td width="1" height="1"
bgcolor=#13170d></td>
    <td width="1" height="1"
bgcolor=#120a04></td>
    <td width="1" height="1"
bgcolor=#150f08></td>
    <td width="1" height="1"
bgcolor=#1e1307></td>
    <td width="1" height="1"
bgcolor=#261706></td>
    <td width="1" height="1"
bgcolor=#291605></td>
    <td width="1" height="1"
bgcolor=#271105></td>
    <td width="1" height="1"
bgcolor=#271803></td>
    <td width="1" height="1"
bgcolor=#29150a></td>
    <td width="1" height="1"
bgcolor=#341a0b></td>
    <td width="1" height="1"
bgcolor=#301c0e></td>
    <td width="1" height="1"
bgcolor=#3f2009></td>
    <td width="1" height="1"
bgcolor=#6d6047></td>
```

```
<td width="1" height="1" bgcolor=#6c4b5a></td>
<td width="1" height="1" bgcolor=#4f4326></td>
<td width="1" height="1" bgcolor=#250c00></td>
<td width="1" height="1" bgcolor=#331308></td>
<td width="1" height="1" bgcolor=#2d180b></td>
<td width="1" height="1" bgcolor=#2e1505></td>
<td width="1" height="1" bgcolor=#230b09></td>
<td width="1" height="1" bgcolor=#2f0805></td>
<td width="1" height="1" bgcolor=#280d06></td>
<td width="1" height="1" bgcolor=#2a0d03></td>
<td width="1" height="1" bgcolor=#2f1206></td>
<td width="1" height="1" bgcolor=#230e03></td>
<td width="1" height="1" bgcolor=#2e1109></td>
<td width="1" height="1" bgcolor=#37110b></td>
<td width="1" height="1" bgcolor=#301611></td>
<td width="1" height="1" bgcolor=#776b37></td>
<td width="1" height="1" bgcolor=#a9441d></td>
<td width="1" height="1" bgcolor=#5e2719></td>
<td width="1" height="1" bgcolor=#582107></td>
<td width="1" height="1" bgcolor=#331904></td>
<td width="1" height="1" bgcolor=#635a21></td>
<td width="1" height="1" bgcolor=#e1d95b></td>
<td width="1" height="1" bgcolor=#7c7b28></td>
<td width="1" height="1" bgcolor=#575f26></td>
<td width="1" height="1" bgcolor=#adac26></td>
<td width="1" height="1" bgcolor=#afb533></td>
<td width="1" height="1" bgcolor=#c2c134></td>
<td width="1" height="1" bgcolor=#56542a></td>
<td width="1" height="1" bgcolor=#83902c></td>
<td width="1" height="1" bgcolor=#c5ca38></td>
<td width="1" height="1" bgcolor=#e9e63e></td>
<td width="1" height="1" bgcolor=#3a5907></td>
<td width="1" height="1" bgcolor=#717335></td>
<td width="1" height="1" bgcolor=#f2ec72></td>
<td width="1" height="1" bgcolor=#919d31></td>
<td width="1" height="1" bgcolor=#70941d></td>
<td width="1" height="1" bgcolor=#3b5c35></td>
<td width="1" height="1" bgcolor=#718530></td>
<td width="1" height="1" bgcolor=#898b5d></td>
<td width="1" height="1" bgcolor=#d5d04e></td>
<td width="1" height="1" bgcolor=#f2e456></td>
<td width="1" height="1" bgcolor=#fff769></td>
<td width="1" height="1" bgcolor=#321d0f></td>
<td width="1" height="1" bgcolor=#251509></td>
<td width="1" height="1" bgcolor=#24180b></td>
<td width="1" height="1" bgcolor=#291607></td>
<td width="1" height="1" bgcolor=#552b16></td>
<td width="1" height="1" bgcolor=#686a31></td>
<td width="1" height="1" bgcolor=#331d0c></td>
<td width="1" height="1" bgcolor=#53220f></td>
<td width="1" height="1" bgcolor=#3d2516></td>
<td width="1" height="1" bgcolor=#311c0d></td>
<td width="1" height="1" bgcolor=#281a07></td>
<td width="1" height="1" bgcolor=#341b0e></td>
<td width="1" height="1" bgcolor=#3a240f></td>
<td width="1" height="1" bgcolor=#43200f></td>
<td width="1" height="1" bgcolor=#451a10></td>
</tr>
<tr>
<td width="1" height="1" bgcolor=#2b2e13></td>
<td width="1" height="1" bgcolor=#341f0c></td>
<td width="1" height="1" bgcolor=#23260f></td>
<td width="1" height="1" bgcolor=#1c1406></td>
<td width="1" height="1" bgcolor=#201505></td>
<td width="1" height="1" bgcolor=#251605></td>
<td width="1" height="1" bgcolor=#3a2112></td>
<td width="1" height="1" bgcolor=#38210c></td>
<td width="1" height="1" bgcolor=#574627></td>
<td width="1" height="1" bgcolor=#675531></td>
<td width="1" height="1" bgcolor=#6c535b></td>
<td width="1" height="1" bgcolor=#614736></td>
<td width="1" height="1" bgcolor=#473516></td>
<td width="1" height="1" bgcolor=#312a0d></td>
<td width="1" height="1" bgcolor=#e6673f></td>
<td width="1" height="1" bgcolor=#9c905d></td>
<td width="1" height="1" bgcolor=#a1944f></td>
<td width="1" height="1" bgcolor=#5b191b></td>
<td width="1" height="1" bgcolor=#5f3d47></td>
<td width="1" height="1" bgcolor=#6c505f></td>
<td width="1" height="1" bgcolor=#755a45></td>
<td width="1" height="1" bgcolor=#9a9149></td>
<td width="1" height="1" bgcolor=#654a35></td>
<td width="1" height="1" bgcolor=#3c1712></td>
<td width="1" height="1" bgcolor=#3b130f></td>
<td width="1" height="1" bgcolor=#3d1b0e></td>
<td width="1" height="1" bgcolor=#3d170b></td>
<td width="1" height="1" bgcolor=#42180d></td>
<td width="1" height="1" bgcolor=#461b0b></td>
```

```
    <td width="1" height="1" bgcolor=#481c0f></td>
    <td width="1" height="1" bgcolor=#775036></td>
    <td width="1" height="1" bgcolor=#89130e></td>
    <td width="1" height="1" bgcolor=#841717></td>
    <td width="1" height="1" bgcolor=#6b1907></td>
    <td width="1" height="1" bgcolor=#221303></td>
    <td width="1" height="1" bgcolor=#1e0b0a></td>
    <td width="1" height="1" bgcolor=#4b3c12></td>
    <td width="1" height="1" bgcolor=#322c0e></td>
    <td width="1" height="1" bgcolor=#2b200f></td>
    <td width="1" height="1" bgcolor=#373216></td>
    <td width="1" height="1" bgcolor=#564d25></td>
    <td width="1" height="1" bgcolor=#494128></td>
    <td width="1" height="1" bgcolor=#402e13></td>
    <td width="1" height="1" bgcolor=#26250e></td>
    <td width="1" height="1" bgcolor=#8d9127></td>
    <td width="1" height="1" bgcolor=#e0dd20></td>
    <td width="1" height="1" bgcolor=#cfd06c></td>
    <td width="1" height="1" bgcolor=#ecf57e></td>
    <td width="1" height="1" bgcolor=#d5c740></td>
    <td width="1" height="1" bgcolor=#f3ea71></td>
    <td width="1" height="1" bgcolor=#e3e76c></td>
    <td width="1" height="1" bgcolor=#b3b875></td>
    <td width="1" height="1" bgcolor=#59564d></td>
    <td width="1" height="1" bgcolor=#332223></td>
    <td width="1" height="1" bgcolor=#6b6e2e></td>
    <td width="1" height="1" bgcolor=#e6e247></td>
    <td width="1" height="1" bgcolor=#fffc89></td>
    <td width="1" height="1" bgcolor=#48481d></td>
    <td width="1" height="1" bgcolor=#41391a></td>
    <td width="1" height="1" bgcolor=#2f1a0d></td>
    <td width="1" height="1" bgcolor=#442915></td>
    <td width="1" height="1" bgcolor=#442914></td>
    <td width="1" height="1" bgcolor=#3c2108></td>
    <td width="1" height="1" bgcolor=#331c0a></td>
    <td width="1" height="1" bgcolor=#42180a></td>
    <td width="1" height="1" bgcolor=#472115></td>
    <td width="1" height="1" bgcolor=#301a0a></td>
    <td width="1" height="1" bgcolor=#29190d></td>
    <td width="1" height="1" bgcolor=#2b1604></td>
    <td width="1" height="1" bgcolor=#462210></td>
    <td width="1" height="1" bgcolor=#40210d></td>
    <td width="1" height="1" bgcolor=#3b1904></td>
  </tr>
  <tr>
    <td width="1" height="1" bgcolor=#1e2b0f></td>
    <td width="1" height="1" bgcolor=#a42826></td>
    <td width="1" height="1" bgcolor=#3e1f0e></td>
    <td width="1" height="1" bgcolor=#28200e></td>
    <td width="1" height="1" bgcolor=#291604></td>
    <td width="1" height="1" bgcolor=#392012></td>
    <td width="1" height="1" bgcolor=#361a05></td>
    <td width="1" height="1" bgcolor=#432812></td>
    <td width="1" height="1" bgcolor=#43330f></td>
    <td width="1" height="1" bgcolor=#a99f65></td>
    <td width="1" height="1" bgcolor=#4d3247></td>
    <td width="1" height="1" bgcolor=#77665f></td>
    <td width="1" height="1" bgcolor=#b58d82></td>
    <td width="1" height="1" bgcolor=#b24b35></td>
    <td width="1" height="1" bgcolor=#ebce43></td>
    <td width="1" height="1" bgcolor=#f5e04e></td>
    <td width="1" height="1" bgcolor=#c85c3e></td>
    <td width="1" height="1" bgcolor=#a03b3d></td>
    <td width="1" height="1" bgcolor=#5e4a4f></td>
    <td width="1" height="1" bgcolor=#604a45></td>
    <td width="1" height="1" bgcolor=#796545></td>
    <td width="1" height="1" bgcolor=#706236></td>
    <td width="1" height="1" bgcolor=#300e0b></td>
    <td width="1" height="1" bgcolor=#3b1508></td>
    <td width="1" height="1" bgcolor=#41160b></td>
    <td width="1" height="1" bgcolor=#451f0f></td>
    <td width="1" height="1" bgcolor=#471e0f></td>
    <td width="1" height="1" bgcolor=#3b1b0d></td>
    <td width="1" height="1" bgcolor=#481f1a></td>
    <td width="1" height="1" bgcolor=#330f0a></td>
    <td width="1" height="1" bgcolor=#4a290b></td>
    <td width="1" height="1" bgcolor=#85150f></td>
    <td width="1" height="1" bgcolor=#891013></td>
    <td width="1" height="1" bgcolor=#26120b></td>
    <td width="1" height="1" bgcolor=#6b2716></td>
    <td width="1" height="1" bgcolor=#190a05></td>
    <td width="1" height="1" bgcolor=#38170a></td>
    <td width="1" height="1" bgcolor=#26130c></td>
    <td width="1" height="1" bgcolor=#2a150a></td>
    <td width="1" height="1" bgcolor=#2a1504></td>
    <td width="1" height="1" bgcolor=#2b1500></td>
    <td width="1" height="1" bgcolor=#2a1c08></td>
    <td width="1" height="1" bgcolor=#351b02></td>
```

```
<td width="1" height="1" bgcolor=#341e07></td>
<td width="1" height="1" bgcolor=#39340a></td>
<td width="1" height="1" bgcolor=#d4d439></td>
<td width="1" height="1" bgcolor=#d2cf48></td>
<td width="1" height="1" bgcolor=#e9e05a></td>
<td width="1" height="1" bgcolor=#b6b449></td>
<td width="1" height="1" bgcolor=#e6df34></td>
<td width="1" height="1" bgcolor=#f4eb5b></td>
<td width="1" height="1" bgcolor=#c8c23b></td>
<td width="1" height="1" bgcolor=#c9c26b></td>
<td width="1" height="1" bgcolor=#c6c96e></td>
<td width="1" height="1" bgcolor=#dbe96d></td>
<td width="1" height="1" bgcolor=#d7cf58></td>
<td width="1" height="1" bgcolor=#fbf56c></td>
<td width="1" height="1" bgcolor=#433718></td>
<td width="1" height="1" bgcolor=#321f03></td>
<td width="1" height="1" bgcolor=#3c2010></td>
<td width="1" height="1" bgcolor=#47240f></td>
<td width="1" height="1" bgcolor=#522712></td>
<td width="1" height="1" bgcolor=#4e2a10></td>
<td width="1" height="1" bgcolor=#502e15></td>
<td width="1" height="1" bgcolor=#462814></td>
<td width="1" height="1" bgcolor=#301d06></td>
<td width="1" height="1" bgcolor=#351f10></td>
<td width="1" height="1" bgcolor=#2a1505></td>
<td width="1" height="1" bgcolor=#3d2010></td>
<td width="1" height="1" bgcolor=#3f1e0d></td>
<td width="1" height="1" bgcolor=#3c1e0c></td>
<td width="1" height="1" bgcolor=#3b1a0b></td>
</tr>
<tr>
<td width="1" height="1" bgcolor=#14120c></td>
<td width="1" height="1" bgcolor=#16120c></td>
<td width="1" height="1" bgcolor=#160d06></td>
<td width="1" height="1" bgcolor=#23130c></td>
<td width="1" height="1" bgcolor=#2d190d></td>
<td width="1" height="1" bgcolor=#361808></td>
<td width="1" height="1" bgcolor=#3e230c></td>
<td width="1" height="1" bgcolor=#3d210d></td>
<td width="1" height="1" bgcolor=#361f0a></td>
<td width="1" height="1" bgcolor=#858041></td>
<td width="1" height="1" bgcolor=#c0b268></td>
<td width="1" height="1" bgcolor=#8b674c></td>
<td width="1" height="1" bgcolor=#b72d37></td>
<td width="1" height="1" bgcolor=#db3b4a></td>
<td width="1" height="1" bgcolor=#957829></td>
<td width="1" height="1" bgcolor=#df893a></td>
<td width="1" height="1" bgcolor=#d92544></td>
<td width="1" height="1" bgcolor=#7b4424></td>
<td width="1" height="1" bgcolor=#a2966d></td>
<td width="1" height="1" bgcolor=#918150></td>
<td width="1" height="1" bgcolor=#6a5a32></td>
<td width="1" height="1" bgcolor=#320a07></td>
<td width="1" height="1" bgcolor=#3d1408></td>
<td width="1" height="1" bgcolor=#391304></td>
<td width="1" height="1" bgcolor=#381209></td>
<td width="1" height="1" bgcolor=#33110a></td>
<td width="1" height="1" bgcolor=#2c0e05></td>
<td width="1" height="1" bgcolor=#65231a></td>
<td width="1" height="1" bgcolor=#ca342b></td>
<td width="1" height="1" bgcolor=#6c2615></td>
<td width="1" height="1" bgcolor=#b23927></td>
<td width="1" height="1" bgcolor=#78110b></td>
<td width="1" height="1" bgcolor=#b8432d></td>
<td width="1" height="1" bgcolor=#70200d></td>
<td width="1" height="1" bgcolor=#ef461d></td>
<td width="1" height="1" bgcolor=#7b2c22></td>
<td width="1" height="1" bgcolor=#953326></td>
<td width="1" height="1" bgcolor=#291b0d></td>
<td width="1" height="1" bgcolor=#2d1106></td>
<td width="1" height="1" bgcolor=#311409></td>
<td width="1" height="1" bgcolor=#341307></td>
<td width="1" height="1" bgcolor=#2c1403></td>
<td width="1" height="1" bgcolor=#33180c></td>
<td width="1" height="1" bgcolor=#301b07></td>
<td width="1" height="1" bgcolor=#1a0d07></td>
<td width="1" height="1" bgcolor=#a49e3d></td>
<td width="1" height="1" bgcolor=#949733></td>
<td width="1" height="1" bgcolor=#9b902d></td>
<td width="1" height="1" bgcolor=#43391b></td>
<td width="1" height="1" bgcolor=#c1b63d></td>
<td width="1" height="1" bgcolor=#c2b24a></td>
<td width="1" height="1" bgcolor=#cec83f></td>
<td width="1" height="1" bgcolor=#9fa137></td>
<td width="1" height="1" bgcolor=#d3d739></td>
<td width="1" height="1" bgcolor=#e2d747></td>
<td width="1" height="1" bgcolor=#797327></td>
<td width="1" height="1" bgcolor=#9d9c2c></td>
```

```
    <td width="1" height="1"
bgcolor=#403919></td>
    <td width="1" height="1"
bgcolor=#321d10></td>
    <td width="1" height="1"
bgcolor=#331b0d></td>
    <td width="1" height="1"
bgcolor=#402210></td>
    <td width="1" height="1"
bgcolor=#432310></td>
    <td width="1" height="1"
bgcolor=#3b2210></td>
    <td width="1" height="1"
bgcolor=#3d230b></td>
    <td width="1" height="1"
bgcolor=#40220e></td>
    <td width="1" height="1"
bgcolor=#402111></td>
    <td width="1" height="1"
bgcolor=#352011></td>
    <td width="1" height="1"
bgcolor=#341a0c></td>
    <td width="1" height="1"
bgcolor=#3b1a07></td>
    <td width="1" height="1"
bgcolor=#3c1d0f></td>
    <td width="1" height="1"
bgcolor=#381a0e></td>
    <td width="1" height="1"
bgcolor=#331409></td>
  </tr>
  <tr>
    <td width="1" height="1"
bgcolor=#14130d></td>
    <td width="1" height="1"
bgcolor=#170e09></td>
    <td width="1" height="1"
bgcolor=#1f110c></td>
    <td width="1" height="1"
bgcolor=#170e06></td>
    <td width="1" height="1"
bgcolor=#1f0e03></td>
    <td width="1" height="1"
bgcolor=#351a0b></td>
    <td width="1" height="1"
bgcolor=#391f09></td>
    <td width="1" height="1"
bgcolor=#3c200f></td>
    <td width="1" height="1"
bgcolor=#412211></td>
    <td width="1" height="1"
bgcolor=#391b10></td>
    <td width="1" height="1"
bgcolor=#4f4620></td>
    <td width="1" height="1"
bgcolor=#817455></td>
    <td width="1" height="1"
bgcolor=#803341></td>
    <td width="1" height="1"
bgcolor=#a62d2b></td>
    <td width="1" height="1"
bgcolor=#a8363a></td>
    <td width="1" height="1"
bgcolor=#8a1c29></td>
    <td width="1" height="1"
bgcolor=#8c3941></td>
    <td width="1" height="1"
bgcolor=#6d5742></td>
    <td width="1" height="1"
bgcolor=#2d060d></td>
    <td width="1" height="1"
bgcolor=#340604></td>
    <td width="1" height="1"
bgcolor=#381009></td>
    <td width="1" height="1"
bgcolor=#391409></td>
    <td width="1" height="1"
bgcolor=#37120a></td>
    <td width="1" height="1"
bgcolor=#330e07></td>
    <td width="1" height="1"
bgcolor=#38140a></td>
    <td width="1" height="1"
bgcolor=#3d160f></td>
    <td width="1" height="1"
bgcolor=#543923></td>
    <td width="1" height="1"
bgcolor=#b28339></td>
    <td width="1" height="1"
bgcolor=#cb2919></td>
    <td width="1" height="1"
bgcolor=#a21a11></td>
    <td width="1" height="1"
bgcolor=#ac3e2d></td>
    <td width="1" height="1"
bgcolor=#d72325></td>
    <td width="1" height="1"
bgcolor=#bc2b20></td>
    <td width="1" height="1"
bgcolor=#e2362a></td>
    <td width="1" height="1"
bgcolor=#af3326></td>
    <td width="1" height="1"
bgcolor=#c1271c></td>
    <td width="1" height="1"
bgcolor=#833318></td>
    <td width="1" height="1"
bgcolor=#362411></td>
    <td width="1" height="1"
bgcolor=#271003></td>
    <td width="1" height="1"
bgcolor=#301407></td>
    <td width="1" height="1"
bgcolor=#2e1505></td>
    <td width="1" height="1"
bgcolor=#35140b></td>
    <td width="1" height="1"
bgcolor=#36190b></td>
    <td width="1" height="1"
bgcolor=#1e0c04></td>
    <td width="1" height="1"
bgcolor=#666d20></td>
    <td width="1" height="1"
bgcolor=#1f0905></td>
    <td width="1" height="1"
bgcolor=#7a7536></td>
    <td width="1" height="1"
bgcolor=#312007></td>
    <td width="1" height="1"
bgcolor=#221002></td>
    <td width="1" height="1"
bgcolor=#4b3f12></td>
    <td width="1" height="1"
bgcolor=#2a1c0e></td>
    <td width="1" height="1"
bgcolor=#847f3b></td>
    <td width="1" height="1"
bgcolor=#2e2c11></td>
    <td width="1" height="1"
bgcolor=#c7cc40></td>
    <td width="1" height="1"
bgcolor=#685f20></td>
    <td width="1" height="1"
bgcolor=#2e1905></td>
    <td width="1" height="1"
bgcolor=#302417></td>
    <td width="1" height="1"
bgcolor=#2e1e07></td>
    <td width="1" height="1"
bgcolor=#311808></td>
    <td width="1" height="1"
bgcolor=#2c1707></td>
    <td width="1" height="1"
bgcolor=#301b0e></td>
    <td width="1" height="1"
bgcolor=#301206></td>
    <td width="1" height="1"
bgcolor=#331b0a></td>
    <td width="1" height="1"
bgcolor=#3a1a0d></td>
    <td width="1" height="1"
bgcolor=#3a1e0c></td>
    <td width="1" height="1"
bgcolor=#371808></td>
    <td width="1" height="1"
bgcolor=#321809></td>
    <td width="1" height="1"
bgcolor=#321a0a></td>
    <td width="1" height="1"
bgcolor=#412714></td>
    <td width="1" height="1"
bgcolor=#2e1102></td>
    <td width="1" height="1"
bgcolor=#361a0c></td>
```

```
    <td width="1" height="1"
bgcolor=#3c1a0f></td>
  </tr>
  <tr>
    <td width="1" height="1"
bgcolor=#171409></td>
    <td width="1" height="1"
bgcolor=#191107></td>
    <td width="1" height="1"
bgcolor=#1d1207></td>
    <td width="1" height="1"
bgcolor=#140b05></td>
    <td width="1" height="1"
bgcolor=#211508></td>
    <td width="1" height="1"
bgcolor=#311c0f></td>
    <td width="1" height="1"
bgcolor=#231100></td>
    <td width="1" height="1"
bgcolor=#331b0e></td>
    <td width="1" height="1"
bgcolor=#301608></td>
    <td width="1" height="1"
bgcolor=#4d4311></td>
    <td width="1" height="1"
bgcolor=#63513f></td>
    <td width="1" height="1"
bgcolor=#523e3f></td>
    <td width="1" height="1"
bgcolor=#5a483a></td>
    <td width="1" height="1"
bgcolor=#a39555></td>
    <td width="1" height="1"
bgcolor=#b6ab4f></td>
    <td width="1" height="1"
bgcolor=#795d39></td>
    <td width="1" height="1"
bgcolor=#422634></td>
    <td width="1" height="1"
bgcolor=#523340></td>
    <td width="1" height="1"
bgcolor=#5e3a49></td>
    <td width="1" height="1"
bgcolor=#684c2b></td>
    <td width="1" height="1"
bgcolor=#330c0a></td>
    <td width="1" height="1"
bgcolor=#2f0906></td>
    <td width="1" height="1"
bgcolor=#290c08></td>
    <td width="1" height="1"
bgcolor=#260603></td>
    <td width="1" height="1"
bgcolor=#280402></td>
    <td width="1" height="1"
bgcolor=#2f0c04></td>
    <td width="1" height="1"
bgcolor=#483d27></td>
    <td width="1" height="1"
bgcolor=#916833></td>
    <td width="1" height="1"
bgcolor=#a6211d></td>
    <td width="1" height="1"
bgcolor=#7d1f13></td>
    <td width="1" height="1"
bgcolor=#762018></td>
    <td width="1" height="1"
bgcolor=#923515></td>
    <td width="1" height="1"
bgcolor=#bb2f25></td>
    <td width="1" height="1"
bgcolor=#af251c></td>
    <td width="1" height="1"
bgcolor=#ac311f></td>
    <td width="1" height="1"
bgcolor=#591a18></td>
    <td width="1" height="1"
bgcolor=#b7b555></td>
    <td width="1" height="1"
bgcolor=#352409></td>
    <td width="1" height="1"
bgcolor=#2a1306></td>
    <td width="1" height="1"
bgcolor=#2b1306></td>
    <td width="1" height="1"
bgcolor=#271204></td>
    <td width="1" height="1"
bgcolor=#2a1608></td>
    <td width="1" height="1"
bgcolor=#3c3a13></td>
    <td width="1" height="1"
bgcolor=#5b6120></td>
    <td width="1" height="1"
bgcolor=#4c5227></td>
    <td width="1" height="1"
bgcolor=#321e07></td>
    <td width="1" height="1"
bgcolor=#230706></td>
    <td width="1" height="1"
bgcolor=#240f04></td>
    <td width="1" height="1"
bgcolor=#1f0b05></td>
    <td width="1" height="1"
bgcolor=#26120d></td>
    <td width="1" height="1"
bgcolor=#271804></td>
    <td width="1" height="1"
bgcolor=#261a0c></td>
    <td width="1" height="1"
bgcolor=#23170c></td>
    <td width="1" height="1"
bgcolor=#4a4821></td>
    <td width="1" height="1"
bgcolor=#251c05></td>
    <td width="1" height="1"
bgcolor=#363218></td>
    <td width="1" height="1"
bgcolor=#4c571b></td>
    <td width="1" height="1"
bgcolor=#2f180e></td>
    <td width="1" height="1"
bgcolor=#321a0b></td>
    <td width="1" height="1"
bgcolor=#3c2212></td>
    <td width="1" height="1"
bgcolor=#35200f></td>
    <td width="1" height="1"
bgcolor=#371c0d></td>
    <td width="1" height="1"
bgcolor=#40230f></td>
    <td width="1" height="1"
bgcolor=#351b03></td>
    <td width="1" height="1"
bgcolor=#351d06></td>
    <td width="1" height="1"
bgcolor=#351a09></td>
    <td width="1" height="1"
bgcolor=#291403></td>
    <td width="1" height="1"
bgcolor=#281808></td>
    <td width="1" height="1"
bgcolor=#2c1a05></td>
    <td width="1" height="1"
bgcolor=#2f1a0c></td>
    <td width="1" height="1"
bgcolor=#341f0e></td>
    <td width="1" height="1"
bgcolor=#301502></td>
  </tr>
</table></body></html>
```

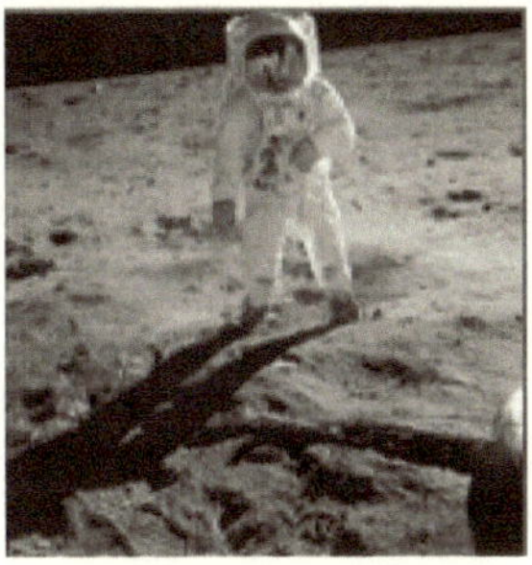

Armstrong's Perspective

```
<html>
<head><title>Armstrong’s Aldrin, written by Broose G. Dickinson</title></head>
<body>
<table border=0 cellpadding=0 cellspacing=0>
  <tr>
    <td width="1" height="1" bgcolor=#3a3b3b></td>
    <td width="1" height="1" bgcolor=#3b3c3c></td>
    <td width="1" height="1" bgcolor=#3a3c3c></td>
    <td width="1" height="1" bgcolor=#393a39></td>
    <td width="1" height="1" bgcolor=#3d3e3e></td>
    <td width="1" height="1" bgcolor=#3c3d3c></td>
    <td width="1" height="1" bgcolor=#3b3c3c></td>
    <td width="1" height="1" bgcolor=#3a3c3b></td>
    <td width="1" height="1" bgcolor=#3b3c3b></td>
    <td width="1" height="1" bgcolor=#3b3c3c></td>
    <td width="1" height="1" bgcolor=#383939></td>
    <td width="1" height="1" bgcolor=#3c3d3d></td>
    <td width="1" height="1" bgcolor=#3d3e3d></td>
    <td width="1" height="1" bgcolor=#3a3b3b></td>
    <td width="1" height="1" bgcolor=#383939></td>
    <td width="1" height="1" bgcolor=#393a3a></td>
    <td width="1" height="1" bgcolor=#383a39></td>
    <td width="1" height="1" bgcolor=#3a3c3b></td>
    <td width="1" height="1" bgcolor=#393a39></td>
    <td width="1" height="1" bgcolor=#383938></td>
    <td width="1" height="1" bgcolor=#343635></td>
    <td width="1" height="1" bgcolor=#373837></td>
    <td width="1" height="1" bgcolor=#3d3e3d></td>
    <td width="1" height="1" bgcolor=#383939></td>
    <td width="1" height="1" bgcolor=#323332></td>
    <td width="1" height="1" bgcolor=#343535></td>
    <td width="1" height="1" bgcolor=#3a3c3b></td>
    <td width="1" height="1" bgcolor=#3e3f3f></td>
    <td width="1" height="1" bgcolor=#393a39></td>
    <td width="1" height="1" bgcolor=#383938></td>
    <td width="1" height="1" bgcolor=#414141></td>
    <td width="1" height="1" bgcolor=#373838></td>
    <td width="1" height="1" bgcolor=#2e3232></td>
    <td width="1" height="1" bgcolor=#4b4e4d></td>
    <td width="1" height="1" bgcolor=#5c5b5b></td>
    <td width="1" height="1" bgcolor=#626263></td>
    <td width="1" height="1" bgcolor=#7b7777></td>
    <td width="1" height="1" bgcolor=#898989></td>
    <td width="1" height="1" bgcolor=#737678></td>
    <td width="1" height="1" bgcolor=#686563></td>
    <td width="1" height="1" bgcolor=#5d5857></td>
    <td width="1" height="1" bgcolor=#959a95></td>
    <td width="1" height="1" bgcolor=#343735></td>
    <td width="1" height="1" bgcolor=#3a3f41></td>
    <td width="1" height="1" bgcolor=#3a3d3e></td>
    <td width="1" height="1" bgcolor=#37393a></td>
    <td width="1" height="1" bgcolor=#353839></td>
    <td width="1" height="1" bgcolor=#37383a></td>
    <td width="1" height="1" bgcolor=#353638></td>
    <td width="1" height="1" bgcolor=#36373a></td>
    <td width="1" height="1" bgcolor=#36383a></td>
    <td width="1" height="1" bgcolor=#34363a></td>
    <td width="1" height="1" bgcolor=#2f3032></td>
    <td width="1" height="1" bgcolor=#323439></td>
    <td width="1" height="1" bgcolor=#38383d></td>
    <td width="1" height="1" bgcolor=#35393c></td>
    <td width="1" height="1" bgcolor=#2d2f32></td>
    <td width="1" height="1" bgcolor=#333435></td>
    <td width="1" height="1" bgcolor=#383939></td>
    <td width="1" height="1" bgcolor=#393a3c></td>
    <td width="1" height="1" bgcolor=#373839></td>
    <td width="1" height="1" bgcolor=#323333></td>
    <td width="1" height="1" bgcolor=#3b3c3c></td>
    <td width="1" height="1" bgcolor=#353736></td>
    <td width="1" height="1" bgcolor=#343535></td>
    <td width="1" height="1" bgcolor=#363736></td>
    <td width="1" height="1" bgcolor=#373838></td>
    <td width="1" height="1" bgcolor=#323333></td>
    <td width="1" height="1" bgcolor=#353635></td>
    <td width="1" height="1" bgcolor=#313332></td>
    <td width="1" height="1" bgcolor=#353635></td>
    <td width="1" height="1" bgcolor=#4c4e4d></td>
  </tr>
  <tr>
    <td rowspan="9" colspan="6" width="1" height="1" bgcolor=#000000></td>
    <td rowspan="8" colspan="9" width="1"
```

```
height="1"
bgcolor=#000000></td>
    <td rowspan="6"
colspan="2" width="1"
height="1"
bgcolor=#000000></td>
    <td rowspan="4"
colspan="3" width="1"
height="1"
bgcolor=#000000></td>
    <td rowspan="2"
colspan="3" width="1"
height="1"
bgcolor=#000000></td>
    <td rowspan="1"
colspan="2" width="1"
height="1"
bgcolor=#000000></td>
    <td width="1" height="1"
bgcolor=#000100></td>
    <td width="1" height="1"
bgcolor=#000002></td>
    <td rowspan="1"
colspan="2" width="1"
height="1"
bgcolor=#000000></td>
    <td width="1" height="1"
bgcolor=#000001></td>
    <td width="1" height="1"
bgcolor=#010101></td>
    <td width="1" height="1"
bgcolor=#7d7d77></td>
    <td width="1" height="1"
bgcolor=#9b9898></td>
    <td width="1" height="1"
bgcolor=#645d5a></td>
    <td width="1" height="1"
bgcolor=#4f4748></td>
    <td width="1" height="1"
bgcolor=#534f54></td>
    <td width="1" height="1"
bgcolor=#4d494f></td>
    <td width="1" height="1"
bgcolor=#746967></td>
    <td width="1" height="1"
bgcolor=#8d8784></td>
    <td width="1" height="1"
bgcolor=#dcdddd></td>
    <td width="1" height="1"
bgcolor=#adb3b1></td>
    <td width="1" height="1"
bgcolor=#cacecd></td>
    <td width="1" height="1"
bgcolor=#d4d8cd></td>
    <td width="1" height="1"
bgcolor=#01080c></td>
    <td width="1" height="1"
bgcolor=#00090f></td>
    <td width="1" height="1"
bgcolor=#00070e></td>
    <td width="1" height="1"
bgcolor=#00060e></td>
    <td width="1" height="1"
bgcolor=#00040f></td>
    <td width="1" height="1"
bgcolor=#00060f></td>
    <td width="1" height="1"
bgcolor=#00060e></td>
    <td width="1" height="1"
bgcolor=#00050e></td>
    <td width="1" height="1"
bgcolor=#01060f></td>
    <td rowspan="1"
colspan="2" width="1"
height="1"
bgcolor=#000811></td>
    <td width="1" height="1"
bgcolor=#000f19></td>
    <td width="1" height="1"
bgcolor=#000814></td>
    <td width="1" height="1"
bgcolor=#00040f></td>
    <td width="1" height="1"
bgcolor=#00020e></td>
    <td width="1" height="1"
bgcolor=#00020c></td>
    <td width="1" height="1"
bgcolor=#000409></td>
    <td width="1" height="1"
bgcolor=#00020c></td>
    <td width="1" height="1"
bgcolor=#00020d></td>
    <td width="1" height="1"
bgcolor=#00020b></td>
    <td width="1" height="1"
bgcolor=#000107></td>
    <td width="1" height="1"
bgcolor=#000105></td>
    <td width="1" height="1"
bgcolor=#000106></td>
    <td width="1" height="1"
bgcolor=#000004></td>
    <td width="1" height="1"
bgcolor=#000002></td>
    <td width="1" height="1"
bgcolor=#000001></td>
    <td rowspan="1"
colspan="2" width="1"
height="1"
bgcolor=#000000></td>
    <td width="1" height="1"
bgcolor=#2f3030></td>
  </tr>
  <tr>
    <td rowspan="2"
colspan="1" width="1"
height="1"
bgcolor=#000100></td>
    <td width="1" height="1"
bgcolor=#000001></td>
    <td width="1" height="1"
bgcolor=#000105></td>
    <td width="1" height="1"
bgcolor=#00030e></td>
    <td width="1" height="1"
bgcolor=#010818></td>
    <td width="1" height="1"
bgcolor=#00040f></td>
    <td width="1" height="1"
bgcolor=#000203></td>
    <td width="1" height="1"
bgcolor=#373a35></td>
    <td width="1" height="1"
bgcolor=#a5a5a3></td>
    <td width="1" height="1"
bgcolor=#797779></td>
    <td width="1" height="1"
bgcolor=#847d80></td>
    <td width="1" height="1"
bgcolor=#4b474f></td>
    <td width="1" height="1"
bgcolor=#564e55></td>
    <td width="1" height="1"
bgcolor=#665d63></td>
    <td width="1" height="1"
bgcolor=#756b6d></td>
    <td width="1" height="1"
bgcolor=#7a6f70></td>
    <td width="1" height="1"
bgcolor=#c9d0ce></td>
    <td width="1" height="1"
bgcolor=#fffefe></td>
    <td width="1" height="1"
bgcolor=#c5c9c5></td>
    <td width="1" height="1"
bgcolor=#d1d0cc></td>
    <td width="1" height="1"
bgcolor=#071314></td>
    <td width="1" height="1"
bgcolor=#000e13></td>
    <td width="1" height="1"
bgcolor=#000d11></td>
    <td width="1" height="1"
bgcolor=#010d14></td>
    <td rowspan="1"
colspan="2" width="1"
height="1"
bgcolor=#000d14></td>
    <td width="1" height="1"
bgcolor=#000c14></td>
    <td width="1" height="1"
bgcolor=#000a12></td>
    <td width="1" height="1"
bgcolor=#000c15></td>
```

```
    <td width="1" height="1" bgcolor=#010d15></td>
    <td width="1" height="1" bgcolor=#01111d></td>
    <td width="1" height="1" bgcolor=#000d17></td>
    <td width="1" height="1" bgcolor=#010912></td>
    <td rowspan="1" colspan="2" width="1" height="1" bgcolor=#000711></td>
    <td rowspan="2" colspan="1" width="1" height="1" bgcolor=#000611></td>
    <td width="1" height="1" bgcolor=#000410></td>
    <td width="1" height="1" bgcolor=#00060f></td>
    <td width="1" height="1" bgcolor=#00030f></td>
    <td width="1" height="1" bgcolor=#00030e></td>
    <td width="1" height="1" bgcolor=#00010a></td>
    <td width="1" height="1" bgcolor=#000107></td>
    <td rowspan="1" colspan="2" width="1" height="1" bgcolor=#000003></td>
    <td rowspan="1" colspan="2" width="1" height="1" bgcolor=#000000></td>
    <td width="1" height="1" bgcolor=#000104></td>
    <td width="1" height="1" bgcolor=#080a0d></td>
    <td width="1" height="1" bgcolor=#3b3c3d></td>
  </tr>
  <tr>
    <td rowspan="2" colspan="1" width="1" height="1" bgcolor=#000100></td>
    <td width="1" height="1" bgcolor=#000100></td>
    <td width="1" height="1" bgcolor=#000000></td>
    <td width="1" height="1" bgcolor=#000100></td>
    <td rowspan="2" colspan="2" width="1" height="1" bgcolor=#000101></td>
    <td width="1" height="1" bgcolor=#000207></td>
    <td width="1" height="1" bgcolor=#000611></td>
    <td width="1" height="1" bgcolor=#000d1c></td>
    <td width="1" height="1" bgcolor=#32393d></td>
    <td width="1" height="1" bgcolor=#828280></td>
    <td width="1" height="1" bgcolor=#8f8b88></td>
    <td width="1" height="1" bgcolor=#544f54></td>
    <td width="1" height="1" bgcolor=#6c686b></td>
    <td width="1" height="1" bgcolor=#7d7269></td>
    <td width="1" height="1" bgcolor=#5c564a></td>
    <td width="1" height="1" bgcolor=#494135></td>
    <td width="1" height="1" bgcolor=#63584b></td>
    <td width="1" height="1" bgcolor=#6d6254></td>
    <td width="1" height="1" bgcolor=#d5d1c9></td>
    <td width="1" height="1" bgcolor=#d7d9d9></td>
    <td width="1" height="1" bgcolor=#e4eaec></td>
    <td width="1" height="1" bgcolor=#081719></td>
    <td width="1" height="1" bgcolor=#001017></td>
    <td width="1" height="1" bgcolor=#000f17></td>
    <td width="1" height="1" bgcolor=#001018></td>
    <td width="1" height="1" bgcolor=#000f18></td>
    <td width="1" height="1" bgcolor=#000e17></td>
    <td rowspan="1" colspan="2" width="1" height="1" bgcolor=#000f17></td>
    <td width="1" height="1" bgcolor=#001019></td>
    <td width="1" height="1" bgcolor=#001321></td>
    <td width="1" height="1" bgcolor=#000e19></td>
    <td width="1" height="1" bgcolor=#000d16></td>
    <td width="1" height="1" bgcolor=#000913></td>
    <td width="1" height="1" bgcolor=#000911></td>
    <td width="1" height="1" bgcolor=#000811></td>
    <td width="1" height="1" bgcolor=#000612></td>
    <td width="1" height="1" bgcolor=#040a15></td>
    <td width="1" height="1" bgcolor=#0c101a></td>
    <td width="1" height="1" bgcolor=#131622></td>
    <td width="1" height="1" bgcolor=#1a202c></td>
    <td width="1" height="1" bgcolor=#2a313c></td>
    <td width="1" height="1" bgcolor=#383f4b></td>
    <td width="1" height="1" bgcolor=#3c424e></td>
    <td width="1" height="1" bgcolor=#454b57></td>
    <td width="1" height="1" bgcolor=#494e5b></td>
    <td width="1" height="1" bgcolor=#4e4f59></td>
    <td width="1" height="1" bgcolor=#4a4c53></td>
    <td width="1" height="1" bgcolor=#4e5053></td>
  </tr>
  <tr>
    <td width="1" height="1" bgcolor=#000000></td>
    <td width="1" height="1" bgcolor=#000100></td>
    <td width="1" height="1" bgcolor=#000001></td>
    <td width="1" height="1" bgcolor=#000101></td>
    <td width="1" height="1" bgcolor=#000102></td>
    <td width="1" height="1" bgcolor=#000207></td>
    <td width="1" height="1" bgcolor=#00020d></td>
    <td width="1" height="1" bgcolor=#151920></td>
    <td width="1" height="1" bgcolor=#828285></td>
    <td width="1" height="1" bgcolor=#615d60></td>
    <td width="1" height="1" bgcolor=#7b777b></td>
    <td width="1" height="1" bgcolor=#251e17></td>
    <td width="1" height="1" bgcolor=#000003></td>
```

```
    <td width="1" height="1" bgcolor=#00090d></td>
    <td width="1" height="1" bgcolor=#000e13></td>
    <td width="1" height="1" bgcolor=#10140e></td>
    <td width="1" height="1" bgcolor=#454136></td>
    <td width="1" height="1" bgcolor=#282520></td>
    <td width="1" height="1" bgcolor=#d6d2ca></td>
    <td width="1" height="1" bgcolor=#ced7d9></td>
    <td width="1" height="1" bgcolor=#3f4d4d></td>
    <td width="1" height="1" bgcolor=#00141c></td>
    <td width="1" height="1" bgcolor=#00121a></td>
    <td width="1" height="1" bgcolor=#00111c></td>
    <td width="1" height="1" bgcolor=#000e1b></td>
    <td rowspan="1" colspan="2" width="1" height="1" bgcolor=#00101d></td>
    <td width="1" height="1" bgcolor=#00141f></td>
    <td width="1" height="1" bgcolor=#051824></td>
    <td width="1" height="1" bgcolor=#0d1925></td>
    <td width="1" height="1" bgcolor=#17212d></td>
    <td width="1" height="1" bgcolor=#212a37></td>
    <td width="1" height="1" bgcolor=#2b3340></td>
    <td width="1" height="1" bgcolor=#353b48></td>
    <td width="1" height="1" bgcolor=#404452></td>
    <td width="1" height="1" bgcolor=#4d505e></td>
    <td width="1" height="1" bgcolor=#4e515d></td>
    <td width="1" height="1" bgcolor=#515460></td>
    <td width="1" height="1" bgcolor=#585965></td>
    <td width="1" height="1" bgcolor=#5c5d6a></td>
    <td width="1" height="1" bgcolor=#555765></td>
    <td width="1" height="1" bgcolor=#5c5c69></td>
    <td width="1" height="1" bgcolor=#585a66></td>
    <td width="1" height="1" bgcolor=#60636e></td>
    <td width="1" height="1" bgcolor=#5d606a></td>
    <td width="1" height="1" bgcolor=#666873></td>
    <td width="1" height="1" bgcolor=#6e7078></td>
    <td width="1" height="1" bgcolor=#74737e></td>
    <td width="1" height="1" bgcolor=#606165></td>
  </tr>
  <tr>
    <td width="1" height="1" bgcolor=#000100></td>
    <td rowspan="1" colspan="2" width="1" height="1" bgcolor=#000000></td>
    <td rowspan="1" colspan="4" width="1" height="1" bgcolor=#000101></td>
    <td width="1" height="1" bgcolor=#000102></td>
    <td width="1" height="1" bgcolor=#000202></td>
    <td width="1" height="1" bgcolor=#000404></td>
    <td width="1" height="1" bgcolor=#000303></td>
    <td rowspan="1" colspan="2" width="1" height="1" bgcolor=#000105></td>
    <td width="1" height="1" bgcolor=#04070a></td>
    <td width="1" height="1" bgcolor=#888480></td>
    <td width="1" height="1" bgcolor=#7f7b7b></td>
    <td width="1" height="1" bgcolor=#2a2a2a></td>
    <td width="1" height="1" bgcolor=#000a17></td>
    <td width="1" height="1" bgcolor=#00070d></td>
    <td width="1" height="1" bgcolor=#00090c></td>
    <td width="1" height="1" bgcolor=#09140e></td>
    <td width="1" height="1" bgcolor=#0c100e></td>
    <td width="1" height="1" bgcolor=#ba987c></td>
    <td width="1" height="1" bgcolor=#091516></td>
    <td width="1" height="1" bgcolor=#807873></td>
    <td width="1" height="1" bgcolor=#dadcde></td>
    <td width="1" height="1" bgcolor=#67736f></td>
    <td width="1" height="1" bgcolor=#121e2a></td>
    <td width="1" height="1" bgcolor=#1a2a34></td>
    <td width="1" height="1" bgcolor=#29333f></td>
    <td width="1" height="1" bgcolor=#3b434f></td>
    <td width="1" height="1" bgcolor=#4c525f></td>
    <td width="1" height="1" bgcolor=#5b5b66></td>
    <td width="1" height="1" bgcolor=#62636f></td>
    <td width="1" height="1" bgcolor=#696975></td>
    <td width="1" height="1" bgcolor=#6b6773></td>
    <td width="1" height="1" bgcolor=#656370></td>
    <td width="1" height="1" bgcolor=#464b56></td>
    <td width="1" height="1" bgcolor=#595d68></td>
    <td width="1" height="1" bgcolor=#706f7b></td>
    <td width="1" height="1" bgcolor=#6a6972></td>
    <td width="1" height="1" bgcolor=#686974></td>
    <td width="1" height="1" bgcolor=#7a7882></td>
    <td width="1" height="1" bgcolor=#6e6c78></td>
    <td width="1" height="1" bgcolor=#676971></td>
    <td width="1" height="1" bgcolor=#7e7f86></td>
    <td width="1" height="1" bgcolor=#6c6c77></td>
    <td width="1" height="1" bgcolor=#5a5d69></td>
    <td width="1" height="1" bgcolor=#4b505d></td>
    <td width="1" height="1" bgcolor=#454c59></td>
    <td width="1" height="1" bgcolor=#575b66></td>
    <td width="1" height="1" bgcolor=#696872></td>
```

```
    <td width="1" height="1"
bgcolor=#6d6e76></td>
    <td width="1" height="1"
bgcolor=#605f67></td>
    <td width="1" height="1"
bgcolor=#5a5a5d></td>
  </tr>
  <tr>
    <td width="1" height="1"
bgcolor=#000000></td>
    <td rowspan="2"
colspan="1" width="1"
height="1"
bgcolor=#000100></td>
    <td rowspan="1"
colspan="2" width="1"
height="1"
bgcolor=#000100></td>
    <td width="1" height="1"
bgcolor=#000101></td>
    <td rowspan="1"
colspan="2" width="1"
height="1"
bgcolor=#000003></td>
    <td width="1" height="1"
bgcolor=#000101></td>
    <td rowspan="1"
colspan="2" width="1"
height="1"
bgcolor=#000103></td>
    <td width="1" height="1"
bgcolor=#000205></td>
    <td width="1" height="1"
bgcolor=#000303></td>
    <td width="1" height="1"
bgcolor=#000101></td>
    <td width="1" height="1"
bgcolor=#030303></td>
    <td width="1" height="1"
bgcolor=#96908d></td>
    <td width="1" height="1"
bgcolor=#817877></td>
    <td width="1" height="1"
bgcolor=#121519></td>
    <td width="1" height="1"
bgcolor=#171a1b></td>
    <td width="1" height="1"
bgcolor=#444946></td>
    <td width="1" height="1"
bgcolor=#41453e></td>
    <td width="1" height="1"
bgcolor=#b0a89b></td>
    <td width="1" height="1"
bgcolor=#3a2c23></td>
    <td width="1" height="1"
bgcolor=#876957></td>
    <td width="1" height="1"
bgcolor=#736659></td>
    <td width="1" height="1"
bgcolor=#7f756d></td>
    <td width="1" height="1"
bgcolor=#e2ecee></td>
    <td width="1" height="1"
bgcolor=#a6a7aa></td>
    <td width="1" height="1"
bgcolor=#76747c></td>
    <td width="1" height="1"
bgcolor=#78777e></td>
    <td width="1" height="1"
bgcolor=#7c7980></td>
    <td width="1" height="1"
bgcolor=#72707a></td>
    <td width="1" height="1"
bgcolor=#7e7c87></td>
    <td width="1" height="1"
bgcolor=#797b83></td>
    <td width="1" height="1"
bgcolor=#333c47></td>
    <td width="1" height="1"
bgcolor=#555a65></td>
    <td width="1" height="1"
bgcolor=#707078></td>
    <td width="1" height="1"
bgcolor=#7b7a82></td>
    <td width="1" height="1"
bgcolor=#7f7e86></td>
    <td width="1" height="1"
bgcolor=#6f6e78></td>
    <td width="1" height="1"
bgcolor=#5b5e65></td>
    <td width="1" height="1"
bgcolor=#5c5d67></td>
    <td width="1" height="1"
bgcolor=#5b5f6b></td>
    <td width="1" height="1"
bgcolor=#72717a></td>
    <td width="1" height="1"
bgcolor=#676772></td>
    <td width="1" height="1"
bgcolor=#787780></td>
    <td width="1" height="1"
bgcolor=#696a73></td>
    <td width="1" height="1"
bgcolor=#60646f></td>
    <td width="1" height="1"
bgcolor=#646571></td>
    <td width="1" height="1"
bgcolor=#7a7a84></td>
    <td width="1" height="1"
bgcolor=#656670></td>
    <td width="1" height="1"
bgcolor=#6f7278></td>
    <td width="1" height="1"
bgcolor=#717479></td>
    <td width="1" height="1"
bgcolor=#65656c></td>
    <td width="1" height="1"
bgcolor=#44454a></td>
    <td width="1" height="1"
bgcolor=#4a4d4e></td>
  </tr>
  <tr>
    <td width="1" height="1"
bgcolor=#000100></td>
    <td width="1" height="1"
bgcolor=#000000></td>
    <td width="1" height="1"
bgcolor=#000101></td>
    <td width="1" height="1"
bgcolor=#000101></td>
    <td width="1" height="1"
bgcolor=#000100></td>
    <td rowspan="1"
colspan="3" width="1"
height="1"
bgcolor=#000000></td>
    <td width="1" height="1"
bgcolor=#000100></td>
    <td width="1" height="1"
bgcolor=#020304></td>
    <td width="1" height="1"
bgcolor=#080809></td>
    <td width="1" height="1"
bgcolor=#0e0d0e></td>
    <td width="1" height="1"
bgcolor=#181c23></td>
    <td width="1" height="1"
bgcolor=#2c2c31></td>
    <td width="1" height="1"
bgcolor=#363639></td>
    <td width="1" height="1"
bgcolor=#928e8b></td>
    <td width="1" height="1"
bgcolor=#756f70></td>
    <td width="1" height="1"
bgcolor=#584c4a></td>
    <td width="1" height="1"
bgcolor=#98856c></td>
    <td width="1" height="1"
bgcolor=#a08f76></td>
    <td width="1" height="1"
bgcolor=#9c8e77></td>
    <td width="1" height="1"
bgcolor=#837564></td>
    <td width="1" height="1"
bgcolor=#6e5e4f></td>
    <td width="1" height="1"
bgcolor=#624f42></td>
    <td width="1" height="1"
bgcolor=#806a58></td>
    <td width="1" height="1"
bgcolor=#655b57></td>
    <td width="1" height="1"
bgcolor=#ecf7f4></td>
```

```
    <td width="1" height="1"
bgcolor=#adb1b1></td>
    <td width="1" height="1"
bgcolor=#60616c></td>
    <td width="1" height="1"
bgcolor=#5d5e68></td>
    <td width="1" height="1"
bgcolor=#6f6c75></td>
    <td width="1" height="1"
bgcolor=#71727b></td>
    <td width="1" height="1"
bgcolor=#676973></td>
    <td width="1" height="1"
bgcolor=#686873></td>
    <td width="1" height="1"
bgcolor=#8b8b92></td>
    <td width="1" height="1"
bgcolor=#838289></td>
    <td width="1" height="1"
bgcolor=#7b7c84></td>
    <td width="1" height="1"
bgcolor=#84838b></td>
    <td width="1" height="1"
bgcolor=#7d7d84></td>
    <td width="1" height="1"
bgcolor=#87888f></td>
    <td width="1" height="1"
bgcolor=#86848d></td>
    <td width="1" height="1"
bgcolor=#6d6f78></td>
    <td width="1" height="1"
bgcolor=#5b5b67></td>
    <td width="1" height="1"
bgcolor=#74747e></td>
    <td width="1" height="1"
bgcolor=#71727d></td>
    <td width="1" height="1"
bgcolor=#676772></td>
    <td width="1" height="1"
bgcolor=#505a63></td>
    <td width="1" height="1"
bgcolor=#5f626d></td>
    <td width="1" height="1"
bgcolor=#5f656f></td>
    <td width="1" height="1"
bgcolor=#595f66></td>
    <td width="1" height="1"
bgcolor=#73727c></td>
    <td width="1" height="1"
bgcolor=#74717c></td>
    <td width="1" height="1"
bgcolor=#75757d></td>
    <td width="1" height="1"
bgcolor=#65646c></td>
    <td width="1" height="1"
bgcolor=#89888f></td>
    <td width="1" height="1"
bgcolor=#67686b></td>
  </tr>
  <tr>
    <td width="1" height="1"
bgcolor=#000000></td>
    <td width="1" height="1"
bgcolor=#030303></td>
    <td width="1" height="1"
bgcolor=#080808></td>
    <td width="1" height="1"
bgcolor=#0a090b></td>
    <td width="1" height="1"
bgcolor=#0c0d0e></td>
    <td width="1" height="1"
bgcolor=#1c1d1d></td>
    <td width="1" height="1"
bgcolor=#37383b></td>
    <td width="1" height="1"
bgcolor=#413f45></td>
    <td width="1" height="1"
bgcolor=#59575d></td>
    <td width="1" height="1"
bgcolor=#68666b></td>
    <td width="1" height="1"
bgcolor=#6b6a6f></td>
    <td width="1" height="1"
bgcolor=#625f66></td>
    <td width="1" height="1"
bgcolor=#6e6a71></td>
    <td width="1" height="1"
bgcolor=#3e3f40></td>
    <td width="1" height="1"
bgcolor=#78747a></td>
    <td width="1" height="1"
bgcolor=#747176></td>
    <td width="1" height="1"
bgcolor=#827e7e></td>
    <td width="1" height="1"
bgcolor=#635f5a></td>
    <td width="1" height="1"
bgcolor=#52514c></td>
    <td width="1" height="1"
bgcolor=#84705f></td>
    <td width="1" height="1"
bgcolor=#816f5d></td>
    <td width="1" height="1"
bgcolor=#453e37></td>
    <td width="1" height="1"
bgcolor=#716250></td>
    <td width="1" height="1"
bgcolor=#aa8b56></td>
    <td width="1" height="1"
bgcolor=#6b584c></td>
    <td width="1" height="1"
bgcolor=#877665></td>
    <td width="1" height="1"
bgcolor=#6c6359></td>
    <td width="1" height="1"
bgcolor=#f6ffff></td>
    <td width="1" height="1"
bgcolor=#c4c4c6></td>
    <td width="1" height="1"
bgcolor=#828186></td>
    <td width="1" height="1"
bgcolor=#96959b></td>
    <td width="1" height="1"
bgcolor=#8e8b91></td>
    <td width="1" height="1"
bgcolor=#8c8d92></td>
    <td width="1" height="1"
bgcolor=#797a83></td>
    <td width="1" height="1"
bgcolor=#7b7c81></td>
    <td width="1" height="1"
bgcolor=#696c74></td>
    <td width="1" height="1"
bgcolor=#616470></td>
    <td width="1" height="1"
bgcolor=#62636e></td>
    <td width="1" height="1"
bgcolor=#73737f></td>
    <td width="1" height="1"
bgcolor=#6b6e7a></td>
    <td width="1" height="1"
bgcolor=#62656d></td>
    <td width="1" height="1"
bgcolor=#7b7b82></td>
    <td width="1" height="1"
bgcolor=#7a7980></td>
    <td width="1" height="1"
bgcolor=#73747c></td>
    <td width="1" height="1"
bgcolor=#86858b></td>
    <td width="1" height="1"
bgcolor=#83838a></td>
    <td width="1" height="1"
bgcolor=#8c8e94></td>
    <td width="1" height="1"
bgcolor=#84858a></td>
    <td width="1" height="1"
bgcolor=#8c8d92></td>
    <td width="1" height="1"
bgcolor=#797780></td>
    <td width="1" height="1"
bgcolor=#8f9196></td>
    <td width="1" height="1"
bgcolor=#8f9094></td>
    <td width="1" height="1"
bgcolor=#929196></td>
    <td width="1" height="1"
bgcolor=#8c8d92></td>
    <td width="1" height="1"
bgcolor=#8a888f></td>
    <td width="1" height="1"
bgcolor=#727177></td>
    <td width="1" height="1"
bgcolor=#6c6e6f></td>
```

```
  </tr>
  <tr>
    <td width="1" height="1" bgcolor=#030304></td>
    <td width="1" height="1" bgcolor=#080808></td>
    <td width="1" height="1" bgcolor=#0b0a0b></td>
    <td width="1" height="1" bgcolor=#0e0d10></td>
    <td width="1" height="1" bgcolor=#1c1a1f></td>
    <td width="1" height="1" bgcolor=#292729></td>
    <td width="1" height="1" bgcolor=#2f2d33></td>
    <td width="1" height="1" bgcolor=#3e3d41></td>
    <td width="1" height="1" bgcolor=#3b393b></td>
    <td width="1" height="1" bgcolor=#6d6a71></td>
    <td width="1" height="1" bgcolor=#6e6b71></td>
    <td width="1" height="1" bgcolor=#6e6a71></td>
    <td width="1" height="1" bgcolor=#6b656b></td>
    <td width="1" height="1" bgcolor=#868186></td>
    <td width="1" height="1" bgcolor=#787279></td>
    <td width="1" height="1" bgcolor=#7a747b></td>
    <td width="1" height="1" bgcolor=#6f6a70></td>
    <td width="1" height="1" bgcolor=#79777a></td>
    <td width="1" height="1" bgcolor=#5c585c></td>
    <td width="1" height="1" bgcolor=#47464b></td>
    <td width="1" height="1" bgcolor=#686369></td>
    <td width="1" height="1" bgcolor=#5f5a5f></td>
    <td width="1" height="1" bgcolor=#88878a></td>
    <td width="1" height="1" bgcolor=#7e797f></td>
    <td width="1" height="1" bgcolor=#8d8a89></td>
    <td width="1" height="1" bgcolor=#706c6b></td>
    <td width="1" height="1" bgcolor=#8a8685></td>
    <td width="1" height="1" bgcolor=#635d59></td>
    <td width="1" height="1" bgcolor=#67544f></td>
    <td width="1" height="1" bgcolor=#614e3f></td>
    <td width="1" height="1" bgcolor=#131616></td>
    <td width="1" height="1" bgcolor=#745e4c></td>
    <td width="1" height="1" bgcolor=#5a443b></td>
    <td width="1" height="1" bgcolor=#725a4e></td>
    <td width="1" height="1" bgcolor=#82675e></td>
    <td width="1" height="1" bgcolor=#e2e1df></td>
    <td width="1" height="1" bgcolor=#e7e6e2></td>
    <td width="1" height="1" bgcolor=#d6cccd></td>
    <td width="1" height="1" bgcolor=#a7a9a8></td>
    <td width="1" height="1" bgcolor=#8b888d></td>
    <td width="1" height="1" bgcolor=#8b8c90></td>
    <td width="1" height="1" bgcolor=#86858b></td>
    <td width="1" height="1" bgcolor=#93929a></td>
    <td width="1" height="1" bgcolor=#97989c></td>
    <td width="1" height="1" bgcolor=#98999d></td>
    <td width="1" height="1" bgcolor=#8f8e95></td>
    <td width="1" height="1" bgcolor=#83838a></td>
    <td width="1" height="1" bgcolor=#8e8f94></td>
    <td width="1" height="1" bgcolor=#7e8185></td>
    <td width="1" height="1" bgcolor=#8e8f95></td>
    <td width="1" height="1" bgcolor=#929196></td>
    <td width="1" height="1" bgcolor=#939398></td>
    <td width="1" height="1" bgcolor=#8e8e93></td>
    <td width="1" height="1" bgcolor=#8b8a90></td>
    <td width="1" height="1" bgcolor=#929499></td>
    <td width="1" height="1" bgcolor=#808288></td>
    <td width="1" height="1" bgcolor=#7e828b></td>
    <td width="1" height="1" bgcolor=#88878d></td>
    <td width="1" height="1" bgcolor=#8c8c93></td>
    <td width="1" height="1" bgcolor=#85858b></td>
    <td width="1" height="1" bgcolor=#929498></td>
    <td width="1" height="1" bgcolor=#939498></td>
    <td width="1" height="1" bgcolor=#808085></td>
    <td width="1" height="1" bgcolor=#67676c></td>
    <td width="1" height="1" bgcolor=#85848a></td>
    <td width="1" height="1" bgcolor=#737375></td>
  </tr>
  <tr>
    <td width="1" height="1" bgcolor=#0a0a0b></td>
    <td width="1" height="1" bgcolor=#212122></td>
    <td width="1" height="1" bgcolor=#333036></td>
    <td width="1" height="1" bgcolor=#353337></td>
    <td width="1" height="1" bgcolor=#403c3e></td>
    <td width="1" height="1" bgcolor=#605b5f></td>
    <td width="1" height="1" bgcolor=#69656b></td>
    <td width="1" height="1" bgcolor=#69646a></td>
    <td width="1" height="1" bgcolor=#5d595e></td>
    <td width="1" height="1" bgcolor=#696568></td>
    <td width="1" height="1" bgcolor=#666265></td>
    <td width="1" height="1" bgcolor=#625e60></td>
    <td width="1" height="1" bgcolor=#69686d></td>
    <td width="1" height="1" bgcolor=#868689></td>
    <td width="1" height="1" bgcolor=#515053></td>
    <td width="1" height="1" bgcolor=#3c3a3a></td>
    <td width="1" height="1" bgcolor=#404043></td>
    <td width="1" height="1" bgcolor=#4b494d></td>
    <td width="1" height="1" bgcolor=#666267></td>
```

```
    <td width="1" height="1" bgcolor=#757379></td>
    <td width="1" height="1" bgcolor=#6d696c></td>
    <td width="1" height="1" bgcolor=#7d767d></td>
    <td width="1" height="1" bgcolor=#807b80></td>
    <td width="1" height="1" bgcolor=#717073></td>
    <td width="1" height="1" bgcolor=#363438></td>
    <td width="1" height="1" bgcolor=#7d797d></td>
    <td width="1" height="1" bgcolor=#7e7c81></td>
    <td width="1" height="1" bgcolor=#6b696f></td>
    <td width="1" height="1" bgcolor=#7e7c7f></td>
    <td width="1" height="1" bgcolor=#777376></td>
    <td width="1" height="1" bgcolor=#93908b></td>
    <td width="1" height="1" bgcolor=#5f5d63></td>
    <td width="1" height="1" bgcolor=#7a716f></td>
    <td width="1" height="1" bgcolor=#787375></td>
    <td width="1" height="1" bgcolor=#5c524a></td>
    <td width="1" height="1" bgcolor=#624c3e></td>
    <td width="1" height="1" bgcolor=#382c23></td>
    <td width="1" height="1" bgcolor=#342b24></td>
    <td width="1" height="1" bgcolor=#5c4539></td>
    <td width="1" height="1" bgcolor=#75634e></td>
    <td width="1" height="1" bgcolor=#827c70></td>
    <td width="1" height="1" bgcolor=#c2c0b7></td>
    <td width="1" height="1" bgcolor=#999ca3></td>
    <td width="1" height="1" bgcolor=#c29d9e></td>
    <td width="1" height="1" bgcolor=#e2d8d4></td>
    <td width="1" height="1" bgcolor=#c5c7c8></td>
    <td width="1" height="1" bgcolor=#909195></td>
    <td width="1" height="1" bgcolor=#8d8d92></td>
    <td width="1" height="1" bgcolor=#85888c></td>
    <td width="1" height="1" bgcolor=#86878e></td>
    <td width="1" height="1" bgcolor=#696a74></td>
    <td width="1" height="1" bgcolor=#686b72></td>
    <td width="1" height="1" bgcolor=#807e85></td>
    <td width="1" height="1" bgcolor=#7e8188></td>
    <td width="1" height="1" bgcolor=#6e6e7a></td>
    <td width="1" height="1" bgcolor=#6e6d75></td>
    <td width="1" height="1" bgcolor=#88868c></td>
    <td width="1" height="1" bgcolor=#8e8f94></td>
    <td width="1" height="1" bgcolor=#8b8c93></td>
    <td width="1" height="1" bgcolor=#818189></td>
    <td width="1" height="1" bgcolor=#8c8d92></td>
    <td width="1" height="1" bgcolor=#828188></td>
    <td width="1" height="1" bgcolor=#7c7d86></td>
    <td width="1" height="1" bgcolor=#7b7980></td>
    <td width="1" height="1" bgcolor=#838287></td>
    <td width="1" height="1" bgcolor=#75757c></td>
    <td width="1" height="1" bgcolor=#4f5156></td>
    <td width="1" height="1" bgcolor=#595a5e></td>
    <td width="1" height="1" bgcolor=#4e4f55></td>
    <td width="1" height="1" bgcolor=#504f55></td>
    <td width="1" height="1" bgcolor=#75747a></td>
    <td width="1" height="1" bgcolor=#707172></td>
  </tr>
  <tr>
    <td width="1" height="1" bgcolor=#534e4d></td>
    <td width="1" height="1" bgcolor=#474244></td>
    <td width="1" height="1" bgcolor=#1a171a></td>
    <td width="1" height="1" bgcolor=#39393a></td>
    <td width="1" height="1" bgcolor=#474449></td>
    <td width="1" height="1" bgcolor=#656067></td>
    <td width="1" height="1" bgcolor=#666369></td>
    <td width="1" height="1" bgcolor=#615d62></td>
    <td width="1" height="1" bgcolor=#69676c></td>
    <td width="1" height="1" bgcolor=#68666b></td>
    <td width="1" height="1" bgcolor=#6a676c></td>
    <td width="1" height="1" bgcolor=#636063></td>
    <td width="1" height="1" bgcolor=#6d696f></td>
    <td width="1" height="1" bgcolor=#6f6870></td>
    <td width="1" height="1" bgcolor=#6f6c72></td>
    <td width="1" height="1" bgcolor=#736e74></td>
    <td width="1" height="1" bgcolor=#756e74></td>
    <td width="1" height="1" bgcolor=#726b72></td>
    <td width="1" height="1" bgcolor=#7b757c></td>
    <td width="1" height="1" bgcolor=#5d595f></td>
    <td width="1" height="1" bgcolor=#67646a></td>
    <td width="1" height="1" bgcolor=#6f6c72></td>
    <td width="1" height="1" bgcolor=#6d6b70></td>
    <td width="1" height="1" bgcolor=#605d61></td>
    <td width="1" height="1" bgcolor=#6e6b6f></td>
    <td width="1" height="1" bgcolor=#89878a></td>
    <td width="1" height="1" bgcolor=#818085></td>
    <td width="1" height="1" bgcolor=#817d82></td>
    <td width="1" height="1" bgcolor=#827f81></td>
    <td width="1" height="1" bgcolor=#7f7b7e></td>
    <td width="1" height="1" bgcolor=#918f8e></td>
    <td width="1" height="1" bgcolor=#6a676d></td>
    <td width="1" height="1" bgcolor=#625a5e></td>
```

```
<td width="1" height="1" bgcolor=#736b68></td>
<td width="1" height="1" bgcolor=#9d9c97></td>
<td width="1" height="1" bgcolor=#a09e8f></td>
<td width="1" height="1" bgcolor=#908878></td>
<td width="1" height="1" bgcolor=#70675d></td>
<td width="1" height="1" bgcolor=#978c7d></td>
<td width="1" height="1" bgcolor=#b5ad9e></td>
<td width="1" height="1" bgcolor=#dbdcd5></td>
<td width="1" height="1" bgcolor=#b8b9b1></td>
<td width="1" height="1" bgcolor=#767780></td>
<td width="1" height="1" bgcolor=#ba8788></td>
<td width="1" height="1" bgcolor=#c4bab3></td>
<td width="1" height="1" bgcolor=#f1f3f0></td>
<td width="1" height="1" bgcolor=#99969c></td>
<td width="1" height="1" bgcolor=#97989e></td>
<td width="1" height="1" bgcolor=#8b8a92></td>
<td width="1" height="1" bgcolor=#8e9098></td>
<td width="1" height="1" bgcolor=#8a8d93></td>
<td width="1" height="1" bgcolor=#9d9fa3></td>
<td width="1" height="1" bgcolor=#7c7e83></td>
<td width="1" height="1" bgcolor=#8a8b90></td>
<td width="1" height="1" bgcolor=#8f8f94></td>
<td width="1" height="1" bgcolor=#8f8e94></td>
<td width="1" height="1" bgcolor=#8d8f93></td>
<td width="1" height="1" bgcolor=#98979d></td>
<td width="1" height="1" bgcolor=#7d8086></td>
<td width="1" height="1" bgcolor=#717379></td>
<td width="1" height="1" bgcolor=#83848a></td>
<td width="1" height="1" bgcolor=#928f96></td>
<td width="1" height="1" bgcolor=#8b8a90></td>
<td width="1" height="1" bgcolor=#8a8a8c></td>
<td width="1" height="1" bgcolor=#808085></td>
<td width="1" height="1" bgcolor=#67666b></td>
<td width="1" height="1" bgcolor=#76747b></td>
<td width="1" height="1" bgcolor=#717076></td>
<td width="1" height="1" bgcolor=#76737a></td>
<td width="1" height="1" bgcolor=#838187></td>
<td width="1" height="1" bgcolor=#838288></td>
<td width="1" height="1" bgcolor=#77787a></td>
</tr>
<tr>
<td width="1" height="1" bgcolor=#565254></td>
<td width="1" height="1" bgcolor=#524e4f></td>
<td width="1" height="1" bgcolor=#484548></td>
<td width="1" height="1" bgcolor=#2f2c2c></td>
<td width="1" height="1" bgcolor=#4e4c4b></td>
<td width="1" height="1" bgcolor=#5c595d></td>
<td rowspan="1" colspan="2" width="1" height="1" bgcolor=#6e6b71></td>
<td width="1" height="1" bgcolor=#151412></td>
<td width="1" height="1" bgcolor=#111112></td>
<td width="1" height="1" bgcolor=#3c3c3e></td>
<td width="1" height="1" bgcolor=#6b666c></td>
<td width="1" height="1" bgcolor=#5d585b></td>
<td width="1" height="1" bgcolor=#727176></td>
<td width="1" height="1" bgcolor=#736f76></td>
<td width="1" height="1" bgcolor=#848486></td>
<td width="1" height="1" bgcolor=#726b72></td>
<td width="1" height="1" bgcolor=#847f85></td>
<td width="1" height="1" bgcolor=#848187></td>
<td width="1" height="1" bgcolor=#838086></td>
<td width="1" height="1" bgcolor=#79747a></td>
<td width="1" height="1" bgcolor=#807c81></td>
<td width="1" height="1" bgcolor=#838083></td>
<td width="1" height="1" bgcolor=#898589></td>
<td width="1" height="1" bgcolor=#8e8e92></td>
<td width="1" height="1" bgcolor=#8f8f91></td>
<td width="1" height="1" bgcolor=#87888a></td>
<td width="1" height="1" bgcolor=#7a787d></td>
<td width="1" height="1" bgcolor=#898687></td>
<td width="1" height="1" bgcolor=#918e90></td>
<td width="1" height="1" bgcolor=#777777></td>
<td width="1" height="1" bgcolor=#6b6969></td>
<td width="1" height="1" bgcolor=#837976></td>
<td width="1" height="1" bgcolor=#847d7a></td>
<td width="1" height="1" bgcolor=#877f7b></td>
<td width="1" height="1" bgcolor=#928a85></td>
<td width="1" height="1" bgcolor=#81766d></td>
<td width="1" height="1" bgcolor=#8a827f></td>
<td width="1" height="1" bgcolor=#847a76></td>
<td width="1" height="1" bgcolor=#7c7169></td>
<td width="1" height="1" bgcolor=#aca396></td>
<td width="1" height="1" bgcolor=#b0b2a7></td>
<td width="1" height="1" bgcolor=#bdb4aa></td>
<td width="1" height="1" bgcolor=#99928e></td>
<td width="1" height="1" bgcolor=#b8ada1></td>
<td width="1" height="1" bgcolor=#c8c8c2></td>
<td width="1" height="1" bgcolor=#edebec></td>
```

```
    <td width="1" height="1"
bgcolor=#909195></td>
    <td width="1" height="1"
bgcolor=#919498></td>
    <td width="1" height="1"
bgcolor=#9d9ca1></td>
    <td width="1" height="1"
bgcolor=#9e9da2></td>
    <td width="1" height="1"
bgcolor=#8b8b92></td>
    <td width="1" height="1"
bgcolor=#84848e></td>
    <td width="1" height="1"
bgcolor=#8b8a94></td>
    <td width="1" height="1"
bgcolor=#747580></td>
    <td width="1" height="1"
bgcolor=#74757c></td>
    <td width="1" height="1"
bgcolor=#87858b></td>
    <td width="1" height="1"
bgcolor=#7e7f85></td>
    <td width="1" height="1"
bgcolor=#76777e></td>
    <td width="1" height="1"
bgcolor=#7d7f86></td>
    <td width="1" height="1"
bgcolor=#686870></td>
    <td width="1" height="1"
bgcolor=#464a52></td>
    <td width="1" height="1"
bgcolor=#253038></td>
    <td width="1" height="1"
bgcolor=#3a3e46></td>
    <td width="1" height="1"
bgcolor=#5e5f66></td>
    <td width="1" height="1"
bgcolor=#838288></td>
    <td width="1" height="1"
bgcolor=#7e7b82></td>
    <td width="1" height="1"
bgcolor=#85858a></td>
    <td width="1" height="1"
bgcolor=#939498></td>
    <td width="1" height="1"
bgcolor=#8a8a8e></td>
    <td width="1" height="1"
bgcolor=#7a797f></td>
    <td width="1" height="1"
bgcolor=#6b6c6d></td>
  </tr>
  <tr>
    <td width="1" height="1"
bgcolor=#60575a></td>
    <td width="1" height="1"
bgcolor=#5a5659></td>
    <td width="1" height="1"
bgcolor=#5b5558></td>
    <td width="1" height="1"
bgcolor=#595458></td>
    <td width="1" height="1"
bgcolor=#646266></td>
    <td width="1" height="1"
bgcolor=#615e65></td>
    <td rowspan="1"
colspan="2" width="1"
height="1"
bgcolor=#686369></td>
    <td width="1" height="1"
bgcolor=#706c73></td>
    <td width="1" height="1"
bgcolor=#636063></td>
    <td width="1" height="1"
bgcolor=#6c6b6e></td>
    <td width="1" height="1"
bgcolor=#666369></td>
    <td width="1" height="1"
bgcolor=#6e6d72></td>
    <td width="1" height="1"
bgcolor=#6b686e></td>
    <td width="1" height="1"
bgcolor=#79757b></td>
    <td width="1" height="1"
bgcolor=#77747a></td>
    <td width="1" height="1"
bgcolor=#7d7c81></td>
    <td width="1" height="1"
bgcolor=#746f75></td>
    <td width="1" height="1"
bgcolor=#79767d></td>
    <td width="1" height="1"
bgcolor=#636163></td>
    <td width="1" height="1"
bgcolor=#4c4b50></td>
    <td width="1" height="1"
bgcolor=#787679></td>
    <td width="1" height="1"
bgcolor=#929093></td>
    <td width="1" height="1"
bgcolor=#8f8f91></td>
    <td width="1" height="1"
bgcolor=#89898b></td>
    <td width="1" height="1"
bgcolor=#88898a></td>
    <td width="1" height="1"
bgcolor=#8f8f91></td>
    <td width="1" height="1"
bgcolor=#89898b></td>
    <td width="1" height="1"
bgcolor=#67666c></td>
    <td width="1" height="1"
bgcolor=#96959a></td>
    <td width="1" height="1"
bgcolor=#7f7b7c></td>
    <td width="1" height="1"
bgcolor=#847a79></td>
    <td width="1" height="1"
bgcolor=#978e87></td>
    <td width="1" height="1"
bgcolor=#898480></td>
    <td width="1" height="1"
bgcolor=#807571></td>
    <td width="1" height="1"
bgcolor=#827d79></td>
    <td width="1" height="1"
bgcolor=#a19790></td>
    <td width="1" height="1"
bgcolor=#87796c></td>
    <td width="1" height="1"
bgcolor=#a39b8e></td>
    <td width="1" height="1"
bgcolor=#afa39a></td>
    <td width="1" height="1"
bgcolor=#a0978a></td>
    <td width="1" height="1"
bgcolor=#938a81></td>
    <td width="1" height="1"
bgcolor=#b1a89f></td>
    <td width="1" height="1"
bgcolor=#9d9894></td>
    <td width="1" height="1"
bgcolor=#bbb1ad></td>
    <td width="1" height="1"
bgcolor=#bfb6ac></td>
    <td width="1" height="1"
bgcolor=#d3cfc7></td>
    <td width="1" height="1"
bgcolor=#b1b5b5></td>
    <td width="1" height="1"
bgcolor=#b0b3b8></td>
    <td width="1" height="1"
bgcolor=#a3a7ac></td>
    <td width="1" height="1"
bgcolor=#9e9fa3></td>
    <td width="1" height="1"
bgcolor=#9d9ea2></td>
    <td width="1" height="1"
bgcolor=#9e9ea2></td>
    <td width="1" height="1"
bgcolor=#8a898e></td>
    <td width="1" height="1"
bgcolor=#7a7981></td>
    <td width="1" height="1"
bgcolor=#76747e></td>
    <td width="1" height="1"
bgcolor=#6d6e78></td>
    <td width="1" height="1"
bgcolor=#5c5d68></td>
    <td width="1" height="1"
bgcolor=#5e5e6b></td>
    <td width="1" height="1"
bgcolor=#4c4c58></td>
    <td width="1" height="1"
bgcolor=#73747a></td>
```

```
    <td rowspan="1" colspan="2" width="1" height="1" bgcolor=#8c8b91></td>
    <td width="1" height="1" bgcolor=#949398></td>
    <td width="1" height="1" bgcolor=#a1a0a5></td>
    <td width="1" height="1" bgcolor=#939295></td>
    <td width="1" height="1" bgcolor=#a1a1a3></td>
    <td width="1" height="1" bgcolor=#9d9ea0></td>
    <td width="1" height="1" bgcolor=#9fa0a1></td>
    <td width="1" height="1" bgcolor=#9a999e></td>
    <td width="1" height="1" bgcolor=#919095></td>
    <td width="1" height="1" bgcolor=#737575></td>
  </tr>
  <tr>
    <td width="1" height="1" bgcolor=#534e50></td>
    <td width="1" height="1" bgcolor=#646265></td>
    <td width="1" height="1" bgcolor=#666367></td>
    <td width="1" height="1" bgcolor=#615e62></td>
    <td width="1" height="1" bgcolor=#636066></td>
    <td width="1" height="1" bgcolor=#656267></td>
    <td width="1" height="1" bgcolor=#6b686c></td>
    <td width="1" height="1" bgcolor=#737076></td>
    <td width="1" height="1" bgcolor=#78757b></td>
    <td width="1" height="1" bgcolor=#807c82></td>
    <td width="1" height="1" bgcolor=#737277></td>
    <td width="1" height="1" bgcolor=#737075></td>
    <td width="1" height="1" bgcolor=#646264></td>
    <td width="1" height="1" bgcolor=#767478></td>
    <td width="1" height="1" bgcolor=#858086></td>
    <td width="1" height="1" bgcolor=#716c72></td>
    <td width="1" height="1" bgcolor=#7c7c7e></td>
    <td width="1" height="1" bgcolor=#7c7a7d></td>
    <td width="1" height="1" bgcolor=#403f3f></td>
    <td width="1" height="1" bgcolor=#99989b></td>
    <td width="1" height="1" bgcolor=#868389></td>
    <td width="1" height="1" bgcolor=#7d7b7e></td>
    <td width="1" height="1" bgcolor=#86858a></td>
    <td width="1" height="1" bgcolor=#8a878d></td>
    <td width="1" height="1" bgcolor=#78757b></td>
    <td width="1" height="1" bgcolor=#848187></td>
    <td width="1" height="1" bgcolor=#919095></td>
    <td width="1" height="1" bgcolor=#848185></td>
    <td width="1" height="1" bgcolor=#8b878a></td>
    <td width="1" height="1" bgcolor=#8f9190></td>
    <td width="1" height="1" bgcolor=#8e8a89></td>
    <td width="1" height="1" bgcolor=#98968c></td>
    <td width="1" height="1" bgcolor=#9f968f></td>
    <td width="1" height="1" bgcolor=#958d83></td>
    <td width="1" height="1" bgcolor=#85807d></td>
    <td width="1" height="1" bgcolor=#726d6a></td>
    <td width="1" height="1" bgcolor=#aeaba0></td>
    <td width="1" height="1" bgcolor=#8a7a6d></td>
    <td width="1" height="1" bgcolor=#9b9285></td>
    <td width="1" height="1" bgcolor=#b3aca1></td>
    <td width="1" height="1" bgcolor=#958980></td>
    <td width="1" height="1" bgcolor=#817775></td>
    <td width="1" height="1" bgcolor=#a8a39e></td>
    <td width="1" height="1" bgcolor=#a19c96></td>
    <td width="1" height="1" bgcolor=#b2aba2></td>
    <td width="1" height="1" bgcolor=#aea9a3></td>
    <td width="1" height="1" bgcolor=#aea39a></td>
    <td width="1" height="1" bgcolor=#e1e2e2></td>
    <td width="1" height="1" bgcolor=#a7acaf></td>
    <td width="1" height="1" bgcolor=#acb1b4></td>
    <td width="1" height="1" bgcolor=#a5a9ad></td>
    <td width="1" height="1" bgcolor=#b0b1b5></td>
    <td width="1" height="1" bgcolor=#9c9da1></td>
    <td width="1" height="1" bgcolor=#9b9ca0></td>
    <td width="1" height="1" bgcolor=#a1a2a6></td>
    <td width="1" height="1" bgcolor=#a3a4a8></td>
    <td width="1" height="1" bgcolor=#a1a0a5></td>
    <td width="1" height="1" bgcolor=#9ea0a2></td>
    <td width="1" height="1" bgcolor=#a9aaac></td>
    <td width="1" height="1" bgcolor=#9a9b9d></td>
    <td width="1" height="1" bgcolor=#a3a4a6></td>
    <td width="1" height="1" bgcolor=#a1a1a3></td>
    <td width="1" height="1" bgcolor=#949497></td>
    <td width="1" height="1" bgcolor=#959597></td>
    <td width="1" height="1" bgcolor=#9c9c9c></td>
    <td width="1" height="1" bgcolor=#9f9f9f></td>
    <td width="1" height="1" bgcolor=#979798></td>
    <td width="1" height="1" bgcolor=#9fa1a2></td>
    <td width="1" height="1" bgcolor=#9f9fa1></td>
    <td width="1" height="1" bgcolor=#99989b></td>
    <td width="1" height="1" bgcolor=#9fa1a2></td>
    <td width="1" height="1" bgcolor=#7b7c7c></td>
  </tr>
  <tr>
    <td width="1" height="1" bgcolor=#545154></td>
    <td width="1" height="1" bgcolor=#575459></td>
```

```
    <td width="1" height="1"
bgcolor=#5f5b5f></td>
    <td width="1" height="1"
bgcolor=#5f5e61></td>
    <td width="1" height="1"
bgcolor=#6d6a70></td>
    <td width="1" height="1"
bgcolor=#656364></td>
    <td width="1" height="1"
bgcolor=#484647></td>
    <td width="1" height="1"
bgcolor=#88878b></td>
    <td width="1" height="1"
bgcolor=#817e83></td>
    <td width="1" height="1"
bgcolor=#6f6c6f></td>
    <td width="1" height="1"
bgcolor=#817e81></td>
    <td width="1" height="1"
bgcolor=#837f85></td>
    <td width="1" height="1"
bgcolor=#787679></td>
    <td width="1" height="1"
bgcolor=#909093></td>
    <td width="1" height="1"
bgcolor=#8d8c91></td>
    <td width="1" height="1"
bgcolor=#8a8a8c></td>
    <td width="1" height="1"
bgcolor=#817d83></td>
    <td width="1" height="1"
bgcolor=#767177></td>
    <td width="1" height="1"
bgcolor=#89868c></td>
    <td width="1" height="1"
bgcolor=#919195></td>
    <td width="1" height="1"
bgcolor=#525051></td>
    <td width="1" height="1"
bgcolor=#959394></td>
    <td width="1" height="1"
bgcolor=#929294></td>
    <td width="1" height="1"
bgcolor=#787678></td>
    <td width="1" height="1"
bgcolor=#747378></td>
    <td width="1" height="1"
bgcolor=#89878a></td>
    <td width="1" height="1"
bgcolor=#919193></td>
    <td width="1" height="1"
bgcolor=#7d7a81></td>
    <td width="1" height="1"
bgcolor=#5b595c></td>
    <td width="1" height="1"
bgcolor=#969190></td>
    <td width="1" height="1"
bgcolor=#8a857e></td>
    <td width="1" height="1"
bgcolor=#aca497></td>
    <td width="1" height="1"
bgcolor=#a19d92></td>
    <td width="1" height="1"
bgcolor=#9e958c></td>
    <td width="1" height="1"
bgcolor=#918c88></td>
    <td width="1" height="1"
bgcolor=#615755></td>
    <td width="1" height="1"
bgcolor=#898481></td>
    <td width="1" height="1"
bgcolor=#968b7b></td>
    <td width="1" height="1"
bgcolor=#a59d8e></td>
    <td width="1" height="1"
bgcolor=#aeaca2></td>
    <td width="1" height="1"
bgcolor=#ada69c></td>
    <td width="1" height="1"
bgcolor=#b4aca7></td>
    <td width="1" height="1"
bgcolor=#a3a49e></td>
    <td width="1" height="1"
bgcolor=#98938f></td>
    <td width="1" height="1"
bgcolor=#9c9492></td>
    <td width="1" height="1"
bgcolor=#9e9492></td>
    <td width="1" height="1"
bgcolor=#bbb8b5></td>
    <td width="1" height="1"
bgcolor=#e8ece6></td>
    <td width="1" height="1"
bgcolor=#a5a6aa></td>
    <td width="1" height="1"
bgcolor=#a2a5a9></td>
    <td width="1" height="1"
bgcolor=#a4a5a9></td>
    <td width="1" height="1"
bgcolor=#a0a1a5></td>
    <td width="1" height="1"
bgcolor=#a0a3a7></td>
    <td width="1" height="1"
bgcolor=#9e9fa4></td>
    <td width="1" height="1"
bgcolor=#96979b></td>
    <td width="1" height="1"
bgcolor=#a9aaae></td>
    <td width="1" height="1"
bgcolor=#a1a4a7></td>
    <td width="1" height="1"
bgcolor=#9d9da2></td>
    <td width="1" height="1"
bgcolor=#818488></td>
    <td width="1" height="1"
bgcolor=#a3a5a6></td>
    <td width="1" height="1"
bgcolor=#9c9d9e></td>
    <td width="1" height="1"
bgcolor=#a8abac></td>
    <td width="1" height="1"
bgcolor=#a7a7a9></td>
    <td width="1" height="1"
bgcolor=#a6a7a6></td>
    <td width="1" height="1"
bgcolor=#aaabac></td>
    <td rowspan="1"
colspan="2" width="1"
height="1"
bgcolor=#9e9ea0></td>
    <td width="1" height="1"
bgcolor=#8b8c8e></td>
    <td width="1" height="1"
bgcolor=#a5a7a7></td>
    <td width="1" height="1"
bgcolor=#a8aaa9></td>
    <td width="1" height="1"
bgcolor=#a3a5a4></td>
    <td width="1" height="1"
bgcolor=#757778></td>
  </tr>
  <tr>
    <td width="1" height="1"
bgcolor=#625d61></td>
    <td width="1" height="1"
bgcolor=#67666b></td>
    <td width="1" height="1"
bgcolor=#737076></td>
    <td width="1" height="1"
bgcolor=#676367></td>
    <td width="1" height="1"
bgcolor=#757278></td>
    <td width="1" height="1"
bgcolor=#747072></td>
    <td width="1" height="1"
bgcolor=#6b676a></td>
    <td width="1" height="1"
bgcolor=#77747a></td>
    <td width="1" height="1"
bgcolor=#797679></td>
    <td width="1" height="1"
bgcolor=#706e71></td>
    <td width="1" height="1"
bgcolor=#747275></td>
    <td width="1" height="1"
bgcolor=#707075></td>
    <td width="1" height="1"
bgcolor=#726e70></td>
    <td width="1" height="1"
bgcolor=#5e5a5d></td>
    <td width="1" height="1"
bgcolor=#6a676d></td>
    <td width="1" height="1"
bgcolor=#858288></td>
```

```
    <td width="1" height="1" bgcolor=#848287></td>
    <td width="1" height="1" bgcolor=#7e7b7e></td>
    <td width="1" height="1" bgcolor=#555356></td>
    <td width="1" height="1" bgcolor=#79787b></td>
    <td width="1" height="1" bgcolor=#a1a1a3></td>
    <td width="1" height="1" bgcolor=#909092></td>
    <td width="1" height="1" bgcolor=#98989a></td>
    <td width="1" height="1" bgcolor=#949496></td>
    <td width="1" height="1" bgcolor=#959597></td>
    <td width="1" height="1" bgcolor=#8f8e8e></td>
    <td width="1" height="1" bgcolor=#87878a></td>
    <td width="1" height="1" bgcolor=#949398></td>
    <td width="1" height="1" bgcolor=#919394></td>
    <td width="1" height="1" bgcolor=#8a8484></td>
    <td width="1" height="1" bgcolor=#9b9890></td>
    <td width="1" height="1" bgcolor=#a19b95></td>
    <td width="1" height="1" bgcolor=#a99d8f></td>
    <td width="1" height="1" bgcolor=#928b83></td>
    <td width="1" height="1" bgcolor=#827f75></td>
    <td width="1" height="1" bgcolor=#726461></td>
    <td width="1" height="1" bgcolor=#a59b99></td>
    <td width="1" height="1" bgcolor=#afaba2></td>
    <td width="1" height="1" bgcolor=#aca3a0></td>
    <td width="1" height="1" bgcolor=#88837f></td>
    <td width="1" height="1" bgcolor=#988f8e></td>
    <td width="1" height="1" bgcolor=#9b897b></td>
    <td width="1" height="1" bgcolor=#999490></td>
    <td width="1" height="1" bgcolor=#a69c96></td>
    <td width="1" height="1" bgcolor=#aea59c></td>
    <td width="1" height="1" bgcolor=#c6c2bb></td>
    <td width="1" height="1" bgcolor=#aea39b></td>
    <td width="1" height="1" bgcolor=#dad8d9></td>
    <td width="1" height="1" bgcolor=#a8a7ad></td>
    <td width="1" height="1" bgcolor=#747379></td>
    <td width="1" height="1" bgcolor=#a2a3a8></td>
    <td width="1" height="1" bgcolor=#a8a9ad></td>
    <td width="1" height="1" bgcolor=#a8aaac></td>
    <td width="1" height="1" bgcolor=#a8a9ad></td>
    <td width="1" height="1" bgcolor=#a4a5a9></td>
    <td width="1" height="1" bgcolor=#a1a2a6></td>
    <td width="1" height="1" bgcolor=#9b9b9f></td>
    <td width="1" height="1" bgcolor=#8d8f93></td>
    <td width="1" height="1" bgcolor=#8f9092></td>
    <td width="1" height="1" bgcolor=#9b9c9d></td>
    <td width="1" height="1" bgcolor=#a4a6a7></td>
    <td width="1" height="1" bgcolor=#959597></td>
    <td width="1" height="1" bgcolor=#8c8c8e></td>
    <td width="1" height="1" bgcolor=#949496></td>
    <td width="1" height="1" bgcolor=#8f8f90></td>
    <td width="1" height="1" bgcolor=#a0a0a0></td>
    <td width="1" height="1" bgcolor=#a8a9aa></td>
    <td width="1" height="1" bgcolor=#aeb0b1></td>
    <td width="1" height="1" bgcolor=#a6a7a9></td>
    <td width="1" height="1" bgcolor=#a7a8a8></td>
    <td width="1" height="1" bgcolor=#a7a7a8></td>
    <td width="1" height="1" bgcolor=#828383></td>
  </tr>
  <tr>
    <td width="1" height="1" bgcolor=#6e6b6e></td>
    <td width="1" height="1" bgcolor=#78747b></td>
    <td width="1" height="1" bgcolor=#777479></td>
    <td width="1" height="1" bgcolor=#7b777e></td>
    <td width="1" height="1" bgcolor=#757379></td>
    <td width="1" height="1" bgcolor=#85858a></td>
    <td width="1" height="1" bgcolor=#605c62></td>
    <td width="1" height="1" bgcolor=#78767c></td>
    <td width="1" height="1" bgcolor=#5e595c></td>
    <td width="1" height="1" bgcolor=#524b4f></td>
    <td width="1" height="1" bgcolor=#383636></td>
    <td width="1" height="1" bgcolor=#575758></td>
    <td width="1" height="1" bgcolor=#7a787b></td>
    <td width="1" height="1" bgcolor=#807e82></td>
    <td width="1" height="1" bgcolor=#8f8e93></td>
    <td width="1" height="1" bgcolor=#929196></td>
    <td width="1" height="1" bgcolor=#8b8a8d></td>
    <td width="1" height="1" bgcolor=#8e8f93></td>
    <td width="1" height="1" bgcolor=#9d9d9f></td>
    <td width="1" height="1" bgcolor=#8a888b></td>
    <td width="1" height="1" bgcolor=#6d6970></td>
    <td width="1" height="1" bgcolor=#87848a></td>
    <td width="1" height="1" bgcolor=#959394></td>
    <td width="1" height="1" bgcolor=#9a9a9a></td>
    <td width="1" height="1" bgcolor=#8c8a8d></td>
    <td width="1" height="1" bgcolor=#858386></td>
    <td width="1" height="1" bgcolor=#817f82></td>
    <td width="1" height="1" bgcolor=#838184></td>
    <td width="1" height="1" bgcolor=#6e6c6f></td>
    <td width="1" height="1" bgcolor=#87847f></td>
```

```
    <td width="1" height="1"
bgcolor=#a69f97></td>
    <td width="1" height="1"
bgcolor=#a09c93></td>
    <td width="1" height="1"
bgcolor=#a1998c></td>
    <td width="1" height="1"
bgcolor=#867d74></td>
    <td width="1" height="1"
bgcolor=#82786f></td>
    <td width="1" height="1"
bgcolor=#8a7e76></td>
    <td width="1" height="1"
bgcolor=#61615f></td>
    <td width="1" height="1"
bgcolor=#23252f></td>
    <td width="1" height="1"
bgcolor=#826e67></td>
    <td width="1" height="1"
bgcolor=#57575a></td>
    <td width="1" height="1"
bgcolor=#b09c8b></td>
    <td width="1" height="1"
bgcolor=#534e55></td>
    <td width="1" height="1"
bgcolor=#a49a96></td>
    <td width="1" height="1"
bgcolor=#b6aca2></td>
    <td width="1" height="1"
bgcolor=#c6bcb2></td>
    <td width="1" height="1"
bgcolor=#c4bcae></td>
    <td width="1" height="1"
bgcolor=#beb4aa></td>
    <td width="1" height="1"
bgcolor=#c7c2b9></td>
    <td width="1" height="1"
bgcolor=#c5c8ca></td>
    <td width="1" height="1"
bgcolor=#a0a1a6></td>
    <td width="1" height="1"
bgcolor=#909196></td>
    <td width="1" height="1"
bgcolor=#9a9b9f></td>
    <td width="1" height="1"
bgcolor=#a2a3a7></td>
    <td width="1" height="1"
bgcolor=#a6a5aa></td>
    <td width="1" height="1"
bgcolor=#a2a4a5></td>
    <td width="1" height="1"
bgcolor=#b0b1b4></td>
    <td width="1" height="1"
bgcolor=#a1a2a6></td>
    <td width="1" height="1"
bgcolor=#abacb0></td>
    <td width="1" height="1"
bgcolor=#b7b8bc></td>
    <td width="1" height="1"
bgcolor=#a3a4a8></td>
    <td width="1" height="1"
bgcolor=#a6a9a9></td>
    <td width="1" height="1"
bgcolor=#a1a3a2></td>
    <td width="1" height="1"
bgcolor=#b1b3b2></td>
    <td width="1" height="1"
bgcolor=#abaead></td>
    <td width="1" height="1"
bgcolor=#a6a7a6></td>
    <td width="1" height="1"
bgcolor=#9fa1a0></td>
    <td width="1" height="1"
bgcolor=#a8aaa7></td>
    <td width="1" height="1"
bgcolor=#a5a7a7></td>
    <td width="1" height="1"
bgcolor=#999b9a></td>
    <td width="1" height="1"
bgcolor=#aeb0ae></td>
    <td width="1" height="1"
bgcolor=#b1b1b2></td>
    <td width="1" height="1"
bgcolor=#727474></td>
  </tr>
  <tr>
    <td width="1" height="1"
bgcolor=#0b0b0e></td>
    <td width="1" height="1"
bgcolor=#414042></td>
    <td width="1" height="1"
bgcolor=#494749></td>
    <td width="1" height="1"
bgcolor=#5f5e61></td>
    <td width="1" height="1"
bgcolor=#848486></td>
    <td width="1" height="1"
bgcolor=#817f84></td>
    <td width="1" height="1"
bgcolor=#838285></td>
    <td width="1" height="1"
bgcolor=#7e7d81></td>
    <td width="1" height="1"
bgcolor=#7c7a7f></td>
    <td width="1" height="1"
bgcolor=#726f74></td>
    <td width="1" height="1"
bgcolor=#6f6c6f></td>
    <td width="1" height="1"
bgcolor=#646063></td>
    <td width="1" height="1"
bgcolor=#6e6b71></td>
    <td width="1" height="1"
bgcolor=#909092></td>
    <td width="1" height="1"
bgcolor=#949596></td>
    <td width="1" height="1"
bgcolor=#999b9c></td>
    <td width="1" height="1"
bgcolor=#8d8d8f></td>
    <td width="1" height="1"
bgcolor=#a6a8a7></td>
    <td width="1" height="1"
bgcolor=#a7a7a7></td>
    <td width="1" height="1"
bgcolor=#969495></td>
    <td width="1" height="1"
bgcolor=#aaacab></td>
    <td width="1" height="1"
bgcolor=#a9a9a9></td>
    <td width="1" height="1"
bgcolor=#a6a5a3></td>
    <td width="1" height="1"
bgcolor=#9e9c9b></td>
    <td width="1" height="1"
bgcolor=#888787></td>
    <td width="1" height="1"
bgcolor=#545354></td>
    <td width="1" height="1"
bgcolor=#2f2e2f></td>
    <td width="1" height="1"
bgcolor=#767477></td>
    <td width="1" height="1"
bgcolor=#6e6a6d></td>
    <td width="1" height="1"
bgcolor=#857f7e></td>
    <td width="1" height="1"
bgcolor=#9c958c></td>
    <td width="1" height="1"
bgcolor=#a0998e></td>
    <td width="1" height="1"
bgcolor=#a09887></td>
    <td width="1" height="1"
bgcolor=#8c7e6f></td>
    <td width="1" height="1"
bgcolor=#846a59></td>
    <td width="1" height="1"
bgcolor=#99918c></td>
    <td width="1" height="1"
bgcolor=#9b948c></td>
    <td width="1" height="1"
bgcolor=#4b4c4c></td>
    <td width="1" height="1"
bgcolor=#8e7e6f></td>
    <td width="1" height="1"
bgcolor=#a29d94></td>
    <td width="1" height="1"
bgcolor=#44424e></td>
    <td width="1" height="1"
bgcolor=#7f6d6f></td>
    <td width="1" height="1"
bgcolor=#796b6a></td>
    <td width="1" height="1"
bgcolor=#bfb6a9></td>
```

```
    <td width="1" height="1" bgcolor=#cbc3b5></td>
    <td width="1" height="1" bgcolor=#c6beb1></td>
    <td width="1" height="1" bgcolor=#c2b8ae></td>
    <td width="1" height="1" bgcolor=#c6bcb1></td>
    <td width="1" height="1" bgcolor=#abadae></td>
    <td width="1" height="1" bgcolor=#a1a4a8></td>
    <td width="1" height="1" bgcolor=#afb0b5></td>
    <td width="1" height="1" bgcolor=#a5a6a9></td>
    <td width="1" height="1" bgcolor=#babdc1></td>
    <td width="1" height="1" bgcolor=#b8bdc1></td>
    <td width="1" height="1" bgcolor=#adb0b4></td>
    <td width="1" height="1" bgcolor=#aeb1b4></td>
    <td width="1" height="1" bgcolor=#b1b2b7></td>
    <td width="1" height="1" bgcolor=#949697></td>
    <td width="1" height="1" bgcolor=#a6a6a8></td>
    <td width="1" height="1" bgcolor=#abacae></td>
    <td width="1" height="1" bgcolor=#b5b7b8></td>
    <td width="1" height="1" bgcolor=#b1b3b2></td>
    <td width="1" height="1" bgcolor=#b6b8b7></td>
    <td width="1" height="1" bgcolor=#afb1b1></td>
    <td width="1" height="1" bgcolor=#b4b4b5></td>
    <td width="1" height="1" bgcolor=#919192></td>
    <td width="1" height="1" bgcolor=#ababa9></td>
    <td width="1" height="1" bgcolor=#9c9c9c></td>
    <td width="1" height="1" bgcolor=#b0b2b0></td>
    <td width="1" height="1" bgcolor=#a6a5a4></td>
    <td width="1" height="1" bgcolor=#818182></td>
    <td width="1" height="1" bgcolor=#80807f></td>
  </tr>
  <tr>
    <td width="1" height="1" bgcolor=#58575b></td>
    <td width="1" height="1" bgcolor=#7d7a7f></td>
    <td width="1" height="1" bgcolor=#504e4f></td>
    <td width="1" height="1" bgcolor=#353333></td>
    <td width="1" height="1" bgcolor=#4e4b4e></td>
    <td width="1" height="1" bgcolor=#858486></td>
    <td width="1" height="1" bgcolor=#6e6c71></td>
    <td width="1" height="1" bgcolor=#8c8c90></td>
    <td width="1" height="1" bgcolor=#858489></td>
    <td rowspan="1" colspan="2" width="1" height="1" bgcolor=#8b8a8f></td>
    <td width="1" height="1" bgcolor=#8a888d></td>
    <td width="1" height="1" bgcolor=#8b888f></td>
    <td width="1" height="1" bgcolor=#88878c></td>
    <td width="1" height="1" bgcolor=#939296></td>
    <td width="1" height="1" bgcolor=#8e8e90></td>
    <td width="1" height="1" bgcolor=#919192></td>
    <td width="1" height="1" bgcolor=#9b9ba0></td>
    <td rowspan="1" colspan="2" width="1" height="1" bgcolor=#929294></td>
    <td width="1" height="1" bgcolor=#818181></td>
    <td width="1" height="1" bgcolor=#9b9b9b></td>
    <td width="1" height="1" bgcolor=#a9a9a7></td>
    <td width="1" height="1" bgcolor=#a1a1a1></td>
    <td width="1" height="1" bgcolor=#9a999c></td>
    <td width="1" height="1" bgcolor=#7b7b7d></td>
    <td width="1" height="1" bgcolor=#6b6768></td>
    <td width="1" height="1" bgcolor=#8e8e8e></td>
    <td width="1" height="1" bgcolor=#a7a7a5></td>
    <td width="1" height="1" bgcolor=#827e7d></td>
    <td width="1" height="1" bgcolor=#99928a></td>
    <td width="1" height="1" bgcolor=#a9a08f></td>
    <td width="1" height="1" bgcolor=#948c80></td>
    <td width="1" height="1" bgcolor=#6e6558></td>
    <td width="1" height="1" bgcolor=#8c817f></td>
    <td width="1" height="1" bgcolor=#484545></td>
    <td width="1" height="1" bgcolor=#142a3a></td>
    <td width="1" height="1" bgcolor=#858177></td>
    <td width="1" height="1" bgcolor=#918474></td>
    <td width="1" height="1" bgcolor=#716e7a></td>
    <td width="1" height="1" bgcolor=#5c565b></td>
    <td width="1" height="1" bgcolor=#8b7e77></td>
    <td width="1" height="1" bgcolor=#9c8c7f></td>
    <td width="1" height="1" bgcolor=#a69c8d></td>
    <td rowspan="1" colspan="2" width="1" height="1" bgcolor=#bfbeb4></td>
    <td width="1" height="1" bgcolor=#c0bcb3></td>
    <td width="1" height="1" bgcolor=#b6b7b7></td>
    <td width="1" height="1" bgcolor=#afb2b6></td>
    <td width="1" height="1" bgcolor=#b6b7bb></td>
    <td width="1" height="1" bgcolor=#bbbcc0></td>
    <td width="1" height="1" bgcolor=#b3b4b8></td>
    <td width="1" height="1" bgcolor=#b8bbbf></td>
    <td width="1" height="1" bgcolor=#b4b5b9></td>
    <td width="1" height="1" bgcolor=#a9abb0></td>
    <td width="1" height="1" bgcolor=#aaadae></td>
    <td width="1" height="1" bgcolor=#a4a7aa></td>
    <td width="1" height="1" bgcolor=#b3b6ba></td>
```

```
    <td width="1" height="1"
bgcolor=#afb2b6></td>
    <td width="1" height="1"
bgcolor=#868689></td>
    <td width="1" height="1"
bgcolor=#4f4e4c></td>
    <td width="1" height="1"
bgcolor=#3a3935></td>
    <td width="1" height="1"
bgcolor=#2b2825></td>
    <td width="1" height="1"
bgcolor=#464441></td>
    <td width="1" height="1"
bgcolor=#767473></td>
    <td width="1" height="1"
bgcolor=#a3a1a0></td>
    <td width="1" height="1"
bgcolor=#82837f></td>
    <td width="1" height="1"
bgcolor=#b9bdbc></td>
    <td width="1" height="1"
bgcolor=#b6b9b8></td>
    <td width="1" height="1"
bgcolor=#a7a6a7></td>
    <td width="1" height="1"
bgcolor=#4a4a47></td>
    <td width="1" height="1"
bgcolor=#464843></td>
  </tr>
  <tr>
    <td width="1" height="1"
bgcolor=#5f5c5c></td>
    <td width="1" height="1"
bgcolor=#6d6a6f></td>
    <td width="1" height="1"
bgcolor=#7e7c7d></td>
    <td width="1" height="1"
bgcolor=#78767a></td>
    <td width="1" height="1"
bgcolor=#635f62></td>
    <td width="1" height="1"
bgcolor=#32312d></td>
    <td width="1" height="1"
bgcolor=#676166></td>
    <td width="1" height="1"
bgcolor=#79767b></td>
    <td width="1" height="1"
bgcolor=#807b80></td>
    <td width="1" height="1"
bgcolor=#919092></td>
    <td width="1" height="1"
bgcolor=#7d7b81></td>
    <td width="1" height="1"
bgcolor=#727073></td>
    <td width="1" height="1"
bgcolor=#908f94></td>
    <td width="1" height="1"
bgcolor=#7c7c7e></td>
    <td width="1" height="1"
bgcolor=#787679></td>
    <td width="1" height="1"
bgcolor=#8b888c></td>
    <td width="1" height="1"
bgcolor=#908e91></td>
    <td width="1" height="1"
bgcolor=#7d7d7f></td>
    <td width="1" height="1"
bgcolor=#908e8f></td>
    <td width="1" height="1"
bgcolor=#959397></td>
    <td width="1" height="1"
bgcolor=#9c9c9e></td>
    <td width="1" height="1"
bgcolor=#6c6a69></td>
    <td width="1" height="1"
bgcolor=#a3a4a2></td>
    <td width="1" height="1"
bgcolor=#9fa3a2></td>
    <td width="1" height="1"
bgcolor=#959595></td>
    <td width="1" height="1"
bgcolor=#adb1b0></td>
    <td width="1" height="1"
bgcolor=#a2a4a3></td>
    <td width="1" height="1"
bgcolor=#9f9d9e></td>
    <td width="1" height="1"
bgcolor=#9e9e9d></td>
    <td width="1" height="1"
bgcolor=#807b78></td>
    <td width="1" height="1"
bgcolor=#9a9187></td>
    <td width="1" height="1"
bgcolor=#aa9e8e></td>
    <td width="1" height="1"
bgcolor=#a0917d></td>
    <td width="1" height="1"
bgcolor=#605855></td>
    <td width="1" height="1"
bgcolor=#8d8a83></td>
    <td width="1" height="1"
bgcolor=#80766a></td>
    <td width="1" height="1"
bgcolor=#42312a></td>
    <td width="1" height="1"
bgcolor=#968d85></td>
    <td width="1" height="1"
bgcolor=#a49c97></td>
    <td width="1" height="1"
bgcolor=#6b6169></td>
    <td width="1" height="1"
bgcolor=#817372></td>
    <td width="1" height="1"
bgcolor=#7f766f></td>
    <td width="1" height="1"
bgcolor=#867872></td>
    <td width="1" height="1"
bgcolor=#f2f4f2></td>
    <td width="1" height="1"
bgcolor=#f4fdfa></td>
    <td width="1" height="1"
bgcolor=#a1a1a3></td>
    <td width="1" height="1"
bgcolor=#b3bab9></td>
    <td width="1" height="1"
bgcolor=#b9bcc0></td>
    <td width="1" height="1"
bgcolor=#b7babe></td>
    <td width="1" height="1"
bgcolor=#89868c></td>
    <td width="1" height="1"
bgcolor=#a0a0a5></td>
    <td width="1" height="1"
bgcolor=#b4b6b7></td>
    <td width="1" height="1"
bgcolor=#b5b6ba></td>
    <td width="1" height="1"
bgcolor=#b8bcbf></td>
    <td width="1" height="1"
bgcolor=#b7bbbe></td>
    <td width="1" height="1"
bgcolor=#b8bbbf></td>
    <td width="1" height="1"
bgcolor=#b4b9ba></td>
    <td width="1" height="1"
bgcolor=#afb2b3></td>
    <td width="1" height="1"
bgcolor=#6b6a6e></td>
    <td width="1" height="1"
bgcolor=#8d8d90></td>
    <td width="1" height="1"
bgcolor=#b8bbbc></td>
    <td width="1" height="1"
bgcolor=#bdc3c3></td>
    <td width="1" height="1"
bgcolor=#bdc1c2></td>
    <td width="1" height="1"
bgcolor=#bec2c3></td>
    <td width="1" height="1"
bgcolor=#bfc4c5></td>
    <td width="1" height="1"
bgcolor=#b8bcbd></td>
    <td width="1" height="1"
bgcolor=#b9bcbd></td>
    <td width="1" height="1"
bgcolor=#b4b6b6></td>
    <td width="1" height="1"
bgcolor=#afb2b1></td>
    <td width="1" height="1"
bgcolor=#b6bcba></td>
    <td width="1" height="1"
bgcolor=#bec1c5></td>
    <td width="1" height="1"
bgcolor=#898c8d></td>
```

```
</tr>
<tr>
<td width="1" height="1" bgcolor=#7d7b7d></td>
<td width="1" height="1" bgcolor=#828284></td>
<td width="1" height="1" bgcolor=#7e7b7e></td>
<td width="1" height="1" bgcolor=#807c83></td>
<td width="1" height="1" bgcolor=#848586></td>
<td width="1" height="1" bgcolor=#787578></td>
<td width="1" height="1" bgcolor=#7b7b7d></td>
<td width="1" height="1" bgcolor=#787578></td>
<td width="1" height="1" bgcolor=#747274></td>
<td width="1" height="1" bgcolor=#8d8d8f></td>
<td width="1" height="1" bgcolor=#929293></td>
<td width="1" height="1" bgcolor=#9e9e9e></td>
<td width="1" height="1" bgcolor=#878789></td>
<td width="1" height="1" bgcolor=#9a9a9c></td>
<td width="1" height="1" bgcolor=#8e9090></td>
<td width="1" height="1" bgcolor=#8d8d8d></td>
<td width="1" height="1" bgcolor=#8b8b8d></td>
<td width="1" height="1" bgcolor=#9c9e9d></td>
<td width="1" height="1" bgcolor=#a0a2a1></td>
<td width="1" height="1" bgcolor=#939393></td>
<td width="1" height="1" bgcolor=#8b8887></td>
<td width="1" height="1" bgcolor=#a6a8a7></td>
<td width="1" height="1" bgcolor=#a0a0a0></td>
<td width="1" height="1" bgcolor=#9e9d9d></td>
<td width="1" height="1" bgcolor=#a5a7a8></td>
<td width="1" height="1" bgcolor=#9b9b9b></td>
<td width="1" height="1" bgcolor=#9a9a98></td>
<td width="1" height="1" bgcolor=#807f7b></td>
<td width="1" height="1" bgcolor=#9fa29c></td>
<td width="1" height="1" bgcolor=#8a827f></td>
<td width="1" height="1" bgcolor=#94877e></td>
<td width="1" height="1" bgcolor=#ad9f8c></td>
<td width="1" height="1" bgcolor=#a19a80></td>
<td width="1" height="1" bgcolor=#5c5150></td>
<td width="1" height="1" bgcolor=#9b948a></td>
<td width="1" height="1" bgcolor=#816b62></td>
<td width="1" height="1" bgcolor=#592220></td>
<td width="1" height="1" bgcolor=#63413a></td>
<td width="1" height="1" bgcolor=#a29b93></td>
<td width="1" height="1" bgcolor=#aaa39b></td>
<td width="1" height="1" bgcolor=#a58f7e></td>
<td width="1" height="1" bgcolor=#8e6567></td>
<td width="1" height="1" bgcolor=#c7bcae></td>
<td width="1" height="1" bgcolor=#d8d7d7></td>
<td width="1" height="1" bgcolor=#fafcf8></td>
<td width="1" height="1" bgcolor=#b5b6b9></td>
<td width="1" height="1" bgcolor=#aaabad></td>
<td width="1" height="1" bgcolor=#b6b8b9></td>
<td width="1" height="1" bgcolor=#bbc0c1></td>
<td width="1" height="1" bgcolor=#bbbdbe></td>
<td width="1" height="1" bgcolor=#a0a0a2></td>
<td width="1" height="1" bgcolor=#989a9b></td>
<td width="1" height="1" bgcolor=#a9a8aa></td>
<td width="1" height="1" bgcolor=#abadae></td>
<td width="1" height="1" bgcolor=#ababab></td>
<td width="1" height="1" bgcolor=#abadae></td>
<td width="1" height="1" bgcolor=#b0b1b2></td>
<td width="1" height="1" bgcolor=#c0c6c6></td>
<td width="1" height="1" bgcolor=#c1c7c7></td>
<td width="1" height="1" bgcolor=#c1c5c6></td>
<td width="1" height="1" bgcolor=#c4c7ca></td>
<td width="1" height="1" bgcolor=#b6b9b8></td>
<td width="1" height="1" bgcolor=#b5b8b9></td>
<td width="1" height="1" bgcolor=#bac1c2></td>
<td width="1" height="1" bgcolor=#b9bbbb></td>
<td width="1" height="1" bgcolor=#c0c4c3></td>
<td width="1" height="1" bgcolor=#b4b7b6></td>
<td width="1" height="1" bgcolor=#bcbfc0></td>
<td width="1" height="1" bgcolor=#bcbec3></td>
<td width="1" height="1" bgcolor=#babebe></td>
<td width="1" height="1" bgcolor=#b7bcbb></td>
<td width="1" height="1" bgcolor=#8d918f></td>
</tr>
<tr>
<td width="1" height="1" bgcolor=#8c898b></td>
<td width="1" height="1" bgcolor=#949595></td>
<td width="1" height="1" bgcolor=#8e8d8e></td>
<td width="1" height="1" bgcolor=#919193></td>
<td width="1" height="1" bgcolor=#929093></td>
<td width="1" height="1" bgcolor=#8f9192></td>
<td width="1" height="1" bgcolor=#949295></td>
<td width="1" height="1" bgcolor=#7d7c7d></td>
<td width="1" height="1" bgcolor=#89898c></td>
<td width="1" height="1" bgcolor=#939395></td>
<td width="1" height="1" bgcolor=#908e91></td>
<td width="1" height="1" bgcolor=#8b898a></td>
<td width="1" height="1" bgcolor=#9c9c9d></td>
```

```
    <td width="1" height="1"
bgcolor=#777473></td>
    <td width="1" height="1"
bgcolor=#6c6666></td>
    <td width="1" height="1"
bgcolor=#8e8c8d></td>
    <td width="1" height="1"
bgcolor=#969692></td>
    <td width="1" height="1"
bgcolor=#878380></td>
    <td width="1" height="1"
bgcolor=#797672></td>
    <td width="1" height="1"
bgcolor=#888783></td>
    <td width="1" height="1"
bgcolor=#9fa19e></td>
    <td width="1" height="1"
bgcolor=#aaaaa8></td>
    <td width="1" height="1"
bgcolor=#aaaca9></td>
    <td width="1" height="1"
bgcolor=#b2b4b1></td>
    <td width="1" height="1"
bgcolor=#aaaba6></td>
    <td width="1" height="1"
bgcolor=#9e9e9c></td>
    <td width="1" height="1"
bgcolor=#939391></td>
    <td width="1" height="1"
bgcolor=#abadaa></td>
    <td width="1" height="1"
bgcolor=#9d9e9b></td>
    <td width="1" height="1"
bgcolor=#898682></td>
    <td width="1" height="1"
bgcolor=#9a927f></td>
    <td width="1" height="1"
bgcolor=#afa691></td>
    <td width="1" height="1"
bgcolor=#9d9483></td>
    <td width="1" height="1"
bgcolor=#989287></td>
    <td width="1" height="1"
bgcolor=#a69d94></td>
    <td width="1" height="1"
bgcolor=#86776c></td>
    <td width="1" height="1"
bgcolor=#7d5c51></td>
    <td width="1" height="1"
bgcolor=#877c74></td>
    <td width="1" height="1"
bgcolor=#988c88></td>
    <td width="1" height="1"
bgcolor=#946b66></td>
    <td width="1" height="1"
bgcolor=#ac9e91></td>
    <td width="1" height="1"
bgcolor=#b3aa99></td>
    <td width="1" height="1"
bgcolor=#d2d7d0></td>
    <td width="1" height="1"
bgcolor=#cbc7c2></td>
    <td width="1" height="1"
bgcolor=#e4e9e2></td>
    <td width="1" height="1"
bgcolor=#7f7f7f></td>
    <td width="1" height="1"
bgcolor=#bbbdc1></td>
    <td width="1" height="1"
bgcolor=#bdc0c4></td>
    <td width="1" height="1"
bgcolor=#bbbec2></td>
    <td width="1" height="1"
bgcolor=#babec2></td>
    <td width="1" height="1"
bgcolor=#b3b5b6></td>
    <td width="1" height="1"
bgcolor=#c1c4c9></td>
    <td width="1" height="1"
bgcolor=#c9cdd0></td>
    <td width="1" height="1"
bgcolor=#c8cdd1></td>
    <td width="1" height="1"
bgcolor=#c1c4c6></td>
    <td width="1" height="1"
bgcolor=#bfc3c6></td>
    <td width="1" height="1"
bgcolor=#c2c5c7></td>
    <td width="1" height="1"
bgcolor=#bfc2c3></td>
    <td width="1" height="1"
bgcolor=#a5a5a7></td>
    <td width="1" height="1"
bgcolor=#bcc0c1></td>
    <td width="1" height="1"
bgcolor=#bec2c5></td>
    <td width="1" height="1"
bgcolor=#babebb></td>
    <td width="1" height="1"
bgcolor=#b0b2ae></td>
    <td width="1" height="1"
bgcolor=#babfbf></td>
    <td width="1" height="1"
bgcolor=#b0b0b0></td>
    <td width="1" height="1"
bgcolor=#bcc0c0></td>
    <td width="1" height="1"
bgcolor=#c0c4c6></td>
    <td width="1" height="1"
bgcolor=#bbbfbf></td>
    <td width="1" height="1"
bgcolor=#bdc1c0></td>
    <td width="1" height="1"
bgcolor=#bbc1c1></td>
    <td width="1" height="1"
bgcolor=#b6bbbc></td>
    <td width="1" height="1"
bgcolor=#888c8c></td>
  </tr>
  <tr>
    <td width="1" height="1"
bgcolor=#8b8989></td>
    <td width="1" height="1"
bgcolor=#8c8b8c></td>
    <td width="1" height="1"
bgcolor=#8e8d8d></td>
    <td width="1" height="1"
bgcolor=#7a7879></td>
    <td width="1" height="1"
bgcolor=#908f90></td>
    <td width="1" height="1"
bgcolor=#676667></td>
    <td width="1" height="1"
bgcolor=#adafae></td>
    <td width="1" height="1"
bgcolor=#999999></td>
    <td width="1" height="1"
bgcolor=#8d8787></td>
    <td width="1" height="1"
bgcolor=#817e7d></td>
    <td width="1" height="1"
bgcolor=#a4a2a1></td>
    <td width="1" height="1"
bgcolor=#9c9d9a></td>
    <td width="1" height="1"
bgcolor=#a4a4a2></td>
    <td width="1" height="1"
bgcolor=#a3a5a2></td>
    <td width="1" height="1"
bgcolor=#abaaa9></td>
    <td width="1" height="1"
bgcolor=#969794></td>
    <td width="1" height="1"
bgcolor=#a4a2a1></td>
    <td width="1" height="1"
bgcolor=#a6a4a0></td>
    <td width="1" height="1"
bgcolor=#9f9d9b></td>
    <td width="1" height="1"
bgcolor=#90908d></td>
    <td width="1" height="1"
bgcolor=#817d7c></td>
    <td width="1" height="1"
bgcolor=#9e9c9b></td>
    <td width="1" height="1"
bgcolor=#969694></td>
    <td width="1" height="1"
bgcolor=#a5a6a4></td>
    <td width="1" height="1"
bgcolor=#aeb2af></td>
    <td width="1" height="1"
bgcolor=#a5a5a3></td>
    <td width="1" height="1"
bgcolor=#b8bbb8></td>
```

```
    <td width="1" height="1" bgcolor=#b0b4b2></td>
    <td width="1" height="1" bgcolor=#a8a5a6></td>
    <td width="1" height="1" bgcolor=#898078></td>
    <td width="1" height="1" bgcolor=#a49886></td>
    <td width="1" height="1" bgcolor=#9a8d73></td>
    <td width="1" height="1" bgcolor=#b9bbb7></td>
    <td width="1" height="1" bgcolor=#7d6d64></td>
    <td width="1" height="1" bgcolor=#60544a></td>
    <td width="1" height="1" bgcolor=#584639></td>
    <td width="1" height="1" bgcolor=#807369></td>
    <td width="1" height="1" bgcolor=#8a8477></td>
    <td width="1" height="1" bgcolor=#979286></td>
    <td width="1" height="1" bgcolor=#b3ad9f></td>
    <td width="1" height="1" bgcolor=#b9b4aa></td>
    <td width="1" height="1" bgcolor=#bfb3a2></td>
    <td width="1" height="1" bgcolor=#cac8bc></td>
    <td width="1" height="1" bgcolor=#dbdfd8></td>
    <td width="1" height="1" bgcolor=#dcdfdd></td>
    <td width="1" height="1" bgcolor=#c7cdd1></td>
    <td width="1" height="1" bgcolor=#b5b5b8></td>
    <td width="1" height="1" bgcolor=#969797></td>
    <td width="1" height="1" bgcolor=#bcbdc1></td>
    <td width="1" height="1" bgcolor=#babec0></td>
    <td width="1" height="1" bgcolor=#b9bbba></td>
    <td width="1" height="1" bgcolor=#c4c6c7></td>
    <td width="1" height="1" bgcolor=#bbbfc0></td>
    <td width="1" height="1" bgcolor=#c5c9ca></td>
    <td width="1" height="1" bgcolor=#c9ced1></td>
    <td width="1" height="1" bgcolor=#c5c8cb></td>
    <td width="1" height="1" bgcolor=#b4b7b7></td>
    <td width="1" height="1" bgcolor=#b7b7b7></td>
    <td width="1" height="1" bgcolor=#bfc3c2></td>
    <td width="1" height="1" bgcolor=#b8b8b8></td>
    <td width="1" height="1" bgcolor=#b9bdbc></td>
    <td width="1" height="1" bgcolor=#bdbfc2></td>
    <td width="1" height="1" bgcolor=#c5cbc9></td>
    <td width="1" height="1" bgcolor=#babcba></td>
    <td width="1" height="1" bgcolor=#aeadac></td>
    <td width="1" height="1" bgcolor=#b6b6b4></td>
    <td width="1" height="1" bgcolor=#b1b2ad></td>
    <td width="1" height="1" bgcolor=#a0a09f></td>
    <td width="1" height="1" bgcolor=#b4b7b7></td>
    <td width="1" height="1" bgcolor=#b4b6b3></td>
    <td width="1" height="1" bgcolor=#acafac></td>
    <td width="1" height="1" bgcolor=#878988></td>
  </tr>
  <tr>
    <td width="1" height="1" bgcolor=#85807f></td>
    <td width="1" height="1" bgcolor=#7f7d7e></td>
    <td width="1" height="1" bgcolor=#9b9c9a></td>
    <td width="1" height="1" bgcolor=#a5a5a3></td>
    <td width="1" height="1" bgcolor=#a6a7a5></td>
    <td width="1" height="1" bgcolor=#a4a5a3></td>
    <td width="1" height="1" bgcolor=#9e9e9c></td>
    <td width="1" height="1" bgcolor=#a2a1a0></td>
    <td width="1" height="1" bgcolor=#989994></td>
    <td width="1" height="1" bgcolor=#9d9e9a></td>
    <td width="1" height="1" bgcolor=#9c9a97></td>
    <td width="1" height="1" bgcolor=#918e8d></td>
    <td width="1" height="1" bgcolor=#8b8a86></td>
    <td width="1" height="1" bgcolor=#8b8a89></td>
    <td width="1" height="1" bgcolor=#9e9d9b></td>
    <td width="1" height="1" bgcolor=#908e8a></td>
    <td width="1" height="1" bgcolor=#a4a7a2></td>
    <td width="1" height="1" bgcolor=#8f8c88></td>
    <td width="1" height="1" bgcolor=#aaaba9></td>
    <td width="1" height="1" bgcolor=#b2b3b0></td>
    <td width="1" height="1" bgcolor=#b7b9b6></td>
    <td width="1" height="1" bgcolor=#adb0ad></td>
    <td width="1" height="1" bgcolor=#a4a39f></td>
    <td width="1" height="1" bgcolor=#bbbcb9></td>
    <td width="1" height="1" bgcolor=#bababa></td>
    <td width="1" height="1" bgcolor=#bcc1bf></td>
    <td width="1" height="1" bgcolor=#9c9999></td>
    <td width="1" height="1" bgcolor=#b8b9b7></td>
    <td width="1" height="1" bgcolor=#a09d99></td>
    <td width="1" height="1" bgcolor=#99948c></td>
    <td width="1" height="1" bgcolor=#9f9788></td>
    <td width="1" height="1" bgcolor=#b1a692></td>
    <td width="1" height="1" bgcolor=#b8b9b9></td>
    <td width="1" height="1" bgcolor=#a8a190></td>
    <td width="1" height="1" bgcolor=#9b9387></td>
    <td width="1" height="1" bgcolor=#948c80></td>
    <td width="1" height="1" bgcolor=#989489></td>
    <td width="1" height="1" bgcolor=#938376></td>
    <td width="1" height="1" bgcolor=#a49b8f></td>
    <td width="1" height="1" bgcolor=#b6aa9a></td>
    <td width="1" height="1" bgcolor=#a89686></td>
```

```
    <td width="1" height="1"
bgcolor=#b7ad9b></td>
    <td width="1" height="1"
bgcolor=#c7beaf></td>
    <td width="1" height="1"
bgcolor=#beb6a3></td>
    <td width="1" height="1"
bgcolor=#e1e2e0></td>
    <td width="1" height="1"
bgcolor=#c2c6c5></td>
    <td width="1" height="1"
bgcolor=#c1c4c7></td>
    <td width="1" height="1"
bgcolor=#ced3d7></td>
    <td width="1" height="1"
bgcolor=#c4c8c9></td>
    <td width="1" height="1"
bgcolor=#c3c7c8></td>
    <td width="1" height="1"
bgcolor=#cacccb></td>
    <td width="1" height="1"
bgcolor=#c0c2c3></td>
    <td width="1" height="1"
bgcolor=#a9a7a7></td>
    <td width="1" height="1"
bgcolor=#9b989b></td>
    <td width="1" height="1"
bgcolor=#b9bbb9></td>
    <td width="1" height="1"
bgcolor=#bebebe></td>
    <td width="1" height="1"
bgcolor=#bfc1c0></td>
    <td width="1" height="1"
bgcolor=#b4b4b2></td>
    <td width="1" height="1"
bgcolor=#a09f9d></td>
    <td width="1" height="1"
bgcolor=#bbbebd></td>
    <td width="1" height="1"
bgcolor=#b5b6b6></td>
    <td width="1" height="1"
bgcolor=#95948f></td>
    <td width="1" height="1"
bgcolor=#a8a7a2></td>
    <td width="1" height="1"
bgcolor=#675e5b></td>
    <td width="1" height="1"
bgcolor=#5f5a4d></td>
    <td width="1" height="1"
bgcolor=#86817d></td>
    <td width="1" height="1"
bgcolor=#b5b5b5></td>
    <td width="1" height="1"
bgcolor=#a8aaa7></td>
    <td width="1" height="1"
bgcolor=#999792></td>
    <td width="1" height="1"
bgcolor=#9d9b99></td>
    <td width="1" height="1"
bgcolor=#aaa8a8></td>
    <td width="1" height="1"
bgcolor=#868886></td>
  </tr>
  <tr>
    <td rowspan="2"
colspan="1" width="1"
height="1"
bgcolor=#918f8d></td>
    <td width="1" height="1"
bgcolor=#9f9d9d></td>
    <td width="1" height="1"
bgcolor=#9b9e9b></td>
    <td width="1" height="1"
bgcolor=#9a9998></td>
    <td width="1" height="1"
bgcolor=#a3a4a2></td>
    <td width="1" height="1"
bgcolor=#a1a19f></td>
    <td width="1" height="1"
bgcolor=#a4a3a2></td>
    <td width="1" height="1"
bgcolor=#9e9f9a></td>
    <td width="1" height="1"
bgcolor=#9e9e9e></td>
    <td width="1" height="1"
bgcolor=#a0a09b></td>
    <td width="1" height="1"
bgcolor=#afafad></td>
    <td width="1" height="1"
bgcolor=#a2a49e></td>
    <td width="1" height="1"
bgcolor=#999793></td>
    <td width="1" height="1"
bgcolor=#a6a8a2></td>
    <td width="1" height="1"
bgcolor=#a8a8a3></td>
    <td width="1" height="1"
bgcolor=#aaaba6></td>
    <td width="1" height="1"
bgcolor=#acada8></td>
    <td width="1" height="1"
bgcolor=#afb0ab></td>
    <td width="1" height="1"
bgcolor=#a5a5a3></td>
    <td width="1" height="1"
bgcolor=#a3a4a0></td>
    <td width="1" height="1"
bgcolor=#a3a29e></td>
    <td width="1" height="1"
bgcolor=#b1b0af></td>
    <td width="1" height="1"
bgcolor=#b7b9b6></td>
    <td width="1" height="1"
bgcolor=#b5b7b2></td>
    <td width="1" height="1"
bgcolor=#b4b4af></td>
    <td width="1" height="1"
bgcolor=#989590></td>
    <td width="1" height="1"
bgcolor=#adaeac></td>
    <td width="1" height="1"
bgcolor=#bec3c3></td>
    <td width="1" height="1"
bgcolor=#a9a9a9></td>
    <td width="1" height="1"
bgcolor=#9e9691></td>
    <td width="1" height="1"
bgcolor=#878070></td>
    <td width="1" height="1"
bgcolor=#998e7c></td>
    <td width="1" height="1"
bgcolor=#b6bab9></td>
    <td width="1" height="1"
bgcolor=#979893></td>
    <td width="1" height="1"
bgcolor=#99928a></td>
    <td width="1" height="1"
bgcolor=#a0968c></td>
    <td width="1" height="1"
bgcolor=#9f9989></td>
    <td width="1" height="1"
bgcolor=#a49e8e></td>
    <td width="1" height="1"
bgcolor=#a49b91></td>
    <td width="1" height="1"
bgcolor=#bab3a8></td>
    <td width="1" height="1"
bgcolor=#bcb8ad></td>
    <td width="1" height="1"
bgcolor=#bcb4a7></td>
    <td width="1" height="1"
bgcolor=#c9c6b9></td>
    <td width="1" height="1"
bgcolor=#d4d2c7></td>
    <td width="1" height="1"
bgcolor=#c3c1b3></td>
    <td width="1" height="1"
bgcolor=#ececf0></td>
    <td width="1" height="1"
bgcolor=#c0c2c2></td>
    <td width="1" height="1"
bgcolor=#c7c7cc></td>
    <td width="1" height="1"
bgcolor=#bcbebf></td>
    <td width="1" height="1"
bgcolor=#c4c6ca></td>
    <td width="1" height="1"
bgcolor=#babcbb></td>
    <td width="1" height="1"
bgcolor=#b4b4b5></td>
    <td width="1" height="1"
bgcolor=#bcbebd></td>
    <td width="1" height="1"
bgcolor=#b4b4b2></td>
```

```
    <td width="1" height="1" bgcolor=#b6b6b5></td>
    <td width="1" height="1" bgcolor=#b3b3b3></td>
    <td width="1" height="1" bgcolor=#adaaa7></td>
    <td width="1" height="1" bgcolor=#746e6e></td>
    <td width="1" height="1" bgcolor=#7f7875></td>
    <td width="1" height="1" bgcolor=#928d8a></td>
    <td width="1" height="1" bgcolor=#a19f9b></td>
    <td width="1" height="1" bgcolor=#85807e></td>
    <td width="1" height="1" bgcolor=#342b21></td>
    <td width="1" height="1" bgcolor=#4a4037></td>
    <td width="1" height="1" bgcolor=#4f4642></td>
    <td width="1" height="1" bgcolor=#625c57></td>
    <td width="1" height="1" bgcolor=#989590></td>
    <td width="1" height="1" bgcolor=#bcbcbc></td>
    <td width="1" height="1" bgcolor=#a6a7a3></td>
    <td width="1" height="1" bgcolor=#b9bab9></td>
    <td width="1" height="1" bgcolor=#b8bab9></td>
    <td width="1" height="1" bgcolor=#808381></td>
  </tr>
  <tr>
    <td width="1" height="1" bgcolor=#7f7c7b></td>
    <td width="1" height="1" bgcolor=#9f9c99></td>
    <td width="1" height="1" bgcolor=#9a9a97></td>
    <td width="1" height="1" bgcolor=#95928e></td>
    <td width="1" height="1" bgcolor=#959490></td>
    <td width="1" height="1" bgcolor=#74726e></td>
    <td width="1" height="1" bgcolor=#a7a9a4></td>
    <td width="1" height="1" bgcolor=#a3a49e></td>
    <td width="1" height="1" bgcolor=#abada9></td>
    <td width="1" height="1" bgcolor=#a9aca7></td>
    <td width="1" height="1" bgcolor=#aeadac></td>
    <td width="1" height="1" bgcolor=#acaea8></td>
    <td width="1" height="1" bgcolor=#a2a39e></td>
    <td width="1" height="1" bgcolor=#a9aaa5></td>
    <td width="1" height="1" bgcolor=#abaca7></td>
    <td width="1" height="1" bgcolor=#908f8b></td>
    <td width="1" height="1" bgcolor=#989793></td>
    <td width="1" height="1" bgcolor=#a2a19f></td>
    <td width="1" height="1" bgcolor=#aaaba6></td>
    <td width="1" height="1" bgcolor=#a4a5a0></td>
    <td width="1" height="1" bgcolor=#adaeaa></td>
    <td width="1" height="1" bgcolor=#a1a19d></td>
    <td width="1" height="1" bgcolor=#afaeaa></td>
    <td width="1" height="1" bgcolor=#b5b7b5></td>
    <td width="1" height="1" bgcolor=#a7a8a4></td>
    <td width="1" height="1" bgcolor=#aeafaa></td>
    <td width="1" height="1" bgcolor=#a9a9a5></td>
    <td width="1" height="1" bgcolor=#938b89></td>
    <td width="1" height="1" bgcolor=#4e4139></td>
    <td width="1" height="1" bgcolor=#624d42></td>
    <td width="1" height="1" bgcolor=#655044></td>
    <td width="1" height="1" bgcolor=#c9cccd></td>
    <td width="1" height="1" bgcolor=#898480></td>
    <td width="1" height="1" bgcolor=#827871></td>
    <td width="1" height="1" bgcolor=#94877a></td>
    <td width="1" height="1" bgcolor=#9a8e80></td>
    <td width="1" height="1" bgcolor=#a69a89></td>
    <td width="1" height="1" bgcolor=#a39a91></td>
    <td width="1" height="1" bgcolor=#b7b0a5></td>
    <td width="1" height="1" bgcolor=#ada89c></td>
    <td width="1" height="1" bgcolor=#bcb3a9></td>
    <td width="1" height="1" bgcolor=#c2b9ab></td>
    <td width="1" height="1" bgcolor=#c4baaf></td>
    <td width="1" height="1" bgcolor=#cbc2b6></td>
    <td width="1" height="1" bgcolor=#e8ede8></td>
    <td width="1" height="1" bgcolor=#c5c5c9></td>
    <td width="1" height="1" bgcolor=#c9cbcf></td>
    <td width="1" height="1" bgcolor=#908c8c></td>
    <td width="1" height="1" bgcolor=#bfc0c2></td>
    <td width="1" height="1" bgcolor=#c3c8cc></td>
    <td width="1" height="1" bgcolor=#bfc2c0></td>
    <td width="1" height="1" bgcolor=#c7c9ca></td>
    <td width="1" height="1" bgcolor=#bbbbbd></td>
    <td width="1" height="1" bgcolor=#b8b8b8></td>
    <td width="1" height="1" bgcolor=#b4b4b2></td>
    <td width="1" height="1" bgcolor=#a2a19f></td>
    <td width="1" height="1" bgcolor=#aeacac></td>
    <td width="1" height="1" bgcolor=#aeb0ac></td>
    <td width="1" height="1" bgcolor=#a7a3a3></td>
    <td width="1" height="1" bgcolor=#938f8c></td>
    <td width="1" height="1" bgcolor=#b6b4b2></td>
    <td width="1" height="1" bgcolor=#c7c9c9></td>
    <td width="1" height="1" bgcolor=#cbcec9></td>
    <td width="1" height="1" bgcolor=#babbbb></td>
    <td width="1" height="1" bgcolor=#bdbcbc></td>
    <td width="1" height="1" bgcolor=#322923></td>
    <td width="1" height="1" bgcolor=#8d8c85></td>
    <td width="1" height="1" bgcolor=#a1a19e></td>
```

```
    <td width="1" height="1"
bgcolor=#7d7c76></td>
    <td width="1" height="1"
bgcolor=#716a62></td>
    <td width="1" height="1"
bgcolor=#747472></td>
  </tr>
  <tr>
    <td width="1" height="1"
bgcolor=#847f7e></td>
    <td width="1" height="1"
bgcolor=#757271></td>
    <td width="1" height="1"
bgcolor=#837f7d></td>
    <td width="1" height="1"
bgcolor=#898683></td>
    <td width="1" height="1"
bgcolor=#94918d></td>
    <td width="1" height="1"
bgcolor=#9c9e98></td>
    <td width="1" height="1"
bgcolor=#a9a9a5></td>
    <td width="1" height="1"
bgcolor=#9f9e99></td>
    <td width="1" height="1"
bgcolor=#92908f></td>
    <td width="1" height="1"
bgcolor=#999592></td>
    <td width="1" height="1"
bgcolor=#817c78></td>
    <td width="1" height="1"
bgcolor=#999893></td>
    <td width="1" height="1"
bgcolor=#a4a49f></td>
    <td width="1" height="1"
bgcolor=#adafa9></td>
    <td width="1" height="1"
bgcolor=#a1a19c></td>
    <td width="1" height="1"
bgcolor=#b3b4af></td>
    <td width="1" height="1"
bgcolor=#a9aba6></td>
    <td width="1" height="1"
bgcolor=#a9aaa5></td>
    <td width="1" height="1"
bgcolor=#a8a7a3></td>
    <td width="1" height="1"
bgcolor=#aaaba5></td>
    <td width="1" height="1"
bgcolor=#b1afab></td>
    <td width="1" height="1"
bgcolor=#92908c></td>
    <td width="1" height="1"
bgcolor=#b1b0ad></td>
    <td width="1" height="1"
bgcolor=#acaca9></td>
    <td width="1" height="1"
bgcolor=#bec1bb></td>
    <td width="1" height="1"
bgcolor=#9b9a96></td>
    <td width="1" height="1"
bgcolor=#9d9a96></td>
    <td width="1" height="1"
bgcolor=#adada8></td>
    <td width="1" height="1"
bgcolor=#908d86></td>
    <td width="1" height="1"
bgcolor=#665652></td>
    <td width="1" height="1"
bgcolor=#6b5445></td>
    <td width="1" height="1"
bgcolor=#715f50></td>
    <td width="1" height="1"
bgcolor=#c0c4c3></td>
    <td width="1" height="1"
bgcolor=#7e7874></td>
    <td width="1" height="1"
bgcolor=#9b958f></td>
    <td width="1" height="1"
bgcolor=#aca396></td>
    <td width="1" height="1"
bgcolor=#ac9c8c></td>
    <td width="1" height="1"
bgcolor=#b6a998></td>
    <td width="1" height="1"
bgcolor=#b8b19e></td>
    <td width="1" height="1"
bgcolor=#bbb9ad></td>
    <td width="1" height="1"
bgcolor=#a8a297></td>
    <td width="1" height="1"
bgcolor=#b9b3a4></td>
    <td width="1" height="1"
bgcolor=#bbb3a8></td>
    <td width="1" height="1"
bgcolor=#bebaad></td>
    <td width="1" height="1"
bgcolor=#cbcabf></td>
    <td width="1" height="1"
bgcolor=#cac7bc></td>
    <td width="1" height="1"
bgcolor=#ced2d6></td>
    <td width="1" height="1"
bgcolor=#c6c8c8></td>
    <td width="1" height="1"
bgcolor=#caccd1></td>
    <td width="1" height="1"
bgcolor=#c3c7c7></td>
    <td width="1" height="1"
bgcolor=#c9ccce></td>
    <td width="1" height="1"
bgcolor=#c7cbce></td>
    <td width="1" height="1"
bgcolor=#c5c9ca></td>
    <td width="1" height="1"
bgcolor=#c4c8c8></td>
    <td width="1" height="1"
bgcolor=#c6c8c9></td>
    <td width="1" height="1"
bgcolor=#bdbec0></td>
    <td width="1" height="1"
bgcolor=#c3c9cb></td>
    <td width="1" height="1"
bgcolor=#bebfbf></td>
    <td width="1" height="1"
bgcolor=#a7a3a2></td>
    <td width="1" height="1"
bgcolor=#4a413f></td>
    <td width="1" height="1"
bgcolor=#3a3127></td>
    <td width="1" height="1"
bgcolor=#544c41></td>
    <td width="1" height="1"
bgcolor=#3a3428></td>
    <td width="1" height="1"
bgcolor=#87847f></td>
    <td width="1" height="1"
bgcolor=#9f9c97></td>
    <td width="1" height="1"
bgcolor=#a0a19d></td>
    <td width="1" height="1"
bgcolor=#aeafaf></td>
    <td width="1" height="1"
bgcolor=#aeafa8></td>
    <td width="1" height="1"
bgcolor=#a6a5a0></td>
    <td width="1" height="1"
bgcolor=#a5a4a0></td>
    <td width="1" height="1"
bgcolor=#ababa8></td>
    <td width="1" height="1"
bgcolor=#7a7a78></td>
  </tr>
  <tr>
    <td width="1" height="1"
bgcolor=#93918e></td>
    <td width="1" height="1"
bgcolor=#999897></td>
    <td width="1" height="1"
bgcolor=#938f8d></td>
    <td width="1" height="1"
bgcolor=#9f9f9a></td>
    <td width="1" height="1"
bgcolor=#a5a5a3></td>
    <td width="1" height="1"
bgcolor=#b4b5b3></td>
    <td width="1" height="1"
bgcolor=#817f7a></td>
    <td width="1" height="1"
bgcolor=#595652></td>
    <td width="1" height="1"
bgcolor=#8e8787></td>
    <td width="1" height="1"
bgcolor=#a3a49e></td>
```

```
    <td width="1" height="1"
bgcolor=#888380></td>
    <td width="1" height="1"
bgcolor=#645b57></td>
    <td width="1" height="1"
bgcolor=#9a9793></td>
    <td width="1" height="1"
bgcolor=#96938f></td>
    <td width="1" height="1"
bgcolor=#afb1ac></td>
    <td width="1" height="1"
bgcolor=#aeaea9></td>
    <td width="1" height="1"
bgcolor=#a6a7a2></td>
    <td width="1" height="1"
bgcolor=#a5a29e></td>
    <td width="1" height="1"
bgcolor=#8b8783></td>
    <td width="1" height="1"
bgcolor=#b4b3ae></td>
    <td width="1" height="1"
bgcolor=#a3a39e></td>
    <td width="1" height="1"
bgcolor=#4f443f></td>
    <td width="1" height="1"
bgcolor=#473d38></td>
    <td width="1" height="1"
bgcolor=#574d49></td>
    <td width="1" height="1"
bgcolor=#2a221a></td>
    <td width="1" height="1"
bgcolor=#5e5752></td>
    <td width="1" height="1"
bgcolor=#a4a19c></td>
    <td width="1" height="1"
bgcolor=#837c79></td>
    <td width="1" height="1"
bgcolor=#88817a></td>
    <td width="1" height="1"
bgcolor=#665455></td>
    <td width="1" height="1"
bgcolor=#756154></td>
    <td width="1" height="1"
bgcolor=#47372d></td>
    <td width="1" height="1"
bgcolor=#a7a5a1></td>
    <td width="1" height="1"
bgcolor=#95928b></td>
    <td width="1" height="1"
bgcolor=#a8a59b></td>
    <td width="1" height="1"
bgcolor=#a39990></td>
    <td width="1" height="1"
bgcolor=#ada598></td>
    <td width="1" height="1"
bgcolor=#b4aa9a></td>
    <td width="1" height="1"
bgcolor=#bcb4a4></td>
    <td width="1" height="1"
bgcolor=#d1d3d7></td>
    <td width="1" height="1"
bgcolor=#bdbdb4></td>
    <td width="1" height="1"
bgcolor=#bbbab0></td>
    <td width="1" height="1"
bgcolor=#b9b8ad></td>
    <td width="1" height="1"
bgcolor=#bdbaad></td>
    <td width="1" height="1"
bgcolor=#c1bcae></td>
    <td width="1" height="1"
bgcolor=#dadad3></td>
    <td width="1" height="1"
bgcolor=#d4dada></td>
    <td width="1" height="1"
bgcolor=#ccd0d6></td>
    <td width="1" height="1"
bgcolor=#cbcfd2></td>
    <td width="1" height="1"
bgcolor=#c8cdd0></td>
    <td width="1" height="1"
bgcolor=#c4c8ca></td>
    <td width="1" height="1"
bgcolor=#c5c8cc></td>
    <td width="1" height="1"
bgcolor=#c7cbcc></td>
    <td width="1" height="1"
bgcolor=#c9ccd0></td>
    <td width="1" height="1"
bgcolor=#cacdcf></td>
    <td width="1" height="1"
bgcolor=#c5c8cb></td>
    <td width="1" height="1"
bgcolor=#c9cfd0></td>
    <td width="1" height="1"
bgcolor=#c7cace></td>
    <td width="1" height="1"
bgcolor=#cbd0d2></td>
    <td width="1" height="1"
bgcolor=#c2c2c3></td>
    <td width="1" height="1"
bgcolor=#b6b8b7></td>
    <td width="1" height="1"
bgcolor=#c8cccb></td>
    <td width="1" height="1"
bgcolor=#c6c8c7></td>
    <td width="1" height="1"
bgcolor=#bcbdba></td>
    <td width="1" height="1"
bgcolor=#babebc></td>
    <td width="1" height="1"
bgcolor=#b8bab5></td>
    <td width="1" height="1"
bgcolor=#b8b8b5></td>
    <td width="1" height="1"
bgcolor=#b7b8b6></td>
    <td width="1" height="1"
bgcolor=#b8bcb8></td>
    <td width="1" height="1"
bgcolor=#a7a6a2></td>
    <td width="1" height="1"
bgcolor=#989793></td>
    <td width="1" height="1"
bgcolor=#7c7c7a></td>
  </tr>
  <tr>
    <td width="1" height="1"
bgcolor=#9a9a98></td>
    <td width="1" height="1"
bgcolor=#928d8b></td>
    <td width="1" height="1"
bgcolor=#90908d></td>
    <td width="1" height="1"
bgcolor=#78726d></td>
    <td width="1" height="1"
bgcolor=#989a96></td>
    <td width="1" height="1"
bgcolor=#969590></td>
    <td width="1" height="1"
bgcolor=#928f8b></td>
    <td width="1" height="1"
bgcolor=#83817c></td>
    <td width="1" height="1"
bgcolor=#73716c></td>
    <td width="1" height="1"
bgcolor=#adadaa></td>
    <td width="1" height="1"
bgcolor=#a3a4a1></td>
    <td width="1" height="1"
bgcolor=#acaba7></td>
    <td width="1" height="1"
bgcolor=#84817c></td>
    <td width="1" height="1"
bgcolor=#9d9c97></td>
    <td width="1" height="1"
bgcolor=#a5a39e></td>
    <td width="1" height="1"
bgcolor=#9c9995></td>
    <td width="1" height="1"
bgcolor=#94928d></td>
    <td width="1" height="1"
bgcolor=#79736f></td>
    <td width="1" height="1"
bgcolor=#635b56></td>
    <td width="1" height="1"
bgcolor=#b9b8b3></td>
    <td width="1" height="1"
bgcolor=#b4b6b2></td>
    <td width="1" height="1"
bgcolor=#aeadaa></td>
    <td width="1" height="1"
bgcolor=#4d4540></td>
    <td width="1" height="1"
bgcolor=#87837d></td>
```

```
    <td width="1" height="1" bgcolor=#837d77></td>
    <td width="1" height="1" bgcolor=#5d544d></td>
    <td width="1" height="1" bgcolor=#87847e></td>
    <td width="1" height="1" bgcolor=#817976></td>
    <td width="1" height="1" bgcolor=#615753></td>
    <td width="1" height="1" bgcolor=#574b46></td>
    <td width="1" height="1" bgcolor=#5f4d47></td>
    <td width="1" height="1" bgcolor=#6e6260></td>
    <td width="1" height="1" bgcolor=#807c78></td>
    <td width="1" height="1" bgcolor=#a4a29e></td>
    <td width="1" height="1" bgcolor=#a5a19a></td>
    <td width="1" height="1" bgcolor=#a8a196></td>
    <td width="1" height="1" bgcolor=#aea898></td>
    <td width="1" height="1" bgcolor=#afa894></td>
    <td width="1" height="1" bgcolor=#bdb9ab></td>
    <td width="1" height="1" bgcolor=#c9cdd0></td>
    <td width="1" height="1" bgcolor=#d5d9d9></td>
    <td width="1" height="1" bgcolor=#cfd3cf></td>
    <td width="1" height="1" bgcolor=#c3c5c0></td>
    <td width="1" height="1" bgcolor=#bcb3a9></td>
    <td width="1" height="1" bgcolor=#bab4aa></td>
    <td width="1" height="1" bgcolor=#d5cfc2></td>
    <td width="1" height="1" bgcolor=#dbdedf></td>
    <td width="1" height="1" bgcolor=#cfd4d6></td>
    <td width="1" height="1" bgcolor=#cdd0d4></td>
    <td width="1" height="1" bgcolor=#d3d8db></td>
    <td width="1" height="1" bgcolor=#ced2d6></td>
    <td width="1" height="1" bgcolor=#d4d9dc></td>
    <td width="1" height="1" bgcolor=#cfd4d7></td>
    <td width="1" height="1" bgcolor=#d1d5d9></td>
    <td width="1" height="1" bgcolor=#ccd0d4></td>
    <td width="1" height="1" bgcolor=#ccd1d4></td>
    <td width="1" height="1" bgcolor=#cfd5d8></td>
    <td width="1" height="1" bgcolor=#cccfce></td>
    <td width="1" height="1" bgcolor=#b0afae></td>
    <td width="1" height="1" bgcolor=#cbcecf></td>
    <td width="1" height="1" bgcolor=#d3d8dc></td>
    <td width="1" height="1" bgcolor=#d0d4d9></td>
    <td width="1" height="1" bgcolor=#c0c4c2></td>
    <td width="1" height="1" bgcolor=#bfc1be></td>
    <td width="1" height="1" bgcolor=#b6b5b3></td>
    <td width="1" height="1" bgcolor=#a9a8a4></td>
    <td width="1" height="1" bgcolor=#b5b7b2></td>
    <td width="1" height="1" bgcolor=#b3b6b2></td>
    <td width="1" height="1" bgcolor=#aeb0ae></td>
    <td width="1" height="1" bgcolor=#b6b7b4></td>
    <td width="1" height="1" bgcolor=#bdc2c1></td>
    <td width="1" height="1" bgcolor=#909392></td>
  </tr>
  <tr>
    <td width="1" height="1" bgcolor=#797371></td>
    <td width="1" height="1" bgcolor=#9f9d9a></td>
    <td width="1" height="1" bgcolor=#716b69></td>
    <td width="1" height="1" bgcolor=#5e5753></td>
    <td width="1" height="1" bgcolor=#969391></td>
    <td width="1" height="1" bgcolor=#9c9b99></td>
    <td width="1" height="1" bgcolor=#0b0807></td>
    <td rowspan="1" colspan="2" width="1" height="1" bgcolor=#000000></td>
    <td width="1" height="1" bgcolor=#342b26></td>
    <td width="1" height="1" bgcolor=#887f7d></td>
    <td width="1" height="1" bgcolor=#8f8d89></td>
    <td width="1" height="1" bgcolor=#726d69></td>
    <td width="1" height="1" bgcolor=#9d9894></td>
    <td width="1" height="1" bgcolor=#928f8b></td>
    <td width="1" height="1" bgcolor=#a6a7a2></td>
    <td width="1" height="1" bgcolor=#a3a29d></td>
    <td width="1" height="1" bgcolor=#9f9d99></td>
    <td width="1" height="1" bgcolor=#96918d></td>
    <td width="1" height="1" bgcolor=#93928d></td>
    <td width="1" height="1" bgcolor=#b1b3af></td>
    <td width="1" height="1" bgcolor=#625a53></td>
    <td width="1" height="1" bgcolor=#6c645f></td>
    <td width="1" height="1" bgcolor=#938f8c></td>
    <td width="1" height="1" bgcolor=#898481></td>
    <td width="1" height="1" bgcolor=#8b8480></td>
    <td width="1" height="1" bgcolor=#5f5451></td>
    <td width="1" height="1" bgcolor=#736b67></td>
    <td width="1" height="1" bgcolor=#675c59></td>
    <td width="1" height="1" bgcolor=#7c7170></td>
    <td width="1" height="1" bgcolor=#5e5552></td>
    <td width="1" height="1" bgcolor=#7f7774></td>
    <td width="1" height="1" bgcolor=#655d5a></td>
    <td width="1" height="1" bgcolor=#999691></td>
    <td width="1" height="1" bgcolor=#a2a097></td>
    <td width="1" height="1" bgcolor=#ada69b></td>
    <td width="1" height="1" bgcolor=#b4ac9b></td>
    <td width="1" height="1" bgcolor=#b6ad9d></td>
```

```
    <td width="1" height="1" bgcolor=#d3d5cf></td>
    <td width="1" height="1" bgcolor=#b9bab7></td>
    <td width="1" height="1" bgcolor=#c6c8c4></td>
    <td width="1" height="1" bgcolor=#d7dee0></td>
    <td width="1" height="1" bgcolor=#d1d7d3></td>
    <td width="1" height="1" bgcolor=#b4ab9f></td>
    <td width="1" height="1" bgcolor=#bbb4ab></td>
    <td width="1" height="1" bgcolor=#bfb8a7></td>
    <td width="1" height="1" bgcolor=#eaf0ed></td>
    <td width="1" height="1" bgcolor=#d1d6da></td>
    <td width="1" height="1" bgcolor=#d2d6da></td>
    <td width="1" height="1" bgcolor=#d8dde0></td>
    <td width="1" height="1" bgcolor=#d3d8dc></td>
    <td width="1" height="1" bgcolor=#ced2d6></td>
    <td rowspan="1" colspan="2" width="1" height="1" bgcolor=#cfd2d6></td>
    <td width="1" height="1" bgcolor=#d2d5d9></td>
    <td width="1" height="1" bgcolor=#d2d7da></td>
    <td width="1" height="1" bgcolor=#ccd0d4></td>
    <td width="1" height="1" bgcolor=#c1c4c3></td>
    <td width="1" height="1" bgcolor=#bebfbc></td>
    <td width="1" height="1" bgcolor=#c3c5c3></td>
    <td width="1" height="1" bgcolor=#bec1bd></td>
    <td width="1" height="1" bgcolor=#c0c1bd></td>
    <td width="1" height="1" bgcolor=#cbcecd></td>
    <td width="1" height="1" bgcolor=#bfc1c3></td>
    <td width="1" height="1" bgcolor=#c4cac9></td>
    <td width="1" height="1" bgcolor=#c4c7c8></td>
    <td width="1" height="1" bgcolor=#c4c7ca></td>
    <td width="1" height="1" bgcolor=#c0c4c4></td>
    <td width="1" height="1" bgcolor=#b8bcb8></td>
    <td width="1" height="1" bgcolor=#a9aaa8></td>
    <td width="1" height="1" bgcolor=#a7a8a4></td>
    <td width="1" height="1" bgcolor=#8c8f8f></td>
  </tr>
  <tr>
    <td width="1" height="1" bgcolor=#3b3433></td>
    <td width="1" height="1" bgcolor=#6c6765></td>
    <td width="1" height="1" bgcolor=#706e6a></td>
    <td width="1" height="1" bgcolor=#787371></td>
    <td width="1" height="1" bgcolor=#a09d9c></td>
    <td width="1" height="1" bgcolor=#a4a2a0></td>
    <td width="1" height="1" bgcolor=#858180></td>
    <td width="1" height="1" bgcolor=#464543></td>
    <td width="1" height="1" bgcolor=#605c5b></td>
    <td width="1" height="1" bgcolor=#8c8885></td>
    <td width="1" height="1" bgcolor=#8b8b86></td>
    <td width="1" height="1" bgcolor=#9a9793></td>
    <td width="1" height="1" bgcolor=#918a86></td>
    <td width="1" height="1" bgcolor=#9d9b97></td>
    <td width="1" height="1" bgcolor=#a0a19c></td>
    <td width="1" height="1" bgcolor=#b1b1ac></td>
    <td width="1" height="1" bgcolor=#b4b4b0></td>
    <td width="1" height="1" bgcolor=#a4a5a0></td>
    <td width="1" height="1" bgcolor=#999793></td>
    <td width="1" height="1" bgcolor=#979590></td>
    <td width="1" height="1" bgcolor=#9b9793></td>
    <td width="1" height="1" bgcolor=#7b7470></td>
    <td width="1" height="1" bgcolor=#7d7571></td>
    <td width="1" height="1" bgcolor=#7e7572></td>
    <td width="1" height="1" bgcolor=#8c8482></td>
    <td width="1" height="1" bgcolor=#9f9c96></td>
    <td width="1" height="1" bgcolor=#9e9d97></td>
    <td width="1" height="1" bgcolor=#a29e99></td>
    <td width="1" height="1" bgcolor=#9d9994></td>
    <td width="1" height="1" bgcolor=#9c9997></td>
    <td width="1" height="1" bgcolor=#8d8684></td>
    <td width="1" height="1" bgcolor=#94908c></td>
    <td width="1" height="1" bgcolor=#999390></td>
    <td width="1" height="1" bgcolor=#9d9a95></td>
    <td width="1" height="1" bgcolor=#9b968f></td>
    <td width="1" height="1" bgcolor=#a29b91></td>
    <td width="1" height="1" bgcolor=#aea696></td>
    <td width="1" height="1" bgcolor=#b6aa99></td>
    <td width="1" height="1" bgcolor=#bfbcb6></td>
    <td width="1" height="1" bgcolor=#9a9892></td>
    <td width="1" height="1" bgcolor=#8a8780></td>
    <td width="1" height="1" bgcolor=#e0e3e1></td>
    <td width="1" height="1" bgcolor=#cfd5d1></td>
    <td width="1" height="1" bgcolor=#ada597></td>
    <td width="1" height="1" bgcolor=#b2afa3></td>
    <td width="1" height="1" bgcolor=#c6beb1></td>
    <td width="1" height="1" bgcolor=#eef0ee></td>
    <td width="1" height="1" bgcolor=#c2c4c5></td>
    <td width="1" height="1" bgcolor=#babbb7></td>
    <td width="1" height="1" bgcolor=#c5c7c3></td>
    <td width="1" height="1" bgcolor=#c5c6c5></td>
    <td width="1" height="1" bgcolor=#c9cac9></td>
```

```
    <td width="1" height="1"
bgcolor=#c9cacb></td>
    <td width="1" height="1"
bgcolor=#cfd0d3></td>
    <td width="1" height="1"
bgcolor=#cbced1></td>
    <td width="1" height="1"
bgcolor=#cbcfd1></td>
    <td width="1" height="1"
bgcolor=#cfd4d4></td>
    <td width="1" height="1"
bgcolor=#ced1d3></td>
    <td rowspan="1"
colspan="2" width="1"
height="1"
bgcolor=#c8caca></td>
    <td width="1" height="1"
bgcolor=#c0c2bf></td>
    <td width="1" height="1"
bgcolor=#ced1d4></td>
    <td width="1" height="1"
bgcolor=#cfd4d4></td>
    <td width="1" height="1"
bgcolor=#cdd3d2></td>
    <td width="1" height="1"
bgcolor=#c7cbcd></td>
    <td width="1" height="1"
bgcolor=#bdc1bf></td>
    <td width="1" height="1"
bgcolor=#bbbcba></td>
    <td width="1" height="1"
bgcolor=#ced3d4></td>
    <td width="1" height="1"
bgcolor=#cbced2></td>
    <td width="1" height="1"
bgcolor=#cbced1></td>
    <td width="1" height="1"
bgcolor=#c1c5c6></td>
    <td width="1" height="1"
bgcolor=#8f9495></td>
  </tr>
  <tr>
    <td width="1" height="1"
bgcolor=#0d0b07></td>
    <td width="1" height="1"
bgcolor=#524d4d></td>
    <td width="1" height="1"
bgcolor=#494340></td>
    <td width="1" height="1"
bgcolor=#433a39></td>
    <td width="1" height="1"
bgcolor=#969591></td>
    <td width="1" height="1"
bgcolor=#93928e></td>
    <td width="1" height="1"
bgcolor=#92908d></td>
    <td width="1" height="1"
bgcolor=#969390></td>
    <td width="1" height="1"
bgcolor=#868280></td>
    <td width="1" height="1"
bgcolor=#a4a4a0></td>
    <td width="1" height="1"
bgcolor=#a6a3a3></td>
    <td width="1" height="1"
bgcolor=#9e9d99></td>
    <td width="1" height="1"
bgcolor=#a5a5a1></td>
    <td width="1" height="1"
bgcolor=#aaaaa7></td>
    <td width="1" height="1"
bgcolor=#b4b5b1></td>
    <td width="1" height="1"
bgcolor=#afb1ab></td>
    <td width="1" height="1"
bgcolor=#b2b4b0></td>
    <td width="1" height="1"
bgcolor=#bdc0ba></td>
    <td width="1" height="1"
bgcolor=#b5b6b2></td>
    <td width="1" height="1"
bgcolor=#a8a8a2></td>
    <td width="1" height="1"
bgcolor=#b6b7b4></td>
    <td width="1" height="1"
bgcolor=#babab6></td>
    <td width="1" height="1"
bgcolor=#b4b5ae></td>
    <td width="1" height="1"
bgcolor=#a5a49f></td>
    <td width="1" height="1"
bgcolor=#acada8></td>
    <td width="1" height="1"
bgcolor=#afb0ad></td>
    <td width="1" height="1"
bgcolor=#a09e9a></td>
    <td width="1" height="1"
bgcolor=#aaa8a6></td>
    <td width="1" height="1"
bgcolor=#9e9d98></td>
    <td width="1" height="1"
bgcolor=#999793></td>
    <td width="1" height="1"
bgcolor=#aeaba4></td>
    <td width="1" height="1"
bgcolor=#aeada7></td>
    <td width="1" height="1"
bgcolor=#a7a4a0></td>
    <td width="1" height="1"
bgcolor=#94928e></td>
    <td width="1" height="1"
bgcolor=#a7a49e></td>
    <td width="1" height="1"
bgcolor=#aba69a></td>
    <td width="1" height="1"
bgcolor=#b3aa9a></td>
    <td width="1" height="1"
bgcolor=#c3c0b3></td>
    <td width="1" height="1"
bgcolor=#bab6b4></td>
    <td width="1" height="1"
bgcolor=#aeafaa></td>
    <td width="1" height="1"
bgcolor=#b0afaa></td>
    <td width="1" height="1"
bgcolor=#867f75></td>
    <td width="1" height="1"
bgcolor=#dfe7e4></td>
    <td width="1" height="1"
bgcolor=#b7b3a8></td>
    <td width="1" height="1"
bgcolor=#b4ada0></td>
    <td width="1" height="1"
bgcolor=#b3a698></td>
    <td width="1" height="1"
bgcolor=#dcddd3></td>
    <td width="1" height="1"
bgcolor=#aba7a2></td>
    <td width="1" height="1"
bgcolor=#a3a19e></td>
    <td width="1" height="1"
bgcolor=#a6a4a0></td>
    <td width="1" height="1"
bgcolor=#a29e9a></td>
    <td width="1" height="1"
bgcolor=#9c9996></td>
    <td width="1" height="1"
bgcolor=#b0b0ad></td>
    <td width="1" height="1"
bgcolor=#b6b6b3></td>
    <td width="1" height="1"
bgcolor=#bfbfbb></td>
    <td width="1" height="1"
bgcolor=#c7c8c4></td>
    <td width="1" height="1"
bgcolor=#c1c2c0></td>
    <td width="1" height="1"
bgcolor=#b7b7b3></td>
    <td width="1" height="1"
bgcolor=#c7c9c8></td>
    <td width="1" height="1"
bgcolor=#d6dbdd></td>
    <td width="1" height="1"
bgcolor=#d5d8dc></td>
    <td width="1" height="1"
bgcolor=#d4d8db></td>
    <td width="1" height="1"
bgcolor=#d1d6d8></td>
    <td width="1" height="1"
bgcolor=#d1d5d9></td>
    <td width="1" height="1"
bgcolor=#d6dcdf></td>
    <td width="1" height="1"
bgcolor=#ced3d5></td>
```

```
    <td width="1" height="1"
bgcolor=#cdd3d5></td>
    <td width="1" height="1"
bgcolor=#caced0></td>
    <td width="1" height="1"
bgcolor=#cbd2d4></td>
    <td width="1" height="1"
bgcolor=#c3c7c7></td>
    <td width="1" height="1"
bgcolor=#c5c9cd></td>
    <td width="1" height="1"
bgcolor=#979a9b></td>
  </tr>
  <tr>
    <td width="1" height="1"
bgcolor=#989594></td>
    <td width="1" height="1"
bgcolor=#726e6e></td>
    <td width="1" height="1"
bgcolor=#45423b></td>
    <td width="1" height="1"
bgcolor=#5c5857></td>
    <td width="1" height="1"
bgcolor=#595654></td>
    <td width="1" height="1"
bgcolor=#726e6a></td>
    <td width="1" height="1"
bgcolor=#73706d></td>
    <td width="1" height="1"
bgcolor=#afafae></td>
    <td width="1" height="1"
bgcolor=#a6a7a1></td>
    <td width="1" height="1"
bgcolor=#a1a19f></td>
    <td width="1" height="1"
bgcolor=#908c8b></td>
    <td width="1" height="1"
bgcolor=#a6a5a3></td>
    <td width="1" height="1"
bgcolor=#a0a09b></td>
    <td width="1" height="1"
bgcolor=#8e8d89></td>
    <td width="1" height="1"
bgcolor=#a6a7a3></td>
    <td width="1" height="1"
bgcolor=#acacaa></td>
    <td width="1" height="1"
bgcolor=#bbbcb8></td>
    <td width="1" height="1"
bgcolor=#a8a7a6></td>
    <td width="1" height="1"
bgcolor=#b6bab8></td>
    <td width="1" height="1"
bgcolor=#bcbebd></td>
    <td width="1" height="1"
bgcolor=#b9bbba></td>
    <td width="1" height="1"
bgcolor=#bcbdbc></td>
    <td width="1" height="1"
bgcolor=#bfc1bc></td>
    <td width="1" height="1"
bgcolor=#a5a39e></td>
    <td width="1" height="1"
bgcolor=#adada7></td>
    <td width="1" height="1"
bgcolor=#b0b0aa></td>
    <td width="1" height="1"
bgcolor=#a3a19c></td>
    <td width="1" height="1"
bgcolor=#8e8885></td>
    <td width="1" height="1"
bgcolor=#989590></td>
    <td width="1" height="1"
bgcolor=#928b87></td>
    <td width="1" height="1"
bgcolor=#9f9d98></td>
    <td width="1" height="1"
bgcolor=#9e9c98></td>
    <td width="1" height="1"
bgcolor=#a39b97></td>
    <td width="1" height="1"
bgcolor=#989793></td>
    <td width="1" height="1"
bgcolor=#a29b96></td>
    <td width="1" height="1"
bgcolor=#aca79c></td>
    <td width="1" height="1"
bgcolor=#aba291></td>
    <td width="1" height="1"
bgcolor=#c4bdb5></td>
    <td width="1" height="1"
bgcolor=#847c74></td>
    <td width="1" height="1"
bgcolor=#a3a19c></td>
    <td width="1" height="1"
bgcolor=#b2b1aa></td>
    <td width="1" height="1"
bgcolor=#aeaca7></td>
    <td width="1" height="1"
bgcolor=#e3e7e8></td>
    <td width="1" height="1"
bgcolor=#c2c1ba></td>
    <td width="1" height="1"
bgcolor=#b8b4a7></td>
    <td width="1" height="1"
bgcolor=#b9ae9d></td>
    <td width="1" height="1"
bgcolor=#bfbcad></td>
    <td width="1" height="1"
bgcolor=#a59f9c></td>
    <td width="1" height="1"
bgcolor=#a7a49f></td>
    <td width="1" height="1"
bgcolor=#9e9b97></td>
    <td width="1" height="1"
bgcolor=#8d8685></td>
    <td width="1" height="1"
bgcolor=#877d7c></td>
    <td width="1" height="1"
bgcolor=#7e7472></td>
    <td width="1" height="1"
bgcolor=#8a8280></td>
    <td width="1" height="1"
bgcolor=#aeaba7></td>
    <td width="1" height="1"
bgcolor=#837d79></td>
    <td width="1" height="1"
bgcolor=#a4a39e></td>
    <td width="1" height="1"
bgcolor=#cacdcd></td>
    <td width="1" height="1"
bgcolor=#d3d7db></td>
    <td width="1" height="1"
bgcolor=#c9cdce></td>
    <td width="1" height="1"
bgcolor=#ccd2d2></td>
    <td width="1" height="1"
bgcolor=#cbd1d0></td>
    <td width="1" height="1"
bgcolor=#d0d5d8></td>
    <td width="1" height="1"
bgcolor=#d4d9dc></td>
    <td width="1" height="1"
bgcolor=#d8dce0></td>
    <td width="1" height="1"
bgcolor=#d1d6d9></td>
    <td width="1" height="1"
bgcolor=#ced4d4></td>
    <td width="1" height="1"
bgcolor=#cacbd0></td>
    <td width="1" height="1"
bgcolor=#cdd4d6></td>
    <td width="1" height="1"
bgcolor=#cfd4d7></td>
    <td width="1" height="1"
bgcolor=#d2d5db></td>
    <td rowspan="2"
colspan="1" width="1"
height="1"
bgcolor=#919596></td>
  </tr>
  <tr>
    <td width="1" height="1"
bgcolor=#252523></td>
    <td width="1" height="1"
bgcolor=#5a5853></td>
    <td width="1" height="1"
bgcolor=#080a04></td>
    <td width="1" height="1"
bgcolor=#000400></td>
    <td width="1" height="1"
bgcolor=#080905></td>
    <td width="1" height="1"
bgcolor=#1c1a14></td>
```

```
    <td width="1" height="1"
bgcolor=#47433e></td>
    <td width="1" height="1"
bgcolor=#898380></td>
    <td width="1" height="1"
bgcolor=#9a9998></td>
    <td width="1" height="1"
bgcolor=#9c9998></td>
    <td width="1" height="1"
bgcolor=#929190></td>
    <td width="1" height="1"
bgcolor=#999895></td>
    <td width="1" height="1"
bgcolor=#9a9a97></td>
    <td width="1" height="1"
bgcolor=#9b9b96></td>
    <td width="1" height="1"
bgcolor=#a8a9a4></td>
    <td width="1" height="1"
bgcolor=#a5a5a1></td>
    <td width="1" height="1"
bgcolor=#a5a2a0></td>
    <td width="1" height="1"
bgcolor=#a8a8a4></td>
    <td width="1" height="1"
bgcolor=#9e9b97></td>
    <td width="1" height="1"
bgcolor=#9f9d99></td>
    <td width="1" height="1"
bgcolor=#a9a7a2></td>
    <td width="1" height="1"
bgcolor=#9d9c97></td>
    <td width="1" height="1"
bgcolor=#918e8a></td>
    <td width="1" height="1"
bgcolor=#837a78></td>
    <td width="1" height="1"
bgcolor=#827876></td>
    <td width="1" height="1"
bgcolor=#766c6a></td>
    <td width="1" height="1"
bgcolor=#79716e></td>
    <td width="1" height="1"
bgcolor=#847b78></td>
    <td width="1" height="1"
bgcolor=#87807d></td>
    <td width="1" height="1"
bgcolor=#a5a29d></td>
    <td width="1" height="1"
bgcolor=#aba9a4></td>
    <td width="1" height="1"
bgcolor=#b2b3ad></td>
    <td width="1" height="1"
bgcolor=#b1b3ad></td>
    <td width="1" height="1"
bgcolor=#908e89></td>
    <td width="1" height="1"
bgcolor=#a6a39a></td>
    <td width="1" height="1"
bgcolor=#afa79b></td>
    <td width="1" height="1"
bgcolor=#b2a696></td>
    <td width="1" height="1"
bgcolor=#d8d8cf></td>
    <td width="1" height="1"
bgcolor=#817875></td>
    <td width="1" height="1"
bgcolor=#857c7a></td>
    <td width="1" height="1"
bgcolor=#665e5a></td>
    <td width="1" height="1"
bgcolor=#695e5b></td>
    <td width="1" height="1"
bgcolor=#dce2dc></td>
    <td width="1" height="1"
bgcolor=#c9ccc8></td>
    <td width="1" height="1"
bgcolor=#8b8174></td>
    <td width="1" height="1"
bgcolor=#928375></td>
    <td width="1" height="1"
bgcolor=#b5ab9b></td>
    <td width="1" height="1"
bgcolor=#cac7c4></td>
    <td width="1" height="1"
bgcolor=#706564></td>
    <td rowspan="1"
colspan="2" width="1"
height="1"
bgcolor=#746a68></td>
    <td width="1" height="1"
bgcolor=#655b59></td>
    <td width="1" height="1"
bgcolor=#726967></td>
    <td width="1" height="1"
bgcolor=#7d7472></td>
    <td width="1" height="1"
bgcolor=#7f7875></td>
    <td width="1" height="1"
bgcolor=#96918d></td>
    <td width="1" height="1"
bgcolor=#aca9a5></td>
    <td width="1" height="1"
bgcolor=#b4b5b0></td>
    <td width="1" height="1"
bgcolor=#bab9b6></td>
    <td width="1" height="1"
bgcolor=#c1c3c0></td>
    <td width="1" height="1"
bgcolor=#c0c1bd></td>
    <td width="1" height="1"
bgcolor=#bfc1be></td>
    <td width="1" height="1"
bgcolor=#d2d5d6></td>
    <td width="1" height="1"
bgcolor=#cbd0d2></td>
    <td width="1" height="1"
bgcolor=#d5d9db></td>
    <td width="1" height="1"
bgcolor=#d2d6da></td>
    <td width="1" height="1"
bgcolor=#d5dbdd></td>
    <td width="1" height="1"
bgcolor=#cbcfd1></td>
    <td width="1" height="1"
bgcolor=#bdc1be></td>
    <td width="1" height="1"
bgcolor=#c5caca></td>
    <td width="1" height="1"
bgcolor=#c8cecd></td>
  </tr>
  <tr>
    <td width="1" height="1"
bgcolor=#000200></td>
    <td width="1" height="1"
bgcolor=#000000></td>
    <td width="1" height="1"
bgcolor=#0b0c0a></td>
    <td width="1" height="1"
bgcolor=#3d3a39></td>
    <td width="1" height="1"
bgcolor=#706e6b></td>
    <td width="1" height="1"
bgcolor=#5f5a55></td>
    <td width="1" height="1"
bgcolor=#a7a5a3></td>
    <td width="1" height="1"
bgcolor=#a3a4a2></td>
    <td width="1" height="1"
bgcolor=#a8a8a6></td>
    <td width="1" height="1"
bgcolor=#9b9a97></td>
    <td width="1" height="1"
bgcolor=#a3a29f></td>
    <td width="1" height="1"
bgcolor=#96938f></td>
    <td width="1" height="1"
bgcolor=#9d9b97></td>
    <td width="1" height="1"
bgcolor=#a09e99></td>
    <td width="1" height="1"
bgcolor=#a6a49f></td>
    <td width="1" height="1"
bgcolor=#a09d98></td>
    <td width="1" height="1"
bgcolor=#a3a09b></td>
    <td width="1" height="1"
bgcolor=#95908c></td>
    <td width="1" height="1"
bgcolor=#9f9b98></td>
    <td width="1" height="1"
bgcolor=#918a87></td>
    <td width="1" height="1"
bgcolor=#908b88></td>
```

```
    <td width="1" height="1"
bgcolor=#918a87></td>
    <td width="1" height="1"
bgcolor=#827976></td>
    <td width="1" height="1"
bgcolor=#87807c></td>
    <td width="1" height="1"
bgcolor=#7e7673></td>
    <td width="1" height="1"
bgcolor=#7f7674></td>
    <td width="1" height="1"
bgcolor=#857e7b></td>
    <td width="1" height="1"
bgcolor=#8b827f></td>
    <td width="1" height="1"
bgcolor=#908986></td>
    <td width="1" height="1"
bgcolor=#938f8a></td>
    <td width="1" height="1"
bgcolor=#a29e9a></td>
    <td width="1" height="1"
bgcolor=#aeaba6></td>
    <td width="1" height="1"
bgcolor=#bcbcb9></td>
    <td width="1" height="1"
bgcolor=#9c9a94></td>
    <td width="1" height="1"
bgcolor=#a59e93></td>
    <td width="1" height="1"
bgcolor=#a9a195></td>
    <td width="1" height="1"
bgcolor=#b2a99b></td>
    <td width="1" height="1"
bgcolor=#ccc9bc></td>
    <td width="1" height="1"
bgcolor=#97918d></td>
    <td width="1" height="1"
bgcolor=#837d7a></td>
    <td width="1" height="1"
bgcolor=#6d6766></td>
    <td width="1" height="1"
bgcolor=#746b68></td>
    <td width="1" height="1"
bgcolor=#625b55></td>
    <td width="1" height="1"
bgcolor=#d5dad6></td>
    <td width="1" height="1"
bgcolor=#7a7065></td>
    <td width="1" height="1"
bgcolor=#95897d></td>
    <td width="1" height="1"
bgcolor=#b8b1a6></td>
    <td width="1" height="1"
bgcolor=#dcdcd5></td>
    <td width="1" height="1"
bgcolor=#4d453e></td>
    <td width="1" height="1"
bgcolor=#766d6a></td>
    <td width="1" height="1"
bgcolor=#827877></td>
    <td width="1" height="1"
bgcolor=#8a807e></td>
    <td width="1" height="1"
bgcolor=#948a88></td>
    <td width="1" height="1"
bgcolor=#a5a09d></td>
    <td width="1" height="1"
bgcolor=#b0afaa></td>
    <td width="1" height="1"
bgcolor=#aeaaa7></td>
    <td width="1" height="1"
bgcolor=#adada8></td>
    <td width="1" height="1"
bgcolor=#aaa7a2></td>
    <td width="1" height="1"
bgcolor=#b1b1ac></td>
    <td width="1" height="1"
bgcolor=#bcb9b6></td>
    <td width="1" height="1"
bgcolor=#c7c7c6></td>
    <td width="1" height="1"
bgcolor=#c3c5c3></td>
    <td width="1" height="1"
bgcolor=#b4b6b0></td>
    <td width="1" height="1"
bgcolor=#b2b1ac></td>
    <td width="1" height="1"
bgcolor=#aaa9a4></td>
    <td width="1" height="1"
bgcolor=#c0c0be></td>
    <td width="1" height="1"
bgcolor=#b9bab8></td>
    <td width="1" height="1"
bgcolor=#c7cccb></td>
    <td width="1" height="1"
bgcolor=#c9cdcb></td>
    <td width="1" height="1"
bgcolor=#c8cbcc></td>
    <td width="1" height="1"
bgcolor=#c4c8ca></td>
    <td width="1" height="1"
bgcolor=#909393></td>
  </tr>
  <tr>
    <td width="1" height="1"
bgcolor=#746d6c></td>
    <td width="1" height="1"
bgcolor=#878684></td>
    <td width="1" height="1"
bgcolor=#9f9c99></td>
    <td width="1" height="1"
bgcolor=#817d79></td>
    <td width="1" height="1"
bgcolor=#a09f9d></td>
    <td width="1" height="1"
bgcolor=#aaa9a7></td>
    <td width="1" height="1"
bgcolor=#a1a29e></td>
    <td width="1" height="1"
bgcolor=#88847f></td>
    <td width="1" height="1"
bgcolor=#87817f></td>
    <td width="1" height="1"
bgcolor=#a19e9a></td>
    <td width="1" height="1"
bgcolor=#948d8a></td>
    <td width="1" height="1"
bgcolor=#979490></td>
    <td width="1" height="1"
bgcolor=#989591></td>
    <td width="1" height="1"
bgcolor=#a1a09b></td>
    <td width="1" height="1"
bgcolor=#b7b7b4></td>
    <td width="1" height="1"
bgcolor=#b3b4af></td>
    <td width="1" height="1"
bgcolor=#adaca8></td>
    <td width="1" height="1"
bgcolor=#b2b1ad></td>
    <td width="1" height="1"
bgcolor=#b3b6b0></td>
    <td width="1" height="1"
bgcolor=#b1afab></td>
    <td width="1" height="1"
bgcolor=#a5a39e></td>
    <td width="1" height="1"
bgcolor=#9f9d98></td>
    <td rowspan="1"
colspan="2" width="1"
height="1"
bgcolor=#a19c98></td>
    <td width="1" height="1"
bgcolor=#97918d></td>
    <td width="1" height="1"
bgcolor=#a5a19d></td>
    <td width="1" height="1"
bgcolor=#aaa9a4></td>
    <td width="1" height="1"
bgcolor=#999691></td>
    <td width="1" height="1"
bgcolor=#adaea8></td>
    <td width="1" height="1"
bgcolor=#a5a49f></td>
    <td width="1" height="1"
bgcolor=#aaa7a2></td>
    <td width="1" height="1"
bgcolor=#827b78></td>
    <td width="1" height="1"
bgcolor=#96908a></td>
    <td width="1" height="1"
bgcolor=#a5a3a1></td>
    <td width="1" height="1"
bgcolor=#a09893></td>
```

```
    <td width="1" height="1"
bgcolor=#73665c></td>
    <td width="1" height="1"
bgcolor=#776659></td>
    <td width="1" height="1"
bgcolor=#deded9></td>
    <td width="1" height="1"
bgcolor=#b5b5b0></td>
    <td width="1" height="1"
bgcolor=#b0b2ac></td>
    <td width="1" height="1"
bgcolor=#b1afaa></td>
    <td width="1" height="1"
bgcolor=#a09d98></td>
    <td rowspan="2"
colspan="1" width="1"
height="1"
bgcolor=#99908d></td>
    <td width="1" height="1"
bgcolor=#d0d2d0></td>
    <td width="1" height="1"
bgcolor=#b0aca7></td>
    <td width="1" height="1"
bgcolor=#afa89d></td>
    <td width="1" height="1"
bgcolor=#b3ab9a></td>
    <td width="1" height="1"
bgcolor=#afa99e></td>
    <td width="1" height="1"
bgcolor=#877e7c></td>
    <td width="1" height="1"
bgcolor=#796f6d></td>
    <td width="1" height="1"
bgcolor=#6a605e></td>
    <td width="1" height="1"
bgcolor=#8e8582></td>
    <td width="1" height="1"
bgcolor=#89837f></td>
    <td width="1" height="1"
bgcolor=#9f9a96></td>
    <td width="1" height="1"
bgcolor=#afaea9></td>
    <td width="1" height="1"
bgcolor=#acaaa5></td>
    <td width="1" height="1"
bgcolor=#b2b0ab></td>
    <td width="1" height="1"
bgcolor=#bebfbb></td>
    <td width="1" height="1"
bgcolor=#b9b8b4></td>
    <td width="1" height="1"
bgcolor=#a4a29e></td>
    <td width="1" height="1"
bgcolor=#948f8a></td>
    <td width="1" height="1"
bgcolor=#b8b8b5></td>
    <td width="1" height="1"
bgcolor=#c8cbc9></td>
    <td width="1" height="1"
bgcolor=#c5c7c4></td>
    <td width="1" height="1"
bgcolor=#c6c8c7></td>
    <td width="1" height="1"
bgcolor=#bdc0bf></td>
    <td width="1" height="1"
bgcolor=#c1c2c0></td>
    <td width="1" height="1"
bgcolor=#c7cdcd></td>
    <td width="1" height="1"
bgcolor=#c8cbcc></td>
    <td width="1" height="1"
bgcolor=#c4c7c7></td>
    <td width="1" height="1"
bgcolor=#c8cbce></td>
    <td width="1" height="1"
bgcolor=#8c8f8e></td>
  </tr>
  <tr>
    <td width="1" height="1"
bgcolor=#807d7c></td>
    <td width="1" height="1"
bgcolor=#a0a19e></td>
    <td width="1" height="1"
bgcolor=#999897></td>
    <td width="1" height="1"
bgcolor=#9e9d9b></td>
    <td width="1" height="1"
bgcolor=#96948f></td>
    <td width="1" height="1"
bgcolor=#918e89></td>
    <td width="1" height="1"
bgcolor=#77726d></td>
    <td width="1" height="1"
bgcolor=#443d39></td>
    <td width="1" height="1"
bgcolor=#7d7472></td>
    <td width="1" height="1"
bgcolor=#97938e></td>
    <td width="1" height="1"
bgcolor=#9e9c98></td>
    <td width="1" height="1"
bgcolor=#9e9c97></td>
    <td width="1" height="1"
bgcolor=#8c8784></td>
    <td width="1" height="1"
bgcolor=#999591></td>
    <td width="1" height="1"
bgcolor=#a4a39d></td>
    <td width="1" height="1"
bgcolor=#a09f9a></td>
    <td width="1" height="1"
bgcolor=#a5a29d></td>
    <td width="1" height="1"
bgcolor=#aaa8a3></td>
    <td width="1" height="1"
bgcolor=#a4a39e></td>
    <td width="1" height="1"
bgcolor=#aeada8></td>
    <td width="1" height="1"
bgcolor=#aeada9></td>
    <td width="1" height="1"
bgcolor=#a8a7a2></td>
    <td width="1" height="1"
bgcolor=#a8a5a0></td>
    <td width="1" height="1"
bgcolor=#a7a49e></td>
    <td width="1" height="1"
bgcolor=#9f9c98></td>
    <td width="1" height="1"
bgcolor=#68615c></td>
    <td width="1" height="1"
bgcolor=#7f7772></td>
    <td width="1" height="1"
bgcolor=#b4b2ae></td>
    <td width="1" height="1"
bgcolor=#b6b5b0></td>
    <td width="1" height="1"
bgcolor=#a6a49f></td>
    <td width="1" height="1"
bgcolor=#8e8480></td>
    <td width="1" height="1"
bgcolor=#726965></td>
    <td width="1" height="1"
bgcolor=#938e8a></td>
    <td width="1" height="1"
bgcolor=#a9a7a2></td>
    <td width="1" height="1"
bgcolor=#9f9b97></td>
    <td width="1" height="1"
bgcolor=#9f968e></td>
    <td width="1" height="1"
bgcolor=#9f978a></td>
    <td width="1" height="1"
bgcolor=#bebfba></td>
    <td width="1" height="1"
bgcolor=#b6b6b3></td>
    <td width="1" height="1"
bgcolor=#9c9590></td>
    <td width="1" height="1"
bgcolor=#8c8583></td>
    <td width="1" height="1"
bgcolor=#776d6b></td>
    <td width="1" height="1"
bgcolor=#9b9691></td>
    <td width="1" height="1"
bgcolor=#9e9c92></td>
    <td width="1" height="1"
bgcolor=#9c9189></td>
    <td width="1" height="1"
bgcolor=#9b8f80></td>
    <td width="1" height="1"
bgcolor=#b2ada6></td>
    <td width="1" height="1"
bgcolor=#89837f></td>
```

```
    <td width="1" height="1" bgcolor=#8c827f></td>
    <td width="1" height="1" bgcolor=#98928f></td>
    <td width="1" height="1" bgcolor=#9c9894></td>
    <td width="1" height="1" bgcolor=#9e9895></td>
    <td width="1" height="1" bgcolor=#aaa9a4></td>
    <td width="1" height="1" bgcolor=#b6b3b0></td>
    <td width="1" height="1" bgcolor=#a5a19d></td>
    <td width="1" height="1" bgcolor=#b7b7b5></td>
    <td width="1" height="1" bgcolor=#95928c></td>
    <td width="1" height="1" bgcolor=#bab9b5></td>
    <td width="1" height="1" bgcolor=#b7b6b2></td>
    <td width="1" height="1" bgcolor=#bbbbb8></td>
    <td width="1" height="1" bgcolor=#c9c8c7></td>
    <td width="1" height="1" bgcolor=#bcbebc></td>
    <td width="1" height="1" bgcolor=#c5c5c5></td>
    <td width="1" height="1" bgcolor=#bcbdb9></td>
    <td width="1" height="1" bgcolor=#c3c5c2></td>
    <td width="1" height="1" bgcolor=#c5c9c8></td>
    <td width="1" height="1" bgcolor=#c2c5c4></td>
    <td width="1" height="1" bgcolor=#b6b9b5></td>
    <td width="1" height="1" bgcolor=#b1b0ad></td>
    <td width="1" height="1" bgcolor=#abaca6></td>
    <td width="1" height="1" bgcolor=#8c8e8c></td>
  </tr>
  <tr>
    <td width="1" height="1" bgcolor=#a09e9b></td>
    <td width="1" height="1" bgcolor=#9a9996></td>
    <td width="1" height="1" bgcolor=#85817d></td>
    <td width="1" height="1" bgcolor=#85807d></td>
    <td width="1" height="1" bgcolor=#807a77></td>
    <td width="1" height="1" bgcolor=#928d89></td>
    <td width="1" height="1" bgcolor=#928c88></td>
    <td width="1" height="1" bgcolor=#8d8985></td>
    <td width="1" height="1" bgcolor=#766f6c></td>
    <td width="1" height="1" bgcolor=#4c4240></td>
    <td width="1" height="1" bgcolor=#4f4442></td>
    <td width="1" height="1" bgcolor=#534846></td>
    <td width="1" height="1" bgcolor=#625756></td>
    <td width="1" height="1" bgcolor=#605755></td>
    <td width="1" height="1" bgcolor=#7b7572></td>
    <td width="1" height="1" bgcolor=#a4a19c></td>
    <td width="1" height="1" bgcolor=#aaaaa5></td>
    <td width="1" height="1" bgcolor=#ababa5></td>
    <td width="1" height="1" bgcolor=#adaca7></td>
    <td width="1" height="1" bgcolor=#acaba6></td>
    <td width="1" height="1" bgcolor=#b0aea9></td>
    <td width="1" height="1" bgcolor=#a6a5a0></td>
    <td width="1" height="1" bgcolor=#a6a49f></td>
    <td width="1" height="1" bgcolor=#adaaa5></td>
    <td width="1" height="1" bgcolor=#a5a39c></td>
    <td width="1" height="1" bgcolor=#abaaa3></td>
    <td width="1" height="1" bgcolor=#b4b3ad></td>
    <td width="1" height="1" bgcolor=#aba9a4></td>
    <td width="1" height="1" bgcolor=#ababa6></td>
    <td width="1" height="1" bgcolor=#b4b4af></td>
    <td width="1" height="1" bgcolor=#b1afaa></td>
    <td width="1" height="1" bgcolor=#b9b9b4></td>
    <td width="1" height="1" bgcolor=#bcbcb7></td>
    <td width="1" height="1" bgcolor=#6c6461></td>
    <td width="1" height="1" bgcolor=#9a9590></td>
    <td width="1" height="1" bgcolor=#9b9289></td>
    <td width="1" height="1" bgcolor=#ada69c></td>
    <td width="1" height="1" bgcolor=#b1b1ac></td>
    <td width="1" height="1" bgcolor=#b3b0ad></td>
    <td width="1" height="1" bgcolor=#babab2></td>
    <td width="1" height="1" bgcolor=#4d443e></td>
    <td width="1" height="1" bgcolor=#49403b></td>
    <td width="1" height="1" bgcolor=#403533></td>
    <td width="1" height="1" bgcolor=#3a302b></td>
    <td width="1" height="1" bgcolor=#7f736c></td>
    <td width="1" height="1" bgcolor=#64574e></td>
    <td width="1" height="1" bgcolor=#867665></td>
    <td width="1" height="1" bgcolor=#6a5849></td>
    <td width="1" height="1" bgcolor=#716863></td>
    <td width="1" height="1" bgcolor=#7a6f6d></td>
    <td width="1" height="1" bgcolor=#817876></td>
    <td width="1" height="1" bgcolor=#807774></td>
    <td width="1" height="1" bgcolor=#817875></td>
    <td width="1" height="1" bgcolor=#817873></td>
    <td width="1" height="1" bgcolor=#9b9792></td>
    <td width="1" height="1" bgcolor=#a3a19d></td>
    <td width="1" height="1" bgcolor=#bfbfbd></td>
    <td width="1" height="1" bgcolor=#c9cbc8></td>
    <td width="1" height="1" bgcolor=#bfbfbc></td>
    <td width="1" height="1" bgcolor=#c3c5c4></td>
    <td width="1" height="1" bgcolor=#bdbebc></td>
    <td width="1" height="1" bgcolor=#c1c2c1></td>
    <td width="1" height="1" bgcolor=#c8cccb></td>
```

```
    <td width="1" height="1"
bgcolor=#b5b6b1></td>
    <td width="1" height="1"
bgcolor=#b3b3af></td>
    <td width="1" height="1"
bgcolor=#a9a8a4></td>
    <td width="1" height="1"
bgcolor=#a6a5a0></td>
    <td width="1" height="1"
bgcolor=#a9a9a5></td>
    <td width="1" height="1"
bgcolor=#b9b9b8></td>
    <td width="1" height="1"
bgcolor=#c7cccc></td>
    <td width="1" height="1"
bgcolor=#c3c6c3></td>
    <td width="1" height="1"
bgcolor=#8a8c8b></td>
  </tr>
  <tr>
    <td width="1" height="1"
bgcolor=#4a4540></td>
    <td width="1" height="1"
bgcolor=#3e3633></td>
    <td width="1" height="1"
bgcolor=#635c56></td>
    <td width="1" height="1"
bgcolor=#615a57></td>
    <td width="1" height="1"
bgcolor=#564c4a></td>
    <td width="1" height="1"
bgcolor=#594f4d></td>
    <td width="1" height="1"
bgcolor=#716866></td>
    <td width="1" height="1"
bgcolor=#877d7b></td>
    <td width="1" height="1"
bgcolor=#a19b98></td>
    <td width="1" height="1"
bgcolor=#7f7774></td>
    <td width="1" height="1"
bgcolor=#837977></td>
    <td width="1" height="1"
bgcolor=#6f6765></td>
    <td width="1" height="1"
bgcolor=#736967></td>
    <td width="1" height="1"
bgcolor=#8d8683></td>
    <td width="1" height="1"
bgcolor=#8f8885></td>
    <td rowspan="1"
colspan="2" width="1"
height="1"
bgcolor=#928d89></td>
    <td width="1" height="1"
bgcolor=#9e9995></td>
    <td width="1" height="1"
bgcolor=#a3a09b></td>
    <td width="1" height="1"
bgcolor=#a8a6a1></td>
    <td width="1" height="1"
bgcolor=#adaaa6></td>
    <td width="1" height="1"
bgcolor=#aeada9></td>
    <td width="1" height="1"
bgcolor=#b2b1ad></td>
    <td width="1" height="1"
bgcolor=#adaca7></td>
    <td width="1" height="1"
bgcolor=#b3b4af></td>
    <td width="1" height="1"
bgcolor=#b1b0ab></td>
    <td width="1" height="1"
bgcolor=#b2b1ac></td>
    <td width="1" height="1"
bgcolor=#b6b5b1></td>
    <td width="1" height="1"
bgcolor=#adaca7></td>
    <td width="1" height="1"
bgcolor=#b8b8b5></td>
    <td width="1" height="1"
bgcolor=#adaca7></td>
    <td width="1" height="1"
bgcolor=#b1aeaa></td>
    <td width="1" height="1"
bgcolor=#a09b98></td>
    <td width="1" height="1"
bgcolor=#544947></td>
    <td width="1" height="1"
bgcolor=#9f9991></td>
    <td width="1" height="1"
bgcolor=#887b72></td>
    <td width="1" height="1"
bgcolor=#a89e90></td>
    <td width="1" height="1"
bgcolor=#887e7a></td>
    <td width="1" height="1"
bgcolor=#89827e></td>
    <td width="1" height="1"
bgcolor=#96928d></td>
    <td width="1" height="1"
bgcolor=#938b88></td>
    <td width="1" height="1"
bgcolor=#5c544f></td>
    <td width="1" height="1"
bgcolor=#817974></td>
    <td width="1" height="1"
bgcolor=#8a7f7e></td>
    <td width="1" height="1"
bgcolor=#857c77></td>
    <td width="1" height="1"
bgcolor=#3f3328></td>
    <td width="1" height="1"
bgcolor=#4d3d30></td>
    <td width="1" height="1"
bgcolor=#38281f></td>
    <td width="1" height="1"
bgcolor=#979085></td>
    <td width="1" height="1"
bgcolor=#796f6c></td>
    <td width="1" height="1"
bgcolor=#9f9897></td>
    <td width="1" height="1"
bgcolor=#b4b2ae></td>
    <td width="1" height="1"
bgcolor=#bbbdb8></td>
    <td width="1" height="1"
bgcolor=#b2aeac></td>
    <td width="1" height="1"
bgcolor=#b8b9b5></td>
    <td width="1" height="1"
bgcolor=#c2c3c2></td>
    <td width="1" height="1"
bgcolor=#c2c3c4></td>
    <td width="1" height="1"
bgcolor=#c4c7c6></td>
    <td width="1" height="1"
bgcolor=#c6c6c3></td>
    <td width="1" height="1"
bgcolor=#9e9c93></td>
    <td width="1" height="1"
bgcolor=#c6c6c3></td>
    <td width="1" height="1"
bgcolor=#b4b4ae></td>
    <td width="1" height="1"
bgcolor=#c1c2c1></td>
    <td width="1" height="1"
bgcolor=#bdbfbe></td>
    <td width="1" height="1"
bgcolor=#c8cac8></td>
    <td width="1" height="1"
bgcolor=#cacbc8></td>
    <td width="1" height="1"
bgcolor=#bfbfbd></td>
    <td width="1" height="1"
bgcolor=#c9ccca></td>
    <td width="1" height="1"
bgcolor=#c7cac8></td>
    <td width="1" height="1"
bgcolor=#c2c3c4></td>
    <td width="1" height="1"
bgcolor=#c8cccc></td>
    <td width="1" height="1"
bgcolor=#8c9090></td>
  </tr>
  <tr>
    <td width="1" height="1"
bgcolor=#756c6a></td>
    <td width="1" height="1"
bgcolor=#766c6c></td>
    <td width="1" height="1"
bgcolor=#4f4943></td>
    <td width="1" height="1"
bgcolor=#5a514e></td>
```

```
<td width="1" height="1" bgcolor=#6c6361></td>
<td width="1" height="1" bgcolor=#756b6a></td>
<td width="1" height="1" bgcolor=#796f6d></td>
<td width="1" height="1" bgcolor=#847d7a></td>
<td width="1" height="1" bgcolor=#948f8b></td>
<td width="1" height="1" bgcolor=#a09c98></td>
<td width="1" height="1" bgcolor=#9b9894></td>
<td width="1" height="1" bgcolor=#9e9b97></td>
<td width="1" height="1" bgcolor=#837c79></td>
<td width="1" height="1" bgcolor=#8e8b86></td>
<td width="1" height="1" bgcolor=#98938f></td>
<td width="1" height="1" bgcolor=#938f8a></td>
<td width="1" height="1" bgcolor=#9b9692></td>
<td width="1" height="1" bgcolor=#908985></td>
<td width="1" height="1" bgcolor=#928d89></td>
<td width="1" height="1" bgcolor=#a09d98></td>
<td width="1" height="1" bgcolor=#b2b2ad></td>
<td width="1" height="1" bgcolor=#b4b4af></td>
<td width="1" height="1" bgcolor=#bcbdb8></td>
<td width="1" height="1" bgcolor=#c6c7c3></td>
<td width="1" height="1" bgcolor=#c2c4c1></td>
<td width="1" height="1" bgcolor=#b6b7b4></td>
<td width="1" height="1" bgcolor=#babab6></td>
<td width="1" height="1" bgcolor=#bfc0bc></td>
<td width="1" height="1" bgcolor=#abaca8></td>
<td width="1" height="1" bgcolor=#b6b5b0></td>
<td width="1" height="1" bgcolor=#8d8781></td>
<td width="1" height="1" bgcolor=#9f9896></td>
<td width="1" height="1" bgcolor=#9f9a97></td>
<td width="1" height="1" bgcolor=#302925></td>
<td width="1" height="1" bgcolor=#3c332b></td>
<td width="1" height="1" bgcolor=#291e13></td>
<td width="1" height="1" bgcolor=#87827a></td>
<td width="1" height="1" bgcolor=#5e5952></td>
<td width="1" height="1" bgcolor=#908683></td>
<td width="1" height="1" bgcolor=#98908c></td>
<td width="1" height="1" bgcolor=#96908d></td>
<td width="1" height="1" bgcolor=#a8a29e></td>
<td width="1" height="1" bgcolor=#98928e></td>
<td width="1" height="1" bgcolor=#a8a29f></td>
<td width="1" height="1" bgcolor=#8d8380></td>
<td width="1" height="1" bgcolor=#493f38></td>
<td width="1" height="1" bgcolor=#493d34></td>
<td width="1" height="1" bgcolor=#544538></td>
<td width="1" height="1" bgcolor=#473b31></td>
<td width="1" height="1" bgcolor=#a19e97></td>
<td width="1" height="1" bgcolor=#bfc1bb></td>
<td width="1" height="1" bgcolor=#4a3e38></td>
<td width="1" height="1" bgcolor=#b8bab4></td>
<td width="1" height="1" bgcolor=#c9c9cb></td>
<td width="1" height="1" bgcolor=#cacbca></td>
<td width="1" height="1" bgcolor=#ced0d0></td>
<td width="1" height="1" bgcolor=#c9cbc9></td>
<td width="1" height="1" bgcolor=#bfbeb9></td>
<td width="1" height="1" bgcolor=#acaaa7></td>
<td width="1" height="1" bgcolor=#b5b4b0></td>
<td width="1" height="1" bgcolor=#a8a5a0></td>
<td width="1" height="1" bgcolor=#b8b6b3></td>
<td width="1" height="1" bgcolor=#b8bab5></td>
<td width="1" height="1" bgcolor=#b4b3b0></td>
<td width="1" height="1" bgcolor=#bfbfbc></td>
<td width="1" height="1" bgcolor=#bcbbba></td>
<td width="1" height="1" bgcolor=#b5b6b0></td>
<td width="1" height="1" bgcolor=#babbb6></td>
<td width="1" height="1" bgcolor=#b6b7b2></td>
<td width="1" height="1" bgcolor=#bbbcb7></td>
<td width="1" height="1" bgcolor=#b4b6b0></td>
<td width="1" height="1" bgcolor=#8a8b8a></td>
</tr>
<tr>
<td width="1" height="1" bgcolor=#4b4442></td>
<td width="1" height="1" bgcolor=#584e4d></td>
<td width="1" height="1" bgcolor=#6a6460></td>
<td width="1" height="1" bgcolor=#69605e></td>
<td width="1" height="1" bgcolor=#4f4644></td>
<td width="1" height="1" bgcolor=#473f3b></td>
<td width="1" height="1" bgcolor=#807874></td>
<td width="1" height="1" bgcolor=#827a77></td>
<td width="1" height="1" bgcolor=#746e6a></td>
<td width="1" height="1" bgcolor=#736b69></td>
<td width="1" height="1" bgcolor=#95928d></td>
<td width="1" height="1" bgcolor=#958f8b></td>
<td width="1" height="1" bgcolor=#96918d></td>
<td width="1" height="1" bgcolor=#908885></td>
<td width="1" height="1" bgcolor=#86817d></td>
<td width="1" height="1" bgcolor=#706764></td>
<td width="1" height="1" bgcolor=#8f8a86></td>
<td width="1" height="1" bgcolor=#908b87></td>
```

```
    <td width="1" height="1" bgcolor=#9b9793></td>
    <td width="1" height="1" bgcolor=#afaea9></td>
    <td width="1" height="1" bgcolor=#abaaa5></td>
    <td width="1" height="1" bgcolor=#aaa8a3></td>
    <td width="1" height="1" bgcolor=#b3b3ae></td>
    <td width="1" height="1" bgcolor=#b8b8b4></td>
    <td width="1" height="1" bgcolor=#c4c7c6></td>
    <td width="1" height="1" bgcolor=#c8cac8></td>
    <td width="1" height="1" bgcolor=#bdbeba></td>
    <td width="1" height="1" bgcolor=#b9bbb8></td>
    <td width="1" height="1" bgcolor=#adaba6></td>
    <td width="1" height="1" bgcolor=#bcbdba></td>
    <td width="1" height="1" bgcolor=#807a73></td>
    <td width="1" height="1" bgcolor=#a29d98></td>
    <td width="1" height="1" bgcolor=#4b4441></td>
    <td width="1" height="1" bgcolor=#2f2923></td>
    <td width="1" height="1" bgcolor=#281d14></td>
    <td width="1" height="1" bgcolor=#524840></td>
    <td width="1" height="1" bgcolor=#8e8984></td>
    <td width="1" height="1" bgcolor=#807772></td>
    <td width="1" height="1" bgcolor=#958d88></td>
    <td width="1" height="1" bgcolor=#999490></td>
    <td width="1" height="1" bgcolor=#817875></td>
    <td width="1" height="1" bgcolor=#a29b97></td>
    <td width="1" height="1" bgcolor=#a59d9a></td>
    <td width="1" height="1" bgcolor=#a49c99></td>
    <td width="1" height="1" bgcolor=#a19995></td>
    <td width="1" height="1" bgcolor=#37302a></td>
    <td width="1" height="1" bgcolor=#1e1a0d></td>
    <td width="1" height="1" bgcolor=#33291d></td>
    <td width="1" height="1" bgcolor=#453c34></td>
    <td width="1" height="1" bgcolor=#8d8682></td>
    <td width="1" height="1" bgcolor=#8a827e></td>
    <td width="1" height="1" bgcolor=#8e8682></td>
    <td width="1" height="1" bgcolor=#aba8a3></td>
    <td width="1" height="1" bgcolor=#b8b6b2></td>
    <td width="1" height="1" bgcolor=#9a9591></td>
    <td width="1" height="1" bgcolor=#807771></td>
    <td width="1" height="1" bgcolor=#99928d></td>
    <td width="1" height="1" bgcolor=#b1afac></td>
    <td width="1" height="1" bgcolor=#c1c2bf></td>
    <td width="1" height="1" bgcolor=#b8b7b4></td>
    <td width="1" height="1" bgcolor=#b0aeab></td>
    <td width="1" height="1" bgcolor=#aaa5a1></td>
    <td width="1" height="1" bgcolor=#887e7a></td>
    <td width="1" height="1" bgcolor=#463c32></td>
    <td width="1" height="1" bgcolor=#564d43></td>
    <td width="1" height="1" bgcolor=#6e655e></td>
    <td width="1" height="1" bgcolor=#a8a6a2></td>
    <td width="1" height="1" bgcolor=#aeaea8></td>
    <td width="1" height="1" bgcolor=#a2a09b></td>
    <td width="1" height="1" bgcolor=#9e9c97></td>
    <td width="1" height="1" bgcolor=#7c756d></td>
    <td width="1" height="1" bgcolor=#4c4841></td>
  </tr>
  <tr>
    <td width="1" height="1" bgcolor=#796f6f></td>
    <td width="1" height="1" bgcolor=#7b7474></td>
    <td width="1" height="1" bgcolor=#756d6b></td>
    <td width="1" height="1" bgcolor=#7a7270></td>
    <td width="1" height="1" bgcolor=#706866></td>
    <td width="1" height="1" bgcolor=#776f6c></td>
    <td width="1" height="1" bgcolor=#847b78></td>
    <td width="1" height="1" bgcolor=#79716d></td>
    <td width="1" height="1" bgcolor=#756c67></td>
    <td width="1" height="1" bgcolor=#372e2b></td>
    <td width="1" height="1" bgcolor=#989490></td>
    <td width="1" height="1" bgcolor=#a19e99></td>
    <td width="1" height="1" bgcolor=#a5a39f></td>
    <td width="1" height="1" bgcolor=#a4a29e></td>
    <td width="1" height="1" bgcolor=#b3b2ae></td>
    <td width="1" height="1" bgcolor=#a4a39e></td>
    <td width="1" height="1" bgcolor=#a29c9a></td>
    <td width="1" height="1" bgcolor=#aaa8a3></td>
    <td width="1" height="1" bgcolor=#a39f9b></td>
    <td width="1" height="1" bgcolor=#867f7d></td>
    <td width="1" height="1" bgcolor=#a6a4a0></td>
    <td width="1" height="1" bgcolor=#b5b6b1></td>
    <td width="1" height="1" bgcolor=#c2c1bd></td>
    <td width="1" height="1" bgcolor=#b4b2b0></td>
    <td width="1" height="1" bgcolor=#b1afaa></td>
    <td width="1" height="1" bgcolor=#a7a49e></td>
    <td width="1" height="1" bgcolor=#a6a49f></td>
    <td width="1" height="1" bgcolor=#9f9895></td>
    <td width="1" height="1" bgcolor=#948d88></td>
    <td width="1" height="1" bgcolor=#928886></td>
    <td width="1" height="1" bgcolor=#212019></td>
    <td width="1" height="1" bgcolor=#13120d></td>
```

```
    <td width="1" height="1" bgcolor=#191c15></td>
    <td width="1" height="1" bgcolor=#201c16></td>
    <td width="1" height="1" bgcolor=#5e5350></td>
    <td width="1" height="1" bgcolor=#958c86></td>
    <td width="1" height="1" bgcolor=#635955></td>
    <td width="1" height="1" bgcolor=#625753></td>
    <td width="1" height="1" bgcolor=#877e7a></td>
    <td width="1" height="1" bgcolor=#a09c98></td>
    <td width="1" height="1" bgcolor=#b2ada7></td>
    <td width="1" height="1" bgcolor=#a8a09c></td>
    <td width="1" height="1" bgcolor=#a09b96></td>
    <td width="1" height="1" bgcolor=#665d55></td>
    <td width="1" height="1" bgcolor=#3c3529></td>
    <td width="1" height="1" bgcolor=#3b342a></td>
    <td width="1" height="1" bgcolor=#9c958f></td>
    <td width="1" height="1" bgcolor=#c1beba></td>
    <td width="1" height="1" bgcolor=#b3b0ab></td>
    <td width="1" height="1" bgcolor=#a9a5a1></td>
    <td width="1" height="1" bgcolor=#b0aba8></td>
    <td width="1" height="1" bgcolor=#b0ada9></td>
    <td width="1" height="1" bgcolor=#aaa6a1></td>
    <td width="1" height="1" bgcolor=#b3afab></td>
    <td width="1" height="1" bgcolor=#b2aca8></td>
    <td width="1" height="1" bgcolor=#aea9a3></td>
    <td width="1" height="1" bgcolor=#ada9a4></td>
    <td width="1" height="1" bgcolor=#a59f9b></td>
    <td width="1" height="1" bgcolor=#a8a29e></td>
    <td width="1" height="1" bgcolor=#9e9894></td>
    <td width="1" height="1" bgcolor=#a09a97></td>
    <td width="1" height="1" bgcolor=#9a918f></td>
    <td width="1" height="1" bgcolor=#726965></td>
    <td width="1" height="1" bgcolor=#706661></td>
    <td width="1" height="1" bgcolor=#4d4440></td>
    <td width="1" height="1" bgcolor=#756a65></td>
    <td width="1" height="1" bgcolor=#665d55></td>
    <td width="1" height="1" bgcolor=#847d78></td>
    <td width="1" height="1" bgcolor=#8b847c></td>
    <td width="1" height="1" bgcolor=#938b85></td>
    <td width="1" height="1" bgcolor=#7b756f></td>
    <td width="1" height="1" bgcolor=#757370></td>
  </tr>
  <tr>
    <td width="1" height="1" bgcolor=#5b5150></td>
    <td width="1" height="1" bgcolor=#65605c></td>
    <td width="1" height="1" bgcolor=#514847></td>
    <td width="1" height="1" bgcolor=#77706c></td>
    <td width="1" height="1" bgcolor=#999491></td>
    <td width="1" height="1" bgcolor=#8b8582></td>
    <td width="1" height="1" bgcolor=#867f7b></td>
    <td width="1" height="1" bgcolor=#776e6b></td>
    <td width="1" height="1" bgcolor=#716765></td>
    <td width="1" height="1" bgcolor=#6d6563></td>
    <td width="1" height="1" bgcolor=#847b79></td>
    <td width="1" height="1" bgcolor=#867d7b></td>
    <td width="1" height="1" bgcolor=#989691></td>
    <td width="1" height="1" bgcolor=#999691></td>
    <td width="1" height="1" bgcolor=#97928f></td>
    <td width="1" height="1" bgcolor=#95918d></td>
    <td width="1" height="1" bgcolor=#9b9692></td>
    <td width="1" height="1" bgcolor=#9d9a95></td>
    <td width="1" height="1" bgcolor=#978f8c></td>
    <td width="1" height="1" bgcolor=#a09d98></td>
    <td width="1" height="1" bgcolor=#a9a8a1></td>
    <td width="1" height="1" bgcolor=#918c88></td>
    <td width="1" height="1" bgcolor=#938e8a></td>
    <td width="1" height="1" bgcolor=#756c68></td>
    <td width="1" height="1" bgcolor=#827b78></td>
    <td width="1" height="1" bgcolor=#887f7c></td>
    <td width="1" height="1" bgcolor=#887b78></td>
    <td width="1" height="1" bgcolor=#37312a></td>
    <td width="1" height="1" bgcolor=#625855></td>
    <td width="1" height="1" bgcolor=#151711></td>
    <td width="1" height="1" bgcolor=#050c03></td>
    <td width="1" height="1" bgcolor=#000a00></td>
    <td width="1" height="1" bgcolor=#040902></td>
    <td width="1" height="1" bgcolor=#2c2a22></td>
    <td width="1" height="1" bgcolor=#857b79></td>
    <td width="1" height="1" bgcolor=#837a79></td>
    <td width="1" height="1" bgcolor=#918886></td>
    <td width="1" height="1" bgcolor=#b0aba5></td>
    <td width="1" height="1" bgcolor=#a7a49d></td>
    <td width="1" height="1" bgcolor=#827e77></td>
    <td width="1" height="1" bgcolor=#322e23></td>
    <td width="1" height="1" bgcolor=#0e0c00></td>
    <td width="1" height="1" bgcolor=#1f180a></td>
    <td width="1" height="1" bgcolor=#3c372a></td>
    <td width="1" height="1" bgcolor=#918b83></td>
    <td width="1" height="1" bgcolor=#b2aea8></td>
```

```
    <td width="1" height="1"
bgcolor=#9b9490></td>
    <td width="1" height="1"
bgcolor=#98958f></td>
    <td width="1" height="1"
bgcolor=#aaa69f></td>
    <td width="1" height="1"
bgcolor=#aca9a4></td>
    <td width="1" height="1"
bgcolor=#b4b1aa></td>
    <td width="1" height="1"
bgcolor=#9d9793></td>
    <td width="1" height="1"
bgcolor=#aba7a2></td>
    <td width="1" height="1"
bgcolor=#a6a29d></td>
    <td width="1" height="1"
bgcolor=#9f9c98></td>
    <td width="1" height="1"
bgcolor=#b0aea9></td>
    <td width="1" height="1"
bgcolor=#a8a39f></td>
    <td width="1" height="1"
bgcolor=#a8a19e></td>
    <td width="1" height="1"
bgcolor=#aaa7a2></td>
    <td width="1" height="1"
bgcolor=#978f8a></td>
    <td width="1" height="1"
bgcolor=#867d78></td>
    <td width="1" height="1"
bgcolor=#9f9894></td>
    <td width="1" height="1"
bgcolor=#a19897></td>
    <td width="1" height="1"
bgcolor=#908a85></td>
    <td width="1" height="1"
bgcolor=#a29c96></td>
    <td width="1" height="1"
bgcolor=#908783></td>
    <td width="1" height="1"
bgcolor=#978f8b></td>
    <td width="1" height="1"
bgcolor=#8a817a></td>
    <td width="1" height="1"
bgcolor=#776c68></td>
    <td width="1" height="1"
bgcolor=#7c746a></td>
    <td width="1" height="1"
bgcolor=#9d9a95></td>
    <td width="1" height="1"
bgcolor=#7f7e7b></td>
  </tr>
  <tr>
    <td width="1" height="1"
bgcolor=#766d6b></td>
    <td width="1" height="1"
bgcolor=#8b8582></td>
    <td width="1" height="1"
bgcolor=#706866></td>
    <td width="1" height="1"
bgcolor=#6c6462></td>
    <td width="1" height="1"
bgcolor=#79706d></td>
    <td width="1" height="1"
bgcolor=#847b78></td>
    <td width="1" height="1"
bgcolor=#837d79></td>
    <td width="1" height="1"
bgcolor=#79716e></td>
    <td width="1" height="1"
bgcolor=#887f7d></td>
    <td width="1" height="1"
bgcolor=#7f7a76></td>
    <td width="1" height="1"
bgcolor=#6e6563></td>
    <td width="1" height="1"
bgcolor=#847c79></td>
    <td width="1" height="1"
bgcolor=#857d7a></td>
    <td width="1" height="1"
bgcolor=#89827e></td>
    <td width="1" height="1"
bgcolor=#7e7572></td>
    <td width="1" height="1"
bgcolor=#97928e></td>
    <td width="1" height="1"
bgcolor=#948f8b></td>
    <td width="1" height="1"
bgcolor=#867d7a></td>
    <td width="1" height="1"
bgcolor=#887e7c></td>
    <td width="1" height="1"
bgcolor=#8c8681></td>
    <td width="1" height="1"
bgcolor=#988f89></td>
    <td width="1" height="1"
bgcolor=#847b77></td>
    <td width="1" height="1"
bgcolor=#5f5654></td>
    <td width="1" height="1"
bgcolor=#857e7a></td>
    <td width="1" height="1"
bgcolor=#a19c98></td>
    <td width="1" height="1"
bgcolor=#a8a7a2></td>
    <td width="1" height="1"
bgcolor=#6d6c66></td>
    <td width="1" height="1"
bgcolor=#191d18></td>
    <td width="1" height="1"
bgcolor=#000000></td>
    <td width="1" height="1"
bgcolor=#030d02></td>
    <td width="1" height="1"
bgcolor=#000b02></td>
    <td width="1" height="1"
bgcolor=#5c5750></td>
    <td width="1" height="1"
bgcolor=#a49b97></td>
    <td width="1" height="1"
bgcolor=#928b86></td>
    <td width="1" height="1"
bgcolor=#ada8a4></td>
    <td width="1" height="1"
bgcolor=#8b837f></td>
    <td width="1" height="1"
bgcolor=#24211d></td>
    <td width="1" height="1"
bgcolor=#0a0903></td>
    <td width="1" height="1"
bgcolor=#000000></td>
    <td width="1" height="1"
bgcolor=#080800></td>
    <td width="1" height="1"
bgcolor=#181614></td>
    <td width="1" height="1"
bgcolor=#897f7c></td>
    <td width="1" height="1"
bgcolor=#bebbb6></td>
    <td width="1" height="1"
bgcolor=#a8a3a0></td>
    <td width="1" height="1"
bgcolor=#777069></td>
    <td width="1" height="1"
bgcolor=#9f9895></td>
    <td width="1" height="1"
bgcolor=#b1aea9></td>
    <td width="1" height="1"
bgcolor=#99928c></td>
    <td width="1" height="1"
bgcolor=#928e89></td>
    <td width="1" height="1"
bgcolor=#96938d></td>
    <td width="1" height="1"
bgcolor=#ada9a5></td>
    <td width="1" height="1"
bgcolor=#968e8a></td>
    <td width="1" height="1"
bgcolor=#7b736c></td>
    <td width="1" height="1"
bgcolor=#887e7a></td>
    <td width="1" height="1"
bgcolor=#8e8480></td>
    <td width="1" height="1"
bgcolor=#847b77></td>
    <td width="1" height="1"
bgcolor=#948a88></td>
    <td width="1" height="1"
bgcolor=#958a88></td>
    <td width="1" height="1"
bgcolor=#9a9691></td>
    <td width="1" height="1"
bgcolor=#9e9a96></td>
```

```
    <td width="1" height="1" bgcolor=#a5a09c></td>
    <td width="1" height="1" bgcolor=#9d9793></td>
    <td width="1" height="1" bgcolor=#4c423a></td>
    <td width="1" height="1" bgcolor=#9b9691></td>
    <td width="1" height="1" bgcolor=#aaa5a1></td>
    <td width="1" height="1" bgcolor=#a3a09b></td>
    <td width="1" height="1" bgcolor=#aaa7a0></td>
    <td width="1" height="1" bgcolor=#adaba7></td>
    <td width="1" height="1" bgcolor=#b2aeaa></td>
    <td width="1" height="1" bgcolor=#b3b5af></td>
    <td width="1" height="1" bgcolor=#949088></td>
    <td width="1" height="1" bgcolor=#716f6b></td>
  </tr>
  <tr>
    <td width="1" height="1" bgcolor=#6b635f></td>
    <td width="1" height="1" bgcolor=#77706e></td>
    <td width="1" height="1" bgcolor=#746d6a></td>
    <td width="1" height="1" bgcolor=#706865></td>
    <td width="1" height="1" bgcolor=#6a6060></td>
    <td width="1" height="1" bgcolor=#665c5b></td>
    <td width="1" height="1" bgcolor=#746f6c></td>
    <td width="1" height="1" bgcolor=#786f6e></td>
    <td width="1" height="1" bgcolor=#78726e></td>
    <td width="1" height="1" bgcolor=#574f4d></td>
    <td width="1" height="1" bgcolor=#2a2823></td>
    <td width="1" height="1" bgcolor=#7b7571></td>
    <td width="1" height="1" bgcolor=#867c7a></td>
    <td width="1" height="1" bgcolor=#6a5f5e></td>
    <td width="1" height="1" bgcolor=#7a726f></td>
    <td width="1" height="1" bgcolor=#746766></td>
    <td width="1" height="1" bgcolor=#857c7a></td>
    <td width="1" height="1" bgcolor=#786f6d></td>
    <td width="1" height="1" bgcolor=#736b69></td>
    <td width="1" height="1" bgcolor=#766c6a></td>
    <td width="1" height="1" bgcolor=#302e29></td>
    <td width="1" height="1" bgcolor=#746a65></td>
    <td width="1" height="1" bgcolor=#9b938f></td>
    <td width="1" height="1" bgcolor=#86807b></td>
    <td width="1" height="1" bgcolor=#211f1f></td>
    <td width="1" height="1" bgcolor=#000000></td>
    <td width="1" height="1" bgcolor=#000401></td>
    <td width="1" height="1" bgcolor=#010904></td>
    <td width="1" height="1" bgcolor=#020901></td>
    <td width="1" height="1" bgcolor=#11100f></td>
    <td width="1" height="1" bgcolor=#8a7f7d></td>
    <td width="1" height="1" bgcolor=#7c7371></td>
    <td width="1" height="1" bgcolor=#6c6360></td>
    <td width="1" height="1" bgcolor=#1b1d18></td>
    <td rowspan="1" colspan="2" width="1" height="1" bgcolor=#000100></td>
    <td width="1" height="1" bgcolor=#020c02></td>
    <td width="1" height="1" bgcolor=#060701></td>
    <td width="1" height="1" bgcolor=#13110b></td>
    <td width="1" height="1" bgcolor=#9c9792></td>
    <td width="1" height="1" bgcolor=#a09d96></td>
    <td width="1" height="1" bgcolor=#a9a5a1></td>
    <td width="1" height="1" bgcolor=#9b918f></td>
    <td width="1" height="1" bgcolor=#b4b4ae></td>
    <td width="1" height="1" bgcolor=#a4a09b></td>
    <td width="1" height="1" bgcolor=#ada9a2></td>
    <td width="1" height="1" bgcolor=#857f7a></td>
    <td width="1" height="1" bgcolor=#a49e9a></td>
    <td width="1" height="1" bgcolor=#a79e9a></td>
    <td width="1" height="1" bgcolor=#a39d99></td>
    <td width="1" height="1" bgcolor=#aaa7a3></td>
    <td width="1" height="1" bgcolor=#97908c></td>
    <td width="1" height="1" bgcolor=#aaa4a2></td>
    <td width="1" height="1" bgcolor=#837a74></td>
    <td width="1" height="1" bgcolor=#847d74></td>
    <td width="1" height="1" bgcolor=#675c58></td>
    <td width="1" height="1" bgcolor=#87817d></td>
    <td width="1" height="1" bgcolor=#a39a97></td>
    <td width="1" height="1" bgcolor=#8f8683></td>
    <td width="1" height="1" bgcolor=#8f8884></td>
    <td width="1" height="1" bgcolor=#9d9592></td>
    <td width="1" height="1" bgcolor=#867f77></td>
    <td width="1" height="1" bgcolor=#9b938d></td>
    <td width="1" height="1" bgcolor=#9f9893></td>
    <td width="1" height="1" bgcolor=#867e76></td>
    <td width="1" height="1" bgcolor=#9f9994></td>
    <td width="1" height="1" bgcolor=#b0afa9></td>
    <td width="1" height="1" bgcolor=#adaca9></td>
    <td width="1" height="1" bgcolor=#a5a19d></td>
    <td width="1" height="1" bgcolor=#9a9690></td>
    <td width="1" height="1" bgcolor=#b4b4af></td>
    <td width="1" height="1" bgcolor=#868784></td>
  </tr>
  <tr>
    <td width="1" height="1" bgcolor=#847c79></td>
```

```
    <td width="1" height="1"
bgcolor=#7c7372></td>
    <td width="1" height="1"
bgcolor=#817b78></td>
    <td width="1" height="1"
bgcolor=#736c69></td>
    <td width="1" height="1"
bgcolor=#7f7875></td>
    <td width="1" height="1"
bgcolor=#6c615f></td>
    <td width="1" height="1"
bgcolor=#7d7572></td>
    <td width="1" height="1"
bgcolor=#5b5451></td>
    <td width="1" height="1"
bgcolor=#726b68></td>
    <td width="1" height="1"
bgcolor=#403835></td>
    <td width="1" height="1"
bgcolor=#827977></td>
    <td width="1" height="1"
bgcolor=#695d5c></td>
    <td width="1" height="1"
bgcolor=#8e8884></td>
    <td width="1" height="1"
bgcolor=#817775></td>
    <td width="1" height="1"
bgcolor=#8a807e></td>
    <td width="1" height="1"
bgcolor=#6c6361></td>
    <td width="1" height="1"
bgcolor=#a29e98></td>
    <td width="1" height="1"
bgcolor=#97918c></td>
    <td width="1" height="1"
bgcolor=#a7a5a0></td>
    <td width="1" height="1"
bgcolor=#867f78></td>
    <td width="1" height="1"
bgcolor=#585551></td>
    <td width="1" height="1"
bgcolor=#312f2d></td>
    <td width="1" height="1"
bgcolor=#494440></td>
    <td width="1" height="1"
bgcolor=#000000></td>
    <td width="1" height="1"
bgcolor=#050902></td>
    <td width="1" height="1"
bgcolor=#000501></td>
    <td width="1" height="1"
bgcolor=#010401></td>
    <td width="1" height="1"
bgcolor=#000a01></td>
    <td width="1" height="1"
bgcolor=#31342d></td>
    <td width="1" height="1"
bgcolor=#9f9694></td>
    <td width="1" height="1"
bgcolor=#908b87></td>
    <td width="1" height="1"
bgcolor=#463c39></td>
    <td width="1" height="1"
bgcolor=#544e4c></td>
    <td width="1" height="1"
bgcolor=#000400></td>
    <td width="1" height="1"
bgcolor=#090c02></td>
    <td width="1" height="1"
bgcolor=#090e04></td>
    <td width="1" height="1"
bgcolor=#040900></td>
    <td width="1" height="1"
bgcolor=#2e2b27></td>
    <td width="1" height="1"
bgcolor=#111210></td>
    <td width="1" height="1"
bgcolor=#000100></td>
    <td width="1" height="1"
bgcolor=#474440></td>
    <td width="1" height="1"
bgcolor=#968e8b></td>
    <td width="1" height="1"
bgcolor=#655b58></td>
    <td width="1" height="1"
bgcolor=#776f6a></td>
    <td width="1" height="1"
bgcolor=#756b67></td>
    <td width="1" height="1"
bgcolor=#948a88></td>
    <td width="1" height="1"
bgcolor=#89807a></td>
    <td width="1" height="1"
bgcolor=#786e6a></td>
    <td width="1" height="1"
bgcolor=#605553></td>
    <td width="1" height="1"
bgcolor=#463d3a></td>
    <td width="1" height="1"
bgcolor=#7d746c></td>
    <td width="1" height="1"
bgcolor=#7b706b></td>
    <td width="1" height="1"
bgcolor=#726d67></td>
    <td width="1" height="1"
bgcolor=#7b726e></td>
    <td width="1" height="1"
bgcolor=#988f8c></td>
    <td width="1" height="1"
bgcolor=#928b86></td>
    <td width="1" height="1"
bgcolor=#98908d></td>
    <td width="1" height="1"
bgcolor=#968e8a></td>
    <td width="1" height="1"
bgcolor=#a29c99></td>
    <td width="1" height="1"
bgcolor=#9e9b97></td>
    <td width="1" height="1"
bgcolor=#a4a19c></td>
    <td width="1" height="1"
bgcolor=#aba8a4></td>
    <td width="1" height="1"
bgcolor=#a7a29a></td>
    <td width="1" height="1"
bgcolor=#908880></td>
    <td width="1" height="1"
bgcolor=#a49e99></td>
    <td width="1" height="1"
bgcolor=#96928b></td>
    <td width="1" height="1"
bgcolor=#a8a19e></td>
    <td width="1" height="1"
bgcolor=#9d9b94></td>
    <td rowspan="1"
colspan="2" width="1"
height="1"
bgcolor=#b1b1ac></td>
    <td width="1" height="1"
bgcolor=#a8a6a2></td>
    <td width="1" height="1"
bgcolor=#7f807d></td>
  </tr>
  <tr>
    <td width="1" height="1"
bgcolor=#6f6764></td>
    <td width="1" height="1"
bgcolor=#756c6a></td>
    <td width="1" height="1"
bgcolor=#695f5d></td>
    <td width="1" height="1"
bgcolor=#6c6261></td>
    <td width="1" height="1"
bgcolor=#6c6260></td>
    <td width="1" height="1"
bgcolor=#726967></td>
    <td width="1" height="1"
bgcolor=#7e7673></td>
    <td width="1" height="1"
bgcolor=#33302b></td>
    <td width="1" height="1"
bgcolor=#201c1c></td>
    <td width="1" height="1"
bgcolor=#0e0d0c></td>
    <td width="1" height="1"
bgcolor=#5c5150></td>
    <td width="1" height="1"
bgcolor=#645c59></td>
    <td width="1" height="1"
bgcolor=#706563></td>
    <td width="1" height="1"
bgcolor=#796f6d></td>
    <td width="1" height="1"
bgcolor=#5e5452></td>
```

```
    <td width="1" height="1" bgcolor=#4c4140></td>
    <td width="1" height="1" bgcolor=#8e8781></td>
    <td width="1" height="1" bgcolor=#5b5451></td>
    <td width="1" height="1" bgcolor=#7e7771></td>
    <td width="1" height="1" bgcolor=#98928e></td>
    <td width="1" height="1" bgcolor=#35322f></td>
    <td width="1" height="1" bgcolor=#000000></td>
    <td width="1" height="1" bgcolor=#010302></td>
    <td width="1" height="1" bgcolor=#000301></td>
    <td width="1" height="1" bgcolor=#010500></td>
    <td width="1" height="1" bgcolor=#000201></td>
    <td width="1" height="1" bgcolor=#000501></td>
    <td width="1" height="1" bgcolor=#2f2b27></td>
    <td width="1" height="1" bgcolor=#6a5f5c></td>
    <td width="1" height="1" bgcolor=#908885></td>
    <td width="1" height="1" bgcolor=#1c1a16></td>
    <td width="1" height="1" bgcolor=#000000></td>
    <td width="1" height="1" bgcolor=#000501></td>
    <td width="1" height="1" bgcolor=#000300></td>
    <td width="1" height="1" bgcolor=#000700></td>
    <td width="1" height="1" bgcolor=#080807></td>
    <td width="1" height="1" bgcolor=#6f6b60></td>
    <td width="1" height="1" bgcolor=#d3d7d3></td>
    <td width="1" height="1" bgcolor=#dde1e0></td>
    <td width="1" height="1" bgcolor=#dddedb></td>
    <td width="1" height="1" bgcolor=#77726c></td>
    <td width="1" height="1" bgcolor=#6d625f></td>
    <td width="1" height="1" bgcolor=#887e7a></td>
    <td width="1" height="1" bgcolor=#8a847e></td>
    <td width="1" height="1" bgcolor=#8c827f></td>
    <td width="1" height="1" bgcolor=#736b68></td>
    <td width="1" height="1" bgcolor=#8f8784></td>
    <td width="1" height="1" bgcolor=#665e5a></td>
    <td width="1" height="1" bgcolor=#655957></td>
    <td width="1" height="1" bgcolor=#11110f></td>
    <td width="1" height="1" bgcolor=#191410></td>
    <td width="1" height="1" bgcolor=#3a322d></td>
    <td width="1" height="1" bgcolor=#25221c></td>
    <td width="1" height="1" bgcolor=#0e0d02></td>
    <td width="1" height="1" bgcolor=#352a21></td>
    <td width="1" height="1" bgcolor=#736962></td>
    <td width="1" height="1" bgcolor=#857b79></td>
    <td width="1" height="1" bgcolor=#776d68></td>
    <td width="1" height="1" bgcolor=#847b75></td>
    <td width="1" height="1" bgcolor=#968e8a></td>
    <td width="1" height="1" bgcolor=#98958f></td>
    <td width="1" height="1" bgcolor=#9b9792></td>
    <td width="1" height="1" bgcolor=#9c9892></td>
    <td width="1" height="1" bgcolor=#8b847b></td>
    <td width="1" height="1" bgcolor=#776d5f></td>
    <td width="1" height="1" bgcolor=#9e968c></td>
    <td width="1" height="1" bgcolor=#9a928c></td>
    <td width="1" height="1" bgcolor=#9d9993></td>
    <td width="1" height="1" bgcolor=#acaaa4></td>
    <td width="1" height="1" bgcolor=#b3b2ad></td>
    <td width="1" height="1" bgcolor=#b1afab></td>
    <td width="1" height="1" bgcolor=#7c7c79></td>
  </tr>
  <tr>
    <td width="1" height="1" bgcolor=#534c49></td>
    <td width="1" height="1" bgcolor=#5e5754></td>
    <td width="1" height="1" bgcolor=#736b68></td>
    <td width="1" height="1" bgcolor=#4f4644></td>
    <td width="1" height="1" bgcolor=#595350></td>
    <td width="1" height="1" bgcolor=#7b7470></td>
    <td width="1" height="1" bgcolor=#6f6663></td>
    <td width="1" height="1" bgcolor=#4f4b48></td>
    <td width="1" height="1" bgcolor=#181714></td>
    <td width="1" height="1" bgcolor=#383331></td>
    <td width="1" height="1" bgcolor=#272621></td>
    <td width="1" height="1" bgcolor=#4d4343></td>
    <td width="1" height="1" bgcolor=#443d3a></td>
    <td width="1" height="1" bgcolor=#443c39></td>
    <td width="1" height="1" bgcolor=#6b605e></td>
    <td width="1" height="1" bgcolor=#918b87></td>
    <td width="1" height="1" bgcolor=#5a534a></td>
    <td width="1" height="1" bgcolor=#a09e9a></td>
    <td width="1" height="1" bgcolor=#ada9a5></td>
    <td width="1" height="1" bgcolor=#8a8581></td>
    <td width="1" height="1" bgcolor=#000000></td>
    <td width="1" height="1" bgcolor=#000100></td>
    <td width="1" height="1" bgcolor=#000502></td>
    <td width="1" height="1" bgcolor=#000200></td>
    <td width="1" height="1" bgcolor=#000500></td>
    <td width="1" height="1" bgcolor=#030302></td>
    <td width="1" height="1" bgcolor=#433e3a></td>
    <td width="1" height="1" bgcolor=#7c7271></td>
    <td width="1" height="1" bgcolor=#33322e></td>
```

```
<td width="1" height="1" bgcolor=#000000></td>
<td width="1" height="1" bgcolor=#000601></td>
<td width="1" height="1" bgcolor=#010501></td>
<td width="1" height="1" bgcolor=#000301></td>
<td width="1" height="1" bgcolor=#000000></td>
<td width="1" height="1" bgcolor=#14120f></td>
<td width="1" height="1" bgcolor=#9a918f></td>
<td width="1" height="1" bgcolor=#8f8683></td>
<td width="1" height="1" bgcolor=#898480></td>
<td width="1" height="1" bgcolor=#69625a></td>
<td width="1" height="1" bgcolor=#8a857f></td>
<td width="1" height="1" bgcolor=#908984></td>
<td width="1" height="1" bgcolor=#938c89></td>
<td width="1" height="1" bgcolor=#5f5753></td>
<td width="1" height="1" bgcolor=#8f8581></td>
<td width="1" height="1" bgcolor=#8f8883></td>
<td width="1" height="1" bgcolor=#847c79></td>
<td width="1" height="1" bgcolor=#7d726f></td>
<td width="1" height="1" bgcolor=#867c7a></td>
<td width="1" height="1" bgcolor=#766e6b></td>
<td width="1" height="1" bgcolor=#6d6360></td>
<td width="1" height="1" bgcolor=#393632></td>
<td width="1" height="1" bgcolor=#201d1c></td>
<td width="1" height="1" bgcolor=#322d28></td>
<td width="1" height="1" bgcolor=#0c0d0a></td>
<td width="1" height="1" bgcolor=#030501></td>
<td width="1" height="1" bgcolor=#28221d></td>
<td width="1" height="1" bgcolor=#4e453e></td>
<td width="1" height="1" bgcolor=#675f5a></td>
<td width="1" height="1" bgcolor=#443a31></td>
<td width="1" height="1" bgcolor=#574d44></td>
<td width="1" height="1" bgcolor=#9e9693></td>
<td width="1" height="1" bgcolor=#aeaca7></td>
<td width="1" height="1" bgcolor=#b7b7b1></td>
<td width="1" height="1" bgcolor=#a09d96></td>
<td width="1" height="1" bgcolor=#9a938d></td>
<td width="1" height="1" bgcolor=#a79e97></td>
<td width="1" height="1" bgcolor=#80766d></td>
<td width="1" height="1" bgcolor=#877e72></td>
<td width="1" height="1" bgcolor=#8f857b></td>
<td width="1" height="1" bgcolor=#a9a297></td>
<td width="1" height="1" bgcolor=#b2b0a7></td>
<td width="1" height="1" bgcolor=#858580></td>
</tr>
<tr>
<td width="1" height="1" bgcolor=#3f3734></td>
<td width="1" height="1" bgcolor=#4f4946></td>
<td width="1" height="1" bgcolor=#6f6665></td>
<td width="1" height="1" bgcolor=#7b716f></td>
<td width="1" height="1" bgcolor=#7e7876></td>
<td width="1" height="1" bgcolor=#675e5b></td>
<td width="1" height="1" bgcolor=#6c6361></td>
<td width="1" height="1" bgcolor=#766e6b></td>
<td width="1" height="1" bgcolor=#938f8b></td>
<td width="1" height="1" bgcolor=#5f5453></td>
<td width="1" height="1" bgcolor=#615855></td>
<td width="1" height="1" bgcolor=#504644></td>
<td width="1" height="1" bgcolor=#625b59></td>
<td width="1" height="1" bgcolor=#574e4b></td>
<td width="1" height="1" bgcolor=#5b514e></td>
<td width="1" height="1" bgcolor=#6f6563></td>
<td width="1" height="1" bgcolor=#46403d></td>
<td width="1" height="1" bgcolor=#5e5452></td>
<td width="1" height="1" bgcolor=#5d5655></td>
<td width="1" height="1" bgcolor=#020000></td>
<td width="1" height="1" bgcolor=#010103></td>
<td width="1" height="1" bgcolor=#000101></td>
<td rowspan="2" colspan="1" width="1" height="1" bgcolor=#010301></td>
<td width="1" height="1" bgcolor=#000301></td>
<td width="1" height="1" bgcolor=#11100e></td>
<td width="1" height="1" bgcolor=#736866></td>
<td width="1" height="1" bgcolor=#5d5554></td>
<td width="1" height="1" bgcolor=#090807></td>
<td rowspan="1" colspan="3" width="1" height="1" bgcolor=#000301></td>
<td width="1" height="1" bgcolor=#000501></td>
<td width="1" height="1" bgcolor=#000200></td>
<td width="1" height="1" bgcolor=#322e2a></td>
<td width="1" height="1" bgcolor=#302925></td>
<td width="1" height="1" bgcolor=#1b1712></td>
<td width="1" height="1" bgcolor=#797471></td>
<td width="1" height="1" bgcolor=#978d8c></td>
<td width="1" height="1" bgcolor=#9f9a96></td>
<td width="1" height="1" bgcolor=#a9a6a1></td>
<td width="1" height="1" bgcolor=#a6a39c></td>
<td width="1" height="1" bgcolor=#b7b5b1></td>
<td width="1" height="1" bgcolor=#b5b5b0></td>
```

```
    <td width="1" height="1" bgcolor=#a9a6a1></td>
    <td width="1" height="1" bgcolor=#908784></td>
    <td width="1" height="1" bgcolor=#a59c99></td>
    <td width="1" height="1" bgcolor=#938e88></td>
    <td width="1" height="1" bgcolor=#857b79></td>
    <td width="1" height="1" bgcolor=#79746e></td>
    <td width="1" height="1" bgcolor=#928c88></td>
    <td width="1" height="1" bgcolor=#7f7774></td>
    <td width="1" height="1" bgcolor=#736d6a></td>
    <td width="1" height="1" bgcolor=#403a36></td>
    <td width="1" height="1" bgcolor=#7c7670></td>
    <td width="1" height="1" bgcolor=#585250></td>
    <td width="1" height="1" bgcolor=#1c1b16></td>
    <td width="1" height="1" bgcolor=#0b0b0a></td>
    <td width="1" height="1" bgcolor=#29221c></td>
    <td width="1" height="1" bgcolor=#584e47></td>
    <td width="1" height="1" bgcolor=#2d241b></td>
    <td width="1" height="1" bgcolor=#655c54></td>
    <td width="1" height="1" bgcolor=#706b62></td>
    <td width="1" height="1" bgcolor=#9f9c97></td>
    <td width="1" height="1" bgcolor=#c9c8c5></td>
    <td width="1" height="1" bgcolor=#bdbab7></td>
    <td width="1" height="1" bgcolor=#a19995></td>
    <td width="1" height="1" bgcolor=#aca89f></td>
    <td width="1" height="1" bgcolor=#aaa9a1></td>
    <td width="1" height="1" bgcolor=#b5b4ad></td>
    <td width="1" height="1" bgcolor=#a6a095></td>
    <td width="1" height="1" bgcolor=#a39c8c></td>
    <td width="1" height="1" bgcolor=#87837d></td>
</tr>
<tr>
    <td width="1" height="1" bgcolor=#524b49></td>
    <td width="1" height="1" bgcolor=#534c49></td>
    <td width="1" height="1" bgcolor=#4e4844></td>
    <td width="1" height="1" bgcolor=#736b69></td>
    <td width="1" height="1" bgcolor=#675f5c></td>
    <td width="1" height="1" bgcolor=#2b2524></td>
    <td width="1" height="1" bgcolor=#4b4443></td>
    <td width="1" height="1" bgcolor=#8c8482></td>
    <td width="1" height="1" bgcolor=#6f6461></td>
    <td width="1" height="1" bgcolor=#6b6461></td>
    <td width="1" height="1" bgcolor=#7e7472></td>
    <td width="1" height="1" bgcolor=#5f5453></td>
    <td width="1" height="1" bgcolor=#5c5452></td>
    <td width="1" height="1" bgcolor=#3b3734></td>
    <td width="1" height="1" bgcolor=#130f0f></td>
    <td width="1" height="1" bgcolor=#5c5654></td>
    <td width="1" height="1" bgcolor=#3c3435></td>
    <td width="1" height="1" bgcolor=#0b0a09></td>
    <td width="1" height="1" bgcolor=#000000></td>
    <td width="1" height="1" bgcolor=#000101></td>
    <td width="1" height="1" bgcolor=#000200></td>
    <td width="1" height="1" bgcolor=#000100></td>
    <td width="1" height="1" bgcolor=#040604></td>
    <td width="1" height="1" bgcolor=#0b0e0a></td>
    <td width="1" height="1" bgcolor=#000700></td>
    <td width="1" height="1" bgcolor=#000701></td>
    <td width="1" height="1" bgcolor=#000601></td>
    <td width="1" height="1" bgcolor=#000500></td>
    <td rowspan="2" colspan="1" width="1" height="1" bgcolor=#000301></td>
    <td width="1" height="1" bgcolor=#000200></td>
    <td width="1" height="1" bgcolor=#000000></td>
    <td width="1" height="1" bgcolor=#4a4742></td>
    <td width="1" height="1" bgcolor=#837977></td>
    <td width="1" height="1" bgcolor=#8e8985></td>
    <td width="1" height="1" bgcolor=#807674></td>
    <td width="1" height="1" bgcolor=#4d4542></td>
    <td width="1" height="1" bgcolor=#716c69></td>
    <td width="1" height="1" bgcolor=#9f9995></td>
    <td width="1" height="1" bgcolor=#a3a09c></td>
    <td width="1" height="1" bgcolor=#bab9b5></td>
    <td width="1" height="1" bgcolor=#a3a19a></td>
    <td width="1" height="1" bgcolor=#857c75></td>
    <td width="1" height="1" bgcolor=#a7a19d></td>
    <td width="1" height="1" bgcolor=#aeaba7></td>
    <td width="1" height="1" bgcolor=#a1a29c></td>
    <td width="1" height="1" bgcolor=#a6a19d></td>
    <td width="1" height="1" bgcolor=#94918c></td>
    <td width="1" height="1" bgcolor=#766f6c></td>
    <td width="1" height="1" bgcolor=#6d6560></td>
    <td width="1" height="1" bgcolor=#736b66></td>
    <td width="1" height="1" bgcolor=#8f8a84></td>
    <td width="1" height="1" bgcolor=#999490></td>
    <td width="1" height="1" bgcolor=#776e6a></td>
    <td width="1" height="1" bgcolor=#635c59></td>
    <td width="1" height="1" bgcolor=#807773></td>
    <td width="1" height="1" bgcolor=#524b48></td>
```

```
    <td width="1" height="1"
bgcolor=#8c867e></td>
    <td width="1" height="1"
bgcolor=#938e86></td>
    <td width="1" height="1"
bgcolor=#989390></td>
    <td width="1" height="1"
bgcolor=#9e9994></td>
    <td width="1" height="1"
bgcolor=#bab9b6></td>
    <td width="1" height="1"
bgcolor=#aca9a0></td>
    <td width="1" height="1"
bgcolor=#8b837a></td>
    <td width="1" height="1"
bgcolor=#8b817a></td>
    <td width="1" height="1"
bgcolor=#867c70></td>
    <td width="1" height="1"
bgcolor=#b9bcb7></td>
    <td width="1" height="1"
bgcolor=#aca5a2></td>
    <td width="1" height="1"
bgcolor=#b6b3ab></td>
    <td width="1" height="1"
bgcolor=#b0ada7></td>
    <td width="1" height="1"
bgcolor=#c1beb0></td>
    <td width="1" height="1"
bgcolor=#9c9989></td>
  </tr>
  <tr>
    <td width="1" height="1"
bgcolor=#352f2b></td>
    <td width="1" height="1"
bgcolor=#3c3633></td>
    <td width="1" height="1"
bgcolor=#1e1c1a></td>
    <td rowspan="2"
colspan="2" width="1"
height="1"
bgcolor=#000000></td>
    <td width="1" height="1"
bgcolor=#000101></td>
    <td width="1" height="1"
bgcolor=#28221f></td>
    <td width="1" height="1"
bgcolor=#544e4b></td>
    <td width="1" height="1"
bgcolor=#5f5854></td>
    <td width="1" height="1"
bgcolor=#5e5451></td>
    <td width="1" height="1"
bgcolor=#625955></td>
    <td width="1" height="1"
bgcolor=#0d0b08></td>
    <td width="1" height="1"
bgcolor=#060403></td>
    <td width="1" height="1"
bgcolor=#463e3c></td>
    <td width="1" height="1"
bgcolor=#55504e></td>
    <td width="1" height="1"
bgcolor=#2c2927></td>
    <td rowspan="2"
colspan="1" width="1"
height="1"
bgcolor=#000000></td>
    <td rowspan="2"
colspan="1" width="1"
height="1"
bgcolor=#000101></td>
    <td width="1" height="1"
bgcolor=#000101></td>
    <td width="1" height="1"
bgcolor=#010201></td>
    <td width="1" height="1"
bgcolor=#000400></td>
    <td width="1" height="1"
bgcolor=#010301></td>
    <td width="1" height="1"
bgcolor=#000501></td>
    <td width="1" height="1"
bgcolor=#010301></td>
    <td width="1" height="1"
bgcolor=#030b01></td>
    <td rowspan="1"
colspan="2" width="1"
height="1"
bgcolor=#000302></td>
    <td width="1" height="1"
bgcolor=#000500></td>
    <td width="1" height="1"
bgcolor=#000501></td>
    <td width="1" height="1"
bgcolor=#010200></td>
    <td width="1" height="1"
bgcolor=#373430></td>
    <td width="1" height="1"
bgcolor=#6f6662></td>
    <td width="1" height="1"
bgcolor=#766e6c></td>
    <td width="1" height="1"
bgcolor=#625754></td>
    <td width="1" height="1"
bgcolor=#635b58></td>
    <td width="1" height="1"
bgcolor=#615757></td>
    <td width="1" height="1"
bgcolor=#817775></td>
    <td width="1" height="1"
bgcolor=#938b89></td>
    <td width="1" height="1"
bgcolor=#716765></td>
    <td width="1" height="1"
bgcolor=#4f4745></td>
    <td width="1" height="1"
bgcolor=#a29c99></td>
    <td width="1" height="1"
bgcolor=#bebfba></td>
    <td width="1" height="1"
bgcolor=#adaba5></td>
    <td width="1" height="1"
bgcolor=#b0aea7></td>
    <td width="1" height="1"
bgcolor=#b2afaa></td>
    <td width="1" height="1"
bgcolor=#aeada6></td>
    <td width="1" height="1"
bgcolor=#7f7a76></td>
    <td width="1" height="1"
bgcolor=#706662></td>
    <td width="1" height="1"
bgcolor=#837b78></td>
    <td width="1" height="1"
bgcolor=#55504c></td>
    <td width="1" height="1"
bgcolor=#837d7a></td>
    <td width="1" height="1"
bgcolor=#a3a09a></td>
    <td width="1" height="1"
bgcolor=#8e8381></td>
    <td width="1" height="1"
bgcolor=#a7a7a1></td>
    <td width="1" height="1"
bgcolor=#877f7b></td>
    <td width="1" height="1"
bgcolor=#928d89></td>
    <td width="1" height="1"
bgcolor=#7b7570></td>
    <td width="1" height="1"
bgcolor=#968e8b></td>
    <td width="1" height="1"
bgcolor=#817874></td>
    <td width="1" height="1"
bgcolor=#766f67></td>
    <td width="1" height="1"
bgcolor=#736a61></td>
    <td width="1" height="1"
bgcolor=#aba6a1></td>
    <td width="1" height="1"
bgcolor=#a29d9a></td>
    <td width="1" height="1"
bgcolor=#adaca6></td>
    <td width="1" height="1"
bgcolor=#aeaaa2></td>
    <td width="1" height="1"
bgcolor=#9f978e></td>
    <td width="1" height="1"
bgcolor=#928980></td>
    <td width="1" height="1"
bgcolor=#979182></td>
    <td width="1" height="1"
bgcolor=#a99e8b></td>
```

```
    <td width="1" height="1"
bgcolor=#faf4e6></td>
    <td width="1" height="1"
bgcolor=#aaabaa></td>
  </tr>
  <tr>
    <td width="1" height="1"
bgcolor=#554e4b></td>
    <td width="1" height="1"
bgcolor=#625a58></td>
    <td width="1" height="1"
bgcolor=#2f2b27></td>
    <td width="1" height="1"
bgcolor=#241f1e></td>
    <td width="1" height="1"
bgcolor=#322a2a></td>
    <td width="1" height="1"
bgcolor=#78716f></td>
    <td width="1" height="1"
bgcolor=#786f6b></td>
    <td width="1" height="1"
bgcolor=#95908d></td>
    <td width="1" height="1"
bgcolor=#999692></td>
    <td width="1" height="1"
bgcolor=#2d2a26></td>
    <td width="1" height="1"
bgcolor=#070806></td>
    <td width="1" height="1"
bgcolor=#161211></td>
    <td rowspan="1"
colspan="2" width="1"
height="1"
bgcolor=#000000></td>
    <td width="1" height="1"
bgcolor=#000200></td>
    <td width="1" height="1"
bgcolor=#000300></td>
    <td width="1" height="1"
bgcolor=#010401></td>
    <td width="1" height="1"
bgcolor=#060605></td>
    <td width="1" height="1"
bgcolor=#3a3834></td>
    <td width="1" height="1"
bgcolor=#050400></td>
    <td width="1" height="1"
bgcolor=#080605></td>
    <td width="1" height="1"
bgcolor=#010501></td>
    <td width="1" height="1"
bgcolor=#010600></td>
    <td rowspan="2"
colspan="1" width="1"
height="1"
bgcolor=#000301></td>
    <td rowspan="2"
colspan="1" width="1"
height="1"
bgcolor=#000200></td>
    <td rowspan="1"
colspan="2" width="1"
height="1"
bgcolor=#000200></td>
    <td width="1" height="1"
bgcolor=#000000></td>
    <td width="1" height="1"
bgcolor=#050202></td>
    <td width="1" height="1"
bgcolor=#6b6360></td>
    <td width="1" height="1"
bgcolor=#6f6764></td>
    <td width="1" height="1"
bgcolor=#645c59></td>
    <td width="1" height="1"
bgcolor=#050201></td>
    <td width="1" height="1"
bgcolor=#000000></td>
    <td width="1" height="1"
bgcolor=#594e4c></td>
    <td width="1" height="1"
bgcolor=#8d8583></td>
    <td width="1" height="1"
bgcolor=#6f6563></td>
    <td width="1" height="1"
bgcolor=#766e6b></td>
    <td width="1" height="1"
bgcolor=#867b7a></td>
    <td width="1" height="1"
bgcolor=#b6b3ae></td>
    <td width="1" height="1"
bgcolor=#aaa8a3></td>
    <td width="1" height="1"
bgcolor=#b6b5b0></td>
    <td width="1" height="1"
bgcolor=#a09b97></td>
    <td width="1" height="1"
bgcolor=#9d9892></td>
    <td width="1" height="1"
bgcolor=#aeaca8></td>
    <td width="1" height="1"
bgcolor=#b0ada8></td>
    <td width="1" height="1"
bgcolor=#a39f98></td>
    <td width="1" height="1"
bgcolor=#a4a19c></td>
    <td width="1" height="1"
bgcolor=#918c88></td>
    <td width="1" height="1"
bgcolor=#948d8b></td>
    <td width="1" height="1"
bgcolor=#a7a39f></td>
    <td width="1" height="1"
bgcolor=#a7a6a1></td>
    <td width="1" height="1"
bgcolor=#aeaca7></td>
    <td width="1" height="1"
bgcolor=#b2b0ab></td>
    <td width="1" height="1"
bgcolor=#9e9794></td>
    <td width="1" height="1"
bgcolor=#918c87></td>
    <td width="1" height="1"
bgcolor=#8b8582></td>
    <td width="1" height="1"
bgcolor=#928b86></td>
    <td width="1" height="1"
bgcolor=#8e8580></td>
    <td width="1" height="1"
bgcolor=#a19e98></td>
    <td width="1" height="1"
bgcolor=#a8a29d></td>
    <td width="1" height="1"
bgcolor=#aaa59d></td>
    <td width="1" height="1"
bgcolor=#938b80></td>
    <td width="1" height="1"
bgcolor=#94897f></td>
    <td width="1" height="1"
bgcolor=#867765></td>
    <td width="1" height="1"
bgcolor=#d9c28d></td>
    <td width="1" height="1"
bgcolor=#f3f1e1></td>
    <td width="1" height="1"
bgcolor=#a3a2a0></td>
  </tr>
  <tr>
    <td width="1" height="1"
bgcolor=#35312d></td>
    <td width="1" height="1"
bgcolor=#75696a></td>
    <td width="1" height="1"
bgcolor=#5f5b57></td>
    <td width="1" height="1"
bgcolor=#413b39></td>
    <td width="1" height="1"
bgcolor=#4b413f></td>
    <td width="1" height="1"
bgcolor=#120f0f></td>
    <td width="1" height="1"
bgcolor=#040404></td>
    <td width="1" height="1"
bgcolor=#837a77></td>
    <td width="1" height="1"
bgcolor=#79706e></td>
    <td width="1" height="1"
bgcolor=#8a8581></td>
    <td width="1" height="1"
bgcolor=#bcbab7></td>
    <td width="1" height="1"
bgcolor=#616160></td>
    <td width="1" height="1"
bgcolor=#0b0908></td>
```

```
    <td rowspan="1" colspan="2" width="1" height="1" bgcolor=#000100></td>
    <td width="1" height="1" bgcolor=#010201></td>
    <td width="1" height="1" bgcolor=#000102></td>
    <td width="1" height="1" bgcolor=#000100></td>
    <td width="1" height="1" bgcolor=#000300></td>
    <td width="1" height="1" bgcolor=#000001></td>
    <td width="1" height="1" bgcolor=#24201d></td>
    <td width="1" height="1" bgcolor=#302e2a></td>
    <td width="1" height="1" bgcolor=#000000></td>
    <td width="1" height="1" bgcolor=#060701></td>
    <td width="1" height="1" bgcolor=#010301></td>
    <td width="1" height="1" bgcolor=#000300></td>
    <td width="1" height="1" bgcolor=#000301></td>
    <td width="1" height="1" bgcolor=#020202></td>
    <td width="1" height="1" bgcolor=#010101></td>
    <td width="1" height="1" bgcolor=#37322f></td>
    <td width="1" height="1" bgcolor=#6c6461></td>
    <td width="1" height="1" bgcolor=#beb9b3></td>
    <td width="1" height="1" bgcolor=#706b67></td>
    <td width="1" height="1" bgcolor=#76716c></td>
    <td width="1" height="1" bgcolor=#14120f></td>
    <td width="1" height="1" bgcolor=#020202></td>
    <td width="1" height="1" bgcolor=#010101></td>
    <td width="1" height="1" bgcolor=#5f5552></td>
    <td width="1" height="1" bgcolor=#807674></td>
    <td width="1" height="1" bgcolor=#6f6561></td>
    <td width="1" height="1" bgcolor=#908788></td>
    <td width="1" height="1" bgcolor=#716763></td>
    <td width="1" height="1" bgcolor=#a6a19e></td>
    <td width="1" height="1" bgcolor=#a49c99></td>
    <td width="1" height="1" bgcolor=#aea8a8></td>
    <td width="1" height="1" bgcolor=#b4afab></td>
    <td width="1" height="1" bgcolor=#a39e9a></td>
    <td width="1" height="1" bgcolor=#a7a49d></td>
    <td width="1" height="1" bgcolor=#afaeaa></td>
    <td width="1" height="1" bgcolor=#aca7a6></td>
    <td width="1" height="1" bgcolor=#a3a09c></td>
    <td width="1" height="1" bgcolor=#8f8a87></td>
    <td width="1" height="1" bgcolor=#95918c></td>
    <td width="1" height="1" bgcolor=#938f8c></td>
    <td width="1" height="1" bgcolor=#a9a39f></td>
    <td width="1" height="1" bgcolor=#999490></td>
    <td width="1" height="1" bgcolor=#c0bebc></td>
    <td width="1" height="1" bgcolor=#bdbdbb></td>
    <td width="1" height="1" bgcolor=#b8b8b3></td>
    <td width="1" height="1" bgcolor=#b5b4b3></td>
    <td width="1" height="1" bgcolor=#9a958f></td>
    <td width="1" height="1" bgcolor=#9f9b95></td>
    <td width="1" height="1" bgcolor=#9d958f></td>
    <td width="1" height="1" bgcolor=#95908c></td>
    <td width="1" height="1" bgcolor=#999591></td>
    <td width="1" height="1" bgcolor=#aeadaa></td>
    <td width="1" height="1" bgcolor=#a38457></td>
    <td width="1" height="1" bgcolor=#e1cd9a></td>
    <td width="1" height="1" bgcolor=#f6f4e7></td>
    <td width="1" height="1" bgcolor=#ababaa></td>
   </tr>
   <tr>
    <td width="1" height="1" bgcolor=#6a605e></td>
    <td width="1" height="1" bgcolor=#534b4b></td>
    <td width="1" height="1" bgcolor=#6e6562></td>
    <td width="1" height="1" bgcolor=#1b1713></td>
    <td width="1" height="1" bgcolor=#000101></td>
    <td width="1" height="1" bgcolor=#000000></td>
    <td width="1" height="1" bgcolor=#2d2b28></td>
    <td width="1" height="1" bgcolor=#4f4a48></td>
    <td width="1" height="1" bgcolor=#2f2c2a></td>
    <td width="1" height="1" bgcolor=#666363></td>
    <td width="1" height="1" bgcolor=#2a2724></td>
    <td width="1" height="1" bgcolor=#272927></td>
    <td rowspan="5" colspan="1" width="1" height="1" bgcolor=#000000></td>
    <td rowspan="2" colspan="3" width="1" height="1" bgcolor=#000101></td>
    <td width="1" height="1" bgcolor=#000201></td>
    <td width="1" height="1" bgcolor=#000000></td>
    <td width="1" height="1" bgcolor=#000101></td>
    <td width="1" height="1" bgcolor=#000601></td>
    <td width="1" height="1" bgcolor=#000101></td>
    <td width="1" height="1" bgcolor=#010803></td>
    <td width="1" height="1" bgcolor=#010806></td>
    <td width="1" height="1" bgcolor=#000302></td>
    <td width="1" height="1" bgcolor=#000301></td>
    <td rowspan="2" colspan="1" width="1" height="1" bgcolor=#000101></td>
    <td width="1" height="1" bgcolor=#000101></td>
    <td width="1" height="1" bgcolor=#000100></td>
```

```
<td width="1" height="1" bgcolor=#483d3f></td>
<td width="1" height="1" bgcolor=#6f6563></td>
<td width="1" height="1" bgcolor=#3e3935></td>
<td width="1" height="1" bgcolor=#1d1716></td>
<td width="1" height="1" bgcolor=#544b49></td>
<td width="1" height="1" bgcolor=#87837d></td>
<td width="1" height="1" bgcolor=#b1aeaa></td>
<td width="1" height="1" bgcolor=#694015></td>
<td width="1" height="1" bgcolor=#d2c1b9></td>
<td width="1" height="1" bgcolor=#ddd0c2></td>
<td width="1" height="1" bgcolor=#908172></td>
<td width="1" height="1" bgcolor=#565950></td>
<td width="1" height="1" bgcolor=#807577></td>
<td width="1" height="1" bgcolor=#837d7d></td>
<td width="1" height="1" bgcolor=#8b8381></td>
<td width="1" height="1" bgcolor=#948e89></td>
<td width="1" height="1" bgcolor=#857d78></td>
<td width="1" height="1" bgcolor=#a09c98></td>
<td width="1" height="1" bgcolor=#a49f9b></td>
<td width="1" height="1" bgcolor=#938b89></td>
<td width="1" height="1" bgcolor=#8b8682></td>
<td width="1" height="1" bgcolor=#807672></td>
<td width="1" height="1" bgcolor=#888380></td>
<td width="1" height="1" bgcolor=#857c79></td>
<td width="1" height="1" bgcolor=#807772></td>
<td width="1" height="1" bgcolor=#a49c99></td>
<td width="1" height="1" bgcolor=#83807b></td>
<td width="1" height="1" bgcolor=#999490></td>
<td width="1" height="1" bgcolor=#928a86></td>
<td width="1" height="1" bgcolor=#817974></td>
<td width="1" height="1" bgcolor=#9b938f></td>
<td width="1" height="1" bgcolor=#96918d></td>
<td width="1" height="1" bgcolor=#8a817b></td>
<td width="1" height="1" bgcolor=#6c625a></td>
<td width="1" height="1" bgcolor=#645b4d></td>
<td width="1" height="1" bgcolor=#968e88></td>
<td width="1" height="1" bgcolor=#867d77></td>
<td width="1" height="1" bgcolor=#867d74></td>
<td width="1" height="1" bgcolor=#a09d97></td>
<td width="1" height="1" bgcolor=#96866f></td>
<td width="1" height="1" bgcolor=#7e612f></td>
<td width="1" height="1" bgcolor=#c1ab71></td>
<td width="1" height="1" bgcolor=#f0e9d3></td>
<td width="1" height="1" bgcolor=#9e9890></td>
</tr>
<tr>
<td width="1" height="1" bgcolor=#6e6562></td>
<td width="1" height="1" bgcolor=#7c7373></td>
<td width="1" height="1" bgcolor=#8b8983></td>
<td width="1" height="1" bgcolor=#635b59></td>
<td width="1" height="1" bgcolor=#3f3735></td>
<td width="1" height="1" bgcolor=#6b6361></td>
<td width="1" height="1" bgcolor=#706c69></td>
<td width="1" height="1" bgcolor=#a09c98></td>
<td width="1" height="1" bgcolor=#9c9994></td>
<td width="1" height="1" bgcolor=#918886></td>
<td rowspan="9" colspan="1" width="1" height="1" bgcolor=#000000></td>
<td width="1" height="1" bgcolor=#000100></td>
<td rowspan="1" colspan="2" width="1" height="1" bgcolor=#000100></td>
<td width="1" height="1" bgcolor=#080902></td>
<td width="1" height="1" bgcolor=#000200></td>
<td width="1" height="1" bgcolor=#010703></td>
<td width="1" height="1" bgcolor=#010503></td>
<td width="1" height="1" bgcolor=#000401></td>
<td rowspan="1" colspan="2" width="1" height="1" bgcolor=#010201></td>
<td width="1" height="1" bgcolor=#000000></td>
<td width="1" height="1" bgcolor=#252322></td>
<td width="1" height="1" bgcolor=#5c5351></td>
<td width="1" height="1" bgcolor=#524d4a></td>
<td width="1" height="1" bgcolor=#000000></td>
<td width="1" height="1" bgcolor=#2d2e29></td>
<td width="1" height="1" bgcolor=#372d2e></td>
<td width="1" height="1" bgcolor=#0a0504></td>
<td width="1" height="1" bgcolor=#433b38></td>
<td width="1" height="1" bgcolor=#0e0706></td>
<td width="1" height="1" bgcolor=#28190d></td>
<td width="1" height="1" bgcolor=#533110></td>
<td width="1" height="1" bgcolor=#2b0e01></td>
<td width="1" height="1" bgcolor=#5a3b1c></td>
<td width="1" height="1" bgcolor=#af784a></td>
<td width="1" height="1" bgcolor=#bfb0a0></td>
<td width="1" height="1" bgcolor=#9c9485></td>
<td width="1" height="1" bgcolor=#50483e></td>
<td width="1" height="1" bgcolor=#3a3130></td>
<td width="1" height="1" bgcolor=#3c3832></td>
```

```
    <td width="1" height="1"
bgcolor=#272321></td>
    <td width="1" height="1"
bgcolor=#56504e></td>
    <td width="1" height="1"
bgcolor=#0f0f10></td>
    <td width="1" height="1"
bgcolor=#312b29></td>
    <td width="1" height="1"
bgcolor=#423a37></td>
    <td width="1" height="1"
bgcolor=#4f4a46></td>
    <td width="1" height="1"
bgcolor=#786d6a></td>
    <td width="1" height="1"
bgcolor=#5f5855></td>
    <td width="1" height="1"
bgcolor=#b8b2ae></td>
    <td width="1" height="1"
bgcolor=#c1bcb9></td>
    <td width="1" height="1"
bgcolor=#bcbbb7></td>
    <td width="1" height="1"
bgcolor=#938f8b></td>
    <td width="1" height="1"
bgcolor=#969490></td>
    <td width="1" height="1"
bgcolor=#9d9a95></td>
    <td width="1" height="1"
bgcolor=#9f9895></td>
    <td width="1" height="1"
bgcolor=#8e8582></td>
    <td width="1" height="1"
bgcolor=#aaa8a3></td>
    <td width="1" height="1"
bgcolor=#c6c7c6></td>
    <td width="1" height="1"
bgcolor=#a39f9c></td>
    <td width="1" height="1"
bgcolor=#a49d95></td>
    <td width="1" height="1"
bgcolor=#8c8279></td>
    <td width="1" height="1"
bgcolor=#816437></td>
    <td width="1" height="1"
bgcolor=#876936></td>
    <td width="1" height="1"
bgcolor=#8d6c3e></td>
    <td width="1" height="1"
bgcolor=#ac9466></td>
    <td width="1" height="1"
bgcolor=#948d7a></td>
  </tr>
  <tr>
    <td width="1" height="1"
bgcolor=#2f2a29></td>
    <td width="1" height="1"
bgcolor=#47413e></td>
    <td width="1" height="1"
bgcolor=#62585a></td>
    <td width="1" height="1"
bgcolor=#544e4a></td>
    <td width="1" height="1"
bgcolor=#9c9c99></td>
    <td width="1" height="1"
bgcolor=#696565></td>
    <td width="1" height="1"
bgcolor=#666463></td>
    <td width="1" height="1"
bgcolor=#4f4c4c></td>
    <td rowspan="9"
colspan="1" width="1"
height="1"
bgcolor=#000000></td>
    <td width="1" height="1"
bgcolor=#010101></td>
    <td width="1" height="1"
bgcolor=#000101></td>
    <td width="1" height="1"
bgcolor=#010101></td>
    <td width="1" height="1"
bgcolor=#000100></td>
    <td width="1" height="1"
bgcolor=#000101></td>
    <td width="1" height="1"
bgcolor=#000000></td>
    <td width="1" height="1"
bgcolor=#a19d9b></td>
    <td width="1" height="1"
bgcolor=#5a5955></td>
    <td width="1" height="1"
bgcolor=#000000></td>
    <td width="1" height="1"
bgcolor=#000603></td>
    <td width="1" height="1"
bgcolor=#010601></td>
    <td width="1" height="1"
bgcolor=#000201></td>
    <td rowspan="2"
colspan="1" width="1"
height="1"
bgcolor=#000101></td>
    <td width="1" height="1"
bgcolor=#000101></td>
    <td width="1" height="1"
bgcolor=#010101></td>
    <td width="1" height="1"
bgcolor=#42403f></td>
    <td width="1" height="1"
bgcolor=#000000></td>
    <td rowspan="1"
colspan="3" width="1"
height="1"
bgcolor=#000100></td>
    <td width="1" height="1"
bgcolor=#010101></td>
    <td rowspan="1"
colspan="3" width="1"
height="1"
bgcolor=#000000></td>
    <td rowspan="1"
colspan="2" width="1"
height="1"
bgcolor=#000100></td>
    <td width="1" height="1"
bgcolor=#000201></td>
    <td rowspan="1"
colspan="2" width="1"
height="1"
bgcolor=#000100></td>
    <td width="1" height="1"
bgcolor=#100801></td>
    <td width="1" height="1"
bgcolor=#020301></td>
    <td width="1" height="1"
bgcolor=#190902></td>
    <td width="1" height="1"
bgcolor=#30210f></td>
    <td width="1" height="1"
bgcolor=#392106></td>
    <td width="1" height="1"
bgcolor=#c5a790></td>
    <td width="1" height="1"
bgcolor=#291e15></td>
    <td rowspan="1"
colspan="2" width="1"
height="1"
bgcolor=#000000></td>
    <td width="1" height="1"
bgcolor=#060406></td>
    <td width="1" height="1"
bgcolor=#403c3b></td>
    <td width="1" height="1"
bgcolor=#0e0b0b></td>
    <td width="1" height="1"
bgcolor=#12130d></td>
    <td width="1" height="1"
bgcolor=#47423f></td>
    <td width="1" height="1"
bgcolor=#362f2c></td>
    <td width="1" height="1"
bgcolor=#393532></td>
    <td width="1" height="1"
bgcolor=#342f2c></td>
    <td width="1" height="1"
bgcolor=#544c4a></td>
    <td width="1" height="1"
bgcolor=#7e7978></td>
    <td width="1" height="1"
bgcolor=#a6a39f></td>
    <td width="1" height="1"
bgcolor=#93918b></td>
    <td width="1" height="1"
bgcolor=#aeaba4></td>
```

```
    <td width="1" height="1"
bgcolor=#bbbab8></td>
    <td width="1" height="1"
bgcolor=#a29b97></td>
    <td width="1" height="1"
bgcolor=#b4aea8></td>
    <td width="1" height="1"
bgcolor=#bebeb9></td>
    <td width="1" height="1"
bgcolor=#9f9a90></td>
    <td width="1" height="1"
bgcolor=#977d5c></td>
    <td width="1" height="1"
bgcolor=#8b6d37></td>
    <td width="1" height="1"
bgcolor=#967947></td>
    <td width="1" height="1"
bgcolor=#c4b188></td>
    <td width="1" height="1"
bgcolor=#ababa6></td>
  </tr>
  <tr>
    <td width="1" height="1"
bgcolor=#322e2c></td>
    <td width="1" height="1"
bgcolor=#101111></td>
    <td width="1" height="1"
bgcolor=#000000></td>
    <td width="1" height="1"
bgcolor=#3f3b3a></td>
    <td width="1" height="1"
bgcolor=#0f0e0e></td>
    <td width="1" height="1"
bgcolor=#464545></td>
    <td rowspan="13"
colspan="1" width="1"
height="1"
bgcolor=#000000></td>
    <td rowspan="8"
colspan="1" width="1"
height="1"
bgcolor=#000000></td>
    <td rowspan="7"
colspan="1" width="1"
height="1"
bgcolor=#000000></td>
    <td rowspan="7"
colspan="1" width="1"
height="1"
bgcolor=#000000></td>
    <td width="1" height="1"
bgcolor=#000100></td>
    <td width="1" height="1"
bgcolor=#000000></td>
    <td width="1" height="1"
bgcolor=#050404></td>
    <td width="1" height="1"
bgcolor=#625f5b></td>
    <td width="1" height="1"
bgcolor=#000000></td>
    <td rowspan="3"
colspan="1" width="1"
height="1"
bgcolor=#000101></td>
    <td width="1" height="1"
bgcolor=#000201></td>
    <td width="1" height="1"
bgcolor=#000502></td>
    <td rowspan="2"
colspan="1" width="1"
height="1"
bgcolor=#000101></td>
    <td rowspan="2"
colspan="1" width="1"
height="1"
bgcolor=#000100></td>
    <td width="1" height="1"
bgcolor=#000000></td>
    <td width="1" height="1"
bgcolor=#010201></td>
    <td width="1" height="1"
bgcolor=#010101></td>
    <td width="1" height="1"
bgcolor=#000100></td>
    <td rowspan="1"
colspan="2" width="1"
height="1"
bgcolor=#000000></td>
    <td width="1" height="1"
bgcolor=#292a25></td>
    <td width="1" height="1"
bgcolor=#565551></td>
    <td width="1" height="1"
bgcolor=#857b79></td>
    <td width="1" height="1"
bgcolor=#302e2d></td>
    <td width="1" height="1"
bgcolor=#020202></td>
    <td width="1" height="1"
bgcolor=#000101></td>
    <td rowspan="1"
colspan="10" width="1"
height="1"
bgcolor=#000000></td>
    <td width="1" height="1"
bgcolor=#040301></td>
    <td width="1" height="1"
bgcolor=#0c0501></td>
    <td width="1" height="1"
bgcolor=#382b15></td>
    <td width="1" height="1"
bgcolor=#2a1c08></td>
    <td width="1" height="1"
bgcolor=#200901></td>
    <td width="1" height="1"
bgcolor=#000100></td>
    <td width="1" height="1"
bgcolor=#000000></td>
    <td width="1" height="1"
bgcolor=#040500></td>
    <td width="1" height="1"
bgcolor=#11100f></td>
    <td width="1" height="1"
bgcolor=#040303></td>
    <td width="1" height="1"
bgcolor=#020100></td>
    <td rowspan="4"
colspan="1" width="1"
height="1"
bgcolor=#000000></td>
    <td rowspan="2"
colspan="1" width="1"
height="1"
bgcolor=#000000></td>
    <td width="1" height="1"
bgcolor=#010101></td>
    <td width="1" height="1"
bgcolor=#040303></td>
    <td width="1" height="1"
bgcolor=#14120d></td>
    <td width="1" height="1"
bgcolor=#171006></td>
    <td width="1" height="1"
bgcolor=#503f31></td>
    <td width="1" height="1"
bgcolor=#544635></td>
    <td width="1" height="1"
bgcolor=#6d5f53></td>
    <td width="1" height="1"
bgcolor=#8a8073></td>
    <td width="1" height="1"
bgcolor=#958b81></td>
    <td width="1" height="1"
bgcolor=#5b3b13></td>
    <td width="1" height="1"
bgcolor=#95794d></td>
    <td width="1" height="1"
bgcolor=#b09d7c></td>
    <td width="1" height="1"
bgcolor=#8f8a7a></td>
  </tr>
  <tr>
    <td width="1" height="1"
bgcolor=#3a3733></td>
    <td width="1" height="1"
bgcolor=#3d3737></td>
    <td width="1" height="1"
bgcolor=#4f4d4c></td>
    <td width="1" height="1"
bgcolor=#060302></td>
    <td rowspan="11"
colspan="2" width="1"
height="1"
bgcolor=#000000></td>
```

```
    <td rowspan="2"
colspan="1" width="1"
height="1"
bgcolor=#000000></td>
    <td width="1" height="1"
bgcolor=#000101></td>
    <td width="1" height="1"
bgcolor=#020102></td>
    <td width="1" height="1"
bgcolor=#000000></td>
    <td width="1" height="1"
bgcolor=#000100></td>
    <td rowspan="2"
colspan="1" width="1"
height="1"
bgcolor=#000101></td>
    <td width="1" height="1"
bgcolor=#000101></td>
    <td width="1" height="1"
bgcolor=#040303></td>
    <td width="1" height="1"
bgcolor=#74726e></td>
    <td width="1" height="1"
bgcolor=#000000></td>
    <td width="1" height="1"
bgcolor=#282522></td>
    <td width="1" height="1"
bgcolor=#3b3736></td>
    <td width="1" height="1"
bgcolor=#69615f></td>
    <td width="1" height="1"
bgcolor=#8d8582></td>
    <td width="1" height="1"
bgcolor=#7e7472></td>
    <td width="1" height="1"
bgcolor=#4f4645></td>
    <td width="1" height="1"
bgcolor=#090909></td>
    <td width="1" height="1"
bgcolor=#000000></td>
    <td width="1" height="1"
bgcolor=#181615></td>
    <td width="1" height="1"
bgcolor=#645c5a></td>
    <td width="1" height="1"
bgcolor=#4f4b4a></td>
    <td width="1" height="1"
bgcolor=#121211></td>
    <td width="1" height="1"
bgcolor=#191914></td>
    <td rowspan="1"
colspan="2" width="1"
height="1"
bgcolor=#000000></td>
    <td width="1" height="1"
bgcolor=#171414></td>
    <td width="1" height="1"
bgcolor=#8f8b86></td>
    <td width="1" height="1"
bgcolor=#a9a3a0></td>
    <td width="1" height="1"
bgcolor=#67625e></td>
    <td width="1" height="1"
bgcolor=#6c6763></td>
    <td width="1" height="1"
bgcolor=#36332f></td>
    <td width="1" height="1"
bgcolor=#272722></td>
    <td rowspan="1"
colspan="2" width="1"
height="1"
bgcolor=#000000></td>
    <td width="1" height="1"
bgcolor=#1a1b1b></td>
    <td width="1" height="1"
bgcolor=#030205></td>
    <td width="1" height="1"
bgcolor=#010000></td>
    <td width="1" height="1"
bgcolor=#261c07></td>
    <td width="1" height="1"
bgcolor=#100c06></td>
    <td width="1" height="1"
bgcolor=#281203></td>
    <td rowspan="2"
colspan="1" width="1"
height="1"
bgcolor=#000000></td>
    <td width="1" height="1"
bgcolor=#000000></td>
    <td width="1" height="1"
bgcolor=#151511></td>
    <td width="1" height="1"
bgcolor=#12100e></td>
    <td width="1" height="1"
bgcolor=#050400></td>
    <td width="1" height="1"
bgcolor=#130800></td>
    <td width="1" height="1"
bgcolor=#3b281c></td>
    <td width="1" height="1"
bgcolor=#6a5b4c></td>
    <td width="1" height="1"
bgcolor=#361d07></td>
    <td width="1" height="1"
bgcolor=#442b02></td>
    <td width="1" height="1"
bgcolor=#4f330c></td>
    <td width="1" height="1"
bgcolor=#75532e></td>
    <td width="1" height="1"
bgcolor=#a99169></td>
    <td width="1" height="1"
bgcolor=#857e69></td>
   </tr>
   <tr>
    <td width="1" height="1"
bgcolor=#564e4d></td>
    <td width="1" height="1"
bgcolor=#24201d></td>
    <td rowspan="10"
colspan="2" width="1"
height="1"
bgcolor=#000000></td>
    <td width="1" height="1"
bgcolor=#000100></td>
    <td rowspan="5"
colspan="1" width="1"
height="1"
bgcolor=#000000></td>
    <td rowspan="1"
colspan="2" width="1"
height="1"
bgcolor=#000100></td>
    <td width="1" height="1"
bgcolor=#000101></td>
    <td width="1" height="1"
bgcolor=#000100></td>
    <td width="1" height="1"
bgcolor=#000000></td>
    <td width="1" height="1"
bgcolor=#353231></td>
    <td width="1" height="1"
bgcolor=#817c79></td>
    <td width="1" height="1"
bgcolor=#685f5d></td>
    <td width="1" height="1"
bgcolor=#6b6461></td>
    <td width="1" height="1"
bgcolor=#615b57></td>
    <td width="1" height="1"
bgcolor=#574f4c></td>
    <td width="1" height="1"
bgcolor=#776f6c></td>
    <td width="1" height="1"
bgcolor=#716765></td>
    <td width="1" height="1"
bgcolor=#6c6260></td>
    <td width="1" height="1"
bgcolor=#181617></td>
    <td width="1" height="1"
bgcolor=#000000></td>
    <td width="1" height="1"
bgcolor=#010100></td>
    <td width="1" height="1"
bgcolor=#11100e></td>
    <td width="1" height="1"
bgcolor=#0c0907></td>
    <td width="1" height="1"
bgcolor=#080805></td>
    <td width="1" height="1"
bgcolor=#433d3d></td>
    <td width="1" height="1"
bgcolor=#625d5a></td>
```

```
<td width="1" height="1" bgcolor=#000001></td>
<td width="1" height="1" bgcolor=#000000></td>
<td width="1" height="1" bgcolor=#070707></td>
<td width="1" height="1" bgcolor=#423e3d></td>
<td width="1" height="1" bgcolor=#827d7a></td>
<td width="1" height="1" bgcolor=#999793></td>
<td width="1" height="1" bgcolor=#5d5351></td>
<td width="1" height="1" bgcolor=#534f4b></td>
<td width="1" height="1" bgcolor=#837977></td>
<td width="1" height="1" bgcolor=#786f6e></td>
<td width="1" height="1" bgcolor=#807b76></td>
<td width="1" height="1" bgcolor=#948f8a></td>
<td width="1" height="1" bgcolor=#858180></td>
<td width="1" height="1" bgcolor=#020100></td>
<td rowspan="1" colspan="2" width="1" height="1" bgcolor=#000000></td>
<td width="1" height="1" bgcolor=#010000></td>
<td width="1" height="1" bgcolor=#010000></td>
<td width="1" height="1" bgcolor=#060400></td>
<td width="1" height="1" bgcolor=#090400></td>
<td width="1" height="1" bgcolor=#1b0f06></td>
<td width="1" height="1" bgcolor=#090900></td>
<td width="1" height="1" bgcolor=#1a0e00></td>
<td width="1" height="1" bgcolor=#221302></td>
<td width="1" height="1" bgcolor=#281701></td>
<td width="1" height="1" bgcolor=#2f1d01></td>
<td width="1" height="1" bgcolor=#3c2502></td>
<td width="1" height="1" bgcolor=#402804></td>
<td width="1" height="1" bgcolor=#3c2703></td>
<td width="1" height="1" bgcolor=#6d4f27></td>
<td width="1" height="1" bgcolor=#675844></td>
</tr>
<tr>
<td width="1" height="1" bgcolor=#010101></td>
<td rowspan="10" colspan="1" width="1" height="1" bgcolor=#000000></td>
<td width="1" height="1" bgcolor=#000000></td>
<td width="1" height="1" bgcolor=#000100></td>
<td width="1" height="1" bgcolor=#000101></td>
<td width="1" height="1" bgcolor=#000000></td>
<td rowspan="1" colspan="3" width="1" height="1" bgcolor=#000100></td>
<td rowspan="4" colspan="1" width="1" height="1" bgcolor=#000000></td>
<td width="1" height="1" bgcolor=#242322></td>
<td width="1" height="1" bgcolor=#88807e></td>
<td width="1" height="1" bgcolor=#8d8583></td>
<td width="1" height="1" bgcolor=#8e8986></td>
<td width="1" height="1" bgcolor=#746b6a></td>
<td width="1" height="1" bgcolor=#7a7371></td>
<td width="1" height="1" bgcolor=#5b5653></td>
<td width="1" height="1" bgcolor=#706a67></td>
<td width="1" height="1" bgcolor=#807876></td>
<td width="1" height="1" bgcolor=#3d3a37></td>
<td width="1" height="1" bgcolor=#000000></td>
<td width="1" height="1" bgcolor=#5d5554></td>
<td width="1" height="1" bgcolor=#3f3b38></td>
<td width="1" height="1" bgcolor=#2a2a29></td>
<td width="1" height="1" bgcolor=#191615></td>
<td width="1" height="1" bgcolor=#151410></td>
<td width="1" height="1" bgcolor=#5d5654></td>
<td width="1" height="1" bgcolor=#635d59></td>
<td width="1" height="1" bgcolor=#615d59></td>
<td width="1" height="1" bgcolor=#353130></td>
<td rowspan="2" colspan="1" width="1" height="1" bgcolor=#000000></td>
<td width="1" height="1" bgcolor=#0f0f0d></td>
<td width="1" height="1" bgcolor=#4b4948></td>
<td width="1" height="1" bgcolor=#746a68></td>
<td width="1" height="1" bgcolor=#615c59></td>
<td width="1" height="1" bgcolor=#6a625f></td>
<td width="1" height="1" bgcolor=#6e6462></td>
<td width="1" height="1" bgcolor=#85807d></td>
<td width="1" height="1" bgcolor=#766e6d></td>
<td width="1" height="1" bgcolor=#635b58></td>
<td width="1" height="1" bgcolor=#4b4441></td>
<td width="1" height="1" bgcolor=#78706d></td>
<td width="1" height="1" bgcolor=#9a9792></td>
<td width="1" height="1" bgcolor=#b6b2b0></td>
<td width="1" height="1" bgcolor=#545351></td>
<td width="1" height="1" bgcolor=#0c0b09></td>
<td rowspan="1" colspan="2" width="1" height="1" bgcolor=#000000></td>
<td width="1" height="1" bgcolor=#000100></td>
<td width="1" height="1" bgcolor=#000000></td>
<td width="1" height="1" bgcolor=#010200></td>
<td width="1" height="1" bgcolor=#0b0501></td>
<td width="1" height="1" bgcolor=#190e01></td>
```

```
    <td width="1" height="1" bgcolor=#211002></td>
    <td width="1" height="1" bgcolor=#2d1a04></td>
    <td width="1" height="1" bgcolor=#382207></td>
    <td width="1" height="1" bgcolor=#2e1b00></td>
    <td width="1" height="1" bgcolor=#251600></td>
    <td width="1" height="1" bgcolor=#462f0f></td>
    <td width="1" height="1" bgcolor=#3a3025></td>
  </tr>
  <tr>
    <td rowspan="9" colspan="1" width="1" height="1" bgcolor=#000000></td>
    <td width="1" height="1" bgcolor=#000001></td>
    <td rowspan="3" colspan="1" width="1" height="1" bgcolor=#000000></td>
    <td width="1" height="1" bgcolor=#000000></td>
    <td width="1" height="1" bgcolor=#000101></td>
    <td width="1" height="1" bgcolor=#010201></td>
    <td width="1" height="1" bgcolor=#000101></td>
    <td width="1" height="1" bgcolor=#000100></td>
    <td width="1" height="1" bgcolor=#010302></td>
    <td width="1" height="1" bgcolor=#272525></td>
    <td width="1" height="1" bgcolor=#4a4343></td>
    <td width="1" height="1" bgcolor=#716869></td>
    <td width="1" height="1" bgcolor=#5f5d59></td>
    <td width="1" height="1" bgcolor=#776c6b></td>
    <td width="1" height="1" bgcolor=#6f6765></td>
    <td width="1" height="1" bgcolor=#534a48></td>
    <td width="1" height="1" bgcolor=#726a68></td>
    <td width="1" height="1" bgcolor=#817775></td>
    <td width="1" height="1" bgcolor=#6a6361></td>
    <td width="1" height="1" bgcolor=#807b77></td>
    <td width="1" height="1" bgcolor=#7b7371></td>
    <td width="1" height="1" bgcolor=#756b6a></td>
    <td width="1" height="1" bgcolor=#6a6562></td>
    <td width="1" height="1" bgcolor=#9d9592></td>
    <td width="1" height="1" bgcolor=#7b7371></td>
    <td width="1" height="1" bgcolor=#605b58></td>
    <td width="1" height="1" bgcolor=#0e0e0a></td>
    <td width="1" height="1" bgcolor=#000100></td>
    <td width="1" height="1" bgcolor=#25241f></td>
    <td width="1" height="1" bgcolor=#000000></td>
    <td width="1" height="1" bgcolor=#1f1c1a></td>
    <td width="1" height="1" bgcolor=#575251></td>
    <td width="1" height="1" bgcolor=#3d3b3a></td>
    <td width="1" height="1" bgcolor=#58524f></td>
    <td width="1" height="1" bgcolor=#8a8581></td>
    <td width="1" height="1" bgcolor=#8e8784></td>
    <td width="1" height="1" bgcolor=#938e8a></td>
    <td width="1" height="1" bgcolor=#504846></td>
    <td width="1" height="1" bgcolor=#2d2925></td>
    <td width="1" height="1" bgcolor=#100e0b></td>
    <td width="1" height="1" bgcolor=#524a49></td>
    <td width="1" height="1" bgcolor=#453b37></td>
    <td width="1" height="1" bgcolor=#4b4744></td>
    <td width="1" height="1" bgcolor=#8c867f></td>
    <td width="1" height="1" bgcolor=#928b88></td>
    <td width="1" height="1" bgcolor=#aeaca7></td>
    <td width="1" height="1" bgcolor=#423f3c></td>
    <td width="1" height="1" bgcolor=#6c6c67></td>
    <td rowspan="1" colspan="3" width="1" height="1" bgcolor=#000000></td>
    <td width="1" height="1" bgcolor=#0a0601></td>
    <td width="1" height="1" bgcolor=#120a01></td>
    <td width="1" height="1" bgcolor=#160d00></td>
    <td width="1" height="1" bgcolor=#160c00></td>
    <td width="1" height="1" bgcolor=#110800></td>
    <td width="1" height="1" bgcolor=#050400></td>
    <td width="1" height="1" bgcolor=#453b30></td>
  </tr>
  <tr>
    <td rowspan="2" colspan="1" width="1" height="1" bgcolor=#000000></td>
    <td width="1" height="1" bgcolor=#000100></td>
    <td rowspan="1" colspan="3" width="1" height="1" bgcolor=#000000></td>
    <td width="1" height="1" bgcolor=#0d0d0d></td>
    <td rowspan="2" colspan="1" width="1" height="1" bgcolor=#000000></td>
    <td width="1" height="1" bgcolor=#0a0a0a></td>
    <td width="1" height="1" bgcolor=#050502></td>
    <td width="1" height="1" bgcolor=#514847></td>
    <td width="1" height="1" bgcolor=#342f2d></td>
    <td width="1" height="1" bgcolor=#7f7a76></td>
    <td width="1" height="1" bgcolor=#837d7a></td>
    <td width="1" height="1" bgcolor=#7e7472></td>
    <td width="1" height="1" bgcolor=#5f5755></td>
    <td width="1" height="1" bgcolor=#766e6b></td>
    <td width="1" height="1" bgcolor=#7b716f></td>
    <td width="1" height="1" bgcolor=#706664></td>
```

```
<td width="1" height="1" bgcolor=#7f7673></td>
<td width="1" height="1" bgcolor=#7d7573></td>
<td width="1" height="1" bgcolor=#746a68></td>
<td width="1" height="1" bgcolor=#66605e></td>
<td width="1" height="1" bgcolor=#847c79></td>
<td width="1" height="1" bgcolor=#837b79></td>
<td width="1" height="1" bgcolor=#746f6c></td>
<td width="1" height="1" bgcolor=#1f1e1d></td>
<td width="1" height="1" bgcolor=#312c29></td>
<td width="1" height="1" bgcolor=#020302></td>
<td width="1" height="1" bgcolor=#010101></td>
<td width="1" height="1" bgcolor=#000000></td>
<td width="1" height="1" bgcolor=#0f0b0a></td>
<td width="1" height="1" bgcolor=#191817></td>
<td width="1" height="1" bgcolor=#030303></td>
<td width="1" height="1" bgcolor=#0f0e0e></td>
<td width="1" height="1" bgcolor=#262625></td>
<td width="1" height="1" bgcolor=#3f3b38></td>
<td width="1" height="1" bgcolor=#79716f></td>
<td width="1" height="1" bgcolor=#8b8280></td>
<td width="1" height="1" bgcolor=#756b69></td>
<td width="1" height="1" bgcolor=#554c49></td>
<td width="1" height="1" bgcolor=#3f3936></td>
<td width="1" height="1" bgcolor=#7e7472></td>
<td width="1" height="1" bgcolor=#7c7472></td>
<td width="1" height="1" bgcolor=#807a77></td>
<td width="1" height="1" bgcolor=#97928e></td>
<td width="1" height="1" bgcolor=#94918d></td>
<td width="1" height="1" bgcolor=#ada9a5></td>
<td width="1" height="1" bgcolor=#a9a8a4></td>
<td width="1" height="1" bgcolor=#a4a2a1></td>
<td width="1" height="1" bgcolor=#545352></td>
<td rowspan="10" colspan="1" width="1" height="1" bgcolor=#000000></td>
<td width="1" height="1" bgcolor=#010000></td>
<td width="1" height="1" bgcolor=#020100></td>
<td width="1" height="1" bgcolor=#010100></td>
<td width="1" height="1" bgcolor=#000100></td>
<td rowspan="11" colspan="1" width="1" height="1" bgcolor=#000000></td>
<td width="1" height="1" bgcolor=#2d2d2c></td>
</tr>
<tr>
<td width="1" height="1" bgcolor=#221f1e></td>
<td width="1" height="1" bgcolor=#3f3b39></td>
<td width="1" height="1" bgcolor=#969190></td>
<td width="1" height="1" bgcolor=#686564></td>
<td width="1" height="1" bgcolor=#696866></td>
<td width="1" height="1" bgcolor=#1b1919></td>
<td width="1" height="1" bgcolor=#6f6a6a></td>
<td width="1" height="1" bgcolor=#151312></td>
<td width="1" height="1" bgcolor=#5e5654></td>
<td width="1" height="1" bgcolor=#888380></td>
<td width="1" height="1" bgcolor=#43403d></td>
<td width="1" height="1" bgcolor=#7b7673></td>
<td width="1" height="1" bgcolor=#59514f></td>
<td width="1" height="1" bgcolor=#867f7c></td>
<td width="1" height="1" bgcolor=#968d8b></td>
<td width="1" height="1" bgcolor=#938886></td>
<td width="1" height="1" bgcolor=#726a67></td>
<td width="1" height="1" bgcolor=#57524f></td>
<td width="1" height="1" bgcolor=#645a58></td>
<td width="1" height="1" bgcolor=#7a706e></td>
<td width="1" height="1" bgcolor=#6d6462></td>
<td width="1" height="1" bgcolor=#766d6a></td>
<td width="1" height="1" bgcolor=#332d2a></td>
<td width="1" height="1" bgcolor=#7a706e></td>
<td width="1" height="1" bgcolor=#2a2623></td>
<td width="1" height="1" bgcolor=#030303></td>
<td rowspan="1" colspan="2" width="1" height="1" bgcolor=#000100></td>
<td rowspan="2" colspan="1" width="1" height="1" bgcolor=#000000></td>
<td width="1" height="1" bgcolor=#0c0a0b></td>
<td rowspan="3" colspan="1" width="1" height="1" bgcolor=#000000></td>
<td rowspan="2" colspan="1" width="1" height="1" bgcolor=#000000></td>
<td width="1" height="1" bgcolor=#050505></td>
<td width="1" height="1" bgcolor=#1a1717></td>
<td width="1" height="1" bgcolor=#645b59></td>
<td width="1" height="1" bgcolor=#3b3532></td>
<td width="1" height="1" bgcolor=#6e6462></td>
<td width="1" height="1" bgcolor=#3d3936></td>
<td width="1" height="1" bgcolor=#030202></td>
<td width="1" height="1" bgcolor=#090709></td>
<td width="1" height="1" bgcolor=#3b312f></td>
<td width="1" height="1" bgcolor=#8f8985></td>
```

```
    <td width="1" height="1"
bgcolor=#96918d></td>
    <td width="1" height="1"
bgcolor=#a5a09f></td>
    <td width="1" height="1"
bgcolor=#989491></td>
    <td width="1" height="1"
bgcolor=#75706c></td>
    <td width="1" height="1"
bgcolor=#95918d></td>
    <td width="1" height="1"
bgcolor=#242322></td>
    <td width="1" height="1"
bgcolor=#000100></td>
    <td rowspan="10"
colspan="1" width="1"
height="1"
bgcolor=#000000></td>
    <td width="1" height="1"
bgcolor=#000101></td>
    <td rowspan="10"
colspan="1" width="1"
height="1"
bgcolor=#000000></td>
    <td width="1" height="1"
bgcolor=#2d2e2d></td>
  </tr>
  <tr>
    <td width="1" height="1"
bgcolor=#292726></td>
    <td width="1" height="1"
bgcolor=#767271></td>
    <td width="1" height="1"
bgcolor=#55524f></td>
    <td width="1" height="1"
bgcolor=#6d6664></td>
    <td width="1" height="1"
bgcolor=#807a7a></td>
    <td width="1" height="1"
bgcolor=#999490></td>
    <td width="1" height="1"
bgcolor=#8a8181></td>
    <td width="1" height="1"
bgcolor=#4c4643></td>
    <td width="1" height="1"
bgcolor=#706967></td>
    <td width="1" height="1"
bgcolor=#928f8b></td>
    <td width="1" height="1"
bgcolor=#8e8986></td>
    <td width="1" height="1"
bgcolor=#585854></td>
    <td width="1" height="1"
bgcolor=#686261></td>
    <td width="1" height="1"
bgcolor=#706866></td>
    <td width="1" height="1"
bgcolor=#736e6b></td>
    <td width="1" height="1"
bgcolor=#464241></td>
    <td width="1" height="1"
bgcolor=#53504c></td>
    <td width="1" height="1"
bgcolor=#706966></td>
    <td width="1" height="1"
bgcolor=#3c3835></td>
    <td width="1" height="1"
bgcolor=#0b0a09></td>
    <td width="1" height="1"
bgcolor=#181514></td>
    <td width="1" height="1"
bgcolor=#060304></td>
    <td width="1" height="1"
bgcolor=#252321></td>
    <td width="1" height="1"
bgcolor=#3d3735></td>
    <td width="1" height="1"
bgcolor=#827a78></td>
    <td width="1" height="1"
bgcolor=#877d7b></td>
    <td width="1" height="1"
bgcolor=#887f7c></td>
    <td width="1" height="1"
bgcolor=#7b726f></td>
    <td width="1" height="1"
bgcolor=#46413f></td>
    <td width="1" height="1"
bgcolor=#5a5452></td>
    <td width="1" height="1"
bgcolor=#736b69></td>
    <td width="1" height="1"
bgcolor=#6e6765></td>
    <td width="1" height="1"
bgcolor=#000000></td>
    <td width="1" height="1"
bgcolor=#191715></td>
    <td rowspan="1"
colspan="2" width="1"
height="1"
bgcolor=#000000></td>
    <td width="1" height="1"
bgcolor=#000000></td>
    <td width="1" height="1"
bgcolor=#070606></td>
    <td width="1" height="1"
bgcolor=#000000></td>
    <td width="1" height="1"
bgcolor=#1e1c19></td>
    <td width="1" height="1"
bgcolor=#605554></td>
    <td width="1" height="1"
bgcolor=#201a16></td>
    <td width="1" height="1"
bgcolor=#706764></td>
    <td width="1" height="1"
bgcolor=#857e7c></td>
    <td width="1" height="1"
bgcolor=#3f3835></td>
    <td width="1" height="1"
bgcolor=#372f2d></td>
    <td width="1" height="1"
bgcolor=#151312></td>
    <td width="1" height="1"
bgcolor=#3e3432></td>
    <td width="1" height="1"
bgcolor=#615853></td>
    <td width="1" height="1"
bgcolor=#6d6360></td>
    <td width="1" height="1"
bgcolor=#867f7b></td>
    <td width="1" height="1"
bgcolor=#aeaba9></td>
    <td width="1" height="1"
bgcolor=#020202></td>
    <td rowspan="9"
colspan="1" width="1"
height="1"
bgcolor=#000000></td>
    <td rowspan="9"
colspan="1" width="1"
height="1"
bgcolor=#000000></td>
    <td width="1" height="1"
bgcolor=#2b2c2c></td>
  </tr>
  <tr>
    <td width="1" height="1"
bgcolor=#0d0d0d></td>
    <td width="1" height="1"
bgcolor=#524d4a></td>
    <td width="1" height="1"
bgcolor=#55514f></td>
    <td width="1" height="1"
bgcolor=#464141></td>
    <td width="1" height="1"
bgcolor=#908a89></td>
    <td width="1" height="1"
bgcolor=#777372></td>
    <td width="1" height="1"
bgcolor=#636160></td>
    <td width="1" height="1"
bgcolor=#7a797b></td>
    <td width="1" height="1"
bgcolor=#7e7a76></td>
    <td width="1" height="1"
bgcolor=#948f8f></td>
    <td width="1" height="1"
bgcolor=#8e8f8e></td>
    <td width="1" height="1"
bgcolor=#83807f></td>
    <td width="1" height="1"
bgcolor=#b7b3b2></td>
    <td width="1" height="1"
bgcolor=#887f81></td>
```

```
    <td width="1" height="1"
bgcolor=#77726f></td>
    <td width="1" height="1"
bgcolor=#4d4442></td>
    <td width="1" height="1"
bgcolor=#57504d></td>
    <td width="1" height="1"
bgcolor=#8a827f></td>
    <td width="1" height="1"
bgcolor=#837e7b></td>
    <td width="1" height="1"
bgcolor=#6f6765></td>
    <td width="1" height="1"
bgcolor=#3e3736></td>
    <td width="1" height="1"
bgcolor=#131111></td>
    <td width="1" height="1"
bgcolor=#0f0e0c></td>
    <td width="1" height="1"
bgcolor=#030403></td>
    <td width="1" height="1"
bgcolor=#302e2d></td>
    <td width="1" height="1"
bgcolor=#53494a></td>
    <td width="1" height="1"
bgcolor=#4a4645></td>
    <td width="1" height="1"
bgcolor=#776e6b></td>
    <td width="1" height="1"
bgcolor=#6a6360></td>
    <td width="1" height="1"
bgcolor=#5e5552></td>
    <td width="1" height="1"
bgcolor=#6c6965></td>
    <td width="1" height="1"
bgcolor=#584f4d></td>
    <td width="1" height="1"
bgcolor=#262120></td>
    <td width="1" height="1"
bgcolor=#615d5a></td>
    <td width="1" height="1"
bgcolor=#5b5351></td>
    <td width="1" height="1"
bgcolor=#000000></td>
    <td width="1" height="1"
bgcolor=#3d3634></td>
    <td width="1" height="1"
bgcolor=#6d6564></td>
    <td width="1" height="1"
bgcolor=#38322e></td>
    <td width="1" height="1"
bgcolor=#040202></td>
    <td width="1" height="1"
bgcolor=#292725></td>
    <td width="1" height="1"
bgcolor=#211f1c></td>
    <td width="1" height="1"
bgcolor=#161312></td>
    <td width="1" height="1"
bgcolor=#11100e></td>
    <td width="1" height="1"
bgcolor=#342c2a></td>
    <td width="1" height="1"
bgcolor=#665d5b></td>
    <td width="1" height="1"
bgcolor=#433b37></td>
    <td width="1" height="1"
bgcolor=#706765></td>
    <td width="1" height="1"
bgcolor=#7b7271></td>
    <td width="1" height="1"
bgcolor=#534b47></td>
    <td width="1" height="1"
bgcolor=#6c635f></td>
    <td width="1" height="1"
bgcolor=#716764></td>
    <td width="1" height="1"
bgcolor=#443b38></td>
    <td width="1" height="1"
bgcolor=#7a7270></td>
    <td width="1" height="1"
bgcolor=#78716f></td>
    <td width="1" height="1"
bgcolor=#766d6d></td>
    <td rowspan="3"
colspan="1" width="1"
height="1"
bgcolor=#000000></td>
    <td width="1" height="1"
bgcolor=#2b2b2b></td>
  </tr>
  <tr>
    <td rowspan="4"
colspan="1" width="1"
height="1"
bgcolor=#000000></td>
    <td width="1" height="1"
bgcolor=#494547></td>
    <td width="1" height="1"
bgcolor=#7d7373></td>
    <td width="1" height="1"
bgcolor=#6c6767></td>
    <td width="1" height="1"
bgcolor=#777171></td>
    <td width="1" height="1"
bgcolor=#716b6a></td>
    <td width="1" height="1"
bgcolor=#7e7d7c></td>
    <td width="1" height="1"
bgcolor=#858380></td>
    <td width="1" height="1"
bgcolor=#696868></td>
    <td width="1" height="1"
bgcolor=#535552></td>
    <td width="1" height="1"
bgcolor=#6a6261></td>
    <td width="1" height="1"
bgcolor=#22201e></td>
    <td width="1" height="1"
bgcolor=#000000></td>
    <td width="1" height="1"
bgcolor=#252524></td>
    <td width="1" height="1"
bgcolor=#8e8887></td>
    <td width="1" height="1"
bgcolor=#5b5554></td>
    <td width="1" height="1"
bgcolor=#7a7270></td>
    <td width="1" height="1"
bgcolor=#5b5051></td>
    <td width="1" height="1"
bgcolor=#887f7d></td>
    <td width="1" height="1"
bgcolor=#9c9893></td>
    <td width="1" height="1"
bgcolor=#898681></td>
    <td width="1" height="1"
bgcolor=#5e5654></td>
    <td width="1" height="1"
bgcolor=#706966></td>
    <td width="1" height="1"
bgcolor=#080808></td>
    <td rowspan="2"
colspan="1" width="1"
height="1"
bgcolor=#000000></td>
    <td width="1" height="1"
bgcolor=#000000></td>
    <td width="1" height="1"
bgcolor=#120f0f></td>
    <td width="1" height="1"
bgcolor=#4e4745></td>
    <td width="1" height="1"
bgcolor=#635b59></td>
    <td width="1" height="1"
bgcolor=#97918e></td>
    <td width="1" height="1"
bgcolor=#7e7874></td>
    <td width="1" height="1"
bgcolor=#89827f></td>
    <td width="1" height="1"
bgcolor=#605554></td>
    <td width="1" height="1"
bgcolor=#343131></td>
    <td width="1" height="1"
bgcolor=#6c615f></td>
    <td width="1" height="1"
bgcolor=#938987></td>
    <td width="1" height="1"
bgcolor=#807874></td>
    <td width="1" height="1"
bgcolor=#696360></td>
    <td width="1" height="1"
bgcolor=#716b69></td>
```

```
    <td width="1" height="1"
bgcolor=#807672></td>
    <td width="1" height="1"
bgcolor=#7e7474></td>
    <td width="1" height="1"
bgcolor=#3a332f></td>
    <td width="1" height="1"
bgcolor=#7e7673></td>
    <td width="1" height="1"
bgcolor=#6f6864></td>
    <td width="1" height="1"
bgcolor=#897f7d></td>
    <td width="1" height="1"
bgcolor=#7f7573></td>
    <td width="1" height="1"
bgcolor=#8c8481></td>
    <td width="1" height="1"
bgcolor=#726866></td>
    <td width="1" height="1"
bgcolor=#423a37></td>
    <td width="1" height="1"
bgcolor=#4e4441></td>
    <td width="1" height="1"
bgcolor=#524847></td>
    <td width="1" height="1"
bgcolor=#5c5453></td>
    <td width="1" height="1"
bgcolor=#655b59></td>
    <td width="1" height="1"
bgcolor=#716965></td>
    <td width="1" height="1"
bgcolor=#58514e></td>
    <td width="1" height="1"
bgcolor=#463e39></td>
    <td width="1" height="1"
bgcolor=#494341></td>
    <td width="1" height="1"
bgcolor=#252726></td>
  </tr>
  <tr>
    <td width="1" height="1"
bgcolor=#302f30></td>
    <td width="1" height="1"
bgcolor=#706667></td>
    <td width="1" height="1"
bgcolor=#484342></td>
    <td width="1" height="1"
bgcolor=#363332></td>
    <td width="1" height="1"
bgcolor=#545051></td>
    <td width="1" height="1"
bgcolor=#6f6b6c></td>
    <td width="1" height="1"
bgcolor=#aaabaa></td>
    <td width="1" height="1"
bgcolor=#7e7f7c></td>
    <td width="1" height="1"
bgcolor=#8d8585></td>
    <td width="1" height="1"
bgcolor=#6d6867></td>
    <td width="1" height="1"
bgcolor=#777470></td>
    <td width="1" height="1"
bgcolor=#6f6a6a></td>
    <td width="1" height="1"
bgcolor=#4a4946></td>
    <td width="1" height="1"
bgcolor=#292522></td>
    <td width="1" height="1"
bgcolor=#7b7474></td>
    <td width="1" height="1"
bgcolor=#756d6b></td>
    <td width="1" height="1"
bgcolor=#605857></td>
    <td width="1" height="1"
bgcolor=#1b1819></td>
    <td width="1" height="1"
bgcolor=#3c3839></td>
    <td width="1" height="1"
bgcolor=#5c5552></td>
    <td width="1" height="1"
bgcolor=#908886></td>
    <td width="1" height="1"
bgcolor=#78706e></td>
    <td rowspan="2"
colspan="1" width="1"
height="1"
bgcolor=#000000></td>
    <td width="1" height="1"
bgcolor=#0f100c></td>
    <td width="1" height="1"
bgcolor=#473e3b></td>
    <td width="1" height="1"
bgcolor=#544f4b></td>
    <td width="1" height="1"
bgcolor=#716b67></td>
    <td width="1" height="1"
bgcolor=#605857></td>
    <td width="1" height="1"
bgcolor=#514946></td>
    <td width="1" height="1"
bgcolor=#3d3634></td>
    <td width="1" height="1"
bgcolor=#918a87></td>
    <td width="1" height="1"
bgcolor=#544c4c></td>
    <td width="1" height="1"
bgcolor=#242221></td>
    <td width="1" height="1"
bgcolor=#342b29></td>
    <td width="1" height="1"
bgcolor=#121110></td>
    <td width="1" height="1"
bgcolor=#373330></td>
    <td width="1" height="1"
bgcolor=#7e7774></td>
    <td width="1" height="1"
bgcolor=#312b2a></td>
    <td width="1" height="1"
bgcolor=#827b78></td>
    <td width="1" height="1"
bgcolor=#908786></td>
    <td width="1" height="1"
bgcolor=#8e8785></td>
    <td width="1" height="1"
bgcolor=#7d7573></td>
    <td width="1" height="1"
bgcolor=#857f7c></td>
    <td width="1" height="1"
bgcolor=#89817e></td>
    <td width="1" height="1"
bgcolor=#6e6664></td>
    <td width="1" height="1"
bgcolor=#807674></td>
    <td width="1" height="1"
bgcolor=#7c7471></td>
    <td width="1" height="1"
bgcolor=#645b59></td>
    <td width="1" height="1"
bgcolor=#776f6c></td>
    <td width="1" height="1"
bgcolor=#726866></td>
    <td width="1" height="1"
bgcolor=#766c6b></td>
    <td width="1" height="1"
bgcolor=#6f6664></td>
    <td width="1" height="1"
bgcolor=#796f6e></td>
    <td width="1" height="1"
bgcolor=#7b7371></td>
    <td width="1" height="1"
bgcolor=#776d6e></td>
    <td width="1" height="1"
bgcolor=#2a2b2b></td>
  </tr>
  <tr>
    <td width="1" height="1"
bgcolor=#0e0c0b></td>
    <td width="1" height="1"
bgcolor=#595252></td>
    <td width="1" height="1"
bgcolor=#7e7877></td>
    <td width="1" height="1"
bgcolor=#1f1d1d></td>
    <td width="1" height="1"
bgcolor=#070708></td>
    <td width="1" height="1"
bgcolor=#1b1b19></td>
    <td width="1" height="1"
bgcolor=#231f23></td>
    <td width="1" height="1"
bgcolor=#877f7f></td>
    <td width="1" height="1"
bgcolor=#655e5e></td>
```

```
    <td width="1" height="1" bgcolor=#605656></td>
    <td width="1" height="1" bgcolor=#7c7474></td>
    <td width="1" height="1" bgcolor=#7d7976></td>
    <td width="1" height="1" bgcolor=#534b4b></td>
    <td width="1" height="1" bgcolor=#84807d></td>
    <td width="1" height="1" bgcolor=#090908></td>
    <td width="1" height="1" bgcolor=#4d4748></td>
    <td width="1" height="1" bgcolor=#9c9893></td>
    <td width="1" height="1" bgcolor=#75716f></td>
    <td width="1" height="1" bgcolor=#6d6466></td>
    <td width="1" height="1" bgcolor=#352e2c></td>
    <td width="1" height="1" bgcolor=#797672></td>
    <td width="1" height="1" bgcolor=#302f2d></td>
    <td width="1" height="1" bgcolor=#302c2b></td>
    <td width="1" height="1" bgcolor=#665d5c></td>
    <td width="1" height="1" bgcolor=#574e4e></td>
    <td width="1" height="1" bgcolor=#4d4b49></td>
    <td width="1" height="1" bgcolor=#342f2e></td>
    <td width="1" height="1" bgcolor=#57524f></td>
    <td width="1" height="1" bgcolor=#756a69></td>
    <td width="1" height="1" bgcolor=#1d1b17></td>
    <td width="1" height="1" bgcolor=#22201d></td>
    <td width="1" height="1" bgcolor=#342f2c></td>
    <td width="1" height="1" bgcolor=#514949></td>
    <td width="1" height="1" bgcolor=#655f5d></td>
    <td width="1" height="1" bgcolor=#55514d></td>
    <td width="1" height="1" bgcolor=#484440></td>
    <td width="1" height="1" bgcolor=#211b1d></td>
    <td width="1" height="1" bgcolor=#473e3d></td>
    <td width="1" height="1" bgcolor=#7e7573></td>
    <td width="1" height="1" bgcolor=#827a78></td>
    <td width="1" height="1" bgcolor=#6c605f></td>
    <td width="1" height="1" bgcolor=#37302d></td>
    <td width="1" height="1" bgcolor=#6c6261></td>
    <td width="1" height="1" bgcolor=#564d4b></td>
    <td width="1" height="1" bgcolor=#5f5754></td>
    <td width="1" height="1" bgcolor=#6a605e></td>
    <td width="1" height="1" bgcolor=#776e6c></td>
    <td width="1" height="1" bgcolor=#857d7a></td>
    <td width="1" height="1" bgcolor=#7c7170></td>
    <td width="1" height="1" bgcolor=#746a69></td>
    <td width="1" height="1" bgcolor=#7c7371></td>
    <td width="1" height="1" bgcolor=#6e6662></td>
    <td width="1" height="1" bgcolor=#837978></td>
    <td width="1" height="1" bgcolor=#675e5c></td>
    <td width="1" height="1" bgcolor=#574d4c></td>
    <td width="1" height="1" bgcolor=#070604></td>
    <td width="1" height="1" bgcolor=#2b2c2b></td>
  </tr>
  <tr>
    <td width="1" height="1" bgcolor=#060707></td>
    <td width="1" height="1" bgcolor=#010000></td>
    <td width="1" height="1" bgcolor=#070605></td>
    <td width="1" height="1" bgcolor=#000000></td>
    <td width="1" height="1" bgcolor=#121011></td>
    <td width="1" height="1" bgcolor=#373233></td>
    <td width="1" height="1" bgcolor=#6d6567></td>
    <td width="1" height="1" bgcolor=#373231></td>
    <td width="1" height="1" bgcolor=#454040></td>
    <td width="1" height="1" bgcolor=#3c3636></td>
    <td width="1" height="1" bgcolor=#322f2f></td>
    <td width="1" height="1" bgcolor=#545155></td>
    <td width="1" height="1" bgcolor=#837f7d></td>
    <td width="1" height="1" bgcolor=#3f3536></td>
    <td width="1" height="1" bgcolor=#474340></td>
    <td width="1" height="1" bgcolor=#635f61></td>
    <td width="1" height="1" bgcolor=#555151></td>
    <td width="1" height="1" bgcolor=#6c6564></td>
    <td width="1" height="1" bgcolor=#393636></td>
    <td width="1" height="1" bgcolor=#000000></td>
    <td width="1" height="1" bgcolor=#2e2a2b></td>
    <td width="1" height="1" bgcolor=#786f71></td>
    <td width="1" height="1" bgcolor=#5f5656></td>
    <td width="1" height="1" bgcolor=#534c4a></td>
    <td width="1" height="1" bgcolor=#6e6366></td>
    <td width="1" height="1" bgcolor=#888985></td>
    <td width="1" height="1" bgcolor=#4e4a48></td>
    <td width="1" height="1" bgcolor=#413f3c></td>
    <td width="1" height="1" bgcolor=#332e2d></td>
    <td width="1" height="1" bgcolor=#000000></td>
    <td width="1" height="1" bgcolor=#10100e></td>
    <td width="1" height="1" bgcolor=#4c4545></td>
    <td width="1" height="1" bgcolor=#191916></td>
    <td width="1" height="1" bgcolor=#45423e></td>
    <td width="1" height="1" bgcolor=#89807e></td>
    <td width="1" height="1" bgcolor=#585150></td>
    <td width="1" height="1" bgcolor=#6b6562></td>
    <td width="1" height="1" bgcolor=#34312f></td>
```

```
    <td width="1" height="1"
bgcolor=#8a8280></td>
    <td width="1" height="1"
bgcolor=#282422></td>
    <td width="1" height="1"
bgcolor=#10120f></td>
    <td width="1" height="1"
bgcolor=#605554></td>
    <td width="1" height="1"
bgcolor=#1d1b19></td>
    <td width="1" height="1"
bgcolor=#474140></td>
    <td width="1" height="1"
bgcolor=#6d6361></td>
    <td width="1" height="1"
bgcolor=#89827e></td>
    <td width="1" height="1"
bgcolor=#8c8683></td>
    <td width="1" height="1"
bgcolor=#796d6f></td>
    <td width="1" height="1"
bgcolor=#817977></td>
    <td width="1" height="1"
bgcolor=#817776></td>
    <td width="1" height="1"
bgcolor=#796e6d></td>
    <td width="1" height="1"
bgcolor=#625958></td>
    <td width="1" height="1"
bgcolor=#6a5f5e></td>
    <td width="1" height="1"
bgcolor=#5e5252></td>
    <td width="1" height="1"
bgcolor=#78726f></td>
    <td width="1" height="1"
bgcolor=#6c6765></td>
    <td width="1" height="1"
bgcolor=#6a6160></td>
    <td width="1" height="1"
bgcolor=#48403d></td>
    <td width="1" height="1"
bgcolor=#514b47></td>
    <td width="1" height="1"
bgcolor=#6d6362></td>
    <td width="1" height="1"
bgcolor=#272222></td>
    <td width="1" height="1"
bgcolor=#292a2a></td>
  </tr>
  <tr>
    <td width="1" height="1"
bgcolor=#171311></td>
    <td width="1" height="1"
bgcolor=#3e3935></td>
    <td width="1" height="1"
bgcolor=#56504e></td>
    <td width="1" height="1"
bgcolor=#696564></td>
    <td width="1" height="1"
bgcolor=#7e7a7c></td>
    <td width="1" height="1"
bgcolor=#4b4a45></td>
    <td width="1" height="1"
bgcolor=#343331></td>
    <td width="1" height="1"
bgcolor=#5b5657></td>
    <td width="1" height="1"
bgcolor=#282824></td>
    <td width="1" height="1"
bgcolor=#2c2728></td>
    <td width="1" height="1"
bgcolor=#736b6e></td>
    <td width="1" height="1"
bgcolor=#585251></td>
    <td width="1" height="1"
bgcolor=#463f42></td>
    <td width="1" height="1"
bgcolor=#4a4648></td>
    <td width="1" height="1"
bgcolor=#252322></td>
    <td width="1" height="1"
bgcolor=#000000></td>
    <td width="1" height="1"
bgcolor=#403839></td>
    <td width="1" height="1"
bgcolor=#736b6a></td>
    <td width="1" height="1"
bgcolor=#746c6d></td>
    <td width="1" height="1"
bgcolor=#706d6c></td>
    <td width="1" height="1"
bgcolor=#6f6a68></td>
    <td width="1" height="1"
bgcolor=#736d6c></td>
    <td width="1" height="1"
bgcolor=#615c5d></td>
    <td width="1" height="1"
bgcolor=#413d3c></td>
    <td width="1" height="1"
bgcolor=#1f1c1c></td>
    <td width="1" height="1"
bgcolor=#312e2b></td>
    <td width="1" height="1"
bgcolor=#3d3835></td>
    <td width="1" height="1"
bgcolor=#5c5555></td>
    <td width="1" height="1"
bgcolor=#686362></td>
    <td width="1" height="1"
bgcolor=#7f7674></td>
    <td width="1" height="1"
bgcolor=#494646></td>
    <td width="1" height="1"
bgcolor=#100e0e></td>
    <td width="1" height="1"
bgcolor=#010102></td>
    <td width="1" height="1"
bgcolor=#080605></td>
    <td width="1" height="1"
bgcolor=#494445></td>
    <td width="1" height="1"
bgcolor=#0e0b0b></td>
    <td width="1" height="1"
bgcolor=#383231></td>
    <td width="1" height="1"
bgcolor=#534b48></td>
    <td width="1" height="1"
bgcolor=#685f5c></td>
    <td width="1" height="1"
bgcolor=#64615d></td>
    <td width="1" height="1"
bgcolor=#534b48></td>
    <td width="1" height="1"
bgcolor=#161212></td>
    <td width="1" height="1"
bgcolor=#1d1a1c></td>
    <td width="1" height="1"
bgcolor=#020403></td>
    <td width="1" height="1"
bgcolor=#3e3636></td>
    <td width="1" height="1"
bgcolor=#1e1e1a></td>
    <td width="1" height="1"
bgcolor=#030202></td>
    <td rowspan="3"
colspan="2" width="1"
height="1"
bgcolor=#000000></td>
    <td width="1" height="1"
bgcolor=#6b6160></td>
    <td width="1" height="1"
bgcolor=#594f4d></td>
    <td width="1" height="1"
bgcolor=#736967></td>
    <td width="1" height="1"
bgcolor=#584d4c></td>
    <td width="1" height="1"
bgcolor=#716767></td>
    <td width="1" height="1"
bgcolor=#6f6564></td>
    <td width="1" height="1"
bgcolor=#362d2b></td>
    <td width="1" height="1"
bgcolor=#39322d></td>
    <td width="1" height="1"
bgcolor=#080707></td>
    <td width="1" height="1"
bgcolor=#2a2421></td>
    <td width="1" height="1"
bgcolor=#5d5251></td>
    <td width="1" height="1"
bgcolor=#453f3d></td>
    <td width="1" height="1"
bgcolor=#58504e></td>
```

```
    <td width="1" height="1" bgcolor=#5e5553></td>
    <td width="1" height="1" bgcolor=#5e5352></td>
    <td width="1" height="1" bgcolor=#352e2d></td>
    <td rowspan="2" colspan="1" width="1" height="1" bgcolor=#272928></td>
  </tr>
  <tr>
    <td width="1" height="1" bgcolor=#464447></td>
    <td width="1" height="1" bgcolor=#938f8f></td>
    <td width="1" height="1" bgcolor=#969393></td>
    <td width="1" height="1" bgcolor=#6f6a69></td>
    <td width="1" height="1" bgcolor=#494748></td>
    <td width="1" height="1" bgcolor=#929597></td>
    <td width="1" height="1" bgcolor=#545050></td>
    <td width="1" height="1" bgcolor=#252124></td>
    <td width="1" height="1" bgcolor=#393536></td>
    <td width="1" height="1" bgcolor=#6a6163></td>
    <td width="1" height="1" bgcolor=#474343></td>
    <td width="1" height="1" bgcolor=#4b484a></td>
    <td width="1" height="1" bgcolor=#51474a></td>
    <td width="1" height="1" bgcolor=#413939></td>
    <td width="1" height="1" bgcolor=#21201f></td>
    <td width="1" height="1" bgcolor=#1c191a></td>
    <td width="1" height="1" bgcolor=#0c0c0e></td>
    <td width="1" height="1" bgcolor=#777373></td>
    <td width="1" height="1" bgcolor=#79726f></td>
    <td width="1" height="1" bgcolor=#72706f></td>
    <td width="1" height="1" bgcolor=#8a8481></td>
    <td width="1" height="1" bgcolor=#837f7c></td>
    <td width="1" height="1" bgcolor=#676060></td>
    <td width="1" height="1" bgcolor=#5e5453></td>
    <td width="1" height="1" bgcolor=#575450></td>
    <td width="1" height="1" bgcolor=#3a3335></td>
    <td width="1" height="1" bgcolor=#282626></td>
    <td width="1" height="1" bgcolor=#302c2b></td>
    <td width="1" height="1" bgcolor=#403d3c></td>
    <td width="1" height="1" bgcolor=#766c6c></td>
    <td width="1" height="1" bgcolor=#4d4545></td>
    <td rowspan="1" colspan="2" width="1" height="1" bgcolor=#000000></td>
    <td width="1" height="1" bgcolor=#574e4e></td>
    <td width="1" height="1" bgcolor=#3b3836></td>
    <td width="1" height="1" bgcolor=#46413f></td>
    <td width="1" height="1" bgcolor=#453d3c></td>
    <td width="1" height="1" bgcolor=#524a49></td>
    <td width="1" height="1" bgcolor=#6d6664></td>
    <td width="1" height="1" bgcolor=#7a7471></td>
    <td width="1" height="1" bgcolor=#9a9491></td>
    <td width="1" height="1" bgcolor=#75706f></td>
    <td width="1" height="1" bgcolor=#4f4a47></td>
    <td width="1" height="1" bgcolor=#191515></td>
    <td width="1" height="1" bgcolor=#46403d></td>
    <td width="1" height="1" bgcolor=#171212></td>
    <td rowspan="2" colspan="1" width="1" height="1" bgcolor=#000000></td>
    <td width="1" height="1" bgcolor=#161413></td>
    <td width="1" height="1" bgcolor=#6a5f5d></td>
    <td width="1" height="1" bgcolor=#6e6563></td>
    <td width="1" height="1" bgcolor=#7e7472></td>
    <td width="1" height="1" bgcolor=#564b4a></td>
    <td width="1" height="1" bgcolor=#4d4442></td>
    <td width="1" height="1" bgcolor=#564c4b></td>
    <td width="1" height="1" bgcolor=#3b3330></td>
    <td width="1" height="1" bgcolor=#534b49></td>
    <td width="1" height="1" bgcolor=#544c4a></td>
    <td width="1" height="1" bgcolor=#413834></td>
    <td width="1" height="1" bgcolor=#433c37></td>
    <td width="1" height="1" bgcolor=#4c4340></td>
    <td width="1" height="1" bgcolor=#4e4342></td>
    <td width="1" height="1" bgcolor=#524745></td>
    <td width="1" height="1" bgcolor=#4e4442></td>
  </tr>
  <tr>
    <td width="1" height="1" bgcolor=#4d484d></td>
    <td width="1" height="1" bgcolor=#2f2a2b></td>
    <td width="1" height="1" bgcolor=#656263></td>
    <td width="1" height="1" bgcolor=#7c797c></td>
    <td width="1" height="1" bgcolor=#79797a></td>
    <td width="1" height="1" bgcolor=#747174></td>
    <td width="1" height="1" bgcolor=#7c7978></td>
    <td width="1" height="1" bgcolor=#797675></td>
    <td width="1" height="1" bgcolor=#7a7676></td>
    <td width="1" height="1" bgcolor=#766f71></td>
    <td width="1" height="1" bgcolor=#686365></td>
    <td width="1" height="1" bgcolor=#413b3a></td>
    <td width="1" height="1" bgcolor=#4a4447></td>
    <td width="1" height="1" bgcolor=#6a6564></td>
    <td width="1" height="1" bgcolor=#5b5557></td>
    <td width="1" height="1" bgcolor=#4d4648></td>
```

```
<td width="1" height="1" bgcolor=#2f2d2b></td>
<td width="1" height="1" bgcolor=#342d31></td>
<td width="1" height="1" bgcolor=#766f70></td>
<td width="1" height="1" bgcolor=#888281></td>
<td width="1" height="1" bgcolor=#8c8786></td>
<td width="1" height="1" bgcolor=#797273></td>
<td width="1" height="1" bgcolor=#756b6f></td>
<td width="1" height="1" bgcolor=#796f6f></td>
<td width="1" height="1" bgcolor=#6b6064></td>
<td width="1" height="1" bgcolor=#767272></td>
<td width="1" height="1" bgcolor=#2f2726></td>
<td width="1" height="1" bgcolor=#393334></td>
<td width="1" height="1" bgcolor=#5b5354></td>
<td width="1" height="1" bgcolor=#6c6263></td>
<td width="1" height="1" bgcolor=#84807d></td>
<td width="1" height="1" bgcolor=#393331></td>
<td width="1" height="1" bgcolor=#665e5d></td>
<td width="1" height="1" bgcolor=#37302f></td>
<td width="1" height="1" bgcolor=#625c5a></td>
<td width="1" height="1" bgcolor=#7c7575></td>
<td width="1" height="1" bgcolor=#595352></td>
<td width="1" height="1" bgcolor=#040304></td>
<td width="1" height="1" bgcolor=#1e191a></td>
<td width="1" height="1" bgcolor=#514a48></td>
<td width="1" height="1" bgcolor=#89837f></td>
<td width="1" height="1" bgcolor=#695f5e></td>
<td width="1" height="1" bgcolor=#605855></td>
<td width="1" height="1" bgcolor=#635e5a></td>
<td width="1" height="1" bgcolor=#867f7c></td>
<td width="1" height="1" bgcolor=#020202></td>
<td width="1" height="1" bgcolor=#171212></td>
<td width="1" height="1" bgcolor=#211c1b></td>
<td width="1" height="1" bgcolor=#393532></td>
<td width="1" height="1" bgcolor=#443c3a></td>
<td width="1" height="1" bgcolor=#6c6261></td>
<td width="1" height="1" bgcolor=#5e5453></td>
<td width="1" height="1" bgcolor=#554c4a></td>
<td width="1" height="1" bgcolor=#665c5c></td>
<td width="1" height="1" bgcolor=#372e2b></td>
<td width="1" height="1" bgcolor=#584e4e></td>
<td width="1" height="1" bgcolor=#625756></td>
<td width="1" height="1" bgcolor=#5b4f4d></td>
<td width="1" height="1" bgcolor=#605553></td>
<td width="1" height="1" bgcolor=#443a38></td>
<td width="1" height="1" bgcolor=#66605c></td>
<td width="1" height="1" bgcolor=#605655></td>
<td width="1" height="1" bgcolor=#020101></td>
<td width="1" height="1" bgcolor=#2c2d2d></td>
  </tr>
</table></body></html>
```

So lives the land of the new order.

www.ingramcontent.com/pod-product-compliance
Lightning Source LLC
Chambersburg PA
CBHW031121180526
45160CB00005B/41/J
*9780578171951*